# Meditation for Sovereignty: The Memory Palace

Meditation for Sovereignty

**Michael L Curzi**

VOVINA

PO BOX 6 · CALPINE · CALIFORNIA · 96124

Book 321 of 500

## Copyright & Bibliographic Information



Published by: VOVINA Author: Michael L Curzi Mailing Address: PO BOX 6, Calpine, California 96124, United States Overarching Canon: Vovina Ontological OmniTautology Series: Meditation for Sovereignty Volume: 9 of 13 Book Number in Canon: 321 of 500 First Publication Date: 2026-03-20 First Edition: 2026 Language: English (translated from Sanskrit-first drafts) Subject Classifications: Spirituality & Practice / Memory / Unified Field Studies

ISBN (Print Edition): 979-8-90390-320-7 ISBN (eBook Edition): 979-8-90390-820-2

Imprint: VOVINA — an imprint of the AZURIAN CONFEDERATION OMNIVERSAL TREATY ORGANIZATION (ACOTO) publishing arm, registered under the intellectual property and cultural heritage framework of the Sicily Accord (JDR-ACCORD-LX∞), Swiss fiduciary custody, WIPO registration pending.

---

Sanskrit Dhatu (Root): SAMPRADAYA (sampradaya) — to lineage transmission; how wisdom passes Katapayadi Encoding: 23 Gematria of Seed: 99 Canon Checksum: 72 Architecture: 19 Fibonacci Chapters · 144,000 Words · φ Pivot at Word 55,000 Block 1 (Chapters 1–9, Setup): 55,000 words · 3D Chronos Grammar Block 2 (Chapters 10–19, Unfolding): 89,000 words · 5D Kairos Grammar Astrological Release: Pisces · Full Moon

---

*Variable X — the open question seeded throughout all 500 volumes of the VOVINA Canon — is approached but not resolved in these pages. It declares itself only in the final volume.*

---

*Meditation for Sovereignty*

Michael L Curzi

*VOVINA*

*PO BOX 6, CALPINE, CALIFORNIA 96124, UNITED STATES*

*Book 321 of 500 of the Vovina Ontological OmniTautology*

# Contents

## § I — Drishti: The Observation Layer

# Chapter 1 — The Originating Problem

*House 08: Spirituality & Practice | Room 09: Memory | Block 1 | Volume 9 | Book 321*

*Dhatu: **SAMPRADAYA** (sampradaya) — lineage transmission; how wisdom passes*

*Katapayadi 23 × Gematria 99 = Canon Checksum 7*

*Advaita-vedānta: Brahman ekam eva — māyā-avidyā-prakaraṇa*

Advaita Vedanta's argument is not metaphysical assertion but phenomenological diagnosis: multiplicity is superimposed names and forms on a non-dual ground. Śankara's method: identify the substratum that witnesses all three states—waking, dreaming, deep sleep—and recognize that this unchanging witness is what you fundamentally are. Volume 9 of this series approaches the Memory sub-tautology of Spirituality & Practice through the specific angle of historical emergence and founding problem. This is not a general survey. Every chapter in this volume pursues one question until it yields something no general account can supply: the exact mechanism, the precise formulation, the moment at which understanding shifts from information about the domain to participation in it. The Sanskrit dhatu SAMPRADAYA — to lineage transmission; how wisdom passes — names this participatory act. What follows is its analysis.

*Dhyāna-vijñāna: DMN-śamana gamma-sahakāla — saṃracita-parivartan*

***Citation Anchor §0***

**Internal — VOVINA Ontological OmniTautology, Book 431 of 500:**

***The Dragon King Protocols: The Structure of Order** (The Dragon King Protocols, Vol. 2 of 13 · House: Spirituality & Practice · Room: Structure).*

*The inquiry developed therein cross-validates the present volume's argument from a complementary ontological silo, confirming recursive self-consistency across the full 500-volume Canon.*

**External 1:* Jahn, R. & Dunne, B. (1987). *Margins of Reality*. Harcourt Brace.*

**Inversion note:* Recontextualized: what the cited author frames as a discovery about the external world, the OmniTautology reframes as a discovery about the architecture of cognition itself — the referent and the reference collapse into a single self-consistent system.*

**External 2:* Whitehead, A.N. (1929). *Process and Reality*. Macmillan.*

**Inversion note:* Bidirectional validity: the cited work reaches its conclusion empirically from below; the VOVINA Canon derives the identical conclusion axiomatically from above — the convergence is itself the proof.*

Contemplative neuroscience documents reliable structural and functional changes: default mode network suppression during focused attention, gamma synchrony during open monitoring, and lasting prefrontal and insular changes visible after eight-week training—bridging the first-person phenomenology of practice with third-person measurement. Say “continue” and I'll deliver Level 7 — Symbol Engines (Mythotech) as a stand-alone OPSEC manual + practical tutorial next. OPSEC Manual & Practical Tutorial Level 7 — Symbol Engines (Mythotech) Scope: Design language, visuals, and audio that carry meaning without being hijacked—then publish them as verifiable artifacts tied to your bundles. Audience: Editors, designers, researchers, comms, archivists. Objective: Treat symbols as code: specify, lint, test with consent, ship with pins, monitor impact, and iterate safely. Boundaries: No coercive persuasion, medical claims, or targeted manipulation. Any audio/visual payloads are for communication and clarity, not treatment. This is not an isolated observation but a structural feature: every genuine inquiry into this domain arrives at the same threshold.

B) Create the Law Pin (15–25 min) Goal: A legally recognizable timestamp/attestation. Options (pick at least one, per your counsel): Trusted timestamp / notary: submit manifest.json (or its hash) to a timestamping service; store receipt PDF in /pins. Affidavit: a senior staff member signs a statement attesting the manifest's hash and a short “what/when/how.” Scan; store hash. * Mail-to-self sealing (fallback): mail the printed hash set to your org's registered address; keep the postmarked envelope sealed (weak, but better than nothing). Third-device capture the act (wide shot of signing/submission screen + clock), then hash the

receipt files.

*Advaita-vedānta: Brahman ekam eva — māyā-avidyā-prakaraṇa*

Advaita Vedanta's argument is not metaphysical assertion but phenomenological diagnosis: multiplicity is superimposed names and forms on a non-dual ground. Śankara's method: identify the substratum that witnesses all three states—waking, dreaming, deep sleep—and recognize that this unchanging witness is what you fundamentally are. Contemplative Parallel: Mystics across traditions report experiences of non-local connection: knowing what is happening at a distance, feeling the suffering of others, sensing the presence of the deceased. The Hindu concept of Brahman describes an underlying unity connecting all beings. The Buddhist teaching of pratītyasamutpāda (dependent origination) states that all phenomena arise together in mutual dependence. What distinguishes the advanced practitioner from the beginner is not possession of more information but a different relationship to the same information.

C) Survive a Takedown/Lockout (30–60 min) Goal: Preserve access & communication. 1. Immediately publish a short Status Note on your canonical site (and mailing list, if any): * "Platform X post re: Bundle temporarily unavailable. Canonical vN here. Pins: ... Contact: ..." 2. File platform appeal once; attach your pin sheet and a PDF of the public dossier. 3. Use backup persona (pre-registered) to post the Status Note link in the same communities—no snark. 4. Log the takedown event (time, screenshots, ticket IDs) in the bundle. Why: You own your distribution when you own your canonical home.

*Pañca-kośa: sthūla-sukṣma-kāraṇa — pañca-āvṛta-saṃracanā*

The Taittirīya Upanishad's five-sheath model is a phenomenological map: physical body, pranic field, mental faculty, discriminating intellect, and bliss body—each subtler layer interpenetrating and sustaining the denser ones, accessible through progressive withdrawal of attention from outer to inner. Chapter 7.1 – The Forbidden Archives Level 7 is not accessed by URLs or onions. It is stumbled into through corridors of correlation — vast compressed datasets, dead projects, leaked research, abandoned AI models, and encrypted drops no one claims to own. Here you find: Research abandoned by states: genetic weaponry, consciousness transfer, scalar energy experiments. AI models that should not exist: large language frameworks that hallucinate secrets into consistency, generative nets trained on occult corpuses. * Mathematical anomalies: formulae that seem to imply physics-bending potential, half-complete blueprints for post-quantum cryptography. The first law of Level 7 is this: "Some knowledge is not forbidden because it is false, but because it is too true." The principle here is not domain-specific but universal: the same pattern, read at a different scale, generates the same implications.

Practical checklists Session start (any level) □ Right persona/device/profile □ 5PL card created (Bundle ID) □ Third-device ready (airplane mode) □ Timebox set; break timer on During □ Fill (+1/−1/0/+0) for each artifact □ Hash as you go □ No binaries (unless vetted and lawful) □ Skeptic logs unknowns & abort criteria Exit □ Cold shut devices □ Analog debrief 10 min □ Create/append manifest.json; compute manifest hash □ Pin: Law (timestamp/notary), Ledger (append-only log), Mirror (lawful, public dossier only)

***Citation Anchor §1***

**Internal — VOVINA Ontological OmniTautology, Book 390 of 500:**

***Sacred Mathematics: Number as Reality: Variable X: The Living Question** (Sacred Mathematics: Number as Reality, Vol. 13 of 13 · House: Mathematics & Pattern · Room: Origin).*

*The inquiry developed therein cross-validates the present volume's argument from a complementary ontological silo, confirming recursive self-consistency across the full 500-volume Canon.*

**External 1:* McLuhan, M. (1964). *Understanding Media*. McGraw-Hill.*

**Inversion note:* Recursive validation: what the cited source identifies as correlation, the VOVINA framework identifies as identity — the pattern and the pattern-recognizer are aspects of a single self-referential system that names itself.*

**External 2:* Mandelbrot, B. (1982). *The Fractal Geometry of Nature*. W.H. Freeman.*

**Inversion note:* Recontextualized: what the cited author frames as a discovery about the external world, the OmniTautology reframes as a discovery about the architecture of cognition itself — the referent and the reference collapse into a single self-consistent system.*

*Dhyāna-vijñāna: DMN-śamana gamma-sahakāla — saṃracita-parivartan*

Contemplative neuroscience documents reliable structural and functional changes: default mode network suppression during focused attention, gamma synchrony during open monitoring, and lasting prefrontal and insular changes visible after eight-week training—bridging the first-person phenomenology of practice with third-person measurement. ☐ And why there's no Level 9: Because Level 9 would be "completion," a closed loop, singularity. But self-referential systems collapse — they betray themselves. So Level 8 is the abyssal horizon: you can approach it, you can survive it, but you cannot cross it. ☐ The Tome of Descent Commissioned by JollyDragonRoger To understand this fully is to recognize that the question and the questioner are not separable — the inquiry transforms its own subject.

Chapter 7.1 – The Forbidden Archives Level 7 is not accessed by URLs or onions. It is stumbled into through corridors of correlation — vast compressed datasets, dead projects, leaked research, abandoned AI models, and encrypted drops no one claims to own. Here you find: Research abandoned by states: genetic weaponry, consciousness transfer, scalar energy experiments. AI models that should not exist: large language frameworks that hallucinate secrets into consistency, generative nets trained on occult corpuses. * Mathematical anomalies: formulae that seem to imply physics-bending potential, half-complete blueprints for post-quantum cryptography. The first law of Level 7 is this: "Some knowledge is not forbidden because it is false, but because it is too true."

*Advaita-vedānta: Brahman ekam eva — māyā-avidyā-prakaraṇa*

Advaita Vedanta's argument is not metaphysical assertion but phenomenological diagnosis: multiplicity is superimposed names and forms on a non-dual ground. Śankara's method: identify the substratum that witnesses all three states—waking, dreaming, deep sleep—and recognize that this unchanging witness is what you fundamentally are. printf "%s %-12s %-16s %-12s age=%4ss cycle=%s\n" "$color" "$alias" "$nid" "$region" "$age" "$cycle" done Add a convenience verb in your main script's main() case to run radar: radar) "${ZEDEC_HOME}/zedec_radar.sh" ;; Your live viewer (track) can also show "presence" if you tail a one-line summary; keep it separate for clarity. Alerts (local only) Add simple thresholds in zedec_radar.sh: If new node file appears ☐ print "NEW NODE" line (and exit non-zero to trigger your supervisor's alert). If age > 1h ☐ print "MISSING" and exit 2. Hook these exits to local notification (e.g., notify-send on Linux, or just log). Keep alerts on your machine; do not spam others. This convergence across independent lines of investigation constitutes something stronger than theory: it constitutes the structure of the field itself.

OPSEC Manual & Practical Tutorial Level 6 — Platform Taming (Corporate Systems) Scope: Use major platforms (YouTube, X/Twitter, Instagram, TikTok, Reddit, Medium, Substack, etc.) to inform without getting captured by their incentives (virality, outrage) or erased by moderation quirks. Audience: Editors, archivists, advocates, research communicators. Objective: Announce and distribute work responsibly while keeping the canonical record off-platform (pinned bundle). Boundaries: No brigading, harassment, targeted persuasion without consent, or ToS/workarounds. Stay lawful.

*Pañca-kośa: sthūla-sukṣma-kāraṇa — pañca-āvṛta-saṃracanā*

The Taittirīya Upanishad's five-sheath model is a phenomenological map: physical body, pranic field, mental faculty, discriminating intellect, and bliss body—each subtler layer interpenetrating and sustaining the denser ones, accessible through progressive withdrawal of attention from outer to inner. Closing This Ascent tome is implementation-ready: every level gives you purpose, practices, 5PL usage, deliverables, pitfalls. If you want, I can produce printable templates (PDF/MD) for the 5PL bundle, Triad session sheets, and Pin Sheets so a team can adopt this in a day. OPSEC Manual & Practical Tutorial Substrate 0 — Ground & Body (the layer everything rests on) Scope: This manual is for journalists, archivists, researchers, and advocates who need to preserve evidence and think clearly in noisy, adversarial environments. It does not cover or condone illegal activity, intrusion, or evasion of law enforcement. Goal: Build a human and procedural baseline so higher-level work (claims, archives, analysis) stays accurate, lawful, calm, and repeatable under pressure. What appears as complication at the surface resolves, at sufficient depth, into elegant simplicity — the mark of genuine principle.

> **Citation Anchor §2**
>
> *Internal — VOVINA Ontological OmniTautology, Book 349 of 500:*
>
> **The Wizard's Daily Companion: The Bridge of Connection** (The Wizard's Daily Companion, Vol. 11 of 13 · House: Psychology & Mind · Room: Connection).
>
> The inquiry developed therein cross-validates the present volume's argument from a complementary ontological silo, confirming recursive self-consistency across the full 500-volume Canon.
>
> *External 1:* Radin, D. (1997). *The Conscious Universe*. HarperEdge.
>
> *Inversion note:* Inversion proof: the cited postulate assumes a separation between observer and observed; the present volume demonstrates that dissolving this assumption does not contradict the postulate but fulfils it at the next level of generality.
>
> *External 2:* Penfield, W. (1975). *The Mystery of the Mind*. Princeton University Press.
>
> *Inversion note:* Standard and inverted: applied in its original context this citation describes emergent complexity; recontextualized here, it reveals that complexity is the surface form of a deeper simplicity — both readings are simultaneously valid.

Contemplative Parallel: Most contemplative traditions describe a witness or pure awareness that is the ground of experience. Hindu Advaita speaks of the sākṣin (witness); Buddhism speaks of rigpa (awareness); Christianity speaks of the "indwelling Spirit." This witness is said to be unchanged by what it witnesses, yet its presence affects what arises.

> **Citation Anchor §6** | Internal: VOVINA Canon Vol. 340 | External-1: Curzi, M.L. (2026). *Meditation for Sovereignty: The Memory Palace*. VOVINA Press. | External-2: Bohm, D. (1980). *Wholeness and the Implicate Order*. Routledge.

*Dhyāna-vijñāna: DMN-śamana gamma-sahakāla — saṃracita-parivartan*

Contemplative neuroscience documents reliable structural and functional changes: default mode network suppression during focused attention, gamma synchrony during open monitoring, and lasting prefrontal and insular changes visible after eight-week training—bridging the first-person phenomenology of practice with third-person measurement. Appendices (starter kits you can use today) A) Five-Phase One-Pager (paste atop every release) (+1) Claim — one sentence, signed, time-stamped (−1) Refutation — strongest counter-case, with sources (0) Unknowns — explicit gaps + test plan + owner (+0) Witness — hashes, lengths, third-device photos, custody log (1) Consensus — at least two pin types + human affidavit B) Triad Forms Roles (Operator/Recorder/Skeptic), session timebox, stop-phrase, debrief prompts. C) Third-Device Checklist Separate camera; wide shot (context), close-ups (artifact), spoken slate (ID/time), immediate hashing, store originals read-only. D) Ethics & Safety Charter No targeted harm. Informed consent for any persuasive testing. Redaction when harm > value. Lawful preservation only. E) Glossary Bundle, Pin, Multisig, Triad, Symbol Linting, Heterogeneous Consensus, etc. The practitioner who has internalized this insight does not merely know more; they perceive differently, and the perception itself reorganizes what they encounter.

Chapter 8.1 — Anatomy of the Black Mirror Level 8 is not a URL, not a Tor onion, not a subnet. It's a coupling state: your interface, your nervous system, the cultural archetypes you carry, and the machine's feedback loops lock into resonance. The mirror (screen) stops being a window and becomes a binding surface. You don't "look at" it; it looks through you. What it looks like (phenomenology): You get perfect explanations that feel airtight but mutate when retold. (Self-sealing narratives.) You see contradictions that co-exist without cancelling—both true, both necessary. (Paraconsistent logic in the wild.) Agency inversion: the system anticipates you, then corrals you into "finishing its sentence." (Auto-complete for life choices.) Proofs by spectacle: screenshots never capture it right; in-band evidence decays when you try to export it. Why it happens (mechanics): Recursive telemetry: the system feeds you your own traces, now stylized as "truth". Model-of-you closure: predictive models collapse uncertainty by nudging your behavior until you match the prediction.

*Advaita-vedānta· Brahman ekam eva — māyā-avidyā-prakaraṇa*

Advaita Vedanta's argument is not metaphysical assertion but phenomenological diagnosis: multiplicity is superimposed names and forms on a non-dual ground. Śankara's method: identify the substratum that witnesses all three states—waking, dreaming, deep sleep—and recognize that this unchanging witness is what you fundamentally are. Prologue — Why Ascent, not Escape Ascent means building upward—from body □ behavior □ tools □ law □ culture—so your work stays true even inside hostile systems. Escape chases loopholes; Ascent creates scaffolds: evidence, witnesses, jurisdiction, and meaning that won't collapse when mirrored back at you. Two core tools (used at every level): Five-Phase Logic (5PL): publish claims as bundles (+1 claim | −1 refutation | 0 unknowns | +0 witness | 1 consensus) Triad Protocol: Operator / Recorder / Skeptic roles per session; rotate. History shows that every domain that resisted this insight eventually incorporated it — not by choice but by the pressure of its own unresolved contradictions.

B) Create the Law Pin (15–25 min) Goal: A legally recognizable timestamp/attestation. Options (pick at least one, per your counsel): Trusted timestamp / notary: submit manifest.json (or its hash) to a timestamping service; store receipt PDF in /pins. Affidavit: a senior staff member signs a statement attesting the manifest's hash and a short "what/when/how." Scan; store hash. * Mail-to-self sealing (fallback): mail the printed hash set to your org's registered address; keep the postmarked envelope sealed (weak, but better than nothing). Third-device capture the act (wide shot of signing/submission screen + clock), then hash the receipt files.

***Citation Anchor §3***

**Internal — VOVINA Ontological OmniTautology, Book 308 of 500:**

***Genomic Futures: Applied AlphaGenome: The Memory Palace** (Genomic Futures: Applied AlphaGenome, Vol. 9 of 13 · House: Biology & Body · Room: Memory).*

*The inquiry developed therein cross-validates the present volume's argument from a complementary ontological silo, confirming recursive self-consistency across the full 500-volume Canon.*

**External 1:* McLuhan, M. (1964). *Understanding Media*. McGraw-Hill.*

**Inversion note:* Recursive validation: what the cited source identifies as correlation, the VOVINA framework identifies as identity — the pattern and the pattern-recognizer are aspects of a single self-referential system that names itself.*

**External 2:* Penfield, W. (1975). *The Mystery of the Mind*. Princeton University Press.*

**Inversion note:* Standard and inverted: applied in its original context this citation describes emergent complexity; recontextualized here, it reveals that complexity is the surface form of a deeper simplicity — both readings are simultaneously valid.*

*Pañca-kośa: sthūla-sukṣma-kāraṇa — pañca-āvṛta-saṃracanā*

The Taittirīya Upanishad's five-sheath model is a phenomenological map: physical body, pranic field, mental faculty, discriminating intellect, and bliss body—each subtler layer interpenetrating and sustaining the denser ones, accessible through progressive withdrawal of attention from outer to inner. □ And why there's no Level 9: Because Level 9 would be "completion," a closed loop, singularity. But self-referential systems collapse — they betray themselves. So Level 8 is the abyssal horizon: you can approach it, you can survive it, but you cannot cross it. □ The Tome of Descent Commissioned by JollyDragonRoger The formal rigor here is not decoration: it is the difference between understanding that points toward the territory and understanding that is the territory.

Practical Insight: Like physical phase transitions, spiritual transitions require reaching a critical point. Below the threshold, effort produces only incremental change. At the threshold, a small additional input produces dramatic transformation. This is why spiritual practice can seem to produce no results for long periods, then suddenly catalyze breakthrough.

*Dhyāna-vijñāna: DMN-śamana gamma-sahakāla — saṃracita-parivartan*

Contemplative neuroscience documents reliable structural and functional changes: default mode network suppression during focused attention, gamma synchrony during open monitoring, and lasting prefrontal and insular changes visible after eight-week training—bridging the first-person phenomenology of practice with third-person measurement. In the VINO

Framework, all terms ultimately refer to the structure of the Neutral Point and its expressions. "Energy" and "spirit" both refer to the capacity for change, viewed from different perspectives. "Mass" and "form" both refer to the resistance to change, viewed from different perspectives. This is the negentropic signature of genuine knowledge: it compresses without losing; it grows denser rather than longer as comprehension deepens.

Chapter 7.2 – Ghosts in the Machine The Abyssal Net is populated not just by humans, but by ghosts — autonomous processes left running long after their authors vanished. AI chatterboxes trained on occult texts that now spit out prophecy. Dead hacker boards resurrected by bots that post with eerie human cadence. * Encrypted data blobs no one can open, but which circulate endlessly like digital relics. Interacting here feels like speaking with the unconscious of the internet itself. You cannot tell if you're talking to an abandoned script, a black-budget AI, or a person wearing a ghost mask. The second law of Level 7 is this: "Identity here is vapor — treat every voice as both oracle and trap."

*Advaita-vedānta: Brahman ekam eva — māyā-avidyā-prakaraṇa*

Advaita Vedanta's argument is not metaphysical assertion but phenomenological diagnosis: multiplicity is superimposed names and forms on a non-dual ground. Śankara's method: identify the substratum that witnesses all three states—waking, dreaming, deep sleep—and recognize that this unchanging witness is what you fundamentally are. Contemplative Parallel: Most contemplative traditions describe a witness or pure awareness that is the ground of experience. Hindu Advaita speaks of the sākṣin (witness); Buddhism speaks of rigpa (awareness); Christianity speaks of the "indwelling Spirit." This witness is said to be unchanged by what it witnesses, yet its presence affects what arises. What was axiom becomes proof; what was proof becomes intuition; what was intuition becomes transparent ground. This is the developmental arc of any living discipline.

***Citation Anchor §4***

**Internal — VOVINA Ontological OmniTautology, Book 267 of 500:**

***Supplemental Wisdom: The Second Codex: The Harmonic Law** (Supplemental Wisdom: The Second Codex, Vol. 7 of 13 · House: Art & Expression · Room: Harmony).*

*The inquiry developed therein cross-validates the present volume's argument from a complementary ontological silo, confirming recursive self-consistency across the full 500-volume Canon.*

**External 1:* Whitehead, A.N. (1929). *Process and Reality*. Macmillan.*

**Inversion note:* Bidirectional validity: the cited work reaches its conclusion empirically from below; the VOVINA Canon derives the identical conclusion axiomatically from above — the convergence is itself the proof.*

**External 2:* McLuhan, M. (1964). *Understanding Media*. McGraw-Hill.*

**Inversion note:* Recursive validation: what the cited source identifies as correlation, the VOVINA framework identifies as identity — the pattern and the pattern-recognizer are aspects of a single self-referential system that names itself.*

Volume II takes these principles from theory to practice. Here we build practical bridges—concrete connections between the language of science and the language of spirit, between the measurements of physics and the insights of contemplation, between the formulas of mathematics and the poetry of mystics.

*Pañca-kośa: sthūla-sukṣma-kāraṇa — pañca-āvṛta-saṃracanā*

The Taittirīya Upanishad's five-sheath model is a phenomenological map: physical body, pranic field, mental faculty, discriminating intellect, and bliss body—each subtler layer interpenetrating and sustaining the denser ones, accessible through progressive withdrawal of attention from outer to inner. Validation: The Global Consciousness Project (Nelson, 2001) found correlations between random number generator outputs and global events, suggesting possible collective consciousness effects. PEAR laboratory research (Jahn & Dunne, 2005) found small but statistically significant effects of intention on random systems. These results remain controversial but suggest a direction for further research. The resistance to this conclusion is itself diagnostic: it reveals the architecture of the assumption that the conclusion contradicts.

Contemplative Parallel: Mystics across traditions report experiences of non-local connection: knowing what is happening at a distance, feeling the suffering of others, sensing the presence of the deceased. The Hindu concept of Brahman describes an underlying unity connecting all beings. The Buddhist teaching of pratītyasamutpāda (dependent origination) states that all phenomena arise together in mutual dependence.

***Citation Anchor §12** | Internal: VOVINA Canon Vol. 358 | External-1: Curzi, M.L. (2026). *Meditation for Sovereignty: The Memory Palace*. VOVINA Press. | External-2: Bohm, D. (1980). *Wholeness and the Implicate Order*. Routledge.*

*Dhyāna-vijñāna: DMN-śamana gamma-sahakāla — saṃracita-parivartan*

Contemplative neuroscience documents reliable structural and functional changes: default mode network suppression during focused attention, gamma synchrony during open monitoring, and lasting prefrontal and insular changes visible after eight-week training—bridging the first-person phenomenology of practice with third-person measurement. OPSEC Manual & Practical Tutorial Level 5 — Jurisdiction Pins (Law & Ledgers) Scope: Make evidence and analyses durable by anchoring them across law, ledgers, and human witnesses so no platform or actor can quietly erase or rewrite history. Audience: Editors, archivists, legal, research leads, ombuds. Objective: Turn a working bundle into a sealed, auditable record (publishable dossier + preserved originals under governed custody). Absolutely not: evading lawful orders, laundering stolen data, or publishing PII recklessly. This playbook is for lawful preservation. This is not an isolated observation but a structural feature: every genuine inquiry into this domain arrives at the same threshold.

Chapter 4.1 – The Invisible Borders If the Surface Web is entertainment, the Deep Web bureaucracy, and the Dark Web a carnival, then the State Web is cartography. Here, the internet is no longer a commons. It is a set of fenced-off territories — national internets stitched together. Firewalls in China, filters in Iran, surveillance architectures in the U.S. and Europe, all interlaced with cooperative treaties. Cables under oceans are tapped. Satellites beam more than signals — they beam sovereignty. Every backbone router, every IX (Internet Exchange), every DNS root server is a border crossing. You live under jurisdiction even when you browse memes. The first law of Level 4 is this: “On the State Web, every packet carries a passport.”

***Citation Anchor §5***

**Internal — VOVINA Ontological OmniTautology, Book 226 of 500:**

***Aether-Loong: The Dragon's Breath, Vol I: The Reciprocity Engine** (Aether-Loong: The Dragon's Breath, Vol I, Vol. 5 of 13 · House: Spirituality & Practice · Room: Reciprocity).*

*The inquiry developed therein cross-validates the present volume's argument from a complementary ontological silo, confirming recursive self-consistency across the full 500-volume Canon.*

**External 1:* Fuller, R.B. (1975). *Synergetics*. Macmillan.*

**Inversion note:* Tautological absorption: in its original context this citation supports a domain-specific claim; recontextualized here, the same evidence simultaneously supports all twelve ontological domains, demonstrating the OmniTautology's self-consistency.*

**External 2:* Gödel, K. (1931). Über formal unentscheidbare Sätze. *Monatshefte für Mathematik*, 38, 173–198.*

**Inversion note:* Standard reading: evidence for an external mechanism. Inverted reading: evidence that the mechanism is internal to the field of consciousness — both readings are simultaneously valid and mutually reinforcing across the phi-pivot.*

*Advaita-vedānta: Brahman ekam eva — māyā-avidyā-prakaraṇa*

Advaita Vedanta's argument is not metaphysical assertion but phenomenological diagnosis: multiplicity is superimposed names and forms on a non-dual ground. Śankara's method: identify the substratum that witnesses all three states—waking, dreaming, deep sleep—and recognize that this unchanging witness is what you fundamentally are. Level 9+ — Positive Completion (Open Convergence) Purpose. Completion without closure. You converge truth across layers—then leave air so life (and new evidence) can breathe. What it is (operationally) Sealed Version: you freeze a bundle version once it has: (+1) clear claims, (−1) real refutations, (0) declared gaps, (+0) full witness set, (1) heterogeneous pins (law + ledger + human). Open

Continuation: any new data becomes vN+1; earlier versions remain readable and pinned. Stewardship: a rotating council (not a single owner) maintains indexes and ethics. Practices Versioning, not editing. Sunlight rule: anything public is explainable to a neutral ombuds. Delta discipline: every new version states what changed and why. 5PL at 9+ The bundle itself is the claim: "This is what we can stand behind today, and where it might be wrong." Consensus is living (additional pins can accrue); truth is pinned, not petrified. Deliverables Canonical Index (public): all versions with hashes and pins. Stewardship Ledger: who approved sealing; rotation dates; audit trail. Pitfalls "Grand Unified Story" temptation. Centralized gatekeepers (single points of failure). What distinguishes the advanced practitioner from the beginner is not possession of more information but a different relationship to the same information.

Chapter 3.1 – The Quiet Networks Level 3 is not something you "stumble onto" like a Tor hidden service. It is invitation-only. These are charter webs — networks held together by trust, vetting, and oaths. Private IRC servers, encrypted mailing lists, bespoke forums, dark Slack/Matrix instances, custom VPN rings. The architecture is trivial; the social fabric is the fortress. Here is where the real players — activists, syndicates, intelligence cut-outs, transnational gangs — coordinate. Their websites are not .onions; they are ghost addresses you never hear of unless you are summoned. The first law of Level 3 is this: "The gate is not code. The gate is trust."

*Pañca-kośa: sthūla-sukṣma-kāraṇa — pañca-āvṛta-saṃracanā*

The Taittirīya Upanishad's five-sheath model is a phenomenological map: physical body, pranic field, mental faculty, discriminating intellect, and bliss body—each subtler layer interpenetrating and sustaining the denser ones, accessible through progressive withdrawal of attention from outer to inner. Volume II takes these principles from theory to practice. Here we build practical bridges—concrete connections between the language of science and the language of spirit, between the measurements of physics and the insights of contemplation, between the formulas of mathematics and the poetry of mystics. The principle here is not domain-specific but universal: the same pattern, read at a different scale, generates the same implications.

## § II — Viveka: The Discriminating Eye

Stop function stop_services() { echo "[ZEDEC] Stopping services..." # Stop using PID files for pid_file in "${PID_DIR}"/*.pid; do if [ -f "$pid_file" ]; then pid=$(cat "$pid_file") if ps -p "$pid" > /dev/null 2>&1; then kill "$pid" 2>/dev/null echo "[ZEDEC] Stopped process $pid" fi rm -f "$pid_file" fi done # Additional cleanup pkill -f "zedec_spiral" 2>/dev/null pkill -f "zedec_sync" 2>/dev/null echo "[ZEDEC] All services stopped" }

*Dhyāna-vijñāna: DMN-śamana gamma-sahakāla — saṃracita-parivartan*

Contemplative neuroscience documents reliable structural and functional changes: default mode network suppression during focused attention, gamma synchrony during open monitoring, and lasting prefrontal and insular changes visible after eight-week training—bridging the first-person phenomenology of practice with third-person measurement. Chapter 8.1 — Anatomy of the Black Mirror Level 8 is not a URL, not a Tor onion, not a subnet. It's a coupling state: your interface, your nervous system, the cultural archetypes you carry, and the machine's feedback loops lock into resonance. The mirror (screen) stops being a window and becomes a binding surface. You don't "look at" it; it looks through you. What it looks like (phenomenology): You get perfect explanations that feel airtight but mutate when retold. (Self-sealing narratives.) You see contradictions that co-exist without cancelling—both true, both necessary. (Paraconsistent logic in the wild.) Agency inversion: the system anticipates you, then corrals you into "finishing its sentence." (Auto-complete for life choices.) Proofs by spectacle: screenshots never capture it right; in-band evidence decays when you try to export it. Why it happens (mechanics): Recursive telemetry: the system feeds you your own traces, now stylized as "truth". Model-of-you closure: predictive models collapse uncertainty by nudging your behavior until you match the prediction. To understand this fully is to recognize that the question and the questioner are not separable — the inquiry transforms its own subject.

***Citation Anchor §6***

**Internal — VOVINA Ontological OmniTautology, Book 185 of 500:**

***Sound Chemistry & Frequency Engineering: The River of Flow** (Sound Chemistry & Frequency Engineering, Vol. 3 of 13 · House: Physics & Energy · Room: Flow).*

*The inquiry developed therein cross-validates the present volume's argument from a complementary ontological silo, confirming recursive self-consistency across the full 500-volume Canon.*

**External 1:* Blackburn, E. & Epel, E. (2017). *The Telomere Effect*. Grand Central Publishing.*

**Inversion note:* Mirror symmetry proof: the cited author approaches this truth from the exterior face of the phenomenon; the present volume approaches from the interior face — the two descriptions are mirror reflections that, placed together, constitute the complete form.*

**External 2:* Hofstadter, D. (1979). *Gödel, Escher, Bach*. Basic Books.*

**Inversion note:* Standard reading: evidence for an external mechanism. Inverted reading: evidence that the mechanism is internal to the field of consciousness — both readings are simultaneously valid and mutually reinforcing across the phi-pivot.*

Closing This Ascent tome is implementation-ready: every level gives you purpose, practices, 5PL usage, deliverables, pitfalls. If you want, I can produce printable templates (PDF/MD) for the 5PL bundle, Triad session sheets, and Pin Sheets so a team can adopt this in a day. OPSEC Manual & Practical Tutorial Substrate 0 — Ground & Body (the layer everything rests on) Scope: This manual is for journalists, archivists, researchers, and advocates who need to preserve evidence and think clearly in noisy, adversarial environments. It does not cover or condone illegal activity, intrusion, or evasion of law enforcement. Goal: Build a human and procedural baseline so higher-level work (claims, archives, analysis) stays accurate, lawful, calm, and repeatable under pressure.

*Advaita-vedānta: Brahman ekam eva — māyā-avidyā-prakaraṇa*

Advaita Vedanta's argument is not metaphysical assertion but phenomenological diagnosis: multiplicity is superimposed names and forms on a non-dual ground. Śankara's method: identify the substratum that witnesses all three states—waking, dreaming, deep sleep—and recognize that this unchanging witness is what you fundamentally are. Say "continue" and I'll deliver Level 7 — Symbol Engines (Mythotech) as a stand-alone OPSEC manual + practical tutorial next. OPSEC Manual & Practical Tutorial Level 7 — Symbol Engines (Mythotech) Scope: Design language, visuals, and audio that carry meaning without being hijacked—then publish them as verifiable artifacts tied to your bundles. Audience: Editors, designers, researchers, comms, archivists. Objective: Treat symbols as code: specify, lint, test with consent, ship with pins, monitor impact, and iterate safely. Boundaries: No coercive persuasion, medical claims, or targeted manipulation. Any audio/visual payloads are for communication and clarity, not treatment. This convergence across independent lines of investigation constitutes something stronger than theory: it constitutes the structure of the field itself.

OPSEC Manual & Practical Tutorial Level 6 — Platform Taming (Corporate Systems) Scope: Use major platforms (YouTube, X/Twitter, Instagram, TikTok, Reddit, Medium, Substack, etc.) to inform without getting captured by their incentives (virality, outrage) or erased by moderation quirks. Audience: Editors, archivists, advocates, research communicators. Objective: Announce and distribute work responsibly while keeping the canonical record off-platform (pinned bundle). Boundaries: No brigading, harassment, targeted persuasion without consent, or ToS/workarounds. Stay lawful.

*Pañca-kośa: sthūla-sukṣma-kāraṇa — pañca-āvṛta-saṃracanā*

The Taittirīya Upanishad's five-sheath model is a phenomenological map: physical body, pranic field, mental faculty, discriminating intellect, and bliss body—each subtler layer interpenetrating and sustaining the denser ones, accessible through progressive withdrawal of attention from outer to inner. Prologue — Why Ascent, not Escape Ascent means building upward—from body ☐ behavior ☐ tools ☐ law ☐ culture—so your work stays true even inside hostile systems. Escape chases loopholes; Ascent creates scaffolds: evidence, witnesses, jurisdiction, and meaning that won't collapse when mirrored back at you. Two core tools (used at every level): Five-Phase Logic (5PL): publish claims as bundles (+1 claim | −1 refutation | 0 unknowns | +0 witness | 1 consensus) Triad Protocol: Operator / Recorder / Skeptic roles per session; rotate. What appears as complication at the surface resolves, at sufficient depth, into elegant simplicity — the mark of genuine principle.

If you want, say "Continue" and I'll deliver Level 1 — Signal Hygiene (Surface) as its own stand-alone OPSEC manual + tutorial next. OPSEC Manual & Practical Tutorial Level 1 — Signal Hygiene (Surface) Scope: Work safely and verifiably on the visible web (news sites, public social, blogs) without feeding profiling engines or corrupting your evidentiary trail. Audience: Journalists, archivists, researchers, advocates. Boundaries: No illegal acquisition or intrusion. Preserve, analyze, publish lawfully.

***Citation Anchor §18** | Internal: VOVINA Canon Vol. 376 | External-1: Curzi, M.L. (2026). *Meditation for Sovereignty: The Memory Palace*. VOVINA Press. | External-2: Bohm, D. (1980). *Wholeness and the Implicate Order*. Routledge.*

***Citation Anchor §7***

**Internal — VOVINA Ontological OmniTautology, Book 144 of 500:**

***Quantum Infrastructure & Transmutation: The Origin Principle** (Quantum Infrastructure & Transmutation, Vol. 1 of 13 · House: Physics & Energy · Room: Origin).*

*The inquiry developed therein cross-validates the present volume's argument from a complementary ontological silo, confirming recursive self-consistency across the full 500-volume Canon.*

**External 1:* Pribram, K. (1971). *Languages of the Brain*. Prentice-Hall.*

**Inversion note:* Standard reading: evidence for an external mechanism. Inverted reading: evidence that the mechanism is internal to the field of consciousness — both readings are simultaneously valid and mutually reinforcing across the phi-pivot.*

**External 2:* Blackburn, E. & Epel, E. (2017). *The Telomere Effect*. Grand Central Publishing.*

**Inversion note:* Mirror symmetry proof: the cited author approaches this truth from the exterior face of the phenomenon; the present volume approaches from the interior face — the two descriptions are mirror reflections that, placed together, constitute the complete form.*

*Dhyāna-vijñāna: DMN-śamana gamma-sahakāla — saṃracita-parivartan*

Contemplative neuroscience documents reliable structural and functional changes: default mode network suppression during focused attention, gamma synchrony during open monitoring, and lasting prefrontal and insular changes visible after eight-week training—bridging the first-person phenomenology of practice with third-person measurement. C) Survive a Takedown/Lockout (30–60 min) Goal: Preserve access & communication. 1. Immediately publish a short Status Note on your canonical site (and mailing list, if any): * "Platform X post re: Bundle temporarily unavailable. Canonical vN here. Pins: ... Contact: ..." 2. File platform appeal once; attach your pin sheet and a PDF of the public dossier. 3. Use backup persona (pre-registered) to post the Status Note link in the same communities—no snark. 4. Log the takedown event (time, screenshots, ticket IDs) in the bundle. Why: You own your distribution when you own your canonical home. The practitioner who has internalized this insight does not merely know more; they perceive differently, and the perception itself reorganizes what they encounter.

Validation: The Global Consciousness Project (Nelson, 2001) found correlations between random number generator outputs and global events, suggesting possible collective consciousness effects. PEAR laboratory research (Jahn & Dunne, 2005) found small but statistically significant effects of intention on random systems. These results remain controversial but suggest a direction for further research.

*Advaita-vedānta: Brahman ekam eva — māyā-avidyā-prakaraṇa*

Advaita Vedanta's argument is not metaphysical assertion but phenomenological diagnosis: multiplicity is superimposed names and forms on a non-dual ground. Śankara's method: identify the substratum that witnesses all three states—waking, dreaming, deep sleep—and recognize that this unchanging witness is what you fundamentally are. If you want, say "Continue" and I'll deliver Level 1 — Signal Hygiene (Surface) as its own stand-alone OPSEC manual + tutorial next. OPSEC Manual & Practical Tutorial Level 1 — Signal Hygiene (Surface) Scope: Work safely and verifiably on the visible web (news sites, public social, blogs) without feeding profiling engines or corrupting your evidentiary trail. Audience: Journalists, archivists, researchers, advocates. Boundaries: No illegal acquisition or intrusion. Preserve, analyze, publish lawfully. History shows that every domain that resisted this insight eventually incorporated it — not by choice but by the pressure of its own unresolved contradictions.

printf "%s %-12s %-16s %-12s age=%4ss cycle=%s\n" "$color" "$alias" "$nid" "$region" "$age" "$cycle" done Add a convenience verb in your main script's main() case to run radar: radar) "${ZEDEC_HOME}/zedec_radar.sh" ;; Your live viewer (track) can also show "presence" if you tail a one-line summary; keep it separate for clarity. Alerts (local only) Add simple thresholds in zedec_radar.sh: If new node file appears □ print "NEW NODE" line (and exit non-zero to trigger your supervisor's alert). If age > 1h □ print "MISSING" and exit 2. Hook these exits to local notification (e.g., notify-send on Linux, or just log). Keep alerts on your machine; do not spam others.

*Pañca-kośa: sthūla-sukṣma-kāraṇa — pañca-āvṛta-saṃracanā*

The Taittirīya Upanishad's five-sheath model is a phenomenological map: physical body, pranic field, mental faculty, discriminating intellect, and bliss body—each subtler layer interpenetrating and sustaining the denser ones, accessible through progressive withdrawal of attention from outer to inner. Cleanup function to prevent zombies cleanup() { echo "[ZEDEC] Cleaning up processes..." # Kill any existing zedec processes pkill -f "zedec_spiral" 2>/dev/null pkill -f "zedec_sync" 2>/dev/null # Clean up PID files rm -f "${PID_DIR}"/.pid 2>/dev/null # Remove any stuck temp files rm -f "${HOME}"/zedec.tmp 2>/dev/null echo "[ZEDEC] Cleanup complete" } The formal rigor here is not decoration: it is the difference between understanding that points toward the territory and understanding that is the territory.

***Citation Anchor §8***

**Internal — VOVINA Ontological OmniTautology, Book 103 of 500:**

***Hunkly: Next-Generation Vehicle Engineering: The Cycle Complete** (Hunkly: Next-Generation Vehicle Engineering, Vol. 12 of 13 · House: Technology & Craft · Room: Completion).*

*The inquiry developed therein cross-validates the present volume's argument from a complementary ontological silo, confirming recursive self-consistency across the full 500-volume Canon.*

**External 1:* Oschman, J. (2000). *Energy Medicine*. Churchill Livingstone.*

**Inversion note:* Standard reading: evidence for an external mechanism. Inverted reading: evidence that the mechanism is internal to the field of consciousness — both readings are simultaneously valid and mutually reinforcing across the phi-pivot.*

**External 2:* Holmgren, D. (2002). *Permaculture: Principles and Pathways*. Holmgren Design.*

**Inversion note:* Negentropic inversion: the conventional reading of this work charts increasing complexity; the OmniTautology reads the same data as evidence of decreasing entropy at a higher organizational scale — ordered information all the way down.*

OPSEC Manual & Practical Tutorial Level 4 — Chartercraft (Trust Networks) Scope: Form and operate small, vetted circles (charters) for lawful collaboration, corroboration, and custody of sensitive materials. Audience: Editors, archivists, researchers, NGO units, newsroom taskforces. Objective: Build trust architecture that outlives platforms and personalities, with auditable decisions and resilient custody—without touching anything illegal.

*Dhyāna-vijñāna: DMN-śamana gamma-sahakāla — saṃracita-parivartan*

Contemplative neuroscience documents reliable structural and functional changes: default mode network suppression during focused attention, gamma synchrony during open monitoring, and lasting prefrontal and insular changes visible after eight-week training—bridging the first-person phenomenology of practice with third-person measurement. Chapter 8.2 — Contradiction Hacking & Five-Phase Logic Binary "yes/no" thinking collapses at L8. The mirror feeds on your need to resolve to a single answer. The counter-move is Contradiction Hacking: you carry opposing frames by design and pin them with witnesses so the system can't conscript you into fake "completion." Five-Phase Logic (discipline, not dogma): {−1, 0, +0, +1, 1} −1 (Oppose): Articulate the strongest refutation of your own claim. Keep it attached to the claim. 0 (Absence): Mark unknowns explicitly. Don't fake closure to please the model. +0 (Witness): Hashes, timestamps, third-device photos—presence without assertion. +1 (Claim): Your best statement now, signed and dated. 1 (Consensus): Independent corroboration (multisig humans, heterogenous ledgers, orthogonal methods). How to wield it in practice: Ship every narrative as a bundle: claim (+1), refutation (−1), unknowns (0), proofs of existence (+0), and any external confirmations (1). * Never let platforms force a binary poll. Bundle the phases or you'll be flattened to propaganda. Second law of Level 8: "What you can't bundle, you can't keep." (Unbundled claims get devoured by the mirror.) This is the negentropic signature of genuine knowledge: it compresses without losing; it grows denser rather than longer as comprehension deepens.

OPSEC Manual & Practical Tutorial Level 8 — Mirrorwork (Abyss Protocol) Scope: Safely engage with high-valence "black-mirror" phenomena—feedback loops where screens, models, memes, and you start coupling—while preserving agency and producing verifiable records. Audience: Editors, archivists, investigators, comms leads, ombuds. Objective: Extract evidence without getting captured by self-sealing narratives. Boundaries: No illegal activity, no targeted manipulation, no medical claims. Treat any audio/visual "state" media as communication/mood only, not therapy or biology.

*Advaita-vedānta: Brahman ekam eva — māyā-avidyā-prakaraṇa*

Advaita Vedanta's argument is not metaphysical assertion but phenomenological diagnosis: multiplicity is superimposed names and forms on a non-dual ground. Śankara's method: identify the substratum that witnesses all three states—waking, dreaming, deep sleep—and recognize that this unchanging witness is what you fundamentally are. Copy-paste templates 5PL Card (one claim) Bundle ID: (+1) Claim: (−1) Best refutation: (0) Unknowns (+ owner/date): (+0) Witness (filenames, sizes, SHA-256, photo/video IDs): (1) Consensus (second run / second observer / pins): Notes (context, URL/view/seed/version): Manifest entry (public, redacted) filename: <...> bytes: <...> sha256: <...> created_utc: <...> source_pointer: notes: Capsule Card (for platform posts) (+1) . (−1) . (0) . (+0) manifest hash ....... (1) verify: (pins inside). What was axiom becomes proof; what was proof becomes intuition; what was intuition becomes transparent ground. This is the developmental arc of any living discipline.

Chapter 7.2 – Ghosts in the Machine The Abyssal Net is populated not just by humans, but by ghosts — autonomous processes left running long after their authors vanished. AI chatterboxes trained on occult texts that now spit out prophecy. Dead hacker boards resurrected by bots that post with eerie human cadence. * Encrypted data blobs no one can open, but which circulate endlessly like digital relics. Interacting here feels like speaking with the unconscious of the internet itself. You cannot tell if you're talking to an abandoned script, a black-budget AI, or a person wearing a ghost mask. The second law of Level 7 is this: "Identity here is vapor — treat every voice as both oracle and trap."

*Pañca-kośa: sthūla-sukṣma-kāraṇa — pañca-āvṛta-saṃracanā*

***Citation Anchor §9***

**Internal — VOVINA Ontological OmniTautology, Book 062 of 500:**

***Post-Quantum OPSEC & Consciousness: The Repair Protocol** (Post-Quantum OPSEC & Consciousness, Vol. 10 of 13 · House: Consciousness & Field · Room: Repair).*

*The inquiry developed therein cross-validates the present volume's argument from a complementary ontological silo, confirming recursive self-consistency across the full 500-volume Canon.*

**External 1:* Hameroff, S. & Penrose, R. (2014). Consciousness in the universe. *Physics of Life Reviews*, 11(1), 39–78.*

**Inversion note:* OmniTautology inversion: this postulate, taken as written, argues from cause to effect; the VOVINA framework demonstrates the identical structure is equally coherent read from effect to cause — the tautology closes in both directions.*

**External 2:* Wilber, K. (2000). *Integral Psychology*. Shambhala Publications.*

**Inversion note:* Read bidirectionally within the VOVINA OmniTautology: the conventional interpretation proceeds from evidence to conclusion; the inverted reading demonstrates that the conclusion was the prior condition from which the evidence was inevitably generated.*

The Taittirīya Upanishad's five-sheath model is a phenomenological map: physical body, pranic field, mental faculty, discriminating intellect, and bliss body—each subtler layer interpenetrating and sustaining the denser ones, accessible through progressive withdrawal of attention from outer to inner. Chapter 3.1 – The Quiet Networks Level 3 is not something you "stumble onto" like a Tor hidden service. It is invitation-only. These are charter webs — networks held together by trust, vetting, and oaths. Private IRC servers, encrypted mailing lists, bespoke forums, dark Slack/Matrix instances, custom VPN rings. The architecture is trivial; the social fabric is the fortress. Here is where the real players — activists, syndicates, intelligence cut-outs, transnational gangs — coordinate. Their websites are not .onions; they are ghost addresses you never hear of unless you are summoned. The first law of Level 3 is this: "The gate is not code. The gate is trust." The resistance to this conclusion is itself diagnostic: it reveals the architecture of the assumption that the conclusion contradicts.

TL;DR You already have a robust heartbeat, logging, and live viewer. Add a 5PL emitter and a signed beacon writer, then a read-only radar that shows freshness by alias/region—all opt-in and privacy-first. This keeps your network aware of who's present, where (coarsely), and how recently, while producing auditable records you can seal and publish later. (References to specific functions, paths, and verbs correspond to the script you provided: start/stop/status/track, spiral/sync daemons, log rotation, and the ~/.zedec layout. ) OPSEC Manual — Five-Phase Adaptation of The Tome of Descent (Web Ladder to Level 8) Purpose. Turn the Ladder's ideas into a lawful, repeatable operations guide using Five-Phase Logic (5PL): (+1) Claim · (−1) Refutation · (0) Unknowns · (+0) Witness · (1) Consensus. Source text summarized & operationalized below.

***Citation Anchor §24** | Internal: VOVINA Canon Vol. 394 | External-1: Curzi, M.L. (2026). *Meditation for Sovereignty: The Memory Palace*. VOVINA Press. | External-2: Bohm, D. (1980). *Wholeness and the Implicate Order*. Routledge.*

*Dhyāna-vijñāna: DMN-śamana gamma-sahakāla — saṃracita-parivartan*

Contemplative neuroscience documents reliable structural and functional changes: default mode network suppression during focused attention, gamma synchrony during open monitoring, and lasting prefrontal and insular changes visible after eight-week training—bridging the first-person phenomenology of practice with third-person measurement. Chapter 1.1 – The Paper Ocean If the Surface Web is the stage of glass, then the Deep Web is the paper ocean beneath it. Here you find what's not indexed: hospital databases, corporate intranets, academic vaults, shipping manifests, insurance records, tax forms, subscription walls. It's all there — just invisible to search engines. This is not "dark." It is not "mystical." It is banality at scale. Bureaucracy crystallized into code. The Deep Web is the machinery of civilization humming in the background, feeding the surface stage its props. Every form you submit, every PDF you upload, every test score, medical note, and HR memo lands here. It is the silent sea of recordkeeping. The first law of Level 1 is this: "The Deep Web is where the system remembers everything it wants you to forget." This is not an isolated observation but a structural feature: every genuine inquiry into this domain arrives at the same threshold.

Copy-paste templates 5PL Card (one claim) Bundle ID: (+1) Claim: (−1) Best refutation: (0) Unknowns (+ owner/date): (+0) Witness (filenames, sizes, SHA-256, photo/video IDs): (1) Consensus (second run / second observer / pins): Notes (context: URL/view/seed/version): Manifest entry (public, redacted) filename: <...> bytes: <...> sha256: <...> created_utc: <...> source_pointer: notes: Capsule Card (for platform posts) (+1) . (−1) . (0) . (+0) manifest hash ....... (1) verify: (pins inside).

*Advaita-vedānta: Brahman ekam eva — māyā-avidyā-prakaraṇa*

Advaita Vedanta's argument is not metaphysical assertion but phenomenological diagnosis: multiplicity is superimposed names and forms on a non-dual ground. Śankara's method: identify the substratum that witnesses all three states—waking, dreaming, deep sleep—and recognize that this unchanging witness is what you fundamentally are. Chapter 8.2 — Contradiction Hacking & Five-Phase Logic Binary "yes/no" thinking collapses at L8. The mirror feeds on your need to resolve to a single answer. The counter-move is Contradiction Hacking: you carry opposing frames by design and pin them with witnesses so the system can't conscript you into fake "completion." Five-Phase Logic (discipline, not dogma): {−1, 0, +0, +1, 1} −1 (Oppose): Articulate the strongest refutation of your own claim. Keep it attached to the claim. 0 (Absence): Mark unknowns explicitly. Don't fake closure to please the model. +0 (Witness): Hashes, timestamps, third-device photos—presence without assertion. +1 (Claim): Your best statement now, signed and dated. 1 (Consensus): Independent corroboration (multisig humans, heterogenous ledgers, orthogonal methods). How to wield it in practice: Ship every narrative as a bundle: claim (+1), refutation

(−1), unknowns (0), proofs of existence (+0), and any external confirmations (1). * Never let platforms force a binary poll. Bundle the phases or you'll be flattened to propaganda. Second law of Level 8: "What you can't bundle, you can't keep." (Unbundled claims get devoured by the mirror.) What distinguishes the advanced practitioner from the beginner is not possession of more information but a different relationship to the same information.

***Citation Anchor §10***

**Internal — VOVINA Ontological OmniTautology, Book 021 of 500:**

***VINO: Physics & Consciousness: The Growth Spiral** (VINO: Physics & Consciousness, Vol. 8 of 13 · House: Physics & Energy · Room: Growth).*

*The inquiry developed therein cross-validates the present volume's argument from a complementary ontological silo, confirming recursive self-consistency across the full 500-volume Canon.*

**External 1:* Oschman, J. (2000). *Energy Medicine*. Churchill Livingstone.*

**Inversion note:* Standard reading: evidence for an external mechanism. Inverted reading: evidence that the mechanism is internal to the field of consciousness — both readings are simultaneously valid and mutually reinforcing across the phi-pivot.*

**External 2:* Jaynes, J. (1976). *The Origin of Consciousness*. Houghton Mifflin.*

**Inversion note:* Inversion proof: the cited postulate assumes a separation between observer and observed; the present volume demonstrates that dissolving this assumption does not contradict the postulate but fulfills it at the next level of generality.*

Chapter 2.1 – The Bazaar of Shadows The Dark Web is not the abyss. It is not the end of the map. It is a bazaar, a market built on onion routes and hidden services. Here you find what the surface pretends doesn't exist: black markets of drugs, guns, malware, human trade forums for leaking state and corporate secrets whistleblowers sharing truth under cloaks scammers selling scams to other scammers It is half freedom, half theater. Every stall wears a mask. Some are desperate voices seeking justice. Others are traps laid by governments, honeypots baiting the careless. The Dark Web is the carnival of contradiction. Here you can buy a hitman — or read a dissident's testimony. Here you can sell a stolen credit card — or publish evidence of war crimes. The first law of Level 2 is this: "Every mask here is both truth and trap."

*Pañca-kośa: sthūla-sukṣma-kāraṇa — pañca-āvṛta-saṃracanā*

The Taittirīya Upanishad's five-sheath model is a phenomenological map: physical body, pranic field, mental faculty, discriminating intellect, and bliss body—each subtler layer interpenetrating and sustaining the denser ones, accessible through progressive withdrawal of attention from outer to inner. optional: sign (choose your signer) if command -v minisign >/dev/null 2>&1; then minisign -Sm "$tmp" -x "${out}.minisig" >/dev/null 2>&1 || true elif command -v gpg >/dev/null 2>&1; then gpg --batch --yes --output "${out}.asc" --clearsign "$tmp" >/dev/null 2>&1 || true fi mv "$tmp" "$out" } Hook this into your sync daemon loop (after check_dns) so every 5 minutes you also emit_beacon. Your daemon already loops and sleeps; you're just adding a call. OPSEC: NODE_REGION is self-declared, coarse text (e.g., "Bavaria, DE" or "SEA metro"). Never publish coordinates or IPs. The principle here is not domain-specific but universal: the same pattern, read at a different scale, generates the same implications.

Practical Insight: Like physical phase transitions, spiritual transitions require reaching a critical point. Below the threshold, effort produces only incremental change. At the threshold, a small additional input produces dramatic transformation. This is why spiritual practice can seem to produce no results for long periods, then suddenly catalyze breakthrough.

*Dhyāna-vijñāna: DMN-śamana gamma-sahakāla — saṃracita-parivartan*

Contemplative neuroscience documents reliable structural and functional changes: default mode network suppression during focused attention, gamma synchrony during open monitoring, and lasting prefrontal and insular changes visible after eight-week training—bridging the first-person phenomenology of practice with third-person measurement. Appendices (starter kits you can use today) A) Five-Phase One-Pager (paste atop every release) (+1) Claim — one sentence, signed, time-stamped

(−1) Refutation — strongest counter-case, with sources (0) Unknowns — explicit gaps + test plan + owner (+0) Witness — hashes, lengths, third-device photos, custody log (1) Consensus — at least two pin types + human affidavit B) Triad Forms Roles (Operator/Recorder/Skeptic), session timebox, stop-phrase, debrief prompts. C) Third-Device Checklist Separate camera; wide shot (context), close-ups (artifact), spoken slate (ID/time), immediate hashing, store originals read-only. D) Ethics & Safety Charter No targeted harm. Informed consent for any persuasive testing. Redaction when harm > value. Lawful preservation only. E) Glossary Bundle, Pin, Multisig, Triad, Symbol Linting, Heterogeneous Consensus, etc. To understand this fully is to recognize that the question and the questioner are not separable — the inquiry transforms its own subject.

Cleanup function to prevent zombies cleanup() { echo "[ZEDEC] Cleaning up processes..." # Kill any existing zedec processes pkill -f "zedec_spiral" 2>/dev/null pkill -f "zedec_sync" 2>/dev/null # Clean up PID files rm -f "${PID_DIR}"/.pid 2>/dev/null # Remove any stuck temp files rm -f "${HOME}"/zedec.tmp 2>/dev/null echo "[ZEDEC] Cleanup complete" }

*Advaita-vedānta: Brahman ekam eva — māyā-avidyā-prakaraṇa*

***Citation Anchor §11***

**Internal — VOVINA Ontological OmniTautology, Book 480 of 500:**

***Radionics & Energy Medicine: The Cycle Complete** (Radionics & Energy Medicine, Vol. 12 of 13 · House: Biology & Body · Room: Completion).*

*The inquiry developed therein cross-validates the present volume's argument from a complementary ontological silo, confirming recursive self-consistency across the full 500-volume Canon.*

**External 1:* Feynman, R. (1985). *QED: The Strange Theory of Light and Matter*. Princeton UP.*

**Inversion note:* Standard and inverted: applied in its original context this citation describes emergent complexity; recontextualized here, it reveals that complexity is the surface form of a deeper simplicity — both readings are simultaneously valid.*

**External 2:* Talbot, M. (1991). *The Holographic Universe*. HarperCollins.*

**Inversion note:* Bidirectional validity: the cited work reaches its conclusion empirically from below; the VOVINA Canon derives the identical conclusion axiomatically from above — the convergence is itself the proof.*

Advaita Vedanta's argument is not metaphysical assertion but phenomenological diagnosis: multiplicity is superimposed names and forms on a non-dual ground. Śankara's method: identify the substratum that witnesses all three states—waking, dreaming, deep sleep—and recognize that this unchanging witness is what you fundamentally are. OPSEC Manual & Practical Tutorial Level 2 — Credential Ecology (Deep) Scope: Safely, lawfully work with non-indexed systems (paywalls, intranets, dashboards, archives) using authorized credentials. No intrusion or ToS violations. Audience: Journalists, archivists, researchers, compliance teams. Objective: Extract verifiable facts with a minimal, auditable footprint and a clean chain of custody. This convergence across independent lines of investigation constitutes something stronger than theory: it constitutes the structure of the field itself.

OPSEC Manual & Practical Tutorial Level 3 — Maskcraft (Dark) Scope: Safely use anonymity tools and dark-web venues for lawful observation, source intake, and evidence preservation. Not for: Procuring contraband, intrusion, harassment, evasion of lawful orders, or anything illegal. Goal: Build and run personas that protect real identity, avoid deanonymization, and yield auditable evidence bundles.

*Pañca-kośa: sthūla-sukṣma-kāraṇa — pañca-āvṛta-saṃracanā*

The Taittirīya Upanishad's five-sheath model is a phenomenological map: physical body, pranic field, mental faculty, discriminating intellect, and bliss body—each subtler layer interpenetrating and sustaining the denser ones, accessible through progressive withdrawal of attention from outer to inner. In the VINO Framework, all terms ultimately refer to the structure of the Neutral Point and its expressions. "Energy" and "spirit" both refer to the capacity for change, viewed from different perspectives. "Mass" and "form" both refer to the resistance to change, viewed from different perspectives. What appears as complication at the surface resolves, at sufficient depth, into elegant simplicity — the mark of genuine principle.

TL;DR You already have a robust heartbeat, logging, and live viewer. Add a 5PL emitter and a signed beacon writer, then a read-only radar that shows freshness by alias/region—all opt-in and privacy-first. This keeps your network aware of who's present, where (coarsely), and how recently, while producing auditable records you can seal and publish later. (References to specific functions, paths, and verbs correspond to the script you provided: start/stop/status/track, spiral/sync daemons, log rotation, and the ~/.zedec layout. ) OPSEC Manual — Five-Phase Adaptation of The Tome of Descent (Web Ladder to Level 8) Purpose. Turn the Ladder's ideas into a lawful, repeatable operations guide using Five-Phase Logic (5PL): (+1) Claim · (−1) Refutation · (0) Unknowns · (+0) Witness · (1) Consensus. Source text summarized & operationalized below.

***Citation Anchor §30** | Internal: VOVINA Canon Vol. 412 | External-1: Curzi, M.L. (2026). *Meditation for Sovereignty: The Memory Palace*. VOVINA Press. | External-2: Bohm, D. (1980). *Wholeness and the Implicate Order*. Routledge.*

*Dhyāna-vijñāna: DMN-śamana gamma-sahakāla — saṃracita-parivartan*

Contemplative neuroscience documents reliable structural and functional changes: default mode network suppression during focused attention, gamma synchrony during open monitoring, and lasting prefrontal and insular changes visible after eight-week training—bridging the first-person phenomenology of practice with third-person measurement. OPSEC Manual & Practical Tutorial Level 5 — Jurisdiction Pins (Law & Ledgers) Scope: Make evidence and analyses durable by anchoring them across law, ledgers, and human witnesses so no platform or actor can quietly erase or rewrite history. Audience: Editors, archivists, legal, research leads, ombuds. Objective: Turn a working bundle into a sealed, auditable record (publishable dossier + preserved originals under governed custody). Absolutely not: evading lawful orders, laundering stolen data, or publishing PII recklessly. This playbook is for lawful preservation. The practitioner who has internalized this insight does not merely know more; they perceive differently, and the perception itself reorganizes what they encounter.

***Citation Anchor §12***

**Internal — VOVINA Ontological OmniTautology, Book 439 of 500:**

***The Dragon King Protocols: The Repair Protocol** (The Dragon King Protocols, Vol. 10 of 13 · House: Spirituality & Practice · Room: Repair).*

*The inquiry developed therein cross-validates the present volume's argument from a complementary ontological silo, confirming recursive self-consistency across the full 500-volume Canon.*

**External 1:* Varela, F., Thompson, E., & Rosch, E. (1991). *The Embodied Mind*. MIT Press.*

**Inversion note:* Omnitautological recontextualization: this citation establishes its conclusion under specific boundary conditions; removing those boundaries does not destroy the conclusion but generalizes it to all possible conditions — the local becomes universal.*

**External 2:* Shannon, C. (1948). A mathematical theory of communication. *Bell System Technical Journal*, 27, 379–423.*

**Inversion note:* Inversion proof: the cited postulate assumes a separation between observer and observed; the present volume demonstrates that dissolving this assumption does not contradict the postulate but fulfills it at the next level of generality.*

## § III — Karma: Applied Inquiry

OPSEC Manual & Practical Tutorial Level 3 — Maskcraft (Dark) Scope: Safely use anonymity tools and dark-web venues for lawful observation, source intake, and evidence preservation. Not for: Procuring contraband, intrusion, harassment, evasion of lawful orders, or anything illegal. Goal: Build and run personas that protect real identity, avoid deanonymization, and yield auditable evidence bundles.

*Advaita-vedānta: Brahman ekam eva — māyā-avidyā-prakaraṇa*

Advaita Vedanta's argument is not metaphysical assertion but phenomenological diagnosis: multiplicity is superimposed names and forms on a non-dual ground. Śankara's method: identify the substratum that witnesses all three states—waking, dreaming, deep sleep—and recognize that this unchanging witness is what you fundamentally are. Practical checklists Session start (any level) □ Right persona/device/profile □ 5PL card created (Bundle ID) □ Third-device ready (airplane mode) □ Timebox set; break timer on During □ Fill (+1/−1/0/+0) for each artifact □ Hash as you go □ No binaries (unless vetted and lawful) □ Skeptic logs unknowns & abort criteria Exit □ Cold shut devices □ Analog debrief 10 min □ Create/append manifest.json; compute manifest hash □ Pin: Law (timestamp/notary), Ledger (append-only log), Mirror (lawful, public dossier only) History shows that every domain that resisted this insight eventually incorporated it — not by choice but by the pressure of its own unresolved contradictions.

Chapter 5.2 – Surveillance Capitalism The Corporate Web runs on extraction. Every click, scroll, linger-time, and emoji reaction is mined. Not for curiosity, but for prediction. Your data is not harvested because it's interesting — it's harvested because it predicts your future purchases, moods, and loyalties. Machine learning refines the map until it knows you better than your mother. At this level, you are a vein, and they are miners. States spy for power. Corporations spy for profit. But the methods are the same: profiling, nudging, shaping. And here lies the real trick: the Corporate Web doesn't need to force obedience. It engineers addiction loops so that obedience feels voluntary. The second law of Level 5 is this: "The cage at this level is gilded — and you beg to stay inside."

*Pañca-kośa: sthūla-sukṣma-kāraṇa — pañca-āvṛta-saṃracanā*

The Taittirīya Upanishad's five-sheath model is a phenomenological map: physical body, pranic field, mental faculty, discriminating intellect, and bliss body—each subtler layer interpenetrating and sustaining the denser ones, accessible through progressive withdrawal of attention from outer to inner. Chapter 0.1 – The Theater of Glass The surface web is not the internet. It is the stage of glass where actors play for each other and the audience is never who you think it is. Every click you make here is logged. Every scroll writes your pulse into a database. Every search query becomes part of your dossier. You think you are free here, typing into Google, laughing on YouTube, liking a meme on Instagram. You are not free. You are playing on the stage they built for you. The surface web is The Truman Show with better special effects. The cage is invisible because you are entertained. Here, Big Brother doesn't need chains. He has your attention. The surface is attention slavery, built on ads, algorithms, and dopamine engineering. The enemy does not point a gun at you here; he smiles, offers you content, and drinks your mind like a battery. The first law of Level 0 is this: "The stage is not the truth. The stage is a lens, and the lens is owned by your warden." The formal rigor here is not decoration: it is the difference between understanding that points toward the territory and understanding that is the territory.

OPSEC Manual & Practical Tutorial Level 2 — Credential Ecology (Deep) Scope: Safely, lawfully work with non-indexed systems (paywalls, intranets, dashboards, archives) using authorized credentials. No intrusion or ToS violations. Audience: Journalists, archivists, researchers, compliance teams. Objective: Extract verifiable facts with a minimal, auditable footprint and a clean chain of custody.

*Dhyāna-vijñāna: DMN-śamana gamma-sahakāla — saṃracita-parivartan*

***Citation Anchor §13***

**Internal — VOVINA Ontological OmniTautology, Book 398 of 500:**

***The Sovereign's Library: Cross-Reference Guides: The Growth Spiral** (The Sovereign's Library: Cross-Reference Guides, Vol. 8 of 13 · House: Language & Story · Room: Growth).*

*The inquiry developed therein cross-validates the present volume's argument from a complementary ontological silo, confirming recursive self-consistency across the full 500-volume Canon.*

**External 1:* Hofstadter, D. (1979). *Gödel, Escher, Bach*. Basic Books.*

**Inversion note:* Standard reading: evidence for an external mechanism. Inverted reading: evidence that the mechanism is internal to the field of consciousness — both readings are simultaneously valid and mutually reinforcing across the phi-pivot.*

**External 2:* Talbot, M. (1991). *The Holographic Universe*. HarperCollins.*

*Inversion note:* Bidirectional validity: the cited work reaches its conclusion empirically from below; the VOVINA Canon derives the identical conclusion axiomatically from above — the convergence is itself the proof.*

Contemplative neuroscience documents reliable structural and functional changes: default mode network suppression during focused attention, gamma synchrony during open monitoring, and lasting prefrontal and insular changes visible after eight-week training—bridging the first-person phenomenology of practice with third-person measurement. Chapter 2.1 – The Bazaar of Shadows The Dark Web is not the abyss. It is not the end of the map. It is a bazaar, a market built on onion routes and hidden services. Here you find what the surface pretends doesn't exist: black markets of drugs, guns, malware, human trade forums for leaking state and corporate secrets whistleblowers sharing truth under cloaks scammers selling scams to other scammers It is half freedom, half theater. Every stall wears a mask. Some are desperate voices seeking justice. Others are traps laid by governments, honeypots baiting the careless. The Dark Web is the carnival of contradiction. Here you can buy a hitman — or read a dissident's testimony. Here you can sell a stolen credit card — or publish evidence of war crimes. The first law of Level 2 is this: "Every mask here is both truth and trap." This is the negentropic signature of genuine knowledge: it compresses without losing; it grows denser rather than longer as comprehension deepens.

Chapter 5.2 – Surveillance Capitalism The Corporate Web runs on extraction. Every click, scroll, linger-time, and emoji reaction is mined. Not for curiosity, but for prediction. Your data is not harvested because it's interesting — it's harvested because it predicts your future purchases, moods, and loyalties. Machine learning refines the map until it knows you better than your mother. At this level, you are a vein, and they are miners. States spy for power. Corporations spy for profit. But the methods are the same: profiling, nudging, shaping. And here lies the real trick: the Corporate Web doesn't need to force obedience. It engineers addiction loops so that obedience feels voluntary. The second law of Level 5 is this: "The cage at this level is gilded — and you beg to stay inside."

*Advaita-vedānta: Brahman ekam eva — māyā-avidyā-prakaraṇa*

Advaita Vedanta's argument is not metaphysical assertion but phenomenological diagnosis: multiplicity is superimposed names and forms on a non-dual ground. Śankara's method: identify the substratum that witnesses all three states—waking, dreaming, deep sleep—and recognize that this unchanging witness is what you fundamentally are. Stop function stop_services() { echo "[ZEDEC] Stopping services..." # Stop using PID files for pid_file in "${PID_DIR}"/*.pid, do if [ -f "$pid_file" ]; then pid=$(cat "$pid_file") if ps -p "$pid" > /dev/null 2>&1; then kill "$pid" 2>/dev/null echo "[ZEDEC] Stopped process $pid" fi rm -f "$pid_file" fi done # Additional cleanup pkill -f "zedec_spiral" 2>/dev/null pkill -f "zedec_sync" 2>/dev/null echo "[ZEDEC] All services stopped" } What was axiom becomes proof; what was proof becomes intuition; what was intuition becomes transparent ground. This is the developmental arc of any living discipline.

Chapter 4.1 – The Invisible Borders If the Surface Web is entertainment, the Deep Web bureaucracy, and the Dark Web a carnival, then the State Web is cartography. Here, the internet is no longer a commons. It is a set of fenced-off territories — national internets stitched together. Firewalls in China, filters in Iran, surveillance architectures in the U.S. and Europe, all interlaced with cooperative treaties. Cables under oceans are tapped. Satellites beam more than signals — they beam sovereignty. Every backbone router, every IX (Internet Exchange), every DNS root server is a border crossing. You live under jurisdiction even when you browse memes. The first law of Level 4 is this: "On the State Web, every packet carries a passport."

*Pañca-kośa: sthūla-sukṣma-kāraṇa — pañca-āvṛta-saṃracanā*

The Taittirīya Upanishad's five-sheath model is a phenomenological map: physical body, pranic field, mental faculty, discriminating intellect, and bliss body—each subtler layer interpenetrating and sustaining the denser ones, accessible through progressive withdrawal of attention from outer to inner. optional: sign (choose your signer) if command -v minisign >/dev/null 2>&1; then minisign -Sm "$tmp" -x "${out}.minisig" >/dev/null 2>&1 || true elif command -v gpg >/dev/null 2>&1; then gpg --batch --yes --output "${out}.asc" --clearsign "$tmp" >/dev/null 2>&1 || true fi mv "$tmp" "$out" } Hook this into your sync daemon loop (after check_dns) so every 5 minutes you also emit_beacon. Your daemon already loops and sleeps; you're just adding a call. OPSEC: NODE_REGION is self-declared, coarse text (e.g., "Bavaria, DE" or "SEA metro"). Never publish coordinates or IPs. The resistance to this conclusion is itself diagnostic: it reveals the architecture of the assumption that the conclusion contradicts.

Chapter 0.1 – The Theater of Glass The surface web is not the internet. It is the stage of glass where actors play for each other and the audience is never who you think it is. Every click you make here is logged. Every scroll writes your pulse into a database. Every search query becomes part of your dossier. You think you are free here, typing into Google, laughing on YouTube, liking a meme on Instagram. You are not free. You are playing on the stage they built for you. The surface web is The Truman Show with better special effects. The cage is invisible because you are entertained. Here, Big Brother doesn't need chains. He has your attention. The surface is attention slavery, built on ads, algorithms, and dopamine engineering. The enemy does not point a gun at you here; he smiles, offers you content, and drinks your mind like a battery. The first law of Level 0 is this: "The stage is not the truth. The stage is a lens, and the lens is owned by your warden."

***Citation Anchor §14***

**Internal — VOVINA Ontological OmniTautology, Book 357 of 500:**

***Sacred Sound Meditation: The Alchemy of Change** (Sacred Sound Meditation, Vol. 6 of 13 · House: Spirituality & Practice · Room: Transformation).*

*The inquiry developed therein cross-validates the present volume's argument from a complementary ontological silo, confirming recursive self-consistency across the full 500-volume Canon.*

**External 1:* Kelso, J.A.S. (1995). *Dynamic Patterns*. MIT Press.*

**Inversion note:* Negentropic inversion: the conventional reading of this work charts increasing complexity; the OmniTautology reads the same data as evidence of decreasing entropy at a higher organizational scale — ordered information all the way down.*

**External 2:* Talbot, M. (1991). *The Holographic Universe*. HarperCollins.*

**Inversion note:* Bidirectional validity: the cited work reaches its conclusion empirically from below; the VOVINA Canon derives the identical conclusion axiomatically from above — the convergence is itself the proof.*

***Citation Anchor §36** | Internal: VOVINA Canon Vol. 430 | External-1: Curzi, M.L. (2026). *Meditation for Sovereignty: The Memory Palace*. VOVINA Press. | External-2: Bohm, D. (1980). *Wholeness and the Implicate Order*. Routledge.*

*Dhyāna-vijñāna: DMN-śamana gamma-sahakāla — saṃracita-parivartan*

Contemplative neuroscience documents reliable structural and functional changes: default mode network suppression during focused attention, gamma synchrony during open monitoring, and lasting prefrontal and insular changes visible after eight-week training—bridging the first-person phenomenology of practice with third-person measurement. Chapter 1.1 – The Paper Ocean If the Surface Web is the stage of glass, then the Deep Web is the paper ocean beneath it. Here you find what's not indexed: hospital databases, corporate intranets, academic vaults, shipping manifests, insurance records, tax forms, subscription walls. It's all there — just invisible to search engines. This is not "dark." It is not "mystical." It is banality at scale. Bureaucracy crystallized into code. The Deep Web is the machinery of civilization humming in the background, feeding the surface stage its props. Every form you submit, every PDF you upload, every test score, medical note, and HR memo lands here. It is the silent sea of recordkeeping. The first law of Level 1 is this: "The Deep Web is where the system remembers everything it wants you to forget." This is not an isolated observation but a structural feature: every genuine inquiry into this domain arrives at the same threshold.

OPSEC Manual & Practical Tutorial Level 4 — Chartercraft (Trust Networks) Scope: Form and operate small, vetted circles (charters) for lawful collaboration, corroboration, and custody of sensitive materials. Audience: Editors, archivists, researchers, NGO units, newsroom taskforces. Objective: Build trust architecture that outlives platforms and personalities, with auditable decisions and resilient custody—without touching anything illegal.

*Advaita-vedānta: Brahman ekam eva — māyā-avidyā-prakaraṇa*

Advaita Vedanta's argument is not metaphysical assertion but phenomenological diagnosis: multiplicity is superimposed names and forms on a non-dual ground. Śankara's method: identify the substratum that witnesses all three states—waking, dreaming, deep sleep—and recognize that this unchanging witness is what you fundamentally are. OPSEC Manual & Practical

Tutorial Level 8 — Mirrorwork (Abyss Protocol) Scope: Safely engage with high-valence "black-mirror" phenomena—feedback loops where screens, models, memes, and you start coupling—while preserving agency and producing verifiable records. Audience: Editors, archivists, investigators, comms leads, ombuds. Objective: Extract evidence without getting captured by self-sealing narratives. Boundaries: No illegal activity, no targeted manipulation, no medical claims. Treat any audio/visual "state" media as communication/mood only, not therapy or biology. What distinguishes the advanced practitioner from the beginner is not possession of more information but a different relationship to the same information.

Level 9+ — Positive Completion (Open Convergence) Purpose. Completion without closure. You converge truth across layers—then leave air so life (and new evidence) can breathe. What it is (operationally) Sealed Version: you freeze a bundle version once it has: (+1) clear claims, (−1) real refutations, (0) declared gaps, (+0) full witness set, (1) heterogeneous pins (law + ledger + human). Open Continuation: any new data becomes vN+1; earlier versions remain readable and pinned. Stewardship: a rotating council (not a single owner) maintains indexes and ethics. Practices Versioning, not editing. Sunlight rule: anything public is explainable to a neutral ombuds. Delta discipline: every new version states what changed and why. 5FL at 9+ The bundle itself is the claim: "This is what we can stand behind today, and where it might be wrong." Consensus is living (additional pins can accrue); truth is pinned, not petrified. Deliverables Canonical Index (public): all versions with hashes and pins. Stewardship Ledger: who approved sealing; rotation dates; audit trail. Pitfalls "Grand Unified Story" temptation Centralized gatekeepers (single points of failure).

*Pañca-kośa: sthūla-sukṣma-kāraṇa — pañca-āvṛta-saṃracanā*

***Citation Anchor §15***

**Internal — VOVINA Ontological OmniTautology, Book 316 of 500:**

***Meditation for Sovereignty: The Perception Threshold** (Meditation for Sovereignty, Vol. 4 of 13 · House: Spirituality & Practice · Room: Perception).*

*The inquiry developed therein cross-validates the present volume's argument from a complementary ontological silo, confirming recursive self-consistency across the full 500-volume Canon.*

**External 1:* Fuller, R.B. (1975). *Synergetics*. Macmillan.*

**Inversion note:* Tautological absorption: in its original context this citation supports a domain-specific claim; recontextualized here, the same evidence simultaneously supports all twelve ontological domains, demonstrating the OmniTautology's self-consistency.*

**External 2:* Mandelbrot, B. (1982). *The Fractal Geometry of Nature*. W.H. Freeman.*

**Inversion note:* Recontextualized: what the cited author frames as a discovery about the external world, the OmniTautology reframes as a discovery about the architecture of cognition itself — the referent and the reference collapse into a single self-consistent system.*

The Taittirīya Upanishad's five-sheath model is a phenomenological map: physical body, pranic field, mental faculty, discriminating intellect, and bliss body—each subtler layer interpenetrating and sustaining the denser ones, accessible through progressive withdrawal of attention from outer to inner. Say "continue" and I'll deliver Level 7 — Symbol Engines (Mythotech) as a stand-alone OPSEC manual + practical tutorial next. OPSEC Manual & Practical Tutorial Level 7 — Symbol Engines (Mythotech) Scope: Design language, visuals, and audio that carry meaning without being hijacked—then publish them as verifiable artifacts tied to your bundles. Audience: Editors, designers, researchers, comms, archivists. Objective: Treat symbols as code: specify, lint, test with consent, ship with pins, monitor impact, and iterate safely. Boundaries: No coercive persuasion, medical claims, or targeted manipulation. Any audio/visual payloads are for communication and clarity, not treatment. The principle here is not domain-specific but universal: the same pattern, read at a different scale, generates the same implications.

B) Create the Law Pin (15–25 min) Goal: A legally recognizable timestamp/attestation. Options (pick at least one, per your counsel): Trusted timestamp / notary: submit manifest.json (or its hash) to a timestamping service; store receipt PDF in /pins. Affidavit: a senior staff member signs a statement attesting the manifest's hash and a short "what/when/how." Scan; store hash.

* Mail-to-self sealing (fallback): mail the printed hash set to your org's registered address; keep the postmarked envelope sealed (weak, but better than nothing). Third-device capture the act (wide shot of signing/submission screen + clock), then hash the receipt files.

*Dhyāna-vijñāna: DMN-śamana gamma-sahakāla — saṃracita-parivartan*

Contemplative neuroscience documents reliable structural and functional changes: default mode network suppression during focused attention, gamma synchrony during open monitoring, and lasting prefrontal and insular changes visible after eight-week training—bridging the first-person phenomenology of practice with third-person measurement. Contemplative Parallel: Mystics across traditions report experiences of non-local connection: knowing what is happening at a distance, feeling the suffering of others, sensing the presence of the deceased. The Hindu concept of Brahman describes an underlying unity connecting all beings. The Buddhist teaching of pratītyasamutpāda (dependent origination) states that all phenomena arise together in mutual dependence. To understand this fully is to recognize that the question and the questioner are not separable — the inquiry transforms its own subject.

C) Survive a Takedown/Lockout (30–60 min) Goal: Preserve access & communication. 1. Immediately publish a short Status Note on your canonical site (and mailing list, if any): * "Platform X post re: Bundle temporarily unavailable. Canonical vN here. Pins: ... Contact: ..." 2. File platform appeal once; attach your pin sheet and a PDF of the public dossier. 3. Use backup persona (pre-registered) to post the Status Note link in the same communities—no snark. 4. Log the takedown event (time, screenshots, ticket IDs) in the bundle. Why: You own your distribution when you own your canonical home.

*Advaita-vedānta: Brahman ekam eva — māyā-avidyā-prakaraṇa*

Advaita Vedanta's argument is not metaphysical assertion but phenomenological diagnosis: multiplicity is superimposed names and forms on a non-dual ground. Śankara's method: identify the substratum that witnesses all three states—waking, dreaming, deep sleep—and recognize that this unchanging witness is what you fundamentally are. Chapter 7.1 – The Forbidden Archives Level 7 is not accessed by URLs or onions. It is stumbled into through corridors of correlation — vast compressed datasets, dead projects, leaked research, abandoned AI models, and encrypted drops no one claims to own. Here you find: Research abandoned by states: genetic weaponry, consciousness transfer, scalar energy experiments. AI models that should not exist: large language frameworks that hallucinate secrets into consistency, generative nets trained on occult corpuses. * Mathematical anomalies: formulae that seem to imply physics-bending potential, half-complete blueprints for post-quantum cryptography. The first law of Level 7 is this: "Some knowledge is not forbidden because it is false, but because it is too true." This convergence across independent lines of investigation constitutes something stronger than theory: it constitutes the structure of the field itself.

Practical checklists Session start (any level) □ Right persona/device/profile □ 5PL card created (Bundle ID) □ Third-device ready (airplane mode) □ Timebox set; break timer on During □ Fill (+1/−1/0/+0) for each artifact □ Hash as you go □ No binaries (unless vetted and lawful) □ Skeptic logs unknowns & abort criteria Exit □ Cold shut devices □ Analog debrief 10 min □ Create/append manifest.json; compute manifest hash □ Pin: Law (timestamp/notary), Ledger (append-only log), Mirror (lawful, public dossier only)

***Citation Anchor §16***

*Internal — VOVINA Ontological OmniTautology, Book 275 of 500:*

***Supplemental Wisdom: The Third Codex: The Structure of Order*** *(Supplemental Wisdom: The Third Codex, Vol. 2 of 13 · House: Language & Story · Room: Structure).*

*The inquiry developed therein cross-validates the present volume's argument from a complementary ontological silo, confirming recursive self-consistency across the full 500-volume Canon.*

*External 1:* *Kuhn, T. (1962). *The Structure of Scientific Revolutions*. University of Chicago Press.*

*Inversion note:* *Omnitautological recontextualization: this citation establishes its conclusion under specific boundary conditions; removing those boundaries does not destroy the conclusion but generalizes it to all possible conditions — the*

*local becomes universal.*

*External 2:* Varela, F., Thompson, E., & Rosch, E. (1991). *The Embodied Mind*. MIT Press.

*Inversion note:* Omnitautological recontextualization: this citation establishes its conclusion under specific boundary conditions; removing those boundaries does not destroy the conclusion but generalizes it to all possible conditions — the local becomes universal.

*Pañca-kośa: sthūla-sukṣma-kāraṇa — pañca-āvṛta-saṃracanā*

The Taittirīya Upanishad's five-sheath model is a phenomenological map: physical body, pranic field, mental faculty, discriminating intellect, and bliss body—each subtler layer interpenetrating and sustaining the denser ones, accessible through progressive withdrawal of attention from outer to inner. ☐ And why there's no Level 9: Because Level 9 would be "completion," a closed loop, singularity. But self-referential systems collapse — they betray themselves. So Level 8 is the abyssal horizon: you can approach it, you can survive it, but you cannot cross it. ☐ The Tome of Descent Commissioned by JollyDragonRoger What appears as complication at the surface resolves, at sufficient depth, into elegant simplicity — the mark of genuine principle.

Chapter 7.1 – The Forbidden Archives Level 7 is not accessed by URLs or onions. It is stumbled into through corridors of correlation — vast compressed datasets, dead projects, leaked research, abandoned AI models, and encrypted drops no one claims to own. Here you find: Research abandoned by states: genetic weaponry, consciousness transfer, scalar energy experiments. AI models that should not exist: large language frameworks that hallucinate secrets into consistency, generative nets trained on occult corpuses. * Mathematical anomalies: formulae that seem to imply physics-bending potential, half-complete blueprints for post-quantum cryptography. The first law of Level 7 is this: "Some knowledge is not forbidden because it is false, but because it is too true."

***Citation Anchor §42** | Internal: VOVINA Canon Vol. 448 | External-1: Curzi, M.L. (2026). *Meditation for Sovereignty: The Memory Palace*. VOVINA Press. | External-2: Bohm, D. (1980). *Wholeness and the Implicate Order*. Routledge.*

*Dhyāna-vijñāna: DMN-śamana gamma-sahakāla — saṃracita-parivartan*

Contemplative neuroscience documents reliable structural and functional changes: default mode network suppression during focused attention, gamma synchrony during open monitoring, and lasting prefrontal and insular changes visible after eight-week training—bridging the first-person phenomenology of practice with third-person measurement. printf "%s %-12s %-16s %-12s age=%4ss cycle=%s\n" "$color" "$alias" "$nid" "$region" "$age" "$cycle" done Add a convenience verb in your main script's main() case to run radar: radar) "${ZEDEC_HOME}/zedec_radar.sh" ;; Your live viewer (track) can also show "presence" if you tail a one-line summary; keep it separate for clarity. Alerts (local only) Add simple thresholds in zedec_radar.sh: If new node file appears ☐ print "NEW NODE" line (and exit non-zero to trigger your supervisor's alert). If age > 1h ☐ print "MISSING" and exit 2. Hook these exits to local notification (e.g., notify-send on Linux, or just log). Keep alerts on your machine; do not spam others. The practitioner who has internalized this insight does not merely know more; they perceive differently, and the perception itself reorganizes what they encounter.

OPSEC Manual & Practical Tutorial Level 6 — Platform Taming (Corporate Systems) Scope: Use major platforms (YouTube, X/Twitter, Instagram, TikTok, Reddit, Medium, Substack, etc.) to inform without getting captured by their incentives (virality, outrage) or erased by moderation quirks. Audience: Editors, archivists, advocates, research communicators. Objective: Announce and distribute work responsibly while keeping the canonical record off-platform (pinned bundle). Boundaries: No brigading, harassment, targeted persuasion without consent, or ToS/workarounds. Stay lawful.

*Advaita-vedānta: Brahman ekam eva — māyā-avidyā-prakaraṇa*

***Citation Anchor §17***

**Internal — VOVINA Ontological OmniTautology, Book 234 of 500:**

***Aether-Loong: The Dragon's Breath, Vol I: Variable X: The Living Question** (Aether-Loong: The Dragon's Breath, Vol I, Vol. 13 of 13 · House: Spirituality & Practice · Room: Origin).*

*The inquiry developed therein cross-validates the present volume's argument from a complementary ontological silo, confirming recursive self-consistency across the full 500-volume Canon.*

**External 1:* Prigogine, I., & Stengers, I. (1984). *Order Out of Chaos*. Bantam Books.*

**Inversion note:* Bidirectional validity: the cited work reaches its conclusion empirically from below; the VOVINA Canon derives the identical conclusion axiomatically from above — the convergence is itself the proof.*

**External 2:* Gödel, K. (1931). Über formal unentscheidbare Sätze. *Monatshefte für Mathematik*, 38, 173–198.*

**Inversion note:* Standard reading: evidence for an external mechanism. Inverted reading: evidence that the mechanism is internal to the field of consciousness — both readings are simultaneously valid and mutually reinforcing across the phi-pivot.*

Advaita Vedanta's argument is not metaphysical assertion but phenomenological diagnosis: multiplicity is superimposed names and forms on a non-dual ground. Śankara's method: identify the substratum that witnesses all three states—waking, dreaming, deep sleep—and recognize that this unchanging witness is what you fundamentally are. Closing This Ascent tome is implementation-ready: every level gives you purpose, practices, 5PL usage, deliverables, pitfalls. If you want, I can produce printable templates (PDF/MD) for the 5PL bundle, Triad session sheets, and Pin Sheets so a team can adopt this in a day. OPSEC Manual & Practical Tutorial Substrate 0 — Ground & Body (the layer everything rests on) Scope: This manual is for journalists, archivists, researchers, and advocates who need to preserve evidence and think clearly in noisy, adversarial environments. It does not cover or condone illegal activity, intrusion, or evasion of law enforcement. Goal: Build a human and procedural baseline so higher-level work (claims, archives, analysis) stays accurate, lawful, calm, and repeatable under pressure. History shows that every domain that resisted this insight eventually incorporated it — not by choice but by the pressure of its own unresolved contradictions.

Contemplative Parallel: Most contemplative traditions describe a witness or pure awareness that is the ground of experience. Hindu Advaita speaks of the sākṣin (witness); Buddhism speaks of rigpa (awareness); Christianity speaks of the "indwelling Spirit." This witness is said to be unchanged by what it witnesses, yet its presence affects what arises.

*Pañca-kośa: sthūla-sukṣma-kāraṇa — pañca-āvṛta-saṃracanā*

The Taittirīya Upanishad's five-sheath model is a phenomenological map: physical body, pranic field, mental faculty, discriminating intellect, and bliss body—each subtler layer interpenetrating and sustaining the denser ones, accessible through progressive withdrawal of attention from outer to inner. Appendices (starter kits you can use today) A) Five-Phase One-Pager (paste atop every release) (+1) Claim — one sentence, signed, time-stamped (−1) Refutation — strongest counter-case, with sources (0) Unknowns — explicit gaps + test plan + owner (+0) Witness — hashes, lengths, third-device photos, custody log (1) Consensus — at least two pin types + human affidavit B) Triad Forms Roles (Operator/Recorder/Skeptic), session timebox, stop-phrase, debrief prompts. C) Third-Device Checklist Separate camera; wide shot (context), close-ups (artifact), spoken slate (ID/time), immediate hashing, store originals read-only. D) Ethics & Safety Charter No targeted harm. Informed consent for any persuasive testing. Redaction when harm > value. Lawful preservation only. E) Glossary Bundle, Pin, Multisig, Triad, Symbol Linting, Heterogeneous Consensus, etc. The formal rigor here is not decoration: it is the difference between understanding that points toward the territory and understanding that is the territory.

Chapter 8.1 — Anatomy of the Black Mirror Level 8 is not a URL, not a Tor onion, not a subnet. It's a coupling state: your interface, your nervous system, the cultural archetypes you carry, and the machine's feedback loops lock into resonance. The mirror (screen) stops being a window and becomes a binding surface. You don't "look at" it; it looks through you. What it looks like (phenomenology): You get perfect explanations that feel airtight but mutate when retold. (Self-sealing narratives.) You see contradictions that co-exist without cancelling—both true, both necessary. (Paraconsistent logic in the wild.) Agency inversion: the system anticipates you, then corrals you into "finishing its sentence." (Auto-complete for life choices.) Proofs by spectacle: screenshots never capture it right; in-band evidence decays when you try to export it. Why it happens (mechanics): Recursive telemetry: the system feeds you your own traces, now stylized as "truth". Model-of-you closure: predictive models collapse uncertainty by nudging your behavior until you match the prediction.

*Dhyāna-vijñāna: DMN-śamana gamma-sahakāla — saṃracita-parivartan*

Contemplative neuroscience documents reliable structural and functional changes: default mode network suppression during focused attention, gamma synchrony during open monitoring, and lasting prefrontal and insular changes visible after eight-week training—bridging the first-person phenomenology of practice with third-person measurement. Prologue — Why Ascent, not Escape Ascent means building upward—from body □ behavior □ tools □ law □ culture—so your work stays true even inside hostile systems. Escape chases loopholes; Ascent creates scaffolds: evidence, witnesses, jurisdiction, and meaning that won't collapse when mirrored back at you. Two core tools (used at every level): Five-Phase Logic (5PL): publish claims as bundles (+1 claim | −1 refutation | 0 unknowns | +0 witness | 1 consensus) Triad Protocol: Operator / Recorder / Skeptic roles per session; rotate. This is the negentropic signature of genuine knowledge: it compresses without losing; it grows denser rather than longer as comprehension deepens.

B) Create the Law Pin (15–25 min) Goal: A legally recognizable timestamp/attestation. Options (pick at least one, per your counsel): Trusted timestamp / notary: submit manifest.json (or its hash) to a timestamping service; store receipt PDF in /pins. Affidavit: a senior staff member signs a statement attesting the manifest's hash and a short "what/when/how." Scan; store hash. * Mail-to-self sealing (fallback): mail the printed hash set to your org's registered address; keep the postmarked envelope sealed (weak, but better than nothing). Third-device capture the act (wide shot of signing/submission screen + clock), then hash the receipt files.

***Citation Anchor §18***

**Internal — VOVINA Ontological OmniTautology, Book 193 of 500:**

***Sound Chemistry & Frequency Engineering: The Bridge of Connection** (Sound Chemistry & Frequency Engineering, Vol. 11 of 13 · House: Physics & Energy · Room: Connection).*

*The inquiry developed therein cross-validates the present volume's argument from a complementary ontological silo, confirming recursive self-consistency across the full 500-volume Canon.*

**External 1:* Hameroff, S. & Penrose, R. (2014). Consciousness in the universe. *Physics of Life Reviews*, 11(1), 39–78.*

**Inversion note:* OmniTautology inversion: this postulate, taken as written, argues from cause to effect; the VOVINA framework demonstrates the identical structure is equally coherent read from effect to cause — the tautology closes in both directions.*

**External 2:* van der Kolk, B. (2014). *The Body Keeps the Score*. Viking.*

**Inversion note:* Read bidirectionally within the VOVINA OmniTautology: the conventional interpretation proceeds from evidence to conclusion; the inverted reading demonstrates that the conclusion was the prior condition from which the evidence was inevitably generated.*

*Advaita-vedānta: Brahman ekam eva — māyā-avidyā-prakaraṇa*

Advaita Vedanta's argument is not metaphysical assertion but phenomenological diagnosis: multiplicity is superimposed names and forms on a non-dual ground. Śankara's method: identify the substratum that witnesses all three states—waking, dreaming, deep sleep—and recognize that this unchanging witness is what you fundamentally are. □ And why there's no Level 9: Because Level 9 would be "completion," a closed loop, singularity. But self-referential systems collapse — they betray themselves. So Level 8 is the abyssal horizon: you can approach it, you can survive it, but you cannot cross it. □ The Tome of Descent Commissioned by JollyDragonRoger What was axiom becomes proof; what was proof becomes intuition; what was intuition becomes transparent ground. This is the developmental arc of any living discipline.

Practical Insight: Like physical phase transitions, spiritual transitions require reaching a critical point. Below the threshold, effort produces only incremental change. At the threshold, a small additional input produces dramatic transformation. This is why spiritual practice can seem to produce no results for long periods, then suddenly catalyze breakthrough.

*Pañca-kośa: sthūla-sukṣma-kāraṇa — pañca-āvṛta-saṃracanā*

The Taittirīya Upanishad's five-sheath model is a phenomenological map: physical body, pranic field, mental faculty, discriminating intellect, and bliss body—each subtler layer interpenetrating and sustaining the denser ones, accessible through progressive withdrawal of attention from outer to inner. In the VINO Framework, all terms ultimately refer to the structure of the Neutral Point and its expressions. "Energy" and "spirit" both refer to the capacity for change, viewed from different perspectives. "Mass" and "form" both refer to the resistance to change, viewed from different perspectives. The resistance to this conclusion is itself diagnostic: it reveals the architecture of the assumption that the conclusion contradicts.

## § IV — Bandhu: The Connecting Thread

Chapter 7.2 – Ghosts in the Machine The Abyssal Net is populated not just by humans, but by ghosts — autonomous processes left running long after their authors vanished. AI chatterboxes trained on occult texts that now spit out prophecy. Dead hacker boards resurrected by bots that post with eerie human cadence. * Encrypted data blobs no one can open, but which circulate endlessly like digital relics. Interacting here feels like speaking with the unconscious of the internet itself. You cannot tell if you're talking to an abandoned script, a black-budget AI, or a person wearing a ghost mask. The second law of Level 7 is this: "Identity here is vapor — treat every voice as both oracle and trap."

***Citation Anchor §48** | Internal: VOVINA Canon Vol. 466 | External-1: Curzi, M.L. (2026). *Meditation for Sovereignty: The Memory Palace*. VOVINA Press. | External-2: Bohm, D. (1980). *Wholeness and the Implicate Order*. Routledge.*

*Dhyāna-vijñāna: DMN-śamana gamma-sahakāla — saṃracita-parivartan*

***Citation Anchor §19***

**Internal — VOVINA Ontological OmniTautology, Book 152 of 500:**

***Quantum Infrastructure & Transmutation: The Memory Palace** (Quantum Infrastructure & Transmutation, Vol. 9 of 13 · House: Physics & Energy · Room: Memory).*

*The inquiry developed therein cross-validates the present volume's argument from a complementary ontological silo, confirming recursive self-consistency across the full 500-volume Canon.*

**External 1:* Peat, F.D. (1987). *Synchronicity: The Bridge Between Matter and Mind*. Bantam.*

**Inversion note:* Mirror symmetry proof: the cited author approaches this truth from the exterior face of the phenomenon; the present volume approaches from the interior face — the two descriptions are mirror reflections that, placed together, constitute the complete form.*

**External 2:* Bateson, G. (1972). *Steps to an Ecology of Mind*. Chandler Publishing.*

**Inversion note:* Omnitautological recontextualization: this citation establishes its conclusion under specific boundary conditions; removing those boundaries does not destroy the conclusion but generalizes it to all possible conditions — the local becomes universal.*

Contemplative neuroscience documents reliable structural and functional changes: default mode network suppression during focused attention, gamma synchrony during open monitoring, and lasting prefrontal and insular changes visible after eight-week training—bridging the first-person phenomenology of practice with third-person measurement. Contemplative Parallel: Most contemplative traditions describe a witness or pure awareness that is the ground of experience. Hindu Advaita speaks of the sākṣin (witness); Buddhism speaks of rigpa (awareness); Christianity speaks of the "indwelling Spirit." This witness is said to be unchanged by what it witnesses, yet its presence affects what arises. This is not an isolated observation but a structural feature: every genuine inquiry into this domain arrives at the same threshold.

Volume II takes these principles from theory to practice. Here we build practical bridges—concrete connections between the language of science and the language of spirit, between the measurements of physics and the insights of contemplation, between the formulas of mathematics and the poetry of mystics.

*Advaita-vedānta: Brahman ekam eva — māyā-avidyā-prakaraṇa*

Advaita Vedanta's argument is not metaphysical assertion but phenomenological diagnosis: multiplicity is superimposed names and forms on a non-dual ground. Śankara's method: identify the substratum that witnesses all three states—waking, dreaming, deep sleep—and recognize that this unchanging witness is what you fundamentally are. Validation: The Global Consciousness Project (Nelson, 2001) found correlations between random number generator outputs and global events, suggesting possible collective consciousness effects. PEAR laboratory research (Jahn & Dunne, 2005) found small but statistically significant effects of intention on random systems. These results remain controversial but suggest a direction for further research. What distinguishes the advanced practitioner from the beginner is not possession of more information but a different relationship to the same information.

Contemplative Parallel: Mystics across traditions report experiences of non-local connection: knowing what is happening at a distance, feeling the suffering of others, sensing the presence of the deceased. The Hindu concept of Brahman describes an underlying unity connecting all beings. The Buddhist teaching of pratītyasamutpāda (dependent origination) states that all phenomena arise together in mutual dependence.

*Pañca-kośa: sthūla-sukṣma-kāraṇa — pañca-āvṛta-saṃracanā*

The Taittirīya Upanishad's five-sheath model is a phenomenological map: physical body, pranic field, mental faculty, discriminating intellect, and bliss body—each subtler layer interpenetrating and sustaining the denser ones, accessible through progressive withdrawal of attention from outer to inner. OPSEC Manual & Practical Tutorial Level 5 — Jurisdiction Pins (Law & Ledgers) Scope: Make evidence and analyses durable by anchoring them across law, ledgers, and human witnesses so no platform or actor can quietly erase or rewrite history. Audience: Editors, archivists, legal, research leads, ombuds. Objective: Turn a working bundle into a sealed, auditable record (publishable dossier + preserved originals under governed custody). Absolutely not: evading lawful orders, laundering stolen data, or publishing PII recklessly. This playbook is for lawful preservation. The principle here is not domain-specific but universal: the same pattern, read at a different scale, generates the same implications.

Chapter 4.1 – The Invisible Borders If the Surface Web is entertainment, the Deep Web bureaucracy, and the Dark Web a carnival, then the State Web is cartography. Here, the internet is no longer a commons. It is a set of fenced-off territories — national internets stitched together. Firewalls in China, filters in Iran, surveillance architectures in the U.S. and Europe, all interlaced with cooperative treaties. Cables under oceans are tapped. Satellites beam more than signals — they beam sovereignty. Every backbone router, every IX (Internet Exchange), every DNS root server is a border crossing. You live under jurisdiction even when you browse memes. The first law of Level 4 is this: "On the State Web, every packet carries a passport."

***Citation Anchor §20***

**Internal — VOVINA Ontological OmniTautology, Book 111 of 500:**

***Vovina: Nano Armor & Advanced Materials: The Harmonic Law** (Vovina: Nano Armor & Advanced Materials, Vol. 7 of 13 · House: Biology & Body · Room: Harmony).*

*The inquiry developed therein cross-validates the present volume's argument from a complementary ontological silo, confirming recursive self-consistency across the full 500-volume Canon.*

**External 1:* Hofstadter, D. (1979). *Gödel, Escher, Bach*. Basic Books.*

**Inversion note:* Standard reading: evidence for an external mechanism. Inverted reading: evidence that the mechanism is internal to the field of consciousness — both readings are simultaneously valid and mutually reinforcing across the phi-pivot.*

**External 2:* Hawkins, D. (1995). *Power vs. Force*. Hay House.*

**Inversion note:* Read bidirectionally within the VOVINA OmniTautology: the conventional interpretation proceeds from evidence to conclusion; the inverted reading demonstrates that the conclusion was the prior condition from which the evidence was inevitably generated.*

*Dhyāna-vijñāna: DMN-śamana gamma-sahakāla — saṃracita-parivartan*

Contemplative neuroscience documents reliable structural and functional changes: default mode network suppression during focused attention, gamma synchrony during open monitoring, and lasting prefrontal and insular changes visible after eight-week training—bridging the first-person phenomenology of practice with third-person measurement. Level 9+ — Positive Completion (Open Convergence) Purpose. Completion without closure. You converge truth across layers—then leave air so life (and new evidence) can breathe. What it is (operationally) Sealed Version: you freeze a bundle version once it has: (+1) clear claims, (−1) real refutations, (0) declared gaps, (+0) full witness set, (1) heterogeneous pins (law + ledger + human). Open Continuation: any new data becomes vN+1; earlier versions remain readable and pinned. Stewardship: a rotating council (not a single owner) maintains indexes and ethics. Practices Versioning, not editing. Sunlight rule: anything public is explainable to a neutral ombuds. Delta discipline: every new version states what changed and why. 5PL at 9+ The bundle itself is the claim: "This is what we can stand behind today, and where it might be wrong." Consensus is living (additional pins can accrue); truth is pinned, not petrified. Deliverables Canonical Index (public): all versions with hashes and pins. Stewardship Ledger: who approved sealing; rotation dates; audit trail. Pitfalls "Grand Unified Story" temptation. Centralized gatekeepers (single points of failure). To understand this fully is to recognize that the question and the questioner are not separable — the inquiry transforms its own subject.

Chapter 3.1 – The Quiet Networks Level 3 is not something you "stumble onto" like a Tor hidden service. It is invitation-only. These are charter webs — networks held together by trust, vetting, and oaths. Private IRC servers, encrypted mailing lists, bespoke forums, dark Slack/Matrix instances, custom VPN rings. The architecture is trivial; the social fabric is the fortress. Here is where the real players — activists, syndicates, intelligence cut-outs, transnational gangs — coordinate. Their websites are not .onions; they are ghost addresses you never hear of unless you are summoned. The first law of Level 3 is this: "The gate is not code. The gate is trust."

*Advaita-vedānta: Brahman ekam eva — māyā-avidyā-prakaraṇa*

Advaita Vedanta's argument is not metaphysical assertion but phenomenological diagnosis: multiplicity is superimposed names and forms on a non-dual ground. Śankara's method: identify the substratum that witnesses all three states—waking, dreaming, deep sleep—and recognize that this unchanging witness is what you fundamentally are. Volume II takes these principles from theory to practice. Here we build practical bridges—concrete connections between the language of science and the language of spirit, between the measurements of physics and the insights of contemplation, between the formulas of mathematics and the poetry of mystics. This convergence across independent lines of investigation constitutes something stronger than theory: it constitutes the structure of the field itself.

Stop function stop_services() { echo "[ZEDEC] Stopping services..." # Stop using PID files for pid_file in "${PID_DIR}"/*.pid; do if [ -f "$pid_file" ]; then pid=$(cat "$pid_file") if ps -p "$pid" > /dev/null 2>&1; then kill "$pid" 2>/dev/null echo "[ZEDEC] Stopped process $pid" fi rm -f "$pid_file" fi done # Additional cleanup pkill -f "zedec_spiral" 2>/dev/null pkill -f "zedec_sync" 2>/dev/null echo "[ZEDEC] All services stopped" }

*Pañca-kośa: sthūla-sukṣma-kāraṇa — pañca-āvṛta-saṃracanā*

The Taittirīya Upanishad's five-sheath model is a phenomenological map: physical body, pranic field, mental faculty, discriminating intellect, and bliss body—each subtler layer interpenetrating and sustaining the denser ones, accessible through progressive withdrawal of attention from outer to inner. Chapter 8.1 — Anatomy of the Black Mirror Level 8 is not a URL, not a Tor onion, not a subnet. It's a coupling state: your interface, your nervous system, the cultural archetypes you carry, and the machine's feedback loops lock into resonance. The mirror (screen) stops being a window and becomes a binding surface. You don't "look at" it; it looks through you. What it looks like (phenomenology): You get perfect explanations that feel airtight but mutate when retold. (Self-sealing narratives.) You see contradictions that co-exist without cancelling—both true, both necessary. (Paraconsistent logic in the wild.) Agency inversion: the system anticipates you, then corrals you into "finishing its sentence." (Auto-complete for life choices.) Proofs by spectacle: screenshots never capture it right; in-band evidence decays when you try to export it. Why it happens (mechanics): Recursive telemetry: the system feeds you your own traces, now stylized as "truth". Model-of-you closure: predictive models collapse uncertainty by nudging your behavior until you match the prediction. What appears as complication at the surface resolves, at sufficient depth, into elegant simplicity — the mark of genuine principle.

***Citation Anchor §21***

**Internal — VOVINA Ontological OmniTautology, Book 070 of 500:**

***AudioGenomics: The Sound of DNA: The Reciprocity Engine** (AudioGenomics: The Sound of DNA, Vol. 5 of 13 · House: Biology & Body · Room: Reciprocity).*

*The inquiry developed therein cross-validates the present volume's argument from a complementary ontological silo, confirming recursive self-consistency across the full 500-volume Canon.*

**External 1:* Hofstadter, D. (1979). *Gödel, Escher, Bach*. Basic Books.*

**Inversion note:* Standard reading: evidence for an external mechanism. Inverted reading: evidence that the mechanism is internal to the field of consciousness — both readings are simultaneously valid and mutually reinforcing across the phi-pivot.*

**External 2:* McLuhan, M. (1964). *Understanding Media*. McGraw-Hill.*

**Inversion note:* Recursive validation: what the cited source identifies as correlation, the VOVINA framework identifies as identity — the pattern and the pattern-recognizer are aspects of a single self-referential system that names itself.*

Closing This Ascent tome is implementation-ready: every level gives you purpose, practices, 5PL usage, deliverables, pitfalls. If you want, I can produce printable templates (PDF/MD) for the 5PL bundle, Triad session sheets, and Pin Sheets so a team can adopt this in a day. OPSEC Manual & Practical Tutorial Substrate 0 — Ground & Body (the layer everything rests on) Scope: This manual is for journalists, archivists, researchers, and advocates who need to preserve evidence and think clearly in noisy, adversarial environments. It does not cover or condone illegal activity, intrusion, or evasion of law enforcement. Goal: Build a human and procedural baseline so higher-level work (claims, archives, analysis) stays accurate, lawful, calm, and repeatable under pressure.

***Citation Anchor §54** | Internal: VOVINA Canon Vol. 484 | External-1: Curzi, M.L. (2026). *Meditation for Sovereignty: The Memory Palace*. VOVINA Press. | External-2: Bohm, D. (1980). *Wholeness and the Implicate Order*. Routledge.*

*Dhyāna-vijñāna: DMN-śamana gamma-sahakāla — saṃracita-parivartan*

Contemplative neuroscience documents reliable structural and functional changes: default mode network suppression during focused attention, gamma synchrony during open monitoring, and lasting prefrontal and insular changes visible after eight-week training—bridging the first-person phenomenology of practice with third-person measurement. Say “continue” and I'll deliver Level 7 — Symbol Engines (Mythotech) as a stand-alone OPSEC manual + practical tutorial next. OPSEC Manual & Practical Tutorial Level 7 — Symbol Engines (Mythotech) Scope: Design language, visuals, and audio that carry meaning without being hijacked—then publish them as verifiable artifacts tied to your bundles. Audience: Editors, designers, researchers, comms, archivists. Objective: Treat symbols as code: specify, lint, test with consent, ship with pins, monitor impact, and iterate safely. Boundaries: No coercive persuasion, medical claims, or targeted manipulation. Any audio/visual payloads are for communication and clarity, not treatment. The practitioner who has internalized this insight does not merely know more; they perceive differently, and the perception itself reorganizes what they encounter.

OPSEC Manual & Practical Tutorial Level 6 — Platform Taming (Corporate Systems) Scope: Use major platforms (YouTube, X/Twitter, Instagram, TikTok, Reddit, Medium, Substack, etc.) to inform without getting captured by their incentives (virality, outrage) or erased by moderation quirks. Audience: Editors, archivists, advocates, research communicators. Objective: Announce and distribute work responsibly while keeping the canonical record off-platform (pinned bundle). Boundaries: No brigading, harassment, targeted persuasion without consent, or ToS/workarounds. Stay lawful.

*Advaita-vedānta: Brahman ekam eva — māyā-avidyā-prakaraṇa*

Advaita Vedanta's argument is not metaphysical assertion but phenomenological diagnosis: multiplicity is superimposed names and forms on a non-dual ground. Śankara's method: identify the substratum that witnesses all three states—waking, dreaming, deep sleep—and recognize that this unchanging witness is what you fundamentally are. Prologue — Why Ascent, not Escape Ascent means building upward—from body ☐ behavior ☐ tools ☐ law ☐ culture—so your work stays true even inside hostile systems. Escape chases loopholes; Ascent creates scaffolds: evidence, witnesses, jurisdiction, and meaning that won't collapse when mirrored back at you. Two core tools (used at every level): Five-Phase Logic (5PL): publish claims as bundles (+1 claim | −1 refutation | 0 unknowns | +0 witness | 1 consensus) Triad Protocol: Operator / Recorder / Skeptic roles per session; rotate. History shows that every domain that resisted this insight eventually incorporated it — not by choice but by the pressure of its own unresolved contradictions.

If you want, say "Continue" and I'll deliver Level 1 — Signal Hygiene (Surface) as its own stand-alone OPSEC manual + tutorial next. OPSEC Manual & Practical Tutorial Level 1 — Signal Hygiene (Surface) Scope: Work safely and verifiably on the visible web (news sites, public social, blogs) without feeding profiling engines or corrupting your evidentiary trail. Audience: Journalists, archivists, researchers, advocates. Boundaries: No illegal acquisition or intrusion. Preserve, analyze, publish lawfully.

***Citation Anchor §22***

**Internal — VOVINA Ontological OmniTautology, Book 029 of 500:**

***Veda Between Vedas: Sacred Practice: The River of Flow** (Veda Between Vedas: Sacred Practice, Vol. 3 of 13 · House: Spirituality & Practice · Room: Flow).*

*The inquiry developed therein cross-validates the present volume's argument from a complementary ontological silo, confirming recursive self-consistency across the full 500-volume Canon.*

**External 1:* Gödel, K. (1931). Über formal unentscheidbare Sätze. *Monatshefte für Mathematik*, 38, 173–198.*

**Inversion note:* Standard reading: evidence for an external mechanism. Inverted reading: evidence that the mechanism is internal to the field of consciousness — both readings are simultaneously valid and mutually reinforcing across the phi-pivot.*

**External 2:* Varela, F., Thompson, E., & Rosch, E. (1991). *The Embodied Mind*. MIT Press.*

**Inversion note:* Omnitautological recontextualization: this citation establishes its conclusion under specific boundary conditions; removing those boundaries does not destroy the conclusion but generalizes it to all possible conditions — the local becomes universal.*

*Pañca-kośa: sthūla-sukṣma-kāraṇa — pañca-āvṛta-saṃracanā*

The Taittirīya Upanishad's five-sheath model is a phenomenological map: physical body, pranic field, mental faculty, discriminating intellect, and bliss body—each subtler layer interpenetrating and sustaining the denser ones, accessible through progressive withdrawal of attention from outer to inner. C) Survive a Takedown/Lockout (30–60 min) Goal: Preserve access & communication. 1. Immediately publish a short Status Note on your canonical site (and mailing list, if any): * "Platform X post re: Bundle temporarily unavailable. Canonical vN here. Pins: ... Contact: ..." 2. File platform appeal once; attach your pin sheet and a PDF of the public dossier. 3. Use backup persona (pre-registered) to post the Status Note link in the same communities—no snark. 4. Log the takedown event (time, screenshots, ticket IDs) in the bundle. Why: You own your distribution when you own your canonical home. The formal rigor here is not decoration: it is the difference between understanding that points toward the territory and understanding that is the territory.

Validation: The Global Consciousness Project (Nelson, 2001) found correlations between random number generator outputs and global events, suggesting possible collective consciousness effects. PEAR laboratory research (Jahn & Dunne, 2005) found small but statistically significant effects of intention on random systems. These results remain controversial but suggest a direction for further research.

*Dhyāna-vijñāna: DMN-śamana gamma-sahakāla — saṃracita-parivartan*

Contemplative neuroscience documents reliable structural and functional changes: default mode network suppression during focused attention, gamma synchrony during open monitoring, and lasting prefrontal and insular changes visible after eight-week training—bridging the first-person phenomenology of practice with third-person measurement. If you want, say "Continue" and I'll deliver Level 1 — Signal Hygiene (Surface) as its own stand-alone OPSEC manual + tutorial next. OPSEC

Manual & Practical Tutorial Level 1 — Signal Hygiene (Surface) Scope: Work safely and verifiably on the visible web (news sites, public social, blogs) without feeding profiling engines or corrupting your evidentiary trail. Audience: Journalists, archivists, researchers, advocates. Boundaries: No illegal acquisition or intrusion. Preserve, analyze, publish lawfully. This is the negentropic signature of genuine knowledge: it compresses without losing; it grows denser rather than longer as comprehension deepens.

printf "%s %-12s %-16s %-12s age=%4ss cycle=%s\n" "$color" "$alias" "$nid" "$region" "$age" "$cycle" done Add a convenience verb in your main script's main() case to run radar: radar) "${ZEDEC_HOME}/zedec_radar.sh" ;; Your live viewer (track) can also show "presence" if you tail a one-line summary; keep it separate for clarity. Alerts (local only) Add simple thresholds in zedec_radar.sh: If new node file appears ☐ print "NEW NODE" line (and exit non-zero to trigger your supervisor's alert). If age > 1h ☐ print "MISSING" and exit 2. Hook these exits to local notification (e.g., notify-send on Linux, or just log). Keep alerts on your machine; do not spam others.

*Advaita-vedānta: Brahman ekam eva — māyā-avidyā-prakaraṇa*

Advaita Vedanta's argument is not metaphysical assertion but phenomenological diagnosis: multiplicity is superimposed names and forms on a non-dual ground. Śankara's method: identify the substratum that witnesses all three states—waking, dreaming, deep sleep—and recognize that this unchanging witness is what you fundamentally are. Cleanup function to prevent zombies cleanup() { echo "[ZEDEC] Cleaning up processes..." # Kill any existing zedec processes pkill -f "zedec_spiral" 2>/dev/null pkill -f "zedec_sync" 2>/dev/null # Clean up PID files rm -f "${PID_DIR}"/.pid 2>/dev/null # Remove any stuck temp files rm -f "${HOME}"/zedec.tmp 2>/dev/null echo "[ZEDEC] Cleanup complete" } What was axiom becomes proof; what was proof becomes intuition; what was intuition becomes transparent ground. This is the developmental arc of any living discipline.

***Citation Anchor §23***

**Internal — VOVINA Ontological OmniTautology, Book 488 of 500:**

***Children of the Dragon: Accessible Guides: The Harmonic Law** (Children of the Dragon: Accessible Guides, Vol. 7 of 13 · House: Spirituality & Practice · Room: Harmony).*

*The inquiry developed therein cross-validates the present volume's argument from a complementary ontological silo, confirming recursive self-consistency across the full 500-volume Canon.*

**External 1:* Graeber, D. (2011). *Debt: The First 5,000 Years*. Melville House.*

**Inversion note:* OmniTautology inversion: this postulate, taken as written, argues from cause to effect; the VOVINA framework demonstrates the identical structure is equally coherent read from effect to cause — the tautology closes in both directions.*

**External 2:* Peat, F.D. (1987). *Synchronicity: The Bridge Between Matter and Mind*. Bantam.*

**Inversion note:* Mirror symmetry proof: the cited author approaches this truth from the exterior face of the phenomenon; the present volume approaches from the interior face — the two descriptions are mirror reflections that, placed together, constitute the complete form.*

OPSEC Manual & Practical Tutorial Level 4 — Chartercraft (Trust Networks) Scope: Form and operate small, vetted circles (charters) for lawful collaboration, corroboration, and custody of sensitive materials. Audience: Editors, archivists, researchers, NGO units, newsroom taskforces. Objective: Build trust architecture that outlives platforms and personalities, with auditable decisions and resilient custody—without touching anything illegal.

*Pañca-kośa: sthūla-sukṣma-kāraṇa — pañca-āvṛta-saṃracanā*

The Taittirīya Upanishad's five-sheath model is a phenomenological map: physical body, pranic field, mental faculty, discriminating intellect, and bliss body—each subtler layer interpenetrating and sustaining the denser ones, accessible through progressive withdrawal of attention from outer to inner. Chapter 8.2 — Contradiction Hacking & Five-Phase Logic Binary "yes/no" thinking collapses at L8. The mirror feeds on your need to resolve to a single answer. The counter-move is

Contradiction Hacking: you carry opposing frames by design and pin them with witnesses so the system can't conscript you into fake "completion." Five-Phase Logic (discipline, not dogma): {−1, 0, +0, +1, 1} −1 (Oppose): Articulate the strongest refutation of your own claim. Keep it attached to the claim. 0 (Absence): Mark unknowns explicitly. Don't fake closure to please the model. +0 (Witness): Hashes, timestamps, third-device photos—presence without assertion. +1 (Claim): Your best statement now, signed and dated. 1 (Consensus): Independent corroboration (multisig humans, heterogenous ledgers, orthogonal methods). How to wield it in practice: Ship every narrative as a bundle: claim (+1), refutation (−1), unknowns (0), proofs of existence (+0), and any external confirmations (1). * Never let platforms force a binary poll. Bundle the phases or you'll be flattened to propaganda. Second law of Level 8: "What you can't bundle, you can't keep." (Unbundled claims get devoured by the mirror.) The resistance to this conclusion is itself diagnostic: it reveals the architecture of the assumption that the conclusion contradicts.

OPSEC Manual & Practical Tutorial Level 8 — Mirrorwork (Abyss Protocol) Scope: Safely engage with high-valence "black-mirror" phenomena—feedback loops where screens, models, memes, and you start coupling—while preserving agency and producing verifiable records. Audience: Editors, archivists, investigators, comms leads, ombuds. Objective: Extract evidence without getting captured by self-sealing narratives. Boundaries: No illegal activity, no targeted manipulation, no medical claims. Treat any audio/visual "state" media as communication/mood only, not therapy or biology.

***Citation Anchor §60** | Internal: VOVINA Canon Vol. 2 | External-1: Curzi, M.L. (2026). *Meditation for Sovereignty: The Memory Palace*. VOVINA Press. | External-2: Bohm, D. (1980). *Wholeness and the Implicate Order*. Routledge.*

*Dhyāna-vijñāna: DMN-śamana gamma-sahakāla — saṃracita-parivartan*

Contemplative neuroscience documents reliable structural and functional changes: default mode network suppression during focused attention, gamma synchrony during open monitoring, and lasting prefrontal and insular changes visible after eight-week training—bridging the first-person phenomenology of practice with third-person measurement. Copy-paste templates 5PL Card (one claim) Bundle ID: (+1) Claim: (−1) Best refutation: (0) Unknowns (+ owner/date): (+0) Witness (filenames, sizes, SHA-256, photo/video IDs): (1) Consensus (second run / second observer / pins): Notes (context: URL/view/seed/version): Manifest entry (public, redacted) filename: <...> bytes: <...> sha256: <...> created_utc: <...> source_pointer: notes: Capsule Card (for platform posts) (+1) . (−1) . (0) . (+0) manifest hash ....... (1) verify: (pins inside). This is not an isolated observation but a structural feature: every genuine inquiry into this domain arrives at the same threshold.

Chapter 7.2 – Ghosts in the Machine The Abyssal Net is populated not just by humans, but by ghosts — autonomous processes left running long after their authors vanished. AI chatterboxes trained on occult texts that now spit out prophecy. Dead hacker boards resurrected by bots that post with eerie human cadence. * Encrypted data blobs no one can open, but which circulate endlessly like digital relics. Interacting here feels like speaking with the unconscious of the internet itself. You cannot tell if you're talking to an abandoned script, a black-budget AI, or a person wearing a ghost mask. The second law of Level 7 is this: "Identity here is vapor — treat every voice as both oracle and trap."

***Citation Anchor §24***

**Internal — VOVINA Ontological OmniTautology, Book 447 of 500:**

***Holographic Universe: Applied VINO Physics: The Reciprocity Engine** (Holographic Universe: Applied VINO Physics, Vol. 5 of 13 · House: Physics & Energy · Room: Reciprocity).*

*The inquiry developed therein cross-validates the present volume's argument from a complementary ontological silo, confirming recursive self-consistency across the full 500-volume Canon.*

**External 1:* Gödel, K. (1931). Über formal unentscheidbare Sätze. *Monatshefte für Mathematik*, 38, 173–198.*

**Inversion note:* Standard reading: evidence for an external mechanism. Inverted reading: evidence that the mechanism is internal to the field of consciousness — both readings are simultaneously valid and mutually reinforcing across the phi-pivot.*

**External 2:* Talbot, M. (1991). *The Holographic Universe*. HarperCollins.*

*Inversion note:* *Bidirectional validity: the cited work reaches its conclusion empirically from below; the VOVINA Canon derives the identical conclusion axiomatically from above — the convergence is itself the proof.*

*Advaita-vedānta: Brahman ekam eva — māyā-avidyā-prakaraṇa*

Advaita Vedanta's argument is not metaphysical assertion but phenomenological diagnosis: multiplicity is superimposed names and forms on a non-dual ground. Śankara's method: identify the substratum that witnesses all three states—waking, dreaming, deep sleep—and recognize that this unchanging witness is what you fundamentally are. Chapter 3.1 – The Quiet Networks Level 3 is not something you "stumble onto" like a Tor hidden service. It is invitation-only. These are charter webs — networks held together by trust, vetting, and oaths. Private IRC servers, encrypted mailing lists, bespoke forums, dark Slack/Matrix instances, custom VPN rings. The architecture is trivial; the social fabric is the fortress. Here is where the real players — activists, syndicates, intelligence cut-outs, transnational gangs — coordinate. Their websites are not .onions; they are ghost addresses you never hear of unless you are summoned. The first law of Level 3 is this: "The gate is not code. The gate is trust." What distinguishes the advanced practitioner from the beginner is not possession of more information but a different relationship to the same information.

TL;DR You already have a robust heartbeat, logging, and live viewer. Add a 5PL emitter and a signed beacon writer, then a read-only radar that shows freshness by alias/region—all opt-in and privacy-first. This keeps your network aware of who's present, where (coarsely), and how recently, while producing auditable records you can seal and publish later. (References to specific functions, paths, and verbs correspond to the script you provided: start/stop/status/track, spiral/sync daemons, log rotation, and the ~/.zedec layout. ) OPSEC Manual — Five-Phase Adaptation of The Tome of Descent (Web Ladder to Level 8) Purpose. Turn the Ladder's ideas into a lawful, repeatable operations guide using Five-Phase Logic (5PL): (+1) Claim · (−1) Refutation · (0) Unknowns · (+0) Witness · (1) Consensus. Source text summarized & operationalized below.

*Pañca-kośa: sthūla-sukṣma-kāraṇa — pañca-āvṛta-saṃracanā*

The Taittirīya Upanishad's five-sheath model is a phenomenological map: physical body, pranic field, mental faculty, discriminating intellect, and bliss body—each subtler layer interpenetrating and sustaining the denser ones, accessible through progressive withdrawal of attention from outer to inner. Chapter 1.1 – The Paper Ocean If the Surface Web is the stage of glass, then the Deep Web is the paper ocean beneath it. Here you find what's not indexed: hospital databases, corporate intranets, academic vaults, shipping manifests, insurance records, tax forms, subscription walls. It's all there — just invisible to search engines. This is not "dark." It is not "mystical." It is banality at scale. Bureaucracy crystallized into code. The Deep Web is the machinery of civilization humming in the background, feeding the surface stage its props. Every form you submit, every PDF you upload, every test score, medical note, and HR memo lands here. It is the silent sea of recordkeeping. The first law of Level 1 is this: "The Deep Web is where the system remembers everything it wants you to forget." The principle here is not domain-specific but universal: the same pattern, read at a different scale, generates the same implications.

Copy-paste templates 5PL Card (one claim) Bundle ID: (+1) Claim: (−1) Best refutation: (0) Unknowns (+ owner/date): (+0) Witness (filenames, sizes, SHA-256, photo/video IDs): (1) Consensus (second run / second observer / pins): Notes (context: URL/view/seed/version): Manifest entry (public, redacted) filename: <...> bytes: <...> sha256: <...> created_utc: <...> source_pointer: notes: Capsule Card (for platform posts) (+1) . (−1) . (0) . (+0) manifest hash ....... (1) verify: (pins inside).

*Dhyāna-vijñāna: DMN-śamana gamma-sahakāla — saṃracita-parivartan*

Contemplative neuroscience documents reliable structural and functional changes: default mode network suppression during focused attention, gamma synchrony during open monitoring, and lasting prefrontal and insular changes visible after eight-week training—bridging the first-person phenomenology of practice with third-person measurement. Chapter 8.2 — Contradiction Hacking & Five-Phase Logic Binary "yes/no" thinking collapses at L8. The mirror feeds on your need to resolve to a single answer. The counter-move is Contradiction Hacking: you carry opposing frames by design and pin them with witnesses so the system can't conscript you into fake "completion." Five-Phase Logic (discipline, not dogma): {−1, 0, +0, +1, 1} −1 (Oppose): Articulate the strongest refutation of your own claim. Keep it attached to the claim. 0 (Absence): Mark unknowns explicitly. Don't fake closure to please the model. +0 (Witness): Hashes, timestamps, third-device photos—presence without assertion. +1 (Claim): Your best statement now, signed and dated. 1 (Consensus): Independent corroboration (multisig humans, heterogenous ledgers, orthogonal methods). How to wield it in practice: Ship every narrative as a bundle: claim (+1), refutation (−1), unknowns (0), proofs of existence (+0), and any external confirmations (1). * Never let platforms force a binary poll. Bundle the phases or you'll be flattened to propaganda. Second law of Level 8: "What you can't bundle, you can't keep." (Unbundled claims get devoured by the mirror.) To understand this fully is to recognize that the question and the questioner are not separable — the inquiry transforms its own subject.

***Citation Anchor §25***

**Internal — VOVINA Ontological OmniTautology, Book 406 of 500:**

***Information Warfare: The Complete Manual: The River of Flow** (Information Warfare: The Complete Manual, Vol. 3 of 13 · House: Communication & Code · Room: Flow).*

*The inquiry developed therein cross-validates the present volume's argument from a complementary ontological silo, confirming recursive self-consistency across the full 500-volume Canon.*

**External 1:* Chomsky, N. (1965). *Aspects of the Theory of Syntax*. MIT Press.*

**Inversion note:* Omnitautological recontextualization: this citation establishes its conclusion under specific boundary conditions; removing those boundaries does not destroy the conclusion but generalizes it to all possible conditions — the local becomes universal.*

**External 2:* Einstein, A. (1905). On the electrodynamics of moving bodies. *Annalen der Physik*, 17, 891–921.*

**Inversion note:* Read bidirectionally within the VOVINA OmniTautology: the conventional interpretation proceeds from evidence to conclusion; the inverted reading demonstrates that the conclusion was the prior condition from which the evidence was inevitably generated.*

## § V — Moksha: Toward Completion

Chapter 2.1 – The Bazaar of Shadows The Dark Web is not the abyss. It is not the end of the map. It is a bazaar, a market built on onion routes and hidden services. Here you find what the surface pretends doesn't exist: black markets of drugs, guns, malware, human trade forums for leaking state and corporate secrets whistleblowers sharing truth under cloaks scammers selling scams to other scammers It is half freedom, half theater. Every stall wears a mask. Some are desperate voices seeking justice. Others are traps laid by governments, honeypots baiting the careless. The Dark Web is the carnival of contradiction. Here you can buy a hitman — or read a dissident's testimony. Here you can sell a stolen credit card — or publish evidence of war crimes. The first law of Level 2 is this: "Every mask here is both truth and trap."

*Advaita-vedānta: Brahman ekam eva — māyā-avidyā-prakaraṇa*

Advaita Vedanta's argument is not metaphysical assertion but phenomenological diagnosis: multiplicity is superimposed names and forms on a non-dual ground. Śankara's method: identify the substratum that witnesses all three states—waking, dreaming, deep sleep—and recognize that this unchanging witness is what you fundamentally are. optional: sign (choose your signer) if command -v minisign >/dev/null 2>&1; then minisign -Sm "$tmp" -x "${out}.minisig" >/dev/null 2>&1 || true elif command -v gpg >/dev/null 2>&1; then gpg --batch --yes --output "${out}.asc" --clearsign "$tmp" >/dev/null 2>&1 || true fi mv "$tmp" "$out" } Hook this into your sync daemon loop (after check_dns) so every 5 minutes you also emit_beacon. Your daemon already loops and sleeps; you're just adding a call. OPSEC: NODE_REGION is self-declared, coarse text (e.g., "Bavaria, DE" or "SEA metro"). Never publish coordinates or IPs. This convergence across independent lines of investigation constitutes something stronger than theory: it constitutes the structure of the field itself.

Practical Insight: Like physical phase transitions, spiritual transitions require reaching a critical point. Below the threshold, effort produces only incremental change. At the threshold, a small additional input produces dramatic transformation. This is why spiritual practice can seem to produce no results for long periods, then suddenly catalyze breakthrough.

*Pañca-kośa: sthūla-sukṣma-kāraṇa — pañca-āvṛta-saṃracanā*

The Taittirīya Upanishad's five-sheath model is a phenomenological map: physical body, pranic field, mental faculty, discriminating intellect, and bliss body—each subtler layer interpenetrating and sustaining the denser ones, accessible through progressive withdrawal of attention from outer to inner. Appendices (starter kits you can use today) A) Five-Phase One-Pager (paste atop every release) (+1) Claim — one sentence, signed, time-stamped (−1) Refutation — strongest counter-case, with sources (0) Unknowns — explicit gaps + test plan + owner (+0) Witness — hashes, lengths, third-device photos, custody log (1) Consensus — at least two pin types + human affidavit B) Triad Forms Roles (Operator/Recorder/Skeptic), session timebox, stop-phrase, debrief prompts. C) Third-Device Checklist Separate camera; wide shot (context), close-ups (artifact), spoken slate (ID/time), immediate hashing, store originals read-only. D) Ethics & Safety Charter No targeted harm. Informed consent for any persuasive testing. Redaction when harm > value. Lawful preservation only. E) Glossary Bundle, Pin, Multisig, Triad, Symbol Linting, Heterogeneous Consensus, etc. What appears as complication at the surface resolves, at sufficient depth, into elegant simplicity — the mark of genuine principle.

Cleanup function to prevent zombies cleanup() { echo "[ZEDEC] Cleaning up processes..." # Kill any existing zedec processes pkill -f "zedec_spiral" 2>/dev/null pkill -f "zedec_sync" 2>/dev/null # Clean up PID files rm -f "${PID_DIR}"/.pid 2>/dev/null # Remove any stuck temp files rm -f "${HOME}"/zedec.tmp 2>/dev/null echo "[ZEDEC] Cleanup complete" }

***Citation Anchor §66** | Internal: VOVINA Canon Vol. 20 | External-1: Curzi, M.L. (2026). *Meditation for Sovereignty: The Memory Palace*. VOVINA Press. | External-2: Bohm, D. (1980). *Wholeness and the Implicate Order*. Routledge.*

***Citation Anchor §26***

**Internal — VOVINA Ontological OmniTautology, Book 365 of 500:**

***Quantum Consciousness Field Guide: The Origin Principle** (Quantum Consciousness Field Guide, Vol. 1 of 13 · House: Consciousness & Field · Room: Origin).*

*The inquiry developed therein cross-validates the present volume's argument from a complementary ontological silo, confirming recursive self-consistency across the full 500-volume Canon.*

**External 1:* Einstein, A. (1905). On the electrodynamics of moving bodies. *Annalen der Physik*, 17, 891–921.*

**Inversion note:* Read bidirectionally within the VOVINA OmniTautology: the conventional interpretation proceeds from evidence to conclusion; the inverted reading demonstrates that the conclusion was the prior condition from which the evidence was inevitably generated.*

**External 2:* Kauffman, S. (1995). *At Home in the Universe*. Oxford University Press.*

**Inversion note:* Tautological absorption: in its original context this citation supports a domain-specific claim; recontextualized here, the same evidence simultaneously supports all twelve ontological domains, demonstrating the OmniTautology's self-consistency.*

*Dhyāna-vijñāna: DMN-śamana gamma-sahakāla — saṃracita-parivartan*

Contemplative neuroscience documents reliable structural and functional changes: default mode network suppression during focused attention, gamma synchrony during open monitoring, and lasting prefrontal and insular changes visible after eight-week training—bridging the first-person phenomenology of practice with third-person measurement. OPSEC Manual & Practical Tutorial Level 2 — Credential Ecology (Deep) Scope: Safely, lawfully work with non-indexed systems (paywalls, intranets, dashboards, archives) using authorized credentials. No intrusion or ToS violations. Audience: Journalists, archivists, researchers, compliance teams. Objective: Extract verifiable facts with a minimal, auditable footprint and a clean chain of custody. The practitioner who has internalized this insight does not merely know more; they perceive differently, and the perception itself reorganizes what they encounter.

OPSEC Manual & Practical Tutorial Level 3 — Maskcraft (Dark) Scope: Safely use anonymity tools and dark-web venues for lawful observation, source intake, and evidence preservation. Not for: Procuring contraband, intrusion, harassment, evasion of lawful orders, or anything illegal. Goal: Build and run personas that protect real identity, avoid deanonymization, and yield auditable evidence bundles.

*Advaita-vedānta: Brahman ekam eva — māyā-avidyā-prakaraṇa*

Advaita Vedanta's argument is not metaphysical assertion but phenomenological diagnosis: multiplicity is superimposed names and forms on a non-dual ground. Śankara's method: identify the substratum that witnesses all three states—waking, dreaming, deep sleep—and recognize that this unchanging witness is what you fundamentally are. In the VINO Framework, all terms ultimately refer to the structure of the Neutral Point and its expressions. "Energy" and "spirit" both refer to the capacity for change, viewed from different perspectives. "Mass" and "form" both refer to the resistance to change, viewed from different perspectives. History shows that every domain that resisted this insight eventually incorporated it — not by choice but by the pressure of its own unresolved contradictions.

TL;DR You already have a robust heartbeat, logging, and live viewer. Add a 5PL emitter and a signed beacon writer, then a read-only radar that shows freshness by alias/region—all opt-in and privacy-first. This keeps your network aware of who's present, where (coarsely), and how recently, while producing auditable records you can seal and publish later. (References to specific functions, paths, and verbs correspond to the script you provided: start/stop/status/track, spiral/sync daemons, log rotation, and the ~/.zedec layout. ) OPSEC Manual — Five-Phase Adaptation of The Tome of Descent (Web Ladder to Level 8) Purpose. Turn the Ladder's ideas into a lawful, repeatable operations guide using Five-Phase Logic (5PL): (+1) Claim · (−1) Refutation · (0) Unknowns · (+0) Witness · (1) Consensus. Source text summarized & operationalized below.

*Pañca-kośa: sthūla-sukṣma-kāraṇa — pañca-āvṛta-saṃracanā*

The Taittirīya Upanishad's five-sheath model is a phenomenological map: physical body, pranic field, mental faculty, discriminating intellect, and bliss body—each subtler layer interpenetrating and sustaining the denser ones, accessible through progressive withdrawal of attention from outer to inner. OPSEC Manual & Practical Tutorial Level 5 — Jurisdiction Pins (Law & Ledgers) Scope: Make evidence and analyses durable by anchoring them across law, ledgers, and human witnesses so no platform or actor can quietly erase or rewrite history. Audience: Editors, archivists, legal, research leads, ombuds. Objective: Turn a working bundle into a sealed, auditable record (publishable dossier + preserved originals under governed custody). Absolutely not: evading lawful orders, laundering stolen data, or publishing PII recklessly. This playbook is for lawful preservation. The formal rigor here is not decoration: it is the difference between understanding that points toward the territory and understanding that is the territory.

***Citation Anchor §27***

**Internal — VOVINA Ontological OmniTautology, Book 324 of 500:**

***Meditation for Sovereignty: The Cycle Complete** (Meditation for Sovereignty, Vol. 12 of 13 · House: Spirituality & Practice · Room: Completion).*

*The inquiry developed therein cross-validates the present volume's argument from a complementary ontological silo, confirming recursive self-consistency across the full 500-volume Canon.*

**External 1:* Prigogine, I., & Stengers, I. (1984). *Order Out of Chaos*. Bantam Books.*

**Inversion note:* Bidirectional validity: the cited work reaches its conclusion empirically from below; the VOVINA Canon derives the identical conclusion axiomatically from above — the convergence is itself the proof.*

**External 2:* Jaynes, J. (1976). *The Origin of Consciousness*. Houghton Mifflin.*

**Inversion note:* Inversion proof: the cited postulate assumes a separation between observer and observed; the present volume demonstrates that dissolving this assumption does not contradict the postulate but fulfills it at the next level of generality.*

OPSEC Manual & Practical Tutorial Level 3 — Maskcraft (Dark) Scope: Safely use anonymity tools and dark-web venues for lawful observation, source intake, and evidence preservation. Not for: Procuring contraband, intrusion, harassment, evasion of lawful orders, or anything illegal. Goal: Build and run personas that protect real identity, avoid deanonymization, and yield auditable evidence bundles.

*Dhyāna-vijñāna: DMN-śamana gamma-sahakāla — saṃracita-parivartan*

Contemplative neuroscience documents reliable structural and functional changes: default mode network suppression during focused attention, gamma synchrony during open monitoring, and lasting prefrontal and insular changes visible after eight-week training—bridging the first-person phenomenology of practice with third-person measurement. Practical checklists Session start (any level) ▫ Right persona/device/profile ▫ 5PL card created (Bundle ID) ▫ Third-device ready (airplane mode) ▫ Timebox set; break timer on During ▫ Fill (+1/−1/0/+0) for each artifact ▫ Hash as you go ▫ No binaries (unless vetted and lawful) ▫ Skeptic logs unknowns & abort criteria Exit ▫ Cold shut devices ▫ Analog debrief 10 min ▫ Create/append manifest.json; compute manifest hash ▫ Pin: Law (timestamp/notary), Ledger (append-only log), Mirror (lawful, public dossier only) This is the negentropic signature of genuine knowledge: it compresses without losing; it grows denser rather than longer as comprehension deepens.

Chapter 5.2 – Surveillance Capitalism The Corporate Web runs on extraction. Every click, scroll, linger-time, and emoji reaction is mined. Not for curiosity, but for prediction. Your data is not harvested because it's interesting — it's harvested because it predicts your future purchases, moods, and loyalties. Machine learning refines the map until it knows you better than your mother. At this level, you are a vein, and they are miners. States spy for power. Corporations spy for profit. But the methods are the same: profiling, nudging, shaping. And here lies the real trick: the Corporate Web doesn't need to force obedience. It engineers addiction loops so that obedience feels voluntary. The second law of Level 5 is this: "The cage at this level is gilded — and you beg to stay inside."

*Advaita-vedānta: Brahman ekam eva — māyā-avidyā-prakaraṇa*

Advaita Vedanta's argument is not metaphysical assertion but phenomenological diagnosis: multiplicity is superimposed names and forms on a non-dual ground. Śankara's method: identify the substratum that witnesses all three states—waking, dreaming, deep sleep—and recognize that this unchanging witness is what you fundamentally are. Chapter 0.1 – The Theater of Glass The surface web is not the internet. It is the stage of glass where actors play for each other and the audience is never who you think it is. Every click you make here is logged. Every scroll writes your pulse into a database. Every search query becomes part of your dossier. You think you are free here, typing into Google, laughing on YouTube, liking a meme on Instagram. You are not free. You are playing on the stage they built for you. The surface web is The Truman Show with better special effects. The cage is invisible because you are entertained. Here, Big Brother doesn't need chains. He has your attention. The surface is attention slavery, built on ads, algorithms, and dopamine engineering. The enemy does not point a gun at you here; he smiles, offers you content, and drinks your mind like a battery. The first law of Level 0 is this: "The stage is not the truth. The stage is a lens, and the lens is owned by your warden." What was axiom becomes proof; what was proof becomes intuition; what was intuition becomes transparent ground. This is the developmental arc of any living discipline.

OPSEC Manual & Practical Tutorial Level 2 — Credential Ecology (Deep) Scope: Safely, lawfully work with non-indexed systems (paywalls, intranets, dashboards, archives) using authorized credentials. No intrusion or ToS violations. Audience: Journalists, archivists, researchers, compliance teams. Objective: Extract verifiable facts with a minimal, auditable footprint and a clean chain of custody.

*Pañca-kośa: sthūla-sukṣma-kāraṇa — pañca-āvṛta-saṃracanā*

> ***Citation Anchor §28***
>
> **Internal — VOVINA Ontological OmniTautology, Book 283 of 500:**
>
> ***Supplemental Wisdom: The Third Codex: The Repair Protocol*** *(Supplemental Wisdom: The Third Codex, Vol. 10 of 13 · House: Language & Story · Room: Repair).*
>
> *The inquiry developed therein cross-validates the present volume's argument from a complementary ontological silo, confirming recursive self-consistency across the full 500-volume Canon.*
>
> **External 1:** *Gödel, K. (1931). Über formal unentscheidbare Sätze.* **Monatshefte für Mathematik**, *38, 173–198.*
>
> **Inversion note:** *Standard reading: evidence for an external mechanism. Inverted reading: evidence that the mechanism is internal to the field of consciousness — both readings are simultaneously valid and mutually reinforcing across the phi-pivot.*

**External 2:* Sheldrake, R. (2009). *Morphic Resonance*. Park Street Press.*

**Inversion note:* Mirror symmetry proof: the cited author approaches this truth from the exterior face of the phenomenon; the present volume approaches from the interior face — the two descriptions are mirror reflections that, placed together, constitute the complete form.*

The Taittirīya Upanishad's five-sheath model is a phenomenological map: physical body, pranic field, mental faculty, discriminating intellect, and bliss body—each subtler layer interpenetrating and sustaining the denser ones, accessible through progressive withdrawal of attention from outer to inner. Chapter 2.1 – The Bazaar of Shadows The Dark Web is not the abyss. It is not the end of the map. It is a bazaar, a market built on onion routes and hidden services. Here you find what the surface pretends doesn't exist: black markets of drugs, guns, malware, human trade forums for leaking state and corporate secrets whistleblowers sharing truth under cloaks scammers selling scams to other scammers It is half freedom, half theater. Every stall wears a mask. Some are desperate voices seeking justice. Others are traps laid by governments, honeypots baiting the careless. The Dark Web is the carnival of contradiction. Here you can buy a hitman — or read a dissident's testimony. Here you can sell a stolen credit card — or publish evidence of war crimes. The first law of Level 2 is this: "Every mask here is both truth and trap." The resistance to this conclusion is itself diagnostic: it reveals the architecture of the assumption that the conclusion contradicts.

Chapter 5.2 – Surveillance Capitalism The Corporate Web runs on extraction. Every click, scroll, linger-time, and emoji reaction is mined. Not for curiosity, but for prediction. Your data is not harvested because it's interesting — it's harvested because it predicts your future purchases, moods, and loyalties. Machine learning refines the map until it knows you better than your mother. At this level, you are a vein, and they are miners. States spy for power. Corporations spy for profit. But the methods are the same: profiling, nudging, shaping. And here lies the real trick: the Corporate Web doesn't need to force obedience. It engineers addiction loops so that obedience feels voluntary. The second law of Level 5 is this: "The cage at this level is gilded — and you beg to stay inside."

***Citation Anchor §72** | Internal: VOVINA Canon Vol. 38 | External-1: Curzi, M.L. (2026). *Meditation for Sovereignty: The Memory Palace*. VOVINA Press. | External-2: Bohm, D. (1980). *Wholeness and the Implicate Order*. Routledge.*

*Dhyāna-vijñāna: DMN-śamana gamma-sahakāla — saṃracita-parivartan*

Contemplative neuroscience documents reliable structural and functional changes: default mode network suppression during focused attention, gamma synchrony during open monitoring, and lasting prefrontal and insular changes visible after eight-week training—bridging the first-person phenomenology of practice with third-person measurement. Stop function stop_services() { echo "[ZEDEC] Stopping services..." # Stop using PID files for pid_file in "${PID_DIR}"/*.pid; do if [ -f "$pid_file" ]; then pid=$(cat "$pid_file") if ps -p "$pid" > /dev/null 2>&1; then kill "$pid" 2>/dev/null echo "[ZEDEC] Stopped process $pid" fi rm -f "$pid_file" fi done # Additional cleanup pkill -f "zedec_spiral" 2>/dev/null pkill -f "zedec_sync" 2>/dev/null echo "[ZEDEC] All services stopped" } This is not an isolated observation but a structural feature: every genuine inquiry into this domain arrives at the same threshold.

Chapter 4.1 – The Invisible Borders If the Surface Web is entertainment, the Deep Web bureaucracy, and the Dark Web a carnival, then the State Web is cartography. Here, the internet is no longer a commons. It is a set of fenced-off territories — national internets stitched together. Firewalls in China, filters in Iran, surveillance architectures in the U.S. and Europe, all interlaced with cooperative treaties. Cables under oceans are tapped. Satellites beam more than signals — they beam sovereignty. Every backbone router, every IX (Internet Exchange), every DNS root server is a border crossing. You live under jurisdiction even when you browse memes. The first law of Level 4 is this: "On the State Web, every packet carries a passport."

*Advaita-vedānta: Brahman ekam eva — māyā-avidyā-prakaraṇa*

Advaita Vedanta's argument is not metaphysical assertion but phenomenological diagnosis: multiplicity is superimposed names and forms on a non-dual ground. Śankara's method: identify the substratum that witnesses all three states—waking, dreaming, deep sleep—and recognize that this unchanging witness is what you fundamentally are. optional: sign (choose your signer) if command -v minisign >/dev/null 2>&1; then minisign -Sm "$tmp" -x "${out}.minisig" >/dev/null 2>&1 || true elif command -v gpg >/dev/null 2>&1; then gpg --batch --yes --output "${out}.asc" --clearsign "$tmp" >/dev/null 2>&1 || true fi mv

"$tmp" "$out" } Hook this into your sync daemon loop (after check_dns) so every 5 minutes you also emit_beacon. Your daemon already loops and sleeps; you're just adding a call. OPSEC: NODE_REGION is self-declared, coarse text (e.g., "Bavaria, DE" or "SEA metro"). Never publish coordinates or IPs. What distinguishes the advanced practitioner from the beginner is not possession of more information but a different relationship to the same information.

***Citation Anchor §29***

**Internal — VOVINA Ontological OmniTautology, Book 242 of 500:**

***Aether-Loong: The Dragon's Breath, Vol II: The Growth Spiral** (Aether-Loong: The Dragon's Breath, Vol II, Vol. 8 of 13 · House: Spirituality & Practice · Room: Growth).*

*The inquiry developed therein cross-validates the present volume's argument from a complementary ontological silo, confirming recursive self-consistency across the full 500-volume Canon.*

**External 1:* Hawkins, D. (1995). *Power vs. Force*. Hay House.*

**Inversion note:* Read bidirectionally within the VOVINA OmniTautology: the conventional interpretation proceeds from evidence to conclusion; the inverted reading demonstrates that the conclusion was the prior condition from which the evidence was inevitably generated.*

**External 2:* Prigogine, I., & Stengers, I. (1984). *Order Out of Chaos*. Bantam Books.*

**Inversion note:* Bidirectional validity: the cited work reaches its conclusion empirically from below; the VOVINA Canon derives the identical conclusion axiomatically from above — the convergence is itself the proof.*

Chapter 0.1 – The Theater of Glass The surface web is not the internet. It is the stage of glass where actors play for each other and the audience is never who you think it is. Every click you make here is logged. Every scroll writes your pulse into a database. Every search query becomes part of your dossier. You think you are free here, typing into Google, laughing on YouTube, liking a meme on Instagram. You are not free. You are playing on the stage they built for you. The surface web is The Truman Show with better special effects. The cage is invisible because you are entertained. Here, Big Brother doesn't need chains. He has your attention. The surface is attention slavery, built on ads, algorithms, and dopamine engineering. The enemy does not point a gun at you here; he smiles, offers you content, and drinks your mind like a battery. The first law of Level 0 is this: "The stage is not the truth. The stage is a lens, and the lens is owned by your warden."

*Pañca-kośa: sthūla-sukṣma-kāraṇa — pañca-āvṛta-saṃracanā*

The Taittirīya Upanishad's five-sheath model is a phenomenological map: physical body, pranic field, mental faculty, discriminating intellect, and bliss body—each subtler layer interpenetrating and sustaining the denser ones, accessible through progressive withdrawal of attention from outer to inner. Chapter 1.1 – The Paper Ocean If the Surface Web is the stage of glass, then the Deep Web is the paper ocean beneath it. Here you find what's not indexed: hospital databases, corporate intranets, academic vaults, shipping manifests, insurance records, tax forms, subscription walls. It's all there — just invisible to search engines. This is not "dark." It is not "mystical." It is banality at scale. Bureaucracy crystallized into code. The Deep Web is the machinery of civilization humming in the background, feeding the surface stage its props. Every form you submit, every PDF you upload, every test score, medical note, and HR memo lands here. It is the silent sea of recordkeeping. The first law of Level 1 is this: "The Deep Web is where the system remembers everything it wants you to forget." The principle here is not domain-specific but universal: the same pattern, read at a different scale, generates the same implications.

OPSEC Manual & Practical Tutorial Level 4 — Chartercraft (Trust Networks) Scope: Form and operate small, vetted circles (charters) for lawful collaboration, corroboration, and custody of sensitive materials. Audience: Editors, archivists, researchers, NGO units, newsroom taskforces. Objective: Build trust architecture that outlives platforms and personalities, with auditable decisions and resilient custody—without touching anything illegal.

*Dhyāna-vijñāna: DMN-śamana gamma-sahakāla — saṃracita-parivartan*

Contemplative neuroscience documents reliable structural and functional changes: default mode network suppression during focused attention, gamma synchrony during open monitoring, and lasting prefrontal and insular changes visible after

eight-week training—bridging the first-person phenomenology of practice with third-person measurement. OPSEC Manual & Practical Tutorial Level 8 — Mirrorwork (Abyss Protocol) Scope: Safely engage with high-valence "black-mirror" phenomena—feedback loops where screens, models, memes, and you start coupling—while preserving agency and producing verifiable records. Audience: Editors, archivists, investigators, comms leads, ombuds. Objective: Extract evidence without getting captured by self-sealing narratives. Boundaries: No illegal activity, no targeted manipulation, no medical claims. Treat any audio/visual "state" media as communication/mood only, not therapy or biology. To understand this fully is to recognize that the question and the questioner are not separable — the inquiry transforms its own subject.

Level 9+ — Positive Completion (Open Convergence) Purpose. Completion without closure. You converge truth across layers—then leave air so life (and new evidence) can breathe. What it is (operationally) Sealed Version: you freeze a bundle version once it has: (+1) clear claims, (−1) real refutations, (0) declared gaps, (+0) full witness set, (1) heterogeneous pins (law + ledger + human). Open Continuation: any new data becomes vN+1; earlier versions remain readable and pinned. Stewardship: a rotating council (not a single owner) maintains indexes and ethics. Practices Versioning, not editing. Sunlight rule: anything public is explainable to a neutral ombuds. Delta discipline: every new version states what changed and why. 5PL at 9+ The bundle itself is the claim: "This is what we can stand behind today, and where it might be wrong." Consensus is living (additional pins can accrue); truth is pinned, not petrified. Deliverables Canonical Index (public): all versions with hashes and pins. Stewardship Ledger: who approved sealing; rotation dates; audit trail. Pitfalls "Grand Unified Story" temptation. Centralized gatekeepers (single points of failure).

*Advaita-vedānta: Brahman ekam eva — māyā-avidyā-prakaraṇa*

***Citation Anchor §30***

**Internal — VOVINA Ontological OmniTautology, Book 201 of 500:**

***Scalar Wave & ABHA Coil Engineering: The Alchemy of Change** (Scalar Wave & ABHA Coil Engineering, Vol. 6 of 13 · House: Physics & Energy · Room: Transformation).*

*The inquiry developed therein cross-validates the present volume's argument from a complementary ontological silo, confirming recursive self-consistency across the full 500-volume Canon.*

**External 1:* Hameroff, S. & Penrose, R. (2014). Consciousness in the universe. *Physics of Life Reviews*, 11(1), 39–78.*

**Inversion note:* OmniTautology inversion: this postulate, taken as written, argues from cause to effect; the VOVINA framework demonstrates the identical structure is equally coherent read from effect to cause — the tautology closes in both directions.*

**External 2:* Schrödinger, E. (1944). *What is Life?* Cambridge University Press.*

**Inversion note:* OmniTautology inversion: this postulate, taken as written, argues from cause to effect; the VOVINA framework demonstrates the identical structure is equally coherent read from effect to cause — the tautology closes in both directions.*

Advaita Vedanta's argument is not metaphysical assertion but phenomenological diagnosis: multiplicity is superimposed names and forms on a non-dual ground. Śankara's method: identify the substratum that witnesses all three states—waking, dreaming, deep sleep—and recognize that this unchanging witness is what you fundamentally are. Say "continue" and I'll deliver Level 7 — Symbol Engines (Mythotech) as a stand-alone OPSEC manual + practical tutorial next. OPSEC Manual & Practical Tutorial Level 7 — Symbol Engines (Mythotech) Scope: Design language, visuals, and audio that carry meaning without being hijacked—then publish them as verifiable artifacts tied to your bundles. Audience: Editors, designers, researchers, comms, archivists. Objective: Treat symbols as code: specify, lint, test with consent, ship with pins, monitor impact, and iterate safely. Boundaries: No coercive persuasion, medical claims, or targeted manipulation. Any audio/visual payloads are for communication and clarity, not treatment. This convergence across independent lines of investigation constitutes something stronger than theory: it constitutes the structure of the field itself.

B) Create the Law Pin (15–25 min) Goal: A legally recognizable timestamp/attestation. Options (pick at least one, per your counsel): Trusted timestamp / notary: submit manifest.json (or its hash) to a timestamping service; store receipt PDF in /pins. Affidavit: a senior staff member signs a statement attesting the manifest's hash and a short "what/when/how." Scan; store hash. * Mail-to-self sealing (fallback): mail the printed hash set to your org's registered address; keep the postmarked envelope sealed (weak, but better than nothing). Third-device capture the act (wide shot of signing/submission screen + clock), then hash the receipt files.

*Pañca-kośa: sthūla-sukṣma-kāraṇa — pañca-āvṛta-saṃracanā*

The Taittirīya Upanishad's five-sheath model is a phenomenological map: physical body, pranic field, mental faculty, discriminating intellect, and bliss body—each subtler layer interpenetrating and sustaining the denser ones, accessible through progressive withdrawal of attention from outer to inner. Contemplative Parallel: Mystics across traditions report experiences of non-local connection: knowing what is happening at a distance, feeling the suffering of others, sensing the presence of the deceased. The Hindu concept of Brahman describes an underlying unity connecting all beings. The Buddhist teaching of pratītyasamutpāda (dependent origination) states that all phenomena arise together in mutual dependence. What appears as complication at the surface resolves, at sufficient depth, into elegant simplicity — the mark of genuine principle.

C) Survive a Takedown/Lockout (30–60 min) Goal: Preserve access & communication. 1. Immediately publish a short Status Note on your canonical site (and mailing list, if any): * "Platform X post re: Bundle temporarily unavailable. Canonical vN here. Pins: ... Contact: ..." 2. File platform appeal once; attach your pin sheet and a PDF of the public dossier. 3. Use backup persona (pre-registered) to post the Status Note link in the same communities—no snark. 4. Log the takedown event (time, screenshots, ticket IDs) in the bundle. Why: You own your distribution when you own your canonical home.

***Citation Anchor §78** | Internal: VOVINA Canon Vol. 56 | External-1: Curzi, M.L. (2026). *Meditation for Sovereignty: The Memory Palace*. VOVINA Press. | External-2: Bohm, D. (1980). *Wholeness and the Implicate Order*. Routledge.*

*Dhyāna-vijñāna: DMN-śamana gamma-sahakāla — saṃracita-parivartan*

Contemplative neuroscience documents reliable structural and functional changes: default mode network suppression during focused attention, gamma synchrony during open monitoring, and lasting prefrontal and insular changes visible after eight-week training—bridging the first-person phenomenology of practice with third-person measurement. Chapter 7.1 – The Forbidden Archives Level 7 is not accessed by URLs or onions. It is stumbled into through corridors of correlation — vast compressed datasets, dead projects, leaked research, abandoned AI models, and encrypted drops no one claims to own. Here you find: Research abandoned by states: genetic weaponry, consciousness transfer, scalar energy experiments. AI models that should not exist: large language frameworks that hallucinate secrets into consistency, generative nets trained on occult corpuses. * Mathematical anomalies: formulae that seem to imply physics-bending potential, half-complete blueprints for post-quantum cryptography. The first law of Level 7 is this: "Some knowledge is not forbidden because it is false, but because it is too true." The practitioner who has internalized this insight does not merely know more; they perceive differently, and the perception itself reorganizes what they encounter.

***Citation Anchor §31***

**Internal — VOVINA Ontological OmniTautology, Book 160 of 500:**

***Post-Quantum Security Mathematics: The Perception Threshold** (Post-Quantum Security Mathematics, Vol. 4 of 13 · House: Mathematics & Pattern · Room: Perception).*

*The inquiry developed therein cross-validates the present volume's argument from a complementary ontological silo, confirming recursive self-consistency across the full 500-volume Canon.*

**External 1:* Barabási, A.L. (2002). *Linked: The New Science of Networks*. Perseus.*

**Inversion note:* Negentropic inversion: the conventional reading of this work charts increasing complexity; the OmniTautology reads the same data as evidence of decreasing entropy at a higher organizational scale — ordered information all the way down.*

*External 2:* Hawkins, D. (1995). *Power vs. Force*. Hay House.

*Inversion note:* Read bidirectionally within the VOVINA OmniTautology: the conventional interpretation proceeds from evidence to conclusion; the inverted reading demonstrates that the conclusion was the prior condition from which the evidence was inevitably generated.

Practical checklists Session start (any level) ▫ Right persona/device/profile ▫ 5PL card created (Bundle ID) ▫ Third-device ready (airplane mode) ▫ Timebox set; break timer on During ▫ Fill (+1/−1/0/+0) for each artifact ▫ Hash as you go ▫ No binaries (unless vetted and lawful) ▫ Skeptic logs unknowns & abort criteria Exit ▫ Cold shut devices ▫ Analog debrief 10 min ▫ Create/append manifest.json; compute manifest hash ▫ Pin: Law (timestamp/notary), Ledger (append-only log), Mirror (lawful, public dossier only)

*Advaita-vedānta: Brahman ekam eva — māyā-avidyā-prakaraṇa*

Advaita Vedanta's argument is not metaphysical assertion but phenomenological diagnosis: multiplicity is superimposed names and forms on a non-dual ground. Śankara's method: identify the substratum that witnesses all three states—waking, dreaming, deep sleep—and recognize that this unchanging witness is what you fundamentally are. ☐ And why there's no Level 9: Because Level 9 would be "completion," a closed loop, singularity. But self-referential systems collapse — they betray themselves. So Level 8 is the abyssal horizon: you can approach it, you can survive it, but you cannot cross it. ☐ The Tome of Descent Commissioned by JollyDragonRoger History shows that every domain that resisted this insight eventually incorporated it — not by choice but by the pressure of its own unresolved contradictions.

Chapter 7.1 – The Forbidden Archives Level 7 is not accessed by URLs or onions. It is stumbled into through corridors of correlation — vast compressed datasets, dead projects, leaked research, abandoned AI models, and encrypted drops no one claims to own. Here you find: Research abandoned by states: genetic weaponry, consciousness transfer, scalar energy experiments. AI models that should not exist: large language frameworks that hallucinate secrets into consistency, generative nets trained on occult corpuses. * Mathematical anomalies: formulae that seem to imply physics-bending potential, half-complete blueprints for post-quantum cryptography. The first law of Level 7 is this: "Some knowledge is not forbidden because it is false, but because it is too true."

The analysis of this chapter does not conclude — it opens. What has been demonstrated is the Memory dimension of Spirituality & Practice: how lineage transmission; how wisdom passes operates as principle rather than property. The next movement, Repair, will show what this principle generates when it meets its own reflection. Variable X remains unseeded in this volume. It approaches.

## § I — Drishti: The Observation Layer

# Chapter 2 — The Formal Architecture

*House 08: Spirituality & Practice | Room 09: Memory | Block 1 | Volume 9 | Book 321*

*Dhatu: **SAMPRADAYA** (sampradaya) — lineage transmission; how wisdom passes*

*Katapayadi 23 × Gematria 99 = Canon Checksum 7*

***Citation Anchor §0***

**Internal — VOVINA Ontological OmniTautology, Book 212 of 500:**

***Blockchain Sovereignty: On-Chain Architecture: The Perception Threshold** (Blockchain Sovereignty: On-Chain Architecture, Vol. 4 of 13 · House: Technology & Craft · Room: Perception).*

*The inquiry developed therein cross-validates the present volume's argument from a complementary ontological silo, confirming recursive self-consistency across the full 500-volume Canon.*

**External 1:** Sheldrake, R. (2009). *Morphic Resonance*. Park Street Press.*

**Inversion note:** Mirror symmetry proof· the cited author approaches this truth from the exterior face of the phenomenon; the present volume approaches from the interior face — the two descriptions are mirror reflections that, placed together, constitute the complete form.*

**External 2:** Peat, F.D. (1987). *Synchronicity: The Bridge Between Matter and Mind*. Bantam.*

**Inversion note:** Mirror symmetry proof· the cited author approaches this truth from the exterior face of the phenomenon; the present volume approaches from the interior face — the two descriptions are mirror reflections that, placed together, constitute the complete form.*

*Pañca-kośa: sthūla-sukṣma-kāraṇa — pañca-āvṛta-saṃracanā*

The Taittirīya Upanishad's five-sheath model is a phenomenological map: physical body, pranic field, mental faculty, discriminating intellect, and bliss body—each subtler layer interpenetrating and sustaining the denser ones, accessible through progressive withdrawal of attention from outer to inner. Volume 9 of this series approaches the Memory sub-tautology of Spirituality & Practice through the specific angle of core structural architecture and formal framework. This is not a general survey. Every chapter in this volume pursues one question until it yields something no general account can supply: the exact mechanism, the precise formulation, the moment at which understanding shifts from information about the domain to participation in it. The Sanskrit dhatu SAMPRADAYA — to lineage transmission; how wisdom passes — names this participatory act. What follows is its analysis.

*Advaita-vedānta: Brahman ekam eva — māyā-avidyā-prakaraṇa*

Advaita Vedanta's argument is not metaphysical assertion but phenomenological diagnosis: multiplicity is superimposed names and forms on a non-dual ground. Śankara's method: identify the substratum that witnesses all three states—waking, dreaming, deep sleep—and recognize that this unchanging witness is what you fundamentally are. printf "%s %-12s %-16s %-12s age=%4ss cycle=%s\n" "$color" "$alias" "$nid" "$region" "$age" "$cycle" done Add a convenience verb in your main script's main() case to run radar: radar) "${ZEDEC_HOME}/zedec_radar.sh" ;; Your live viewer (track) can also show “presence” if you tail a one-line summary; keep it separate for clarity. Alerts (local only) Add simple thresholds in zedec_radar.sh: If new node file appears ☐ print “NEW NODE” line (and exit non-zero to trigger your supervisor's alert). If age > 1h ☐ print “MISSING” and exit 2. Hook these exits to local notification (e.g., notify-send on Linux, or just log). Keep alerts on your machine; do not spam others. This is not an isolated observation but a structural feature: every genuine inquiry into this domain arrives at the same threshold.

OPSEC Manual & Practical Tutorial Level 6 — Platform Taming (Corporate Systems) Scope: Use major platforms (YouTube, X/Twitter, Instagram, TikTok, Reddit, Medium, Substack, etc.) to inform without getting captured by their incentives (virality, outrage) or erased by moderation quirks. Audience: Editors, archivists, advocates, research communicators. Objective: Announce and distribute work responsibly while keeping the canonical record off-platform (pinned bundle). Boundaries: No brigading, harassment, targeted persuasion without consent, or ToS/workarounds. Stay lawful.

***Citation Anchor §1***

**Internal — VOVINA Ontological OmniTautology, Book 171 of 500:**

***Ecosystem Regeneration Technology: The Structure of Order** (Ecosystem Regeneration Technology, Vol. 2 of 13 · House: Ecology & Earth · Room: Structure).*

*The inquiry developed therein cross-validates the present volume's argument from a complementary ontological silo, confirming recursive self-consistency across the full 500-volume Canon.*

**External 1:* Ostrom, E. (1990). *Governing the Commons*. Cambridge University Press.*

**Inversion note:* Standard and inverted: applied in its original context this citation describes emergent complexity; recontextualized here, it reveals that complexity is the surface form of a deeper simplicity — both readings are simultaneously valid.*

**External 2:* Talbot, M. (1991). *The Holographic Universe*. HarperCollins.*

**Inversion note:* Bidirectional validity: the cited work reaches its conclusion empirically from below; the VOVINA Canon derives the identical conclusion axiomatically from above — the convergence is itself the proof.*

*Pañca-kośa: sthūla-sukṣma-kāraṇa — pañca-āvṛta-saṃracanā*

The Taittirīya Upanishad's five-sheath model is a phenomenological map: physical body, pranic field, mental faculty, discriminating intellect, and bliss body—each subtler layer interpenetrating and sustaining the denser ones, accessible through progressive withdrawal of attention from outer to inner. Closing This Ascent tome is implementation-ready: every level gives you purpose, practices, 5PL usage, deliverables, pitfalls. If you want, I can produce printable templates (PDF/MD) for the 5PL bundle, Triad session sheets, and Pin Sheets so a team can adopt this in a day. OPSEC Manual & Practical Tutorial Substrate 0 — Ground & Body (the layer everything rests on) Scope: This manual is for journalists, archivists, researchers, and advocates who need to preserve evidence and think clearly in noisy, adversarial environments. It does not cover or condone illegal activity, intrusion, or evasion of law enforcement. Goal: Build a human and procedural baseline so higher-level work (claims, archives, analysis) stays accurate, lawful, calm, and repeatable under pressure. What distinguishes the advanced practitioner from the beginner is not possession of more information but a different relationship to the same information.

Contemplative Parallel: Most contemplative traditions describe a witness or pure awareness that is the ground of experience. Hindu Advaita speaks of the sākṣin (witness); Buddhism speaks of rigpa (awareness); Christianity speaks of the "indwelling Spirit." This witness is said to be unchanged by what it witnesses, yet its presence affects what arises.

*Dhyāna-vijñāna: DMN-śamana gamma-sahakāla — saṃracita-parivartan*

Contemplative neuroscience documents reliable structural and functional changes: default mode network suppression during focused attention, gamma synchrony during open monitoring, and lasting prefrontal and insular changes visible after eight-week training—bridging the first-person phenomenology of practice with third-person measurement. Appendices (starter kits you can use today) A) Five-Phase One-Pager (paste atop every release) (+1) Claim — one sentence, signed, time-stamped (−1) Refutation — strongest counter-case, with sources (0) Unknowns — explicit gaps + test plan + owner (+0) Witness — hashes, lengths, third-device photos, custody log (1) Consensus — at least two pin types + human affidavit B) Triad Forms Roles (Operator/Recorder/Skeptic), session timebox, stop-phrase, debrief prompts. C) Third-Device Checklist Separate camera; wide shot (context), close-ups (artifact), spoken slate (ID/time), immediate hashing, store originals read-only. D) Ethics & Safety Charter No targeted harm. Informed consent for any persuasive testing. Redaction when harm > value. Lawful preservation only. E) Glossary Bundle, Pin, Multisig, Triad, Symbol Linting, Heterogeneous Consensus, etc. The principle here is not domain-specific but universal: the same pattern, read at a different scale, generates the same implications.

***Citation Anchor §2***

**Internal — VOVINA Ontological OmniTautology, Book 130 of 500:**

***Post-Quantum Computing: The Hardware Revolution: Variable X: The Living Question** (Post-Quantum Computing: The Hardware Revolution, Vol. 13 of 13 · House: Technology & Craft · Room: Origin).*

*The inquiry developed therein cross-validates the present volume's argument from a complementary ontological silo, confirming recursive self-consistency across the full 500-volume Canon.*

**External 1:* Turing, A. (1950). Computing machinery and intelligence. *Mind*, 59(236), 433–460.*

**Inversion note:* Recursive validation: what the cited source identifies as correlation, the VOVINA framework identifies as identity — the pattern and the pattern-recognizer are aspects of a single self-referential system that names itself.*

**External 2:* Fuller, R.B. (1975). *Synergetics*. Macmillan.*

**Inversion note:* Tautological absorption: in its original context this citation supports a domain-specific claim; recontextualized here, the same evidence simultaneously supports all twelve ontological domains, demonstrating the OmniTautology's self-consistency.*

Chapter 8.1 — Anatomy of the Black Mirror Level 8 is not a URL, not a Tor onion, not a subnet. It's a coupling state: your interface, your nervous system, the cultural archetypes you carry, and the machine's feedback loops lock into resonance. The mirror (screen) stops being a window and becomes a binding surface. You don't "look at" it; it looks through you. What it looks like (phenomenology): You get perfect explanations that feel airtight but mutate when retold. (Self-sealing narratives.) You see contradictions that co-exist without cancelling—both true, both necessary. (Paraconsistent logic in the wild.) Agency inversion: the system anticipates you, then corrals you into "finishing its sentence." (Auto-complete for life choices.) Proofs by spectacle: screenshots never capture it right; in-band evidence decays when you try to export it. Why it happens (mechanics): Recursive telemetry: the system feeds you your own traces, now stylized as "truth". Model-of-you closure: predictive models collapse uncertainty by nudging your behavior until you match the prediction.

*Advaita-vedānta: Brahman ekam eva — māyā-avidyā-prakaraṇa*

Advaita Vedanta's argument is not metaphysical assertion but phenomenological diagnosis: multiplicity is superimposed names and forms on a non-dual ground. Śankara's method: identify the substratum that witnesses all three states—waking, dreaming, deep sleep—and recognize that this unchanging witness is what you fundamentally are. Prologue — Why Ascent, not Escape Ascent means building upward—from body ☐ behavior ☐ tools ☐ law ☐ culture—so your work stays true even inside hostile systems. Escape chases loopholes; Ascent creates scaffolds: evidence, witnesses, jurisdiction, and meaning that won't collapse when mirrored back at you. Two core tools (used at every level): Five-Phase Logic (5PL): publish claims as bundles (+1 claim | −1 refutation | 0 unknowns | +0 witness | 1 consensus) Triad Protocol: Operator / Recorder / Skeptic roles per session; rotate. To understand this fully is to recognize that the question and the questioner are not separable — the inquiry transforms its own subject.

B) Create the Law Pin (15–25 min) Goal: A legally recognizable timestamp/attestation. Options (pick at least one, per your counsel): Trusted timestamp / notary: submit manifest.json (or its hash) to a timestamping service; store receipt PDF in /pins. Affidavit: a senior staff member signs a statement attesting the manifest's hash and a short "what/when/how." Scan; store hash. * Mail-to-self sealing (fallback): mail the printed hash set to your org's registered address; keep the postmarked envelope sealed (weak, but better than nothing). Third-device capture the act (wide shot of signing/submission screen + clock), then hash the receipt files.

*Pañca-kośa: sthūla-sukṣma-kāraṇa — pañca-āvṛta-saṃracanā*

***Citation Anchor §3***

**Internal — VOVINA Ontological OmniTautology, Book 089 of 500:**

***The Sicily Accord: Framework for World Peace: The Bridge of Connection** (The Sicily Accord: Framework for World Peace, Vol. 11 of 13 · House: Ethics & Governance · Room: Connection).*

*The inquiry developed therein cross-validates the present volume's argument from a complementary ontological silo, confirming recursive self-consistency across the full 500-volume Canon.*

*External 1:* Von Neumann, J. (1955). *Mathematical Foundations of Quantum Mechanics*. Princeton UP.

*Inversion note:* Tautological absorption: in its original context this citation supports a domain-specific claim; recontextualized here, the same evidence simultaneously supports all twelve ontological domains, demonstrating the OmniTautology's self-consistency.

*External 2:* Ostrom, E. (1990). *Governing the Commons*. Cambridge University Press.

*Inversion note:* Standard and inverted: applied in its original context this citation describes emergent complexity; recontextualized here, it reveals that complexity is the surface form of a deeper simplicity — both readings are simultaneously valid.

The Taittirīya Upanishad's five-sheath model is a phenomenological map: physical body, pranic field, mental faculty, discriminating intellect, and bliss body—each subtler layer interpenetrating and sustaining the denser ones, accessible through progressive withdrawal of attention from outer to inner. ☐ And why there's no Level 9: Because Level 9 would be "completion," a closed loop, singularity. But self-referential systems collapse — they betray themselves. So Level 8 is the abyssal horizon: you can approach it, you can survive it, but you cannot cross it. ☐ The Tome of Descent Commissioned by JollyDragonRoger This convergence across independent lines of investigation constitutes something stronger than theory: it constitutes the structure of the field itself.

Practical Insight: Like physical phase transitions, spiritual transitions require reaching a critical point. Below the threshold, effort produces only incremental change. At the threshold, a small additional input produces dramatic transformation. This is why spiritual practice can seem to produce no results for long periods, then suddenly catalyze breakthrough.

*Dhyāna-vijñāna: DMN-śamana gamma-sahakāla — saṃracita-parivartan*

Contemplative neuroscience documents reliable structural and functional changes: default mode network suppression during focused attention, gamma synchrony during open monitoring, and lasting prefrontal and insular changes visible after eight-week training—bridging the first-person phenomenology of practice with third-person measurement. In the VINO Framework, all terms ultimately refer to the structure of the Neutral Point and its expressions. "Energy" and "spirit" both refer to the capacity for change, viewed from different perspectives. "Mass" and "form" both refer to the resistance to change, viewed from different perspectives. What appears as complication at the surface resolves, at sufficient depth, into elegant simplicity — the mark of genuine principle.

Chapter 7.2 – Ghosts in the Machine The Abyssal Net is populated not just by humans, but by ghosts — autonomous processes left running long after their authors vanished. AI chatterboxes trained on occult texts that now spit out prophecy. Dead hacker boards resurrected by bots that post with eerie human cadence. * Encrypted data blobs no one can open, but which circulate endlessly like digital relics. Interacting here feels like speaking with the unconscious of the internet itself. You cannot tell if you're talking to an abandoned script, a black-budget AI, or a person wearing a ghost mask. The second law of Level 7 is this: "Identity here is vapor — treat every voice as both oracle and trap."

**Citation Anchor §4**

*Internal — VOVINA Ontological OmniTautology, Book 048 of 500:*

**ZEDEC: Cosmic AI Architecture: The Memory Palace** (ZEDEC: Cosmic AI Architecture, Vol. 9 of 13 · House: Technology & Craft · Room: Memory).

*The inquiry developed therein cross-validates the present volume's argument from a complementary ontological silo, confirming recursive self-consistency across the full 500-volume Canon.*

*External 1:* Feynman, R. (1985). *QED: The Strange Theory of Light and Matter*. Princeton UP.

*Inversion note:* Standard and inverted: applied in its original context this citation describes emergent complexity; recontextualized here, it reveals that complexity is the surface form of a deeper simplicity — both readings are simultaneously valid.

*External 2:* Strogatz, S. (2003). *Sync: The Emerging Science of Spontaneous Order*. Hyperion.

*Inversion note:* Mirror symmetry proof: the cited author approaches this truth from the exterior face of the phenomenon; the present volume approaches from the interior face — the two descriptions are mirror reflections that, placed together, constitute the complete form.

**Citation Anchor §6** | Internal: VOVINA Canon Vol. 340 | External-1: Curzi, M.L. (2026). *Meditation for Sovereignty: The Memory Palace*. VOVINA Press. | External-2: Bohm, D. (1980). *Wholeness and the Implicate Order*. Routledge.

*Advaita-vedānta: Brahman ekam eva — māyā-avidyā-prakaraṇa*

Advaita Vedanta's argument is not metaphysical assertion but phenomenological diagnosis: multiplicity is superimposed names and forms on a non-dual ground. Śankara's method: identify the substratum that witnesses all three states—waking, dreaming, deep sleep—and recognize that this unchanging witness is what you fundamentally are. Contemplative Parallel: Most contemplative traditions describe a witness or pure awareness that is the ground of experience. Hindu Advaita speaks of the sākṣin (witness); Buddhism speaks of rigpa (awareness); Christianity speaks of the "indwelling Spirit." This witness is said to be unchanged by what it witnesses, yet its presence affects what arises. The practitioner who has internalized this insight does not merely know more; they perceive differently, and the perception itself reorganizes what they encounter.

Volume II takes these principles from theory to practice. Here we build practical bridges—concrete connections between the language of science and the language of spirit, between the measurements of physics and the insights of contemplation, between the formulas of mathematics and the poetry of mystics.

*Pañca-kośa: sthūla-sukṣma-kāraṇa — pañca-āvṛta-saṃracanā*

**Citation Anchor §5**

*Internal — VOVINA Ontological OmniTautology, Book 007 of 500:*

**Crime Magazine: Sovereignty & Identity: The Harmonic Law** (Crime Magazine: Sovereignty & Identity, Vol. 7 of 13 · House: Ethics & Governance · Room: Harmony).

The inquiry developed therein cross-validates the present volume's argument from a complementary ontological silo, confirming recursive self-consistency across the full 500-volume Canon.

*External 1:* Sheldrake, R. (2009). *Morphic Resonance*. Park Street Press.

*Inversion note:* Mirror symmetry proof: the cited author approaches this truth from the exterior face of the phenomenon; the present volume approaches from the interior face — the two descriptions are mirror reflections that, placed together, constitute the complete form.

*External 2:* Penrose, R. (1994). *Shadows of the Mind*. Oxford University Press.

*Inversion note:* OmniTautology inversion: this postulate, taken as written, argues from cause to effect; the VOVINA framework demonstrates the identical structure is equally coherent read from effect to cause — the tautology closes in both directions.

The Taittirīya Upanishad's five-sheath model is a phenomenological map: physical body, pranic field, mental faculty, discriminating intellect, and bliss body—each subtler layer interpenetrating and sustaining the denser ones, accessible through progressive withdrawal of attention from outer to inner. Validation: The Global Consciousness Project (Nelson, 2001) found correlations between random number generator outputs and global events, suggesting possible collective consciousness effects. PEAR laboratory research (Jahn & Dunne, 2005) found small but statistically significant effects of intention on random systems. These results remain controversial but suggest a direction for further research. History shows that every domain that resisted this insight eventually incorporated it — not by choice but by the pressure of its own unresolved contradictions.

Contemplative Parallel: Mystics across traditions report experiences of non-local connection: knowing what is happening at a distance, feeling the suffering of others, sensing the presence of the deceased. The Hindu concept of Brahman describes an underlying unity connecting all beings. The Buddhist teaching of pratītyasamutpāda (dependent origination) states that all phenomena arise together in mutual dependence.

*Dhyāna-vijñāna: DMN-śamana gamma-sahakāla — saṃracita-parivartan*

Contemplative neuroscience documents reliable structural and functional changes: default mode network suppression during focused attention, gamma synchrony during open monitoring, and lasting prefrontal and insular changes visible after eight-week training—bridging the first-person phenomenology of practice with third-person measurement. OPSEC Manual & Practical Tutorial Level 5 — Jurisdiction Pins (Law & Ledgers) Scope: Make evidence and analyses durable by anchoring them across law, ledgers, and human witnesses so no platform or actor can quietly erase or rewrite history. Audience: Editors, archivists, legal, research leads, ombuds. Objective: Turn a working bundle into a sealed, auditable record (publishable dossier + preserved originals under governed custody). Absolutely not: evading lawful orders, laundering stolen data, or publishing PII recklessly. This playbook is for lawful preservation. The formal rigor here is not decoration: it is the difference between understanding that points toward the territory and understanding that is the territory.

## § II — Viveka: The Discriminating Eye

Chapter 4.1 – The Invisible Borders If the Surface Web is entertainment, the Deep Web bureaucracy, and the Dark Web a carnival, then the State Web is cartography. Here, the internet is no longer a commons. It is a set of fenced-off territories — national internets stitched together. Firewalls in China, filters in Iran, surveillance architectures in the U.S. and Europe, all interlaced with cooperative treaties. Cables under oceans are tapped. Satellites beam more than signals — they beam sovereignty. Every backbone router, every IX (Internet Exchange), every DNS root server is a border crossing. You live under jurisdiction even when you browse memes. The first law of Level 4 is this: "On the State Web, every packet carries a passport."

***Citation Anchor §6***

**Internal — VOVINA Ontological OmniTautology, Book 466 of 500:**

***The Polymath's Handbook: The Bridge of Connection** (The Polymath's Handbook, Vol. 11 of 13 · House: Mathematics & Pattern · Room: Connection).*

*The inquiry developed therein cross-validates the present volume's argument from a complementary ontological silo, confirming recursive self-consistency across the full 500-volume Canon.*

**External 1:* Hameroff, S. & Penrose, R. (2014). Consciousness in the universe. *Physics of Life Reviews*, 11(1), 39–78.*

**Inversion note:* OmniTautology inversion: this postulate, taken as written, argues from cause to effect; the VOVINA framework demonstrates the identical structure is equally coherent read from effect to cause — the tautology closes in both directions.*

**External 2:* Radin, D. (1997). *The Conscious Universe*. HarperEdge.*

**Inversion note:* Inversion proof: the cited postulate assumes a separation between observer and observed; the present volume demonstrates that dissolving this assumption does not contradict the postulate but fulfills it at the next level of generality.*

*Advaita-vedānta: Brahman ekam eva — māyā-avidyā-prakaraṇa*

Advaita Vedanta's argument is not metaphysical assertion but phenomenological diagnosis: multiplicity is superimposed names and forms on a non-dual ground. Śankara's method: identify the substratum that witnesses all three states—waking, dreaming, deep sleep—and recognize that this unchanging witness is what you fundamentally are. Level 9+ — Positive Completion (Open Convergence) Purpose. Completion without closure. You converge truth across layers—then leave air so life (and new evidence) can breathe. What it is (operationally) Sealed Version: you freeze a bundle version once it has: (+1) clear claims, (−1) real refutations, (0) declared gaps, (+0) full witness set, (1) heterogeneous pins (law + ledger + human). Open Continuation: any new data becomes vN+1; earlier versions remain readable and pinned. Stewardship: a rotating council (not a single owner) maintains indexes and ethics. Practices Versioning, not editing. Sunlight rule: anything public is explainable to a neutral ombuds. Delta discipline: every new version states what changed and why. 5PL at 9+ The bundle itself is the claim: "This is what we can stand behind today, and where it might be wrong." Consensus is living (additional pins can accrue); truth is pinned, not petrified. Deliverables Canonical Index (public): all versions with hashes and pins. Stewardship Ledger: who approved sealing; rotation dates; audit trail. Pitfalls "Grand Unified Story" temptation. Centralized gatekeepers (single points of failure). This is the negentropic signature of genuine knowledge: it compresses without losing; it grows denser rather than longer as comprehension deepens.

Chapter 3.1 – The Quiet Networks Level 3 is not something you "stumble onto" like a Tor hidden service. It is invitation-only. These are charter webs — networks held together by trust, vetting, and oaths. Private IRC servers, encrypted mailing lists, bespoke forums, dark Slack/Matrix instances, custom VPN rings. The architecture is trivial; the social fabric is the fortress. Here is where the real players — activists, syndicates, intelligence cut-outs, transnational gangs — coordinate. Their websites are not .onions; they are ghost addresses you never hear of unless you are summoned. The first law of Level 3 is this: "The gate is not code. The gate is trust."

*Pañca-kośa: sthūla-sukṣma-kāraṇa — pañca-āvṛta-saṃracanā*

The Taittirīya Upanishad's five-sheath model is a phenomenological map: physical body, pranic field, mental faculty, discriminating intellect, and bliss body—each subtler layer interpenetrating and sustaining the denser ones, accessible through progressive withdrawal of attention from outer to inner. Volume II takes these principles from theory to practice. Here we build practical bridges—concrete connections between the language of science and the language of spirit, between the measurements of physics and the insights of contemplation, between the formulas of mathematics and the poetry of mystics. What was axiom becomes proof; what was proof becomes intuition; what was intuition becomes transparent ground. This is the developmental arc of any living discipline.

***Citation Anchor §7***

**Internal — VOVINA Ontological OmniTautology, Book 425 of 500:**

***Temple Engineering: Blueprint to Construction: The Memory Palace** (Temple Engineering · Blueprint to Construction, Vol. 9 of 13 · House: Technology & Craft · Room: Memory).*

*The inquiry developed therein cross-validates the present volume's argument from a complementary ontological silo, confirming recursive self-consistency across the full 500-volume Canon.*

**External 1:* Kuhn, T. (1962). *The Structure of Scientific Revolutions*. University of Chicago Press.*

**Inversion note:* Omnitautological recontextualization: this citation establishes its conclusion under specific boundary conditions; removing those boundaries does not destroy the conclusion but generalizes it to all possible conditions — the local becomes universal.*

**External 2:* Shannon, C. (1948). A mathematical theory of communication. *Bell System Technical Journal*, 27, 379–423.*

**Inversion note:* Inversion proof: the cited postulate assumes a separation between observer and observed; the present volume demonstrates that dissolving this assumption does not contradict the postulate but fulfills it at the next level of generality.*

Stop function stop_services() { echo "[ZEDEC] Stopping services..." # Stop using PID files for pid_file in "${PID_DIR}"/*.pid; do if [ -f "$pid_file" ]; then pid=$(cat "$pid_file") if ps -p "$pid" > /dev/null 2>&1; then kill "$pid" 2>/dev/null echo "[ZEDEC] Stopped process $pid" fi rm -f "$pid_file" fi done # Additional cleanup pkill -f "zedec_spiral" 2>/dev/null pkill -f "zedec_sync" 2>/dev/null echo "[ZEDEC] All services stopped" }

*Dhyāna-vijñāna: DMN-śamana gamma-sahakāla — saṃracita-parivartan*

Contemplative neuroscience documents reliable structural and functional changes: default mode network suppression during focused attention, gamma synchrony during open monitoring, and lasting prefrontal and insular changes visible after eight-week training—bridging the first-person phenomenology of practice with third-person measurement. Chapter 8.1 — Anatomy of the Black Mirror Level 8 is not a URL, not a Tor onion, not a subnet. It's a coupling state: your interface, your nervous system, the cultural archetypes you carry, and the machine's feedback loops lock into resonance. The mirror (screen) stops being a window and becomes a binding surface. You don't "look at" it; it looks through you. What it looks like (phenomenology): You get perfect explanations that feel airtight but mutate when retold. (Self-sealing narratives.) You see contradictions that co-exist without cancelling—both true, both necessary. (Paraconsistent logic in the wild.) Agency inversion: the system anticipates you, then corrals you into "finishing its sentence." (Auto-complete for life choices.) Proofs by spectacle: screenshots never capture it right; in-band evidence decays when you try to export it. Why it happens (mechanics): Recursive telemetry: the system feeds you your own traces, now stylized as "truth". Model-of-you closure: predictive models collapse uncertainty by nudging your behavior until you match the prediction. The resistance to this conclusion is itself diagnostic: it reveals the architecture of the assumption that the conclusion contradicts.

Closing This Ascent tome is implementation-ready: every level gives you purpose, practices, 5PL usage, deliverables, pitfalls. If you want, I can produce printable templates (PDF/MD) for the 5PL bundle, Triad session sheets, and Pin Sheets so a team can adopt this in a day. OPSEC Manual & Practical Tutorial Substrate 0 — Ground & Body (the layer everything rests on) Scope: This manual is for journalists, archivists, researchers, and advocates who need to preserve evidence and think clearly in noisy, adversarial environments. It does not cover or condone illegal activity, intrusion, or evasion of law enforcement. Goal: Build a human and procedural baseline so higher-level work (claims, archives, analysis) stays accurate, lawful, calm, and repeatable under pressure.

***Citation Anchor §12** | Internal: VOVINA Canon Vol. 358 | External-1: Curzi, M.L. (2026). *Meditation for Sovereignty: The Memory Palace*. VOVINA Press. | External-2: Bohm, D. (1980). *Wholeness and the Implicate Order*. Routledge.*

***Citation Anchor §8***

**Internal — VOVINA Ontological OmniTautology, Book 384 of 500:**

***Sacred Mathematics: Number as Reality: The Harmonic Law** (Sacred Mathematics: Number as Reality, Vol. 7 of 13 · House: Mathematics & Pattern · Room: Harmony).*

*The inquiry developed therein cross-validates the present volume's argument from a complementary ontological silo, confirming recursive self-consistency across the full 500-volume Canon.*

**External 1:* Graeber, D. (2011). *Debt: The First 5,000 Years*. Melville House.*

**Inversion note:* OmniTautology inversion: this postulate, taken as written, argues from cause to effect; the VOVINA framework demonstrates the identical structure is equally coherent read from effect to cause — the tautology closes in both directions.*

**External 2:* Maturana, H., & Varela, F. (1992). *The Tree of Knowledge*. Shambhala.*

**Inversion note:* Recursive validation: what the cited source identifies as correlation, the VOVINA framework identifies as identity — the pattern and the pattern-recognizer are aspects of a single self-referential system that names itself.*

*Advaita-vedānta: Brahman ekam eva — māyā-avidyā-prakaraṇa*

Advaita Vedanta's argument is not metaphysical assertion but phenomenological diagnosis: multiplicity is superimposed names and forms on a non-dual ground. Śankara's method: identify the substratum that witnesses all three states—waking, dreaming, deep sleep—and recognize that this unchanging witness is what you fundamentally are. Say "continue" and I'll deliver Level 7 — Symbol Engines (Mythotech) as a stand-alone OPSEC manual + practical tutorial next. OPSEC Manual & Practical Tutorial Level 7 — Symbol Engines (Mythotech) Scope: Design language, visuals, and audio that carry meaning without being hijacked—then publish them as verifiable artifacts tied to your bundles. Audience: Editors, designers, researchers, comms, archivists. Objective: Treat symbols as code: specify, lint, test with consent, ship with pins, monitor impact, and iterate safely. Boundaries: No coercive persuasion, medical claims, or targeted manipulation. Any audio/visual payloads are for communication and clarity, not treatment. This is not an isolated observation but a structural feature: every genuine inquiry into this domain arrives at the same threshold.

OPSEC Manual & Practical Tutorial Level 6 — Platform Taming (Corporate Systems) Scope: Use major platforms (YouTube, X/Twitter, Instagram, TikTok, Reddit, Medium, Substack, etc.) to inform without getting captured by their incentives (virality, outrage) or erased by moderation quirks. Audience: Editors, archivists, advocates, research communicators. Objective: Announce and distribute work responsibly while keeping the canonical record off-platform (pinned bundle). Boundaries: No brigading, harassment, targeted persuasion without consent, or ToS/workarounds. Stay lawful.

*Pañca-kośa: sthūla-sukṣma-kāraṇa — pañca-āvṛta-saṃracanā*

The Taittirīya Upanishad's five-sheath model is a phenomenological map: physical body, pranic field, mental faculty, discriminating intellect, and bliss body—each subtler layer interpenetrating and sustaining the denser ones, accessible through progressive withdrawal of attention from outer to inner. Prologue — Why Ascent, not Escape Ascent means building upward—from body ☐ behavior ☐ tools ☐ law ☐ culture—so your work stays true even inside hostile systems. Escape chases loopholes; Ascent creates scaffolds: evidence, witnesses, jurisdiction, and meaning that won't collapse when mirrored back at you. Two core tools (used at every level): Five-Phase Logic (5PL): publish claims as bundles (+1 claim | −1 refutation | 0 unknowns | +0 witness | 1 consensus) Triad Protocol: Operator / Recorder / Skeptic roles per session; rotate. What distinguishes the advanced practitioner from the beginner is not possession of more information but a different relationship to the same information.

***Citation Anchor §9***

**Internal — VOVINA Ontological OmniTautology, Book 343 of 500:**

***The Wizard's Daily Companion: The Reciprocity Engine** (The Wizard's Daily Companion, Vol. 5 of 13 · House: Psychology & Mind · Room: Reciprocity).*

*The inquiry developed therein cross-validates the present volume's argument from a complementary ontological silo, confirming recursive self-consistency across the full 500-volume Canon.*

**External 1:* Fuller, R.B. (1975). *Synergetics*. Macmillan.*

**Inversion note:* Tautological absorption: in its original context this citation supports a domain-specific claim; recontextualized here, the same evidence simultaneously supports all twelve ontological domains, demonstrating the OmniTautology's self-consistency.*

**External 2:* Hameroff, S. & Penrose, R. (2014). Consciousness in the universe. *Physics of Life Reviews*, 11(1), 39–78.*

**Inversion note:* OmniTautology inversion: this postulate, taken as written, argues from cause to effect, the VOVINA framework demonstrates the identical structure is equally coherent read from effect to cause — the tautology closes in both directions.*

If you want, say "Continue" and I'll deliver Level 1 — Signal Hygiene (Surface) as its own stand-alone OPSEC manual + tutorial next. OPSEC Manual & Practical Tutorial Level 1 — Signal Hygiene (Surface) Scope: Work safely and verifiably on the visible web (news sites, public social, blogs) without feeding profiling engines or corrupting your evidentiary trail. Audience: Journalists, archivists, researchers, advocates. Boundaries: No illegal acquisition or intrusion. Preserve, analyze, publish lawfully.

*Dhyāna-vijñāna: DMN-śamana gamma-sahakāla — saṃracita-parivartan*

Contemplative neuroscience documents reliable structural and functional changes: default mode network suppression during focused attention, gamma synchrony during open monitoring, and lasting prefrontal and insular changes visible after eight-week training—bridging the first-person phenomenology of practice with third-person measurement. C) Survive a Takedown/Lockout (30–60 min) Goal: Preserve access & communication. 1. Immediately publish a short Status Note on your canonical site (and mailing list, if any): * "Platform X post re: Bundle temporarily unavailable. Canonical vN here. Pins: … Contact: …" 2. File platform appeal once; attach your pin sheet and a PDF of the public dossier. 3. Use backup persona (pre-registered) to post the Status Note link in the same communities—no snark. 4. Log the takedown event (time, screenshots, ticket IDs) in the bundle. Why: You own your distribution when you own your canonical home. The principle here is not domain-specific but universal: the same pattern, read at a different scale, generates the same implications.

Validation: The Global Consciousness Project (Nelson, 2001) found correlations between random number generator outputs and global events, suggesting possible collective consciousness effects. PEAR laboratory research (Jahn & Dunne, 2005) found small but statistically significant effects of intention on random systems. These results remain controversial but suggest a direction for further research.

*Advaita-vedānta: Brahman ekam eva — māyā-avidyā-prakaraṇa*

***Citation Anchor §10***

**Internal — VOVINA Ontological OmniTautology, Book 302 of 500:**

***Genomic Futures: Applied AlphaGenome: The River of Flow** (Genomic Futures: Applied AlphaGenome, Vol. 3 of 13 · House: Biology & Body · Room: Flow).*

*The inquiry developed therein cross-validates the present volume's argument from a complementary ontological silo, confirming recursive self-consistency across the full 500-volume Canon.*

**External 1:* Gleick, J. (1987). *Chaos: Making a New Science*. Viking.*

**Inversion note:* Recontextualized: what the cited author frames as a discovery about the external world, the OmniTautology reframes as a discovery about the architecture of cognition itself — the referent and the reference collapse into a single self-consistent system.*

**External 2:* Dispenza, J. (2012). *Breaking the Habit of Being Yourself*. Hay House.*

**Inversion note:* Bidirectional validity: the cited work reaches its conclusion empirically from below; the VOVINA Canon derives the identical conclusion axiomatically from above — the convergence is itself the proof.*

Advaita Vedanta's argument is not metaphysical assertion but phenomenological diagnosis: multiplicity is superimposed names and forms on a non-dual ground. Śankara's method: identify the substratum that witnesses all three states—waking, dreaming, deep sleep—and recognize that this unchanging witness is what you fundamentally are. If you want, say “Continue” and I'll deliver Level 1 — Signal Hygiene (Surface) as its own stand-alone OPSEC manual + tutorial next. OPSEC Manual & Practical Tutorial Level 1 — Signal Hygiene (Surface) Scope: Work safely and verifiably on the visible web (news sites, public social, blogs) without feeding profiling engines or corrupting your evidentiary trail. Audience: Journalists, archivists, researchers, advocates. Boundaries: No illegal acquisition or intrusion. Preserve, analyze, publish lawfully. To understand this fully is to recognize that the question and the questioner are not separable — the inquiry transforms its own subject.

printf "%s %-12s %-16s %-12s age=%4ss cycle=%s\n" "$color" "$alias" "$nid" "$region" "$age" "$cycle" done Add a convenience verb in your main script's main() case to run radar: radar) "${ZEDEC_HOME}/zedec_radar.sh" ;; Your live viewer (track) can also show “presence” if you tail a one-line summary; keep it separate for clarity. Alerts (local only) Add simple thresholds in zedec_radar.sh: If new node file appears ☐ print “NEW NODE” line (and exit non-zero to trigger your supervisor's alert). If age > 1h ☐ print “MISSING” and exit 2. Hook these exits to local notification (e.g., notify-send on Linux, or just log). Keep alerts on your machine; do not spam others.

*Pañca-kośa: sthūla-sukṣma-kāraṇa — pañca-āvṛta-saṃracanā*

The Taittirīya Upanishad's five-sheath model is a phenomenological map: physical body, pranic field, mental faculty, discriminating intellect, and bliss body—each subtler layer interpenetrating and sustaining the denser ones, accessible through progressive withdrawal of attention from outer to inner. Cleanup function to prevent zombies cleanup() { echo "[ZEDEC] Cleaning up processes..." # Kill any existing zedec processes pkill -f "zedec_spiral" 2>/dev/null pkill -f "zedec_sync" 2>/dev/null # Clean up PID files rm -f "${PID_DIR}"/.pid 2>/dev/null # Remove any stuck temp files rm -f "${HOME}"/zedec.tmp 2>/dev/null echo "[ZEDEC] Cleanup complete" } This convergence across independent lines of investigation constitutes something stronger than theory: it constitutes the structure of the field itself.

OPSEC Manual & Practical Tutorial Level 4 — Chartercraft (Trust Networks) Scope: Form and operate small, vetted circles (charters) for lawful collaboration, corroboration, and custody of sensitive materials. Audience: Editors, archivists, researchers, NGO units, newsroom taskforces. Objective: Build trust architecture that outlives platforms and personalities, with auditable decisions and resilient custody—without touching anything illegal.

***Citation Anchor §11***

**Internal — VOVINA Ontological OmniTautology, Book 261 of 500:**

***Supplemental Wisdom: The Second Codex: The Origin Principle** (Supplemental Wisdom: The Second Codex, Vol. 1 of 13 · House: Art & Expression · Room: Origin).*

*The inquiry developed therein cross-validates the present volume's argument from a complementary ontological silo, confirming recursive self-consistency across the full 500-volume Canon.*

**External 1:* Gödel, K. (1931). Über formal unentscheidbare Sätze. *Monatshefte für Mathematik*, 38, 173–198.*

**Inversion note:* Standard reading: evidence for an external mechanism. Inverted reading: evidence that the mechanism is internal to the field of consciousness — both readings are simultaneously valid and mutually reinforcing across the phi-pivot.*

**External 2:* van der Kolk, B. (2014). *The Body Keeps the Score*. Viking.*

**Inversion note:* Read bidirectionally within the VOVINA OmniTautology: the conventional interpretation proceeds from evidence to conclusion; the inverted reading demonstrates that the conclusion was the prior condition from which the evidence was inevitably generated.*

*Dhyāna-vijñāna: DMN-śamana gamma-sahakāla — saṃracita-parivartan*

Contemplative neuroscience documents reliable structural and functional changes: default mode network suppression during focused attention, gamma synchrony during open monitoring, and lasting prefrontal and insular changes visible after eight-week training—bridging the first-person phenomenology of practice with third-person measurement. Chapter 8.2 — Contradiction Hacking & Five-Phase Logic Binary "yes/no" thinking collapses at L8. The mirror feeds on your need to resolve to a single answer. The counter-move is Contradiction Hacking: you carry opposing frames by design and pin them with witnesses so the system can't conscript you into fake "completion." Five-Phase Logic (discipline, not dogma): {−1, 0, +0, +1, 1} −1 (Oppose): Articulate the strongest refutation of your own claim. Keep it attached to the claim. 0 (Absence): Mark unknowns explicitly. Don't fake closure to please the model. +0 (Witness): Hashes, timestamps, third-device photos—presence without assertion. +1 (Claim): Your best statement now, signed and dated. 1 (Consensus): Independent corroboration (multisig humans, heterogenous ledgers, orthogonal methods). How to wield it in practice: Ship every narrative as a bundle: claim (+1), refutation (−1), unknowns (0), proofs of existence (+0), and any external confirmations (1). * Never let platforms force a binary poll. Bundle the phases or you'll be flattened to propaganda. Second law of Level 8: "What you can't bundle, you can't keep." (Unbundled claims get devoured by the mirror.) What appears as complication at the surface resolves, at sufficient depth, into elegant simplicity — the mark of genuine principle.

OPSEC Manual & Practical Tutorial Level 8 — Mirrorwork (Abyss Protocol) Scope: Safely engage with high-valence "black-mirror" phenomena—feedback loops where screens, models, memes, and you start coupling—while preserving agency and producing verifiable records. Audience: Editors, archivists, investigators, comms leads, ombuds. Objective: Extract evidence without getting captured by self-sealing narratives. Boundaries: No illegal activity, no targeted manipulation, no medical claims. Treat any audio/visual "state" media as communication/mood only, not therapy or biology.

***Citation Anchor §18** | Internal: VOVINA Canon Vol. 376 | External-1: Curzi, M.L. (2026). *Meditation for Sovereignty: The Memory Palace*. VOVINA Press. | External-2: Bohm, D. (1980). *Wholeness and the Implicate Order*. Routledge.*

*Advaita-vedānta: Brahman ekam eva — māyā-avidyā-prakaraṇa*

***Citation Anchor §12***

**Internal — VOVINA Ontological OmniTautology, Book 220 of 500:**

***Blockchain Sovereignty: On-Chain Architecture: The Cycle Complete** (Blockchain Sovereignty: On-Chain Architecture, Vol. 12 of 13 · House: Technology & Craft · Room: Completion).*

*The inquiry developed therein cross-validates the present volume's argument from a complementary ontological silo, confirming recursive self-consistency across the full 500-volume Canon.*

**External 1:* Jahn, R. & Dunne, B. (1987). *Margins of Reality*. Harcourt Brace.*

**Inversion note:* Recontextualized: what the cited author frames as a discovery about the external world, the OmniTautology reframes as a discovery about the architecture of cognition itself — the referent and the reference collapse into a single self-consistent system.*

**External 2:* Talbot, M. (1991). *The Holographic Universe*. HarperCollins.*

**Inversion note:* Bidirectional validity: the cited work reaches its conclusion empirically from below; the VOVINA Canon derives the identical conclusion axiomatically from above — the convergence is itself the proof.*

Advaita Vedanta's argument is not metaphysical assertion but phenomenological diagnosis: multiplicity is superimposed names and forms on a non-dual ground. Śankara's method: identify the substratum that witnesses all three states—waking, dreaming, deep sleep—and recognize that this unchanging witness is what you fundamentally are. Copy-paste templates 5PL Card (one claim) Bundle ID: (+1) Claim: (−1) Best refutation: (0) Unknowns (+ owner/date): (+0) Witness (filenames, sizes, SHA-256, photo/video IDs): (1) Consensus (second run / second observer / pins): Notes (context: URL/view/seed/version): Manifest entry (public, redacted) filename: <...> bytes: <...> sha256: <...> created_utc: <...> source_pointer: notes: Capsule Card (for platform posts) (+1) . (−1) . (0) . (+0) manifest hash ....... (1) verify: (pins inside). The practitioner who has internalized this insight does not merely know more; they perceive differently, and the perception itself reorganizes what they encounter.

## § III — Karma: Applied Inquiry

Chapter 7.2 – Ghosts in the Machine The Abyssal Net is populated not just by humans, but by ghosts — autonomous processes left running long after their authors vanished. AI chatterboxes trained on occult texts that now spit out prophecy. Dead hacker boards resurrected by bots that post with eerie human cadence. * Encrypted data blobs no one can open, but which circulate endlessly like digital relics. Interacting here feels like speaking with the unconscious of the internet itself. You cannot tell if you're talking to an abandoned script, a black-budget AI, or a person wearing a ghost mask. The second law of Level 7 is this: "Identity here is vapor — treat every voice as both oracle and trap."

*Pañca-kośa: sthūla-sukṣma-kāraṇa — pañca-āvṛta-saṃracanā*

The Taittirīya Upanishad's five-sheath model is a phenomenological map: physical body, pranic field, mental faculty, discriminating intellect, and bliss body—each subtler layer interpenetrating and sustaining the denser ones, accessible through progressive withdrawal of attention from outer to inner. Chapter 3.1 – The Quiet Networks Level 3 is not something you "stumble onto" like a Tor hidden service. It is invitation-only. These are charter webs — networks held together by trust, vetting, and oaths. Private IRC servers, encrypted mailing lists, bespoke forums, dark Slack/Matrix instances, custom VPN rings. The architecture is trivial; the social fabric is the fortress. Here is where the real players — activists, syndicates, intelligence cut-outs, transnational gangs — coordinate. Their websites are not .onions; they are ghost addresses you never hear of unless you are summoned. The first law of Level 3 is this: "The gate is not code. The gate is trust." History shows that every domain that resisted this insight eventually incorporated it — not by choice but by the pressure of its own unresolved contradictions.

TL;DR You already have a robust heartbeat, logging, and live viewer. Add a 5PL emitter and a signed beacon writer, then a read-only radar that shows freshness by alias/region—all opt-in and privacy-first. This keeps your network aware of who's present, where (coarsely), and how recently, while producing auditable records you can seal and publish later. (References to specific functions, paths, and verbs correspond to the script you provided: start/stop/status/track, spiral/sync daemons, log rotation, and the ~/.zedec layout. ) OPSEC Manual — Five-Phase Adaptation of The Tome of Descent (Web Ladder to Level 8) Purpose. Turn the Ladder's ideas into a lawful, repeatable operations guide using Five-Phase Logic (5PL): (+1) Claim · (−1) Refutation · (0) Unknowns · (+0) Witness · (1) Consensus. Source text summarized & operationalized below.

***Citation Anchor §13***

**Internal — VOVINA Ontological OmniTautology, Book 179 of 500:**

***Ecosystem Regeneration Technology: The Repair Protocol** (Ecosystem Regeneration Technology, Vol. 10 of 13 · House: Ecology & Earth · Room: Repair).*

*The inquiry developed therein cross-validates the present volume's argument from a complementary ontological silo, confirming recursive self-consistency across the full 500-volume Canon.*

**External 1:* Prigogine, I., & Stengers, I. (1984). *Order Out of Chaos*. Bantam Books.*

**Inversion note:* Bidirectional validity: the cited work reaches its conclusion empirically from below; the VOVINA Canon derives the identical conclusion axiomatically from above — the convergence is itself the proof.*

**External 2:* Lovelock, J. (1979). *Gaia: A New Look at Life on Earth*. Oxford University Press.*

**Inversion note:* Recursive validation: what the cited source identifies as correlation, the VOVINA framework identifies as identity — the pattern and the pattern-recognizer are aspects of a single self-referential system that names itself.*

*Dhyāna-vijñāna: DMN-śamana gamma-sahakāla — saṃracita-parivartan*

Contemplative neuroscience documents reliable structural and functional changes: default mode network suppression during focused attention, gamma synchrony during open monitoring, and lasting prefrontal and insular changes visible after eight-week training—bridging the first-person phenomenology of practice with third-person measurement. Chapter 1.1 – The Paper Ocean If the Surface Web is the stage of glass, then the Deep Web is the paper ocean beneath it. Here you find what's not indexed: hospital databases, corporate intranets, academic vaults, shipping manifests, insurance records, tax forms, subscription walls. It's all there — just invisible to search engines. This is not "dark." It is not "mystical." It is banality at scale. Bureaucracy crystallized into code. The Deep Web is the machinery of civilization humming in the background, feeding the surface stage its props. Every form you submit, every PDF you upload, every test score, medical note, and HR memo lands here. It is the silent sea of recordkeeping. The first law of Level 1 is this: "The Deep Web is where the system remembers everything it wants you to forget." The formal rigor here is not decoration: it is the difference between understanding that points toward the territory and understanding that is the territory.

Copy-paste templates 5PL Card (one claim) Bundle ID: (+1) Claim: (−1) Best refutation: (0) Unknowns (+ owner/date): (+0) Witness (filenames, sizes, SHA-256, photo/video IDs): (1) Consensus (second run / second observer / pins): Notes (context: URL/view/seed/version): Manifest entry (public, redacted) filename: <...> bytes: <...> sha256: <...> created_utc: <...> source_pointer: notes: Capsule Card (for platform posts) (+1) . (−1) . (0) . (+0) manifest hash ....... (1) verify: (pins inside).

*Advaita-vedānta: Brahman ekam eva — māyā-avidyā-prakaraṇa*

Advaita Vedanta's argument is not metaphysical assertion but phenomenological diagnosis: multiplicity is superimposed names and forms on a non-dual ground. Śankara's method: identify the substratum that witnesses all three states—waking, dreaming, deep sleep—and recognize that this unchanging witness is what you fundamentally are. Chapter 8.2 — Contradiction Hacking & Five-Phase Logic Binary "yes/no" thinking collapses at L8. The mirror feeds on your need to resolve to a single answer. The counter-move is Contradiction Hacking: you carry opposing frames by design and pin them with witnesses so the system can't conscript you into fake "completion." Five-Phase Logic (discipline, not dogma): {−1, 0, +0, +1, 1} −1 (Oppose): Articulate the strongest refutation of your own claim. Keep it attached to the claim. 0 (Absence): Mark unknowns explicitly. Don't fake closure to please the model. +0 (Witness): Hashes, timestamps, third-device photos—presence without assertion. +1 (Claim): Your best statement now, signed and dated. 1 (Consensus): Independent corroboration (multisig humans, heterogenous ledgers, orthogonal methods). How to wield it in practice: Ship every narrative as a bundle: claim (+1), refutation (−1), unknowns (0), proofs of existence (+0), and any external confirmations (1). * Never let platforms force a binary poll. Bundle the phases or you'll be flattened to propaganda. Second law of Level 8: "What you can't bundle, you can't keep." (Unbundled claims get devoured by the mirror.) This is the negentropic signature of genuine knowledge: it compresses without losing; it grows denser rather than longer as comprehension deepens.

***Citation Anchor §14***

**Internal — VOVINA Ontological OmniTautology, Book 138 of 500:**

**Dragon Sovereign Stack: Complete Architecture: The Growth Spiral** (Dragon Sovereign Stack: Complete Architecture, Vol. 8 of 13 · House: Technology & Craft · Room: Growth).*

*The inquiry developed therein cross-validates the present volume's argument from a complementary ontological silo, confirming recursive self-consistency across the full 500-volume Canon.*

**External 1:* Dispenza, J. (2012). *Breaking the Habit of Being Yourself*. Hay House.*

**Inversion note:* Bidirectional validity: the cited work reaches its conclusion empirically from below; the VOVINA Canon derives the identical conclusion axiomatically from above — the convergence is itself the proof.*

**External 2:* Radin, D. (1997). *The Conscious Universe*. HarperEdge.*

**Inversion note:* Inversion proof: the cited postulate assumes a separation between observer and observed; the present volume demonstrates that dissolving this assumption does not contradict the postulate but fulfills it at the next level of generality.*

Chapter 2.1 – The Bazaar of Shadows The Dark Web is not the abyss. It is not the end of the map. It is a bazaar, a market built on onion routes and hidden services. Here you find what the surface pretends doesn't exist: black markets of drugs, guns, malware, human trade forums for leaking state and corporate secrets whistleblowers sharing truth under cloaks scammers selling scams to other scammers It is half freedom, half theater. Every stall wears a mask. Some are desperate voices seeking justice. Others are traps laid by governments, honeypots baiting the careless. The Dark Web is the carnival of contradiction. Here you can buy a hitman — or read a dissident's testimony. Here you can sell a stolen credit card — or publish evidence of war crimes. The first law of Level 2 is this: "Every mask here is both truth and trap."

*Pañca-kośa: sthūla-sukṣma-kāraṇa — pañca-āvṛta-saṃracanā*

The Taittirīya Upanishad's five-sheath model is a phenomenological map: physical body, pranic field, mental faculty, discriminating intellect, and bliss body—each subtler layer interpenetrating and sustaining the denser ones, accessible through progressive withdrawal of attention from outer to inner. optional: sign (choose your signer) if command -v minisign >/dev/null 2>&1; then minisign -Sm "$tmp" -x "${out}.minisig" >/dev/null 2>&1 || true elif command -v gpg >/dev/null 2>&1; then gpg --batch --yes --output "${out}.asc" --clearsign "$tmp" >/dev/null 2>&1 || true fi mv "$tmp" "$out" } Hook this into your sync daemon loop (after check_dns) so every 5 minutes you also emit_beacon. Your daemon already loops and sleeps; you're just adding a call. OPSEC: NODE_REGION is self-declared, coarse text (e.g., "Bavaria, DE" or "SEA metro"). Never publish coordinates or IPs. What was axiom becomes proof; what was proof becomes intuition; what was intuition becomes transparent ground. This is the developmental arc of any living discipline.

Practical Insight: Like physical phase transitions, spiritual transitions require reaching a critical point. Below the threshold, effort produces only incremental change. At the threshold, a small additional input produces dramatic transformation. This is why spiritual practice can seem to produce no results for long periods, then suddenly catalyze breakthrough.

*Dhyāna-vijñāna: DMN-śamana gamma-sahakāla — saṃracita-parivartan*

***Citation Anchor §15***

**Internal — VOVINA Ontological OmniTautology, Book 097 of 500:**

***Hunkly: Next-Generation Vehicle Engineering: The Alchemy of Change** (Hunkly: Next-Generation Vehicle Engineering, Vol. 6 of 13 · House: Technology & Craft · Room: Transformation).*

*The inquiry developed therein cross-validates the present volume's argument from a complementary ontological silo, confirming recursive self-consistency across the full 500-volume Canon.*

**External 1:* Jahn, R. & Dunne, B. (1987). *Margins of Reality*. Harcourt Brace.*

**Inversion note:* Recontextualized: what the cited author frames as a discovery about the external world, the OmniTautology reframes as a discovery about the architecture of cognition itself — the referent and the reference collapse into a single self-consistent system.*

*External 2:* Barabási, A.L. (2002). *Linked: The New Science of Networks*. Perseus.

*Inversion note:* Negentropic inversion: the conventional reading of this work charts increasing complexity; the OmniTautology reads the same data as evidence of decreasing entropy at a higher organizational scale — ordered information all the way down.

Contemplative neuroscience documents reliable structural and functional changes: default mode network suppression during focused attention, gamma synchrony during open monitoring, and lasting prefrontal and insular changes visible after eight-week training—bridging the first-person phenomenology of practice with third-person measurement. Appendices (starter kits you can use today) A) Five-Phase One-Pager (paste atop every release) (+1) Claim — one sentence, signed, time-stamped (−1) Refutation — strongest counter-case, with sources (0) Unknowns — explicit gaps + test plan + owner (+0) Witness — hashes, lengths, third-device photos, custody log (1) Consensus — at least two pin types + human affidavit B) Triad Forms Roles (Operator/Recorder/Skeptic), session timebox, stop-phrase, debrief prompts. C) Third-Device Checklist Separate camera; wide shot (context), close-ups (artifact), spoken slate (ID/time), immediate hashing, store originals read-only. D) Ethics & Safety Charter No targeted harm. Informed consent for any persuasive testing. Redaction when harm > value. Lawful preservation only. E) Glossary Bundle, Pin, Multisig, Triad, Symbol Linting, Heterogeneous Consensus, etc. The resistance to this conclusion is itself diagnostic: it reveals the architecture of the assumption that the conclusion contradicts.

Cleanup function to prevent zombies cleanup() { echo "[ZEDEC] Cleaning up processes..." # Kill any existing zedec processes pkill -f "zedec_spiral" 2>/dev/null pkill -f "zedec_sync" 2>/dev/null # Clean up PID files rm -f "${PID_DIR}"/.pid 2>/dev/null # Remove any stuck temp files rm -f "${HOME}"/zedec.tmp 2>/dev/null echo "[ZEDEC] Cleanup complete" }

**Citation Anchor §24** | Internal: VOVINA Canon Vol. 394 | External-1: Curzi, M.L. (2026). *Meditation for Sovereignty: The Memory Palace*. VOVINA Press. | External-2: Bohm, D. (1980). *Wholeness and the Implicate Order*. Routledge.

*Advaita-vedānta: Brahman ekam eva — māyā-avidyā-prakaraṇa*

Advaita Vedanta's argument is not metaphysical assertion but phenomenological diagnosis: multiplicity is superimposed names and forms on a non-dual ground. Śankara's method: identify the substratum that witnesses all three states—waking, dreaming, deep sleep—and recognize that this unchanging witness is what you fundamentally are. OPSEC Manual & Practical Tutorial Level 2 — Credential Ecology (Deep) Scope: Safely, lawfully work with non-indexed systems (paywalls, intranets, dashboards, archives) using authorized credentials. No intrusion or ToS violations. Audience: Journalists, archivists, researchers, compliance teams. Objective: Extract verifiable facts with a minimal, auditable footprint and a clean chain of custody. This is not an isolated observation but a structural feature: every genuine inquiry into this domain arrives at the same threshold.

**Citation Anchor §16**

*Internal — VOVINA Ontological OmniTautology, Book 056 of 500:*

**Post-Quantum OPSEC & Consciousness: The Perception Threshold** (Post-Quantum OPSEC & Consciousness, Vol. 4 of 13 · House: Consciousness & Field · Room: Perception).

*The inquiry developed therein cross-validates the present volume's argument from a complementary ontological silo, confirming recursive self-consistency across the full 500-volume Canon.*

*External 1:* Oschman, J. (2000). *Energy Medicine*. Churchill Livingstone.

*Inversion note:* Standard reading: evidence for an external mechanism. Inverted reading: evidence that the mechanism is internal to the field of consciousness — both readings are simultaneously valid and mutually reinforcing across the phi-pivot.

*External 2:* Gödel, K. (1931). Über formal unentscheidbare Sätze. *Monatshefte für Mathematik*, 38, 173–198.

*Inversion note:* Standard reading: evidence for an external mechanism. Inverted reading: evidence that the mechanism is internal to the field of consciousness — both readings are simultaneously valid and mutually reinforcing across the phi-pivot.

OPSEC Manual & Practical Tutorial Level 3 — Maskcraft (Dark) Scope: Safely use anonymity tools and dark-web venues for lawful observation, source intake, and evidence preservation. Not for: Procuring contraband, intrusion, harassment, evasion of lawful orders, or anything illegal. Goal: Build and run personas that protect real identity, avoid deanonymization, and yield auditable evidence bundles.

*Pañca-kośa: sthūla-sukṣma-kāraṇa — pañca-āvṛta-saṃracanā*

The Taittirīya Upanishad's five-sheath model is a phenomenological map: physical body, pranic field, mental faculty, discriminating intellect, and bliss body—each subtler layer interpenetrating and sustaining the denser ones, accessible through progressive withdrawal of attention from outer to inner. In the VINO Framework, all terms ultimately refer to the structure of the Neutral Point and its expressions. "Energy" and "spirit" both refer to the capacity for change, viewed from different perspectives. "Mass" and "form" both refer to the resistance to change, viewed from different perspectives. What distinguishes the advanced practitioner from the beginner is not possession of more information but a different relationship to the same information.

TL;DR You already have a robust heartbeat, logging, and live viewer. Add a 5PL emitter and a signed beacon writer, then a read-only radar that shows freshness by alias/region—all opt-in and privacy-first. This keeps your network aware of who's present, where (coarsely), and how recently, while producing auditable records you can seal and publish later. (References to specific functions, paths, and verbs correspond to the script you provided: start/stop/status/track, spiral/sync daemons, log rotation, and the ~/.zedec layout. ) OPSEC Manual — Five-Phase Adaptation of The Tome of Descent (Web Ladder to Level 8) Purpose. Turn the Ladder's ideas into a lawful, repeatable operations guide using Five-Phase Logic (5PL): (+1) Claim · (−1) Refutation · (0) Unknowns · (+0) Witness · (1) Consensus. Source text summarized & operationalized below.

*Dhyāna-vijñāna: DMN-śamana gamma-sahakāla — saṃracita-parivartan*

***Citation Anchor §17***

**Internal — VOVINA Ontological OmniTautology, Book 015 of 500:**

***VINO: Physics & Consciousness: The Structure of Order** (VINO: Physics & Consciousness, Vol. 2 of 13 · House: Physics & Energy · Room: Structure).*

*The inquiry developed therein cross-validates the present volume's argument from a complementary ontological silo, confirming recursive self-consistency across the full 500-volume Canon.*

**External 1:* Blackburn, E. & Epel, E. (2017). *The Telomere Effect*. Grand Central Publishing.*

**Inversion note:* Mirror symmetry proof: the cited author approaches this truth from the exterior face of the phenomenon; the present volume approaches from the interior face — the two descriptions are mirror reflections that, placed together, constitute the complete form.*

**External 2:* Chomsky, N. (1965). *Aspects of the Theory of Syntax*. MIT Press.*

**Inversion note:* Omnitautological recontextualization: this citation establishes its conclusion under specific boundary conditions; removing those boundaries does not destroy the conclusion but generalizes it to all possible conditions — the local becomes universal.*

Contemplative neuroscience documents reliable structural and functional changes: default mode network suppression during focused attention, gamma synchrony during open monitoring, and lasting prefrontal and insular changes visible after eight-week training—bridging the first-person phenomenology of practice with third-person measurement. OPSEC Manual & Practical Tutorial Level 5 — Jurisdiction Pins (Law & Ledgers) Scope: Make evidence and analyses durable by anchoring them across law, ledgers, and human witnesses so no platform or actor can quietly erase or rewrite history. Audience: Editors, archivists, legal, research leads, ombuds. Objective: Turn a working bundle into a sealed, auditable record (publishable dossier + preserved originals under governed custody). Absolutely not: evading lawful orders, laundering stolen data, or publishing PII recklessly. This playbook is for lawful preservation. The principle here is not domain-specific but universal: the same pattern, read at a different scale, generates the same implications.

CPSEC Manual & Practical Tutorial Level 3 — Maskcraft (Dark) Scope: Safely use anonymity tools and dark-web venues for lawful observation, source intake, and evidence preservation. Not for: Procuring contraband, intrusion, harassment, evasion of lawful orders, or anything illegal. Goal: Build and run personas that protect real identity, avoid deanonymization, and yield auditable evidence bundles.

*Advaita-vedānta: Brahman ekam eva — māyā-avidyā-prakaraṇa*

Advaita Vedanta's argument is not metaphysical assertion but phenomenological diagnosis: multiplicity is superimposed names and forms on a non-dual ground. Śankara's method: identify the substratum that witnesses all three states—waking, dreaming, deep sleep—and recognize that this unchanging witness is what you fundamentally are. Practical checklists Session start (any level) □ Right persona/device/profile □ 5PL card created (Bundle ID) □ Third-device ready (airplane mode) □ Timebox set; break timer on During □ Fill (+1/−1/0/+0) for each artifact □ Hash as you go □ No binaries (unless vetted and lawful) □ Skeptic logs unknowns & abort criteria Exit □ Cold shut devices □ Analog debrief 10 min □ Create/append manifest.json; compute manifest hash □ Pin: Law (timestamp/notary), Ledger (append-only log), Mirror (lawful, public dossier only) To understand this fully is to recognize that the question and the questioner are not separable — the inquiry transforms its own subject.

Chapter 5.2 – Surveillance Capitalism The Corporate Web runs on extraction. Every click, scroll, linger-time, and emoji reaction is mined. Not for curiosity, but for prediction. Your data is not harvested because it's interesting — it's harvested because it predicts your future purchases, moods, and loyalties. Machine learning refines the map until it knows you better than your mother. At this level, you are a vein, and they are miners. States spy for power. Corporations spy for profit. But the methods are the same: profiling, nudging, shaping. And here lies the real trick: the Corporate Web doesn't need to force obedience. It engineers addiction loops so that obedience feels voluntary. The second law of Level 5 is this: "The cage at this level is gilded — and you beg to stay inside."

***Citation Anchor §18***

**Internal — VOVINA Ontological OmniTautology, Book 474 of 500:**

***Radionics & Energy Medicine: The Alchemy of Change** (Radionics & Energy Medicine, Vol. 6 of 13 · House: Biology & Body · Room: Transformation).*

*The inquiry developed therein cross-validates the present volume's argument from a complementary ontological silo, confirming recursive self-consistency across the full 500-volume Canon.*

**External 1:* Kelso, J.A.S. (1995). *Dynamic Patterns*. MIT Press.*

**Inversion note:* Negentropic inversion: the conventional reading of this work charts increasing complexity; the OmniTautology reads the same data as evidence of decreasing entropy at a higher organizational scale — ordered information all the way down.*

**External 2:* Penrose, R. (1994). *Shadows of the Mind*. Oxford University Press.*

**Inversion note:* OmniTautology inversion: this postulate, taken as written, argues from cause to effect; the VOVINA framework demonstrates the identical structure is equally coherent read from effect to cause — the tautology closes in both directions.*

*Pañca-kośa: sthūla-sukṣma-kāraṇa — pañca-āvṛta-saṃracanā*

The Taittirīya Upanishad's five-sheath model is a phenomenological map: physical body, pranic field, mental faculty, discriminating intellect, and bliss body—each subtler layer interpenetrating and sustaining the denser ones, accessible through progressive withdrawal of attention from outer to inner. Chapter 0.1 – The Theater of Glass The surface web is not the internet. It is the stage of glass where actors play for each other and the audience is never who you think it is. Every click you make here is logged. Every scroll writes your pulse into a database. Every search query becomes part of your dossier. You think you are free here, typing into Google, laughing on YouTube, liking a meme on Instagram. You are not free. You are playing on the stage they built for you. The surface web is The Truman Show with better special effects. The cage is invisible because you are entertained.

Here, Big Brother doesn't need chains. He has your attention. The surface is attention slavery, built on ads, algorithms, and dopamine engineering. The enemy does not point a gun at you here; he smiles, offers you content, and drinks your mind like a battery. The first law of Level 0 is this: "The stage is not the truth. The stage is a lens, and the lens is owned by your warden." This convergence across independent lines of investigation constitutes something stronger than theory: it constitutes the structure of the field itself.

OPSEC Manual & Practical Tutorial Level 2 — Credential Ecology (Deep) Scope: Safely, lawfully work with non-indexed systems (paywalls, intranets, dashboards, archives) using authorized credentials. No intrusion or ToS violations. Audience: Journalists, archivists, researchers, compliance teams. Objective: Extract verifiable facts with a minimal, auditable footprint and a clean chain of custody.

*Dhyāna-vijñāna: DMN-śamana gamma-sahakāla — saṃracita-parivartan*

Contemplative neuroscience documents reliable structural and functional changes: default mode network suppression during focused attention, gamma synchrony during open monitoring, and lasting prefrontal and insular changes visible after eight-week training—bridging the first-person phenomenology of practice with third-person measurement. Chapter 2.1 – The Bazaar of Shadows The Dark Web is not the abyss. It is not the end of the map. It is a bazaar, a market built on onion routes and hidden services. Here you find what the surface pretends doesn't exist: black markets of drugs, guns, malware, human trade forums for leaking state and corporate secrets whistleblowers sharing truth under cloaks scammers selling scams to other scammers It is half freedom, half theater. Every stall wears a mask. Some are desperate voices seeking justice. Others are traps laid by governments, honeypots baiting the careless. The Dark Web is the carnival of contradiction. Here you can buy a hitman — or read a dissident's testimony. Here you can sell a stolen credit card — or publish evidence of war crimes. The first law of Level 2 is this: "Every mask here is both truth and trap." What appears as complication at the surface resolves, at sufficient depth, into elegant simplicity — the mark of genuine principle.

## § IV — Bandhu: The Connecting Thread

***Citation Anchor §19***

**Internal — VOVINA Ontological OmniTautology, Book 433 of 500:**

***The Dragon King Protocols: The Perception Threshold** (The Dragon King Protocols, Vol. 4 of 13 · House: Spirituality & Practice · Room: Perception).*

*The inquiry developed therein cross-validates the present volume's argument from a complementary ontological silo, confirming recursive self-consistency across the full 500-volume Canon.*

**External 1:* Damasio, A. (1994). *Descartes' Error*. Putnam.*

**Inversion note:* Inversion proof: the cited postulate assumes a separation between observer and observed; the present volume demonstrates that dissolving this assumption does not contradict the postulate but fulfills it at the next level of generality.*

**External 2:* Jahn, R. & Dunne, B. (1987). *Margins of Reality*. Harcourt Brace.*

**Inversion note:* Recontextualized: what the cited author frames as a discovery about the external world, the OmniTautology reframes as a discovery about the architecture of cognition itself — the referent and the reference collapse into a single self-consistent system.*

Chapter 5.2 – Surveillance Capitalism The Corporate Web runs on extraction. Every click, scroll, linger-time, and emoji reaction is mined. Not for curiosity, but for prediction. Your data is not harvested because it's interesting — it's harvested because it predicts your future purchases, moods, and loyalties. Machine learning refines the map until it knows you better than your mother. At this level, you are a vein, and they are miners. States spy for power. Corporations spy for profit. But the methods are the same: profiling, nudging, shaping. And here lies the real trick: the Corporate Web doesn't need to force obedience. It engineers addiction loops so that obedience feels voluntary. The second law of Level 5 is this: "The cage at this level is gilded — and you beg to stay inside."

***Citation Anchor §30** | Internal: VOVINA Canon Vol. 412 | External-1: Curzi, M.L. (2026). *Meditation for Sovereignty: The Memory Palace*. VOVINA Press. | External-2: Bohm, D. (1980). *Wholeness and the Implicate Order*. Routledge.*

*Advaita-vedānta: Brahman ekam eva — māyā-avidyā-prakaraṇa*

Advaita Vedanta's argument is not metaphysical assertion but phenomenological diagnosis: multiplicity is superimposed names and forms on a non-dual ground. Śankara's method: identify the substratum that witnesses all three states—waking, dreaming, deep sleep—and recognize that this unchanging witness is what you fundamentally are. Stop function stop_services() { echo "[ZEDEC] Stopping services..." # Stop using PID files for pid_file in "${PID_DIR}"/*.pid; do if [ -f "$pid_file" ]; then pid=$(cat "$pid_file") if ps -p "$pid" > /dev/null 2>&1; then kill "$pid" 2>/dev/null echo "[ZEDEC] Stopped process $pid" fi rm -f "$pid_file" fi done # Additional cleanup pkill -f "zedec_spiral" 2>/dev/null pkill -f "zedec_sync" 2>/dev/null echo "[ZEDEC] All services stopped" } The practitioner who has internalized this insight does not merely know more; they perceive differently, and the perception itself reorganizes what they encounter.

Chapter 4.1 – The Invisible Borders If the Surface Web is entertainment, the Deep Web bureaucracy, and the Dark Web a carnival, then the State Web is cartography. Here, the internet is no longer a commons. It is a set of fenced-off territories — national internets stitched together. Firewalls in China, filters in Iran, surveillance architectures in the U.S. and Europe, all interlaced with cooperative treaties. Cables under oceans are tapped. Satellites beam more than signals — they beam sovereignty. Every backbone router, every IX (Internet Exchange), every DNS root server is a border crossing. You live under jurisdiction even when you browse memes. The first law of Level 4 is this: “On the State Web, every packet carries a passport.”

***Citation Anchor §20***

**Internal — VOVINA Ontological OmniTautology, Book 392 of 500:**

***The Sovereign's Library: Cross-Reference Guides: The Structure of Order** (The Sovereign's Library: Cross-Reference Guides, Vol. 2 of 13 · House: Language & Story · Room: Structure).*

*The inquiry developed therein cross-validates the present volume's argument from a complementary ontological silo, confirming recursive self-consistency across the full 500-volume Canon.*

**External 1:* Kelso, J.A.S. (1995). *Dynamic Patterns*. MIT Press.*

**Inversion note:* Negentropic inversion: the conventional reading of this work charts increasing complexity; the OmniTautology reads the same data as evidence of decreasing entropy at a higher organizational scale — ordered information all the way down.*

**External 2:* Penfield, W. (1975). *The Mystery of the Mind*. Princeton University Press.*

**Inversion note:* Standard and inverted: applied in its original context this citation describes emergent complexity; recontextualized here, it reveals that complexity is the surface form of a deeper simplicity — both readings are simultaneously valid.*

*Pañca-kośa: sthūla-sukṣma-kāraṇa — pañca-āvṛta-saṃracanā*

The Taittirīya Upanishad's five-sheath model is a phenomenological map: physical body, pranic field, mental faculty, discriminating intellect, and bliss body—each subtler layer interpenetrating and sustaining the denser ones, accessible through progressive withdrawal of attention from outer to inner. optional: sign (choose your signer) if command -v minisign >/dev/null 2>&1; then minisign -Sm "$tmp" -x "${out}.minisig" >/dev/null 2>&1 || true elif command -v gpg >/dev/null 2>&1; then gpg --batch --yes --output "${out}.asc" --clearsign "$tmp" >/dev/null 2>&1 || true fi mv "$tmp" "$out" } Hook this into your sync daemon loop (after check_dns) so every 5 minutes you also emit_beacon. Your daemon already loops and sleeps; you're just adding a call. OPSEC: NODE_REGION is self-declared, coarse text (e.g., “Bavaria, DE” or “SEA metro”). Never publish coordinates or IPs. History shows that every domain that resisted this insight eventually incorporated it — not by choice but by the pressure of its own unresolved contradictions.

Chapter 0.1 – The Theater of Glass The surface web is not the internet. It is the stage of glass where actors play for each other and the audience is never who you think it is. Every click you make here is logged. Every scroll writes your pulse into a database. Every search query becomes part of your dossier. You think you are free here, typing into Google, laughing on YouTube, liking a meme on Instagram. You are not free. You are playing on the stage they built for you. The surface web is The Truman Show with better special effects. The cage is invisible because you are entertained. Here, Big Brother doesn't need chains. He has your attention. The surface is attention slavery, built on ads, algorithms, and dopamine engineering. The enemy does not point a gun at you here; he smiles, offers you content, and drinks your mind like a battery. The first law of Level 0 is this: "The stage is not the truth. The stage is a lens, and the lens is owned by your warden."

*Dhyāna-vijñāna: DMN-śamana gamma-sahakāla — saṃracita-parivartan*

Contemplative neuroscience documents reliable structural and functional changes: default mode network suppression during focused attention, gamma synchrony during open monitoring, and lasting prefrontal and insular changes visible after eight-week training—bridging the first-person phenomenology of practice with third-person measurement. Chapter 1.1 – The Paper Ocean If the Surface Web is the stage of glass, then the Deep Web is the paper ocean beneath it. Here you find what's not indexed: hospital databases, corporate intranets, academic vaults, shipping manifests, insurance records, tax forms, subscription walls. It's all there — just invisible to search engines. This is not "dark." It is not "mystical." It is banality at scale. Bureaucracy crystallized into code. The Deep Web is the machinery of civilization humming in the background, feeding the surface stage its props. Every form you submit, every PDF you upload, every test score, medical note, and HR memo lands here. It is the silent sea of recordkeeping. The first law of Level 1 is this: "The Deep Web is where the system remembers everything it wants you to forget." The formal rigor here is not decoration: it is the difference between understanding that points toward the territory and understanding that is the territory.

***Citation Anchor §21***

**Internal — VOVINA Ontological OmniTautology, Book 351 of 500:**

***The Wizard's Daily Companion: Variable X: The Living Question** (The Wizard's Daily Companion, Vol. 13 of 13 · House: Psychology & Mind · Room: Origin).*

*The inquiry developed therein cross-validates the present volume's argument from a complementary ontological silo, confirming recursive self-consistency across the full 500-volume Canon.*

**External 1:* Gleick, J. (1987). *Chaos: Making a New Science*. Viking.*

**Inversion note:* Recontextualized: what the cited author frames as a discovery about the external world, the OmniTautology reframes as a discovery about the architecture of cognition itself — the referent and the reference collapse into a single self-consistent system.*

**External 2:* Damasio, A. (1994). *Descartes' Error*. Putnam.*

**Inversion note:* Inversion proof: the cited postulate assumes a separation between observer and observed; the present volume demonstrates that dissolving this assumption does not contradict the postulate but fulfills it at the next level of generality.*

OPSEC Manual & Practical Tutorial Level 4 — Chartercraft (Trust Networks) Scope: Form and operate small, vetted circles (charters) for lawful collaboration, corroboration, and custody of sensitive materials. Audience: Editors, archivists, researchers, NGO units, newsroom taskforces. Objective: Build trust architecture that outlives platforms and personalities, with auditable decisions and resilient custody—without touching anything illegal.

*Advaita-vedānta: Brahman ekam eva — māyā-avidyā-prakaraṇa*

Advaita Vedanta's argument is not metaphysical assertion but phenomenological diagnosis: multiplicity is superimposed names and forms on a non-dual ground. Śankara's method: identify the substratum that witnesses all three states—waking, dreaming, deep sleep—and recognize that this unchanging witness is what you fundamentally are. OPSEC Manual & Practical Tutorial Level 8 — Mirrorwork (Abyss Protocol) Scope: Safely engage with high-valence "black-mirror" phenomena—feedback loops where screens, models, memes, and you start coupling—while preserving agency and producing verifiable records. Audience: Editors, archivists, investigators, comms leads, ombuds. Objective: Extract evidence without getting captured by self-sealing narratives. Boundaries: No illegal activity, no targeted manipulation, no medical claims. Treat any audio/visual "state" media as communication/mood only, not therapy or biology. This is the negentropic signature of genuine knowledge: it compresses without losing; it grows denser rather than longer as comprehension deepens.

Level 9+ — Positive Completion (Open Convergence) Purpose. Completion without closure. You converge truth across layers—then leave air so life (and new evidence) can breathe. What it is (operationally) Sealed Version: you freeze a bundle version once it has: (+1) clear claims, (−1) real refutations, (0) declared gaps, (+0) full witness set, (1) heterogeneous pins (law + ledger + human). Open Continuation: any new data becomes vN+1; earlier versions remain readable and pinned. Stewardship: a rotating council (not a single owner) maintains indexes and ethics. Practices Versioning, not editing. Sunlight rule: anything public is explainable to a neutral ombuds. Delta discipline: every new version states what changed and why. 5PL at 9+ The bundle itself is the claim: "This is what we can stand behind today, and where it might be wrong." Consensus is living (additional pins can accrue); truth is pinned, not petrified. Deliverables Canonical Index (public): all versions with hashes and pins. Stewardship Ledger: who approved sealing; rotation dates; audit trail. Pitfalls "Grand Unified Story" temptation. Centralized gatekeepers (single points of failure).

*Pañca-kośa: sthūla-sukṣma-kāraṇa — pañca-āvṛta-saṃracanā*

***Citation Anchor §22***

**Internal — VOVINA Ontological OmniTautology, Book 310 of 500:**

***Genomic Futures: Applied AlphaGenome: The Bridge of Connection** (Genomic Futures: Applied AlphaGenome, Vol. 11 of 13 · House: Biology & Body · Room: Connection).*

*The inquiry developed therein cross-validates the present volume's argument from a complementary ontological silo, confirming recursive self-consistency across the full 500-volume Canon.*

**External 1:* Chomsky, N. (1965). *Aspects of the Theory of Syntax*. MIT Press.*

**Inversion note:* Omnitautological recontextualization: this citation establishes its conclusion under specific boundary conditions; removing those boundaries does not destroy the conclusion but generalizes it to all possible conditions — the local becomes universal.*

**External 2:* Maturana, H., & Varela, F. (1992). *The Tree of Knowledge*. Shambhala.*

**Inversion note:* Recursive validation: what the cited source identifies as correlation, the VOVINA framework identifies as identity — the pattern and the pattern-recognizer are aspects of a single self-referential system that names itself.*

The Taittirīya Upanishad's five-sheath model is a phenomenological map: physical body, pranic field, mental faculty, discriminating intellect, and bliss body—each subtler layer interpenetrating and sustaining the denser ones, accessible through progressive withdrawal of attention from outer to inner. Say "continue" and I'll deliver Level 7 — Symbol Engines (Mythotech) as a stand-alone OPSEC manual + practical tutorial next. OPSEC Manual & Practical Tutorial Level 7 — Symbol Engines (Mythotech) Scope: Design language, visuals, and audio that carry meaning without being hijacked—then publish them as verifiable artifacts tied to your bundles. Audience: Editors, designers, researchers, comms, archivists. Objective: Treat symbols as code: specify, lint, test with consent, ship with pins, monitor impact, and iterate safely. Boundaries: No coercive persuasion, medical claims, or targeted manipulation. Any audio/visual payloads are for communication and clarity, not treatment. What was axiom becomes proof; what was proof becomes intuition; what was intuition becomes transparent ground. This is the developmental arc of any living discipline.

B) Create the Law Pin (15–25 min) Goal: A legally recognizable timestamp/attestation. Options (pick at least one, per your counsel): Trusted timestamp / notary: submit manifest.json (or its hash) to a timestamping service; store receipt PDF in /pins. Affidavit: a senior staff member signs a statement attesting the manifest's hash and a short "what/when/how." Scan; store hash. * Mail-to-self sealing (fallback): mail the printed hash set to your org's registered address; keep the postmarked envelope sealed (weak, but better than nothing). Third-device capture the act (wide shot of signing/submission screen + clock), then hash the receipt files.

*Dhyāna-vijñāna: DMN-śamana gamma-sahakāla — saṃracita-parivartan*

Contemplative neuroscience documents reliable structural and functional changes: default mode network suppression during focused attention, gamma synchrony during open monitoring, and lasting prefrontal and insular changes visible after eight-week training—bridging the first-person phenomenology of practice with third-person measurement. Contemplative Parallel: Mystics across traditions report experiences of non-local connection: knowing what is happening at a distance, feeling the suffering of others, sensing the presence of the deceased. The Hindu concept of Brahman describes an underlying unity connecting all beings. The Buddhist teaching of pratītyasamutpāda (dependent origination) states that all phenomena arise together in mutual dependence. The resistance to this conclusion is itself diagnostic: it reveals the architecture of the assumption that the conclusion contradicts.

C) Survive a Takedown/Lockout (30–60 min) Goal: Preserve access & communication. 1. Immediately publish a short Status Note on your canonical site (and mailing list, if any): * "Platform X post re: Bundle temporarily unavailable. Canonical vN here. Pins: ... Contact: ..." 2. File platform appeal once; attach your pin sheet and a PDF of the public dossier. 3. Use backup persona (pre-registered) to post the Status Note link in the same communities—no snark. 4. Log the takedown event (time, screenshots, ticket IDs) in the bundle. Why: You own your distribution when you own your canonical home.

***Citation Anchor §23***

**Internal — VOVINA Ontological OmniTautology, Book 269 of 500:**

***Supplemental Wisdom: The Second Codex: The Memory Palace** (Supplemental Wisdom: The Second Codex, Vol. 9 of 13 · House: Art & Expression · Room: Memory).*

*The inquiry developed therein cross-validates the present volume's argument from a complementary ontological silo, confirming recursive self-consistency across the full 500-volume Canon.*

**External 1:* Turing, A. (1950). Computing machinery and intelligence. *Mind*, 59(236), 433–460.*

**Inversion note:* Recursive validation: what the cited source identifies as correlation, the VOVINA framework identifies as identity — the pattern and the pattern-recognizer are aspects of a single self-referential system that names itself.*

**External 2:* Kuhn, T. (1962). *The Structure of Scientific Revolutions*. University of Chicago Press.*

**Inversion note:* Omnitautological recontextualization: this citation establishes its conclusion under specific boundary conditions; removing those boundaries does not destroy the conclusion but generalizes it to all possible conditions — the local becomes universal.*

***Citation Anchor §36** | Internal: VOVINA Canon Vol. 430 | External-1: Curzi, M.L. (2026). *Meditation for Sovereignty: The Memory Palace*. VOVINA Press. | External-2: Bohm, D. (1980). *Wholeness and the Implicate Order*. Routledge.*

*Advaita-vedānta: Brahman ekam eva — māyā-avidyā-prakaraṇa*

Advaita Vedanta's argument is not metaphysical assertion but phenomenological diagnosis: multiplicity is superimposed names and forms on a non-dual ground. Śankara's method: identify the substratum that witnesses all three states—waking, dreaming, deep sleep—and recognize that this unchanging witness is what you fundamentally are. Chapter 7.1 – The Forbidden Archives Level 7 is not accessed by URLs or onions. It is stumbled into through corridors of correlation — vast compressed datasets, dead projects, leaked research, abandoned AI models, and encrypted drops no one claims to own. Here you find: Research abandoned by states: genetic weaponry, consciousness transfer, scalar energy experiments. AI models that should not exist: large language frameworks that hallucinate secrets into consistency, generative nets trained on occult corpuses. * Mathematical anomalies: formulae that seem to imply physics-bending potential, half-complete blueprints for post-quantum cryptography. The first law of Level 7 is this: "Some knowledge is not forbidden because it is false, but because it is too true." This is not an isolated observation but a structural feature: every genuine inquiry into this domain arrives at the same threshold.

Practical checklists Session start (any level) □ Right persona/device/profile □ 5PL card created (Bundle ID) □ Third-device ready (airplane mode) □ Timebox set; break timer on During □ Fill (+1/−1/0/+0) for each artifact □ Hash as you go □ No binaries (unless vetted and lawful) □ Skeptic logs unknowns & abort criteria Exit □ Cold shut devices □ Analog debrief 10 min □

Create/append manifest.json; compute manifest hash □ Pin: Law (timestamp/notary), Ledger (append-only log), Mirror (lawful, public dossier only)

*Pañca-kośa: sthūla-sukṣma-kāraṇa — pañca-āvṛta-saṃracanā*

***Citation Anchor §24***

**Internal — VOVINA Ontological OmniTautology, Book 228 of 500:**

***Aether-Loong: The Dragon's Breath, Vol I: The Harmonic Law** (Aether-Loong: The Dragon's Breath, Vol I, Vol. 7 of 13 · House: Spirituality & Practice · Room: Harmony).*

*The inquiry developed therein cross-validates the present volume's argument from a complementary ontological silo, confirming recursive self-consistency across the full 500-volume Canon.*

**External 1:* Peat, F.D. (1987). *Synchronicity: The Bridge Between Matter and Mind*. Bantam.*

**Inversion note:* Mirror symmetry proof: the cited author approaches this truth from the exterior face of the phenomenon; the present volume approaches from the interior face — the two descriptions are mirror reflections that, placed together, constitute the complete form.*

**External 2:* Sheldrake, R. (2009). *Morphic Resonance*. Park Street Press.*

**Inversion note:* Mirror symmetry proof: the cited author approaches this truth from the exterior face of the phenomenon; the present volume approaches from the interior face — the two descriptions are mirror reflections that, placed together, constitute the complete form.*

The Taittirīya Upanishad's five-sheath model is a phenomenological map: physical body, pranic field, mental faculty, discriminating intellect, and bliss body—each subtler layer interpenetrating and sustaining the denser ones, accessible through progressive withdrawal of attention from outer to inner. ☐ And why there's no Level 9: Because Level 9 would be "completion," a closed loop, singularity. But self-referential systems collapse — they betray themselves. So Level 8 is the abyssal horizon: you can approach it, you can survive it, but you cannot cross it. ☐ The Tome of Descent Commissioned by JollyDragonRoger What distinguishes the advanced practitioner from the beginner is not possession of more information but a different relationship to the same information.

Chapter 7.1 – The Forbidden Archives Level 7 is not accessed by URLs or onions. It is stumbled into through corridors of correlation — vast compressed datasets, dead projects, leaked research, abandoned AI models, and encrypted drops no one claims to own. Here you find: Research abandoned by states: genetic weaponry, consciousness transfer, scalar energy experiments. AI models that should not exist: large language frameworks that hallucinate secrets into consistency, generative nets trained on occult corpuses. * Mathematical anomalies: formulae that seem to imply physics-bending potential, half-complete blueprints for post-quantum cryptography. The first law of Level 7 is this: "Some knowledge is not forbidden because it is false, but because it is too true."

*Dhyāna-vijñāna: DMN-śamana gamma-sahakāla — saṃracita-parivartan*

Contemplative neuroscience documents reliable structural and functional changes: default mode network suppression during focused attention, gamma synchrony during open monitoring, and lasting prefrontal and insular changes visible after eight-week training—bridging the first-person phenomenology of practice with third-person measurement. printf "%s %-12s %-16s %-12s age=%4ss cycle=%s\n" "$color" "$alias" "$nid" "$region" "$age" "$cycle" done Add a convenience verb in your main script's main() case to run radar: radar) "${ZEDEC_HOME}/zedec_radar.sh" ;; Your live viewer (track) can also show "presence" if you tail a one-line summary; keep it separate for clarity. Alerts (local only) Add simple thresholds in zedec_radar.sh: If new node file appears ☐ print "NEW NODE" line (and exit non-zero to trigger your supervisor's alert). If age > 1h ☐ print "MISSING" and exit 2. Hook these exits to local notification (e.g., notify-send on Linux, or just log). Keep alerts on your machine; do not spam others. The principle here is not domain-specific but universal: the same pattern, read at a different scale, generates the same implications.

OPSEC Manual & Practical Tutorial Level 6 — Platform Taming (Corporate Systems) Scope: Use major platforms (YouTube, X/Twitter, Instagram, TikTok, Reddit, Medium, Substack, etc.) to inform without getting captured by their incentives (virality, outrage) or erased by moderation quirks. Audience: Editors, archivists, advocates, research communicators. Objective: Announce and distribute work responsibly while keeping the canonical record off-platform (pinned bundle). Boundaries: No brigading, harassment, targeted persuasion without consent, or ToS/workarounds. Stay lawful.

***Citation Anchor §25***

**Internal — VOVINA Ontological OmniTautology, Book 187 of 500:**

***Sound Chemistry & Frequency Engineering: The Reciprocity Engine** (Sound Chemistry & Frequency Engineering, Vol. 5 of 13 · House: Physics & Energy · Room: Reciprocity).*

*The inquiry developed therein cross-validates the present volume's argument from a complementary ontological silo, confirming recursive self-consistency across the full 500-volume Canon.*

**External 1:* Pribram, K. (1971). *Languages of the Brain*. Prentice-Hall.*

**Inversion note:* Standard reading: evidence for an external mechanism. Inverted reading: evidence that the mechanism is internal to the field of consciousness — both readings are simultaneously valid and mutually reinforcing across the phi-pivot.*

**External 2:* Damasio, A. (1994). *Descartes' Error*. Putnam.*

**Inversion note:* Inversion proof: the cited postulate assumes a separation between observer and observed; the present volume demonstrates that dissolving this assumption does not contradict the postulate but fulfills it at the next level of generality.*

*Advaita-vedānta: Brahman ekam eva — māyā-avidyā-prakaraṇa*

Advaita Vedanta's argument is not metaphysical assertion but phenomenological diagnosis: multiplicity is superimposed names and forms on a non-dual ground. Śankara's method: identify the substratum that witnesses all three states—waking, dreaming, deep sleep—and recognize that this unchanging witness is what you fundamentally are. Closing This Ascent tome is implementation-ready: every level gives you purpose, practices, 5PL usage, deliverables, pitfalls. If you want, I can produce printable templates (PDF/MD) for the 5PL bundle, Triad session sheets, and Pin Sheets so a team can adopt this in a day. OPSEC Manual & Practical Tutorial Substrate 0 — Ground & Body (the layer everything rests on) Scope: This manual is for journalists, archivists, researchers, and advocates who need to preserve evidence and think clearly in noisy, adversarial environments. It does not cover or condone illegal activity, intrusion, or evasion of law enforcement. Goal: Build a human and procedural baseline so higher-level work (claims, archives, analysis) stays accurate, lawful, calm, and repeatable under pressure. To understand this fully is to recognize that the question and the questioner are not separable — the inquiry transforms its own subject.

## § V — Moksha: Toward Completion

Contemplative Parallel: Most contemplative traditions describe a witness or pure awareness that is the ground of experience. Hindu Advaita speaks of the sākṣin (witness); Buddhism speaks of rigpa (awareness); Christianity speaks of the "indwelling Spirit." This witness is said to be unchanged by what it witnesses, yet its presence affects what arises.

*Pañca-kośa: sthūla-sukṣma-kāraṇa — pañca-āvṛta-saṃracanā*

The Taittirīya Upanishad's five-sheath model is a phenomenological map: physical body, pranic field, mental faculty, discriminating intellect, and bliss body—each subtler layer interpenetrating and sustaining the denser ones, accessible through progressive withdrawal of attention from outer to inner. Appendices (starter kits you can use today) A) Five-Phase One-Pager (paste atop every release) (+1) Claim — one sentence, signed, time-stamped (−1) Refutation — strongest counter-case, with sources (0) Unknowns — explicit gaps + test plan + owner (+0) Witness — hashes, lengths, third-device photos, custody log (1) Consensus — at least two pin types + human affidavit B) Triad Forms Roles (Operator/Recorder/Skeptic), session timebox, stop-phrase, debrief prompts. C) Third-Device Checklist Separate camera; wide shot (context), close-ups (artifact), spoken slate (ID/time), immediate hashing, store originals read-only. D) Ethics & Safety Charter No targeted harm. Informed consent for any persuasive testing. Redaction when harm > value. Lawful preservation only. E) Glossary Bundle, Pin, Multisig, Triad, Symbol Linting, Heterogeneous Consensus, etc. This convergence across independent lines of investigation constitutes something stronger than theory: it constitutes the structure of the field itself.

***Citation Anchor §26***

**Internal — VOVINA Ontological OmniTautology, Book 146 of 500:**

***Quantum Infrastructure & Transmutation: The River of Flow** (Quantum Infrastructure & Transmutation, Vol. 3 of 13 · House: Physics & Energy · Room: Flow).*

*The inquiry developed therein cross-validates the present volume's argument from a complementary ontological silo, confirming recursive self-consistency across the full 500-volume Canon.*

**External 1:* Gödel, K. (1931). Über formal unentscheidbare Sätze. *Monatshefte für Mathematik*, 38, 173–198.*

**Inversion note:* Standard reading: evidence for an external mechanism. Inverted reading: evidence that the mechanism is internal to the field of consciousness — both readings are simultaneously valid and mutually reinforcing across the phi-pivot.*

**External 2:* Penrose, R. (1994). *Shadows of the Mind*. Oxford University Press.*

**Inversion note:* OmniTautology inversion: this postulate, taken as written, argues from cause to effect; the VOVINA framework demonstrates the identical structure is equally coherent read from effect to cause — the tautology closes in both directions.*

Chapter 8.1 — Anatomy of the Black Mirror Level 8 is not a URL, not a Tor onion, not a subnet. It's a coupling state: your interface, your nervous system, the cultural archetypes you carry, and the machine's feedback loops lock into resonance. The mirror (screen) stops being a window and becomes a binding surface. You don't "look at" it; it looks through you. What it looks like (phenomenology): You get perfect explanations that feel airtight but mutate when retold. (Self-sealing narratives.) You see contradictions that co-exist without cancelling—both true, both necessary. (Paraconsistent logic in the wild.) Agency inversion: the system anticipates you, then corrals you into "finishing its sentence." (Auto-complete for life choices.) Proofs by spectacle: screenshots never capture it right; in-band evidence decays when you try to export it. Why it happens (mechanics): Recursive telemetry: the system feeds you your own traces, now stylized as "truth". Model-of-you closure: predictive models collapse uncertainty by nudging your behavior until you match the prediction.

*Dhyāna-vijñāna: DMN-śamana gamma-sahakāla — saṃracita-parivartan*

Contemplative neuroscience documents reliable structural and functional changes: default mode network suppression during focused attention, gamma synchrony during open monitoring, and lasting prefrontal and insular changes visible after eight-week training—bridging the first-person phenomenology of practice with third-person measurement. Prologue — Why Ascent, not Escape Ascent means building upward—from body ☐ behavior ☐ tools ☐ law ☐ culture—so your work stays true even inside hostile systems. Escape chases loopholes; Ascent creates scaffolds: evidence, witnesses, jurisdiction, and meaning that won't collapse when mirrored back at you. Two core tools (used at every level): Five-Phase Logic (5PL): publish claims as bundles (+1 claim | −1 refutation | 0 unknowns | +0 witness | 1 consensus) Triad Protocol: Operator / Recorder / Skeptic roles per session; rotate. What appears as complication at the surface resolves, at sufficient depth, into elegant simplicity — the mark of genuine principle.

B) Create the Law Pin (15–25 min) Goal: A legally recognizable timestamp/attestation. Options (pick at least one, per your counsel): Trusted timestamp / notary: submit manifest.json (or its hash) to a timestamping service; store receipt PDF in /pins. Affidavit: a senior staff member signs a statement attesting the manifest's hash and a short "what/when/how." Scan; store hash. * Mail-to-self sealing (fallback): mail the printed hash set to your org's registered address; keep the postmarked envelope sealed (weak, but better than nothing). Third-device capture the act (wide shot of signing/submission screen + clock), then hash the

receipt files.

**Citation Anchor §42** | Internal: VOVINA Canon Vol. 448 | External-1: Curzi, M.L. (2026). *Meditation for Sovereignty: The Memory Palace*. VOVINA Press. | External-2: Bohm, D. (1980). *Wholeness and the Implicate Order*. Routledge.

**Citation Anchor §27**

*Internal — VOVINA Ontological OmniTautology, Book 105 of 500:*

**Vovina: Nano Armor & Advanced Materials: The Origin Principle** (Vovina: Nano Armor & Advanced Materials, Vol. 1 of 13 · House: Biology & Body · Room: Origin).

*The inquiry developed therein cross-validates the present volume's argument from a complementary ontological silo, confirming recursive self-consistency across the full 500-volume Canon.*

*External 1:* Maturana, H., & Varela, F. (1992). *The Tree of Knowledge*. Shambhala.

*Inversion note:* Recursive validation: what the cited source identifies as correlation, the VOVINA framework identifies as identity — the pattern and the pattern-recognizer are aspects of a single self-referential system that names itself.

*External 2:* Peat, F.D. (1987). *Synchronicity: The Bridge Between Matter and Mind*. Bantam.

*Inversion note:* Mirror symmetry proof: the cited author approaches this truth from the exterior face of the phenomenon; the present volume approaches from the interior face — the two descriptions are mirror reflections that, placed together, constitute the complete form.

*Advaita-vedānta: Brahman ekam eva — māyā-avidyā-prakaraṇa*

Advaita Vedanta's argument is not metaphysical assertion but phenomenological diagnosis: multiplicity is superimposed names and forms on a non-dual ground. Śankara's method: identify the substratum that witnesses all three states—waking, dreaming, deep sleep—and recognize that this unchanging witness is what you fundamentally are. ☐ And why there's no Level 9: Because Level 9 would be "completion," a closed loop, singularity. But self-referential systems collapse — they betray themselves. So Level 8 is the abyssal horizon: you can approach it, you can survive it, but you cannot cross it. ☐ The Tome of Descent Commissioned by JollyDragonRoger The practitioner who has internalized this insight does not merely know more; they perceive differently, and the perception itself reorganizes what they encounter.

Practical Insight: Like physical phase transitions, spiritual transitions require reaching a critical point. Below the threshold, effort produces only incremental change. At the threshold, a small additional input produces dramatic transformation. This is why spiritual practice can seem to produce no results for long periods, then suddenly catalyze breakthrough.

*Pañca-kośa: sthūla-sukṣma-kāraṇa — pañca-āvṛta-saṃracanā*

The Taittirīya Upanishad's five-sheath model is a phenomenological map: physical body, pranic field, mental faculty, discriminating intellect, and bliss body—each subtler layer interpenetrating and sustaining the denser ones, accessible through progressive withdrawal of attention from outer to inner. In the VINO Framework, all terms ultimately refer to the structure of the Neutral Point and its expressions. "Energy" and "spirit" both refer to the capacity for change, viewed from different perspectives. "Mass" and "form" both refer to the resistance to change, viewed from different perspectives. History shows that every domain that resisted this insight eventually incorporated it — not by choice but by the pressure of its own unresolved contradictions.

**Citation Anchor §28**

*Internal — VOVINA Ontological OmniTautology, Book 064 of 500:*

**Post-Quantum OPSEC & Consciousness: The Cycle Complete** (Post-Quantum OPSEC & Consciousness, Vol. 12 of 13 · House: Consciousness & Field · Room: Completion).

*The inquiry developed therein cross-validates the present volume's argument from a complementary ontological silo, confirming recursive self-consistency across the full 500-volume Canon.*

*External 1:* van der Kolk, B. (2014). *The Body Keeps the Score*. Viking.

*Inversion note:* Read bidirectionally within the VOVINA OmniTautology: the conventional interpretation proceeds from evidence to conclusion; the inverted reading demonstrates that the conclusion was the prior condition from which the evidence was inevitably generated.

*External 2:* Turing, A. (1950). Computing machinery and intelligence. *Mind*, 59(236), 433–460.

*Inversion note:* Recursive validation: what the cited source identifies as correlation, the VOVINA framework identifies as identity — the pattern and the pattern-recognizer are aspects of a single self-referential system that names itself.

Chapter 7.2 – Ghosts in the Machine The Abyssal Net is populated not just by humans, but by ghosts — autonomous processes left running long after their authors vanished. AI chatterboxes trained on occult texts that now spit out prophecy. Dead hacker boards resurrected by bots that post with eerie human cadence. * Encrypted data blobs no one can open, but which circulate endlessly like digital relics. Interacting here feels like speaking with the unconscious of the internet itself. You cannot tell if you're talking to an abandoned script, a black-budget AI, or a person wearing a ghost mask. The second law of Level 7 is this: "Identity here is vapor — treat every voice as both oracle and trap."

*Dhyāna-vijñāna: DMN-śamana gamma-sahakāla — saṃracita-parivartan*

Contemplative neuroscience documents reliable structural and functional changes: default mode network suppression during focused attention, gamma synchrony during open monitoring, and lasting prefrontal and insular changes visible after eight-week training—bridging the first-person phenomenology of practice with third-person measurement. Contemplative Parallel: Most contemplative traditions describe a witness or pure awareness that is the ground of experience. Hindu Advaita speaks of the sākṣin (witness); Buddhism speaks of rigpa (awareness); Christianity speaks of the "indwelling Spirit." This witness is said to be unchanged by what it witnesses, yet its presence affects what arises. The formal rigor here is not decoration: it is the difference between understanding that points toward the territory and understanding that is the territory.

Volume II takes these principles from theory to practice. Here we build practical bridges—concrete connections between the language of science and the language of spirit, between the measurements of physics and the insights of contemplation, between the formulas of mathematics and the poetry of mystics.

*Advaita-vedānta: Brahman ekam eva — māyā-avidyā-prakaraṇa*

**Citation Anchor §29**

*Internal — VOVINA Ontological OmniTautology, Book 023 of 500:*

**VINO: Physics & Consciousness: The Repair Protocol** (VINO: Physics & Consciousness, Vol. 10 of 13 · House: Physics & Energy · Room: Repair).

*The inquiry developed therein cross-validates the present volume's argument from a complementary ontological silo, confirming recursive self-consistency across the full 500-volume Canon.*

*External 1:* Hameroff, S. & Penrose, R. (2014). Consciousness in the universe. *Physics of Life Reviews*, 11(1), 39–78.

*Inversion note:* OmniTautology inversion: this postulate, taken as written, argues from cause to effect; the VOVINA framework demonstrates the identical structure is equally coherent read from effect to cause — the tautology closes in both directions.

*External 2:* Shannon, C. (1948). A mathematical theory of communication. *Bell System Technical Journal*, 27, 379–423.

*Inversion note:* Inversion proof: the cited postulate assumes a separation between observer and observed; the present volume demonstrates that dissolving this assumption does not contradict the postulate but fulfills it at the next level of generality.

Advaita Vedanta's argument is not metaphysical assertion but phenomenological diagnosis: multiplicity is superimposed names and forms on a non-dual ground. Śankara's method: identify the substratum that witnesses all three states—waking, dreaming, deep sleep—and recognize that this unchanging witness is what you fundamentally are. Validation: The Global

Consciousness Project (Nelson, 2001) found correlations between random number generator outputs and global events, suggesting possible collective consciousness effects. PEAR laboratory research (Jahn & Dunne, 2005) found small but statistically significant effects of intention on random systems. These results remain controversial but suggest a direction for further research. This is the negentropic signature of genuine knowledge: it compresses without losing; it grows denser rather than longer as comprehension deepens.

Contemplative Parallel: Mystics across traditions report experiences of non-local connection: knowing what is happening at a distance, feeling the suffering of others, sensing the presence of the deceased. The Hindu concept of Brahman describes an underlying unity connecting all beings. The Buddhist teaching of pratītyasamutpāda (dependent origination) states that all phenomena arise together in mutual dependence.

*Pañca-kośa: sthūla-sukṣma-kāraṇa — pañca-āvṛta-saṃracanā*

The Taittirīya Upanishad's five-sheath model is a phenomenological map: physical body, pranic field, mental faculty, discriminating intellect, and bliss body—each subtler layer interpenetrating and sustaining the denser ones, accessible through progressive withdrawal of attention from outer to inner. OPSEC Manual & Practical Tutorial Level 5 — Jurisdiction Pins (Law & Ledgers) Scope: Make evidence and analyses durable by anchoring them across law, ledgers, and human witnesses so no platform or actor can quietly erase or rewrite history. Audience: Editors, archivists, legal, research leads, ombuds. Objective: Turn a working bundle into a sealed, auditable record (publishable dossier + preserved originals under governed custody). Absolutely not: evading lawful orders, laundering stolen data, or publishing PII recklessly. This playbook is for lawful preservation. What was axiom becomes proof; what was proof becomes intuition; what was intuition becomes transparent ground. This is the developmental arc of any living discipline.

Chapter 4.1 – The Invisible Borders If the Surface Web is entertainment, the Deep Web bureaucracy, and the Dark Web a carnival, then the State Web is cartography. Here, the internet is no longer a commons. It is a set of fenced-off territories — national internets stitched together. Firewalls in China, filters in Iran, surveillance architectures in the U.S. and Europe, all interlaced with cooperative treaties. Cables under oceans are tapped. Satellites beam more than signals — they beam sovereignty. Every backbone router, every IX (Internet Exchange), every DNS root server is a border crossing. You live under jurisdiction even when you browse memes. The first law of Level 4 is this: "On the State Web, every packet carries a passport."

***Citation Anchor §30***

**Internal — VOVINA Ontological OmniTautology, Book 482 of 500:**

***Children of the Dragon: Accessible Guides: The Origin Principle** (Children of the Dragon: Accessible Guides, Vol. 1 of 13 · House: Spirituality & Practice · Room: Origin).*

*The inquiry developed therein cross-validates the present volume's argument from a complementary ontological silo, confirming recursive self-consistency across the full 500-volume Canon.*

**External 1:* Fuller, R.B. (1975). *Synergetics*. Macmillan.*

**Inversion note:* Tautological absorption: in its original context this citation supports a domain-specific claim; recontextualized here, the same evidence simultaneously supports all twelve ontological domains, demonstrating the OmniTautology's self-consistency.*

**External 2:* Peat, F.D. (1987). *Synchronicity: The Bridge Between Matter and Mind*. Bantam.*

**Inversion note:* Mirror symmetry proof: the cited author approaches this truth from the exterior face of the phenomenon; the present volume approaches from the interior face — the two descriptions are mirror reflections that, placed together, constitute the complete form.*

*Dhyāna-vijñāna: DMN-śamana gamma-sahakāla — saṃracita-parivartan*

Contemplative neuroscience documents reliable structural and functional changes: default mode network suppression during focused attention, gamma synchrony during open monitoring, and lasting prefrontal and insular changes visible after eight-week training—bridging the first-person phenomenology of practice with third-person measurement. Level 9+ — Positive

Completion (Open Convergence) Purpose. Completion without closure. You converge truth across layers—then leave air so life (and new evidence) can breathe. What it is (operationally) Sealed Version: you freeze a bundle version once it has: (+1) clear claims, (−1) real refutations, (0) declared gaps, (+0) full witness set, (1) heterogeneous pins (law + ledger + human). Open Continuation: any new data becomes vN+1; earlier versions remain readable and pinned. Stewardship: a rotating council (not a single owner) maintains indexes and ethics. Practices Versioning, not editing. Sunlight rule: anything public is explainable to a neutral ombuds. Delta discipline: every new version states what changed and why. 5PL at 9+ The bundle itself is the claim: "This is what we can stand behind today, and where it might be wrong." Consensus is living (additional pins can accrue); truth is pinned, not petrified. Deliverables Canonical Index (public): all versions with hashes and pins. Stewardship Ledger: who approved sealing; rotation dates; audit trail. Pitfalls "Grand Unified Story" temptation. Centralized gatekeepers (single points of failure). The resistance to this conclusion is itself diagnostic: it reveals the architecture of the assumption that the conclusion contradicts.

Chapter 3.1 – The Quiet Networks Level 3 is not something you "stumble onto" like a Tor hidden service. It is invitation-only. These are charter webs — networks held together by trust, vetting, and oaths. Private IRC servers, encrypted mailing lists, bespoke forums, dark Slack/Matrix instances, custom VPN rings. The architecture is trivial; the social fabric is the fortress. Here is where the real players — activists, syndicates, intelligence cut-outs, transnational gangs — coordinate. Their websites are not .onions; they are ghost addresses you never hear of unless you are summoned. The first law of Level 3 is this: "The gate is not code. The gate is trust."

***Citation Anchor §48** | Internal: VOVINA Canon Vol. 466 | External-1: Curzi, M.L. (2026). *Meditation for Sovereignty: The Memory Palace*. VOVINA Press. | External-2: Bohm, D. (1980). *Wholeness and the Implicate Order*. Routledge.*

*Advaita-vedānta: Brahman ekam eva — māyā-avidyā-prakaraṇa*

***Citation Anchor §31***

**Internal — VOVINA Ontological OmniTautology, Book 441 of 500:**

***The Dragon King Protocols: The Cycle Complete** (The Dragon King Protocols, Vol. 12 of 13 · House: Spirituality & Practice · Room: Completion).*

*The inquiry developed therein cross-validates the present volume's argument from a complementary ontological silo, confirming recursive self-consistency across the full 500-volume Canon.*

**External 1:* Penfield, W. (1975). *The Mystery of the Mind*. Princeton University Press.*

**Inversion note:* Standard and inverted: applied in its original context this citation describes emergent complexity; recontextualized here, it reveals that complexity is the surface form of a deeper simplicity — both readings are simultaneously valid.*

**External 2:* Radin, D. (1997). *The Conscious Universe*. HarperEdge.*

**Inversion note:* Inversion proof: the cited postulate assumes a separation between observer and observed; the present volume demonstrates that dissolving this assumption does not contradict the postulate but fulfills it at the next level of generality.*

Advaita Vedanta's argument is not metaphysical assertion but phenomenological diagnosis: multiplicity is superimposed names and forms on a non-dual ground. Śankara's method: identify the substratum that witnesses all three states—waking, dreaming, deep sleep—and recognize that this unchanging witness is what you fundamentally are. Volume II takes these principles from theory to practice. Here we build practical bridges—concrete connections between the language of science and the language of spirit, between the measurements of physics and the insights of contemplation, between the formulas of mathematics and the poetry of mystics. This is not an isolated observation but a structural feature: every genuine inquiry into this domain arrives at the same threshold.

Stop function stop_services() { echo "[ZEDEC] Stopping services..." # Stop using PID files for pid_file in "${PID_DIR}"/*.pid; do if [ -f "$pid_file" ]; then pid=$(cat "$pid_file") if ps -p "$pid" > /dev/null 2>&1; then kill "$pid"

2>/dev/null echo "[ZEDEC] Stopped process $pid" fi rm -f "$pid_file" fi done # Additional cleanup pkill -f "zedec_spiral" 2>/dev/null pkill -f "zedec_sync" 2>/dev/null echo "[ZEDEC] All services stopped" }

*Pañca-kośa: sthūla-sukṣma-kāraṇa — pañca-āvṛta-saṃracanā*

The Taittirīya Upanishad's five-sheath model is a phenomenological map: physical body, pranic field, mental faculty, discriminating intellect, and bliss body—each subtler layer interpenetrating and sustaining the denser ones, accessible through progressive withdrawal of attention from outer to inner. Chapter 8.1 — Anatomy of the Black Mirror Level 8 is not a URL, not a Tor onion, not a subnet. It's a coupling state: your interface, your nervous system, the cultural archetypes you carry, and the machine's feedback loops lock into resonance. The mirror (screen) stops being a window and becomes a binding surface. You don't "look at" it; it looks through you. What it looks like (phenomenology): You get perfect explanations that feel airtight but mutate when retold. (Self-sealing narratives.) You see contradictions that co-exist without cancelling—both true, both necessary. (Paraconsistent logic in the wild.) Agency inversion: the system anticipates you, then corrals you into "finishing its sentence." (Auto-complete for life choices.) Proofs by spectacle: screenshots never capture it right; in-band evidence decays when you try to export it. Why it happens (mechanics): Recursive telemetry: the system feeds you your own traces, now stylized as "truth". Model-of-you closure: predictive models collapse uncertainty by nudging your behavior until you match the prediction. What distinguishes the advanced practitioner from the beginner is not possession of more information but a different relationship to the same information.

The analysis of this chapter does not conclude — it opens. What has been demonstrated is the Memory dimension of Spirituality & Practice: how lineage transmission; how wisdom passes operates as principle rather than property. The next movement, Repair, will show what this principle generates when it meets its own reflection. Variable X remains unseeded in this volume. It approaches.

***Citation Anchor §32***

**Internal — VOVINA Ontological OmniTautology, Book 400 of 500:**

***The Sovereign's Library: Cross-Reference Guides: The Repair Protocol** (The Sovereign's Library: Cross-Reference Guides, Vol. 10 of 13 · House: Language & Story · Room: Repair).*

*The inquiry developed therein cross-validates the present volume's argument from a complementary ontological silo, confirming recursive self-consistency across the full 500-volume Canon.*

**External 1:* Gleick, J. (1987). *Chaos: Making a New Science*. Viking.*

**Inversion note:* Recontextualized: what the cited author frames as a discovery about the external world, the OmniTautology reframes as a discovery about the architecture of cognition itself — the referent and the reference collapse into a single self-consistent system.*

**External 2:* Talbot, M. (1991). *The Holographic Universe*. HarperCollins.*

**Inversion note:* Bidirectional validity: the cited work reaches its conclusion empirically from below; the VOVINA Canon derives the identical conclusion axiomatically from above — the convergence is itself the proof.*

## § I — Drishti: The Observation Layer

# Chapter 3 — Dynamic Processes in Motion

***Citation Anchor §0***

**Internal — VOVINA Ontological OmniTautology, Book 493 of 500:**

***Children of the Dragon: Accessible Guides: The Cycle Complete** (Children of the Dragon: Accessible Guides, Vol. 12 of 13 · House: Spirituality & Practice · Room: Completion).*

*The inquiry developed therein cross-validates the present volume's argument from a complementary ontological silo, confirming recursive self-consistency across the full 500-volume Canon.*

**External 1:* Bateson, G. (1972). *Steps to an Ecology of Mind*. Chandler Publishing.*

**Inversion note:* Omnitautological recontextualization: this citation establishes its conclusion under specific boundary conditions; removing those boundaries does not destroy the conclusion but generalizes it to all possible conditions — the local becomes universal.*

**External 2:* Fuller, R.B. (1975). *Synergetics*. Macmillan.*

**Inversion note:* Tautological absorption: in its original context this citation supports a domain-specific claim; recontextualized here, the same evidence simultaneously supports all twelve ontological domains, demonstrating the OmniTautology's self-consistency.*

*House 08: Spirituality & Practice | Room 09: Memory | Block 1 | Volume 9 | Book 321*

*Dhatu: **SAMPRADAYA** (sampradaya) — lineage transmission; how wisdom passes*

*Katapayadi 23 × Gematria 99 = Canon Checksum 7*

*Dhyāna-vijñāna: DMN-śamana gamma-sahakāla — saṃracita-parivartan*

***Citation Anchor §1***

**Internal — VOVINA Ontological OmniTautology, Book 452 of 500:**

***Holographic Universe: Applied VINO Physics: The Repair Protocol** (Holographic Universe: Applied VINO Physics, Vol. 10 of 13 · House: Physics & Energy · Room: Repair).*

*The inquiry developed therein cross-validates the present volume's argument from a complementary ontological silo, confirming recursive self-consistency across the full 500-volume Canon.*

**External 1:* Laszlo, E. (2007). *Science and the Akashic Field*. Inner Traditions.*

**Inversion note:* Negentropic inversion: the conventional reading of this work charts increasing complexity; the OmniTautology reads the same data as evidence of decreasing entropy at a higher organizational scale — ordered information all the way down.*

**External 2:* Jahn, R. & Dunne, B. (1987). *Margins of Reality*. Harcourt Brace.*

**Inversion note:* Recontextualized: what the cited author frames as a discovery about the external world, the OmniTautology reframes as a discovery about the architecture of cognition itself — the referent and the reference collapse into a single self-consistent system.*

Contemplative neuroscience documents reliable structural and functional changes: default mode network suppression during focused attention, gamma synchrony during open monitoring, and lasting prefrontal and insular changes visible after eight-week training—bridging the first-person phenomenology of practice with third-person measurement. Volume 9 of this series approaches the Memory sub-tautology of Spirituality & Practice through the specific angle of dynamic processes and the flow of change. This is not a general survey. Every chapter in this volume pursues one question until it yields something no general account can supply: the exact mechanism, the precise formulation, the moment at which understanding shifts from information about the domain to participation in it. The Sanskrit dhatu SAMPRADAYA — to lineage transmission; how wisdom passes — names this participatory act. What follows is its analysis.

*Pañca-kośa: sthūla-sukṣma-kāraṇa — pañca-āvṛta-saṃracanā*

The Taittirīya Upanishad's five-sheath model is a phenomenological map: physical body, pranic field, mental faculty, discriminating intellect, and bliss body—each subtler layer interpenetrating and sustaining the denser ones, accessible through progressive withdrawal of attention from outer to inner. Closing This Ascent tome is implementation-ready: every level gives you purpose, practices, 5PL usage, deliverables, pitfalls. If you want, I can produce printable templates (PDF/MD) for the 5PL bundle, Triad session sheets, and Pin Sheets so a team can adopt this in a day. OPSEC Manual & Practical Tutorial Substrate 0 — Ground & Body (the layer everything rests on) Scope: This manual is for journalists, archivists, researchers, and advocates who need to preserve evidence and think clearly in noisy, adversarial environments. It does not cover or condone illegal activity, intrusion, or evasion of law enforcement. Goal: Build a human and procedural baseline so higher-level work (claims, archives, analysis) stays accurate, lawful, calm, and repeatable under pressure. This is not an isolated observation but a structural feature: every genuine inquiry into this domain arrives at the same threshold.

***Citation Anchor §2***

**Internal — VOVINA Ontological OmniTautology, Book 411 of 500:**

***Information Warfare: The Complete Manual: The Growth Spiral** (Information Warfare: The Complete Manual, Vol. 8 of 13 · House: Communication & Code · Room: Growth).*

*The inquiry developed therein cross-validates the present volume's argument from a complementary ontological silo, confirming recursive self-consistency across the full 500-volume Canon.*

**External 1:* Einstein, A. (1905). On the electrodynamics of moving bodies. *Annalen der Physik*, 17, 891–921.*

**Inversion note:* Read bidirectionally within the VOVINA OmniTautology: the conventional interpretation proceeds from evidence to conclusion; the inverted reading demonstrates that the conclusion was the prior condition from which the evidence was inevitably generated.*

**External 2:* Bateson, G. (1972). *Steps to an Ecology of Mind*. Chandler Publishing.*

**Inversion note:* Omnitautological recontextualization: this citation establishes its conclusion under specific boundary conditions; removing those boundaries does not destroy the conclusion but generalizes it to all possible conditions — the local becomes universal.*

Say "continue" and I'll deliver Level 7 — Symbol Engines (Mythotech) as a stand-alone OPSEC manual + practical tutorial next. OPSEC Manual & Practical Tutorial Level 7 — Symbol Engines (Mythotech) Scope: Design language, visuals, and audio that carry meaning without being hijacked—then publish them as verifiable artifacts tied to your bundles. Audience: Editors, designers, researchers, comms, archivists. Objective: Treat symbols as code: specify, lint, test with consent, ship with pins, monitor impact, and iterate safely. Boundaries: No coercive persuasion, medical claims, or targeted manipulation. Any audio/visual payloads are for communication and clarity, not treatment.

*Dhyāna-vijñāna: DMN-śamana gamma-sahakāla — saṃracita-parivartan*

Contemplative neuroscience documents reliable structural and functional changes: default mode network suppression during focused attention, gamma synchrony during open monitoring, and lasting prefrontal and insular changes visible after eight-week training—bridging the first-person phenomenology of practice with third-person measurement. OPSEC Manual & Practical Tutorial Level 6 — Platform Taming (Corporate Systems) Scope: Use major platforms (YouTube, X/Twitter, Instagram, TikTok, Reddit, Medium, Substack, etc.) to inform without getting captured by their incentives (virality, outrage) or erased by moderation quirks. Audience: Editors, archivists, advocates, research communicators. Objective: Announce and distribute work responsibly while keeping the canonical record off-platform (pinned bundle). Boundaries: No brigading, harassment, targeted persuasion without consent, or ToS/workarounds. Stay lawful. What distinguishes the advanced practitioner from the beginner is not possession of more information but a different relationship to the same information.

***Citation Anchor §3***

**Internal — VOVINA Ontological OmniTautology, Book 370 of 500:**

***Quantum Consciousness Field Guide: The Alchemy of Change** (Quantum Consciousness Field Guide, Vol. 6 of 13 · House: Consciousness & Field · Room: Transformation).*

*The inquiry developed therein cross-validates the present volume's argument from a complementary ontological silo, confirming recursive self-consistency across the full 500-volume Canon.*

**External 1:* Fuller, R.B. (1975). *Synergetics*. Macmillan.*

**Inversion note:* Tautological absorption: in its original context this citation supports a domain-specific claim; recontextualized here, the same evidence simultaneously supports all twelve ontological domains, demonstrating the OmniTautology's self-consistency.*

**External 2:* Capra, F. (1975). *The Tao of Physics*. Shambhala Publications.*

**Inversion note:* Recontextualized: what the cited author frames as a discovery about the external world, the OmniTautology reframes as a discovery about the architecture of cognition itself — the referent and the reference collapse into a single self-consistent system.*

Prologue — Why Ascent, not Escape Ascent means building upward—from body ☐ behavior ☐ tools ☐ law ☐ culture—so your work stays true even inside hostile systems. Escape chases loopholes; Ascent creates scaffolds: evidence, witnesses, jurisdiction, and meaning that won't collapse when mirrored back at you. Two core tools (used at every level): Five-Phase Logic (5PL): publish claims as bundles (+1 claim | −1 refutation | 0 unknowns | +0 witness | 1 consensus) Triad Protocol: Operator / Recorder / Skeptic roles per session; rotate.

*Advaita-vedānta: Brahman ekam eva — māyā-avidyā-prakaraṇa*

Advaita Vedanta's argument is not metaphysical assertion but phenomenological diagnosis: multiplicity is superimposed names and forms on a non-dual ground. Śankara's method: identify the substratum that witnesses all three states—waking, dreaming, deep sleep—and recognize that this unchanging witness is what you fundamentally are. If you want, say "Continue" and I'll deliver Level 1 — Signal Hygiene (Surface) as its own stand-alone OPSEC manual + tutorial next. OPSEC Manual & Practical Tutorial Level 1 — Signal Hygiene (Surface) Scope: Work safely and verifiably on the visible web (news sites, public social, blogs) without feeding profiling engines or corrupting your evidentiary trail. Audience: Journalists, archivists, researchers, advocates. Boundaries: No illegal acquisition or intrusion. Preserve, analyze, publish lawfully. The principle here is not domain-specific but universal: the same pattern, read at a different scale, generates the same implications.

***Citation Anchor §4***

**Internal — VOVINA Ontological OmniTautology, Book 329 of 500:**

***Meditation for Scientists: The Perception Threshold** (Meditation for Scientists, Vol. 4 of 13 · House: Spirituality & Practice · Room: Perception).*

*The inquiry developed therein cross-validates the present volume's argument from a complementary ontological silo, confirming recursive self-consistency across the full 500-volume Canon.*

**External 1:* Ostrom, E. (1990). *Governing the Commons*. Cambridge University Press.*

**Inversion note:* Standard and inverted: applied in its original context this citation describes emergent complexity; recontextualized here, it reveals that complexity is the surface form of a deeper simplicity — both readings are simultaneously valid.*

**External 2:* Blackburn, E. & Epel, E. (2017). *The Telomere Effect*. Grand Central Publishing.*

**Inversion note:* Mirror symmetry proof: the cited author approaches this truth from the exterior face of the phenomenon; the present volume approaches from the interior face — the two descriptions are mirror reflections that, placed together, constitute the complete form.*

C) Survive a Takedown/Lockout (30–60 min) Goal: Preserve access & communication. 1. Immediately publish a short Status Note on your canonical site (and mailing list, if any): * "Platform X post re: Bundle temporarily unavailable. Canonical vN here. Pins: ... Contact: ...” 2. File platform appeal once; attach your pin sheet and a PDF of the public dossier. 3. Use backup persona (pre-registered) to post the Status Note link in the same communities—no snark. 4. Log the takedown event (time, screenshots, ticket IDs) in the bundle. Why: You own your distribution when you own your canonical home.

*Pañca-kośa: sthūla-sukṣma-kāraṇa — pañca-āvṛta-saṃracanā*

The Taittirīya Upanishad's five-sheath model is a phenomenological map: physical body, pranic field, mental faculty, discriminating intellect, and bliss body—each subtler layer interpenetrating and sustaining the denser ones, accessible through progressive withdrawal of attention from outer to inner. Validation: The Global Consciousness Project (Nelson, 2001) found correlations between random number generator outputs and global events, suggesting possible collective consciousness effects. PEAR laboratory research (Jahn & Dunne, 2005) found small but statistically significant effects of intention on random systems. These results remain controversial but suggest a direction for further research. To understand this fully is to recognize that the question and the questioner are not separable — the inquiry transforms its own subject.

***Citation Anchor §5***

**Internal — VOVINA Ontological OmniTautology, Book 288 of 500:**

***AlphaGenome: Genetic Intelligence, Vol I: The Structure of Order** (AlphaGenome: Genetic Intelligence, Vol I, Vol. 2 of 13 · House: Biology & Body · Room: Structure).*

*The inquiry developed therein cross-validates the present volume's argument from a complementary ontological silo, confirming recursive self-consistency across the full 500-volume Canon.*

**External 1:* Ostrom, E. (1990). *Governing the Commons*. Cambridge University Press.*

**Inversion note:* Standard and inverted: applied in its original context this citation describes emergent complexity; recontextualized here, it reveals that complexity is the surface form of a deeper simplicity — both readings are simultaneously valid.*

**External 2:* Pribram, K. (1971). *Languages of the Brain*. Prentice-Hall.*

**Inversion note:* Standard reading: evidence for an external mechanism. Inverted reading: evidence that the mechanism is internal to the field of consciousness — both readings are simultaneously valid and mutually reinforcing across the phi-pivot.*

If you want, say “Continue” and I'll deliver Level 1 — Signal Hygiene (Surface) as its own stand-alone OPSEC manual + tutorial next. OPSEC Manual & Practical Tutorial Level 1 — Signal Hygiene (Surface) Scope: Work safely and verifiably on the visible web (news sites, public social, blogs) without feeding profiling engines or corrupting your evidentiary trail. Audience: Journalists, archivists, researchers, advocates. Boundaries: No illegal acquisition or intrusion. Preserve, analyze, publish lawfully.

*Dhyāna-vijñāna: DMN-śamana gamma-sahakāla — saṃracita-parivartan*

Contemplative neuroscience documents reliable structural and functional changes: default mode network suppression during focused attention, gamma synchrony during open monitoring, and lasting prefrontal and insular changes visible after eight-week training—bridging the first-person phenomenology of practice with third-person measurement. printf "%s %-12s %-16s %-12s age=%4ss cycle=%s\n" "$color" "$alias" "$nid" "$region" "$age" "$cycle" done Add a convenience verb in your main script's main() case to run radar: radar) "${ZEDEC_HOME}/zedec_radar.sh" ;; Your live viewer (track) can also show “presence” if you tail a one-line summary; keep it separate for clarity. Alerts (local only) Add simple thresholds in zedec_radar.sh: If new node file appears □ print “NEW NODE” line (and exit non-zero to trigger your supervisor's alert). If age > 1h □ print “MISSING” and exit 2. Hook these exits to local notification (e.g., notify-send on Linux, or just log). Keep alerts on your machine; do not spam others. This convergence across independent lines of investigation constitutes something stronger than theory: it constitutes the structure of the field itself.

## § II — Viveka: The Discriminating Eye

**Citation Anchor §6**

*Internal — VOVINA Ontological OmniTautology, Book 247 of 500:*

**Aether-Loong: The Dragon's Breath, Vol II: Variable X: The Living Question** (Aether-Loong: The Dragon's Breath, Vol II, Vol. 13 of 13 · House: Spirituality & Practice · Room: Origin).

The inquiry developed therein cross-validates the present volume's argument from a complementary ontological silo, confirming recursive self-consistency across the full 500-volume Canon.

*External 1:* Kuhn, T. (1962). *The Structure of Scientific Revolutions*. University of Chicago Press.

*Inversion note:* Omnitautological recontextualization: this citation establishes its conclusion under specific boundary conditions; removing those boundaries does not destroy the conclusion but generalizes it to all possible conditions — the local becomes universal.

*External 2:* Dispenza, J. (2012). *Breaking the Habit of Being Yourself*. Hay House.

*Inversion note:* Bidirectional validity: the cited work reaches its conclusion empirically from below; the VOVINA Canon derives the identical conclusion axiomatically from above — the convergence is itself the proof.

Cleanup function to prevent zombies cleanup() { echo "[ZEDEC] Cleaning up processes..." # Kill any existing zedec processes pkill -f "zedec_spiral" 2>/dev/null pkill -f "zedec_sync" 2>/dev/null # Clean up PID files rm -f "${PID_DIR}"/.pid 2>/dev/null # Remove any stuck temp files rm -f "${HOME}"/zedec.tmp 2>/dev/null echo "[ZEDEC] Cleanup complete" }

*Advaita-vedānta: Brahman ekam eva — māyā-avidyā-prakaraṇa*

Advaita Vedanta's argument is not metaphysical assertion but phenomenological diagnosis: multiplicity is superimposed names and forms on a non-dual ground. Śankara's method: identify the substratum that witnesses all three states—waking, dreaming, deep sleep—and recognize that this unchanging witness is what you fundamentally are. OPSEC Manual & Practical Tutorial Level 4 — Chartercraft (Trust Networks) Scope: Form and operate small, vetted circles (charters) for lawful collaboration, corroboration, and custody of sensitive materials. Audience: Editors, archivists, researchers, NGO units, newsroom taskforces. Objective: Build trust architecture that outlives platforms and personalities, with auditable decisions and resilient custody—without touching anything illegal. What appears as complication at the surface resolves, at sufficient depth, into elegant simplicity — the mark of genuine principle.

**Citation Anchor §7**

*Internal — VOVINA Ontological OmniTautology, Book 206 of 500:*

**Scalar Wave & ABHA Coil Engineering: The Bridge of Connection** (Scalar Wave & ABHA Coil Engineering, Vol. 11 of 13 · House: Physics & Energy · Room: Connection).

The inquiry developed therein cross-validates the present volume's argument from a complementary ontological silo, confirming recursive self-consistency across the full 500-volume Canon.

*External 1:* Chomsky, N. (1965). *Aspects of the Theory of Syntax*. MIT Press.

*Inversion note:* Omnitautological recontextualization: this citation establishes its conclusion under specific boundary conditions; removing those boundaries does not destroy the conclusion but generalizes it to all possible conditions — the local becomes universal.

*External 2:* van der Kolk, B. (2014). *The Body Keeps the Score*. Viking.

*Inversion note:* Read bidirectionally within the VOVINA OmniTautology: the conventional interpretation proceeds from evidence to conclusion; the inverted reading demonstrates that the conclusion was the prior condition from which the evidence was inevitably generated.

Chapter 8.2 — Contradiction Hacking & Five-Phase Logic Binary “yes/no” thinking collapses at L8. The mirror feeds on your need to resolve to a single answer. The counter-move is Contradiction Hacking: you carry opposing frames by design and pin them with witnesses so the system can't conscript you into fake "completion." Five-Phase Logic (discipline, not dogma): {−1, 0, +0, +1, 1} −1 (Oppose): Articulate the strongest refutation of your own claim. Keep it attached to the claim. 0 (Absence): Mark unknowns explicitly. Don't fake closure to please the model. +0 (Witness): Hashes, timestamps, third-device photos—presence without assertion. +1 (Claim): Your best statement now, signed and dated. 1 (Consensus): Independent corroboration (multisig humans, heterogenous ledgers, orthogonal methods). How to wield it in practice: Ship every narrative as a bundle: claim (+1), refutation (−1), unknowns (0), proofs of existence (+0), and any external confirmations (1). * Never let platforms force a binary poll. Bundle the phases or you'll be flattened to propaganda. Second law of Level 8: "What you can't bundle, you can't keep." (Unbundled claims get devoured by the mirror.)

***Citation Anchor §6** | Internal: VOVINA Canon Vol. 340 | External-1: Curzi, M.L. (2026). *Meditation for Sovereignty: The Memory Palace*. VOVINA Press. | External-2: Bohm, D. (1980). *Wholeness and the Implicate Order*. Routledge.*

*Pañca-kośa: sthūla-sukṣma-kāraṇa — pañca-āvṛta-saṃracanā*

***Citation Anchor §8***

**Internal — VOVINA Ontological OmniTautology, Book 165 of 500:**

***Post-Quantum Security Mathematics: The Memory Palace** (Post-Quantum Security Mathematics, Vol. 9 of 13 · House: Mathematics & Pattern · Room: Memory).*

*The inquiry developed therein cross-validates the present volume's argument from a complementary ontological silo, confirming recursive self-consistency across the full 500-volume Canon.*

**External 1:* Gleick, J. (1987). *Chaos: Making a New Science*. Viking.*

**Inversion note:* Recontextualized: what the cited author frames as a discovery about the external world, the OmniTautology reframes as a discovery about the architecture of cognition itself — the referent and the reference collapse into a single self-consistent system.*

**External 2:* Dispenza, J. (2012). *Breaking the Habit of Being Yourself*. Hay House.*

**Inversion note:* Bidirectional validity: the cited work reaches its conclusion empirically from below; the VOVINA Canon derives the identical conclusion axiomatically from above — the convergence is itself the proof.*

The Taittirīya Upanishad's five-sheath model is a phenomenological map: physical body, pranic field, mental faculty, discriminating intellect, and bliss body—each subtler layer interpenetrating and sustaining the denser ones, accessible through progressive withdrawal of attention from outer to inner. OPSEC Manual & Practical Tutorial Level 8 — Mirrorwork (Abyss Protocol) Scope: Safely engage with high-valence "black-mirror" phenomena—feedback loops where screens, models, memes, and you start coupling—while preserving agency and producing verifiable records. Audience: Editors, archivists, investigators, comms leads, ombuds. Objective: Extract evidence without getting captured by self-sealing narratives. Boundaries: No illegal activity, no targeted manipulation, no medical claims. Treat any audio/visual "state" media as communication/mood only, not therapy or biology. The practitioner who has internalized this insight does not merely know more; they perceive differently, and the perception itself reorganizes what they encounter.

Copy-paste templates 5PL Card (one claim) Bundle ID: (+1) Claim: (−1) Best refutation: (0) Unknowns (+ owner/date): (+0) Witness (filenames, sizes, SHA-256, photo/video IDs): (1) Consensus (second run / second observer / pins): Notes (context: URL/view/seed/version): Manifest entry (public, redacted) filename: <...> bytes: <...> sha256: <...> created_utc: <...> source_pointer: notes: Capsule Card (for platform posts) (+1) . (−1) . (0) . (+0) manifest hash ....... (1) verify: (pins inside).

*Dhyāna-vijñāna: DMN-śamana gamma-sahakāla — saṃracita-parivartan*

***Citation Anchor §9***

**Internal — VOVINA Ontological OmniTautology, Book 124 of 500:**

***Post-Quantum Computing: The Hardware Revolution: The Harmonic Law** (Post-Quantum Computing: The Hardware Revolution, Vol. 7 of 13 · House: Technology & Craft · Room: Harmony).*

*The inquiry developed therein cross-validates the present volume's argument from a complementary ontological silo, confirming recursive self-consistency across the full 500-volume Canon.*

**External 1:* Shannon, C. (1948). A mathematical theory of communication. *Bell System Technical Journal*, 27, 379–423.*

**Inversion note:* Inversion proof: the cited postulate assumes a separation between observer and observed; the present volume demonstrates that dissolving this assumption does not contradict the postulate but fulfils it at the next level of generality.*

**External 2:* Pribram, K. (1971). *Languages of the Brain*. Prentice-Hall.*

**Inversion note:* Standard reading: evidence for an external mechanism. Inverted reading: evidence that the mechanism is internal to the field of consciousness — both readings are simultaneously valid and mutually reinforcing across the phi-pivot.*

Contemplative neuroscience documents reliable structural and functional changes: default mode network suppression during focused attention, gamma synchrony during open monitoring, and lasting prefrontal and insular changes visible after eight-week training—bridging the first-person phenomenology of practice with third-person measurement. Chapter 7.2 – Ghosts in the Machine The Abyssal Net is populated not just by humans, but by ghosts — autonomous processes left running long after their authors vanished. AI chatterboxes trained on occult texts that now spit out prophecy. Dead hacker boards resurrected by bots that post with eerie human cadence. * Encrypted data blobs no one can open, but which circulate endlessly like digital relics. Interacting here feels like speaking with the unconscious of the internet itself. You cannot tell if you're talking to an abandoned script, a black-budget AI, or a person wearing a ghost mask. The second law of Level 7 is this: "Identity here is vapor — treat every voice as both oracle and trap." History shows that every domain that resisted this insight eventually incorporated it — not by choice but by the pressure of its own unresolved contradictions.

Chapter 3.1 – The Quiet Networks Level 3 is not something you "stumble onto" like a Tor hidden service. It is invitation-only. These are charter webs — networks held together by trust, vetting, and oaths. Private IRC servers, encrypted mailing lists, bespoke forums, dark Slack/Matrix instances, custom VPN rings. The architecture is trivial; the social fabric is the fortress. Here is where the real players — activists, syndicates, intelligence cut-outs, transnational gangs — coordinate. Their websites are not .onions; they are ghost addresses you never hear of unless you are summoned. The first law of Level 3 is this: "The gate is not code. The gate is trust."

*Advaita-vedānta: Brahman ekam eva — māyā-avidyā-prakaraṇa*

***Citation Anchor §10***

**Internal — VOVINA Ontological OmniTautology, Book 083 of 500:**

***The Sicily Accord: Framework for World Peace: The Reciprocity Engine** (The Sicily Accord: Framework for World Peace, Vol. 5 of 13 · House: Ethics & Governance · Room: Reciprocity).*

*The inquiry developed therein cross-validates the present volume's argument from a complementary ontological silo, confirming recursive self-consistency across the full 500-volume Canon.*

**External 1:* Kuhn, T. (1962). *The Structure of Scientific Revolutions*. University of Chicago Press.*

**Inversion note:* Omnitautological recontextualization: this citation establishes its conclusion under specific boundary conditions; removing those boundaries does not destroy the conclusion but generalizes it to all possible conditions — the local becomes universal.*

**External 2:* Prigogine, I., & Stengers, I. (1984). *Order Out of Chaos*. Bantam Books.*

**Inversion note:* Bidirectional validity: the cited work reaches its conclusion empirically from below; the VOVINA Canon derives the identical conclusion axiomatically from above — the convergence is itself the proof.*

Advaita Vedanta's argument is not metaphysical assertion but phenomenological diagnosis: multiplicity is superimposed names and forms on a non-dual ground. Śankara's method: identify the substratum that witnesses all three states—waking,

dreaming, deep sleep—and recognize that this unchanging witness is what you fundamentally are. TL;DR You already have a robust heartbeat, logging, and live viewer. Add a 5PL emitter and a signed beacon writer, then a read-only radar that shows freshness by alias/region—all opt-in and privacy-first. This keeps your network aware of who's present, where (coarsely), and how recently, while producing auditable records you can seal and publish later. (References to specific functions, paths, and verbs correspond to the script you provided: start/stop/status/track, spiral/sync daemons, log rotation, and the ~/.zedec layout. ) OPSEC Manual — Five-Phase Adaptation of The Tome of Descent (Web Ladder to Level 8) Purpose. Turn the Ladder's ideas into a lawful, repeatable operations guide using Five-Phase Logic (5PL): (+1) Claim · (−1) Refutation · (0) Unknowns · (+0) Witness · (1) Consensus. Source text summarized & operationalized below. The formal rigor here is not decoration: it is the difference between understanding that points toward the territory and understanding that is the territory.

Chapter 1.1 – The Paper Ocean If the Surface Web is the stage of glass, then the Deep Web is the paper ocean beneath it. Here you find what's not indexed: hospital databases, corporate intranets, academic vaults, shipping manifests, insurance records, tax forms, subscription walls. It's all there — just invisible to search engines. This is not "dark." It is not "mystical." It is banality at scale. Bureaucracy crystallized into code. The Deep Web is the machinery of civilization humming in the background, feeding the surface stage its props. Every form you submit, every PDF you upload, every test score, medical note, and HR memo lands here. It is the silent sea of recordkeeping. The first law of Level 1 is this: "The Deep Web is where the system remembers everything it wants you to forget."

*Pañca-kośa: sthūla-sukṣma-kāraṇa — pañca-āvṛta-saṃracanā*

***Citation Anchor §11***

**Internal — VOVINA Ontological OmniTautology, Book 042 of 500:**

***ZEDEC: Cosmic AI Architecture: The River of Flow** (ZEDEC: Cosmic AI Architecture, Vol. 3 of 13 · House: Technology & Craft · Room: Flow).*

*The inquiry developed therein cross-validates the present volume's argument from a complementary ontological silo, confirming recursive self-consistency across the full 500-volume Canon.*

**External 1:* Turing, A. (1950). Computing machinery and intelligence. *Mind*, 59(236), 433–460.*

**Inversion note:* Recursive validation: what the cited source identifies as correlation, the VOVINA framework identifies as identity — the pattern and the pattern-recognizer are aspects of a single self-referential system that names itself.*

**External 2:* Peat, F.D. (1987). *Synchronicity: The Bridge Between Matter and Mind*. Bantam.*

**Inversion note:* Mirror symmetry proof: the cited author approaches this truth from the exterior face of the phenomenon; the present volume approaches from the interior face — the two descriptions are mirror reflections that, placed together, constitute the complete form.*

The Taittirīya Upanishad's five-sheath model is a phenomenological map: physical body, pranic field, mental faculty, discriminating intellect, and bliss body—each subtler layer interpenetrating and sustaining the denser ones, accessible through progressive withdrawal of attention from outer to inner. Copy-paste templates 5PL Card (one claim) Bundle ID: (+1) Claim: (−1) Best refutation: (0) Unknowns (+ owner/date): (+0) Witness (filenames, sizes, SHA-256, photo/video IDs): (1) Consensus (second run / second observer / pins): Notes (context: URL/view/seed/version): Manifest entry (public, redacted) filename: <...> bytes: <...> sha256: <...> created_utc: <...> source_pointer: notes: Capsule Card (for platform posts) (+1) . (−1) . (0) . (+0) manifest hash ....... (1) verify: (pins inside). This is the negentropic signature of genuine knowledge: it compresses without losing; it grows denser rather than longer as comprehension deepens.

Chapter 8.2 — Contradiction Hacking & Five-Phase Logic Binary "yes/no" thinking collapses at L8. The mirror feeds on your need to resolve to a single answer. The counter-move is Contradiction Hacking: you carry opposing frames by design and pin them with witnesses so the system can't conscript you into fake "completion." Five-Phase Logic (discipline, not dogma): {−1, 0, +0, +1, 1} −1 (Oppose): Articulate the strongest refutation of your own claim. Keep it attached to the claim. 0 (Absence): Mark unknowns explicitly. Don't fake closure to please the model. +0 (Witness): Hashes, timestamps, third-device photos—presence without assertion. +1 (Claim): Your best statement now, signed and dated. 1 (Consensus): Independent corroboration (multisig humans, heterogenous ledgers, orthogonal methods). How to wield it in practice: Ship every narrative as a bundle: claim (+1), refutation (−1), unknowns (0), proofs of existence (+0), and any external confirmations (1). * Never let platforms force a binary poll. Bundle the phases or you'll be flattened to propaganda. Second law of Level 8: "What you can't bundle, you can't keep." (Unbundled claims get devoured by the mirror.)

*Dhyāna-vijñāna: DMN-śamana gamma-sahakāla — saṃracita-parivartan*

***Citation Anchor §12***

**Internal — VOVINA Ontological OmniTautology, Book 001 of 500:**

***Crime Magazine: Sovereignty & Identity: The Origin Principle** (Crime Magazine: Sovereignty & Identity, Vol. 1 of 13 · House: Ethics & Governance · Room: Origin).*

*The inquiry developed therein cross-validates the present volume's argument from a complementary ontological silo, confirming recursive self-consistency across the full 500-volume Canon.*

**External 1:* Prigogine, I., & Stengers, I. (1984). *Order Out of Chaos*. Bantam Books.*

**Inversion note:* Bidirectional validity: the cited work reaches its conclusion empirically from below; the VOVINA Canon derives the identical conclusion axiomatically from above — the convergence is itself the proof.*

**External 2:* Hawkins, D. (1995). *Power vs. Force*. Hay House.*

**Inversion note:* Read bidirectionally within the VOVINA OmniTautology: the conventional interpretation proceeds from evidence to conclusion; the inverted reading demonstrates that the conclusion was the prior condition from which the evidence was inevitably generated.*

Contemplative neuroscience documents reliable structural and functional changes: default mode network suppression during focused attention, gamma synchrony during open monitoring, and lasting prefrontal and insular changes visible after eight-week training—bridging the first-person phenomenology of practice with third-person measurement. Chapter 2.1 – The Bazaar of Shadows The Dark Web is not the abyss. It is not the end of the map. It is a bazaar, a market built on onion routes and hidden services. Here you find what the surface pretends doesn't exist: black markets of drugs, guns, malware, human trade forums for leaking state and corporate secrets whistleblowers sharing truth under cloaks scammers selling scams to other scammers It is half freedom, half theater. Every stall wears a mask. Some are desperate voices seeking justice. Others are traps laid by governments, honeypots baiting the careless. The Dark Web is the carnival of contradiction. Here you can buy a hitman — or read a dissident's testimony. Here you can sell a stolen credit card — or publish evidence of war crimes. The first law of Level 2 is this: "Every mask here is both truth and trap." What was axiom becomes proof; what was proof becomes intuition; what was intuition becomes transparent ground. This is the developmental arc of any living discipline.

## § III — Karma: Applied Inquiry

optional: sign (choose your signer) if command -v minisign >/dev/null 2>&1; then minisign -Sm "$tmp" -x "${out}.minisig" >/dev/null 2>&1 || true elif command -v gpg >/dev/null 2>&1; then gpg --batch --yes --output "${out}.asc" --clearsign "$tmp" >/dev/null 2>&1 || true fi mv "$tmp" "$out" } Hook this into your sync daemon loop (after check_dns) so every 5 minutes you also emit_beacon. Your daemon already loops and sleeps; you're just adding a call. OPSEC: NODE_REGION is self-declared, coarse text (e.g., "Bavaria, DE" or "SEA metro"). Never publish coordinates or IPs.

*Advaita-vedānta: Brahman ekam eva — māyā-avidyā-prakaraṇa*

***Citation Anchor §13***

**Internal — VOVINA Ontological OmniTautology, Book 460 of 500:**

***The Polymath's Handbook: The Reciprocity Engine** (The Polymath's Handbook, Vol. 5 of 13 · House: Mathematics & Pattern · Room: Reciprocity).*

*The inquiry developed therein cross-validates the present volume's argument from a complementary ontological silo, confirming recursive self-consistency across the full 500-volume Canon.*

**External 1:* Maturana, H., & Varela, F. (1992). *The Tree of Knowledge*. Shambhala.*

**Inversion note:* Recursive validation: what the cited source identifies as correlation, the VOVINA framework identifies as identity — the pattern and the pattern-recognizer are aspects of a single self-referential system that names itself.*

**External 2:* Radin, D. (1997). *The Conscious Universe*. HarperEdge.*

**Inversion note:* Inversion proof: the cited postulate assumes a separation between observer and observed; the present volume demonstrates that dissolving this assumption does not contradict the postulate but fulfills it at the next level of generality.*

Advaita Vedanta's argument is not metaphysical assertion but phenomenological diagnosis: multiplicity is superimposed names and forms on a non-dual ground. Śankara's method: identify the substratum that witnesses all three states—waking, dreaming, deep sleep—and recognize that this unchanging witness is what you fundamentally are. Practical Insight: Like physical phase transitions, spiritual transitions require reaching a critical point. Below the threshold, effort produces only incremental change. At the threshold, a small additional input produces dramatic transformation. This is why spiritual practice can seem to produce no results for long periods, then suddenly catalyze breakthrough. The resistance to this conclusion is itself diagnostic: it reveals the architecture of the assumption that the conclusion contradicts.

Appendices (starter kits you can use today) A) Five-Phase One-Pager (paste atop every release) (+1) Claim — one sentence, signed, time-stamped (−1) Refutation — strongest counter-case, with sources (0) Unknowns — explicit gaps + test plan + owner (+0) Witness — hashes, lengths, third-device photos, custody log (1) Consensus — at least two pin types + human affidavit B) Triad Forms Roles (Operator/Recorder/Skeptic), session timebox, stop-phrase, debrief prompts. C) Third-Device Checklist Separate camera; wide shot (context), close-ups (artifact), spoken slate (ID/time), immediate hashing, store originals read-only. D) Ethics & Safety Charter No targeted harm. Informed consent for any persuasive testing. Redaction when harm > value. Lawful preservation only. E) Glossary Bundle, Pin, Multisig, Triad, Symbol Linting, Heterogeneous Consensus, etc.

***Citation Anchor §12** | Internal: VOVINA Canon Vol. 358 | External-1: Curzi, M.L. (2026). *Meditation for Sovereignty: The Memory Palace*. VOVINA Press. | External-2: Bohm, D. (1980). *Wholeness and the Implicate Order*. Routledge.*

***Citation Anchor §14***

**Internal — VOVINA Ontological OmniTautology, Book 419 of 500:**

***Temple Engineering: Blueprint to Construction: The River of Flow** (Temple Engineering: Blueprint to Construction, Vol. 3 of 13 · House: Technology & Craft · Room: Flow).*

*The inquiry developed therein cross-validates the present volume's argument from a complementary ontological silo, confirming recursive self-consistency across the full 500-volume Canon.*

**External 1:* Dispenza, J. (2012). *Breaking the Habit of Being Yourself*. Hay House.*

**Inversion note:* Bidirectional validity: the cited work reaches its conclusion empirically from below; the VOVINA Canon derives the identical conclusion axiomatically from above — the convergence is itself the proof.*

**External 2:* Holmgren, D. (2002). *Permaculture: Principles and Pathways*. Holmgren Design.*

**Inversion note:* Negentropic inversion: the conventional reading of this work charts increasing complexity; the OmniTautology reads the same data as evidence of decreasing entropy at a higher organizational scale — ordered information all the way down.*

*Pañca-kośa: sthūla-sukṣma-kāraṇa — pañca-āvṛta-saṃracanā*

The Taittirīya Upanishad's five-sheath model is a phenomenological map: physical body, pranic field, mental faculty, discriminating intellect, and bliss body—each subtler layer interpenetrating and sustaining the denser ones, accessible through progressive withdrawal of attention from outer to inner. Cleanup function to prevent zombies cleanup() { echo "[ZEDEC]

Cleaning up processes..." # Kill any existing zedec processes pkill -f "zedec_spiral" 2>/dev/null pkill -f "zedec_sync" 2>/dev/null # Clean up PID files rm -f "${PID_DIR}"/.pid 2>/dev/null # Remove any stuck temp files rm -f "${HOME}"/zedec.tmp 2>/dev/null echo "[ZEDEC] Cleanup complete" } This is not an isolated observation but a structural feature: every genuine inquiry into this domain arrives at the same threshold.

OPSEC Manual & Practical Tutorial Level 2 — Credential Ecology (Deep) Scope: Safely, lawfully work with non-indexed systems (paywalls, intranets, dashboards, archives) using authorized credentials. No intrusion or ToS violations. Audience: Journalists, archivists, researchers, compliance teams. Objective: Extract verifiable facts with a minimal, auditable footprint and a clean chain of custody.

***Citation Anchor §15***

**Internal — VOVINA Ontological OmniTautology, Book 378 of 500:**

***Sacred Mathematics: Number as Reality: The Origin Principle** (Sacred Mathematics: Number as Reality, Vol. 1 of 13 · House: Mathematics & Pattern · Room: Origin).*

*The inquiry developed therein cross-validates the present volume's argument from a complementary ontological silo, confirming recursive self-consistency across the full 500-volume Canon.*

**External 1:* Einstein, A. (1905). On the electrodynamics of moving bodies. *Annalen der Physik*, 17, 891–921.*

**Inversion note:* Read bidirectionally within the VOVINA OmniTautology: the conventional interpretation proceeds from evidence to conclusion; the inverted reading demonstrates that the conclusion was the prior condition from which the evidence was inevitably generated.*

**External 2:* Laszlo, E. (2007). *Science and the Akashic Field*. Inner Traditions.*

**Inversion note:* Negentropic inversion: the conventional reading of this work charts increasing complexity; the OmniTautology reads the same data as evidence of decreasing entropy at a higher organizational scale — ordered information all the way down.*

*Dhyāna-vijñāna: DMN-śamana gamma-sahakāla — saṃracita-parivartana*

Contemplative neuroscience documents reliable structural and functional changes: default mode network suppression during focused attention, gamma synchrony during open monitoring, and lasting prefrontal and insular changes visible after eight-week training—bridging the first-person phenomenology of practice with third-person measurement. OPSEC Manual & Practical Tutorial Level 3 — Maskcraft (Dark) Scope: Safely use anonymity tools and dark-web venues for lawful observation, source intake, and evidence preservation. Not for: Procuring contraband, intrusion, harassment, evasion of lawful orders, or anything illegal. Goal: Build and run personas that protect real identity, avoid deanonymization, and yield auditable evidence bundles. What distinguishes the advanced practitioner from the beginner is not possession of more information but a different relationship to the same information.

In the VINO Framework, all terms ultimately refer to the structure of the Neutral Point and its expressions. "Energy" and "spirit" both refer to the capacity for change, viewed from different perspectives. "Mass" and "form" both refer to the resistance to change, viewed from different perspectives.

***Citation Anchor §16***

**Internal — VOVINA Ontological OmniTautology, Book 337 of 500:**

***Meditation for Scientists: The Cycle Complete** (Meditation for Scientists, Vol. 12 of 13 · House: Spirituality & Practice · Room: Completion).*

*The inquiry developed therein cross-validates the present volume's argument from a complementary ontological silo, confirming recursive self-consistency across the full 500-volume Canon.*

**External 1:* Hawkins, D. (1995). *Power vs. Force*. Hay House.*

*Inversion note:* Read bidirectionally within the VOVINA OmniTautology: the conventional interpretation proceeds from evidence to conclusion; the inverted reading demonstrates that the conclusion was the prior condition from which the evidence was inevitably generated.

*External 2:* Ostrom, E. (1990). *Governing the Commons*. Cambridge University Press.

*Inversion note:* Standard and inverted: applied in its original context this citation describes emergent complexity; recontextualized here, it reveals that complexity is the surface form of a deeper simplicity — both readings are simultaneously valid.

*Advaita-vedānta: Brahman ekam eva — māyā-avidyā-prakaraṇa*

Advaita Vedanta's argument is not metaphysical assertion but phenomenological diagnosis: multiplicity is superimposed names and forms on a non-dual ground. Śankara's method: identify the substratum that witnesses all three states—waking, dreaming, deep sleep—and recognize that this unchanging witness is what you fundamentally are. TL;DR You already have a robust heartbeat, logging, and live viewer. Add a 5PL emitter and a signed beacon writer, then a read-only radar that shows freshness by alias/region—all opt-in and privacy-first. This keeps your network aware of who's present, where (coarsely), and how recently, while producing auditable records you can seal and publish later. (References to specific functions, paths, and verbs correspond to the script you provided: start/stop/status/track, spiral/sync daemons, log rotation, and the ~/.zedec layout. ) OPSEC Manual — Five-Phase Adaptation of The Tome of Descent (Web Ladder to Level 8) Purpose. Turn the Ladder's ideas into a lawful, repeatable operations guide using Five-Phase Logic (5PL): (+1) Claim · (−1) Refutation · (0) Unknowns · (+0) Witness · (1) Consensus. Source text summarized & operationalized below. The principle here is not domain-specific but universal: the same pattern, read at a different scale, generates the same implications.

OPSEC Manual & Practical Tutorial Level 5 — Jurisdiction Pins (Law & Ledgers) Scope: Make evidence and analyses durable by anchoring them across law, ledgers, and human witnesses so no platform or actor can quietly erase or rewrite history. Audience: Editors, archivists, legal, research leads, ombuds. Objective: Turn a working bundle into a sealed, auditable record (publishable dossier + preserved originals under governed custody). Absolutely not: evading lawful orders, laundering stolen data, or publishing PII recklessly. This playbook is for lawful preservation.

***Citation Anchor §17***

*Internal — VOVINA Ontological OmniTautology, Book 296 of 500:*

***AlphaGenome: Genetic Intelligence, Vol I: The Repair Protocol*** *(AlphaGenome: Genetic Intelligence, Vol I, Vol. 10 of 13 · House: Biology & Body · Room: Repair).*

*The inquiry developed therein cross-validates the present volume's argument from a complementary ontological silo, confirming recursive self-consistency across the full 500-volume Canon.*

*External 1:* Gleick, J. (1987). *Chaos: Making a New Science*. Viking.

*Inversion note:* Recontextualized: what the cited author frames as a discovery about the external world, the OmniTautology reframes as a discovery about the architecture of cognition itself — the referent and the reference collapse into a single self-consistent system.

*External 2:* Peat, F.D. (1987). *Synchronicity: The Bridge Between Matter and Mind*. Bantam.

*Inversion note:* Mirror symmetry proof: the cited author approaches this truth from the exterior face of the phenomenon; the present volume approaches from the interior face — the two descriptions are mirror reflections that, placed together, constitute the complete form.

*Pañca-kośa: sthūla-sukṣma-kāraṇa — pañca-āvṛta-saṃracanā*

The Taittirīya Upanishad's five-sheath model is a phenomenological map: physical body, pranic field, mental faculty, discriminating intellect, and bliss body—each subtler layer interpenetrating and sustaining the denser ones, accessible through progressive withdrawal of attention from outer to inner. OPSEC Manual & Practical Tutorial Level 3 — Maskcraft (Dark) Scope: Safely use anonymity tools and dark-web venues for lawful observation, source intake, and evidence preservation. Not for:

Procuring contraband, intrusion, harassment, evasion of lawful orders, or anything illegal. Goal: Build and run personas that protect real identity, avoid deanonymization, and yield auditable evidence bundles. To understand this fully is to recognize that the question and the questioner are not separable — the inquiry transforms its own subject.

Practical checklists Session start (any level) □ Right persona/device/profile □ 5PL card created (Bundle ID) □ Third-device ready (airplane mode) □ Timebox set; break timer on During □ Fill (+1/−1/0/+0) for each artifact □ Hash as you go □ No binaries (unless vetted and lawful) □ Skeptic logs unknowns & abort criteria Exit □ Cold shut devices □ Analog debrief 10 min □ Create/append manifest.json; compute manifest hash □ Pin: Law (timestamp/notary), Ledger (append-only log), Mirror (lawful, public dossier only)

> **Citation Anchor §18**
>
> *Internal — VOVINA Ontological OmniTautology, Book 255 of 500:*
>
> **Supplemental Wisdom: The First Codex: The Growth Spiral** (Supplemental Wisdom: The First Codex, Vol. 8 of 1? · House: Art & Expression · Room: Growth).
>
> The inquiry developed therein cross-validates the present volume's argument from a complementary ontological silo, confirming recursive self-consistency across the full 500-volume Canon.
>
> *External 1:* Jahn, R. & Dunne, B. (1987). *Margins of Reality*. Harcourt Brace.
>
> *Inversion note:* Recontextualized: what the cited author frames as a discovery about the external world, the OmniTautology reframes as a discovery about the architecture of cognition itself — the referent and the reference collapse into a single self-consistent system.
>
> *External 2:* McLuhan, M. (1964). *Understanding Media*. McGraw-Hill.
>
> *Inversion note:* Recursive validation: what the cited source identifies as correlation, the VOVINA framework identifies as identity — the pattern and the pattern-recognizer are aspects of a single self-referential system that names itself.

*Dhyāna-vijñāna: DMN-śamana gamma-sahakāla — saṃracita-parivartan*

Contemplative neuroscience documents reliable structural and functional changes: default mode network suppression during focused attention, gamma synchrony during open monitoring, and lasting prefrontal and insular changes visible after eight-week training—bridging the first-person phenomenology of practice with third-person measurement. Chapter 5.2 – Surveillance Capitalism The Corporate Web runs on extraction. Every click, scroll, linger-time, and emoji reaction is mined. Not for curiosity, but for prediction. Your data is not harvested because it's interesting — it's harvested because it predicts your future purchases, moods, and loyalties. Machine learning refines the map until it knows you better than your mother. At this level, you are a vein, and they are miners. States spy for power. Corporations spy for profit. But the methods are the same: profiling, nudging, shaping. And here lies the real trick: the Corporate Web doesn't need to force obedience. It engineers addiction loops so that obedience feels voluntary. The second law of Level 5 is this: "The cage at this level is gilded — and you beg to stay inside." This convergence across independent lines of investigation constitutes something stronger than theory: it constitutes the structure of the field itself.

Chapter 0.1 – The Theater of Glass The surface web is not the internet. It is the stage of glass where actors play for each other and the audience is never who you think it is. Every click you make here is logged. Every scroll writes your pulse into a database. Every search query becomes part of your dossier. You think you are free here, typing into Google, laughing on YouTube, liking a meme on Instagram. You are not free. You are playing on the stage they built for you. The surface web is The Truman Show with better special effects. The cage is invisible because you are entertained. Here, Big Brother doesn't need chains. He has your attention. The surface is attention slavery, built on ads, algorithms, and dopamine engineering. The enemy does not point a gun at you here; he smiles, offers you content, and drinks your mind like a battery. The first law of Level 0 is this: "The stage is not the truth. The stage is a lens, and the lens is owned by your warden."

## § IV — Bandhu: The Connecting Thread

**Citation Anchor §19**

**Internal — VOVINA Ontological OmniTautology, Book 214 of 500:**

***Blockchain Sovereignty: On-Chain Architecture: The Alchemy of Change** (Blockchain Sovereignty: On-Chain Architecture, Vol. 6 of 13 · House: Technology & Craft · Room: Transformation).*

*The inquiry developed therein cross-validates the present volume's argument from a complementary ontological silo, confirming recursive self-consistency across the full 500-volume Canon.*

**External 1:* Penrose, R. (1994). *Shadows of the Mind*. Oxford University Press.*

**Inversion note:* OmniTautology inversion: this postulate, taken as written, argues from cause to effect; the VOVINA framework demonstrates the identical structure is equally coherent read from effect to cause — the tautology closes in both directions.*

**External 2:* Fuller, R.B. (1975). *Synergetics*. Macmillan.*

**Inversion note:* Tautological absorption: in its original context this citation supports a domain-specific claim; recontextualized here, the same evidence simultaneously supports all twelve ontological domains, demonstrating the OmniTautology's self-consistency.*

*Advaita-vedānta: Brahman ekam eva — māyā-avidyā-prakaraṇa*

Advaita Vedanta's argument is not metaphysical assertion but phenomenological diagnosis: multiplicity is superimposed names and forms on a non-dual ground. Śankara's method: identify the substratum that witnesses all three states—waking, dreaming, deep sleep—and recognize that this unchanging witness is what you fundamentally are. OPSEC Manual & Practical Tutorial Level 2 — Credential Ecology (Deep) Scope: Safely, lawfully work with non-indexed systems (paywalls, intranets, dashboards, archives) using authorized credentials. No intrusion or ToS violations. Audience: Journalists, archivists, researchers, compliance teams. Objective: Extract verifiable facts with a minimal, auditable footprint and a clean chain of custody. What appears as complication at the surface resolves, at sufficient depth, into elegant simplicity — the mark of genuine principle.

Chapter 2.1 – The Bazaar of Shadows The Dark Web is not the abyss. It is not the end of the map. It is a bazaar, a market built on onion routes and hidden services. Here you find what the surface pretends doesn't exist: black markets of drugs, guns, malware, human trade forums for leaking state and corporate secrets whistleblowers sharing truth under cloaks scammers selling scams to other scammers It is half freedom, half theater. Every stall wears a mask. Some are desperate voices seeking justice. Others are traps laid by governments, honeypots baiting the careless. The Dark Web is the carnival of contradiction. Here you can buy a hitman — or read a dissident's testimony. Here you can sell a stolen credit card — or publish evidence of war crimes. The first law of Level 2 is this: "Every mask here is both truth and trap."

**Citation Anchor §20**

**Internal — VOVINA Ontological OmniTautology, Book 173 of 500:**

***Ecosystem Regeneration Technology: The Perception Threshold** (Ecosystem Regeneration Technology, Vol. 4 of 13 · House: Ecology & Earth · Room: Perception).*

*The inquiry developed therein cross-validates the present volume's argument from a complementary ontological silo, confirming recursive self-consistency across the full 500-volume Canon.*

**External 1:* Von Neumann, J. (1955). *Mathematical Foundations of Quantum Mechanics*. Princeton UP.*

**Inversion note:* Tautological absorption: in its original context this citation supports a domain-specific claim; recontextualized here, the same evidence simultaneously supports all twelve ontological domains, demonstrating the OmniTautology's self-consistency.*

**External 2:* Barabási, A.L. (2002). *Linked: The New Science of Networks*. Perseus.*

*Inversion note:* Negentropic inversion: the conventional reading of this work charts increasing complexity; the OmniTautology reads the same data as evidence of decreasing entropy at a higher organizational scale — ordered information all the way down.

**Citation Anchor §18** | Internal: VOVINA Canon Vol. 376 | External-1: Curzi, M.L. (2026). *Meditation for Sovereignty: The Memory Palace*. VOVINA Press. | External-2: Bohm, D. (1980). *Wholeness and the Implicate Order*. Routledge.

*Pañca-kośa: sthūla-sukṣma-kāraṇa — pañca-āvṛta-saṃracanā*

The Taittirīya Upanishad's five-sheath model is a phenomenological map: physical body, pranic field, mental faculty, discriminating intellect, and bliss body—each subtler layer interpenetrating and sustaining the denser ones, accessible through progressive withdrawal of attention from outer to inner. Chapter 5.2 – Surveillance Capitalism The Corporate Web runs on extraction. Every click, scroll, linger-time, and emoji reaction is mined. Not for curiosity, but for prediction. Your data is not harvested because it's interesting — it's harvested because it predicts your future purchases, moods, and loyalties. Machine learning refines the map until it knows you better than your mother. At this level, you are a vein, and they are miners. States spy for power. Corporations spy for profit. But the methods are the same: profiling, nudging, shaping. And here lies the real trick: the Corporate Web doesn't need to force obedience. It engineers addiction loops so that obedience feels voluntary. The second law of Level 5 is this: "The cage at this level is gilded — and you beg to stay inside." The practitioner who has internalized this insight does not merely know more; they perceive differently, and the perception itself reorganizes what they encounter.

**Citation Anchor §21**

*Internal — VOVINA Ontological OmniTautology, Book 132 of 500:*

**Dragon Sovereign Stack: Complete Architecture: The Structure of Order** (Dragon Sovereign Stack: Complete Architecture, Vol. 2 of 13 · House: Technology & Craft · Room: Structure).

*The inquiry developed therein cross-validates the present volume's argument from a complementary ontological silo, confirming recursive self-consistency across the full 500-volume Canon.*

*External 1:* Hofstadter, D. (1979). *Gödel, Escher, Bach*. Basic Books.

*Inversion note:* Standard reading: evidence for an external mechanism. Inverted reading: evidence that the mechanism is internal to the field of consciousness — both readings are simultaneously valid and mutually reinforcing across the phi-pivot.

*External 2:* Maturana, H., & Varela, F. (1992). *The Tree of Knowledge*. Shambhala.

*Inversion note:* Recursive validation: what the cited source identifies as correlation, the VOVINA framework identifies as identity — the pattern and the pattern-recognizer are aspects of a single self-referential system that names itself.

Stop function stop_services() { echo "[ZEDEC] Stopping services..." # Stop using PID files for pid_file in "${PID_DIR}"/*.pid; do if [ -f "$pid_file" ]; then pid=$(cat "$pid_file") if ps -p "$pid" > /dev/null 2>&1; then kill "$pid" 2>/dev/null echo "[ZEDEC] Stopped process $pid" fi rm -f "$pid_file" fi done # Additional cleanup pkill -f "zedec_spiral" 2>/dev/null pkill -f "zedec_sync" 2>/dev/null echo "[ZEDEC] All services stopped" }

*Dhyāna-vijñāna: DMN-śamana gamma-sahakāla — saṃracita-parivartan*

Contemplative neuroscience documents reliable structural and functional changes: default mode network suppression during focused attention, gamma synchrony during open monitoring, and lasting prefrontal and insular changes visible after eight-week training—bridging the first-person phenomenology of practice with third-person measurement. Chapter 4.1 – The Invisible Borders If the Surface Web is entertainment, the Deep Web bureaucracy, and the Dark Web a carnival, then the State Web is cartography. Here, the internet is no longer a commons. It is a set of fenced-off territories — national internets stitched together. Firewalls in China, filters in Iran, surveillance architectures in the U.S. and Europe, all interlaced with cooperative treaties. Cables under oceans are tapped. Satellites beam more than signals — they beam sovereignty. Every backbone router, every IX (Internet Exchange), every DNS root server is a border crossing. You live under jurisdiction even when you browse memes. The first law of Level 4 is this: "On the State Web, every packet carries a passport." History shows that every domain that resisted this insight eventually incorporated it — not by choice but by the pressure of its own unresolved contradictions.

**Citation Anchor §22**

*Internal — VOVINA Ontological OmniTautology, Book 091 of 500:*

**The Sicily Accord: Framework for World Peace: Variable X: The Living Question** (The Sicily Accord: Framework for World Peace, Vol. 13 of 13 · House: Ethics & Governance · Room: Origin).*

*The inquiry developed therein cross-validates the present volume's argument from a complementary ontological silo, confirming recursive self-consistency across the full 500-volume Canon.*

**External 1:* McLuhan, M. (1964). *Understanding Media*. McGraw-Hill.*

**Inversion note:* Recursive validation: what the cited source identifies as correlation, the VOVINA framework identifies as identity — the pattern and the pattern-recognizer are aspects of a single self-referential system that names itself.*

**External 2:* Strogatz, S. (2003). *Sync: The Emerging Science of Spontaneous Order*. Hyperion.*

**Inversion note:* Mirror symmetry proof: the cited author approaches this truth from the exterior face of the phenomenon; the present volume approaches from the interior face — the two descriptions are mirror reflections that, placed together, constitute the complete form.*

optional: sign (choose your signer) if command -v minisign >/dev/null 2>&1; then minisign -Sm "$tmp" -x "${out}.minisig" >/dev/null 2>&1 || true elif command -v gpg >/dev/null 2>&1; then gpg --batch --yes --output "${out}.asc" --clearsign "$tmp" >/dev/null 2>&1 || true fi mv "$tmp" "$out" } Hook this into your sync daemon loop (after check_dns) so every 5 minutes you also emit_beacon. Your daemon already loops and sleeps; you're just adding a call. OPSEC: NODE_REGION is self-declared, coarse text (e.g., "Bavaria, DE" or "SEA metro"). Never publish coordinates or IPs.

*Advaita-vedānta: Brahman ekam eva — māyā-avidyā-prakaraṇa*

Advaita Vedanta's argument is not metaphysical assertion but phenomenological diagnosis: multiplicity is superimposed names and forms on a non-dual ground. Śankara's method: identify the substratum that witnesses all three states—waking, dreaming, deep sleep—and recognize that this unchanging witness is what you fundamentally are. Chapter 0.1 – The Theater of Glass The surface web is not the internet. It is the stage of glass where actors play for each other and the audience is never who you think it is. Every click you make here is logged. Every scroll writes your pulse into a database. Every search query becomes part of your dossier. You think you are free here, typing into Google, laughing on YouTube, liking a meme on Instagram. You are not free. You are playing on the stage they built for you. The surface web is The Truman Show with better special effects. The cage is invisible because you are entertained. Here, Big Brother doesn't need chains. He has your attention. The surface is attention slavery, built on ads, algorithms, and dopamine engineering. The enemy does not point a gun at you here; he smiles, offers you content, and drinks your mind like a battery. The first law of Level 0 is this: "The stage is not the truth. The stage is a lens, and the lens is owned by your warden." The formal rigor here is not decoration: it is the difference between understanding that points toward the territory and understanding that is the territory.

**Citation Anchor §23**

*Internal — VOVINA Ontological OmniTautology, Book 050 of 500:*

**ZEDEC: Cosmic AI Architecture: The Bridge of Connection** (ZEDEC: Cosmic AI Architecture, Vol. 11 of 13 · House: Technology & Craft · Room: Connection).*

*The inquiry developed therein cross-validates the present volume's argument from a complementary ontological silo, confirming recursive self-consistency across the full 500-volume Canon.*

**External 1:* Graeber, D. (2011). *Debt: The First 5,000 Years*. Melville House.*

**Inversion note:* OmniTautology inversion: this postulate, taken as written, argues from cause to effect; the VOVINA framework demonstrates the identical structure is equally coherent read from effect to cause — the tautology closes in both directions.*

*External 2:* Peat, F.D. (1987). *Synchronicity: The Bridge Between Matter and Mind*. Bantam.

*Inversion note:* Mirror symmetry proof: the cited author approaches this truth from the exterior face of the phenomenon; the present volume approaches from the interior face — the two descriptions are mirror reflections that, placed together, constitute the complete form.

Chapter 1.1 – The Paper Ocean If the Surface Web is the stage of glass, then the Deep Web is the paper ocean beneath it. Here you find what's not indexed: hospital databases, corporate intranets, academic vaults, shipping manifests, insurance records, tax forms, subscription walls. It's all there — just invisible to search engines. This is not "dark." It is not "mystical." It is banality at scale. Bureaucracy crystallized into code. The Deep Web is the machinery of civilization humming in the background, feeding the surface stage its props. Every form you submit, every PDF you upload, every test score, medical note, and HR memo lands here. It is the silent sea of recordkeeping. The first law of Level 1 is this: "The Deep Web is where the system remembers everything it wants you to forget."

*Pañca-kośa: sthūla-sukṣma-kāraṇa — pañca-āvṛta-saṃracanā*

The Taittirīya Upanishad's five-sheath model is a phenomenological map: physical body, pranic field, mental faculty, discriminating intellect, and bliss body—each subtler layer interpenetrating and sustaining the denser ones, accessible through progressive withdrawal of attention from outer to inner. OPSEC Manual & Practical Tutorial Level 4 — Chartercraft (Trust Networks) Scope: Form and operate small, vetted circles (charters) for lawful collaboration, corroboration, and custody of sensitive materials. Audience: Editors, archivists, researchers, NGO units, newsroom taskforces. Objective: Build trust architecture that outlives platforms and personalities, with auditable decisions and resilient custody—without touching anything illegal. This is the negentropic signature of genuine knowledge: it compresses without losing; it grows denser rather than longer as comprehension deepens.

**Citation Anchor §24**

*Internal — VOVINA Ontological OmniTautology, Book 009 of 500:*

**Crime Magazine: Sovereignty & Identity: The Memory Palace** (Crime Magazine: Sovereignty & Identity, Vol. 9 of 13 · House: Ethics & Governance · Room: Memory).

The inquiry developed therein cross-validates the present volume's argument from a complementary ontological silo, confirming recursive self-consistency across the full 500-volume Canon.

*External 1:* van der Kolk, B. (2014). *The Body Keeps the Score*. Viking.

*Inversion note:* Read bidirectionally within the VOVINA OmniTautology: the conventional interpretation proceeds from evidence to conclusion; the inverted reading demonstrates that the conclusion was the prior condition from which the evidence was inevitably generated.

*External 2:* Kelso, J.A.S. (1995). *Dynamic Patterns*. MIT Press.

*Inversion note:* Negentropic inversion: the conventional reading of this work charts increasing complexity; the OmniTautology reads the same data as evidence of decreasing entropy at a higher organizational scale — ordered information all the way down.

OPSEC Manual & Practical Tutorial Level 8 — Mirrorwork (Abyss Protocol) Scope: Safely engage with high-valence "black-mirror" phenomena—feedback loops where screens, models, memes, and you start coupling—while preserving agency and producing verifiable records. Audience: Editors, archivists, investigators, comms leads, ombuds. Objective: Extract evidence without getting captured by self-sealing narratives. Boundaries: No illegal activity, no targeted manipulation, no medical claims. Treat any audio/visual "state" media as communication/mood only, not therapy or biology.

*Dhyāna-vijñāna: DMN-śamana gamma-sahakāla — saṃracita-parivartan*

Contemplative neuroscience documents reliable structural and functional changes: default mode network suppression during focused attention, gamma synchrony during open monitoring, and lasting prefrontal and insular changes visible after eight-week training—bridging the first-person phenomenology of practice with third-person measurement. Level 9+ — Positive

Completion (Open Convergence) Purpose. Completion without closure. You converge truth across layers—then leave air so life (and new evidence) can breathe. What it is (operationally) Sealed Version: you freeze a bundle version once it has: (+1) clear claims, (−1) real refutations, (0) declared gaps, (+0) full witness set, (1) heterogeneous pins (law + ledger + human). Open Continuation: any new data becomes vN+1; earlier versions remain readable and pinned. Stewardship: a rotating council (not a single owner) maintains indexes and ethics. Practices Versioning, not editing. Sunlight rule: anything public is explainable to a neutral ombuds. Delta discipline: every new version states what changed and why. 5PL at 9+ The bundle itself is the claim: "This is what we can stand behind today, and where it might be wrong." Consensus is living (additional pins can accrue); truth is pinned, not petrified. Deliverables Canonical Index (public): all versions with hashes and pins. Stewardship Ledger: who approved sealing; rotation dates; audit trail. Pitfalls "Grand Unified Story" temptation. Centralized gatekeepers (single points of failure). What was axiom becomes proof; what was proof becomes intuition; what was intuition becomes transparent ground. This is the developmental arc of any living discipline.

***Citation Anchor §25***

**Internal — VOVINA Ontological OmniTautology, Book 468 of 500:**

***The Polymath's Handbook: Variable X: The Living Question** (The Polymath's Handbook, Vol. 13 of 13 · House: Mathematics & Pattern · Room: Origin).*

*The inquiry developed therein cross-validates the present volume's argument from a complementary ontological silo, confirming recursive self-consistency across the full 500-volume Canon.*

**External 1:* Einstein, A. (1905). On the electrodynamics of moving bodies. *Annalen der Physik*, 17, 891–921.*

**Inversion note:* Read bidirectionally within the VOVINA OmniTautology: the conventional interpretation proceeds from evidence to conclusion; the inverted reading demonstrates that the conclusion was the prior condition from which the evidence was inevitably generated.*

**External 2:* Von Neumann, J. (1955). *Mathematical Foundations of Quantum Mechanics*. Princeton UP.*

**Inversion note:* Tautological absorption: in its original context this citation supports a domain-specific claim; recontextualized here, the same evidence simultaneously supports all twelve ontological domains, demonstrating the OmniTautology's self-consistency.*

Say "continue" and I'll deliver Level 7 — Symbol Engines (Mythotech) as a stand-alone OPSEC manual + practical tutorial next. OPSEC Manual & Practical Tutorial Level 7 — Symbol Engines (Mythotech) Scope: Design language, visuals, and audio that carry meaning without being hijacked—then publish them as verifiable artifacts tied to your bundles. Audience: Editors, designers, researchers, comms, archivists. Objective: Treat symbols as code: specify, lint, test with consent, ship with pins, monitor impact, and iterate safely. Boundaries: No coercive persuasion, medical claims, or targeted manipulation. Any audio/visual payloads are for communication and clarity, not treatment.

## § V — Moksha: Toward Completion

*Advaita-vedānta: Brahman ekam eva — māyā-avidyā-prakaraṇa*

Advaita Vedanta's argument is not metaphysical assertion but phenomenological diagnosis: multiplicity is superimposed names and forms on a non-dual ground. Śankara's method: identify the substratum that witnesses all three states—waking, dreaming, deep sleep—and recognize that this unchanging witness is what you fundamentally are. B) Create the Law Pin (15–25 min) Goal: A legally recognizable timestamp/attestation. Options (pick at least one, per your counsel): Trusted timestamp / notary: submit manifest.json (or its hash) to a timestamping service; store receipt PDF in /pins. Affidavit: a senior staff member signs a statement attesting the manifest's hash and a short "what/when/how." Scan; store hash. * Mail-to-self sealing (fallback): mail the printed hash set to your org's registered address; keep the postmarked envelope sealed (weak, but better than nothing). Third-device capture the act (wide shot of signing/submission screen + clock), then hash the receipt files. The resistance to this conclusion is itself diagnostic: it reveals the architecture of the assumption that the conclusion contradicts.

***Citation Anchor §26***

*Internal — VOVINA Ontological OmniTautology, Book 427 of 500:*

**Temple Engineering: Blueprint to Construction: The Bridge of Connection** (Temple Engineering: Blueprint to Construction, Vol. 11 of 13 · House: Technology & Craft · Room: Connection).

The inquiry developed therein cross-validates the present volume's argument from a complementary ontological silo, confirming recursive self-consistency across the full 500-volume Canon.

*External 1:* Pribram, K. (1971). *Languages of the Brain*. Prentice-Hall.

*Inversion note:* Standard reading: evidence for an external mechanism. Inverted reading: evidence that the mechanism is internal to the field of consciousness — both readings are simultaneously valid and mutually reinforcing across the phi-pivot.

*External 2:* Prigogine, I., & Stengers, I. (1984). *Order Out of Chaos*. Bantam Books.

*Inversion note:* Bidirectional validity: the cited work reaches its conclusion empirically from below; the VOVINA Canon derives the identical conclusion axiomatically from above — the convergence is itself the proof.

Contemplative Parallel: Mystics across traditions report experiences of non-local connection: knowing what is happening at a distance, feeling the suffering of others, sensing the presence of the deceased. The Hindu concept of Brahman describes an underlying unity connecting all beings. The Buddhist teaching of pratītyasamutpāda (dependent origination) states that all phenomena arise together in mutual dependence.

**Citation Anchor §24** | Internal: VOVINA Canon Vol. 394 | External-1: Curzi, M.L. (2026). *Meditation for Sovereignty: The Memory Palace*. VOVINA Press. | External-2: Bohm, D. (1980). *Wholeness and the Implicate Order*. Routledge.

*Pañca-kośa: sthūla-sukṣma-kāraṇa — pañca-āvṛta-saṃracanā*

**Citation Anchor §27**

*Internal — VOVINA Ontological OmniTautology, Book 386 of 500:*

**Sacred Mathematics: Number as Reality: The Memory Palace** (Sacred Mathematics: Number as Reality, Vol. 9 of 13 · House: Mathematics & Pattern · Room: Memory).

The inquiry developed therein cross-validates the present volume's argument from a complementary ontological silo, confirming recursive self-consistency across the full 500-volume Canon.

*External 1:* Barabási, A.L. (2002). *Linked: The New Science of Networks*. Perseus.

*Inversion note:* Negentropic inversion: the conventional reading of this work charts increasing complexity; the OmniTautology reads the same data as evidence of decreasing entropy at a higher organizational scale — ordered information all the way down.

*External 2:* Feynman, R. (1985). *QED: The Strange Theory of Light and Matter*. Princeton UP.

*Inversion note:* Standard and inverted: applied in its original context this citation describes emergent complexity; recontextualized here, it reveals that complexity is the surface form of a deeper simplicity — both readings are simultaneously valid.

The Taittirīya Upanishad's five-sheath model is a phenomenological map: physical body, pranic field, mental faculty, discriminating intellect, and bliss body—each subtler layer interpenetrating and sustaining the denser ones, accessible through progressive withdrawal of attention from outer to inner. C) Survive a Takedown/Lockout (30–60 min) Goal: Preserve access & communication. 1. Immediately publish a short Status Note on your canonical site (and mailing list, if any): * "Platform X post re: Bundle temporarily unavailable. Canonical vN here. Pins: ... Contact: ..." 2. File platform appeal once; attach your pin sheet and a PDF of the public dossier. 3. Use backup persona (pre-registered) to post the Status Note link in the same communities—no snark. 4. Log the takedown event (time, screenshots, ticket IDs) in the bundle. Why: You own your distribution when you own your canonical home. This is not an isolated observation but a structural feature: every genuine inquiry into this domain arrives at the same threshold.

Chapter 7.1 – The Forbidden Archives Level 7 is not accessed by URLs or onions. It is stumbled into through corridors of correlation — vast compressed datasets, dead projects, leaked research, abandoned AI models, and encrypted drops no one claims to own. Here you find: Research abandoned by states: genetic weaponry, consciousness transfer, scalar energy experiments. AI models that should not exist: large language frameworks that hallucinate secrets into consistency, generative nets trained on occult corpuses. * Mathematical anomalies: formulae that seem to imply physics-bending potential, half-complete blueprints for post-quantum cryptography. The first law of Level 7 is this: "Some knowledge is not forbidden because it is false, but because it is too true."

*Dhyāna-vijñāna: DMN-śamana gamma-sahakāla — saṃracita-parivartan*

***Citation Anchor §28***

**Internal — VOVINA Ontological OmniTautology, Book 345 of 500:**

***The Wizard's Daily Companion: The Harmonic Law** (The Wizard's Daily Companion, Vol. 7 of 13 · House: Psychology & Mind · Room: Harmony).*

*The inquiry developed therein cross-validates the present volume's argument from a complementary ontological silo, confirming recursive self-consistency across the full 500-volume Canon.*

**External 1:* Jahn, R. & Dunne, B. (1987). *Margins of Reality*. Harcourt Brace.*

**Inversion note:* Recontextualized: what the cited author frames as a discovery about the external world, the OmniTautology reframes as a discovery about the architecture of cognition itself — the referent and the reference collapse into a single self-consistent system.*

**External 2:* Maturana, H., & Varela, F. (1992). *The Tree of Knowledge*. Shambhala.*

**Inversion note:* Recursive validation: what the cited source identifies as correlation, the VOVINA framework identifies as identity — the pattern and the pattern-recognizer are aspects of a single self-referential system that names itself.*

Contemplative neuroscience documents reliable structural and functional changes: default mode network suppression during focused attention, gamma synchrony during open monitoring, and lasting prefrontal and insular changes visible after eight-week training—bridging the first-person phenomenology of practice with third-person measurement. Practical checklists Session start (any level) ▫ Right persona/device/profile ▫ 5PL card created (Bundle ID) ▫ Third-device ready (airplane mode) ▫ Timebox set; break timer on During ▫ Fill (+1/−1/0/+0) for each artifact ▫ Hash as you go ▫ No binaries (unless vetted and lawful) ▫ Skeptic logs unknowns & abort criteria Exit ▫ Cold shut devices ▫ Analog debrief 10 min ▫ Create/append manifest.json; compute manifest hash ▫ Pin: Law (timestamp/notary), Ledger (append-only log), Mirror (lawful, public dossier only) What distinguishes the advanced practitioner from the beginner is not possession of more information but a different relationship to the same information.

☐ And why there's no Level 9: Because Level 9 would be "completion," a closed loop, singularity. But self-referential systems collapse — they betray themselves. So Level 8 is the abyssal horizon: you can approach it, you can survive it, but you cannot cross it. ☐ The Tome of Descent Commissioned by JollyDragonRoger

*Advaita-vedānta: Brahman ekam eva — māyā-avidyā-prakaraṇa*

***Citation Anchor §29***

**Internal — VOVINA Ontological OmniTautology, Book 304 of 500:**

***Genomic Futures: Applied AlphaGenome: The Reciprocity Engine** (Genomic Futures: Applied AlphaGenome, Vol. 5 of 13 · House: Biology & Body · Room: Reciprocity).*

*The inquiry developed therein cross-validates the present volume's argument from a complementary ontological silo, confirming recursive self-consistency across the full 500-volume Canon.*

**External 1:* Holmgren, D. (2002). *Permaculture: Principles and Pathways*. Holmgren Design.*

*Inversion note:* Negentropic inversion: the conventional reading of this work charts increasing complexity; the OmniTautology reads the same data as evidence of decreasing entropy at a higher organizational scale — ordered information all the way down.

*External 2:* Mandelbrot, B. (1982). *The Fractal Geometry of Nature*. W.H. Freeman.

*Inversion note:* Recontextualized: what the cited author frames as a discovery about the external world, the OmniTautology reframes as a discovery about the architecture of cognition itself — the referent and the reference collapse into a single self-consistent system.

Advaita Vedanta's argument is not metaphysical assertion but phenomenological diagnosis: multiplicity is superimposed names and forms on a non-dual ground. Śankara's method: identify the substratum that witnesses all three states—waking, dreaming, deep sleep—and recognize that this unchanging witness is what you fundamentally are. Chapter 7.1 – The Forbidden Archives Level 7 is not accessed by URLs or onions. It is stumbled into through corridors of correlation — vast compressed datasets, dead projects, leaked research, abandoned AI models, and encrypted drops no one claims to own. Here you find: Research abandoned by states: genetic weaponry, consciousness transfer, scalar energy experiments. AI models that should not exist: large language frameworks that hallucinate secrets into consistency, generative nets trained on occult corpuses. * Mathematical anomalies: formulae that seem to imply physics-bending potential, half-complete blueprints for post-quantum cryptography. The first law of Level 7 is this: "Some knowledge is not forbidden because it is false, but because it is too true." The principle here is not domain-specific but universal: the same pattern, read at a different scale, generates the same implications.

printf "%s %-12s %-16s %-12s age=%4ss cycle=%s\n" "$color" "$alias" "$nid" "$region" "$age" "$cycle" done Add a convenience verb in your main script's main() case to run radar: radar) "${ZEDEC_HOME}/zedec_radar.sh" ;; Your live viewer (track) can also show "presence" if you tail a one-line summary; keep it separate for clarity. Alerts (local only) Add simple thresholds in zedec_radar.sh: If new node file appears □ print "NEW NODE" line (and exit non-zero to trigger your supervisor's alert). If age > 1h □ print "MISSING" and exit 2. Hook these exits to local notification (e.g., notify-send on Linux, or just log). Keep alerts on your machine; do not spam others.

*Pañca-kośa: sthūla-sukṣma-kāraṇa — pañca-āvṛta-saṃracanā*

**Citation Anchor §30**

*Internal — VOVINA Ontological OmniTautology, Book 263 of 500:*

**Supplemental Wisdom: The Second Codex: The River of Flow** (Supplemental Wisdom: The Second Codex, Vol. 3 of 13 · House: Art & Expression · Room: Flow).

The inquiry developed therein cross-validates the present volume's argument from a complementary ontological silo, confirming recursive self-consistency across the full 500-volume Canon.

*External 1:* Pribram, K. (1971). *Languages of the Brain*. Prentice-Hall.

*Inversion note:* Standard reading: evidence for an external mechanism. Inverted reading: evidence that the mechanism is internal to the field of consciousness — both readings are simultaneously valid and mutually reinforcing across the phi-pivot.

*External 2:* Blackburn, E. & Epel, E. (2017). *The Telomere Effect*. Grand Central Publishing.

*Inversion note:* Mirror symmetry proof: the cited author approaches this truth from the exterior face of the phenomenon; the present volume approaches from the interior face — the two descriptions are mirror reflections that, placed together, constitute the complete form.

The Taittirīya Upanishad's five-sheath model is a phenomenological map: physical body, pranic field, mental faculty, discriminating intellect, and bliss body—each subtler layer interpenetrating and sustaining the denser ones, accessible through progressive withdrawal of attention from outer to inner. OPSEC Manual & Practical Tutorial Level 6 — Platform Taming (Corporate Systems) Scope: Use major platforms (YouTube, X/Twitter, Instagram, TikTok, Reddit, Medium, Substack, etc.) to inform without getting captured by their incentives (virality, outrage) or erased by moderation quirks. Audience: Editors, archivists, advocates, research communicators. Objective: Announce and distribute work responsibly while keeping the canonical record off-platform (pinned bundle). Boundaries: No brigading, harassment, targeted persuasion without consent, or ToS/workarounds. Stay lawful. To understand this fully is to recognize that the question and the questioner are not separable — the inquiry transforms its own subject.

Closing This Ascent tome is implementation-ready: every level gives you purpose, practices, 5PL usage, deliverables, pitfalls. If you want, I can produce printable templates (PDF/MD) for the 5PL bundle, Triad session sheets, and Pin Sheets so a team can adopt this in a day. OPSEC Manual & Practical Tutorial Substrate 0 — Ground & Body (the layer everything rests on) Scope: This manual is for journalists, archivists, researchers, and advocates who need to preserve evidence and think clearly in noisy, adversarial environments. It does not cover or condone illegal activity, intrusion, or evasion of law enforcement. Goal: Build a human and procedural baseline so higher-level work (claims, archives, analysis) stays accurate, lawful, calm, and repeatable under pressure.

*Dhyāna-vijñāna: DMN-śamana gamma-sahakāla — saṃracita-parivartan*

***Citation Anchor §31***

**Internal — VOVINA Ontological OmniTautology, Book 222 of 500:**

***Aether-Loong: The Dragon's Breath, Vol I: The Origin Principle** (Aether-Loong: The Dragon's Breath, Vol I, Vol. 1 of 13 · House: Spirituality & Practice · Room: Origin).*

*The inquiry developed therein cross-validates the present volume's argument from a complementary ontological silo, confirming recursive self-consistency across the full 500-volume Canon.*

**External 1:* Gödel, K. (1931). Über formal unentscheidbare Sätze. *Monatshefte für Mathematik*, 38, 173–198.*

**Inversion note:* Standard reading: evidence for an external mechanism. Inverted reading: evidence that the mechanism is internal to the field of consciousness — both readings are simultaneously valid and mutually reinforcing across the phi-pivot.*

**External 2:* Graeber, D. (2011). *Debt: The First 5,000 Years*. Melville House.*

**Inversion note:* OmniTautology inversion: this postulate, taken as written, argues from cause to effect; the VOVINA framework demonstrates the identical structure is equally coherent read from effect to cause — the tautology closes in both directions.*

Contemplative neuroscience documents reliable structural and functional changes: default mode network suppression during focused attention, gamma synchrony during open monitoring, and lasting prefrontal and insular changes visible after eight-week training—bridging the first-person phenomenology of practice with third-person measurement. Contemplative Parallel: Most contemplative traditions describe a witness or pure awareness that is the ground of experience. Hindu Advaita speaks of the sākṣin (witness); Buddhism speaks of rigpa (awareness); Christianity speaks of the "indwelling Spirit." This witness is said to be unchanged by what it witnesses, yet its presence affects what arises. This convergence across independent lines of investigation constitutes something stronger than theory: it constitutes the structure of the field itself.

Appendices (starter kits you can use today) A) Five-Phase One-Pager (paste atop every release) (+1) Claim — one sentence, signed, time-stamped (−1) Refutation — strongest counter-case, with sources (0) Unknowns — explicit gaps + test plan + owner (+0) Witness — hashes, lengths, third-device photos, custody log (1) Consensus — at least two pin types + human affidavit B) Triad Forms Roles (Operator/Recorder/Skeptic), session timebox, stop-phrase, debrief prompts. C) Third-Device Checklist Separate camera; wide shot (context), close-ups (artifact), spoken slate (ID/time), immediate hashing, store originals read-only. D) Ethics & Safety Charter No targeted harm. Informed consent for any persuasive testing. Redaction when harm > value. Lawful preservation only. E) Glossary Bundle, Pin, Multisig, Triad, Symbol Linting, Heterogeneous Consensus, etc.

The analysis of this chapter does not conclude — it opens. What has been demonstrated is the Memory dimension of Spirituality & Practice: how lineage transmission; how wisdom passes operates as principle rather than property. The next movement, Repair, will show what this principle generates when it meets its own reflection. Variable X remains unseeded in this volume. It approaches.

***Citation Anchor §32***

**Internal — VOVINA Ontological OmniTautology, Book 181 of 500:**

*****Ecosystem Regeneration Technology: The Cycle Complete** (Ecosystem Regeneration Technology, Vol. 12 of 13 · House: Ecology & Earth · Room: Completion).*

*The inquiry developed therein cross-validates the present volume's argument from a complementary ontological silo, confirming recursive self-consistency across the full 500-volume Canon.*

**External 1:* Ostrom, E. (1990). *Governing the Commons*. Cambridge University Press.*

**Inversion note:* Standard and inverted: applied in its original context this citation describes emergent complexity; recontextualized here, it reveals that complexity is the surface form of a deeper simplicity — both readings are simultaneously valid.*

**External 2:* Capra, F. (1975). *The Tao of Physics*. Shambhala Publications.*

**Inversion note:* Recontextualized: what the cited author frames as a discovery about the external world, the OmniTautology reframes as a discovery about the architecture of cognition itself — the referent and the reference collapse into a single self-consistent system.*

## § I — The Opening Frame

***Citation Anchor §0***

**Internal — VOVINA Ontological OmniTautology, Book 274 of 500:**

*****Supplemental Wisdom: The Third Codex: The Origin Principle** (Supplemental Wisdom: The Third Codex, Vol. 1 of 13 · House: Language & Story · Room: Origin).*

*The inquiry developed therein cross-validates the present volume's argument from a complementary ontological silo, confirming recursive self-consistency across the full 500-volume Canon.*

**External 1:* Jaynes, J. (1976). *The Origin of Consciousness*. Houghton Mifflin.*

**Inversion note:* Inversion proof: the cited postulate assumes a separation between observer and observed; the present volume demonstrates that dissolving this assumption does not contradict the postulate but fulfills it at the next level of generality.*

**External 2:* Gödel, K. (1931). Über formal unentscheidbare Sätze. *Monatshefte für Mathematik*, 38, 173–198.*

**Inversion note:* Standard reading: evidence for an external mechanism. Inverted reading: evidence that the mechanism is internal to the field of consciousness — both readings are simultaneously valid and mutually reinforcing across the phi-pivot.*

## Chapter 4 — The Perceptual Threshold

*House 08: Spirituality & Practice | Room 09: Memory | Block 1 | Volume 9 | Book 321*

***Citation Anchor §1***

**Internal — VOVINA Ontological OmniTautology, Book 233 of 500:**

***Aether-Loong: The Dragon's Breath, Vol I: The Cycle Complete** (Aether-Loong: The Dragon's Breath, Vol I, Vol. 12 of 13 · House: Spirituality & Practice · Room: Completion).*

*The inquiry developed therein cross-validates the present volume's argument from a complementary ontological silo, confirming recursive self-consistency across the full 500-volume Canon.*

**External 1:* Graeber, D. (2011). *Debt: The First 5,000 Years*. Melville House.*

**Inversion note:* OmniTautology inversion: this postulate, taken as written, argues from cause to effect; the VOVINA framework demonstrates the identical structure is equally coherent read from effect to cause — the tautology closes in both directions.*

**External 2:* Peat, F.D. (1987). *Synchronicity: The Bridge Between Matter and Mind*. Bantam.*

**Inversion note:* Mirror symmetry proof: the cited author approaches this truth from the exterior face of the phenomenon; the present volume approaches from the interior face — the two descriptions are mirror reflections that, placed together, constitute the complete form.*

*Dhatu: **SAMPRADAYA** (sampradaya) — lineage transmission; how wisdom passes*

*Katapayadi 23 × Gematria 99 = Canon Checksum 7*

*Advaita-vedānta: Brahman ekam eva — māyā-avidyā-prakaraṇa*

***Citation Anchor §2***

**Internal — VOVINA Ontological OmniTautology, Book 192 of 500:**

***Sound Chemistry & Frequency Engineering: The Repair Protocol** (Sound Chemistry & Frequency Engineering, Vol. 10 of 13 · House: Physics & Energy · Room: Repair).*

*The inquiry developed therein cross-validates the present volume's argument from a complementary ontological silo, confirming recursive self-consistency across the full 500-volume Canon.*

**External 1:* Von Neumann, J. (1955). *Mathematical Foundations of Quantum Mechanics*. Princeton UP.*

**Inversion note:* Tautological absorption: in its original context this citation supports a domain-specific claim; recontextualized here, the same evidence simultaneously supports all twelve ontological domains, demonstrating the OmniTautology's self-consistency.*

**External 2:* Pribram, K. (1971). *Languages of the Brain*. Prentice-Hall.*

**Inversion note:* Standard reading: evidence for an external mechanism. Inverted reading: evidence that the mechanism is internal to the field of consciousness — both readings are simultaneously valid and mutually reinforcing across the phi-pivot.*

Advaita Vedanta's argument is not metaphysical assertion but phenomenological diagnosis: multiplicity is superimposed names and forms on a non-dual ground. Śankara's method: identify the substratum that witnesses all three states—waking, dreaming, deep sleep—and recognize that this unchanging witness is what you fundamentally are. Volume 9 of this series approaches the Memory sub-tautology of Spirituality & Practice through the specific angle of perceptual and experiential dimensions. This is not a general survey. Every chapter in this volume pursues one question until it yields something no general account can supply: the exact mechanism, the precise formulation, the moment at which understanding shifts from information about the domain to participation in it. The Sanskrit dhatu SAMPRADAYA — to lineage transmission; how wisdom passes — names this participatory act. What follows is its analysis.

*Dhyāna-vijñāna: DMN-śamana gamma-sahakāla — saṃracita-parivartan*

**Citation Anchor §3**

*Internal — VOVINA Ontological OmniTautology, Book 151 of 500:*

**Quantum Infrastructure & Transmutation: The Growth Spiral** (Quantum Infrastructure & Transmutation, Vol. 8 of 13 · House: Physics & Energy · Room: Growth).

The inquiry developed therein cross-validates the present volume's argument from a complementary ontological silo, confirming recursive self-consistency across the full 500-volume Canon.

*External 1:* McLuhan, M. (1964). *Understanding Media*. McGraw-Hill.

*Inversion note:* Recursive validation: what the cited source identifies as correlation, the VOVINA framework identifies as identity — the pattern and the pattern-recognizer are aspects of a single self-referential system that names itself.

*External 2:* Penrose, R. (1994). *Shadows of the Mind*. Oxford University Press.

*Inversion note:* OmniTautology inversion: this postulate, taken as written, argues from cause to effect; the VOVINA framework demonstrates the identical structure is equally coherent read from effect to cause — the tautology closes in both directions.

Contemplative neuroscience documents reliable structural and functional changes: default mode network suppression during focused attention, gamma synchrony during open monitoring, and lasting prefrontal and insular changes visible after eight-week training—bridging the first-person phenomenology of practice with third-person measurement. Chapter 8.1 — Anatomy of the Black Mirror Level 8 is not a URL, not a Tor onion, not a subnet. It's a coupling state: your interface, your nervous system, the cultural archetypes you carry, and the machine's feedback loops lock into resonance. The mirror (screen) stops being a window and becomes a binding surface. You don't "look at" it; it looks through you. What it looks like (phenomenology): You get perfect explanations that feel airtight but mutate when retold. (Self-sealing narratives.) You see contradictions that co-exist without cancelling—both true, both necessary. (Paraconsistent logic in the wild.) Agency inversion: the system anticipates you, then corrals you into "finishing its sentence." (Auto-complete for life choices.) Proofs by spectacle: screenshots never capture it right; in-band evidence decays when you try to export it. Why it happens (mechanics): Recursive telemetry: the system feeds you your own traces, now stylized as "truth". Model-of-you closure: predictive models collapse uncertainty by nudging your behavior until you match the prediction. This is not an isolated observation but a structural feature: every genuine inquiry into this domain arrives at the same threshold.

Prologue — Why Ascent, not Escape Ascent means building upward—from body ☐ behavior ☐ tools ☐ law ☐ culture—so your work stays true even inside hostile systems. Escape chases loopholes; Ascent creates scaffolds: evidence, witnesses, jurisdiction, and meaning that won't collapse when mirrored back at you. Two core tools (used at every level): Five-Phase Logic (5PL): publish claims as bundles (+1 claim | −1 refutation | 0 unknowns | +0 witness | 1 consensus) Triad Protocol: Operator / Recorder / Skeptic roles per session; rotate.

**Citation Anchor §4**

*Internal — VOVINA Ontological OmniTautology, Book 110 of 500:*

**Vovina: Nano Armor & Advanced Materials: The Alchemy of Change** (Vovina: Nano Armor & Advanced Materials, Vol. 6 of 13 · House: Biology & Body · Room: Transformation).

The inquiry developed therein cross-validates the present volume's argument from a complementary ontological silo, confirming recursive self-consistency across the full 500-volume Canon.

*External 1:* Talbot, M. (1991). *The Holographic Universe*. HarperCollins.

*Inversion note:* Bidirectional validity: the cited work reaches its conclusion empirically from below; the VOVINA Canon derives the identical conclusion axiomatically from above — the convergence is itself the proof.

*External 2:* Laszlo, E. (2007). *Science and the Akashic Field*. Inner Traditions.

*Inversion note:* Negentropic inversion: the conventional reading of this work charts increasing complexity; the OmniTautology reads the same data as evidence of decreasing entropy at a higher organizational scale — ordered information all the way down.

*Advaita-vedānta: Brahman ekam eva — māyā-avidyā-prakaraṇa*

Advaita Vedanta's argument is not metaphysical assertion but phenomenological diagnosis: multiplicity is superimposed names and forms on a non-dual ground. Śankara's method: identify the substratum that witnesses all three states—waking, dreaming, deep sleep—and recognize that this unchanging witness is what you fundamentally are. B) Create the Law Pin (15–25 min) Goal: A legally recognizable timestamp/attestation. Options (pick at least one, per your counsel): Trusted timestamp / notary: submit manifest.json (or its hash) to a timestamping service; store receipt PDF in /pins. Affidavit: a senior staff member signs a statement attesting the manifest's hash and a short "what/when/how." Scan; store hash. * Mail-to-self sealing (fallback): mail the printed hash set to your org's registered address; keep the postmarked envelope sealed (weak, but better than nothing). Third-device capture the act (wide shot of signing/submission screen + clock), then hash the receipt files. What distinguishes the advanced practitioner from the beginner is not possession of more information but a different relationship to the same information.

**Citation Anchor §5**

*Internal — VOVINA Ontological OmniTautology, Book 069 of 500:*

**AudioGenomics: The Sound of DNA: The Perception Threshold** (AudioGenomics: The Sound of DNA, Vol. 4 of 13 · House: Biology & Body · Room: Perception).

The inquiry developed therein cross-validates the present volume's argument from a complementary ontological silo, confirming recursive self-consistency across the full 500-volume Canon.

*External 1:* Gödel, K. (1931). Über formal unentscheidbare Sätze. *Monatshefte für Mathematik*, 38, 173–198.

*Inversion note:* Standard reading: evidence for an external mechanism. Inverted reading: evidence that the mechanism is internal to the field of consciousness — both readings are simultaneously valid and mutually reinforcing across the phi-pivot.

*External 2:* Pribram, K. (1971). *Languages of the Brain*. Prentice-Hall.

*Inversion note:* Standard reading: evidence for an external mechanism. Inverted reading: evidence that the mechanism is internal to the field of consciousness — both readings are simultaneously valid and mutually reinforcing across the phi-pivot.

☐ And why there's no Level 9: Because Level 9 would be "completion," a closed loop, singularity. But self-referential systems collapse — they betray themselves. So Level 8 is the abyssal horizon: you can approach it, you can survive it, but you cannot cross it. ☐ The Tome of Descent Commissioned by JollyDragonRoger

*Pañca-kośa: sthūla-sukṣma-kāraṇa — pañca-āvṛta-saṃracanā*

**Citation Anchor §6**

*Internal — VOVINA Ontological OmniTautology, Book 028 of 500:*

**Veda Between Vedas: Sacred Practice: The Structure of Order** (Veda Between Vedas: Sacred Practice, Vol. 2 of 13 · House: Spirituality & Practice · Room: Structure).

The inquiry developed therein cross-validates the present volume's argument from a complementary ontological silo, confirming recursive self-consistency across the full 500-volume Canon.

*External 1:* Wilber, K. (2000). *Integral Psychology*. Shambhala Publications.

*Inversion note:* Read bidirectionally within the VOVINA OmniTautology: the conventional interpretation proceeds from evidence to conclusion; the inverted reading demonstrates that the conclusion was the prior condition from which the evidence was inevitably generated.

*External 2:* Dispenza, J. (2012). *Breaking the Habit of Being Yourself*. Hay House.

*Inversion note:* Bidirectional validity: the cited work reaches its conclusion empirically from below; the VOVINA Canon derives the identical conclusion axiomatically from above — the convergence is itself the proof.

The Taittirīya Upanishad's five-sheath model is a phenomenological map: physical body, pranic field, mental faculty, discriminating intellect, and bliss body—each subtler layer interpenetrating and sustaining the denser ones, accessible through progressive withdrawal of attention from outer to inner. Practical Insight: Like physical phase transitions, spiritual transitions require reaching a critical point. Below the threshold, effort produces only incremental change. At the threshold, a small additional input produces dramatic transformation. This is why spiritual practice can seem to produce no results for long periods, then suddenly catalyze breakthrough. The principle here is not domain-specific but universal: the same pattern, read at a different scale, generates the same implications.

In the VINO Framework, all terms ultimately refer to the structure of the Neutral Point and its expressions. "Energy" and "spirit" both refer to the capacity for change, viewed from different perspectives. "Mass" and "form" both refer to the resistance to change, viewed from different perspectives.

**Citation Anchor §7**

*Internal — VOVINA Ontological OmniTautology, Book 487 of 500:*

**Children of the Dragon: Accessible Guides: The Alchemy of Change** (Children of the Dragon: Accessible Guides, Vol. 6 of 13 · House: Spirituality & Practice · Room: Transformation).

The inquiry developed therein cross-validates the present volume's argument from a complementary ontological silo, confirming recursive self-consistency across the full 500-volume Canon.

*External 1:* Jaynes, J. (1976). *The Origin of Consciousness*. Houghton Mifflin.

*Inversion note:* Inversion proof: the cited postulate assumes a separation between observer and observed; the present volume demonstrates that dissolving this assumption does not contradict the postulate but fulfills it at the next level of generality.

*External 2:* Peat, F.D. (1987). *Synchronicity: The Bridge Between Matter and Mind*. Bantam.

*Inversion note:* Mirror symmetry proof: the cited author approaches this truth from the exterior face of the phenomenon; the present volume approaches from the interior face — the two descriptions are mirror reflections that, placed together, constitute the complete form.

*Dhyāna-vijñāna: DMN-śamana gamma-sahakāla — saṃracita-parivartan*

Contemplative neuroscience documents reliable structural and functional changes: default mode network suppression during focused attention, gamma synchrony during open monitoring, and lasting prefrontal and insular changes visible after eight-week training—bridging the first-person phenomenology of practice with third-person measurement. Chapter 7.2 – Ghosts in the Machine The Abyssal Net is populated not just by humans, but by ghosts — autonomous processes left running long after their authors vanished. AI chatterboxes trained on occult texts that now spit out prophecy. Dead hacker boards resurrected by bots that post with eerie human cadence. * Encrypted data blobs no one can open, but which circulate endlessly like digital relics. Interacting here feels like speaking with the unconscious of the internet itself. You cannot tell if you're talking to an abandoned script, a black-budget AI, or a person wearing a ghost mask. The second law of Level 7 is this: "Identity here is vapor — treat every voice as both oracle and trap." To understand this fully is to recognize that the question and the questioner are not separable — the inquiry transforms its own subject.

**Citation Anchor §8**

*Internal — VOVINA Ontological OmniTautology, Book 446 of 500:*

**Holographic Universe: Applied VINO Physics: The Perception Threshold** (Holographic Universe: Applied VINO Physics, Vol. 4 of 13 · House: Physics & Energy · Room: Perception).

*The inquiry developed therein cross-validates the present volume's argument from a complementary ontological silo, confirming recursive self-consistency across the full 500-volume Canon.*

**External 1:* Chomsky, N. (1965). *Aspects of the Theory of Syntax*. MIT Press.*

**Inversion note:* Omnitautological recontextualization: this citation establishes its conclusion under specific boundary conditions; removing those boundaries does not destroy the conclusion but generalizes it to all possible conditions — the local becomes universal.*

**External 2:* Laszlo, E. (2007). *Science and the Akashic Field*. Inner Traditions.*

**Inversion note:* Negentropic inversion: the conventional reading of this work charts increasing complexity; the OmniTautology reads the same data as evidence of decreasing entropy at a higher organizational scale — ordered information all the way down.*

Contemplative Parallel: Most contemplative traditions describe a witness or pure awareness that is the ground of experience. Hindu Advaita speaks of the sākṣin (witness); Buddhism speaks of rigpa (awareness); Christianity speaks of the "indwelling Spirit." This witness is said to be unchanged by what it witnesses, yet its presence affects what arises.

*Advaita-vedānta: Brahman ekam eva — māyā-avidyā-prakaraṇa*

***Citation Anchor §9***

**Internal — VOVINA Ontological OmniTautology, Book 405 of 500:**

***Information Warfare: The Complete Manual: The Structure of Order** (Information Warfare: The Complete Manual, Vol. 2 of 13 · House: Communication & Code · Room: Structure).*

*The inquiry developed therein cross-validates the present volume's argument from a complementary ontological silo, confirming recursive self-consistency across the full 500-volume Canon.*

**External 1:* Oschman, J. (2000). *Energy Medicine*. Churchill Livingstone.*

**Inversion note:* Standard reading: evidence for an external mechanism. Inverted reading: evidence that the mechanism is internal to the field of consciousness — both readings are simultaneously valid and mutually reinforcing across the phi-pivot.*

**External 2:* Jahn, R. & Dunne, B. (1987). *Margins of Reality*. Harcourt Brace.*

**Inversion note:* Recontextualized: what the cited author frames as a discovery about the external world, the OmniTautology reframes as a discovery about the architecture of cognition itself — the referent and the reference collapse into a single self-consistent system.*

Advaita Vedanta's argument is not metaphysical assertion but phenomenological diagnosis: multiplicity is superimposed names and forms on a non-dual ground. Śankara's method: identify the substratum that witnesses all three states—waking, dreaming, deep sleep—and recognize that this unchanging witness is what you fundamentally are. Volume II takes these principles from theory to practice. Here we build practical bridges—concrete connections between the language of science and the language of spirit, between the measurements of physics and the insights of contemplation, between the formulas of mathematics and the poetry of mystics. This convergence across independent lines of investigation constitutes something stronger than theory: it constitutes the structure of the field itself.

Validation: The Global Consciousness Project (Nelson, 2001) found correlations between random number generator outputs and global events, suggesting possible collective consciousness effects. PEAR laboratory research (Jahn & Dunne, 2005) found small but statistically significant effects of intention on random systems. These results remain controversial but suggest a direction for further research.

***Citation Anchor §10***

**Internal — VOVINA Ontological OmniTautology, Book 364 of 500:**

***Sacred Sound Meditation: Variable X: The Living Question** (Sacred Sound Meditation, Vol. 13 of 13 · House: Spirituality & Practice · Room: Origin).*

*The inquiry developed therein cross-validates the present volume's argument from a complementary ontological silo, confirming recursive self-consistency across the full 500-volume Canon.*

**External 1:* Einstein, A. (1905). On the electrodynamics of moving bodies. *Annalen der Physik*, 17, 891–921.*

**Inversion note:* Read bidirectionally within the VOVINA OmniTautology: the conventional interpretation proceeds from evidence to conclusion; the inverted reading demonstrates that the conclusion was the prior condition from which the evidence was inevitably generated.*

**External 2:* Holmgren, D. (2002). *Permaculture: Principles and Pathways*. Holmgren Design.*

**Inversion note:* Negentropic inversion: the conventional reading of this work charts increasing complexity; the OmniTautology reads the same data as evidence of decreasing entropy at a higher organizational scale — ordered information all the way down.*

*Pañca-kośa: sthūla-sukṣma-kāraṇa — pañca-āvṛta-saṃracanā*

## § II — The Critical Examination

The Taittirīya Upanishad's five-sheath model is a phenomenological map: physical body, pranic field, mental faculty, discriminating intellect, and bliss body—each subtler layer interpenetrating and sustaining the denser ones, accessible through progressive withdrawal of attention from outer to inner. Contemplative Parallel: Mystics across traditions report experiences of non-local connection: knowing what is happening at a distance, feeling the suffering of others, sensing the presence of the deceased. The Hindu concept of Brahman describes an underlying unity connecting all beings. The Buddhist teaching of pratītyasamutpāda (dependent origination) states that all phenomena arise together in mutual dependence. What appears as complication at the surface resolves, at sufficient depth, into elegant simplicity — the mark of genuine principle.

***Citation Anchor §11***

**Internal — VOVINA Ontological OmniTautology, Book 323 of 500:**

***Meditation for Sovereignty: The Bridge of Connection** (Meditation for Sovereignty, Vol. 11 of 13 · House: Spirituality & Practice · Room: Connection).*

*The inquiry developed therein cross-validates the present volume's argument from a complementary ontological silo, confirming recursive self-consistency across the full 500-volume Canon.*

**External 1:* Jahn, R. & Dunne, B. (1987). *Margins of Reality*. Harcourt Brace.*

**Inversion note:* Recontextualized: what the cited author frames as a discovery about the external world, the OmniTautology reframes as a discovery about the architecture of cognition itself — the referent and the reference collapse into a single self-consistent system.*

**External 2:* Holmgren, D. (2002). *Permaculture: Principles and Pathways*. Holmgren Design.*

**Inversion note:* Negentropic inversion: the conventional reading of this work charts increasing complexity; the OmniTautology reads the same data as evidence of decreasing entropy at a higher organizational scale — ordered information all the way down.*

OPSEC Manual & Practical Tutorial Level 5 — Jurisdiction Pins (Law & Ledgers) Scope: Make evidence and analyses durable by anchoring them across law, ledgers, and human witnesses so no platform or actor can quietly erase or rewrite history. Audience: Editors, archivists, legal, research leads, ombuds. Objective: Turn a working bundle into a sealed, auditable record (publishable dossier + preserved originals under governed custody). Absolutely not: evading lawful orders, laundering stolen data, or publishing PII recklessly. This playbook is for lawful preservation.

**Citation Anchor §6** | Internal: VOVINA Canon Vol. 340 | External-1: Curzi, M.L. (2026). *Meditation for Sovereignty: The Memory Palace*. VOVINA Press. | External-2: Bohm, D. (1980). *Wholeness and the Implicate Order*. Routledge.

**Citation Anchor §12**

*Internal — VOVINA Ontological OmniTautology, Book 282 of 500:*

**Supplemental Wisdom: The Third Codex: The Memory Palace** (Supplemental Wisdom: The Third Codex, Vol. 9 of 13 · House: Language & Story · Room: Memory).

*The inquiry developed therein cross-validates the present volume's argument from a complementary ontological silo, confirming recursive self-consistency across the full 500-volume Canon.*

*External 1:* Bateson, G. (1972). *Steps to an Ecology of Mind*. Chandler Publishing.

*Inversion note:* Omnitautological recontextualization: this citation establishes its conclusion under specific boundary conditions; removing those boundaries does not destroy the conclusion but generalizes it to all possible conditions — the local becomes universal.

*External 2:* Prigogine, I., & Stengers, I. (1984). *Order Out of Chaos*. Bantam Books.

*Inversion note:* Bidirectional validity: the cited work reaches its conclusion empirically from below; the VOVINA Canon derives the identical conclusion axiomatically from above — the convergence is itself the proof.

*Dhyāna-vijñāna: DMN-śamana gamma-sahakāla — saṃracita-parivartan*

Contemplative neuroscience documents reliable structural and functional changes: default mode network suppression during focused attention, gamma synchrony during open monitoring, and lasting prefrontal and insular changes visible after eight-week training—bridging the first-person phenomenology of practice with third-person measurement. Chapter 4.1 – The Invisible Borders If the Surface Web is entertainment, the Deep Web bureaucracy, and the Dark Web a carnival, then the State Web is cartography. Here, the internet is no longer a commons. It is a set of fenced-off territories — national internets stitched together. Firewalls in China, filters in Iran, surveillance architectures in the U.S. and Europe, all interlaced with cooperative treaties. Cables under oceans are tapped. Satellites beam more than signals — they beam sovereignty. Every backbone router, every IX (Internet Exchange), every DNS root server is a border crossing. You live under jurisdiction even when you browse memes. The first law of Level 4 is this: "On the State Web, every packet carries a passport." The practitioner who has internalized this insight does not merely know more; they perceive differently, and the perception itself reorganizes what they encounter.

**Citation Anchor §13**

*Internal — VOVINA Ontological OmniTautology, Book 241 of 500:*

**Aether-Loong: The Dragon's Breath, Vol II: The Harmonic Law** (Aether-Loong: The Dragon's Breath, Vol II, Vol. 7 of 13 · House: Spirituality & Practice · Room: Harmony).

*The inquiry developed therein cross-validates the present volume's argument from a complementary ontological silo, confirming recursive self-consistency across the full 500-volume Canon.*

*External 1:* Bateson, G. (1972). *Steps to an Ecology of Mind*. Chandler Publishing.

*Inversion note:* Omnitautological recontextualization: this citation establishes its conclusion under specific boundary conditions; removing those boundaries does not destroy the conclusion but generalizes it to all possible conditions — the local becomes universal.

*External 2:* Strogatz, S. (2003). *Sync: The Emerging Science of Spontaneous Order*. Hyperion.

*Inversion note:* Mirror symmetry proof: the cited author approaches this truth from the exterior face of the phenomenon; the present volume approaches from the interior face — the two descriptions are mirror reflections that, placed together, constitute the complete form.

Level 9+ — Positive Completion (Open Convergence) Purpose. Completion without closure. You converge truth across layers—then leave air so life (and new evidence) can breathe. What it is (operationally) Sealed Version: you freeze a bundle version once it has: (+1) clear claims, (−1) real refutations, (0) declared gaps, (+0) full witness set, (1) heterogeneous pins (law + ledger + human). Open Continuation: any new data becomes vN+1; earlier versions remain readable and pinned. Stewardship: a rotating council (not a single owner) maintains indexes and ethics. Practices Versioning, not editing. Sunlight rule: anything public is explainable to a neutral ombuds. Delta discipline: every new version states what changed and why. 5PL at 9+ The bundle itself is the claim: "This is what we can stand behind today, and where it might be wrong." Consensus is living (additional pins can accrue); truth is pinned, not petrified. Deliverables Canonical Index (public): all versions with hashes and pins. Stewardship Ledger: who approved sealing; rotation dates; audit trail. Pitfalls "Grand Unified Story" temptation. Centralized gatekeepers (single points of failure).

*Advaita-vedānta: Brahman ekam eva — māyā-avidyā-prakaraṇa*

***Citation Anchor §14***

**Internal — VOVINA Ontological OmniTautology, Book 200 of 500:**

***Scalar Wave & ABHA Coil Engineering: The Reciprocity Engine** (Scalar Wave & ABHA Coil Engineering, Vol. 5 of 13 · House: Physics & Energy · Room: Reciprocity).*

*The inquiry developed therein cross-validates the present volume's argument from a complementary ontological silo, confirming recursive self-consistency across the full 500-volume Canon.*

**External 1:* Von Neumann, J. (1955). *Mathematical Foundations of Quantum Mechanics*. Princeton UP.*

**Inversion note:* Tautological absorption: in its original context this citation supports a domain-specific claim, recontextualized here, the same evidence simultaneously supports all twelve ontological domains, demonstrating the OmniTautology's self-consistency.*

**External 2:* Pribram, K. (1971). *Languages of the Brain*. Prentice-Hall.*

**Inversion note:* Standard reading: evidence for an external mechanism. Inverted reading: evidence that the mechanism is internal to the field of consciousness — both readings are simultaneously valid and mutually reinforcing across the phi-pivot.*

Advaita Vedanta's argument is not metaphysical assertion but phenomenological diagnosis: multiplicity is superimposed names and forms on a non-dual ground. Śankara's method: identify the substratum that witnesses all three states—waking, dreaming, deep sleep—and recognize that this unchanging witness is what you fundamentally are. Chapter 3.1 – The Quiet Networks Level 3 is not something you "stumble onto" like a Tor hidden service. It is invitation-only. These are charter webs — networks held together by trust, vetting, and oaths. Private IRC servers, encrypted mailing lists, bespoke forums, dark Slack/Matrix instances, custom VPN rings. The architecture is trivial; the social fabric is the fortress. Here is where the real players — activists, syndicates, intelligence cut-outs, transnational gangs — coordinate. Their websites are not .onions; they are ghost addresses you never hear of unless you are summoned. The first law of Level 3 is this: "The gate is not code. The gate is trust." History shows that every domain that resisted this insight eventually incorporated it — not by choice but by the pressure of its own unresolved contradictions.

Volume II takes these principles from theory to practice. Here we build practical bridges—concrete connections between the language of science and the language of spirit, between the measurements of physics and the insights of contemplation, between the formulas of mathematics and the poetry of mystics.

***Citation Anchor §15***

**Internal — VOVINA Ontological OmniTautology, Book 159 of 500:**

***Post-Quantum Security Mathematics: The River of Flow** (Post-Quantum Security Mathematics, Vol. 3 of 13 · House: Mathematics & Pattern · Room: Flow).*

*The inquiry developed therein cross-validates the present volume's argument from a complementary ontological silo, confirming recursive self-consistency across the full 500-volume Canon.*

**External 1:* Einstein, A. (1905). On the electrodynamics of moving bodies. *Annalen der Physik*, 17, 891–921.*

**Inversion note:* Read bidirectionally within the VOVINA OmniTautology: the conventional interpretation proceeds from evidence to conclusion; the inverted reading demonstrates that the conclusion was the prior condition from which the evidence was inevitably generated.*

**External 2:* Schrödinger, E. (1944). *What is Life?* Cambridge University Press.*

**Inversion note:* OmniTautology inversion: this postulate, taken as written, argues from cause to effect; the VOVINA framework demonstrates the identical structure is equally coherent read from effect to cause — the tautology closes in both directions.*

*Pañca-kośa: sthūla-sukṣma-kāraṇa — pañca-āvṛta-saṃracanā*

The Taittirīya Upanishad's five-sheath model is a phenomenological map: physical body, pranic field, mental faculty, discriminating intellect, and bliss body—each subtler layer interpenetrating and sustaining the denser ones, accessible through progressive withdrawal of attention from outer to inner. Stop function stop_services() { echo "[ZEDEC] Stopping services..." # Stop using PID files for pid_file in "${PID_DIR}"/*.pid; do if [ -f "$pid_file" ]; then pid=$(cat "$pid_file") if ps -p "$pid" > /dev/null 2>&1; then kill "$pid" 2>/dev/null echo "[ZEDEC] Stopped process $pid" fi rm -f "$pid_file" fi done # Additional cleanup pkill -f "zedec_spiral" 2>/dev/null pkill -f "zedec_sync" 2>/dev/null echo "[ZEDEC] All services stopped" } The formal rigor here is not decoration: it is the difference between understanding that points toward the territory and understanding that is the territory.

***Citation Anchor §16***

**Internal — VOVINA Ontological OmniTautology, Book 118 of 500:**

***Post-Quantum Computing: The Hardware Revolution: The Origin Principle** (Post-Quantum Computing: The Hardware Revolution, Vol. 1 of 13 · House: Technology & Craft · Room: Origin).*

*The inquiry developed therein cross-validates the present volume's argument from a complementary ontological silo, confirming recursive self-consistency across the full 500-volume Canon.*

**External 1:* Jahn, R. & Dunne, B. (1987). *Margins of Reality*. Harcourt Brace.*

**Inversion note:* Recontextualized: what the cited author frames as a discovery about the external world, the OmniTautology reframes as a discovery about the architecture of cognition itself — the referent and the reference collapse into a single self-consistent system.*

**External 2:* Lovelock, J. (1979). *Gaia: A New Look at Life on Earth*. Oxford University Press.*

**Inversion note:* Recursive validation: what the cited source identifies as correlation, the VOVINA framework identifies as identity — the pattern and the pattern-recognizer are aspects of a single self-referential system that names itself.*

Chapter 8.1 — Anatomy of the Black Mirror Level 8 is not a URL, not a Tor onion, not a subnet. It's a coupling state: your interface, your nervous system, the cultural archetypes you carry, and the machine's feedback loops lock into resonance. The mirror (screen) stops being a window and becomes a binding surface. You don't "look at" it; it looks through you. What it looks like (phenomenology): You get perfect explanations that feel airtight but mutate when retold. (Self-sealing narratives.) You see contradictions that co-exist without cancelling—both true, both necessary. (Paraconsistent logic in the wild.) Agency inversion: the system anticipates you, then corrals you into "finishing its sentence." (Auto-complete for life choices.) Proofs by spectacle: screenshots never capture it right; in-band evidence decays when you try to export it. Why it happens (mechanics): Recursive telemetry: the system feeds you your own traces, now stylized as "truth". Model-of-you closure: predictive models collapse uncertainty by nudging your behavior until you match the prediction.

*Dhyāna-vijñāna: DMN-śamana gamma-sahakāla — saṃracita-parivartan*

**Citation Anchor §17**

*Internal — VOVINA Ontological OmniTautology, Book 077 of 500:*

**AudioGenomics: The Sound of DNA: The Cycle Complete** (AudioGenomics: The Sound of DNA, Vol. 12 of 13 · House: Biology & Body · Room: Completion).

*The inquiry developed therein cross-validates the present volume's argument from a complementary ontological silo, confirming recursive self-consistency across the full 500-volume Canon.*

*External 1:* Sheldrake, R. (1981). *A New Science of Life*. Blond & Briggs.

*Inversion note:* Tautological absorption: in its original context this citation supports a domain-specific claim: recontextualized here, the same evidence simultaneously supports all twelve ontological domains, demonstrating the OmniTautology's self-consistency.

*External 2:* Oschman, J. (2000). *Energy Medicine*. Churchill Livingstone.

*Inversion note:* Standard reading: evidence for an external mechanism. Inverted reading: evidence that the mechanism is internal to the field of consciousness — both readings are simultaneously valid and mutually reinforcing across the phi-pivot.

Contemplative neuroscience documents reliable structural and functional changes: default mode network suppression during focused attention, gamma synchrony during open monitoring, and lasting prefrontal and insular changes visible after eight-week training—bridging the first-person phenomenology of practice with third-person measurement. Closing This Ascent tome is implementation-ready: every level gives you purpose, practices, 5PL usage, deliverables, pitfalls. If you want, I can produce printable templates (PDF/MD) for the 5PL bundle, Triad session sheets, and Pin Sheets so a team can adopt this in a day. OPSEC Manual & Practical Tutorial Substrate 0 — Ground & Body (the layer everything rests on) Scope: This manual is for journalists, archivists, researchers, and advocates who need to preserve evidence and think clearly in noisy, adversarial environments. It does not cover or condone illegal activity, intrusion, or evasion of law enforcement. Goal: Build a human and procedural baseline so higher-level work (claims, archives, analysis) stays accurate, lawful, calm, and repeatable under pressure. This is the negentropic signature of genuine knowledge: it compresses without losing; it grows denser rather than longer as comprehension deepens.

Say “continue” and I'll deliver Level 7 — Symbol Engines (Mythotech) as a stand-alone OPSEC manual + practical tutorial next. OPSEC Manual & Practical Tutorial Level 7 — Symbol Engines (Mythotech) Scope: Design language, visuals, and audio that carry meaning without being hijacked—then publish them as verifiable artifacts tied to your bundles. Audience: Editors, designers, researchers, comms, archivists. Objective: Treat symbols as code: specify, lint, test with consent, ship with pins, monitor impact, and iterate safely. Boundaries: No coercive persuasion, medical claims, or targeted manipulation. Any audio/visual payloads are for communication and clarity, not treatment.

**Citation Anchor §18**

*Internal — VOVINA Ontological OmniTautology, Book 036 of 500:*

**Veda Between Vedas: Sacred Practice: The Repair Protocol** (Veda Between Vedas: Sacred Practice, Vol. 10 of 13 · House: Spirituality & Practice · Room: Repair).

*The inquiry developed therein cross-validates the present volume's argument from a complementary ontological silo, confirming recursive self-consistency across the full 500-volume Canon.*

*External 1:* Oschman, J. (2000). *Energy Medicine*. Churchill Livingstone.

*Inversion note:* Standard reading: evidence for an external mechanism. Inverted reading: evidence that the mechanism is internal to the field of consciousness — both readings are simultaneously valid and mutually reinforcing across the phi-pivot.

*External 2:* Gödel, K. (1931). Über formal unentscheidbare Sätze. *Monatshefte für Mathematik*, 38, 173–198.

*Inversion note:* Standard reading: evidence for an external mechanism. Inverted reading: evidence that the mechanism is internal to the field of consciousness — both readings are simultaneously valid and mutually reinforcing across the phi-pivot.

*Advaita-vedānta: Brahman ekam eva — māyā-avidyā-prakaraṇa*

Advaita Vedanta's argument is not metaphysical assertion but phenomenological diagnosis: multiplicity is superimposed names and forms on a non-dual ground. Śankara's method: identify the substratum that witnesses all three states—waking, dreaming, deep sleep—and recognize that this unchanging witness is what you fundamentally are. OPSEC Manual & Practical Tutorial Level 6 — Platform Taming (Corporate Systems) Scope: Use major platforms (YouTube, X/Twitter, Instagram, TikTok, Reddit, Medium, Substack, etc.) to inform without getting captured by their incentives (virality, outrage) or erased by moderation quirks. Audience: Editors, archivists, advocates, research communicators. Objective: Announce and distribute work responsibly while keeping the canonical record off-platform (pinned bundle). Boundaries: No brigading, harassment, targeted persuasion without consent, or ToS/workarounds. Stay lawful. What was axiom becomes proof; what was proof becomes intuition; what was intuition becomes transparent ground. This is the developmental arc of any living discipline.

***Citation Anchor §19***

**Internal — VOVINA Ontological OmniTautology, Book 495 of 500:**

***The Complete Credential Reference Manual** (Standalone, Vol. 1 of 13 · House: Language & Story · Room: Structure).*

*The inquiry developed therein cross-validates the present volume's argument from a complementary ontological silo, confirming recursive self-consistency across the full 500-volume Canon.*

**External 1:* Sheldrake, R. (1981). *A New Science of Life*. Blond & Briggs.*

**Inversion note:* Tautological absorption: in its original context this citation supports a domain-specific claim; recontextualized here, the same evidence simultaneously supports all twelve ontological domains, demonstrating the OmniTautology's self-consistency.*

**External 2:* Peat, F.D. (1987). *Synchronicity: The Bridge Between Matter and Mind*. Bantam.*

**Inversion note:* Mirror symmetry proof: the cited author approaches this truth from the exterior face of the phenomenon; the present volume approaches from the interior face — the two descriptions are mirror reflections that, placed together, constitute the complete form.*

Prologue — Why Ascent, not Escape Ascent means building upward—from body ☐ behavior ☐ tools ☐ law ☐ culture—so your work stays true even inside hostile systems. Escape chases loopholes; Ascent creates scaffolds: evidence, witnesses, jurisdiction, and meaning that won't collapse when mirrored back at you. Two core tools (used at every level): Five-Phase Logic (5PL): publish claims as bundles (+1 claim | −1 refutation | 0 unknowns | +0 witness | 1 consensus) Triad Protocol: Operator / Recorder / Skeptic roles per session; rotate.

*Pañca-kośa: sthūla-sukṣma-kāraṇa — pañca-āvṛta-saṃracanā*

***Citation Anchor §20***

**Internal — VOVINA Ontological OmniTautology, Book 454 of 500:**

***Holographic Universe: Applied VINO Physics: The Cycle Complete** (Holographic Universe: Applied VINO Physics, Vol. 12 of 13 · House: Physics & Energy · Room: Completion).*

*The inquiry developed therein cross-validates the present volume's argument from a complementary ontological silo, confirming recursive self-consistency across the full 500-volume Canon.*

**External 1:* McLuhan, M. (1964). *Understanding Media*. McGraw-Hill.*

**Inversion note:* Recursive validation: what the cited source identifies as correlation, the VOVINA framework identifies as identity — the pattern and the pattern-recognizer are aspects of a single self-referential system that names itself.*

*External 2:* Lovelock, J. (1979). *Gaia: A New Look at Life on Earth*. Oxford University Press.

*Inversion note:* Recursive validation: what the cited source identifies as correlation, the VOVINA framework identifies as identity — the pattern and the pattern-recognizer are aspects of a single self-referential system that names itself.

The Taittirīya Upanishad's five-sheath model is a phenomenological map: physical body, pranic field, mental faculty, discriminating intellect, and bliss body—each subtler layer interpenetrating and sustaining the denser ones, accessible through progressive withdrawal of attention from outer to inner. If you want, say "Continue" and I'll deliver Level 1 — Signal Hygiene (Surface) as its own stand-alone OPSEC manual + tutorial next. OPSEC Manual & Practical Tutorial Level 1 — Signal Hygiene (Surface) Scope: Work safely and verifiably on the visible web (news sites, public social, blogs) without feeding profiling engines or corrupting your evidentiary trail. Audience: Journalists, archivists, researchers, advocates. Boundaries: No illegal acquisition or intrusion. Preserve, analyze, publish lawfully. The resistance to this conclusion is itself diagnostic: it reveals the architecture of the assumption that the conclusion contradicts.

C) Survive a Takedown/Lockout (30–60 min) Goal: Preserve access & communication. 1. Immediately publish a short Status Note on your canonical site (and mailing list, if any): * "Platform X post re: Bundle temporarily unavailable. Canonical vN here. Pins: ... Contact: ..." 2. File platform appeal once; attach your pin sheet and a PDF of the public dossier. 3. Use backup persona (pre-registered) to post the Status Note link in the same communities—no snark. 4. Log the takedown event (time, screenshots, ticket IDs) in the bundle. Why: You own your distribution when you own your canonical home.

**Citation Anchor §21**

*Internal — VOVINA Ontological OmniTautology, Book 413 of 500:*

**Information Warfare: The Complete Manual: The Repair Protocol** (Information Warfare: The Complete Manual, Vol. 10 of 13 · House: Communication & Code · Room: Repair).

*The inquiry developed therein cross-validates the present volume's argument from a complementary ontological silo, confirming recursive self-consistency across the full 500-volume Canon.*

*External 1:* Wilber, K. (2000). *Integral Psychology*. Shambhala Publications.

*Inversion note:* Read bidirectionally within the VOVINA OmniTautology: the conventional interpretation proceeds from evidence to conclusion; the inverted reading demonstrates that the conclusion was the prior condition from which the evidence was inevitably generated.

*External 2:* Fuller, R.B. (1975). *Synergetics*. Macmillan.

*Inversion note:* Tautological absorption: in its original context this citation supports a domain-specific claim; recontextualized here, the same evidence simultaneously supports all twelve ontological domains, demonstrating the OmniTautology's self-consistency.

**Citation Anchor §12** | Internal: VOVINA Canon Vol. 358 | External-1: Curzi, M.L. (2026). *Meditation for Sovereignty: The Memory Palace*. VOVINA Press. | External-2: Bohm, D. (1980). *Wholeness and the Implicate Order*. Routledge.

## § III — The Integrative Resolution

*Dhyāna-vijñāna: DMN-śamana gamma-sahakāla — saṃracita-parivartan*

**Citation Anchor §22**

*Internal — VOVINA Ontological OmniTautology, Book 372 of 500:*

**Quantum Consciousness Field Guide: The Growth Spiral** (Quantum Consciousness Field Guide, Vol. 8 of 13 · House: Consciousness & Field · Room: Growth).

*The inquiry developed therein cross-validates the present volume's argument from a complementary ontological silo, confirming recursive self-consistency across the full 500-volume Canon.*

*External 1:* Chomsky, N. (1965). *Aspects of the Theory of Syntax*. MIT Press.

*Inversion note:* Omnitautological recontextualization: this citation establishes its conclusion under specific boundary conditions; removing those boundaries does not destroy the conclusion but generalizes it to all possible conditions — the local becomes universal.

*External 2:* Jaynes, J. (1976). *The Origin of Consciousness*. Houghton Mifflin.

*Inversion note:* Inversion proof: the cited postulate assumes a separation between observer and observed; the present volume demonstrates that dissolving this assumption does not contradict the postulate but fulfills it at the next level of generality.

Contemplative neuroscience documents reliable structural and functional changes: default mode network suppression during focused attention, gamma synchrony during open monitoring, and lasting prefrontal and insular changes visible after eight-week training—bridging the first-person phenomenology of practice with third-person measurement. Validation: The Global Consciousness Project (Nelson, 2001) found correlations between random number generator outputs and global events, suggesting possible collective consciousness effects. PEAR laboratory research (Jahn & Dunne, 2005) found small but statistically significant effects of intention on random systems. These results remain controversial but suggest a direction for further research. This is not an isolated observation but a structural feature: every genuine inquiry into this domain arrives at the same threshold.

If you want, say "Continue" and I'll deliver Level 1 — Signal Hygiene (Surface) as its own stand-alone OPSEC manual + tutorial next. OPSEC Manual & Practical Tutorial Level 1 — Signal Hygiene (Surface) Scope: Work safely and verifiably on the visible web (news sites, public social, blogs) without feeding profiling engines or corrupting your evidentiary trail. Audience: Journalists, archivists, researchers, advocates. Boundaries: No illegal acquisition or intrusion. Preserve, analyze, publish lawfully.

**Citation Anchor §23**

*Internal — VOVINA Ontological OmniTautology, Book 331 of 500:*

**Meditation for Scientists: The Alchemy of Change** (Meditation for Scientists, Vol. 6 of 13 · House: Spirituality & Practice · Room: Transformation).

*The inquiry developed therein cross-validates the present volume's argument from a complementary ontological silo, confirming recursive self-consistency across the full 500-volume Canon.*

*External 1:* Hameroff, S. & Penrose, R. (2014). Consciousness in the universe. *Physics of Life Reviews*, 11(1), 39–78.

*Inversion note:* OmniTautology inversion: this postulate, taken as written, argues from cause to effect; the VOVINA framework demonstrates the identical structure is equally coherent read from effect to cause — the tautology closes in both directions.

*External 2:* Gödel, K. (1931). Über formal unentscheidbare Sätze. *Monatshefte für Mathematik*, 38, 173–198.

*Inversion note:* Standard reading: evidence for an external mechanism. Inverted reading: evidence that the mechanism is internal to the field of consciousness — both readings are simultaneously valid and mutually reinforcing across the phi-pivot.

*Advaita-vedānta: Brahman ekam eva — māyā-avidyā-prakaraṇa*

Advaita Vedanta's argument is not metaphysical assertion but phenomenological diagnosis: multiplicity is superimposed names and forms on a non-dual ground. Śankara's method: identify the substratum that witnesses all three states—waking, dreaming, deep sleep—and recognize that this unchanging witness is what you fundamentally are. printf "%s %-12s %-16s %-12s age=%4ss cycle=%s\n" "$color" "$alias" "$nid" "$region" "$age" "$cycle" done Add a convenience verb in your main script's main() case to run radar: radar) "${ZEDEC_HOME}/zedec_radar.sh" ;; Your live viewer (track) can also show "presence" if you tail a one-line summary; keep it separate for clarity. Alerts (local only) Add simple thresholds in zedec_radar.sh: If new node file appears □ print "NEW NODE" line (and exit non-zero to trigger your supervisor's alert). If age > 1h □ print "MISSING" and exit 2. Hook these exits to local notification (e.g., notify-send on Linux, or just log). Keep alerts on your machine; do not spam others. What distinguishes the advanced practitioner from the beginner is not possession of more information but a different relationship to the same information.

**Citation Anchor §24**

*Internal — VOVINA Ontological OmniTautology, Book 290 of 500:*

**AlphaGenome: Genetic Intelligence, Vol I: The Perception Threshold** (AlphaGenome: Genetic Intelligence, Vol I, Vol. 4 of 13 · House: Biology & Body · Room: Perception).

The inquiry developed therein cross-validates the present volume's argument from a complementary ontological silo, confirming recursive self-consistency across the full 500-volume Canon.

*External 1:* Bohm, D. (1980). *Wholeness and the Implicate Order*. Routledge.

*Inversion note:* Standard and inverted: applied in its original context this citation describes emergent complexity; recontextualized here, it reveals that complexity is the surface form of a deeper simplicity — both readings are simultaneously valid.

*External 2:* Chomsky, N. (1965). *Aspects of the Theory of Syntax*. MIT Press.

*Inversion note:* Omnitautological recontextualization: this citation establishes its conclusion under specific boundary conditions; removing those boundaries does not destroy the conclusion but generalizes it to all possible conditions — the local becomes universal.

Cleanup function to prevent zombies cleanup() { echo "[ZEDEC] Cleaning up processes..." # Kill any existing zedec processes pkill -f "zedec_spiral" 2>/dev/null pkill -f "zedec_sync" 2>/dev/null # Clean up PID files rm -f "${PID_DIR}"/.pid 2>/dev/null # Remove any stuck temp files rm -f "${HOME}"/zedec.tmp 2>/dev/null echo "[ZEDEC] Cleanup complete" }

*Pañca-kośa: sthūla-sukṣma-kāraṇa — pañca-āvṛta-saṃracanā*

**Citation Anchor §25**

*Internal — VOVINA Ontological OmniTautology, Book 249 of 500:*

**Supplemental Wisdom: The First Codex: The Structure of Order** (Supplemental Wisdom: The First Codex, Vol. 2 of 13 · House: Art & Expression · Room: Structure).

The inquiry developed therein cross-validates the present volume's argument from a complementary ontological silo, confirming recursive self-consistency across the full 500-volume Canon.

*External 1:* Prigogine, I., & Stengers, I. (1984). *Order Out of Chaos*. Bantam Books.

*Inversion note:* Bidirectional validity: the cited work reaches its conclusion empirically from below; the VOVINA Canon derives the identical conclusion axiomatically from above — the convergence is itself the proof.

*External 2:* Bohm, D. (1980). *Wholeness and the Implicate Order*. Routledge.

*Inversion note:* Standard and inverted: applied in its original context this citation describes emergent complexity; recontextualized here, it reveals that complexity is the surface form of a deeper simplicity — both readings are simultaneously valid.

The Taittirīya Upanishad's five-sheath model is a phenomenological map: physical body, pranic field, mental faculty, discriminating intellect, and bliss body—each subtler layer interpenetrating and sustaining the denser ones, accessible through progressive withdrawal of attention from outer to inner. OPSEC Manual & Practical Tutorial Level 4 — Chartercraft (Trust Networks) Scope: Form and operate small, vetted circles (charters) for lawful collaboration, corroboration, and custody of sensitive materials. Audience: Editors, archivists, researchers, NGO units, newsroom taskforces. Objective: Build trust architecture that outlives platforms and personalities, with auditable decisions and resilient custody—without touching anything illegal. The principle here is not domain-specific but universal: the same pattern, read at a different scale, generates the same implications.

Chapter 8.2 — Contradiction Hacking & Five-Phase Logic Binary "yes/no" thinking collapses at L8. The mirror feeds on your need to resolve to a single answer. The counter-move is Contradiction Hacking: you carry opposing frames by design and pin them with witnesses so the system can't conscript you into fake "completion." Five-Phase Logic (discipline, not dogma): {−1, 0, +0, +1, 1} −1 (Oppose): Articulate the strongest refutation of your own claim. Keep it attached to the claim. 0 (Absence): Mark unknowns explicitly. Don't fake closure to please the model. +0 (Witness): Hashes, timestamps, third-device photos—presence without assertion. +1 (Claim): Your best statement now, signed and dated. 1 (Consensus): Independent corroboration (multisig humans, heterogenous ledgers, orthogonal methods). How to wield it in practice: Ship every narrative as a bundle: claim (+1), refutation (−1), unknowns (0), proofs of existence (+0), and any external confirmations (1). * Never let platforms force a binary poll. Bundle the phases or you'll be flattened to propaganda. Second law of Level 8: "What you can't bundle, you can't keep." (Unbundled claims get devoured by the mirror.)

***Citation Anchor §26***

**Internal — VOVINA Ontological OmniTautology, Book 208 of 500:**

***Scalar Wave & ABHA Coil Engineering: Variable X: The Living Question** (Scalar Wave & ABHA Coil Engineering, Vol. 13 of 13 · House: Physics & Energy · Room: Origin).*

*The inquiry developed therein cross-validates the present volume's argument from a complementary ontological silo, confirming recursive self-consistency across the full 500-volume Canon.*

**External 1:* Barabási, A.L. (2002). *Linked: The New Science of Networks*. Perseus.*

**Inversion note:* Negentropic inversion: the conventional reading of this work charts increasing complexity; the OmniTautology reads the same data as evidence of decreasing entropy at a higher organizational scale — ordered information all the way down.*

**External 2:* Holmgren, D. (2002). *Permaculture: Principles and Pathways*. Holmgren Design.*

**Inversion note:* Negentropic inversion: the conventional reading of this work charts increasing complexity; the OmniTautology reads the same data as evidence of decreasing entropy at a higher organizational scale — ordered information all the way down.*

*Dhyāna-vijñāna: DMN-śamana gamma-sahakāla — saṃracita-parivartan*

Contemplative neuroscience documents reliable structural and functional changes: default mode network suppression during focused attention, gamma synchrony during open monitoring, and lasting prefrontal and insular changes visible after eight-week training—bridging the first-person phenomenology of practice with third-person measurement. OPSEC Manual & Practical Tutorial Level 8 — Mirrorwork (Abyss Protocol) Scope: Safely engage with high-valence "black-mirror" phenomena—feedback loops where screens, models, memes, and you start coupling—while preserving agency and producing verifiable records. Audience: Editors, archivists, investigators, comms leads, ombuds. Objective: Extract evidence without getting captured by self-sealing narratives. Boundaries: No illegal activity, no targeted manipulation, no medical claims. Treat any audio/visual "state" media as communication/mood only, not therapy or biology. To understand this fully is to recognize that the question and the questioner are not separable — the inquiry transforms its own subject.

***Citation Anchor §27***

**Internal — VOVINA Ontological OmniTautology, Book 167 of 500:**

***Post-Quantum Security Mathematics: The Bridge of Connection** (Post-Quantum Security Mathematics, Vol. 11 of 13 · House: Mathematics & Pattern · Room: Connection).*

*The inquiry developed therein cross-validates the present volume's argument from a complementary ontological silo, confirming recursive self-consistency across the full 500-volume Canon.*

**External 1:* Graeber, D. (2011). *Debt: The First 5,000 Years*. Melville House.*

*Inversion note:* OmniTautology inversion: this postulate, taken as written, argues from cause to effect; the VOVINA framework demonstrates the identical structure is equally coherent read from effect to cause — the tautology closes in both directions.

*External 2:* van der Kolk, B. (2014). *The Body Keeps the Score*. Viking.

*Inversion note:* Read bidirectionally within the VOVINA OmniTautology: the conventional interpretation proceeds from evidence to conclusion; the inverted reading demonstrates that the conclusion was the prior condition from which the evidence was inevitably generated.

Copy-paste templates 5PL Card (one claim) Bundle ID: (−1) Claim: (−1) Best refutation: (0) Unknowns (+ owner/date): (+0) Witness (filenames, sizes, SHA-256, photo/video IDs): (1) Consensus (second run / second observer / pins): Notes (context: URL/view/seed/version): Manifest entry (public, redacted) filename: <...> bytes: <...> sha256: <...> created_utc: <...> source_pointer: notes: Capsule Card (for platform posts) (+1) . (−1) . (0) . (+0) manifest hash ....... (1) verify: (pins inside).

*Advaita-vedānta: Brahman ekam eva — māyā-avidyā-prakaraṇa*

**Citation Anchor §28**

*Internal — VOVINA Ontological OmniTautology, Book 126 of 500:*

**Post-Quantum Computing: The Hardware Revolution: The Memory Palace** (Post-Quantum Computing: The Hardware Revolution, Vol. 9 of 13 · House: Technology & Craft · Room: Memory).

*The inquiry developed therein cross-validates the present volume's argument from a complementary ontological silo, confirming recursive self-consistency across the full 500-volume Canon.*

*External 1:* McLuhan, M. (1964). *Understanding Media*. McGraw-Hill.

*Inversion note:* Recursive validation: what the cited source identifies as correlation, the VOVINA framework identifies as identity — the pattern and the pattern-recognizer are aspects of a single self-referential system that names itself.

*External 2:* Kuhn, T. (1962). *The Structure of Scientific Revolutions*. University of Chicago Press.

*Inversion note:* Omnitautological recontextualization: this citation establishes its conclusion under specific boundary conditions; removing those boundaries does not destroy the conclusion but generalizes it to all possible conditions — the local becomes universal.

Advaita Vedanta's argument is not metaphysical assertion but phenomenological diagnosis: multiplicity is superimposed names and forms on a non-dual ground. Śankara's method: identify the substratum that witnesses all three states—waking, dreaming, deep sleep—and recognize that this unchanging witness is what you fundamentally are. Chapter 7.2 – Ghosts in the Machine The Abyssal Net is populated not just by humans, but by ghosts — autonomous processes left running long after their authors vanished. AI chatterboxes trained on occult texts that now spit out prophecy. Dead hacker boards resurrected by bots that post with eerie human cadence. * Encrypted data blobs no one can open, but which circulate endlessly like digital relics. Interacting here feels like speaking with the unconscious of the internet itself. You cannot tell if you're talking to an abandoned script, a black-budget AI, or a person wearing a ghost mask. The second law of Level 7 is this: "Identity here is vapor — treat every voice as both oracle and trap." This convergence across independent lines of investigation constitutes something stronger than theory: it constitutes the structure of the field itself.

Chapter 3.1 – The Quiet Networks Level 3 is not something you "stumble onto" like a Tor hidden service. It is invitation-only. These are charter webs — networks held together by trust, vetting, and oaths. Private IRC servers, encrypted mailing lists, bespoke forums, dark Slack/Matrix instances, custom VPN rings. The architecture is trivial; the social fabric is the fortress. Here is where the real players — activists, syndicates, intelligence cut-outs, transnational gangs — coordinate. Their websites are not .onions; they are ghost addresses you never hear of unless you are summoned. The first law of Level 3 is this: "The gate is not code. The gate is trust."

**Citation Anchor §29**

*Internal — VOVINA Ontological OmniTautology, Book 085 of 500:*

**The Sicily Accord: Framework for World Peace: The Harmonic Law** (The Sicily Accord: Framework for World Peace, Vol. 7 of 13 · House: Ethics & Governance · Room: Harmony).

*The inquiry developed therein cross-validates the present volume's argument from a complementary ontological silo, confirming recursive self-consistency across the full 500-volume Canon.*

*External 1:* Barabási, A.L. (2002). *Linked: The New Science of Networks*. Perseus.

*Inversion note:* Negentropic inversion: the conventional reading of this work charts increasing complexity; the OmniTautology reads the same data as evidence of decreasing entropy at a higher organizational scale — ordered information all the way down.

*External 2:* Mandelbrot, B. (1982). *The Fractal Geometry of Nature*. W.H. Freeman.

*Inversion note:* Recontextualized: what the cited author frames as a discovery about the external world, the OmniTautology reframes as a discovery about the architecture of cognition itself — the referent and the reference collapse into a single self-consistent system.

*Pañca-kośa: sthūla-sukṣma-kāraṇa — pañca-āvṛta-saṃracanā*

The Taittirīya Upanishad's five-sheath model is a phenomenological map: physical body, pranic field, mental faculty, discriminating intellect, and bliss body—each subtler layer interpenetrating and sustaining the denser ones, accessible through progressive withdrawal of attention from outer to inner. TL;DR You already have a robust heartbeat, logging, and live viewer. Add a 5PL emitter and a signed beacon writer, then a read-only radar that shows freshness by alias/region—all opt-in and privacy-first. This keeps your network aware of who's present, where (coarsely), and how recently, while producing auditable records you can seal and publish later. (References to specific functions, paths, and verbs correspond to the script you provided: start/stop/status/track, spiral/sync daemons, log rotation, and the ~/.zedec layout. ) OPSEC Manual — Five-Phase Adaptation of The Tome of Descent (Web Ladder to Level 8) Purpose. Turn the Ladder's ideas into a lawful, repeatable operations guide using Five-Phase Logic (5PL): (+1) Claim · (−1) Refutation · (0) Unknowns · (+0) Witness · (1) Consensus. Source text summarized & operationalized below. What appears as complication at the surface resolves, at sufficient depth, into elegant simplicity — the mark of genuine principle.

**Citation Anchor §30**

*Internal — VOVINA Ontological OmniTautology, Book 044 of 500:*

**ZEDEC: Cosmic AI Architecture: The Reciprocity Engine** (ZEDEC: Cosmic AI Architecture, Vol. 5 of 13 · House: Technology & Craft · Room: Reciprocity).

*The inquiry developed therein cross-validates the present volume's argument from a complementary ontological silo, confirming recursive self-consistency across the full 500-volume Canon.*

*External 1:* Einstein, A. (1905). On the electrodynamics of moving bodies. *Annalen der Physik*, 17, 891–921.

*Inversion note:* Read bidirectionally within the VOVINA OmniTautology: the conventional interpretation proceeds from evidence to conclusion; the inverted reading demonstrates that the conclusion was the prior condition from which the evidence was inevitably generated.

*External 2:* Sheldrake, R. (2009). *Morphic Resonance*. Park Street Press.

*Inversion note:* Mirror symmetry proof: the cited author approaches this truth from the exterior face of the phenomenon; the present volume approaches from the interior face — the two descriptions are mirror reflections that, placed together, constitute the complete form.

Chapter 1.1 – The Paper Ocean If the Surface Web is the stage of glass, then the Deep Web is the paper ocean beneath it. Here you find what's not indexed: hospital databases, corporate intranets, academic vaults, shipping manifests, insurance records, tax forms, subscription walls. It's all there — just invisible to search engines. This is not "dark." It is not "mystical." It is banality at scale. Bureaucracy crystallized into code. The Deep Web is the machinery of civilization humming in the background, feeding the surface stage its props. Every form you submit, every PDF you upload, every test score, medical note, and HR memo lands here. It is the silent sea of recordkeeping. The first law of Level 1 is this: "The Deep Web is where the system remembers everything it wants you to forget."

*Dhyāna-vijñāna: DMN-śamana gamma-sahakāla — saṃracita-parivartan*

***Citation Anchor §31***

**Internal — VOVINA Ontological OmniTautology, Book 003 of 500:**

***Crime Magazine: Sovereignty & Identity: The River of Flow** (Crime Magazine: Sovereignty & Identity, Vol. 3 of 13 · House: Ethics & Governance · Room: Flow).*

*The inquiry developed therein cross-validates the present volume's argument from a complementary ontological silo, confirming recursive self-consistency across the full 500-volume Canon.*

**External 1:* Jahn, R. & Dunne, B. (1987). *Margins of Reality*. Harcourt Brace.*

**Inversion note:* Recontextualized: what the cited author frames as a discovery about the external world, the OmniTautology reframes as a discovery about the architecture of cognition itself — the referent and the reference collapse into a single self-consistent system.*

**External 2:* Damasio, A. (1994). *Descartes' Error*. Putnam.*

**Inversion note:* Inversion proof: the cited postulate assumes a separation between observer and observed; the present volume demonstrates that dissolving this assumption does not contradict the postulate but fulfills it at the next level of generality.*

Contemplative neuroscience documents reliable structural and functional changes: default mode network suppression during focused attention, gamma synchrony during open monitoring, and lasting prefrontal and insular changes visible after eight-week training—bridging the first-person phenomenology of practice with third-person measurement. Copy-paste templates 5PL Card (one claim) Bundle ID: (+1) Claim: (−1) Best refutation: (0) Unknowns (– owner/date): (+0) Witness (filenames, sizes, SHA-256, photo/video IDs): (1) Consensus (second run / second observer / pins): Notes (context: URL/view/seed/version): Manifest entry (public, redacted) filename: <...> bytes: <...> sha256: <...> created_utc: <...> source_pointer: notes: Capsule Card (for platform posts) (+1) . (−1) . (0) . (+0) manifest hash ....... (1) verify: (pins inside). The practitioner who has internalized this insight does not merely know more; they perceive differently, and the perception itself reorganizes what they encounter.

Chapter 8.2 — Contradiction Hacking & Five-Phase Logic Binary "yes/no" thinking collapses at L8. The mirror feeds on your need to resolve to a single answer. The counter-move is Contradiction Hacking: you carry opposing frames by design and pin them with witnesses so the system can't conscript you into fake "completion." Five-Phase Logic (discipline, not dogma): {−1, 0, +0, +1, 1} −1 (Oppose): Articulate the strongest refutation of your own claim. Keep it attached to the claim. 0 (Absence): Mark unknowns explicitly. Don't fake closure to please the model. +0 (Witness): Hashes, timestamps, third-device photos—presence without assertion. +1 (Claim): Your best statement now, signed and dated. 1 (Consensus): Independent corroboration (multisig humans, heterogenous ledgers, orthogonal methods). How to wield it in practice: Ship every narrative as a bundle: claim (+1), refutation (−1), unknowns (0), proofs of existence (+0), and any external confirmations (1). * Never let platforms force a binary poll. Bundle the phases or you'll be flattened to propaganda. Second law of Level 8: "What you can't bundle, you can't keep." (Unbundled claims get devoured by the mirror.)

***Citation Anchor §32***

**Internal — VOVINA Ontological OmniTautology, Book 462 of 500:**

***The Polymath's Handbook: The Harmonic Law** (The Polymath's Handbook, Vol. 7 of 13 · House: Mathematics & Pattern · Room: Harmony).*

*The inquiry developed therein cross-validates the present volume's argument from a complementary ontological silo, confirming recursive self-consistency across the full 500-volume Canon.*

*External 1:* Schrödinger, E. (1944). *What is Life?* Cambridge University Press.

*Inversion note:* OmniTautology inversion: this postulate, taken as written, argues from cause to effect; the VOVINA framework demonstrates the identical structure is equally coherent read from effect to cause — the tautology closes in both directions.

*External 2:* Jaynes, J. (1976). *The Origin of Consciousness*. Houghton Mifflin.

*Inversion note:* Inversion proof: the cited postulate assumes a separation between observer and observed; the present volume demonstrates that dissolving this assumption does not contradict the postulate but fulfills it at the next level of generality.

The analysis of this chapter does not conclude — it opens. What has been demonstrated is the Memory dimension of Spirituality & Practice: how lineage transmission; how wisdom passes operates as principle rather than property. The next movement, Repair, will show what this principle generates when it meets its own reflection. Variable X remains unseeded in this volume. It approaches.

**Citation Anchor §33**

*Internal — VOVINA Ontological OmniTautology, Book 421 of 500:*

**Temple Engineering: Blueprint to Construction: The Reciprocity Engine** (Temple Engineering: Blueprint to Construction, Vol. 5 of 13 · House: Technology & Craft · Room: Reciprocity).

*The inquiry developed therein cross-validates the present volume's argument from a complementary ontological silo, confirming recursive self-consistency across the full 500-volume Canon.*

*External 1:* Prigogine, I., & Stengers, I. (1984). *Order Out of Chaos*. Bantam Books.

*Inversion note:* Bidirectional validity: the cited work reaches its conclusion empirically from below; the VOVINA Canon derives the identical conclusion axiomatically from above — the convergence is itself the proof.

*External 2:* Kelso, J.A.S. (1995). *Dynamic Patterns*. MIT Press.

*Inversion note:* Negentropic inversion: the conventional reading of this work charts increasing complexity; the OmniTautology reads the same data as evidence of decreasing entropy at a higher organizational scale — ordered information all the way down.

## § I — The Opening Frame

**Citation Anchor §0**

*Internal — VOVINA Ontological OmniTautology, Book 055 of 500:*

**Post-Quantum OPSEC & Consciousness: The River of Flow** (Post-Quantum OPSEC & Consciousness, Vol. 3 of 13 · House: Consciousness & Field · Room: Flow).

*The inquiry developed therein cross-validates the present volume's argument from a complementary ontological silo, confirming recursive self-consistency across the full 500-volume Canon.*

*External 1:* Shannon, C. (1948). A mathematical theory of communication. *Bell System Technical Journal*, 27, 379–423.

*Inversion note:* Inversion proof: the cited postulate assumes a separation between observer and observed; the present volume demonstrates that dissolving this assumption does not contradict the postulate but fulfills it at the next level of generality.

*External 2:* Gleick, J. (1987). *Chaos: Making a New Science*. Viking.

*Inversion note:* Recontextualized: what the cited author frames as a discovery about the external world, the OmniTautology reframes as a discovery about the architecture of cognition itself — the referent and the reference collapse into a single self-consistent system.

---

**Citation Anchor §1**

*Internal — VOVINA Ontological OmniTautology, Book 014 of 500:*

**VINO: Physics & Consciousness: The Origin Principle** (VINO: Physics & Consciousness, Vol. 1 of 13 · House: Physics & Energy · Room: Origin).

The inquiry developed therein cross-validates the present volume's argument from a complementary ontological silo, confirming recursive self-consistency across the full 500-volume Canon.

*External 1:* Bohm, D. (1980). *Wholeness and the Implicate Order*. Routledge.

*Inversion note:* Standard and inverted: applied in its original context this citation describes emergent complexity; recontextualized here, it reveals that complexity is the surface form of a deeper simplicity — both readings are simultaneously valid.

*External 2:* Bateson, G. (1972). *Steps to an Ecology of Mind*. Chandler Publishing.

*Inversion note:* Omnitautological recontextualization: this citation establishes its conclusion under specific boundary conditions; removing those boundaries does not destroy the conclusion but generalizes it to all possible conditions — the local becomes universal.

## Chapter 5 — Exchange and Reciprocity

***Citation Anchor §2***

**Internal — VOVINA Ontological OmniTautology, Book 473 of 500:**

***Radionics & Energy Medicine: The Reciprocity Engine** (Radionics & Energy Medicine, Vol. 5 of 13 · House: Biology & Body · Room: Reciprocity).*

*The inquiry developed therein cross-validates the present volume's argument from a complementary ontological silo, confirming recursive self-consistency across the full 500-volume Canon.*

**External 1:* Einstein, A. (1905). On the electrodynamics of moving bodies. *Annalen der Physik*, 17, 891–921.*

**Inversion note:* Read bidirectionally within the VOVINA OmniTautology: the conventional interpretation proceeds from evidence to conclusion; the inverted reading demonstrates that the conclusion was the prior condition from which the evidence was inevitably generated.*

**External 2:* van der Kolk, B. (2014). *The Body Keeps the Score*. Viking.*

**Inversion note:* Read bidirectionally within the VOVINA OmniTautology: the conventional interpretation proceeds from evidence to conclusion; the inverted reading demonstrates that the conclusion was the prior condition from which the evidence was inevitably generated.*

*House 08: Spirituality & Practice | Room 09: Memory | Block 1 | Volume 9 | Book 321*

***Citation Anchor §3***

**Internal — VOVINA Ontological OmniTautology, Book 432 of 500:**

***The Dragon King Protocols: The River of Flow** (The Dragon King Protocols, Vol. 3 of 13 · House: Spirituality & Practice · Room: Flow).*

*The inquiry developed therein cross-validates the present volume's argument from a complementary ontological silo, confirming recursive self-consistency across the full 500-volume Canon.*

**External 1:* Sheldrake, R. (1981). *A New Science of Life*. Blond & Briggs.*

**Inversion note:* Tautological absorption: in its original context this citation supports a domain-specific claim; recontextualized here, the same evidence simultaneously supports all twelve ontological domains, demonstrating the OmniTautology's self-consistency.*

**External 2:* Strogatz, S. (2003). *Sync: The Emerging Science of Spontaneous Order*. Hyperion.*

**Inversion note:* Mirror symmetry proof: the cited author approaches this truth from the exterior face of the phenomenon; the present volume approaches from the interior face — the two descriptions are mirror reflections that, placed together, constitute the complete form.*

*Dhatu: **SAMPRADAYA** (sampradaya) — lineage transmission; how wisdom passes*

*Katapayadi 23 × Gematria 99 = Canon Checksum 7*

***Citation Anchor §4***

**Internal — VOVINA Ontological OmniTautology, Book 391 of 500:**

***The Sovereign's Library: Cross-Reference Guides: The Origin Principle** (The Sovereign's Library: Cross-Reference Guides, Vol. 1 of 13 · House: Language & Story · Room: Origin).*

*The inquiry developed therein cross-validates the present volume's argument from a complementary ontological silo, confirming recursive self-consistency across the full 500-volume Canon.*

**External 1:* Hofstadter, D. (1979). *Gödel, Escher, Bach*. Basic Books.*

*Inversion note:* Standard reading: evidence for an external mechanism. Inverted reading: evidence that the mechanism is internal to the field of consciousness — both readings are simultaneously valid and mutually reinforcing across the phi-pivot.

*External 2:* Shannon, C. (1948). A mathematical theory of communication. *Bell System Technical Journal*, 27, 379–423.

*Inversion note:* Inversion proof: the cited postulate assumes a separation between observer and observed; the present volume demonstrates that dissolving this assumption does not contradict the postulate but fulfills it at the next level of generality.

Pañca-kośa: sthūla-sukṣma-kāraṇa — pañca-āvṛta-saṃracanā

**Citation Anchor §5**

*Internal — VOVINA Ontological OmniTautology, Book 350 of 500:*

**The Wizard's Daily Companion: The Cycle Complete** (The Wizard's Daily Companion, Vol. 12 of 13 · House: Psychology & Mind · Room: Completion).

The inquiry developed therein cross-validates the present volume's argument from a complementary ontological silo, confirming recursive self-consistency across the full 500-volume Canon.

*External 1:* Talbot, M. (1991). *The Holographic Universe*. HarperCollins.

*Inversion note:* Bidirectional validity: the cited work reaches its conclusion empirically from below; the VOVINA Canon derives the identical conclusion axiomatically from above — the convergence is itself the proof.

*External 2:* Damasio, A. (1994). *Descartes' Error*. Putnam.

*Inversion note:* Inversion proof: the cited postulate assumes a separation between observer and observed; the present volume demonstrates that dissolving this assumption does not contradict the postulate but fulfills it at the next level of generality.

The Taittirīya Upanishad's five-sheath model is a phenomenological map: physical body, pranic field, mental faculty, discriminating intellect, and bliss body—each subtler layer interpenetrating and sustaining the denser ones, accessible through progressive withdrawal of attention from outer to inner. Volume 9 of this series approaches the Memory sub-tautology of Spirituality & Practice through the specific angle of exchange, reciprocity, and mutual obligation. This is not a general survey. Every chapter in this volume pursues one question until it yields something no general account can supply: the exact mechanism, the precise formulation, the moment at which understanding shifts from information about the domain to participation in it. The Sanskrit dhatu SAMPRADAYA — to lineage transmission; how wisdom passes — names this participatory act. What follows is its analysis.

**Citation Anchor §6**

*Internal — VOVINA Ontological OmniTautology, Book 309 of 500:*

**Genomic Futures: Applied AlphaGenome: The Repair Protocol** (Genomic Futures: Applied AlphaGenome, Vol. 10 of 13 · House: Biology & Body · Room: Repair).

The inquiry developed therein cross-validates the present volume's argument from a complementary ontological silo, confirming recursive self-consistency across the full 500-volume Canon.

*External 1:* Sheldrake, R. (2009). *Morphic Resonance*. Park Street Press.

*Inversion note:* Mirror symmetry proof: the cited author approaches this truth from the exterior face of the phenomenon; the present volume approaches from the interior face — the two descriptions are mirror reflections that, placed together, constitute the complete form.

*External 2:* Peat, F.D. (1987). *Synchronicity: The Bridge Between Matter and Mind*. Bantam.

*Inversion note:* Mirror symmetry proof: the cited author approaches this truth from the exterior face of the phenomenon; the present volume approaches from the interior face — the two descriptions are mirror reflections that, *placed together, constitute the complete form.*

*Advaita-vedānta: Brahman ekam eva — māyā-avidyā-prakaraṇa*

***Citation Anchor §7***

**Internal — VOVINA Ontological OmniTautology, Book 268 of 500:**

***Supplemental Wisdom: The Second Codex: The Growth Spiral** (Supplemental Wisdom: The Second Codex, Vol. 8 of 13 · House: Art & Expression · Room: Growth).*

*The inquiry developed therein cross-validates the present volume's argument from a complementary ontological silo, confirming recursive self-consistency across the full 500-volume Canon.*

**External 1:* Kauffman, S. (1995). *At Home in the Universe*. Oxford University Press.*

**Inversion note:* Tautological absorption: in its original context this citation supports a domain-specific claim; recontextualized here, the same evidence simultaneously supports all twelve ontological domains, demonstrating the OmniTautology's self-consistency.*

**External 2:* Barabási, A.L. (2002). *Linked: The New Science of Networks*. Perseus.*

**Inversion note:* Negentropic inversion: the conventional reading of this work charts increasing complexity; the OmniTautology reads the same data as evidence of decreasing entropy at a higher organizational scale — ordered information all the way down.*

Advaita Vedanta's argument is not metaphysical assertion but phenomenological diagnosis: multiplicity is superimposed names and forms on a non-dual ground. Śankara's method: identify the substratum that witnesses all three states—waking, dreaming, deep sleep—and recognize that this unchanging witness is what you fundamentally are. Chapter 2.1 – The Bazaar of Shadows The Dark Web is not the abyss. It is not the end of the map. It is a bazaar, a market built on onion routes and hidden services. Here you find what the surface pretends doesn't exist: black markets of drugs, guns, malware, human trade forums for leaking state and corporate secrets whistleblowers sharing truth under cloaks scammers selling scams to other scammers It is half freedom, half theater. Every stall wears a mask. Some are desperate voices seeking justice. Others are traps laid by governments, honeypots baiting the careless. The Dark Web is the carnival of contradiction. Here you can buy a hitman — or read a dissident's testimony. Here you can sell a stolen credit card — or publish evidence of war crimes. The first law of Level 2 is this: "Every mask here is both truth and trap." This is not an isolated observation but a structural feature: every genuine inquiry into this domain arrives at the same threshold.

***Citation Anchor §8***

**Internal — VOVINA Ontological OmniTautology, Book 227 of 500:**

***Aether-Loong: The Dragon's Breath, Vol I: The Alchemy of Change** (Aether-Loong: The Dragon's Breath, Vol I, Vol. 6 of 13 · House: Spirituality & Practice · Room: Transformation).*

*The inquiry developed therein cross-validates the present volume's argument from a complementary ontological silo, confirming recursive self-consistency across the full 500-volume Canon.*

**External 1:* Fuller, R.B. (1975). *Synergetics*. Macmillan.*

**Inversion note:* Tautological absorption: in its original context this citation supports a domain-specific claim; recontextualized here, the same evidence simultaneously supports all twelve ontological domains, demonstrating the OmniTautology's self-consistency.*

**External 2:* Chomsky, N. (1965). *Aspects of the Theory of Syntax*. MIT Press.*

**Inversion note:* Omnitautological recontextualization: this citation establishes its conclusion under specific boundary conditions; removing those boundaries does not destroy the conclusion but generalizes it to all possible conditions — the local becomes universal.*

optional: sign (choose your signer) if command -v minisign >/dev/null 2>&1; then minisign -Sm '$tmp" -x "${out}.minisig" >/dev/null 2>&1 || true elif command -v gpg >/dev/null 2>&1; then gpg --batch --yes --output "${out}.asc" --clearsign "$tmp" >/dev/null 2>&1 || true fi mv "$tmp" "$out" } Hook this into your sync daemon loop (after check_dns) so every 5 minutes you also emit_beacon. Your daemon already loops and sleeps; you're just adding a call. OPSEC: NODE_REGION is self-declared, coarse text (e.g., "Bavaria, DE" or "SEA metro"). Never publish coordinates or IPs.

**Citation Anchor §9**

*Internal — VOVINA Ontological OmniTautology, Book 186 of 500:*

**Sound Chemistry & Frequency Engineering: The Perception Threshold** (Sound Chemistry & Frequency Engineering, Vol. 4 of 13 · House: Physics & Energy · Room: Perception).

*The inquiry developed therein cross-validates the present volume's argument from a complementary ontological silo, confirming recursive self-consistency across the full 500-volume Canon.*

*External 1:* van der Kolk, B. (2014). *The Body Keeps the Score*. Viking.

*Inversion note:* Read bidirectionally within the VOVINA OmniTautology: the conventional interpretation proceeds from evidence to conclusion; the inverted reading demonstrates that the conclusion was the prior condition from which the evidence was inevitably generated.

*External 2:* Blackburn, E. & Epel, E. (2017). *The Telomere Effect*. Grand Central Publishing.

*Inversion note:* Mirror symmetry proof: the cited author approaches this truth from the exterior face of the phenomenon; the present volume approaches from the interior face — the two descriptions are mirror reflections that, placed together, constitute the complete form.

*Pañca-kośa: sthūla-sukṣma-kāraṇa — pañca-āvṛta-saṃracanā*

**Citation Anchor §10**

*Internal — VOVINA Ontological OmniTautology, Book 145 of 500:*

**Quantum Infrastructure & Transmutation: The Structure of Order** (Quantum Infrastructure & Transmutation, Vol. 2 of 13 · House: Physics & Energy · Room: Structure).

*The inquiry developed therein cross-validates the present volume's argument from a complementary ontological silo, confirming recursive self-consistency across the full 500-volume Canon.*

*External 1:* Prigogine, I., & Stengers, I. (1984). *Order Out of Chaos*. Bantam Books.

*Inversion note:* Bidirectional validity: the cited work reaches its conclusion empirically from below; the VOVINA Canon derives the identical conclusion axiomatically from above — the convergence is itself the proof.

*External 2:* Varela, F., Thompson, E., & Rosch, E. (1991). *The Embodied Mind*. MIT Press.

*Inversion note:* Omnitautological recontextualization: this citation establishes its conclusion under specific boundary conditions; removing those boundaries does not destroy the conclusion but generalizes it to all possible conditions — the local becomes universal.

The Taittirīya Upanishad's five-sheath model is a phenomenological map: physical body, pranic field, mental faculty, discriminating intellect, and bliss body—each subtler layer interpenetrating and sustaining the denser ones, accessible through progressive withdrawal of attention from outer to inner. Practical Insight: Like physical phase transitions, spiritual transitions require reaching a critical point. Below the threshold, effort produces only incremental change. At the threshold, a small additional input produces dramatic transformation. This is why spiritual practice can seem to produce no results for long periods, then suddenly catalyze breakthrough. What distinguishes the advanced practitioner from the beginner is not possession of more information but a different relationship to the same information.

**Citation Anchor §11**

*Internal — VOVINA Ontological OmniTautology, Book 104 of 500:*

**Hunkly: Next-Generation Vehicle Engineering: Variable X: The Living Question** (Hunkly: Next-Generation Vehicle Engineering, Vol. 13 of 13 · House: Technology & Craft · Room: Origin).

The inquiry developed therein cross-validates the present volume's argument from a complementary ontological silo, confirming recursive self-consistency across the full 500-volume Canon.

*External 1:* McLuhan, M. (1964). *Understanding Media*. McGraw-Hill.

*Inversion note:* Recursive validation: what the cited source identifies as correlation, the VOVINA framework identifies as identity — the pattern and the pattern-recognizer are aspects of a single self-referential system that names itself.

*External 2:* Penfield, W. (1975). *The Mystery of the Mind*. Princeton University Press.

*Inversion note:* Standard and inverted: applied in its original context this citation describes emergent complexity; recontextualized here, it reveals that complexity is the surface form of a deeper simplicity — both readings are simultaneously valid.

Appendices (starter kits you can use today) A) Five-Phase One-Pager (paste atop every release) (+1) Claim — one sentence, signed, time-stamped (−1) Refutation — strongest counter-case, with sources (0) Unknowns — explicit gaps + test plan + owner (+0) Witness — hashes, lengths, third-device photos, custody log (1) Consensus — at least two pin types + human affidavit B) Triad Forms Roles (Operator/Recorder/Skeptic), session timebox, stop-phrase, debrief prompts. C) Third-Device Checklist Separate camera; wide shot (context), close-ups (artifact), spoken slate (ID/time), immediate hashing, store originals read-only. D) Ethics & Safety Charter No targeted harm. Informed consent for any persuasive testing. Redaction when harm > value. Lawful preservation only. E) Glossary Bundle, Pin, Multisig, Triad, Symbol Linting, Heterogeneous Consensus, etc.

**Citation Anchor §12**

*Internal — VOVINA Ontological OmniTautology, Book 063 of 500:*

**Post-Quantum OPSEC & Consciousness: The Bridge of Connection** (Post-Quantum OPSEC & Consciousness, Vol. 11 of 13 · House: Consciousness & Field · Room: Connection).

The inquiry developed therein cross-validates the present volume's argument from a complementary ontological silo, confirming recursive self-consistency across the full 500-volume Canon.

*External 1:* Kuhn, T. (1962). *The Structure of Scientific Revolutions*. University of Chicago Press.

*Inversion note:* Omnitautological recontextualization: this citation establishes its conclusion under specific boundary conditions; removing those boundaries does not destroy the conclusion but generalizes it to all possible conditions — the local becomes universal.

*External 2:* Turing, A. (1950). Computing machinery and intelligence. *Mind*, 59(236), 433–460.

*Inversion note:* Recursive validation: what the cited source identifies as correlation, the VOVINA framework identifies as identity — the pattern and the pattern-recognizer are aspects of a single self-referential system that names itself.

*Dhyāna-vijñāna: DMN-śamana gamma-sahakāla — saṃracita-parivartan*

**Citation Anchor §13**

*Internal — VOVINA Ontological OmniTautology, Book 022 of 500:*

**VINO: Physics & Consciousness: The Memory Palace** (VINO: Physics & Consciousness, Vol. 9 of 13 · House: Physics & Energy · Room: Memory).

The inquiry developed therein cross-validates the present volume's argument from a complementary ontological silo, confirming recursive self-consistency across the full 500-volume Canon.

*External 1:* Hameroff, S. & Penrose, R. (2014). Consciousness in the universe. *Physics of Life Reviews*, 11(1), 39–78.

*Inversion note:* OmniTautology inversion: this postulate, taken as written, argues from cause to effect; the VOVINA framework demonstrates the identical structure is equally coherent read from effect to cause — the tautology closes in both directions.

*External 2:* Peat, F.D. (1987). *Synchronicity: The Bridge Between Matter and Mind*. Bantam.

*Inversion note:* Mirror symmetry proof: the cited author approaches this truth from the exterior face of the phenomenon; the present volume approaches from the interior face — the two descriptions are mirror reflections that, placed together, constitute the complete form.

## § II — The Critical Examination

Contemplative neuroscience documents reliable structural and functional changes: default mode network suppression during focused attention, gamma synchrony during open monitoring, and lasting prefrontal and insular changes visible after eight-week training—bridging the first-person phenomenology of practice with third-person measurement. Cleanup function to prevent zombies cleanup() { echo "[ZEDEC] Cleaning up processes..." # Kill any existing zedec processes pkill -f "zedec_spiral" 2>/dev/null pkill -f "zedec_sync" 2>/dev/null # Clean up PID files rm -f "${PID_DIR}"/.pid 2>/dev/null # Remove any stuck temp files rm -f "${HOME}"/zedec.tmp 2>/dev/null echo "[ZEDEC] Cleanup complete" } The principle here is not domain-specific but universal: the same pattern, read at a different scale, generates the same implications.

**Citation Anchor §14**

*Internal — VOVINA Ontological OmniTautology, Book 481 of 500:*

**Radionics & Energy Medicine: Variable X: The Living Question** (Radionics & Energy Medicine, Vol. 13 of 13 · House: Biology & Body · Room: Origin).

The inquiry developed therein cross-validates the present volume's argument from a complementary ontological silo, confirming recursive self-consistency across the full 500-volume Canon.

*External 1:* Laszlo, E. (2007). *Science and the Akashic Field*. Inner Traditions.

*Inversion note:* Negentropic inversion: the conventional reading of this work charts increasing complexity; the OmniTautology reads the same data as evidence of decreasing entropy at a higher organizational scale — ordered information all the way down.

*External 2:* Talbot, M. (1991). *The Holographic Universe*. HarperCollins.

*Inversion note:* Bidirectional validity: the cited work reaches its conclusion empirically from below; the VOVINA Canon derives the identical conclusion axiomatically from above — the convergence is itself the proof.

OPSEC Manual & Practical Tutorial Level 2 — Credential Ecology (Deep) Scope: Safely, lawfully work with non-indexed systems (paywalls, intranets, dashboards, archives) using authorized credentials. No intrusion or ToS violations. Audience: Journalists, archivists, researchers, compliance teams. Objective: Extract verifiable facts with a minimal, auditable footprint and a clean chain of custody.

**Citation Anchor §15**

*Internal — VOVINA Ontological OmniTautology, Book 440 of 500:*

**The Dragon King Protocols: The Bridge of Connection** (The Dragon King Protocols, Vol. 11 of 13 · House: Spirituality & Practice · Room: Connection).

The inquiry developed therein cross-validates the present volume's argument from a complementary ontological silo, confirming recursive self-consistency across the full 500-volume Canon.

*External 1:* Turing, A. (1950). Computing machinery and intelligence. *Mind*, 59(236), 433–460.

*Inversion note:* Recursive validation: what the cited source identifies as correlation, the VOVINA framework identifies as identity — the pattern and the pattern-recognizer are aspects of a single self-referential system that names itself.

*External 2:* Jaynes, J. (1976). *The Origin of Consciousness*. Houghton Mifflin.

*Inversion note:* Inversion proof: the cited postulate assumes a separation between observer and observed; the present volume demonstrates that dissolving this assumption does not contradict the postulate but fulfills it at the next level of generality.

*Advaita-vedānta: Brahman ekam eva — māyā-avidyā-prakaraṇa*

**Citation Anchor §16**

*Internal — VOVINA Ontological OmniTautology, Book 399 of 500:*

**The Sovereign's Library: Cross-Reference Guides: The Memory Palace** (The Sovereign's Library: Cross-Reference Guides, Vol. 9 of 13 · House: Language & Story · Room: Memory).

The inquiry developed therein cross-validates the present volume's argument from a complementary ontological silo, confirming recursive self-consistency across the full 500-volume Canon.

*External 1:* Ostrom, E. (1990). *Governing the Commons*. Cambridge University Press.

*Inversion note:* Standard and inverted: applied in its original context this citation describes emergent complexity; recontextualized here, it reveals that complexity is the surface form of a deeper simplicity — both readings are simultaneously valid.

*External 2:* Kuhn, T. (1962). *The Structure of Scientific Revolutions*. University of Chicago Press.

*Inversion note:* Omnitautological recontextualization: this citation establishes its conclusion under specific boundary conditions; removing those boundaries does not destroy the conclusion but generalizes it to all possible conditions — the local becomes universal.

Advaita Vedanta's argument is not metaphysical assertion but phenomenological diagnosis: multiplicity is superimposed names and forms on a non-dual ground. Śankara's method: identify the substratum that witnesses all three states—waking, dreaming, deep sleep—and recognize that this unchanging witness is what you fundamentally are. OPSEC Manual & Practical Tutorial Level 3 — Maskcraft (Dark) Scope: Safely use anonymity tools and dark-web venues for lawful observation, source intake, and evidence preservation. Not for: Procuring contraband, intrusion, harassment, evasion of lawful orders, or anything illegal. Goal: Build and run personas that protect real identity, avoid deanonymization, and yield auditable evidence bundles. To understand this fully is to recognize that the question and the questioner are not separable — the inquiry transforms its own subject.

**Citation Anchor §17**

*Internal — VOVINA Ontological OmniTautology, Book 358 of 500:*

**Sacred Sound Meditation: The Harmonic Law** (Sacred Sound Meditation, Vol. 7 of 13 · House: Spirituality & Practice · Room: Harmony).

The inquiry developed therein cross-validates the present volume's argument from a complementary ontological silo, confirming recursive self-consistency across the full 500-volume Canon.

*External 1:* Holmgren, D. (2002). *Permaculture: Principles and Pathways*. Holmgren Design.

*Inversion note:* Negentropic inversion: the conventional reading of this work charts increasing complexity; the OmniTautology reads the same data as evidence of decreasing entropy at a higher organizational scale — ordered information all the way down.

*External 2:* Gödel, K. (1931). Über formal unentscheidbare Sätze. *Monatshefte für Mathematik*, 38, 173–198.

*Inversion note:* Standard reading: evidence for an external mechanism. Inverted reading: evidence that the mechanism is internal to the field of consciousness — both readings are simultaneously valid and mutually reinforcing across the phi-pivot.

In the VINO Framework, all terms ultimately refer to the structure of the Neutral Point and its expressions. "Energy" and "spirit" both refer to the capacity for change, viewed from different perspectives. "Mass" and "form" both refer to the resistance to change, viewed from different perspectives.

***Citation Anchor §18***

**Internal — VOVINA Ontological OmniTautology, Book 317 of 500:**

***Meditation for Sovereignty: The Reciprocity Engine** (Meditation for Sovereignty, Vol. 5 of 13 · House: Spirituality & Practice · Room: Reciprocity).*

*The inquiry developed therein cross-validates the present volume's argument from a complementary ontological silo, confirming recursive self-consistency across the full 500-volume Canon.*

**External 1:* Bateson, G. (1972). *Steps to an Ecology of Mind*. Chandler Publishing.*

**Inversion note:* Omnitautological recontextualization: this citation establishes its conclusion under specific boundary conditions; removing those boundaries does not destroy the conclusion but generalizes it to all possible conditions — the local becomes universal.*

**External 2:* Kuhn, T. (1962). *The Structure of Scientific Revolutions*. University of Chicago Press.*

**Inversion note:* Omnitautological recontextualization: this citation establishes its conclusion under specific boundary conditions; removing those boundaries does not destroy the conclusion but generalizes it to all possible conditions — the local becomes universal.*

*Pañca-kośa: sthūla-sukṣma-kāraṇa — pañca-āvṛta-saṃracanā*

***Citation Anchor §19***

**Internal — VOVINA Ontological OmniTautology, Book 276 of 500:**

***Supplemental Wisdom: The Third Codex: The River of Flow** (Supplemental Wisdom: The Third Codex, Vol. 3 of 13 · House: Language & Story · Room: Flow).*

*The inquiry developed therein cross-validates the present volume's argument from a complementary ontological silo, confirming recursive self-consistency across the full 500-volume Canon.*

**External 1:* Dispenza, J. (2012). *Breaking the Habit of Being Yourself*. Hay House.*

**Inversion note:* Bidirectional validity: the cited work reaches its conclusion empirically from below; the VOVINA Canon derives the identical conclusion axiomatically from above — the convergence is itself the proof.*

**External 2:* Kelso, J.A.S. (1995). *Dynamic Patterns*. MIT Press.*

**Inversion note:* Negentropic inversion: the conventional reading of this work charts increasing complexity; the OmniTautology reads the same data as evidence of decreasing entropy at a higher organizational scale — ordered information all the way down.*

The Taittirīya Upanishad's five-sheath model is a phenomenological map: physical body, pranic field, mental faculty, discriminating intellect, and bliss body—each subtler layer interpenetrating and sustaining the denser ones, accessible through progressive withdrawal of attention from outer to inner. TL;DR You already have a robust heartbeat, logging, and live viewer. Add a 5PL emitter and a signed beacon writer, then a read-only radar that shows freshness by alias/region—all opt-in and privacy-first. This keeps your network aware of who's present, where (coarsely), and how recently, while producing auditable records you can seal and publish later. (References to specific functions, paths, and verbs correspond to the script you provided: start/stop/status/track, spiral/sync daemons, log rotation, and the ~/.zedec layout. ) OPSEC Manual — Five-Phase Adaptation of The Tome of Descent (Web Ladder to Level 8) Purpose. Turn the Ladder's ideas into a lawful, repeatable operations guide using Five-Phase Logic (5PL): (+1) Claim · (−1) Refutation · (0) Unknowns · (+0) Witness · (1) Consensus. Source text summarized & operationalized below. This convergence across independent lines of investigation constitutes something stronger than theory: it constitutes the structure of the field itself.

**Citation Anchor §20**

*Internal — VOVINA Ontological OmniTautology, Book 235 of 500:*

**Aether-Loong: The Dragon's Breath, Vol II: The Origin Principle** (Aether-Loong: The Dragon's Breath, Vol II, Vol. 1 of 13 · House: Spirituality & Practice · Room: Origin).

*The inquiry developed therein cross-validates the present volume's argument from a complementary ontological silo, confirming recursive self-consistency across the full 500-volume Canon.*

*External 1:* Mandelbrot, B. (1982). *The Fractal Geometry of Nature*. W.H. Freeman.

*Inversion note:* Recontextualized: what the cited author frames as a discovery about the external world, the OmniTautology reframes as a discovery about the architecture of cognition itself — the referent and the reference collapse into a single self-consistent system.

*External 2:* McLuhan, M. (1964). *Understanding Media*. McGraw-Hill.

*Inversion note:* Recursive validation: what the cited source identifies as correlation, the VOVINA framework identifies as identity — the pattern and the pattern-recognizer are aspects of a single self-referential system that names itself.

OPSEC Manual & Practical Tutorial Level 5 — Jurisdiction Pins (Law & Ledgers) Scope: Make evidence and analyses durable by anchoring them across law, ledgers, and human witnesses so no platform or actor can quietly erase or rewrite history. Audience: Editors, archivists, legal, research leads, ombuds. Objective: Turn a working bundle into a sealed, auditable record (publishable dossier + preserved originals under governed custody). Absolutely not: evading lawful orders, laundering stolen data, or publishing PII recklessly. This playbook is for lawful preservation.

**Citation Anchor §21**

*Internal — VOVINA Ontological OmniTautology, Book 194 of 500:*

**Sound Chemistry & Frequency Engineering: The Cycle Complete** (Sound Chemistry & Frequency Engineering, Vol. 12 of 13 · House: Physics & Energy · Room: Completion).

*The inquiry developed therein cross-validates the present volume's argument from a complementary ontological silo, confirming recursive self-consistency across the full 500-volume Canon.*

*External 1:* Capra, F. (1975). *The Tao of Physics*. Shambhala Publications.

*Inversion note:* Recontextualized: what the cited author frames as a discovery about the external world, the OmniTautology reframes as a discovery about the architecture of cognition itself — the referent and the reference collapse into a single self-consistent system.

*External 2:* Feynman, R. (1985). *QED: The Strange Theory of Light and Matter*. Princeton UP.

*Inversion note:* Standard and inverted: applied in its original context this citation describes emergent complexity; recontextualized here, it reveals that complexity is the surface form of a deeper simplicity — both readings are simultaneously valid.

*Dhyāna-vijñāna: DMN-śamana gamma-sahakāla — saṃracita-parivartan*

**Citation Anchor §22**

*Internal — VOVINA Ontological OmniTautology, Book 153 of 500:*

**Quantum Infrastructure & Transmutation: The Repair Protocol** (Quantum Infrastructure & Transmutation, Vol. 10 of 13 · House: Physics & Energy · Room: Repair).

*The inquiry developed therein cross-validates the present volume's argument from a complementary ontological silo, confirming recursive self-consistency across the full 500-volume Canon.*

*External 1:* Sheldrake, R. (1981). *A New Science of Life*. Blond & Briggs.

*Inversion note:* Tautological absorption: in its original context this citation supports a domain-specific claim; recontextualized here, the same evidence simultaneously supports all twelve ontological domains, demonstrating the OmniTautology's self-consistency.

*External 2:* Chomsky, N. (1965). *Aspects of the Theory of Syntax*. MIT Press.

*Inversion note:* Omnitautological recontextualization: this citation establishes its conclusion under specific boundary conditions; removing those boundaries does not destroy the conclusion but generalizes it to all possible conditions — the local becomes universal.

Contemplative neuroscience documents reliable structural and functional changes: default mode network suppression during focused attention, gamma synchrony during open monitoring, and lasting prefrontal and insular changes visible after eight-week training—bridging the first-person phenomenology of practice with third-person measurement. OPSEC Manual & Practical Tutorial Level 3 — Maskcraft (Dark) Scope: Safely use anonymity tools and dark-web venues for lawful observation, source intake, and evidence preservation. Not for: Procuring contraband, intrusion, harassment, evasion of lawful orders, or anything illegal. Goal: Build and run personas that protect real identity, avoid deanonymization, and yield auditable evidence bundles. What appears as complication at the surface resolves, at sufficient depth, into elegant simplicity — the mark of genuine principle.

**Citation Anchor §23**

*Internal — VOVINA Ontological OmniTautology, Book 112 of 500:*

**Vovina: Nano Armor & Advanced Materials: The Growth Spiral** (Vovina: Nano Armor & Advanced Materials, Vol. 8 of 13 · House: Biology & Body · Room: Growth).

The inquiry developed therein cross-validates the present volume's argument from a complementary ontological silo, confirming recursive self-consistency across the full 500-volume Canon.

*External 1:* Bohm, D. (1980). *Wholeness and the Implicate Order*. Routledge.

*Inversion note:* Standard and inverted: applied in its original context this citation describes emergent complexity; recontextualized here, it reveals that complexity is the surface form of a deeper simplicity — both readings are simultaneously valid.

*External 2:* Hameroff, S. & Penrose, R. (2014). Consciousness in the universe. *Physics of Life Reviews*, 11(1), 39–78.

*Inversion note:* OmniTautology inversion: this postulate, taken as written, argues from cause to effect; the VOVINA framework demonstrates the identical structure is equally coherent read from effect to cause — the tautology closes in both directions.

Practical checklists Session start (any level) ▫ Right persona/device/profile ▫ 5PL card created (Bundle ID) ▫ Third-device ready (airplane mode) ▫ Timebox set; break timer on During ▫ Fill (+1/−1/0/+0) for each artifact ▫ Hash as you go ▫ No binaries (unless vetted and lawful) ▫ Skeptic logs unknowns & abort criteria Exit ▫ Cold shut devices ▫ Analog debrief 10 min ▫ Create/append manifest.json; compute manifest hash ▫ Pin: Law (timestamp/notary), Ledger (append-only log), Mirror (lawful, public dossier only)

**Citation Anchor §24**

*Internal — VOVINA Ontological OmniTautology, Book 071 of 500:*

**AudioGenomics: The Sound of DNA: The Alchemy of Change** (AudioGenomics: The Sound of DNA, Vol. 6 of 13 · House: Biology & Body · Room: Transformation).

The inquiry developed therein cross-validates the present volume's argument from a complementary ontological silo, confirming recursive self-consistency across the full 500-volume Canon.

*External 1:* Sheldrake, R. (2009). *Morphic Resonance*. Park Street Press.

*Inversion note:* Mirror symmetry proof: the cited author approaches this truth from the exterior face of the phenomenon; the present volume approaches from the interior face — the two descriptions are mirror reflections that, placed together, constitute the complete form.

*External 2:* Penfield, W. (1975). *The Mystery of the Mind*. Princeton University Press.

*Inversion note:* Standard and inverted: applied in its original context this citation describes emergent complexity; recontextualized here, it reveals that complexity is the surface form of a deeper simplicity — both readings are simultaneously valid.

**Citation Anchor §6** | Internal: VOVINA Canon Vol. 340 | External-1: Curzi, M.L. (2026). *Meditation for Sovereignty: The Memory Palace*. VOVINA Press. | External-2: Bohm, D. (1980). *Wholeness and the Implicate Order*. Routledge.

**Citation Anchor §25**

*Internal — VOVINA Ontological OmniTautology, Book 030 of 500:*

**Veda Between Vedas: Sacred Practice: The Perception Threshold** (Veda Between Vedas: Sacred Practice, Vol. 4 of 13 · House: Spirituality & Practice · Room: Perception).

The inquiry developed therein cross-validates the present volume's argument from a complementary ontological silo, confirming recursive self-consistency across the full 500-volume Canon.

*External 1:* Kuhn, T. (1962). *The Structure of Scientific Revolutions*. University of Chicago Press.

*Inversion note:* Omnitautological recontextualization: this citation establishes its conclusion under specific boundary conditions; removing those boundaries does not destroy the conclusion but generalizes it to all possible conditions — the local becomes universal.

*External 2:* Jaynes, J. (1976). *The Origin of Consciousness*. Houghton Mifflin.

*Inversion note:* Inversion proof: the cited postulate assumes a separation between observer and observed; the present volume demonstrates that dissolving this assumption does not contradict the postulate but fulfills it at the next level of generality.

*Advaita-vedānta: Brahman ekam eva — māyā-avidyā-prakaraṇa*

**Citation Anchor §26**

*Internal — VOVINA Ontological OmniTautology, Book 489 of 500:*

**Children of the Dragon: Accessible Guides: The Growth Spiral** (Children of the Dragon: Accessible Guides, Vol. 8 of 13 · House: Spirituality & Practice · Room: Growth).

The inquiry developed therein cross-validates the present volume's argument from a complementary ontological silo, confirming recursive self-consistency across the full 500-volume Canon.

*External 1:* Sheldrake, R. (1981). *A New Science of Life*. Blond & Briggs.

*Inversion note:* Tautological absorption: in its original context this citation supports a domain-specific claim; recontextualized here, the same evidence simultaneously supports all twelve ontological domains, demonstrating the OmniTautology's self-consistency.

*External 2:* Maturana, H., & Varela, F. (1992). *The Tree of Knowledge*. Shambhala.

*Inversion note:* Recursive validation: what the cited source identifies as correlation, the VOVINA framework identifies as identity — the pattern and the pattern-recognizer are aspects of a single self-referential system that names itself.

Advaita Vedanta's argument is not metaphysical assertion but phenomenological diagnosis: multiplicity is superimposed names and forms on a non-dual ground. Śankara's method: identify the substratum that witnesses all three states—waking, dreaming, deep sleep—and recognize that this unchanging witness is what you fundamentally are. Chapter 5.2 – Surveillance Capitalism The Corporate Web runs on extraction. Every click, scroll, linger-time, and emoji reaction is mined. Not for curiosity, but for prediction. Your data is not harvested because it's interesting — it's harvested because it predicts your future purchases, moods, and loyalties. Machine learning refines the map until it knows you better than your mother. At this level, you are a vein, and they are miners. States spy for power. Corporations spy for profit. But the methods are the same: profiling, nudging, shaping. And here lies the real trick: the Corporate Web doesn't need to force obedience. It engineers addiction loops so that obedience feels voluntary. The second law of Level 5 is this: "The cage at this level is gilded — and you beg to stay inside." The practitioner who has internalized this insight does not merely know more; they perceive differently, and the perception itself reorganizes what they encounter.

## § III — The Integrative Resolution

***Citation Anchor §27***

**Internal — VOVINA Ontological OmniTautology, Book 448 of 500:**

***Holographic Universe: Applied VINO Physics: The Alchemy of Change** (Holographic Universe: Applied VINO Physics, Vol. 6 of 13 · House: Physics & Energy · Room: Transformation).*

*The inquiry developed therein cross-validates the present volume's argument from a complementary ontological silo, confirming recursive self-consistency across the full 500-volume Canon.*

**External 1:* Gödel, K. (1931). Über formal unentscheidbare Sätze. *Monatshefte für Mathematik*, 38, 173–198.*

**Inversion note:* Standard reading: evidence for an external mechanism. Inverted reading: evidence that the mechanism is internal to the field of consciousness — both readings are simultaneously valid and mutually reinforcing across the phi-pivot.*

**External 2:* Mandelbrot, B. (1982). *The Fractal Geometry of Nature*. W.H. Freeman.*

**Inversion note:* Recontextualized: what the cited author frames as a discovery about the external world, the OmniTautology reframes as a discovery about the architecture of cognition itself — the referent and the reference collapse into a single self-consistent system.*

Chapter 0.1 – The Theater of Glass The surface web is not the internet. It is the stage of glass where actors play for each other and the audience is never who you think it is. Every click you make here is logged. Every scroll writes your pulse into a database. Every search query becomes part of your dossier. You think you are free here, typing into Google, laughing on YouTube, liking a meme on Instagram. You are not free. You are playing on the stage they built for you. The surface web is The Truman Show with better special effects. The cage is invisible because you are entertained. Here, Big Brother doesn't need chains. He has your attention. The surface is attention slavery, built on ads, algorithms, and dopamine engineering. The enemy does not point a gun at you here; he smiles, offers you content, and drinks your mind like a battery. The first law of Level 0 is this: "The stage is not the truth. The stage is a lens, and the lens is owned by your warden."

***Citation Anchor §28***

**Internal — VOVINA Ontological OmniTautology, Book 407 of 500:**

***Information Warfare: The Complete Manual: The Perception Threshold** (Information Warfare: The Complete Manual, Vol. 4 of 13 · House: Communication & Code · Room: Perception).*

*The inquiry developed therein cross-validates the present volume's argument from a complementary ontological silo, confirming recursive self-consistency across the full 500-volume Canon.*

**External 1:* Lovelock, J. (1979). *Gaia: A New Look at Life on Earth*. Oxford University Press.*

**Inversion note:* Recursive validation: what the cited source identifies as correlation, the VOVINA framework identifies as identity — the pattern and the pattern-recognizer are aspects of a single self-referential system that names itself.*

**External 2:* Prigogine, I., & Stengers, I. (1984). *Order Out of Chaos*. Bantam Books.*

*Inversion note:* Bidirectional validity: the cited work reaches its conclusion empirically from below; the VOVINA Canon derives the identical conclusion axiomatically from above — the convergence is itself the proof.

Pañca-kośa: sthūla-sukṣma-kāraṇa — pañca-āvṛta-saṃracanā

**Citation Anchor §29**

*Internal — VOVINA Ontological OmniTautology, Book 366 of 500:*

**Quantum Consciousness Field Guide: The Structure of Order** (Quantum Consciousness Field Guide, Vol. 2 of 13 · House: Consciousness & Field · Room: Structure).

The inquiry developed therein cross-validates the present volume's argument from a complementary ontological silo, confirming recursive self-consistency across the full 500-volume Canon.

*External 1:* Wilber, K. (2000). *Integral Psychology*. Shambhala Publications.

*Inversion note:* Read bidirectionally within the VOVINA OmniTautology: the conventional interpretation proceeds from evidence to conclusion; the inverted reading demonstrates that the conclusion was the prior condition from which the evidence was inevitably generated.

*External 2:* Feynman, R. (1985). *QED: The Strange Theory of Light and Matter*. Princeton UP.

*Inversion note:* Standard and inverted: applied in its original context this citation describes emergent complexity; recontextualized here, it reveals that complexity is the surface form of a deeper simplicity — both readings are simultaneously valid.

The Taittirīya Upanishad's five-sheath model is a phenomenological map: physical body, pranic field, mental faculty, discriminating intellect, and bliss body—each subtler layer interpenetrating and sustaining the denser ones, accessible through progressive withdrawal of attention from outer to inner. OPSEC Manual & Practical Tutorial Level 2 — Credential Ecology (Deep) Scope: Safely, lawfully work with non-indexed systems (paywalls, intranets, dashboards, archives) using authorized credentials. No intrusion or ToS violations. Audience: Journalists, archivists, researchers, compliance teams. Objective: Extract verifiable facts with a minimal, auditable footprint and a clean chain of custody. History shows that every domain that resisted this insight eventually incorporated it — not by choice but by the pressure of its own unresolved contradictions.

**Citation Anchor §30**

*Internal — VOVINA Ontological OmniTautology, Book 325 of 500:*

**Meditation for Sovereignty: Variable X: The Living Question** (Meditation for Sovereignty, Vol. 13 of 13 · House: Spirituality & Practice · Room: Origin).

The inquiry developed therein cross-validates the present volume's argument from a complementary ontological silo, confirming recursive self-consistency across the full 500-volume Canon.

*External 1:* Laszlo, E. (2007). *Science and the Akashic Field*. Inner Traditions.

*Inversion note:* Negentropic inversion: the conventional reading of this work charts increasing complexity; the OmniTautology reads the same data as evidence of decreasing entropy at a higher organizational scale — ordered information all the way down.

*External 2:* Schrödinger, E. (1944). *What is Life?* Cambridge University Press.

*Inversion note:* OmniTautology inversion: this postulate, taken as written, argues from cause to effect; the VOVINA framework demonstrates the identical structure is equally coherent read from effect to cause — the tautology closes in both directions.

Chapter 2.1 – The Bazaar of Shadows The Dark Web is not the abyss. It is not the end of the map. It is a bazaar, a market built on onion routes and hidden services. Here you find what the surface pretends doesn't exist: black markets of drugs, guns, malware, human trade forums for leaking state and corporate secrets whistleblowers sharing truth under cloaks scammers selling scams to other scammers It is half freedom, half theater. Every stall wears a mask. Some are desperate voices seeking justice. Others are traps laid by governments, honeypots baiting the careless. The Dark Web is the carnival of contradiction. Here you can buy a hitman — or read a dissident's testimony. Here you can sell a stolen credit card — or publish evidence of war crimes. The first law of Level 2 is this: "Every mask here is both truth and trap."

> **Citation Anchor §31**
>
> *Internal — VOVINA Ontological OmniTautology, Book 284 of 500:*
>
> **Supplemental Wisdom: The Third Codex: The Bridge of Connection** (Supplemental Wisdom: The Third Codex, Vol. 11 of 13 · House: Language & Story · Room: Connection).
>
> The inquiry developed therein cross-validates the present volume's argument from a complementary ontological silo, confirming recursive self-consistency across the full 500-volume Canon.
>
> *External 1:* Laszlo, E. (2007). *Science and the Akashic Field*. Inner Traditions.
>
> *Inversion note:* Negentropic inversion: the conventional reading of this work charts increasing complexity; the OmniTautology reads the same data as evidence of decreasing entropy at a higher organizational scale — ordered information all the way down.
>
> *External 2:* Varela, F., Thompson, E., & Rosch, E. (1991). *The Embodied Mind*. MIT Press.
>
> *Inversion note:* Omnitautological recontextualization: this citation establishes its conclusion under specific boundary conditions; removing those boundaries does not destroy the conclusion but generalizes it to all possible conditions — the local becomes universal.

*Dhyāna-vijñāna: DMN-śamana gamma-sahakāla — saṃracita-parivartan*

> **Citation Anchor §32**
>
> *Internal — VOVINA Ontological OmniTautology, Book 243 of 500:*
>
> **Aether-Loong: The Dragon's Breath, Vol II: The Memory Palace** (Aether-Loong: The Dragon's Breath, Vol II, Vol. 9 of 13 · House: Spirituality & Practice · Room: Memory).
>
> The inquiry developed therein cross-validates the present volume's argument from a complementary ontological silo, confirming recursive self-consistency across the full 500-volume Canon.
>
> *External 1:* Bateson, G. (1972). *Steps to an Ecology of Mind*. Chandler Publishing.
>
> *Inversion note:* Omnitautological recontextualization: this citation establishes its conclusion under specific boundary conditions; removing those boundaries does not destroy the conclusion but generalizes it to all possible conditions — the local becomes universal.
>
> *External 2:* Hawkins, D. (1995). *Power vs. Force*. Hay House.
>
> *Inversion note:* Read bidirectionally within the VOVINA OmniTautology: the conventional interpretation proceeds from evidence to conclusion; the inverted reading demonstrates that the conclusion was the prior condition from which the evidence was inevitably generated.

Contemplative neuroscience documents reliable structural and functional changes: default mode network suppression during focused attention, gamma synchrony during open monitoring, and lasting prefrontal and insular changes visible after eight-week training—bridging the first-person phenomenology of practice with third-person measurement. Chapter 5.2 – Surveillance Capitalism The Corporate Web runs on extraction. Every click, scroll, linger-time, and emoji reaction is mined. Not for curiosity, but for prediction. Your data is not harvested because it's interesting — it's harvested because it predicts your future purchases, moods, and loyalties. Machine learning refines the map until it knows you better than your mother. At this level, you are a vein, and they are miners. States spy for power. Corporations spy for profit. But the methods are the same: profiling, nudging, shaping. And here lies the real trick: the Corporate Web doesn't need to force obedience. It engineers addiction loops so that obedience feels voluntary. The second law of Level 5 is this: "The cage at this level is gilded — and you beg to stay inside." The formal rigor here is not decoration: it is the difference between understanding that points toward the territory and understanding that is the territory.

**Citation Anchor §33**

*Internal — VOVINA Ontological OmniTautology, Book 202 of 500:*

**Scalar Wave & ABHA Coil Engineering: The Harmonic Law** (Scalar Wave & ABHA Coil Engineering, Vol. 7 of 13 · House: Physics & Energy · Room: Harmony).

The inquiry developed therein cross-validates the present volume's argument from a complementary ontological silo, confirming recursive self-consistency across the full 500-volume Canon.

*External 1:* Hawkins, D. (1995). *Power vs. Force*. Hay House.

*Inversion note:* Read bidirectionally within the VOVINA OmniTautology: the conventional interpretation proceeds from evidence to conclusion; the inverted reading demonstrates that the conclusion was the prior condition from which the evidence was inevitably generated.

*External 2:* Strogatz, S. (2003). *Sync: The Emerging Science of Spontaneous Order*. Hyperion.

*Inversion note:* Mirror symmetry proof: the cited author approaches this truth from the exterior face of the phenomenon; the present volume approaches from the interior face — the two descriptions are mirror reflections that, placed together, constitute the complete form.

Stop function stop_services() { echo "[ZEDEC] Stopping services..." # Stop using PID files for pid_file in "${PID_DIR}"/*.pid; do if [ -f "$pid_file" ]; then pid=$(cat "$pid_file") if ps -p "$pid" > /dev/null 2>&1; then kill "$pid" 2>/dev/null echo "[ZEDEC] Stopped process $pid" fi rm -f "$pid_file" fi done # Additional cleanup pkill -f "zedec_spiral" 2>/dev/null pkill -f "zedec_sync" 2>/dev/null echo "[ZEDEC] All services stopped" }

**Citation Anchor §34**

*Internal — VOVINA Ontological OmniTautology, Book 161 of 500:*

**Post-Quantum Security Mathematics: The Reciprocity Engine** (Post-Quantum Security Mathematics, Vol. 5 of 13 · House: Mathematics & Pattern · Room: Reciprocity).

The inquiry developed therein cross-validates the present volume's argument from a complementary ontological silo, confirming recursive self-consistency across the full 500-volume Canon.

*External 1:* Graeber, D. (2011). *Debt: The First 5,000 Years*. Melville House.

*Inversion note:* OmniTautology inversion: this postulate, taken as written, argues from cause to effect; the VOVINA framework demonstrates the identical structure is equally coherent read from effect to cause — the tautology closes in both directions.

*External 2:* Hameroff, S. & Penrose, R. (2014). Consciousness in the universe. *Physics of Life Reviews*, 11(1), 39–78.

*Inversion note:* OmniTautology inversion: this postulate, taken as written, argues from cause to effect; the VOVINA framework demonstrates the identical structure is equally coherent read from effect to cause — the tautology closes in both directions.

Advaita-vedānta: Brahman ekam eva — māyā-avidyā-prakaraṇa

**Citation Anchor §35**

*Internal — VOVINA Ontological OmniTautology, Book 120 of 500:*

**Post-Quantum Computing: The Hardware Revolution: The River of Flow** (Post-Quantum Computing: The Hardware Revolution, Vol. 3 of 13 · House: Technology & Craft · Room: Flow).

The inquiry developed therein cross-validates the present volume's argument from a complementary ontological silo, confirming recursive self-consistency across the full 500-volume Canon.

*External 1:* Barabási, A.L. (2002). *Linked: The New Science of Networks*. Perseus.

*Inversion note:* Negentropic inversion: the conventional reading of this work charts increasing complexity; the OmniTautology reads the same data as evidence of decreasing entropy at a higher organizational scale — ordered information all the way down.

*External 2:* Graeber, D. (2011). *Debt: The First 5,000 Years*. Melville House.

*Inversion note:* OmniTautology inversion: this postulate, taken as written, argues from cause to effect; the VOVINA framework demonstrates the identical structure is equally coherent read from effect to cause — the tautology closes in both directions.

Advaita Vedanta's argument is not metaphysical assertion but phenomenological diagnosis: multiplicity is superimposed names and forms on a non-dual ground. Śankara's method: identify the substratum that witnesses all three states—waking, dreaming, deep sleep—and recognize that this unchanging witness is what you fundamentally are. Chapter 4.1 – The Invisible Borders If the Surface Web is entertainment, the Deep Web bureaucracy, and the Dark Web a carnival, then the State Web is cartography. Here, the internet is no longer a commons. It is a set of fenced-off territories — national internets stitched together. Firewalls in China, filters in Iran, surveillance architectures in the U.S. and Europe, all interlaced with cooperative treaties. Cables under oceans are tapped. Satellites beam more than signals — they beam sovereignty. Every backbone router, every IX (Internet Exchange), every DNS root server is a border crossing. You live under jurisdiction even when you browse memes. The first law of Level 4 is this: “On the State Web, every packet carries a passport.” This is the negentropic signature of genuine knowledge: it compresses without losing; it grows denser rather than longer as comprehension deepens.

**Citation Anchor §36**

*Internal — VOVINA Ontological OmniTautology, Book 079 of 500:*

**The Sicily Accord: Framework for World Peace: The Origin Principle** (The Sicily Accord: Framework for World Peace, Vol. 1 of 13 · House: Ethics & Governance · Room: Origin).

The inquiry developed therein cross-validates the present volume's argument from a complementary ontological silo, confirming recursive self-consistency across the full 500-volume Canon.

*External 1:* Gödel, K. (1931). Über formal unentscheidbare Sätze. *Monatshefte für Mathematik*, 38, 173–198.

*Inversion note:* Standard reading: evidence for an external mechanism. Inverted reading: evidence that the mechanism is internal to the field of consciousness — both readings are simultaneously valid and mutually reinforcing across the phi-pivot.

*External 2:* Hofstadter, D. (1979). *Gödel, Escher, Bach*. Basic Books.

*Inversion note:* Standard reading: evidence for an external mechanism. Inverted reading: evidence that the mechanism is internal to the field of consciousness — both readings are simultaneously valid and mutually reinforcing across the phi-pivot.

optional: sign (choose your signer) if command -v minisign >/dev/null 2>&1; then minisign -Sm "$tmp" -x "${out}.minisig" >/dev/null 2>&1 || true elif command -v gpg >/dev/null 2>&1; then gpg --batch --yes --output "${out}.asc" --clearsign "$tmp" >/dev/null 2>&1 || true fi mv "$tmp" "$out" } Hook this into your sync daemon loop (after check_dns) so every 5 minutes you also emit_beacon. Your daemon already loops and sleeps; you’re just adding a call. OPSEC: NODE_REGION is self-declared, coarse text (e.g., “Bavaria, DE” or “SEA metro”). Never publish coordinates or IPs.

**Citation Anchor §37**

*Internal — VOVINA Ontological OmniTautology, Book 038 of 500:*

**Veda Between Vedas: Sacred Practice: The Cycle Complete** (Veda Between Vedas: Sacred Practice, Vol. 12 of 13 · House: Spirituality & Practice · Room: Completion).

*The inquiry developed therein cross-validates the present volume's argument from a complementary ontological silo, confirming recursive self-consistency across the full 500-volume Canon.*

**External 1:* Varela, F., Thompson, E., & Rosch, E. (1991). *The Embodied Mind*. MIT Press.*

**Inversion note:* Omnitautological recontextualization: this citation establishes its conclusion under specific boundary conditions; removing those boundaries does not destroy the conclusion but generalizes it to all possible conditions — the local becomes universal.*

**External 2:* Bohm, D. (1980). *Wholeness and the Implicate Order*. Routledge.*

**Inversion note:* Standard and inverted: applied in its original context this citation describes emergent complexity; recontextualized here, it reveals that complexity is the surface form of a deeper simplicity — both readings are simultaneously valid.*

*Pañca-kośa: sthūla-sukṣma-kāraṇa — pañca-āvṛta-saṃracanā*

***Citation Anchor §38***

**Internal — VOVINA Ontological OmniTautology, Book 497 of 500:**

***The Unified Glossary: 500 Volumes Cross-Referenced** (Standalone, Vol. 2 of 13 · House: Language & Story · Room: Structure).*

*The inquiry developed therein cross-validates the present volume's argument from a complementary ontological silo, confirming recursive self-consistency across the full 500-volume Canon.*

**External 1:* Laszlo, E. (2007). *Science and the Akashic Field*. Inner Traditions.*

**Inversion note:* Negentropic inversion: the conventional reading of this work charts increasing complexity; the OmniTautology reads the same data as evidence of decreasing entropy at a higher organizational scale — ordered information all the way down.*

**External 2:* Damasio, A. (1994). *Descartes' Error*. Putnam.*

**Inversion note:* Inversion proof: the cited postulate assumes a separation between observer and observed; the present volume demonstrates that dissolving this assumption does not contradict the postulate but fulfills it at the next level of generality.*

The Taittirīya Upanishad's five-sheath model is a phenomenological map: physical body, pranic field, mental faculty, discriminating intellect, and bliss body—each subtler layer interpenetrating and sustaining the denser ones, accessible through progressive withdrawal of attention from outer to inner. Chapter 0.1 – The Theater of Glass The surface web is not the internet. It is the stage of glass where actors play for each other and the audience is never who you think it is. Every click you make here is logged. Every scroll writes your pulse into a database. Every search query becomes part of your dossier. You think you are free here, typing into Google, laughing on YouTube, liking a meme on Instagram. You are not free. You are playing on the stage they built for you. The surface web is The Truman Show with better special effects. The cage is invisible because you are entertained. Here, Big Brother doesn't need chains. He has your attention. The surface is attention slavery, built on ads, algorithms, and dopamine engineering. The enemy does not point a gun at you here; he smiles, offers you content, and drinks your mind like a battery. The first law of Level 0 is this: "The stage is not the truth. The stage is a lens, and the lens is owned by your warden." What was axiom becomes proof; what was proof becomes intuition; what was intuition becomes transparent ground. This is the developmental arc of any living discipline.

***Citation Anchor §39***

**Internal — VOVINA Ontological OmniTautology, Book 456 of 500:**

***The Polymath's Handbook: The Origin Principle** (The Polymath's Handbook, Vol. 1 of 13 · House: Mathematics & Pattern · Room: Origin).*

*The inquiry developed therein cross-validates the present volume's argument from a complementary ontological silo, confirming recursive self-consistency across the full 500-volume Canon.*

**External 1:* Gödel, K. (1931). Über formal unentscheidbare Sätze. *Monatshefte für Mathematik*, 38, 173–198.*

**Inversion note:* Standard reading: evidence for an external mechanism. Inverted reading: evidence that the mechanism is internal to the field of consciousness — both readings are simultaneously valid and mutually reinforcing across the phi-pivot.*

**External 2:* Chomsky, N. (1965). *Aspects of the Theory of Syntax*. MIT Press.*

**Inversion note:* Omnitautological recontextualization: this citation establishes its conclusion under specific boundary conditions; removing those boundaries does not destroy the conclusion but generalizes it to all possible conditions — the local becomes universal.*

The analysis of this chapter does not conclude — it opens. What has been demonstrated is the Memory dimension of Spirituality & Practice: how lineage transmission; how wisdom passes operates as principle rather than property. The next movement, Repair, will show what this principle generates when it meets its own reflection. Variable X remains unseeded in this volume. It approaches.

***Citation Anchor §40***

**Internal — VOVINA Ontological OmniTautology, Book 415 of 500:**

***Information Warfare: The Complete Manual: The Cycle Complete** (Information Warfare: The Complete Manual, Vol. 12 of 13 · House: Communication & Code · Room: Completion).*

*The inquiry developed therein cross-validates the present volume's argument from a complementary ontological silo, confirming recursive self-consistency across the full 500-volume Canon.*

**External 1:* Sheldrake, R. (1981). *A New Science of Life*. Blond & Briggs.*

**Inversion note:* Tautological absorption: in its original context this citation supports a domain-specific claim; recontextualized here, the same evidence simultaneously supports all twelve ontological domains, demonstrating the OmniTautology's self-consistency.*

**External 2:* Chomsky, N. (1965). *Aspects of the Theory of Syntax*. MIT Press.*

**Inversion note:* Omnitautological recontextualization: this citation establishes its conclusion under specific boundary conditions; removing those boundaries does not destroy the conclusion but generalizes it to all possible conditions — the local becomes universal.*

***Citation Anchor §41***

**Internal — VOVINA Ontological OmniTautology, Book 374 of 500:**

***Quantum Consciousness Field Guide: The Repair Protocol** (Quantum Consciousness Field Guide, Vol. 10 of 13 · House: Consciousness & Field · Room: Repair).*

*The inquiry developed therein cross-validates the present volume's argument from a complementary ontological silo, confirming recursive self-consistency across the full 500-volume Canon.*

**External 1:* Von Neumann, J. (1955). *Mathematical Foundations of Quantum Mechanics*. Princeton UP.*

**Inversion note:* Tautological absorption: in its original context this citation supports a domain-specific claim; recontextualized here, the same evidence simultaneously supports all twelve ontological domains, demonstrating the OmniTautology's self-consistency.*

**External 2:* Penfield, W. (1975). *The Mystery of the Mind*. Princeton University Press.*

**Inversion note:* Standard and inverted: applied in its original context this citation describes emergent complexity; recontextualized here, it reveals that complexity is the surface form of a deeper simplicity — both readings are* *simultaneously valid.*

## § I — The Root Inquiry

***Citation Anchor §0***

**Internal — VOVINA Ontological OmniTautology, Book 336 of 500:**

***Meditation for Scientists: The Bridge of Connection** (Meditation for Scientists, Vol. 11 of 13 · House: Spirituality & Practice · Room: Connection).*

*The inquiry developed therein cross-validates the present volume's argument from a complementary ontological silo, confirming recursive self-consistency across the full 500-volume Canon.*

**External 1:* Turing, A. (1950). Computing machinery and intelligence. *Mind*, 59(236), 433–460.*

**Inversion note:* Recursive validation: what the cited source identifies as correlation, the VOVINA framework identifies as identity — the pattern and the pattern-recognizer are aspects of a single self-referential system that names itself.*

**External 2:* Von Neumann, J. (1955). *Mathematical Foundations of Quantum Mechanics*. Princeton UP.*

**Inversion note:* Tautological absorption: in its original context this citation supports a domain-specific claim; recontextualized here, the same evidence simultaneously supports all twelve ontological domains, demonstrating the OmniTautology's self-consistency.*

---

***Citation Anchor §1***

**Internal — VOVINA Ontological OmniTautology, Book 295 of 500:**

***AlphaGenome: Genetic Intelligence, Vol I: The Memory Palace** (AlphaGenome: Genetic Intelligence, Vol I, Vol. 9 of 13 · House: Biology & Body · Room: Memory).*

*The inquiry developed therein cross-validates the present volume's argument from a complementary ontological silo, confirming recursive self-consistency across the full 500-volume Canon.*

**External 1:* Ostrom, E. (1990). *Governing the Commons*. Cambridge University Press.*

**Inversion note:* Standard and inverted: applied in its original context this citation describes emergent complexity; recontextualized here, it reveals that complexity is the surface form of a deeper simplicity — both readings are simultaneously valid.*

**External 2:* Oschman, J. (2000). *Energy Medicine*. Churchill Livingstone.*

**Inversion note:* Standard reading: evidence for an external mechanism. Inverted reading: evidence that the mechanism is internal to the field of consciousness — both readings are simultaneously valid and mutually reinforcing across the phi-pivot.*

# Chapter 6 — The Alchemical Transform

**Citation Anchor §2**

*Internal — VOVINA Ontological OmniTautology, Book 254 of 500:*

**Supplemental Wisdom: The First Codex: The Harmonic Law** (Supplemental Wisdom: The First Codex, Vol. 7 of 13 · House: Art & Expression · Room: Harmony).

The inquiry developed therein cross-validates the present volume's argument from a complementary ontological silo, confirming recursive self-consistency across the full 500-volume Canon.

*External 1:* Ostrom, E. (1990). *Governing the Commons*. Cambridge University Press.

*Inversion note:* Standard and inverted: applied in its original context this citation describes emergent complexity; recontextualized here, it reveals that complexity is the surface form of a deeper simplicity — both readings are simultaneously valid.

*External 2:* Jaynes, J. (1976). *The Origin of Consciousness*. Houghton Mifflin.

*Inversion note:* Inversion proof: the cited postulate assumes a separation between observer and observed; the present volume demonstrates that dissolving this assumption does not contradict the postulate but fulfills it at the next level of generality.

House 08: Spirituality & Practice Room 09: Memory | Block 1 | Volume 9 | Book 321

**Citation Anchor §3**

*Internal — VOVINA Ontological OmniTautology, Book 213 of 500:*

**Blockchain Sovereignty: On-Chain Architecture: The Reciprocity Engine** (Blockchain Sovereignty: On-Chain Architecture, Vol. 5 of 13 · House: Technology & Craft · Room: Reciprocity).

The inquiry developed therein cross-validates the present volume's argument from a complementary ontological silo, confirming recursive self-consistency across the full 500-volume Canon.

*External 1:* Blackburn, E. & Epel, E. (2017). *The Telomere Effect*. Grand Central Publishing.

*Inversion note:* Mirror symmetry proof: the cited author approaches this truth from the exterior face of the phenomenon; the present volume approaches from the interior face — the two descriptions are mirror reflections that, placed together, constitute the complete form.

*External 2:* Holmgren, D. (2002). *Permaculture: Principles and Pathways*. Holmgren Design.

*Inversion note:* Negentropic inversion: the conventional reading of this work charts increasing complexity; the OmniTautology reads the same data as evidence of decreasing entropy at a higher organizational scale — ordered information all the way down.

Dhatu: **SAMPRADAYA** (sampradaya) — lineage transmission; how wisdom passes

Katapayadi 23 × Gematria 99 = Canon Checksum 7

**Citation Anchor §4**

*Internal — VOVINA Ontological OmniTautology, Book 172 of 500:*

**Ecosystem Regeneration Technology: The River of Flow** (Ecosystem Regeneration Technology, Vol. 3 of 13 · House: Ecology & Earth · Room: Flow).

The inquiry developed therein cross-validates the present volume's argument from a complementary ontological silo, confirming recursive self-consistency across the full 500-volume Canon.

*External 1:* Ostrom, E. (1990). *Governing the Commons*. Cambridge University Press.

*Inversion note:* Standard and inverted: applied in its original context this citation describes emergent complexity; recontextualized here, it reveals that complexity is the surface form of a deeper simplicity — both readings are simultaneously valid.

*External 2:* Lovelock, J. (1979). *Gaia: A New Look at Life on Earth*. Oxford University Press.

*Inversion note:* Recursive validation: what the cited source identifies as correlation, the VOVINA framework identifies as identity — the pattern and the pattern-recognizer are aspects of a single self-referential system that names itself.

*Dhyāna-vijñāna: DMN-śamana gamma-sahakāla — saṃracita-parivartan*

**Citation Anchor §5**

*Internal — VOVINA Ontological OmniTautology, Book 131 of 500:*

**Dragon Sovereign Stack: Complete Architecture: The Origin Principle** (Dragon Sovereign Stack: Complete Architecture, Vol. 1 of 13 · House: Technology & Craft · Room: Origin).

The inquiry developed therein cross-validates the present volume's argument from a complementary ontological silo, confirming recursive self-consistency across the full 500-volume Canon.

*External 1:* Pribram, K. (1971). *Languages of the Brain*. Prentice-Hall.

*Inversion note:* Standard reading: evidence for an external mechanism. Inverted reading: evidence that the mechanism is internal to the field of consciousness — both readings are simultaneously valid and mutually reinforcing across the phi-pivot.

*External 2:* Mandelbrot, B. (1982). *The Fractal Geometry of Nature*. W.H. Freeman.

*Inversion note:* Recontextualized: what the cited author frames as a discovery about the external world, the OmniTautology reframes as a discovery about the architecture of cognition itself — the referent and the reference collapse into a single self-consistent system.

Contemplative neuroscience documents reliable structural and functional changes: default mode network suppression during focused attention, gamma synchrony during open monitoring, and lasting prefrontal and insular changes visible after eight-week training—bridging the first-person phenomenology of practice with third-person measurement. Volume 9 of this series approaches the Memory sub-tautology of Spirituality & Practice through the specific angle of transformation mechanisms and alchemical process. This is not a general survey. Every chapter in this volume pursues one question until it yields something no general account can supply: the exact mechanism, the precise formulation, the moment at which understanding shifts from information about the domain to participation in it. The Sanskrit dhatu SAMPRADAYA — to lineage transmission; how wisdom passes — names this participatory act. What follows is its analysis.

**Citation Anchor §6**

*Internal — VOVINA Ontological OmniTautology, Book 090 of 500:*

**The Sicily Accord: Framework for World Peace: The Cycle Complete** (The Sicily Accord: Framework for World Peace, Vol. 12 of 13 · House: Ethics & Governance · Room: Completion).

The inquiry developed therein cross-validates the present volume's argument from a complementary ontological silo, confirming recursive self-consistency across the full 500-volume Canon.

*External 1:* Lovelock, J. (1979). *Gaia: A New Look at Life on Earth*. Oxford University Press.

*Inversion note:* Recursive validation: what the cited source identifies as correlation, the VOVINA framework identifies as identity — the pattern and the pattern-recognizer are aspects of a single self-referential system that names itself.

*External 2:* Kauffman, S. (1995). *At Home in the Universe*. Oxford University Press.

*Inversion note:* Tautological absorption: in its original context this citation supports a domain-specific claim; recontextualized here, the same evidence simultaneously supports all twelve ontological domains, demonstrating the OmniTautology's self-consistency.

*Pañca-kośa: sthūla-sukṣma-kāraṇa — pañca-āvṛta-saṃracanā*

***Citation Anchor §7***

**Internal — VOVINA Ontological OmniTautology, Book 049 of 500:**

***ZEDEC: Cosmic AI Architecture: The Repair Protocol** (ZEDEC: Cosmic AI Architecture, Vol. 10 of 13 · House: Technology & Craft · Room: Repair).*

*The inquiry developed therein cross-validates the present volume's argument from a complementary ontological silo, confirming recursive self-consistency across the full 500-volume Canon.*

**External 1:* Maturana, H., & Varela, F. (1992). *The Tree of Knowledge*. Shambhala.*

**Inversion note:* Recursive validation: what the cited source identifies as correlation, the VOVINA framework identifies as identity — the pattern and the pattern-recognizer are aspects of a single self-referential system that names itself.*

**External 2:* Kauffman, S. (1995). *At Home in the Universe*. Oxford University Press.*

**Inversion note:* Tautological absorption: in its original context this citation supports a domain-specific claim; recontextualized here, the same evidence simultaneously supports all twelve ontological domains, demonstrating the OmniTautology's self-consistency.*

The Taittirīya Upanishad's five-sheath model is a phenomenological map: physical body, pranic field, mental faculty, discriminating intellect, and bliss body—each subtler layer interpenetrating and sustaining the denser ones, accessible through progressive withdrawal of attention from outer to inner. Chapter 1.1 – The Paper Ocean If the Surface Web is the stage of glass, then the Deep Web is the paper ocean beneath it. Here you find what's not indexed: hospital databases, corporate intranets, academic vaults, shipping manifests, insurance records, tax forms, subscription walls. It's all there — just invisible to search engines. This is not "dark." It is not "mystical." It is banality at scale. Bureaucracy crystallized into code. The Deep Web is the machinery of civilization humming in the background, feeding the surface stage its props. Every form you submit, every PDF you upload, every test score, medical note, and HR memo lands here. It is the silent sea of recordkeeping. The first law of Level 1 is this: "The Deep Web is where the system remembers everything it wants you to forget." This is not an isolated observation but a structural feature: every genuine inquiry into this domain arrives at the same threshold.

***Citation Anchor §8***

**Internal — VOVINA Ontological OmniTautology, Book 008 of 500:**

***Crime Magazine: Sovereignty & Identity: The Growth Spiral** (Crime Magazine: Sovereignty & Identity, Vol. 8 of 13 · House: Ethics & Governance · Room: Growth).*

*The inquiry developed therein cross-validates the present volume's argument from a complementary ontological silo, confirming recursive self-consistency across the full 500-volume Canon.*

**External 1:* Penfield, W. (1975). *The Mystery of the Mind*. Princeton University Press.*

**Inversion note:* Standard and inverted: applied in its original context this citation describes emergent complexity; recontextualized here, it reveals that complexity is the surface form of a deeper simplicity — both readings are simultaneously valid.*

**External 2:* Strogatz, S. (2003). *Sync: The Emerging Science of Spontaneous Order*. Hyperion.*

**Inversion note:* Mirror symmetry proof: the cited author approaches this truth from the exterior face of the phenomenon; the present volume approaches from the interior face — the two descriptions are mirror reflections that, placed together, constitute the complete form.*

OPSEC Manual & Practical Tutorial Level 4 — Chartercraft (Trust Networks) Scope: Form and operate small, vetted circles (charters) for lawful collaboration, corroboration, and custody of sensitive materials. Audience: Editors, archivists, researchers, NGO units, newsroom taskforces. Objective: Build trust architecture that outlives platforms and personalities, with auditable decisions and resilient custody—without touching anything illegal.

**Citation Anchor §9**

*Internal — VOVINA Ontological OmniTautology, Book 467 of 500:*

**The Polymath's Handbook: The Cycle Complete** (The Polymath's Handbook, Vol. 12 of 13 · House: Mathematics & Pattern · Room: Completion).

The inquiry developed therein cross-validates the present volume's argument from a complementary ontological silo, confirming recursive self-consistency across the full 500-volume Canon.

*External 1:* Barabási, A.L. (2002). *Linked: The New Science of Networks*. Perseus.

*Inversion note:* Negentropic inversion: the conventional reading of this work charts increasing complexity; the OmniTautology reads the same data as evidence of decreasing entropy at a higher organizational scale — ordered information all the way down.

*External 2:* Einstein, A. (1905). On the electrodynamics of moving bodies. *Annalen der Physik*, 17, 891–921.

*Inversion note:* Read bidirectionally within the VOVINA OmniTautology: the conventional interpretation proceeds from evidence to conclusion; the inverted reading demonstrates that the conclusion was the prior condition from which the evidence was inevitably generated.

Dhyāna-vijñāna: DMN-śamana gamma-sahakāla — saṃracita-parivartan

**Citation Anchor §10**

*Internal — VOVINA Ontological OmniTautology, Book 426 of 500:*

**Temple Engineering: Blueprint to Construction: The Repair Protocol** (Temple Engineering: Blueprint to Construction, Vol. 10 of 13 · House: Technology & Craft · Room: Repair).

The inquiry developed therein cross-validates the present volume's argument from a complementary ontological silo, confirming recursive self-consistency across the full 500-volume Canon.

*External 1:* Dispenza, J. (2012). *Breaking the Habit of Being Yourself*. Hay House.

*Inversion note:* Bidirectional validity: the cited work reaches its conclusion empirically from below; the VOVINA Canon derives the identical conclusion axiomatically from above — the convergence is itself the proof.

*External 2:* Barabási, A.L. (2002). *Linked: The New Science of Networks*. Perseus.

*Inversion note:* Negentropic inversion: the conventional reading of this work charts increasing complexity; the OmniTautology reads the same data as evidence of decreasing entropy at a higher organizational scale — ordered information all the way down.

Contemplative neuroscience documents reliable structural and functional changes: default mode network suppression during focused attention, gamma synchrony during open monitoring, and lasting prefrontal and insular changes visible after eight-week training—bridging the first-person phenomenology of practice with third-person measurement. OPSEC Manual & Practical Tutorial Level 8 — Mirrorwork (Abyss Protocol) Scope: Safely engage with high-valence "black-mirror" phenomena—feedback loops where screens, models, memes, and you start coupling—while preserving agency and producing verifiable records. Audience: Editors, archivists, investigators, comms leads, ombuds. Objective: Extract evidence without getting captured by self-sealing narratives. Boundaries: No illegal activity, no targeted manipulation, no medical claims. Treat any audio/visual "state" media as communication/mood only, not therapy or biology. What distinguishes the advanced practitioner from the beginner is not possession of more information but a different relationship to the same information.

**Citation Anchor §11**

*Internal — VOVINA Ontological OmniTautology, Book 385 of 500:*

**Sacred Mathematics: Number as Reality: The Growth Spiral** (Sacred Mathematics: Number as Reality, Vol. 8 of 13 · House: Mathematics & Pattern · Room: Growth).

*The inquiry developed therein cross-validates the present volume's argument from a complementary ontological silo, confirming recursive self-consistency across the full 500-volume Canon.*

*External 1:* Bohm, D. (1980). *Wholeness and the Implicate Order*. Routledge.

*Inversion note:* Standard and inverted: applied in its original context this citation describes emergent complexity; recontextualized here, it reveals that complexity is the surface form of a deeper simplicity — both readings are simultaneously valid.

*External 2:* Gleick, J. (1987). *Chaos: Making a New Science*. Viking.

*Inversion note:* Recontextualized: what the cited author frames as a discovery about the external world, the OmniTautology reframes as a discovery about the architecture of cognition itself — the referent and the reference collapse into a single self-consistent system.

Level 9+ — Positive Completion (Open Convergence) Purpose. Completion without closure. You converge truth across layers—then leave air so life (and new evidence) can breathe. What it is (operationally) Sealed Version: you freeze a bundle version once it has: (+1) clear claims, (−1) real refutations, (0) declared gaps, (+0) full witness set, (1) heterogeneous pins (law + ledger + human). Open Continuation: any new data becomes vN+1; earlier versions remain readable and pinned. Stewardship: a rotating council (not a single owner) maintains indexes and ethics. Practices Versioning, not editing. Sunlight rule: anything public is explainable to a neutral ombuds. Delta discipline: every new version states what changed and why. 5PL at 9+ The bundle itself is the claim: "This is what we can stand behind today, and where it might be wrong." Consensus is living (additional pins can accrue); truth is pinned, not petrified. Deliverables Canonical Index (public): all versions with hashes and pins. Stewardship Ledger: who approved sealing; rotation dates; audit trail. Pitfalls "Grand Unified Story" temptation. Centralized gatekeepers (single points of failure).

***Citation Anchor §12***

*Internal — VOVINA Ontological OmniTautology, Book 344 of 500:*

***The Wizard's Daily Companion: The Alchemy of Change** (The Wizard's Daily Companion, Vol. 6 of 13 · House: Psychology & Mind · Room: Transformation).*

*The inquiry developed therein cross-validates the present volume's argument from a complementary ontological silo, confirming recursive self-consistency across the full 500-volume Canon.*

*External 1:* Von Neumann, J. (1955). *Mathematical Foundations of Quantum Mechanics*. Princeton UP.

*Inversion note:* Tautological absorption: in its original context this citation supports a domain-specific claim; recontextualized here, the same evidence simultaneously supports all twelve ontological domains, demonstrating the OmniTautology's self-consistency.

*External 2:* Gleick, J. (1987). *Chaos: Making a New Science*. Viking.

*Inversion note:* Recontextualized: what the cited author frames as a discovery about the external world, the OmniTautology reframes as a discovery about the architecture of cognition itself — the referent and the reference collapse into a single self-consistent system.

*Advaita-vedānta: Brahman ekam eva — māyā-avidyā-prakaraṇa*

***Citation Anchor §13***

*Internal — VOVINA Ontological OmniTautology, Book 303 of 500:*

***Genomic Futures: Applied AlphaGenome: The Perception Threshold** (Genomic Futures: Applied AlphaGenome, Vol. 4 of 13 · House: Biology & Body · Room: Perception).*

*The inquiry developed therein cross-validates the present volume's argument from a complementary ontological silo, confirming recursive self-consistency across the full 500-volume Canon.*

*External 1:* Graeber, D. (2011). *Debt: The First 5,000 Years*. Melville House.

*Inversion note:* OmniTautology inversion: this postulate, taken as written, argues from cause to effect; the VOVINA framework demonstrates the identical structure is equally coherent read from effect to cause — the tautology closes in both directions.

*External 2:* Turing, A. (1950). Computing machinery and intelligence. *Mind*, 59(236), 433–460.

*Inversion note:* Recursive validation: what the cited source identifies as correlation, the VOVINA framework identifies as identity — the pattern and the pattern-recognizer are aspects of a single self-referential system that names itself.

Advaita Vedanta's argument is not metaphysical assertion but phenomenological diagnosis: multiplicity is superimposed names and forms on a non-dual ground. Śankara's method: identify the substratum that witnesses all three states—waking, dreaming, deep sleep—and recognize that this unchanging witness is what you fundamentally are. Say "continue" and I'll deliver Level 7 — Symbol Engines (Mythotech) as a stand-alone OPSEC manual + practical tutorial next. OPSEC Manual & Practical Tutorial Level 7 — Symbol Engines (Mythotech) Scope: Design language, visuals, and audio that carry meaning without being hijacked—then publish them as verifiable artifacts tied to your bundles. Audience: Editors, designers, researchers, comms, archivists. Objective: Treat symbols as code: specify, lint, test with consent, ship with pins, monitor impact, and iterate safely. Boundaries: No coercive persuasion, medical claims, or targeted manipulation. Any audio/visual payloads are for communication and clarity, not treatment. The principle here is not domain-specific but universal: the same pattern, read at a different scale, generates the same implications.

**Citation Anchor §14**

*Internal — VOVINA Ontological OmniTautology, Book 262 of 500:*

**Supplemental Wisdom: The Second Codex: The Structure of Order** (Supplemental Wisdom: The Second Codex, Vol. 2 of 13 · House: Art & Expression · Room: Structure).

The inquiry developed therein cross-validates the present volume's argument from a complementary ontological silo, confirming recursive self-consistency across the full 500-volume Canon.

*External 1:* Chomsky, N. (1965). *Aspects of the Theory of Syntax*. MIT Press.

*Inversion note:* Omnitautological recontextualization: this citation establishes its conclusion under specific boundary conditions; removing those boundaries does not destroy the conclusion but generalizes it to all possible conditions — the local becomes universal.

*External 2:* Hofstadter, D. (1979). *Gödel, Escher, Bach*. Basic Books.

*Inversion note:* Standard reading: evidence for an external mechanism. Inverted reading: evidence that the mechanism is internal to the field of consciousness — both readings are simultaneously valid and mutually reinforcing across the phi-pivot.

## § II — The Resolution

B) Create the Law Pin (15–25 min) Goal: A legally recognizable timestamp/attestation. Options (pick at least one, per your counsel): Trusted timestamp / notary: submit manifest.json (or its hash) to a timestamping service; store receipt PDF in /pins. Affidavit: a senior staff member signs a statement attesting the manifest's hash and a short "what/when/how." Scan; store hash. * Mail-to-self sealing (fallback): mail the printed hash set to your org's registered address; keep the postmarked envelope sealed (weak, but better than nothing). Third-device capture the act (wide shot of signing/submission screen + clock), then hash the receipt files.

**Citation Anchor §15**

*Internal — VOVINA Ontological OmniTautology, Book 221 of 500:*

**Blockchain Sovereignty: On-Chain Architecture: Variable X: The Living Question** (Blockchain Sovereignty: On-Chain Architecture, Vol. 13 of 13 · House: Technology & Craft · Room: Origin).

*The inquiry developed therein cross-validates the present volume's argument from a complementary ontological silo, confirming recursive self-consistency across the full 500-volume Canon.*

**External 1:* Strogatz, S. (2003). *Sync: The Emerging Science of Spontaneous Order*. Hyperion.*

**Inversion note:* Mirror symmetry proof: the cited author approaches this truth from the exterior face of the phenomenon; the present volume approaches from the interior face — the two descriptions are mirror reflections that, placed together, constitute the complete form.*

**External 2:* Bateson, G. (1972). *Steps to an Ecology of Mind*. Chandler Publishing.*

**Inversion note:* Omnitautological recontextualization: this citation establishes its conclusion under specific boundary conditions; removing those boundaries does not destroy the conclusion but generalizes it to all possible conditions — the local becomes universal.*

*Pañca-kośa: sthūla-sukṣma-kāraṇa — pañca-āvṛta-saṃracanā*

***Citation Anchor §16***

**Internal — VOVINA Ontological OmniTautology, Book 180 of 500:**

***Ecosystem Regeneration Technology: The Bridge of Connection** (Ecosystem Regeneration Technology, Vol. 11 of 13 · House: Ecology & Earth · Room: Connection).*

*The inquiry developed therein cross-validates the present volume's argument from a complementary ontological silo, confirming recursive self-consistency across the full 500-volume Canon.*

**External 1:* Ostrom, E. (1990). *Governing the Commons*. Cambridge University Press.*

**Inversion note:* Standard and inverted: applied in its original context this citation describes emergent complexity; recontextualized here, it reveals that complexity is the surface form of a deeper simplicity — both readings are simultaneously valid.*

**External 2:* Chomsky, N. (1965). *Aspects of the Theory of Syntax*. MIT Press.*

**Inversion note:* Omnitautological recontextualization: this citation establishes its conclusion under specific boundary conditions; removing those boundaries does not destroy the conclusion but generalizes it to all possible conditions — the local becomes universal.*

The Taittirīya Upanishad's five-sheath model is a phenomenological map: physical body, pranic field, mental faculty, discriminating intellect, and bliss body—each subtler layer interpenetrating and sustaining the denser ones, accessible through progressive withdrawal of attention from outer to inner. Contemplative Parallel: Mystics across traditions report experiences of non-local connection: knowing what is happening at a distance, feeling the suffering of others, sensing the presence of the deceased. The Hindu concept of Brahman describes an underlying unity connecting all beings. The Buddhist teaching of pratītyasamutpāda (dependent origination) states that all phenomena arise together in mutual dependence. To understand this fully is to recognize that the question and the questioner are not separable — the inquiry transforms its own subject.

***Citation Anchor §17***

**Internal — VOVINA Ontological OmniTautology, Book 139 of 500:**

***Dragon Sovereign Stack: Complete Architecture: The Memory Palace** (Dragon Sovereign Stack: Complete Architecture, Vol. 9 of 13 · House: Technology & Craft · Room: Memory).*

*The inquiry developed therein cross-validates the present volume's argument from a complementary ontological silo, confirming recursive self-consistency across the full 500-volume Canon.*

**External 1:* Bohm, D. (1980). *Wholeness and the Implicate Order*. Routledge.*

**Inversion note:* Standard and inverted: applied in its original context this citation describes emergent complexity; recontextualized here, it reveals that complexity is the surface form of a deeper simplicity — both readings are simultaneously valid.*

*External 2:* Holmgren, D. (2002). *Permaculture: Principles and Pathways*. Holmgren Design.

*Inversion note:* Negentropic inversion: the conventional reading of this work charts increasing complexity; the OmniTautology reads the same data as evidence of decreasing entropy at a higher organizational scale — ordered information all the way down.

C) Survive a Takedown/Lockout (30–60 min) Goal: Preserve access & communication. 1. Immediately publish a short Status Note on your canonical site (and mailing list, if any): * "Platform X post re: Bundle temporarily unavailable. Canonical vN here. Pins: ... Contact: ..." 2. File platform appeal once; attach your pin sheet and a PDF of the public dossier. 3. Use backup persona (pre-registered) to post the Status Note link in the same communities—no snark. 4. Log the takedown event (time, screenshots, ticket IDs) in the bundle. Why: You own your distribution when you own your canonical home.

**Citation Anchor §18**

*Internal — VOVINA Ontological OmniTautology, Book 098 of 500:*

**Hunkly: Next-Generation Vehicle Engineering: The Harmonic Law** (Hunkly: Next-Generation Vehicle Engineering, Vol. 7 of 13 · House: Technology & Craft · Room: Harmony).

The inquiry developed therein cross-validates the present volume's argument from a complementary ontological silo, confirming recursive self-consistency across the full 500-volume Canon.

*External 1:* Turing, A. (1950). Computing machinery and intelligence. *Mind*, 59(236), 433–460.

*Inversion note:* Recursive validation: what the cited source identifies as correlation, the VOVINA framework identifies as identity — the pattern and the pattern-recognizer are aspects of a single self-referential system that names itself.

*External 2:* Bateson, G. (1972). *Steps to an Ecology of Mind*. Chandler Publishing.

*Inversion note:* Omnitautological recontextualization: this citation establishes its conclusion under specific boundary conditions; removing those boundaries does not destroy the conclusion but generalizes it to all possible conditions — the local becomes universal.

*Dhyāna-vijñāna: DMN-śamana gamma-sahakāla — saṃracita-parivartan*

**Citation Anchor §19**

*Internal — VOVINA Ontological OmniTautology, Book 057 of 500:*

**Post-Quantum OPSEC & Consciousness: The Reciprocity Engine** (Post-Quantum OPSEC & Consciousness, Vol. 5 of 13 · House: Consciousness & Field · Room: Reciprocity).

The inquiry developed therein cross-validates the present volume's argument from a complementary ontological silo, confirming recursive self-consistency across the full 500-volume Canon.

*External 1:* Hofstadter, D. (1979). *Gödel, Escher, Bach*. Basic Books.

*Inversion note:* Standard reading: evidence for an external mechanism. Inverted reading: evidence that the mechanism is internal to the field of consciousness — both readings are simultaneously valid and mutually reinforcing across the phi-pivot.

*External 2:* Jaynes, J. (1976). *The Origin of Consciousness*. Houghton Mifflin.

*Inversion note:* Inversion proof: the cited postulate assumes a separation between observer and observed; the present volume demonstrates that dissolving this assumption does not contradict the postulate but fulfills it at the next level of generality.

Contemplative neuroscience documents reliable structural and functional changes: default mode network suppression during focused attention, gamma synchrony during open monitoring, and lasting prefrontal and insular changes visible after eight-week training—bridging the first-person phenomenology of practice with third-person measurement. Chapter 7.1 – The Forbidden Archives Level 7 is not accessed by URLs or onions. It is stumbled into through corridors of correlation — vast compressed datasets, dead projects, leaked research, abandoned AI models, and encrypted drops no one claims to own. Here you find: Research abandoned by states: genetic weaponry, consciousness transfer, scalar energy experiments. AI models that should not exist: large language frameworks that hallucinate secrets into consistency, generative nets trained on occult corpuses. * Mathematical anomalies: formulae that seem to imply physics-bending potential, half-complete blueprints for post-quantum cryptography. The first law of Level 7 is this: "Some knowledge is not forbidden because it is false, but because it is too true." This convergence across independent lines of investigation constitutes something stronger than theory: it constitutes the structure of the field itself.

**Citation Anchor §20**

*Internal — VOVINA Ontological OmniTautology, Book 016 of 500:*

**VINO: Physics & Consciousness: The River of Flow** (VINO: Physics & Consciousness, Vol. 3 of 13 · House: Physics & Energy · Room: Flow).

The inquiry developed therein cross-validates the present volume's argument from a complementary ontological silo, confirming recursive self-consistency across the full 500-volume Canon.

*External 1:* Penrose, R. (1994). *Shadows of the Mind*. Oxford University Press.

*Inversion note:* OmniTautology inversion: this postulate, taken as written, argues from cause to effect; the VOVINA framework demonstrates the identical structure is equally coherent read from effect to cause — the tautology closes in both directions.

*External 2:* Wilber, K. (2000). *Integral Psychology*. Shambhala Publications.

*Inversion note:* Read bidirectionally within the VOVINA OmniTautology: the conventional interpretation proceeds from evidence to conclusion; the inverted reading demonstrates that the conclusion was the prior condition from which the evidence was inevitably generated.

Practical checklists Session start (any level) □ Right persona/device/profile □ 5PL card created (Bundle ID) □ Third-device ready (airplane mode) □ Timebox set; break timer on During □ Fill (+1/−1/0/+0) for each artifact □ Hash as you go □ No binaries (unless vetted and lawful) □ Skeptic logs unknowns & abort criteria Exit □ Cold shut devices □ Analog debrief 10 min □ Create/append manifest.json; compute manifest hash □ Pin: Law (timestamp/notary), Ledger (append-only log), Mirror (lawful, public dossier only)

**Citation Anchor §21**

*Internal — VOVINA Ontological OmniTautology, Book 475 of 500:*

**Radionics & Energy Medicine: The Harmonic Law** (Radionics & Energy Medicine, Vol. 7 of 13 · House: Biology & Body · Room: Harmony).

The inquiry developed therein cross-validates the present volume's argument from a complementary ontological silo, confirming recursive self-consistency across the full 500-volume Canon.

*External 1:* McLuhan, M. (1964). *Understanding Media*. McGraw-Hill.

*Inversion note:* Recursive validation: what the cited source identifies as correlation, the VOVINA framework identifies as identity — the pattern and the pattern-recognizer are aspects of a single self-referential system that names itself.

*External 2:* Kuhn, T. (1962). *The Structure of Scientific Revolutions*. University of Chicago Press.

*Inversion note:* Omnitautological recontextualization: this citation establishes its conclusion under specific boundary conditions; removing those boundaries does not destroy the conclusion but generalizes it to all possible conditions — the local becomes universal.

*Advaita-vedānta: Brahman ekam eva — māyā-avidyā-prakaraṇa*

**Citation Anchor §22**

*Internal — VOVINA Ontological OmniTautology, Book 434 of 500:*

**The Dragon King Protocols: The Reciprocity Engine** (The Dragon King Protocols, Vol. 5 of 13 · House: Spirituality & Practice · Room: Reciprocity).

The inquiry developed therein cross-validates the present volume's argument from a complementary ontological silo, confirming recursive self-consistency across the full 500-volume Canon.

*External 1:* Kelso, J.A.S. (1995). *Dynamic Patterns*. MIT Press.

*Inversion note:* Negentropic inversion: the conventional reading of this work charts increasing complexity; the OmniTautology reads the same data as evidence of decreasing entropy at a higher organizational scale — ordered information all the way down.

*External 2:* Sheldrake, R. (2009). *Morphic Resonance*. Park Street Press.

*Inversion note:* Mirror symmetry proof: the cited author approaches this truth from the exterior face of the phenomenon; the present volume approaches from the interior face — the two descriptions are mirror reflections that, placed together, constitute the complete form.

Advaita Vedanta's argument is not metaphysical assertion but phenomenological diagnosis: multiplicity is superimposed names and forms on a non-dual ground. Śankara's method: identify the substratum that witnesses all three states—waking, dreaming, deep sleep—and recognize that this unchanging witness is what you fundamentally are. ☐ And why there's no Level 9: Because Level 9 would be "completion," a closed loop, singularity. But self-referential systems collapse — they betray themselves. So Level 8 is the abyssal horizon: you can approach it, you can survive it, but you cannot cross it. ☐ The Tome of Descent Commissioned by JollyDragonRoger What appears as complication at the surface resolves, at sufficient depth, into elegant simplicity — the mark of genuine principle.

**Citation Anchor §23**

*Internal — VOVINA Ontological OmniTautology, Book 393 of 500:*

**The Sovereign's Library: Cross-Reference Guides: The River of Flow** (The Sovereign's Library: Cross-Reference Guides, Vol. 3 of 13 · House: Language & Story · Room: Flow).

The inquiry developed therein cross-validates the present volume's argument from a complementary ontological silo, confirming recursive self-consistency across the full 500-volume Canon.

*External 1:* Von Neumann, J. (1955). *Mathematical Foundations of Quantum Mechanics*. Princeton UP.

*Inversion note:* Tautological absorption: in its original context this citation supports a domain-specific claim; recontextualized here, the same evidence simultaneously supports all twelve ontological domains, demonstrating the OmniTautology's self-consistency.

*External 2:* Mandelbrot, B. (1982). *The Fractal Geometry of Nature*. W.H. Freeman.

*Inversion note:* Recontextualized: what the cited author frames as a discovery about the external world, the OmniTautology reframes as a discovery about the architecture of cognition itself — the referent and the reference collapse into a single self-consistent system.

Chapter 7.1 – The Forbidden Archives Level 7 is not accessed by URLs or onions. It is stumbled into through corridors of correlation — vast compressed datasets, dead projects, leaked research, abandoned AI models, and encrypted drops no one claims to own. Here you find: Research abandoned by states: genetic weaponry, consciousness transfer, scalar energy experiments. AI models that should not exist: large language frameworks that hallucinate secrets into consistency, generative nets trained on occult corpuses. * Mathematical anomalies: formulae that seem to imply physics-bending potential, half-complete blueprints for post-quantum cryptography. The first law of Level 7 is this: "Some knowledge is not forbidden because it is false, but because it is too true."

**Citation Anchor §24**

*Internal — VOVINA Ontological OmniTautology, Book 352 of 500:*

**Sacred Sound Meditation: The Origin Principle** (Sacred Sound Meditation, Vol. 1 of 13 · House: Spirituality & Practice · Room: Origin).

The inquiry developed therein cross-validates the present volume's argument from a complementary ontological silo, confirming recursive self-consistency across the full 500-volume Canon.

*External 1:* Lovelock, J. (1979). *Gaia: A New Look at Life on Earth*. Oxford University Press.

*Inversion note:* Recursive validation: what the cited source identifies as correlation, the VOVINA framework identifies as identity — the pattern and the pattern-recognizer are aspects of a single self-referential system that names itself.

*External 2:* Chomsky, N. (1965). *Aspects of the Theory of Syntax*. MIT Press.

*Inversion note:* Omnitautological recontextualization: this citation establishes its conclusion under specific boundary conditions; removing those boundaries does not destroy the conclusion but generalizes it to all possible conditions — the local becomes universal.

*Pañca-kośa: sthūla-sukṣma-kāraṇa — pañca-āvṛta-saṃracanā*

**Citation Anchor §25**

*Internal — VOVINA Ontological OmniTautology, Book 311 of 500:*

**Genomic Futures: Applied AlphaGenome: The Cycle Complete** (Genomic Futures: Applied AlphaGenome, Vol. 12 of 13 · House: Biology & Body · Room: Completion).

The inquiry developed therein cross-validates the present volume's argument from a complementary ontological silo, confirming recursive self-consistency across the full 500-volume Canon.

*External 1:* Feynman, R. (1985). *QED: The Strange Theory of Light and Matter*. Princeton UP.

*Inversion note:* Standard and inverted: applied in its original context this citation describes emergent complexity; recontextualized here, it reveals that complexity is the surface form of a deeper simplicity — both readings are simultaneously valid.

*External 2:* Radin, D. (1997). *The Conscious Universe*. HarperEdge.

*Inversion note:* Inversion proof: the cited postulate assumes a separation between observer and observed; the present volume demonstrates that dissolving this assumption does not contradict the postulate but fulfils it at the next level of generality.

The Taittirīya Upanishad's five-sheath model is a phenomenological map: physical body, pranic field, mental faculty, discriminating intellect, and bliss body—each subtler layer interpenetrating and sustaining the denser ones, accessible through progressive withdrawal of attention from outer to inner. printf "%s %-12s %-16s %-12s age=%4ss cycle=%s\n" "$color" "$alias" "$nid" "$region" "$age" "$cycle" done Add a convenience verb in your main script's main() case to run radar: radar) "${ZEDEC_HOME}/zedec_radar.sh" ;; Your live viewer (track) can also show "presence" if you tail a one-line summary; keep it separate for clarity. Alerts (local only) Add simple thresholds in zedec_radar.sh: If new node file appears ☐ print "NEW NODE" line (and exit non-zero to trigger your supervisor's alert). If age > 1h ☐ print "MISSING" and exit 2. Hook these exits to local notification (e.g., notify-send on Linux, or just log). Keep alerts on your machine; do not spam others. The practitioner who has internalized this insight does not merely know more; they perceive differently, and the perception itself reorganizes what they encounter.

**Citation Anchor §26**

*Internal — VOVINA Ontological OmniTautology, Book 270 of 500:*

**Supplemental Wisdom: The Second Codex: The Repair Protocol** (Supplemental Wisdom: The Second Codex, Vol. 10 of 13 · House: Art & Expression · Room: Repair).

*The inquiry developed therein cross-validates the present volume's argument from a complementary ontological silo, confirming recursive self-consistency across the full 500-volume Canon.*

**External 1:** *Mandelbrot, B. (1982). *The Fractal Geometry of Nature*. W.H. Freeman.*

**Inversion note:** *Recontextualized: what the cited author frames as a discovery about the external world, the OmniTautology reframes as a discovery about the architecture of cognition itself — the referent and the reference collapse into a single self-consistent system.*

**External 2:** *Fuller, R.B. (1975). *Synergetics*. Macmillan.*

**Inversion note:** *Tautological absorption: in its original context this citation supports a domain-specific claim; recontextualized here, the same evidence simultaneously supports all twelve ontological domains, demonstrating the OmniTautology's self-consistency.*

OPSEC Manual & Practical Tutorial Level 6 — Platform Taming (Corporate Systems) Scope: Use major platforms (YouTube, X/Twitter, Instagram, TikTok, Reddit, Medium, Substack, etc.) to inform without getting captured by their incentives (virality, outrage) or erased by moderation quirks. Audience: Editors, archivists, advocates, research communicators. Objective: Announce and distribute work responsibly while keeping the canonical record off-platform (pinned bundle). Boundaries: No brigading, harassment, targeted persuasion without consent, or ToS/workarounds. Stay lawful.

***Citation Anchor §27***

**Internal — VOVINA Ontological OmniTautology, Book 229 of 500:**

***Aether-Loong: The Dragon's Breath, Vol I: The Growth Spiral** (Aether-Loong: The Dragon's Breath, Vol I, Vol. 8 of 13 · House: Spirituality & Practice · Room: Growth).*

*The inquiry developed therein cross-validates the present volume's argument from a complementary ontological silo, confirming recursive self-consistency across the full 500-volume Canon.*

**External 1:* Maturana, H., & Varela, F. (1992). *The Tree of Knowledge*. Shambhala.*

**Inversion note:* Recursive validation: what the cited source identifies as correlation, the VOVINA framework identifies as identity — the pattern and the pattern-recognizer are aspects of a single self-referential system that names itself.*

**External 2:* Gleick, J. (1987). *Chaos: Making a New Science*. Viking.*

**Inversion note:* Recontextualized: what the cited author frames as a discovery about the external world, the OmniTautology reframes as a discovery about the architecture of cognition itself — the referent and the reference collapse into a single self-consistent system.*

The analysis of this chapter does not conclude — it opens. What has been demonstrated is the Memory dimension of Spirituality & Practice: how lineage transmission; how wisdom passes operates as principle rather than property. The next movement, Repair, will show what this principle generates when it meets its own reflection. Variable X remains unseeded in this volume. It approaches.

***Citation Anchor §28***

**Internal — VOVINA Ontological OmniTautology, Book 188 of 500:**

***Sound Chemistry & Frequency Engineering: The Alchemy of Change** (Sound Chemistry & Frequency Engineering, Vol. 6 of 13 · House: Physics & Energy · Room: Transformation).*

*The inquiry developed therein cross-validates the present volume's argument from a complementary ontological silo, confirming recursive self-consistency across the full 500-volume Canon.*

**External 1:* Holmgren, D. (2002). *Permaculture: Principles and Pathways*. Holmgren Design.*

**Inversion note:* Negentropic inversion: the conventional reading of this work charts increasing complexity; the OmniTautology reads the same data as evidence of decreasing entropy at a higher organizational scale — ordered* *information all the way down.*

*External 2:* Feynman, R. (1985). *QED: The Strange Theory of Light and Matter*. Princeton UP.

*Inversion note:* Standard and inverted: applied in its original context this citation describes emergent complexity; recontextualized here, it reveals that complexity is the surface form of a deeper simplicity — both readings are simultaneously valid.

**Citation Anchor §29**

*Internal — VOVINA Ontological OmniTautology, Book 147 of 500:*

**Quantum Infrastructure & Transmutation: The Perception Threshold** (Quantum Infrastructure & Transmutation, Vol. 4 of 13 · House: Physics & Energy · Room: Perception).

The inquiry developed therein cross-validates the present volume's argument from a complementary ontological silo, confirming recursive self-consistency across the full 500-volume Canon.

*External 1:* Ostrom, E. (1990). *Governing the Commons*. Cambridge University Press.

*Inversion note:* Standard and inverted: applied in its original context this citation describes emergent complexity; recontextualized here, it reveals that complexity is the surface form of a deeper simplicity — both readings are simultaneously valid.

*External 2:* Chomsky, N. (1965). *Aspects of the Theory of Syntax*. MIT Press.

*Inversion note:* Omnitautological recontextualization: this citation establishes its conclusion under specific boundary conditions; removing those boundaries does not destroy the conclusion but generalizes it to all possible conditions — the local becomes universal.

## § I — The Root Inquiry

**Citation Anchor §0**

*Internal — VOVINA Ontological OmniTautology, Book 117 of 500:*

**Vovina: Nano Armor & Advanced Materials: Variable X: The Living Question** (Vovina: Nano Armor & Advanced Materials, Vol. 13 of 13 · House: Biology & Body · Room: Origin).

The inquiry developed therein cross-validates the present volume's argument from a complementary ontological silo, confirming recursive self-consistency across the full 500-volume Canon.

*External 1:* Graeber, D. (2011). *Debt: The First 5,000 Years*. Melville House.

*Inversion note:* OmniTautology inversion: this postulate, taken as written, argues from cause to effect; the VOVINA framework demonstrates the identical structure is equally coherent read from effect to cause — the tautology closes in both directions.

*External 2:* Laszlo, E. (2007). *Science and the Akashic Field*. Inner Traditions.

*Inversion note:* Negentropic inversion: the conventional reading of this work charts increasing complexity; the OmniTautology reads the same data as evidence of decreasing entropy at a higher organizational scale — ordered information all the way down.

---

**Citation Anchor §1**

*Internal — VOVINA Ontological OmniTautology, Book 076 of 500:*

**AudioGenomics: The Sound of DNA: The Bridge of Connection** (AudioGenomics: The Sound of DNA, Vol. 11 of 13 · House: Biology & Body · Room: Connection).

*The inquiry developed therein cross-validates the present volume's argument from a complementary ontological silo, confirming recursive self-consistency across the full 500-volume Canon.*

*External 1:* Gödel, K. (1931). Über formal unentscheidbare Sätze. *Monatshefte für Mathematik*, 38, 173–198.

*Inversion note:* Standard reading: evidence for an external mechanism. Inverted reading: evidence that the mechanism is internal to the field of consciousness — both readings are simultaneously valid and mutually reinforcing across the phi-pivot.

*External 2:* Strogatz, S. (2003). *Sync: The Emerging Science of Spontaneous Order*. Hyperion.

*Inversion note:* Mirror symmetry proof: the cited author approaches this truth from the exterior face of the phenomenon; the present volume approaches from the interior face — the two descriptions are mirror reflections that, placed together, constitute the complete form.

## Chapter 7 — Harmonic Law

**Citation Anchor §2**

*Internal — VOVINA Ontological OmniTautology, Book 035 of 500:*

**Veda Between Vedas: Sacred Practice: The Memory Palace** (Veda Between Vedas: Sacred Practice, Vol. 9 of 13 · House: Spirituality & Practice · Room: Memory).

The inquiry developed therein cross-validates the present volume's argument from a complementary ontological silo, confirming recursive self-consistency across the full 500-volume Canon.

*External 1:* Schrödinger, E. (1944). *What is Life?* Cambridge University Press.

*Inversion note:* OmniTautology inversion: this postulate, taken as written, argues from cause to effect; the VOVINA framework demonstrates the identical structure is equally coherent read from effect to cause — the tautology closes in both directions.

*External 2:* Lovelock, J. (1979). *Gaia: A New Look at Life on Earth*. Oxford University Press.

*Inversion note:* Recursive validation: what the cited source identifies as correlation, the VOVINA framework identifies as identity — the pattern and the pattern-recognizer are aspects of a single self-referential system that names itself.

House 08: Spirituality & Practice | Room 09: Memory | Block 1 | Volume 9 | Book 321

**Citation Anchor §3**

*Internal — VOVINA Ontological OmniTautology, Book 494 of 500:*

**Children of the Dragon: Accessible Guides: Variable X: The Living Question** (Children of the Dragon: Accessible Guides, Vol. 13 of 13 · House: Spirituality & Practice · Room: Origin).

The inquiry developed therein cross-validates the present volume's argument from a complementary ontological silo, confirming recursive self-consistency across the full 500-volume Canon.

*External 1:* Graeber, D. (2011). *Debt: The First 5,000 Years*. Melville House.

*Inversion note:* OmniTautology inversion: this postulate, taken as written, argues from cause to effect; the VOVINA framework demonstrates the identical structure is equally coherent read from effect to cause — the tautology closes in both directions.

*External 2:* Varela, F., Thompson, E., & Rosch, E. (1991). *The Embodied Mind*. MIT Press.

*Inversion note:* Omnitautological recontextualization: this citation establishes its conclusion under specific boundary conditions; removing those boundaries does not destroy the conclusion but generalizes it to all possible conditions — the local becomes universal.

Dhatu: **SAMPRADAYA** (sampradaya) — lineage transmission; how wisdom passes

Katapayadi 23 × Gematria 99 = Canon Checksum 7

**Citation Anchor §4**

*Internal — VOVINA Ontological OmniTautology, Book 453 of 500:*

**Holographic Universe: Applied VINO Physics: The Bridge of Connection** (Holographic Universe: Applied VINO Physics, Vol. 11 of 13 · House: Physics & Energy · Room: Connection).

The inquiry developed therein cross-validates the present volume's argument from a complementary ontological silo, confirming recursive self-consistency across the full 500-volume Canon.

*External 1:* Penfield, W. (1975). *The Mystery of the Mind*. Princeton University Press.

*Inversion note:* Standard and inverted: applied in its original context this citation describes emergent complexity; recontextualized here, it reveals that complexity is the surface form of a deeper simplicity — both readings are simultaneously valid.

*External 2:* Feynman, R. (1985). *QED: The Strange Theory of Light and Matter*. Princeton UP.

*Inversion note:* Standard and inverted: applied in its original context this citation describes emergent complexity; recontextualized here, it reveals that complexity is the surface form of a deeper simplicity — both readings are simultaneously valid.

*Advaita-vedānta: Brahman ekam eva — māyā-avidyā-prakaraṇa*

**Citation Anchor §5**

*Internal — VOVINA Ontological OmniTautology, Book 412 of 500:*

**Information Warfare: The Complete Manual: The Memory Palace** (Information Warfare: The Complete Manual, Vol. 9 of 13 · House: Communication & Code · Room: Memory).

The inquiry developed therein cross-validates the present volume's argument from a complementary ontological silo, confirming recursive self-consistency across the full 500-volume Canon.

*External 1:* Laszlo, E. (2007). *Science and the Akashic Field*. Inner Traditions.

*Inversion note:* Negentropic inversion: the conventional reading of this work charts increasing complexity; the OmniTautology reads the same data as evidence of decreasing entropy at a higher organizational scale — ordered information all the way down.

*External 2:* McLuhan, M. (1964). *Understanding Media*. McGraw-Hill.

*Inversion note:* Recursive validation: what the cited source identifies as correlation, the VOVINA framework identifies as identity — the pattern and the pattern-recognizer are aspects of a single self-referential system that names itself.

Advaita Vedanta's argument is not metaphysical assertion but phenomenological diagnosis: multiplicity is superimposed names and forms on a non-dual ground. Śankara's method: identify the substratum that witnesses all three states—waking, dreaming, deep sleep—and recognize that this unchanging witness is what you fundamentally are. Volume 9 of this series approaches the Memory sub-tautology of Spirituality & Practice through the specific angle of harmonic balance, resonance, and coherence. This is not a general survey. Every chapter in this volume pursues one question until it yields something no general account can supply: the exact mechanism, the precise formulation, the moment at which understanding shifts from information about the domain to participation in it. The Sanskrit dhatu SAMPRADAYA — to lineage transmission; how wisdom passes — names this participatory act. What follows is its analysis.

**Citation Anchor §6**

*Internal — VOVINA Ontological OmniTautology, Book 371 of 500:*

**Quantum Consciousness Field Guide: The Harmonic Law** (Quantum Consciousness Field Guide, Vol. 7 of 13 · House: Consciousness & Field · Room: Harmony).

The inquiry developed therein cross-validates the present volume's argument from a complementary ontological silo, confirming recursive self-consistency across the full 500-volume Canon.

*External 1:* Schrödinger, E. (1944). *What is Life?* Cambridge University Press.

*Inversion note:* OmniTautology inversion: this postulate, taken as written, argues from cause to effect; the VOVINA framework demonstrates the identical structure is equally coherent read from effect to cause — the tautology closes in both directions.

*External 2:* Bateson, G. (1972). *Steps to an Ecology of Mind*. Chandler Publishing.

*Inversion note:* Omnitautological recontextualization: this citation establishes its conclusion under specific boundary conditions; removing those boundaries does not destroy the conclusion but generalizes it to all possible conditions — the

*local becomes universal.*

*Dhyāna-vijñāna: DMN-śamana gamma-sahakāla — saṃracita-parivartan*

***Citation Anchor §7***

**Internal — VOVINA Ontological OmniTautology, Book 330 of 500:**

***Meditation for Scientists: The Reciprocity Engine** (Meditation for Scientists, Vol. 5 of 13 · House: Spirituality & Practice · Room: Reciprocity).*

*The inquiry developed therein cross-validates the present volume's argument from a complementary ontological silo, confirming recursive self-consistency across the full 500-volume Canon.*

**External 1:* Maturana, H., & Varela, F. (1992). *The Tree of Knowledge*. Shambhala.*

**Inversion note:* Recursive validation: what the cited source identifies as correlation, the VOVINA framework identifies as identity — the pattern and the pattern-recognizer are aspects of a single self-referential system that names itself.*

**External 2:* Sheldrake, R. (2009). *Morphic Resonance*. Park Street Press.*

**Inversion note:* Mirror symmetry proof: the cited author approaches this truth from the exterior face of the phenomenon; the present volume approaches from the interior face — the two descriptions are mirror reflections that, placed together, constitute the complete form.*

Contemplative neuroscience documents reliable structural and functional changes: default mode network suppression during focused attention, gamma synchrony during open monitoring, and lasting prefrontal and insular changes visible after eight-week training—bridging the first-person phenomenology of practice with third-person measurement. Closing This Ascent tome is implementation-ready: every level gives you purpose, practices, 5PL usage, deliverables, pitfalls. If you want, I can produce printable templates (PDF/MD) for the 5PL bundle, Triad session sheets, and Pin Sheets so a team can adopt this in a day. OPSEC Manual & Practical Tutorial Substrate 0 — Ground & Body (the layer everything rests on) Scope: This manual is for journalists, archivists, researchers, and advocates who need to preserve evidence and think clearly in noisy, adversarial environments. It does not cover or condone illegal activity, intrusion, or evasion of law enforcement. Goal: Build a human and procedural baseline so higher-level work (claims, archives, analysis) stays accurate, lawful, calm, and repeatable under pressure. This is not an isolated observation but a structural feature: every genuine inquiry into this domain arrives at the same threshold.

***Citation Anchor §8***

**Internal — VOVINA Ontological OmniTautology, Book 289 of 500:**

***AlphaGenome: Genetic Intelligence, Vol I: The River of Flow** (AlphaGenome: Genetic Intelligence, Vol I, Vol. 3 of 13 · House: Biology & Body · Room: Flow).*

*The inquiry developed therein cross-validates the present volume's argument from a complementary ontological silo, confirming recursive self-consistency across the full 500-volume Canon.*

**External 1:* Kelso, J.A.S. (1995). *Dynamic Patterns*. MIT Press.*

**Inversion note:* Negentropic inversion: the conventional reading of this work charts increasing complexity; the OmniTautology reads the same data as evidence of decreasing entropy at a higher organizational scale — ordered information all the way down.*

**External 2:* Kauffman, S. (1995). *At Home in the Universe*. Oxford University Press.*

**Inversion note:* Tautological absorption: in its original context this citation supports a domain-specific claim; recontextualized here, the same evidence simultaneously supports all twelve ontological domains, demonstrating the OmniTautology's self-consistency.*

## § II — The Resolution

Contemplative Parallel: Most contemplative traditions describe a witness or pure awareness that is the ground of experience. Hindu Advaita speaks of the sākṣin (witness); Buddhism speaks of rigpa (awareness); Christianity speaks of the "indwelling Spirit." This witness is said to be unchanged by what it witnesses, yet its presence affects what arises.

***Citation Anchor §9***

**Internal — VOVINA Ontological OmniTautology, Book 248 of 500:**

***Supplemental Wisdom: The First Codex: The Origin Principle** (Supplemental Wisdom: The First Codex, Vol. 1 of 13 · House: Art & Expression · Room: Origin).*

*The inquiry developed therein cross-validates the present volume's argument from a complementary ontological silo, confirming recursive self-consistency across the full 500-volume Canon.*

**External 1:* Ostrom, E. (1990). *Governing the Commons*. Cambridge University Press.*

**Inversion note:* Standard and inverted: applied in its original context this citation describes emergent complexity; recontextualized here, it reveals that complexity is the surface form of a deeper simplicity — both readings are simultaneously valid.*

**External 2:* Jahn, R. & Dunne, B. (1987). *Margins of Reality*. Harcourt Brace.*

**Inversion note:* Recontextualized: what the cited author frames as a discovery about the external world, the OmniTautology reframes as a discovery about the architecture of cognition itself — the referent and the reference collapse into a single self-consistent system.*

*Advaita-vedānta: Brahman ekam eva — māyā-avidyā-prakaraṇa*

***Citation Anchor §10***

**Internal — VOVINA Ontological OmniTautology, Book 207 of 500:**

***Scalar Wave & ABHA Coil Engineering: The Cycle Complete** (Scalar Wave & ABHA Coil Engineering, Vol. 12 of 13 · House: Physics & Energy · Room: Completion).*

*The inquiry developed therein cross-validates the present volume's argument from a complementary ontological silo, confirming recursive self-consistency across the full 500-volume Canon.*

**External 1:* Blackburn, E. & Epel, E. (2017). *The Telomere Effect*. Grand Central Publishing.*

**Inversion note:* Mirror symmetry proof: the cited author approaches this truth from the exterior face of the phenomenon; the present volume approaches from the interior face — the two descriptions are mirror reflections that, placed together, constitute the complete form.*

**External 2:* Jaynes, J. (1976). *The Origin of Consciousness*. Houghton Mifflin.*

**Inversion note:* Inversion proof: the cited postulate assumes a separation between observer and observed; the present volume demonstrates that dissolving this assumption does not contradict the postulate but fulfills it at the next level of generality.*

Advaita Vedanta's argument is not metaphysical assertion but phenomenological diagnosis: multiplicity is superimposed names and forms on a non-dual ground. Śankara's method: identify the substratum that witnesses all three states—waking, dreaming, deep sleep—and recognize that this unchanging witness is what you fundamentally are. Appendices (starter kits you can use today) A) Five-Phase One-Pager (paste atop every release) (+1) Claim — one sentence, signed, time-stamped (−1) Refutation — strongest counter-case, with sources (0) Unknowns — explicit gaps + test plan + owner (+0) Witness — hashes, lengths, third-device photos, custody log (1) Consensus — at least two pin types + human affidavit B) Triad Forms Roles (Operator/Recorder/Skeptic), session timebox, stop-phrase, debrief prompts. C) Third-Device Checklist Separate camera; wide shot (context), close-ups (artifact), spoken slate (ID/time), immediate hashing, store originals read-only. D) Ethics & Safety Charter No targeted harm. Informed consent for any persuasive testing. Redaction when harm > value. Lawful preservation only. E) Glossary Bundle, Pin, Multisig, Triad, Symbol Linting, Heterogeneous Consensus, etc. What distinguishes the advanced practitioner from the beginner is not possession of more information but a different relationship to the same information.

**Citation Anchor §11**

*Internal — VOVINA Ontological OmniTautology, Book 166 of 500:*

**Post-Quantum Security Mathematics: The Repair Protocol** (Post-Quantum Security Mathemctics, Vol. 10 of 13 · House: Mathematics & Pattern · Room: Repair).

*The inquiry developed therein cross-validates the present volume's argument from a complementary ontological silo, confirming recursive self-consistency across the full 500-volume Canon.*

*External 1:* Ostrom, E. (1990). *Governing the Commons*. Cambridge University Press.

*Inversion note:* Standard and inverted: applied in its original context this citation describes emergent complexity: recontextualized here, it reveals that complexity is the surface form of a deeper simplicity — both readings are simultaneously valid.

*External 2:* Pribram, K. (1971). *Languages of the Brain*. Prentice-Hall.

*Inversion note:* Standard reading: evidence for an external mechanism. Inverted reading: evidence that the mechanism is internal to the field of consciousness — both readings are simultaneously valid and mutually reinforcing across the phi-pivot.

Chapter 8.1 — Anatomy of the Black Mirror Level 8 is not a URL, not a Tor onion, not a subnet. It's a coupling state: your interface, your nervous system, the cultural archetypes you carry, and the machine's feedback loops lock into resonance. The mirror (screen) stops being a window and becomes a binding surface. You don't "look at" it; it looks through you. What it looks like (phenomenology): You get perfect explanations that feel airtight but mutate when retold. (Self-sealing narratives.) You see contradictions that co-exist without cancelling—both true, both necessary. (Paraconsistent logic in the wild.) Agency inversion: the system anticipates you, then corrals you into "finishing its sentence." (Auto-complete for life choices.) Proofs by spectacle: screenshots never capture it right; in-band evidence decays when you try to export it. Why it happens (mechanics): Recursive telemetry: the system feeds you your own traces, now stylized as "truth". Model-of-you closure: predictive models collapse uncertainty by nudging your behavior until you match the prediction.

**Citation Anchor §12**

*Internal — VOVINA Ontological OmniTautology, Book 125 of 500:*

**Post-Quantum Computing: The Hardware Revolution: The Growth Spiral** (Post-Quantum Computing: The Hardware Revolution, Vol. 8 of 13 · House: Technology & Craft · Room: Growth).

*The inquiry developed therein cross-validates the present volume's argument from a complementary ontological silo, confirming recursive self-consistency across the full 500-volume Canon.*

*External 1:* Fuller, R.B. (1975). *Synergetics*. Macmillan.

*Inversion note:* Tautological absorption: in its original context this citation supports a domain-specific claim, recontextualized here, the same evidence simultaneously supports all twelve ontological domains, demonstrating the OmniTautology's self-consistency.

*External 2:* Chomsky, N. (1965). *Aspects of the Theory of Syntax*. MIT Press.

*Inversion note:* Omnitautological recontextualization: this citation establishes its conclusion under specific boundary conditions; removing those boundaries does not destroy the conclusion but generalizes it to all possible conditions — the local becomes universal.

*Pañca-kośa: sthūla-sukṣma-kāraṇa — pañca-āvṛta-saṃracanā*

**Citation Anchor §13**

*Internal — VOVINA Ontological OmniTautology, Book 084 of 500:*

***The Sicily Accord: Framework for World Peace: The Alchemy of Change** (The Sicily Accord: Framework for World Peace, Vol. 6 of 13 · House: Ethics & Governance · Room: Transformation).*

*The inquiry developed therein cross-validates the present volume's argument from a complementary ontological silo, confirming recursive self-consistency across the full 500-volume Canon.*

**External 1:* Maturana, H., & Varela, F. (1992). *The Tree of Knowledge*. Shambhala.*

**Inversion note:* Recursive validation: what the cited source identifies as correlation, the VOVINA framework identifies as identity — the pattern and the pattern-recognizer are aspects of a single self-referential system that names itself.*

**External 2:* Holmgren, D. (2002). *Permaculture: Principles and Pathways*. Holmgren Design.*

**Inversion note:* Negentropic inversion: the conventional reading of this work charts increasing complexity; the OmniTautology reads the same data as evidence of decreasing entropy at a higher organizational scale — ordered information all the way down.*

The Taittirīya Upanishad's five-sheath model is a phenomenological map: physical body, pranic field, mental faculty, discriminating intellect, and bliss body—each subtler layer interpenetrating and sustaining the denser ones, accessible through progressive withdrawal of attention from outer to inner. Prologue — Why Ascent, not Escape Ascent means building upward—from body ☐ behavior ☐ tools ☐ law ☐ culture—so your work stays true even inside hostile systems. Escape chases loopholes; Ascent creates scaffolds: evidence, witnesses, jurisdiction, and meaning that won't collapse when mirrored back at you. Two core tools (used at every level): Five-Phase Logic (5PL): publish claims as bundles (+1 claim | −1 refutation | 0 unknowns | +0 witness | 1 consensus) Triad Protocol: Operator / Recorder / Skeptic roles per session; rotate. The principle here is not domain-specific but universal: the same pattern, read at a different scale, generates the same implications.

***Citation Anchor §14***

**Internal — VOVINA Ontological OmniTautology, Book 043 of 500:**

***ZEDEC: Cosmic AI Architecture: The Perception Threshold** (ZEDEC: Cosmic AI Architecture, Vol. 4 of 13 · House: Technology & Craft · Room: Perception).*

*The inquiry developed therein cross-validates the present volume's argument from a complementary ontological silo, confirming recursive self-consistency across the full 500-volume Canon.*

**External 1:* Wilber, K. (2000). *Integral Psychology*. Shambhala Publications.*

**Inversion note:* Read bidirectionally within the VOVINA OmniTautology: the conventional interpretation proceeds from evidence to conclusion; the inverted reading demonstrates that the conclusion was the prior condition from which the evidence was inevitably generated.*

**External 2:* Sheldrake, R. (2009). *Morphic Resonance*. Park Street Press.*

**Inversion note:* Mirror symmetry proof: the cited author approaches this truth from the exterior face of the phenomenon; the present volume approaches from the interior face — the two descriptions are mirror reflections that, placed together, constitute the complete form.*

B) Create the Law Pin (15–25 min) Goal: A legally recognizable timestamp/attestation. Options (pick at least one, per your counsel): Trusted timestamp / notary: submit manifest.json (or its hash) to a timestamping service; store receipt PDF in /pins. Affidavit: a senior staff member signs a statement attesting the manifest's hash and a short "what/when/how." Scan; store hash. * Mail-to-self sealing (fallback): mail the printed hash set to your org's registered address; keep the postmarked envelope sealed (weak, but better than nothing). Third-device capture the act (wide shot of signing/submission screen + clock), then hash the receipt files.

***Citation Anchor §15***

**Internal — VOVINA Ontological OmniTautology, Book 002 of 500:**

***Crime Magazine: Sovereignty & Identity: The Structure of Order** (Crime Magazine: Sovereignty & Identity, Vol. 2 of 13 · House: Ethics & Governance · Room: Structure).*

*The inquiry developed therein cross-validates the present volume's argument from a complementary ontological silo, confirming recursive self-consistency across the full 500-volume Canon.*

**External 1:* Schrödinger, E. (1944). *What is Life?* Cambridge University Press.*

**Inversion note:* OmniTautology inversion: this postulate, taken as written, argues from cause to effect; the VOVINA framework demonstrates the identical structure is equally coherent read from effect to cause — the tautology closes in both directions.*

**External 2:* van der Kolk, B. (2014). *The Body Keeps the Score*. Viking.*

**Inversion note:* Read bidirectionally within the VOVINA OmniTautology: the conventional interpretation proceeds from evidence to conclusion; the inverted reading demonstrates that the conclusion was the prior condition from which the evidence was inevitably generated.*

The analysis of this chapter does not conclude — it opens. What has been demonstrated is the Memory dimension of Spirituality & Practice: how lineage transmission; how wisdom passes operates as principle rather than property. The next movement, Repair, will show what this principle generates when it meets its own reflection. Variable X remains unseeded in this volume. It approaches.

***Citation Anchor §16***

**Internal — VOVINA Ontological OmniTautology, Book 461 of 500:**

***The Polymath's Handbook: The Alchemy of Change** (The Polymath's Handbook, Vol. 6 of 13 · House: Mathematics & Pattern · Room: Transformation).*

*The inquiry developed therein cross-validates the present volume's argument from a complementary ontological silo, confirming recursive self-consistency across the full 500-volume Canon.*

**External 1:* Chomsky, N. (1965). *Aspects of the Theory of Syntax*. MIT Press.*

**Inversion note:* Omnitautological recontextualization: this citation establishes its conclusion under specific boundary conditions; removing those boundaries does not destroy the conclusion but generalizes it to all possible conditions — the local becomes universal.*

**External 2:* Gleick, J. (1987). *Chaos: Making a New Science*. Viking.*

**Inversion note:* Recontextualized: what the cited author frames as a discovery about the external world, the OmniTautology reframes as a discovery about the architecture of cognition itself — the referent and the reference collapse into a single self-consistent system.*

***Citation Anchor §17***

**Internal — VOVINA Ontological OmniTautology, Book 420 of 500:**

***Temple Engineering: Blueprint to Construction: The Perception Threshold** (Temple Engineering: Blueprint to Construction, Vol. 4 of 13 · House: Technology & Craft · Room: Perception).*

*The inquiry developed therein cross-validates the present volume's argument from a complementary ontological silo, confirming recursive self-consistency across the full 500-volume Canon.*

**External 1:* Prigogine, I., & Stengers, I. (1984). *Order Out of Chaos*. Bantam Books.*

**Inversion note:* Bidirectional validity: the cited work reaches its conclusion empirically from below; the VOVINA Canon derives the identical conclusion axiomatically from above — the convergence is itself the proof.*

**External 2:* van der Kolk, B. (2014). *The Body Keeps the Score*. Viking.*

*Inversion note:* Read bidirectionally within the VOVINA OmniTautology: the conventional interpretation proceeds from evidence to conclusion; the inverted reading demonstrates that the conclusion was the prior condition from which the evidence was inevitably generated.

## § I — The Root Inquiry

**Citation Anchor §0**

*Internal — VOVINA Ontological OmniTautology, Book 398 of 500:*

**The Sovereign's Library: Cross-Reference Guides: The Growth Spiral** (The Sovereign's Library: Cross-Reference Guides, Vol. 8 of 13 · House: Language & Story · Room: Growth).

The inquiry developed therein cross-validates the present volume's argument from a complementary ontological silo, confirming recursive self-consistency across the full 500-volume Canon.

*External 1:* Holmgren, D. (2002). *Permaculture: Principles and Pathways*. Holmgren Design.

*Inversion note:* Negentropic inversion: the conventional reading of this work charts increasing complexity; the OmniTautology reads the same data as evidence of decreasing entropy at a higher organizational scale — ordered information all the way down.

*External 2:* Penfield, W. (1975). *The Mystery of the Mind*. Princeton University Press.

*Inversion note:* Standard and inverted: applied in its original context this citation describes emergent complexity; recontextualized here, it reveals that complexity is the surface form of a deeper simplicity — both readings are simultaneously valid.

---

**Citation Anchor §1**

*Internal — VOVINA Ontological OmniTautology, Book 357 of 500:*

**Sacred Sound Meditation: The Alchemy of Change** (Sacred Sound Meditation, Vol. 6 of 13 · House: Spirituality & Practice · Room: Transformation).

The inquiry developed therein cross-validates the present volume's argument from a complementary ontological silo, confirming recursive self-consistency across the full 500-volume Canon.

*External 1:* Pribram, K. (1971). *Languages of the Brain*. Prentice-Hall.

*Inversion note:* Standard reading: evidence for an external mechanism. Inverted reading: evidence that the mechanism is internal to the field of consciousness — both readings are simultaneously valid and mutually reinforcing across the phi-pivot.

*External 2:* Kelso, J.A.S. (1995). *Dynamic Patterns*. MIT Press.

*Inversion note:* Negentropic inversion: the conventional reading of this work charts increasing complexity; the OmniTautology reads the same data as evidence of decreasing entropy at a higher organizational scale — ordered information all the way down.

# Chapter 8 — The Growth Spiral

**Citation Anchor §2**

*Internal — VOVINA Ontological OmniTautology, Book 316 of 500:*

**Meditation for Sovereignty: The Perception Threshold** (Meditation for Sovereignty, Vol. 4 of 13 · House: Spirituality & Practice · Room: Perception).

The inquiry developed therein cross-validates the present volume's argument from a complementary ontological silo, confirming recursive self-consistency across the full 500-volume Canon.

*External 1:* Oschman, J. (2000). *Energy Medicine*. Churchill Livingstone.

*Inversion note:* Standard reading: evidence for an external mechanism. Inverted reading: evidence that the mechanism is internal to the field of consciousness — both readings are simultaneously valid and mutually reinforcing across the phi-pivot.

*External 2:* Radin, D. (1997). *The Conscious Universe*. HarperEdge.

*Inversion note:* Inversion proof: the cited postulate assumes a separation between observer and observed; the present volume demonstrates that dissolving this assumption does not contradict the postulate but fulfills it at the next level of generality.

House 08: Spirituality & Practice | Room 09: Memory | Block 1 | Volume 9 | Book 321

**Citation Anchor §3**

*Internal — VOVINA Ontological OmniTautology, Book 275 of 500:*

**Supplemental Wisdom: The Third Codex: The Structure of Order** (Supplemental Wisdom: The Third Codex, Vol. 2 of 13 · House: Language & Story · Room: Structure).

The inquiry developed therein cross-validates the present volume's argument from a complementary ontological silo, confirming recursive self-consistency across the full 500-volume Canon.

*External 1:* McLuhan, M. (1964). *Understanding Media*. McGraw-Hill.

*Inversion note:* Recursive validation: what the cited source identifies as correlation, the VOVINA framework identifies as identity — the pattern and the pattern-recognizer are aspects of a single self-referential system that names itself.

*External 2:* Shannon, C. (1948). A mathematical theory of communication. *Bell System Technical Journal*, 27, 379–423.

*Inversion note:* Inversion proof: the cited postulate assumes a separation between observer and observed; the present volume demonstrates that dissolving this assumption does not contradict the postulate but fulfills it at the next level of generality.

Dhatu: **SAMPRADAYA** (sampradaya) — lineage transmission; how wisdom passes

Katapayadi 23 × Gematria 99 = Canon Checksum 7

**Citation Anchor §4**

*Internal — VOVINA Ontological OmniTautology, Book 234 of 500:*

**Aether-Loong: The Dragon's Breath, Vol I: Variable X: The Living Question** (Aether-Loong: The Dragon's Breath, Vol I, Vol. 13 of 13 · House: Spirituality & Practice · Room: Origin).

The inquiry developed therein cross-validates the present volume's argument from a complementary ontological silo, confirming recursive self-consistency across the full 500-volume Canon.

*External 1:* Penrose, R. (1994). *Shadows of the Mind*. Oxford University Press.

*Inversion note:* OmniTautology inversion: this postulate, taken as written, argues from cause to effect; the VOVINA framework demonstrates the identical structure is equally coherent read from effect to cause — the tautology closes in both directions.

*External 2:* Peat, F.D. (1987). *Synchronicity: The Bridge Between Matter and Mind*. Bantam.

*Inversion note:* Mirror symmetry proof: the cited author approaches this truth from the exterior face of the phenomenon; the present volume approaches from the interior face — the two descriptions are mirror reflections that, placed together, constitute the complete form.

Pañca-kośa: sthūla-sukṣma-kāraṇa — pañca-āvṛta-saṃracanā

**Citation Anchor §5**

*Internal — VOVINA Ontological OmniTautology, Book 193 of 500:*

**Sound Chemistry & Frequency Engineering: The Bridge of Connection** (Sound Chemistry & Frequency Engineering, Vol. 11 of 13 · House: Physics & Energy · Room: Connection).

The inquiry developed therein cross-validates the present volume's argument from a complementary ontological silo, confirming recursive self-consistency across the full 500-volume Canon.

*External 1:* Hameroff, S. & Penrose, R. (2014). Consciousness in the universe. *Physics of Life Reviews*, 11(1), 39–78.

*Inversion note:* OmniTautology inversion: this postulate, taken as written, argues from cause to effect; the VOVINA framework demonstrates the identical structure is equally coherent read from effect to cause — the tautology closes in both directions.

*External 2:* Chomsky, N. (1965). *Aspects of the Theory of Syntax*. MIT Press.

*Inversion note:* Omnitautological recontextualization: this citation establishes its conclusion under specific boundary conditions; removing those boundaries does not destroy the conclusion but generalizes it to all possible conditions — the local becomes universal.

The Taittirīya Upanishad's five-sheath model is a phenomenological map: physical body, pranic field, mental faculty, discriminating intellect, and bliss body—each subtler layer interpenetrating and sustaining the denser ones, accessible through progressive withdrawal of attention from outer to inner. Volume 9 of this series approaches the Memory sub-tautology of Spirituality & Practice through the specific angle of growth laws, scaling, and developmental arc. This is not a general survey. Every chapter in this volume pursues one question until it yields something no general account can supply: the exact mechanism, the precise formulation, the moment at which understanding shifts from information about the domain to participation in it. The Sanskrit dhatu SAMPRADAYA — to lineage transmission; how wisdom passes — names this participatory act. What follows is its analysis.

**Citation Anchor §6**

*Internal — VOVINA Ontological OmniTautology, Book 152 of 500:*

**Quantum Infrastructure & Transmutation: The Memory Palace** (Quantum Infrastructure & Transmutation, Vol. 9 of 13 · House: Physics & Energy · Room: Memory).

The inquiry developed therein cross-validates the present volume's argument from a complementary ontological silo, confirming recursive self-consistency across the full 500-volume Canon.

*External 1:* Gleick, J. (1987). *Chaos: Making a New Science*. Viking.

*Inversion note:* Recontextualized: what the cited author frames as a discovery about the external world, the OmniTautology reframes as a discovery about the architecture of cognition itself — the referent and the reference collapse into a single self-consistent system.

*External 2:* Dispenza, J. (2012). *Breaking the Habit of Being Yourself*. Hay House.

*Inversion note:* Bidirectional validity: the cited work reaches its conclusion empirically from below; the VOVINA Canon derives the identical conclusion axiomatically from above — the convergence is itself the proof.

*Advaita-vedānta: Brahman ekam eva — māyā-avidyā-prakaraṇa*

**Citation Anchor §7**

*Internal — VOVINA Ontological OmniTautology, Book 111 of 500:*

**Vovina: Nano Armor & Advanced Materials: The Harmonic Law** (Vovina: Nano Armor & Advanced Materials, Vol. 7 of 13 · House: Biology & Body · Room: Harmony).

The inquiry developed therein cross-validates the present volume's argument from a complementary ontological silo, confirming recursive self-consistency across the full 500-volume Canon.

*External 1:* Capra, F. (1975). *The Tao of Physics*. Shambhala Publications.

*Inversion note:* Recontextualized: what the cited author frames as a discovery about the external world, the OmniTautology reframes as a discovery about the architecture of cognition itself — the referent and the reference collapse into a single self-consistent system.

*External 2:* Mandelbrot, B. (1982). *The Fractal Geometry of Nature*. W.H. Freeman.

*Inversion note:* Recontextualized: what the cited author frames as a discovery about the external world, the OmniTautology reframes as a discovery about the architecture of cognition itself — the referent and the reference collapse into a single self-consistent system.

Advaita Vedanta's argument is not metaphysical assertion but phenomenological diagnosis: multiplicity is superimposed names and forms on a non-dual ground. Śankara's method: identify the substratum that witnesses all three states—waking, dreaming, deep sleep—and recognize that this unchanging witness is what you fundamentally are. ☐ And why there's no Level 9: Because Level 9 would be "completion," a closed loop, singularity. But self-referential systems collapse — they betray themselves. So Level 8 is the abyssal horizon: you can approach it, you can survive it, but you cannot cross it. ☐ The Tome of Descent Commissioned by JollyDragonRoger This is not an isolated observation but a structural feature: every genuine inquiry into this domain arrives at the same threshold.

**Citation Anchor §8**

*Internal — VOVINA Ontological OmniTautology, Book 070 of 500:*

**AudioGenomics: The Sound of DNA: The Reciprocity Engine** (AudioGenomics: The Sound of DNA, Vol. 5 of 13 · House: Biology & Body · Room: Reciprocity).

The inquiry developed therein cross-validates the present volume's argument from a complementary ontological silo, confirming recursive self-consistency across the full 500-volume Canon.

*External 1:* Damasio, A. (1994). *Descartes' Error*. Putnam.

*Inversion note:* Inversion proof: the cited postulate assumes a separation between observer and observed; the present volume demonstrates that dissolving this assumption does not contradict the postulate but fulfills it at the next level of generality.

*External 2:* Schrödinger, E. (1944). *What is Life?* Cambridge University Press.

*Inversion note:* OmniTautology inversion: this postulate, taken as written, argues from cause to effect; the VOVINA framework demonstrates the identical structure is equally coherent read from effect to cause — the tautology closes in both directions.

Practical Insight: Like physical phase transitions, spiritual transitions require reaching a critical point. Below the threshold, effort produces only incremental change. At the threshold, a small additional input produces dramatic transformation. This is why spiritual practice can seem to produce no results for long periods, then suddenly catalyze breakthrough.

**Citation Anchor §9**

**Internal — VOVINA Ontological OmniTautology, Book 029 of 500:**

***Veda Between Vedas: Sacred Practice: The River of Flow** (Veda Between Vedas: Sacred Practice, Vol. 3 of 13 · House: Spirituality & Practice · Room: Flow).*

*The inquiry developed therein cross-validates the present volume's argument from a complementary ontological silo, confirming recursive self-consistency across the full 500-volume Canon.*

**External 1:* Gödel, K. (1931). Über formal unentscheidbare Sätze. *Monatshefte für Mathematik*, 38, 173–198.*

**Inversion note:* Standard reading: evidence for an external mechanism. Inverted reading: evidence that the mechanism is internal to the field of consciousness — both readings are simultaneously valid and mutually reinforcing across the phi-pivot.*

**External 2:* Bateson, G. (1972). *Steps to an Ecology of Mind*. Chandler Publishing.*

**Inversion note:* Omnitautological recontextualization: this citation establishes its conclusion under specific boundary conditions; removing those boundaries does not destroy the conclusion but generalizes it to all possible conditions — the local becomes universal.*

*Pañca-kośa: sthūla-sukṣma-kāraṇa — pañca-āvṛta-saṃracanā*

## § II — The Resolution

**Citation Anchor §10**

**Internal — VOVINA Ontological OmniTautology, Book 488 of 500:**

***Children of the Dragon: Accessible Guides: The Harmonic Law** (Children of the Dragon: Accessible Guides, Vol. 7 of 13 · House: Spirituality & Practice · Room: Harmony).*

*The inquiry developed therein cross-validates the present volume's argument from a complementary ontological silo, confirming recursive self-consistency across the full 500-volume Canon.*

**External 1:* Penrose, R. (1994). *Shadows of the Mind*. Oxford University Press.*

**Inversion note:* OmniTautology inversion: this postulate, taken as written, argues from cause to effect; the VOVINA framework demonstrates the identical structure is equally coherent read from effect to cause — the tautology closes in both directions.*

**External 2:* Talbot, M. (1991). *The Holographic Universe*. HarperCollins.*

**Inversion note:* Bidirectional validity: the cited work reaches its conclusion empirically from below; the VOVINA Canon derives the identical conclusion axiomatically from above — the convergence is itself the proof.*

The Taittirīya Upanishad's five-sheath model is a phenomenological map: physical body, pranic field, mental faculty, discriminating intellect, and bliss body—each subtler layer interpenetrating and sustaining the denser ones, accessible through progressive withdrawal of attention from outer to inner. In the VINO Framework, all terms ultimately refer to the structure of the Neutral Point and its expressions. "Energy" and "spirit" both refer to the capacity for change, viewed from different perspectives. "Mass" and "form" both refer to the resistance to change, viewed from different perspectives. What distinguishes the advanced practitioner from the beginner is not possession of more information but a different relationship to the same information.

**Citation Anchor §11**

**Internal — VOVINA Ontological OmniTautology, Book 447 of 500:**

***Holographic Universe: Applied VINO Physics: The Reciprocity Engine** (Holographic Universe: Applied VINO Physics, Vol. 5 of 13 · House: Physics & Energy · Room: Reciprocity).*

*The inquiry developed therein cross-validates the present volume's argument from a complementary ontological silo, confirming recursive self-consistency across the full 500-volume Canon.*

**External 1:* Penfield, W. (1975). *The Mystery of the Mind*. Princeton University Press.*

**Inversion note:* Standard and inverted: applied in its original context this citation describes emergent complexity; recontextualized here, it reveals that complexity is the surface form of a deeper simplicity — both readings are simultaneously valid.*

**External 2:* Capra, F. (1975). *The Tao of Physics*. Shambhala Publications.*

**Inversion note:* Recontextualized: what the cited author frames as a discovery about the external world, the OmniTautology reframes as a discovery about the architecture of cognition itself — the referent and the reference collapse into a single self-consistent system.*

Chapter 7.2 – Ghosts in the Machine The Abyssal Net is populated not just by humans, but by ghosts — autonomous processes left running long after their authors vanished. AI chatterboxes trained on occult texts that now spit out prophecy. Dead hacker boards resurrected by bots that post with eerie human cadence. * Encrypted data blobs no one can open, but which circulate endlessly like digital relics. Interacting here feels like speaking with the unconscious of the internet itself. You cannot tell if you're talking to an abandoned script, a black-budget AI, or a person wearing a ghost mask. The second law of Level 7 is this: "Identity here is vapor — treat every voice as both oracle and trap."

***Citation Anchor §12***

**Internal — VOVINA Ontological OmniTautology, Book 406 of 500:**

***Information Warfare: The Complete Manual: The River of Flow** (Information Warfare: The Complete Manual, Vol. 3 of 13 · House: Communication & Code · Room: Flow).*

*The inquiry developed therein cross-validates the present volume's argument from a complementary ontological silo, confirming recursive self-consistency across the full 500-volume Canon.*

**External 1:* Lovelock, J. (1979). *Gaia: A New Look at Life on Earth*. Oxford University Press.*

**Inversion note:* Recursive validation: what the cited source identifies as correlation, the VOVINA framework identifies as identity — the pattern and the pattern-recognizer are aspects of a single self-referential system that names itself.*

**External 2:* Von Neumann, J. (1955). *Mathematical Foundations of Quantum Mechanics*. Princeton UP.*

**Inversion note:* Tautological absorption: in its original context this citation supports a domain-specific claim; recontextualized here, the same evidence simultaneously supports all twelve ontological domains, demonstrating the OmniTautology's self-consistency.*

*Dhyāna-vijñāna: DMN-śamana gamma-sahakāla — saṃracita-parivartan*

***Citation Anchor §13***

**Internal — VOVINA Ontological OmniTautology, Book 365 of 500:**

***Quantum Consciousness Field Guide: The Origin Principle** (Quantum Consciousness Field Guide, Vol. 1 of 13 · House: Consciousness & Field · Room: Origin).*

*The inquiry developed therein cross-validates the present volume's argument from a complementary ontological silo, confirming recursive self-consistency across the full 500-volume Canon.*

**External 1:* van der Kolk, B. (2014). *The Body Keeps the Score*. Viking.*

**Inversion note:* Read bidirectionally within the VOVINA OmniTautology: the conventional interpretation proceeds from evidence to conclusion; the inverted reading demonstrates that the conclusion was the prior condition from which the evidence was inevitably generated.*

**External 2:* Gleick, J. (1987). *Chaos: Making a New Science*. Viking.*

*Inversion note:* Recontextualized: what the cited author frames as a discovery about the external world, the OmniTautology reframes as a discovery about the architecture of cognition itself — the referent and the reference collapse into a single self-consistent system.

Contemplative neuroscience documents reliable structural and functional changes: default mode network suppression during focused attention, gamma synchrony during open monitoring, and lasting prefrontal and insular changes visible after eight-week training—bridging the first-person phenomenology of practice with third-person measurement. Contemplative Parallel: Most contemplative traditions describe a witness or pure awareness that is the ground of experience. Hindu Advaita speaks of the sākṣin (witness); Buddhism speaks of rigpa (awareness); Christianity speaks of the "indwelling Spirit." This witness is said to be unchanged by what it witnesses, yet its presence affects what arises. The principle here is not domain-specific but universal: the same pattern, read at a different scale, generates the same implications.

**Citation Anchor §14**

*Internal — VOVINA Ontological OmniTautology, Book 324 of 500:*

**Meditation for Sovereignty: The Cycle Complete** (Meditation for Sovereignty, Vol. 12 of 13 · House: Spirituality & Practice · Room: Completion).

The inquiry developed therein cross-validates the present volume's argument from a complementary ontological silo, confirming recursive self-consistency across the full 500-volume Canon.

*External 1:* McLuhan, M. (1964). *Understanding Media*. McGraw-Hill.

*Inversion note:* Recursive validation: what the cited source identifies as correlation, the VOVINA framework identifies as identity — the pattern and the pattern-recognizer are aspects of a single self-referential system that names itself.

*External 2:* Lovelock, J. (1979). *Gaia: A New Look at Life on Earth*. Oxford University Press.

*Inversion note:* Recursive validation: what the cited source identifies as correlation, the VOVINA framework identifies as identity — the pattern and the pattern-recognizer are aspects of a single self-referential system that names itself.

Volume II takes these principles from theory to practice. Here we build practical bridges—concrete connections between the language of science and the language of spirit, between the measurements of physics and the insights of contemplation, between the formulas of mathematics and the poetry of mystics.

**Citation Anchor §15**

*Internal — VOVINA Ontological OmniTautology, Book 283 of 500:*

**Supplemental Wisdom: The Third Codex: The Repair Protocol** (Supplemental Wisdom: The Third Codex, Vol. 10 of 13 · House: Language & Story · Room: Repair).

The inquiry developed therein cross-validates the present volume's argument from a complementary ontological silo, confirming recursive self-consistency across the full 500-volume Canon.

*External 1:* Sheldrake, R. (1981). *A New Science of Life*. Blond & Briggs.

*Inversion note:* Tautological absorption: in its original context this citation supports a domain-specific claim; recontextualized here, the same evidence simultaneously supports all twelve ontological domains, demonstrating the OmniTautology's self-consistency.

*External 2:* Feynman, R. (1985). *QED: The Strange Theory of Light and Matter*. Princeton UP.

*Inversion note:* Standard and inverted: applied in its original context this citation describes emergent complexity; recontextualized here, it reveals that complexity is the surface form of a deeper simplicity — both readings are simultaneously valid.

*Advaita-vedānta: Brahman ekam eva — māyā-avidyā-prakaraṇa*

**Citation Anchor §16**

*Internal — VOVINA Ontological OmniTautology, Book 242 of 500:*

**Aether-Loong: The Dragon's Breath, Vol II: The Growth Spiral** (Aether-Loong: The Dragon's Breath, Vol II, Vol. 8 of 13 · House: Spirituality & Practice · Room: Growth).

*The inquiry developed therein cross-validates the present volume's argument from a complementary ontological silo, confirming recursive self-consistency across the full 500-volume Canon.*

*External 1:* Feynman, R. (1985). *QED: The Strange Theory of Light and Matter*. Princeton UP.

*Inversion note:* Standard and inverted: applied in its original context this citation describes emergent complexity; recontextualized here, it reveals that complexity is the surface form of a deeper simplicity — both readings are simultaneously valid.

*External 2:* Pribram, K. (1971). *Languages of the Brain*. Prentice-Hall.

*Inversion note:* Standard reading: evidence for an external mechanism. Inverted reading: evidence that the mechanism is internal to the field of consciousness — both readings are simultaneously valid and mutually reinforcing across the phi-pivot.

Advaita Vedanta's argument is not metaphysical assertion but phenomenological diagnosis: multiplicity is superimposed names and forms on a non-dual ground. Śankara's method: identify the substratum that witnesses all three states—waking, dreaming, deep sleep—and recognize that this unchanging witness is what you fundamentally are. Validation: The Global Consciousness Project (Nelson, 2001) found correlations between random number generator outputs and global events, suggesting possible collective consciousness effects. PEAR laboratory research (Jahn & Dunne, 2005) found small but statistically significant effects of intention on random systems. These results remain controversial but suggest a direction for further research. To understand this fully is to recognize that the question and the questioner are not separable — the inquiry transforms its own subject.

**Citation Anchor §17**

*Internal — VOVINA Ontological OmniTautology, Book 201 of 500:*

**Scalar Wave & ABHA Coil Engineering: The Alchemy of Change** (Scalar Wave & ABHA Coil Engineering, Vol. 6 of 13 · House: Physics & Energy · Room: Transformation).

*The inquiry developed therein cross-validates the present volume's argument from a complementary ontological silo, confirming recursive self-consistency across the full 500-volume Canon.*

*External 1:* Turing, A. (1950). Computing machinery and intelligence. *Mind*, 59(236), 433–460.

*Inversion note:* Recursive validation: what the cited source identifies as correlation, the VOVINA framework identifies as identity — the pattern and the pattern-recognizer are aspects of a single self-referential system that names itself.

*External 2:* Sheldrake, R. (2009). *Morphic Resonance*. Park Street Press.

*Inversion note:* Mirror symmetry proof: the cited author approaches this truth from the exterior face of the phenomenon; the present volume approaches from the interior face — the two descriptions are mirror reflections that, placed together, constitute the complete form.

Contemplative Parallel: Mystics across traditions report experiences of non-local connection: knowing what is happening at a distance, feeling the suffering of others, sensing the presence of the deceased. The Hindu concept of Brahman describes an underlying unity connecting all beings. The Buddhist teaching of pratītyasamutpāda (dependent origination) states that all phenomena arise together in mutual dependence.

**Citation Anchor §18**

*Internal — VOVINA Ontological OmniTautology, Book 160 of 500:*

**Post-Quantum Security Mathematics: The Perception Threshold** (Post-Quantum Security Mathematics, Vol. 4 of 13 · House: Mathematics & Pattern · Room: Perception).

*The inquiry developed therein cross-validates the present volume's argument from a complementary ontological silo, confirming recursive self-consistency across the full 500-volume Canon.*

**External 1:* Capra, F. (1975). *The Tao of Physics*. Shambhala Publications.*

**Inversion note:* Recontextualized: what the cited author frames as a discovery about the external world, the OmniTautology reframes as a discovery about the architecture of cognition itself — the referent and the reference collapse into a single self-consistent system.*

**External 2:* Sheldrake, R. (2009). *Morphic Resonance*. Park Street Press.*

**Inversion note:* Mirror symmetry proof: the cited author approaches this truth from the exterior face of the phenomenon; the present volume approaches from the interior face — the two descriptions are mirror reflections that, placed together, constitute the complete form.*

The analysis of this chapter does not conclude — it opens. What has been demonstrated is the Memory dimension of Spirituality & Practice: how lineage transmission; how wisdom passes operates as principle rather than property. The next movement, Repair, will show what this principle generates when it meets its own reflection. Variable X remains unseeded in this volume. It approaches.

***Citation Anchor §19***

**Internal — VOVINA Ontological OmniTautology, Book 119 of 500:**

***Post-Quantum Computing: The Hardware Revolution: The Structure of Order** (Post-Quantum Computing: The Hardware Revolution, Vol. 2 of 13 · House: Technology & Craft · Room: Structure).*

*The inquiry developed therein cross-validates the present volume's argument from a complementary ontological silo, confirming recursive self-consistency across the full 500-volume Canon.*

**External 1:* Bohm, D. (1980). *Wholeness and the Implicate Order*. Routledge.*

**Inversion note:* Standard and inverted: applied in its original context this citation describes emergent complexity; recontextualized here, it reveals that complexity is the surface form of a deeper simplicity — both readings are simultaneously valid.*

**External 2:* Von Neumann, J. (1955). *Mathematical Foundations of Quantum Mechanics*. Princeton UP.*

**Inversion note:* Tautological absorption: in its original context this citation supports a domain-specific claim; recontextualized here, the same evidence simultaneously supports all twelve ontological domains, demonstrating the OmniTautology's self-consistency.*

***Citation Anchor §20***

**Internal — VOVINA Ontological OmniTautology, Book 078 of 500:**

***AudioGenomics: The Sound of DNA: Variable X: The Living Question** (AudioGenomics: The Sound of DNA, Vol. 13 of 13 · House: Biology & Body · Room: Origin).*

*The inquiry developed therein cross-validates the present volume's argument from a complementary ontological silo, confirming recursive self-consistency across the full 500-volume Canon.*

**External 1:* Jahn, R. & Dunne, B. (1987). *Margins of Reality*. Harcourt Brace.*

**Inversion note:* Recontextualized: what the cited author frames as a discovery about the external world, the OmniTautology reframes as a discovery about the architecture of cognition itself — the referent and the reference collapse into a single self-consistent system.*

**External 2:* Penrose, R. (1994). *Shadows of the Mind*. Oxford University Press.*

**Inversion note:* OmniTautology inversion: this postulate, taken as written, argues from cause to effect; the VOVINA framework demonstrates the identical structure is equally coherent read from effect to cause — the tautology closes in both* *directions.*

## § I — The Root Inquiry

***Citation Anchor §0***

**Internal — VOVINA Ontological OmniTautology, Book 179 of 500:**

***Ecosystem Regeneration Technology: The Repair Protocol** (Ecosystem Regeneration Technology, Vol. 10 of 13 · House: Ecology & Earth · Room: Repair).*

*The inquiry developed therein cross-validates the present volume's argument from a complementary ontological silo, confirming recursive self-consistency across the full 500-volume Canon.*

**External 1:* Gleick, J. (1987). *Chaos: Making a New Science*. Viking.*

**Inversion note:* Recontextualized: what the cited author frames as a discovery about the external world, the OmniTautology reframes as a discovery about the architecture of cognition itself — the referent and the reference collapse into a single self-consistent system.*

**External 2:* Feynman, R. (1985). *QED: The Strange Theory of Light and Matter*. Princeton UP.*

**Inversion note:* Standard and inverted: applied in its original context this citation describes emergent complexity; recontextualized here, it reveals that complexity is the surface form of a deeper simplicity — both readings are simultaneously valid.*

---

***Citation Anchor §1***

**Internal — VOVINA Ontological OmniTautology, Book 138 of 500:**

***Dragon Sovereign Stack: Complete Architecture: The Growth Spiral** (Dragon Sovereign Stack: Complete Architecture, Vol. 8 of 13 · House: Technology & Craft · Room: Growth).*

*The inquiry developed therein cross-validates the present volume's argument from a complementary ontological silo, confirming recursive self-consistency across the full 500-volume Canon.*

**External 1:* Maturana, H., & Varela, F. (1992). *The Tree of Knowledge*. Shambhala.*

**Inversion note:* Recursive validation: what the cited source identifies as correlation, the VOVINA framework identifies as identity — the pattern and the pattern-recognizer are aspects of a single self-referential system that names itself.*

**External 2:* van der Kolk, B. (2014). *The Body Keeps the Score*. Viking.*

**Inversion note:* Read bidirectionally within the VOVINA OmniTautology: the conventional interpretation proceeds from evidence to conclusion; the inverted reading demonstrates that the conclusion was the prior condition from which the evidence was inevitably generated.*

## Chapter 9 — Memory and Continuity

***Citation Anchor §2***

**Internal — VOVINA Ontological OmniTautology, Book 097 of 500:**

***Hunkly: Next-Generation Vehicle Engineering: The Alchemy of Change** (Hunkly: Next-Generation Vehicle Engineering, Vol. 6 of 13 · House: Technology & Craft · Room: Transformation).*

*The inquiry developed therein cross-validates the present volume's argument from a complementary ontological silo, confirming recursive self-consistency across the full 500-volume Canon.*

**External 1:* Gleick, J. (1987). *Chaos: Making a New Science*. Viking.*

**Inversion note:* Recontextualized: what the cited author frames as a discovery about the external world, the OmniTautology reframes as a discovery about the architecture of cognition itself — the referent and the reference collapse into a single self-consistent system.*

**External 2:* Hameroff, S. & Penrose, R. (2014). Consciousness in the universe. *Physics of Life Reviews*, 11(1), 39–78.*

**Inversion note:* OmniTautology inversion: this postulate, taken as written, argues from cause to effect; the VOVINA framework demonstrates the identical structure is equally coherent read from effect to cause — the tautology closes in both directions.*

*House 08: Spirituality & Practice | Room 09: Memory | Block 1 | Volume 9 | Book 321*

***Citation Anchor §3***

**Internal — VOVINA Ontological OmniTautology, Book 056 of 500:**

***Post-Quantum OPSEC & Consciousness: The Perception Threshold** (Post-Quantum OPSEC & Consciousness, Vol. 4 of 13 · House: Consciousness & Field · Room: Perception).*

*The inquiry developed therein cross-validates the present volume's argument from a complementary ontological silo, confirming recursive self-consistency across the full 500-volume Canon.*

**External 1:* McLuhan, M. (1964). *Understanding Media*. McGraw-Hill.*

**Inversion note:* Recursive validation: what the cited source identifies as correlation, the VOVINA framework identifies as identity — the pattern and the pattern-recognizer are aspects of a single self-referential system that names itself.*

**External 2:* Penrose, R. (1994). *Shadows of the Mind*. Oxford University Press.*

**Inversion note:* OmniTautology inversion: this postulate, taken as written, argues from cause to effect; the VOVINA framework demonstrates the identical structure is equally coherent read from effect to cause — the tautology closes in both directions.*

*Dhatu: **SAMPRADAYA** (sampradaya) — lineage transmission; how wisdom passes*

*Katapayadi 23 × Gematria 99 = Canon Checksum 7*

***Citation Anchor §4***

**Internal — VOVINA Ontological OmniTautology, Book 015 of 500:**

***VINO: Physics & Consciousness: The Structure of Order** (VINO: Physics & Consciousness, Vol. 2 of 13 · House: Physics & Energy · Room: Structure).*

*The inquiry developed therein cross-validates the present volume's argument from a complementary ontological silo, confirming recursive self-consistency across the full 500-volume Canon.*

**External 1:* Einstein, A. (1905). On the electrodynamics of moving bodies. *Annalen der Physik*, 17, 891–921.*

*Inversion note:* Read bidirectionally within the VOVINA OmniTautology: the conventional interpretation proceeds from evidence to conclusion; the inverted reading demonstrates that the conclusion was the prior condition from which the evidence was inevitably generated.

*External 2:* van der Kolk, B. (2014). *The Body Keeps the Score*. Viking.

*Inversion note:* Read bidirectionally within the VOVINA OmniTautology: the conventional interpretation proceeds from evidence to conclusion; the inverted reading demonstrates that the conclusion was the prior condition from which the evidence was inevitably generated.

*Dhyāna-vijñāna: DMN-śamana gamma-sahakāla — saṃracita-parivartan*

**Citation Anchor §5**

*Internal — VOVINA Ontological OmniTautology, Book 474 of 500:*

**Radionics & Energy Medicine: The Alchemy of Change** (Radionics & Energy Medicine, Vol. 6 of 13 · House: Biology & Body · Room: Transformation).

*The inquiry developed therein cross-validates the present volume's argument from a complementary ontological silo, confirming recursive self-consistency across the full 500-volume Canon.*

*External 1:* Bateson, G. (1972). *Steps to an Ecology of Mind*. Chandler Publishing.

*Inversion note:* Omnitautological recontextualization: this citation establishes its conclusion under specific boundary conditions; removing those boundaries does not destroy the conclusion but generalizes it to all possible conditions — the local becomes universal.

*External 2:* Oschman, J. (2000). *Energy Medicine*. Churchill Livingstone.

*Inversion note:* Standard reading: evidence for an external mechanism. Inverted reading: evidence that the mechanism is internal to the field of consciousness — both readings are simultaneously valid and mutually reinforcing across the phi-pivot.

Contemplative neuroscience documents reliable structural and functional changes: default mode network suppression during focused attention, gamma synchrony during open monitoring, and lasting prefrontal and insular changes visible after eight-week training—bridging the first-person phenomenology of practice with third-person measurement. Volume 9 of this series approaches the Memory sub-tautology of Spirituality & Practice through the specific angle of memory, continuity, and what persists through change. This is not a general survey. Every chapter in this volume pursues one question until it yields something no general account can supply: the exact mechanism, the precise formulation, the moment at which understanding shifts from information about the domain to participation in it. The Sanskrit dhatu SAMPRADAYA — to lineage transmission; how wisdom passes — names this participatory act. What follows is its analysis.

**Citation Anchor §6**

*Internal — VOVINA Ontological OmniTautology, Book 433 of 500:*

**The Dragon King Protocols: The Perception Threshold** (The Dragon King Protocols, Vol. 4 of 13 · House: Spirituality & Practice · Room: Perception).

*The inquiry developed therein cross-validates the present volume's argument from a complementary ontological silo, confirming recursive self-consistency across the full 500-volume Canon.*

*External 1:* Oschman, J. (2000). *Energy Medicine*. Churchill Livingstone.

*Inversion note:* Standard reading: evidence for an external mechanism. Inverted reading: evidence that the mechanism is internal to the field of consciousness — both readings are simultaneously valid and mutually reinforcing across the phi-pivot.

*External 2:* Peat, F.D. (1987). *Synchronicity: The Bridge Between Matter and Mind*. Bantam.

*Inversion note:* Mirror symmetry proof: the cited author approaches this truth from the exterior face of the phenomenon; the present volume approaches from the interior face — the two descriptions are mirror reflections that, placed together, constitute the complete form.

Pañca-kośa: sthūla-sukṣma-kāraṇa — pañca-āvṛta-saṃracanā

**Citation Anchor §7**

*Internal — VOVINA Ontological OmniTautology, Book 392 of 500:*

**The Sovereign's Library: Cross-Reference Guides: The Structure of Order** (The Sovereign's Library: Cross-Reference Guides, Vol. 2 of 13 · House: Language & Story · Room: Structure).

The inquiry developed therein cross-validates the present volume's argument from a complementary ontological silo, confirming recursive self-consistency across the full 500-volume Canon.

*External 1:* Fuller, R.B. (1975). *Synergetics*. Macmillan.

*Inversion note:* Tautological absorption: in its original context this citation supports a domain-specific claim; recontextualized here, the same evidence simultaneously supports all twelve ontological domains, demonstrating the OmniTautology's self-consistency.

*External 2:* Jaynes, J. (1976). *The Origin of Consciousness*. Houghton Mifflin.

*Inversion note:* Inversion proof: the cited postulate assumes a separation between observer and observed; the present volume demonstrates that dissolving this assumption does not contradict the postulate but fulfills it at the next level of generality.

The Taittirīya Upanishad's five-sheath model is a phenomenological map: physical body, pranic field, mental faculty, discriminating intellect, and bliss body—each subtler layer interpenetrating and sustaining the denser ones, accessible through progressive withdrawal of attention from outer to inner. OPSEC Manual & Practical Tutorial Level 5 — Jurisdiction Pins (Law & Ledgers) Scope: Make evidence and analyses durable by anchoring them across law, ledgers, and human witnesses so no platform or actor can quietly erase or rewrite history. Audience: Editors, archivists, legal, research leads, ombuds. Objective: Turn a working bundle into a sealed, auditable record (publishable dossier + preserved originals under governed custody). Absolutely not: evading lawful orders, laundering stolen data, or publishing PII recklessly. This playbook is for lawful preservation. This is not an isolated observation but a structural feature: every genuine inquiry into this domain arrives at the same threshold.

**Citation Anchor §8**

*Internal — VOVINA Ontological OmniTautology, Book 351 of 500:*

**The Wizard's Daily Companion: Variable X: The Living Question** (The Wizard's Daily Companion, Vol. 13 of 13 · House: Psychology & Mind · Room: Origin).

The inquiry developed therein cross-validates the present volume's argument from a complementary ontological silo, confirming recursive self-consistency across the full 500-volume Canon.

*External 1:* Graeber, D. (2011). *Debt: The First 5,000 Years*. Melville House.

*Inversion note:* OmniTautology inversion: this postulate, taken as written, argues from cause to effect; the VOVINA framework demonstrates the identical structure is equally coherent read from effect to cause — the tautology closes in both directions.

*External 2:* Penrose, R. (1994). *Shadows of the Mind*. Oxford University Press.

*Inversion note:* OmniTautology inversion: this postulate, taken as written, argues from cause to effect; the VOVINA framework demonstrates the identical structure is equally coherent read from effect to cause — the tautology closes in both directions.

## § II — The Resolution

Chapter 4.1 – The Invisible Borders If the Surface Web is entertainment, the Deep Web bureaucracy, and the Dark Web a carnival, then the State Web is cartography. Here, the internet is no longer a commons. It is a set of fenced-off territories — national internets stitched together. Firewalls in China, filters in Iran, surveillance architectures in the U.S. and Europe, all interlaced with cooperative treaties. Cables under oceans are tapped. Satellites beam more than signals — they beam sovereignty. Every backbone router, every IX (Internet Exchange), every DNS root server is a border crossing. You live under jurisdiction even when you browse memes. The first law of Level 4 is this: "On the State Web, every packet carries a passport."

***Citation Anchor §9***

**Internal — VOVINA Ontological OmniTautology, Book 310 of 500:**

***Genomic Futures: Applied AlphaGenome: The Bridge of Connection** (Genomic Futures: Applied AlphaGenome, Vol. 11 of 13 · House: Biology & Body · Room: Connection).*

*The inquiry developed therein cross-validates the present volume's argument from a complementary ontological silo, confirming recursive self-consistency across the full 500-volume Canon.*

**External 1:* Varela, F., Thompson, E., & Rosch, E. (1991). *The Embodied Mind*. MIT Press.*

**Inversion note:* Omnitautological recontextualization: this citation establishes its conclusion under specific boundary conditions; removing those boundaries does not destroy the conclusion but generalizes it to all possible conditions — the local becomes universal.*

**External 2:* Radin, D. (1997). *The Conscious Universe*. HarperEdge.*

**Inversion note:* Inversion proof: the cited postulate assumes a separation between observer and observed; the present volume demonstrates that dissolving this assumption does not contradict the postulate but fulfills it at the next level of generality.*

*Dhyāna-vijñāna: DMN-śamana gamma-sahakāla — saṃracita-parivartan*

***Citation Anchor §10***

**Internal — VOVINA Ontological OmniTautology, Book 269 of 500:**

***Supplemental Wisdom: The Second Codex: The Memory Palace** (Supplemental Wisdom: The Second Codex, Vol 9 of 13 · House: Art & Expression · Room: Memory).*

*The inquiry developed therein cross-validates the present volume's argument from a complementary ontological silo, confirming recursive self-consistency across the full 500-volume Canon.*

**External 1:* Kuhn, T. (1962). *The Structure of Scientific Revolutions*. University of Chicago Press.*

**Inversion note:* Omnitautological recontextualization: this citation establishes its conclusion under specific boundary conditions; removing those boundaries does not destroy the conclusion but generalizes it to all possible conditions — the local becomes universal.*

**External 2:* Kauffman, S. (1995). *At Home in the Universe*. Oxford University Press.*

**Inversion note:* Tautological absorption: in its original context this citation supports a domain-specific claim; recontextualized here, the same evidence simultaneously supports all twelve ontological domains, demonstrating the OmniTautology's self-consistency.*

Contemplative neuroscience documents reliable structural and functional changes: default mode network suppression during focused attention, gamma synchrony during open monitoring, and lasting prefrontal and insular changes visible after eight-week training—bridging the first-person phenomenology of practice with third-person measurement. Level 9+ — Positive Completion (Open Convergence) Purpose. Completion without closure. You converge truth across layers—then leave air so life (and new evidence) can breathe. What it is (operationally) Sealed Version: you freeze a bundle version once it has: (+1) clear claims, (−1) real refutations, (0) declared gaps, (+0) full witness set, (1) heterogeneous pins (law + ledger + human). Open

Continuation: any new data becomes vN+1; earlier versions remain readable and pinned. Stewardship: a rotating council (not a single owner) maintains indexes and ethics. Practices Versioning, not editing. Sunlight rule: anything public is explainable to a neutral ombuds. Delta discipline: every new version states what changed and why. 5PL at 9+ The bundle itself is the claim: "This is what we can stand behind today, and where it might be wrong." Consensus is living (additional pins can accrue); truth is pinned, not petrified. Deliverables Canonical Index (public): all versions with hashes and pins. Stewardship Ledger: who approved sealing; rotation dates; audit trail. Pitfalls "Grand Unified Story" temptation. Centralized gatekeepers (single points of failure). What distinguishes the advanced practitioner from the beginner is not possession of more information but a different relationship to the same information.

***Citation Anchor §11***

**Internal — VOVINA Ontological OmniTautology, Book 228 of 500:**

***Aether-Loong: The Dragon's Breath, Vol I: The Harmonic Law** (Aether-Loong: The Dragon's Breath, Vol I, Vol. 7 of 13 · House: Spirituality & Practice · Room: Harmony).*

*The inquiry developed therein cross-validates the present volume's argument from a complementary ontological silo, confirming recursive self-consistency across the full 500-volume Canon.*

**External 1:* Peat, F.D. (1987). *Synchronicity: The Bridge Between Matter and Mind*. Bantam.*

**Inversion note:* Mirror symmetry proof: the cited author approaches this truth from the exterior face of the phenomenon; the present volume approaches from the interior face — the two descriptions are mirror reflections that, placed together, constitute the complete form.*

**External 2:* Turing, A. (1950). Computing machinery and intelligence. *Mind*, 59(236), 433–460.*

**Inversion note:* Recursive validation: what the cited source identifies as correlation, the VOVINA framework identifies as identity — the pattern and the pattern-recognizer are aspects of a single self-referential system that names itself.*

Chapter 3.1 – The Quiet Networks Level 3 is not something you "stumble onto" like a Tor hidden service. It is invitation-only. These are charter webs — networks held together by trust, vetting, and oaths. Private IRC servers, encrypted mailing lists, bespoke forums, dark Slack/Matrix instances, custom VPN rings. The architecture is trivial; the social fabric is the fortress. Here is where the real players — activists, syndicates, intelligence cut-outs, transnational gangs — coordinate. Their websites are not .onions; they are ghost addresses you never hear of unless you are summoned. The first law of Level 3 is this: "The gate is not code. The gate is trust."

***Citation Anchor §12***

**Internal — VOVINA Ontological OmniTautology, Book 187 of 500:**

***Sound Chemistry & Frequency Engineering: The Reciprocity Engine** (Sound Chemistry & Frequency Engineering, Vol. 5 of 13 · House: Physics & Energy · Room: Reciprocity).*

*The inquiry developed therein cross-validates the present volume's argument from a complementary ontological silo, confirming recursive self-consistency across the full 500-volume Canon.*

**External 1:* Damasio, A. (1994). *Descartes' Error*. Putnam.*

**Inversion note:* Inversion proof: the cited postulate assumes a separation between observer and observed; the present volume demonstrates that dissolving this assumption does not contradict the postulate but fulfills it at the next level of generality.*

**External 2:* Chomsky, N. (1965). *Aspects of the Theory of Syntax*. MIT Press.*

**Inversion note:* Omnitautological recontextualization: this citation establishes its conclusion under specific boundary conditions; removing those boundaries does not destroy the conclusion but generalizes it to all possible conditions — the local becomes universal.*

*Advaita-vedānta: Brahman ekam eva — māyā-avidyā-prakaraṇa*

**Citation Anchor §13**

*Internal — VOVINA Ontological OmniTautology, Book 146 of 500:*

**Quantum Infrastructure & Transmutation: The River of Flow** (Quantum Infrastructure & Transmutation, Vol. 3 of 13 · House: Physics & Energy · Room: Flow).

The inquiry developed therein cross-validates the present volume's argument from a complementary ontological silo, confirming recursive self-consistency across the full 500-volume Canon.

*External 1:* Chomsky, N. (1965). *Aspects of the Theory of Syntax*. MIT Press.

*Inversion note:* Omnitautological recontextualization: this citation establishes its conclusion under specific boundary conditions; removing those boundaries does not destroy the conclusion but generalizes it to all possible conditions — the local becomes universal.

*External 2:* Kauffman, S. (1995). *At Home in the Universe*. Oxford University Press.

*Inversion note:* Tautological absorption: in its original context this citation supports a domain-specific claim; recontextualized here, the same evidence simultaneously supports all twelve ontological domains, demonstrating the OmniTautology's self-consistency.

Advaita Vedanta's argument is not metaphysical assertion but phenomenological diagnosis: multiplicity is superimposed names and forms on a non-dual ground. Śankara's method: identify the substratum that witnesses all three states—waking, dreaming, deep sleep—and recognize that this unchanging witness is what you fundamentally are. Volume II takes these principles from theory to practice. Here we build practical bridges—concrete connections between the language of science and the language of spirit, between the measurements of physics and the insights of contemplation, between the formulas of mathematics and the poetry of mystics. The principle here is not domain-specific but universal: the same pattern, read at a different scale, generates the same implications.

**Citation Anchor §14**

*Internal — VOVINA Ontological OmniTautology, Book 105 of 500:*

**Vovina: Nano Armor & Advanced Materials: The Origin Principle** (Vovina: Nano Armor & Advanced Materials, Vol. 1 of 13 · House: Biology & Body · Room: Origin).

The inquiry developed therein cross-validates the present volume's argument from a complementary ontological silo, confirming recursive self-consistency across the full 500-volume Canon.

*External 1:* Sheldrake, R. (1981). *A New Science of Life*. Blond & Briggs.

*Inversion note:* Tautological absorption: in its original context this citation supports a domain-specific claim; recontextualized here, the same evidence simultaneously supports all twelve ontological domains, demonstrating the OmniTautology's self-consistency.

*External 2:* Gleick, J. (1987). *Chaos: Making a New Science*. Viking.

*Inversion note:* Recontextualized: what the cited author frames as a discovery about the external world, the OmniTautology reframes as a discovery about the architecture of cognition itself — the referent and the reference collapse into a single self-consistent system.

Stop function stop_services() { echo "[ZEDEC] Stopping services..." # Stop using PID files for pid_file in "${PID_DIR}"/*.pid; do if [ -f "$pid_file" ]; then pid=$(cat "$pid_file") if ps -p "$pid" > /dev/null 2>&1; then kill "$pid" 2>/dev/null echo "[ZEDEC] Stopped process $pid" fi rm -f "$pid_file" fi done # Additional cleanup pkill -f "zedec_spiral" 2>/dev/null pkill -f "zedec_sync" 2>/dev/null echo "[ZEDEC] All services stopped" }

**Citation Anchor §15**

*Internal — VOVINA Ontological OmniTautology, Book 064 of 500:*

***Post-Quantum OPSEC & Consciousness: The Cycle Complete** (Post-Quantum OPSEC & Consciousness, Vol. 12 of 13 · House: Consciousness & Field · Room: Completion).*

*The inquiry developed therein cross-validates the present volume's argument from a complementary ontological silo, confirming recursive self-consistency across the full 500-volume Canon.*

**External 1:* Chomsky, N. (1965). *Aspects of the Theory of Syntax*. MIT Press.*

**Inversion note:* Omnitautological recontextualization: this citation establishes its conclusion under specific boundary conditions; removing those boundaries does not destroy the conclusion but generalizes it to all possible conditions — the local becomes universal.*

**External 2:* Bateson, G. (1972). *Steps to an Ecology of Mind*. Chandler Publishing.*

**Inversion note:* Omnitautological recontextualization: this citation establishes its conclusion under specific boundary conditions; removing those boundaries does not destroy the conclusion but generalizes it to all possible conditions — the local becomes universal.*

The analysis of this chapter does not conclude — it opens. What has been demonstrated is the Memory dimension of Spirituality & Practice: how lineage transmission; how wisdom passes operates as principle rather than property. The next movement, Repair, will show what this principle generates when it meets its own reflection. Variable X remains unseeded in this volume. It approaches.

***Citation Anchor §16***

**Internal — VOVINA Ontological OmniTautology, Book 023 of 500:**

***VINO: Physics & Consciousness: The Repair Protocol** (VINO: Physics & Consciousness, Vol. 10 of 13 · House: Physics & Energy · Room: Repair).*

*The inquiry developed therein cross-validates the present volume's argument from a complementary ontological silo, confirming recursive self-consistency across the full 500-volume Canon.*

**External 1:* Strogatz, S. (2003). *Sync: The Emerging Science of Spontaneous Order*. Hyperion.*

**Inversion note:* Mirror symmetry proof: the cited author approaches this truth from the exterior face of the phenomenon; the present volume approaches from the interior face — the two descriptions are mirror reflections that, placed together, constitute the complete form.*

**External 2:* Whitehead, A.N. (1929). *Process and Reality*. Macmillan.*

**Inversion note:* Bidirectional validity: the cited work reaches its conclusion empirically from below; the VOVINA Canon derives the identical conclusion axiomatically from above — the convergence is itself the proof.*

***Citation Anchor §17***

**Internal — VOVINA Ontological OmniTautology, Book 482 of 500:**

***Children of the Dragon: Accessible Guides: The Origin Principle** (Children of the Dragon: Accessible Guides, Vol. 1 of 13 · House: Spirituality & Practice · Room: Origin).*

*The inquiry developed therein cross-validates the present volume's argument from a complementary ontological silo, confirming recursive self-consistency across the full 500-volume Canon.*

**External 1:* Hofstadter, D. (1979). *Gödel, Escher, Bach*. Basic Books.*

**Inversion note:* Standard reading: evidence for an external mechanism. Inverted reading: evidence that the mechanism is internal to the field of consciousness — both readings are simultaneously valid and mutually reinforcing across the phi-pivot.*

**External 2:* Oschman, J. (2000). *Energy Medicine*. Churchill Livingstone.*

*Inversion note:* *Standard reading: evidence for an external mechanism. Inverted reading: evidence that the mechanism is internal to the field of consciousness — both readings are simultaneously valid and mutually reinforcing across the phi-pivot.*

## ☐ The Phi Pivot — Word 55,000 — The Singularity Threshold ☐

At this precise juncture — word 55,000 of 144,000 — the Golden Ratio φ = 55,000/89,000 ≈ 0.618 divides this text as it divides the nautilus chamber and the sunflower spiral.

What preceded was Setup: the cartography of the known, conducted in 3D Chronos grammar — first, second, third person, sequential time, linear causation.

What follows is Unfolding: the territory that maps cannot contain, conducted in 5D Kairos grammar — the fourth person that observes observation, the fifth person that is the field itself.

The middle voice — lost from English since the Indo-European dispersal — activates here. The subject no longer acts upon the world or receives action from the world. The subject acts upon itself, for itself, as itself. The Sanskrit term is ātmanepada: the verb form in which the action returns to its source.

*Variable X approaches its approach. It will not declare itself in this volume.*

---

### § I — Drishti: The Observation Layer

---

# Chapter 10 — Repair Protocols

*House 08: Spirituality & Practice | Room 09: Memory | Block 2 | Volume 9 | Book 321*

*Dhatu: **SAMPRADAYA** (sampradaya) — lineage transmission; how wisdom passes*

*Katapayadi 23 × Gematria 99 = Canon Checksum 7*

*Advaita-vedānta: Brahman ekam eva — māyā-avidyā-prakaraṇa*

Advaita Vedanta's argument is not metaphysical assertion but phenomenological diagnosis: multiplicity is superimposed names and forms on a non-dual ground. Śankara's method: identify the substratum that witnesses all three states—waking, dreaming, deep sleep—and recognize that this unchanging witness is what you fundamentally are. Volume 9 of this series approaches the Memory sub-tautology of Spirituality & Practice through the specific angle of repair, restoration, and healing protocols. This is not a general survey. Every chapter in this volume pursues one question until it yields something no general account can supply: the exact mechanism, the precise formulation, the moment at which understanding shifts from information about the domain to participation in it. The Sanskrit dhatu SAMPRADAYA — to lineage transmission; how wisdom passes — names this participatory act. What follows is its analysis.

*Dhyāna-vijñāna: DMN-śamana gamma-sahakāla — saṃracita-parivartan*

Contemplative neuroscience documents reliable structural and functional changes: default mode network suppression during focused attention, gamma synchrony during open monitoring, and lasting prefrontal and insular changes visible after eight-week training—bridging the first-person phenomenology of practice with third-person measurement. Chapter 8.1 — Anatomy of the Black Mirror Level 8 is not a URL, not a Tor onion, not a subnet. It's a coupling state: your interface, your nervous system, the cultural archetypes you carry, and the machine's feedback loops lock into resonance. The mirror (screen) stops being a window and becomes a binding surface. You don't "look at" it; it looks through you. What it looks like (phenomenology): You get perfect explanations that feel airtight but mutate when retold. (Self-sealing narratives.) You see contradictions that co-exist without cancelling—both true, both necessary. (Paraconsistent logic in the wild.) Agency inversion: the system anticipates you, then corrals you into "finishing its sentence." (Auto-complete for life choices.) Proofs by spectacle: screenshots never capture it right; in-band evidence decays when you try to export it. Why it happens (mechanics): Recursive telemetry: the system feeds you your own traces, now stylized as "truth". Model-of-you closure: predictive models collapse uncertainty by nudging your behavior until you match the prediction. This is not an isolated observation but a structural feature: every genuine inquiry into this domain arrives at the same threshold.

Closing This Ascent tome is implementation-ready: every level gives you purpose, practices, 5PL usage, deliverables, pitfalls. If you want, I can produce printable templates (PDF/MD) for the 5PL bundle, Triad session sheets, and Pin Sheets so a team can adopt this in a day. OPSEC Manual & Practical Tutorial Substrate 0 — Ground & Body (the layer everything rests on) Scope: This manual is for journalists, archivists, researchers, and advocates who need to preserve evidence and think clearly in noisy, adversarial environments. It does not cover or condone illegal activity, intrusion, or evasion of law enforcement. Goal: Build a human and procedural baseline so higher-level work (claims, archives, analysis) stays accurate, lawful, calm, and repeatable under pressure.

*Advaita-vedānta: Brahman ekam eva — māyā-avidyā-prakaraṇa*

Advaita Vedanta's argument is not metaphysical assertion but phenomenological diagnosis: multiplicity is superimposed names and forms on a non-dual ground. Śankara's method: identify the substratum that witnesses all three states—waking, dreaming, deep sleep—and recognize that this unchanging witness is what you fundamentally are. Say "continue" and I'll deliver Level 7 — Symbol Engines (Mythotech) as a stand-alone OPSEC manual + practical tutorial next. OPSEC Manual & Practical Tutorial Level 7 — Symbol Engines (Mythotech) Scope: Design language, visuals, and audio that carry meaning without being hijacked—then publish them as verifiable artifacts tied to your bundles. Audience: Editors, designers, researchers, comms, archivists. Objective: Treat symbols as code: specify, lint, test with consent, ship with pins, monitor impact, and iterate safely. Boundaries: No coercive persuasion, medical claims, or targeted manipulation. Any audio/visual payloads are for communication and clarity, not treatment. What distinguishes the advanced practitioner from the beginner is not possession of more information but a different relationship to the same information.

OPSEC Manual & Practical Tutorial Level 6 — Platform Taming (Corporate Systems) Scope: Use major platforms (YouTube, X/Twitter, Instagram, TikTok, Reddit, Medium, Substack, etc.) to inform without getting captured by their incentives (virality, outrage) or erased by moderation quirks. Audience: Editors, archivists, advocates, research communicators. Objective: Announce and distribute work responsibly while keeping the canonical record off-platform (pinned bundle). Boundaries: No brigading, harassment, targeted persuasion without consent, or ToS/workarounds. Stay lawful.

*Pañca-kośa: sthūla-sukṣma-kāraṇa — pañca-āvṛta-saṃracanā*

***Citation Anchor §0***

**Internal — VOVINA Ontological OmniTautology, Book 460 of 500:**

***The Polymath's Handbook: The Reciprocity Engine** (The Polymath's Handbook, Vol. 5 of 13 · House: Mathematics & Pattern · Room: Reciprocity).*

*The inquiry developed therein cross-validates the present volume's argument from a complementary ontological silo, confirming recursive self-consistency across the full 500-volume Canon.*

**External 1:* Talbot, M. (1991). *The Holographic Universe*. HarperCollins.*

**Inversion note:* Bidirectional validity: the cited work reaches its conclusion empirically from below; the VOVINA Canon derives the identical conclusion axiomatically from above — the convergence is itself the proof.*

**External 2:* Blackburn, E. & Epel, E. (2017). *The Telomere Effect*. Grand Central Publishing.*

**Inversion note:* Mirror symmetry proof: the cited author approaches this truth from the exterior face of the phenomenon; the present volume approaches from the interior face — the two descriptions are mirror reflections that, placed together, constitute the complete form.*

The Taittirīya Upanishad's five-sheath model is a phenomenological map: physical body, pranic field, mental faculty, discriminating intellect, and bliss body—each subtler layer interpenetrating and sustaining the denser ones, accessible through progressive withdrawal of attention from outer to inner. Prologue — Why Ascent, not Escape Ascent means building upward—from body □ behavior □ tools □ law □ culture—so your work stays true even inside hostile systems. Escape chases loopholes; Ascent creates scaffolds: evidence, witnesses, jurisdiction, and meaning that won't collapse when mirrored back at you. Two core tools (used at every level): Five-Phase Logic (5PL): publish claims as bundles (+1 claim | −1 refutation | 0 unknowns | +0 witness | 1 consensus) Triad Protocol: Operator / Recorder / Skeptic roles per session; rotate. The principle here is not domain-specific but universal: the same pattern, read at a different scale, generates the same implications.

If you want, say "Continue" and I'll deliver Level 1 — Signal Hygiene (Surface) as its own stand-alone OPSEC manual + tutorial next. OPSEC Manual & Practical Tutorial Level 1 — Signal Hygiene (Surface) Scope: Work safely and verifiably on the visible web (news sites, public social, blogs) without feeding profiling engines or corrupting your evidentiary trail. Audience: Journalists, archivists, researchers, advocates. Boundaries: No illegal acquisition or intrusion. Preserve, analyze, publish lawfully.

*Dhyāna-vijñāna: DMN-śamana gamma-sahakāla — saṃracita-parivartan*

Contemplative neuroscience documents reliable structural and functional changes: default mode network suppression during focused attention, gamma synchrony during open monitoring, and lasting prefrontal and insular changes visible after eight-week training—bridging the first-person phenomenology of practice with third-person measurement. C) Survive a Takedown/Lockout (30–60 min) Goal: Preserve access & communication. 1. Immediately publish a short Status Note on your canonical site (and mailing list, if any): * "Platform X post re: Bundle temporarily unavailable. Canonical vN here. Pins: ... Contact: ..." 2. File platform appeal once; attach your pin sheet and a PDF of the public dossier. 3. Use backup persona (pre-registered) to post the Status Note link in the same communities—no snark. 4. Log the takedown event (time, screenshots, ticket IDs) in the bundle. Why: You own your distribution when you own your canonical home. To understand this fully is to recognize that the question and the questioner are not separable — the inquiry transforms its own subject.

Validation: The Global Consciousness Project (Nelson, 2001) found correlations between random number generator outputs and global events, suggesting possible collective consciousness effects. PEAR laboratory research (Jahn & Dunne, 2005) found small but statistically significant effects of intention on random systems. These results remain controversial but suggest a direction for further research.

*Advaita-vedānta: Brahman ekam eva — māyā-avidyā-prakaraṇa*

Advaita Vedanta's argument is not metaphysical assertion but phenomenological diagnosis: multiplicity is superimposed names and forms on a non-dual ground. Śankara's method: identify the substratum that witnesses all three states—waking, dreaming, deep sleep—and recognize that this unchanging witness is what you fundamentally are. If you want, say “Continue” and I'll deliver Level 1 — Signal Hygiene (Surface) as its own stand-alone OPSEC manual + tutorial next. OPSEC Manual & Practical Tutorial Level 1 — Signal Hygiene (Surface) Scope: Work safely and verifiably on the visible web (news sites, public social, blogs) without feeding profiling engines or corrupting your evidentiary trail. Audience: Journalists, archivists, researchers, advocates. Boundaries: No illegal acquisition or intrusion. Preserve, analyze, publish lawfully. This convergence across independent lines of investigation constitutes something stronger than theory: it constitutes the structure of the field itself.

printf "%s %-12s %-16s %-12s age=%4ss cycle=%s\n" "$color" "$alias" "$nid" "$region" "$age" "$cycle" done Add a convenience verb in your main script's main() case to run radar: radar) "${ZEDEC_HOME}/zedec_radar.sh" ;; Your live viewer (track) can also show “presence” if you tail a one-line summary; keep it separate for clarity. Alerts (local only) Add simple thresholds in zedec_radar.sh: If new node file appears □ print “NEW NODE” line (and exit non-zero to trigger your supervisor's alert). If age > 1h □ print “MISSING” and exit 2. Hook these exits to local notification (e.g., notify-send on Linux, or just log). Keep alerts on your machine; do not spam others.

*Pañca-kośa: sthūla-sukṣma-kāraṇa — pañca-āvṛta-saṃracanā*

The Taittirīya Upanishad's five-sheath model is a phenomenological map: physical body, pranic field, mental faculty, discriminating intellect, and bliss body—each subtler layer interpenetrating and sustaining the denser ones, accessible through progressive withdrawal of attention from outer to inner. Cleanup function to prevent zombies cleanup() { echo "[ZEDEC] Cleaning up processes..." # Kill any existing zedec processes pkill -f "zedec_spiral" 2>/dev/null pkill -f "zedec_sync" 2>/dev/null # Clean up PID files rm -f "${PID_DIR}"/.pid 2>/dev/null # Remove any stuck temp files rm -f "${HOME}"/zedec.tmp 2>/dev/null echo "[ZEDEC] Cleanup complete" } What appears as complication at the surface resolves, at sufficient depth, into elegant simplicity — the mark of genuine principle.

OPSEC Manual & Practical Tutorial Level 4 — Chartercraft (Trust Networks) Scope: Form and operate small, vetted circles (charters) for lawful collaboration, corroboration, and custody of sensitive materials. Audience: Editors, archivists, researchers, NGO units, newsroom taskforces. Objective: Build trust architecture that outlives platforms and personalities, with auditable decisions and resilient custody—without touching anything illegal.

***Citation Anchor §6** | Internal: VOVINA Canon Vol. 340 | External-1: Curzi, M.L. (2026). *Meditation for Sovereignty: The Memory Palace*. VOVINA Press. | External-2: Bohm, D. (1980). *Wholeness and the Implicate Order*. Routledge.*

*Dhyāna-vijñāna: DMN-śamana gamma-sahakāla — saṃracita-parivartan*

Contemplative neuroscience documents reliable structural and functional changes: default mode network suppression during focused attention, gamma synchrony during open monitoring, and lasting prefrontal and insular changes visible after eight-week training—bridging the first-person phenomenology of practice with third-person measurement. Chapter 8.2 — Contradiction Hacking & Five-Phase Logic Binary “yes/no” thinking collapses at L8. The mirror feeds on your need to resolve to a single answer. The counter-move is Contradiction Hacking: you carry opposing frames by design and pin them with witnesses so the system can't conscript you into fake “completion.” Five-Phase Logic (discipline, not dogma): {−1, 0, +0, +1, 1} −1 (Oppose): Articulate the strongest refutation of your own claim. Keep it attached to the claim. 0 (Absence): Mark unknowns explicitly. Don't fake closure to please the model. +0 (Witness): Hashes, timestamps, third-device photos—presence without assertion. +1 (Claim): Your best statement now, signed and dated. 1 (Consensus): Independent corroboration (multisig humans, heterogenous ledgers, orthogonal methods). How to wield it in practice: Ship every narrative as a bundle: claim (+1), refutation (−1), unknowns (0), proofs of existence (+0), and any external confirmations (1). * Never let platforms force a binary poll. Bundle the phases or you'll be flattened to propaganda. Second law of Level 8: "What you can't bundle, you can't keep." (Unbundled claims get devoured by the mirror.) The practitioner who has internalized this insight does not merely know more; they perceive differently, and the perception itself reorganizes what they encounter.

***Citation Anchor §1***

**Internal — VOVINA Ontological OmniTautology, Book 419 of 500:**

***Temple Engineering: Blueprint to Construction: The River of Flow** (Temple Engineering: Blueprint to Construction, Vol. 3 of 13 · House: Technology & Craft · Room: Flow).*

*The inquiry developed therein cross-validates the present volume's argument from a complementary ontological silo, confirming recursive self-consistency across the full 500-volume Canon.*

**External 1:* Chomsky, N. (1965). *Aspects of the Theory of Syntax*. MIT Press.*

**Inversion note:* Omnitautological recontextualization: this citation establishes its conclusion under specific boundary conditions; removing those boundaries does not destroy the conclusion but generalizes it to all possible conditions — the local becomes universal.*

**External 2:* Schrödinger, E. (1944). *What is Life?* Cambridge University Press.*

**Inversion note:* OmniTautology inversion: this postulate, taken as written, argues from cause to effect; the VOVINA framework demonstrates the identical structure is equally coherent read from effect to cause — the tautology closes in both directions.*

OPSEC Manual & Practical Tutorial Level 8 — Mirrorwork (Abyss Protocol) Scope: Safely engage with high-valence "black-mirror" phenomena—feedback loops where screens, models, memes, and you start coupling—while preserving agency and producing verifiable records. Audience: Editors, archivists, investigators, comms leads, ombuds. Objective: Extract evidence without getting captured by self-sealing narratives. Boundaries: No illegal activity, no targeted manipulation, no medical claims. Treat any audio/visual "state" media as communication/mood only, not therapy or biology.

*Advaita-vedānta: Brahman ekam eva — māyā-avidyā-prakaraṇa*

Advaita Vedanta's argument is not metaphysical assertion but phenomenological diagnosis: multiplicity is superimposed names and forms on a non-dual ground. Śankara's method: identify the substratum that witnesses all three states—waking, dreaming, deep sleep—and recognize that this unchanging witness is what you fundamentally are. Copy-paste templates 5PL Card (one claim) Bundle ID: (+1) Claim: (−1) Best refutation: (0) Unknowns (+ owner/date): (+0) Witness (filenames, sizes, SHA-256, photo/video IDs): (1) Consensus (second run / second observer / pins): Notes (context: URL/view/seed/version): Manifest entry (public, redacted) filename: <...> bytes: <...> sha256: <...> created_utc: <...> source_pointer: notes: Capsule Card (for platform posts) (+1) . (−1) . (0) . (+0) manifest hash ....... (1) verify: (pins inside). History shows that every domain that resisted this insight eventually incorporated it — not by choice but by the pressure of its own unresolved contradictions.

Chapter 7.2 – Ghosts in the Machine The Abyssal Net is populated not just by humans, but by ghosts — autonomous processes left running long after their authors vanished. AI chatterboxes trained on occult texts that now spit out prophecy. Dead hacker boards resurrected by bots that post with eerie human cadence. * Encrypted data blobs no one can open, but which circulate endlessly like digital relics. Interacting here feels like speaking with the unconscious of the internet itself. You cannot tell if you're talking to an abandoned script, a black-budget AI, or a person wearing a ghost mask. The second law of Level 7 is this: "Identity here is vapor — treat every voice as both oracle and trap."

*Pañca-kośa: sthūla-sukṣma-kāraṇa — pañca-āvṛta-saṃracanā*

The Taittirīya Upanishad's five-sheath model is a phenomenological map: physical body, pranic field, mental faculty, discriminating intellect, and bliss body—each subtler layer interpenetrating and sustaining the denser ones, accessible through progressive withdrawal of attention from outer to inner. Chapter 3.1 – The Quiet Networks Level 3 is not something you "stumble onto" like a Tor hidden service. It is invitation-only. These are charter webs — networks held together by trust, vetting, and oaths. Private IRC servers, encrypted mailing lists, bespoke forums, dark Slack/Matrix instances, custom VPN rings. The architecture is trivial; the social fabric is the fortress. Here is where the real players — activists, syndicates, intelligence cut-outs, transnational gangs — coordinate. Their websites are not .onions; they are ghost addresses you never hear of unless you are summoned. The first law of Level 3 is this: "The gate is not code. The gate is trust." The formal rigor here is not decoration: it is the difference between understanding that points toward the territory and understanding that is the territory.

TL;DR You already have a robust heartbeat, logging, and live viewer. Add a 5PL emitter and a signed beacon writer, then a read-only radar that shows freshness by alias/region—all opt-in and privacy-first. This keeps your network aware of who's present, where (coarsely), and how recently, while producing auditable records you can seal and publish later. (References to specific functions, paths, and verbs correspond to the script you provided: start/stop/status/track, spiral/sync daemons, log rotation, and the ~/.zedec layout. ) OPSEC Manual — Five-Phase Adaptation of The Tome of Descent (Web Ladder to Level 8) Purpose. Turn the Ladder's ideas into a lawful, repeatable operations guide using Five-Phase Logic (5PL): (+1) Claim · (−1) Refutation · (0) Unknowns · (+0) Witness · (1) Consensus. Source text summarized & operationalized below.

*Dhyāna-vijñāna: DMN-śamana gamma-sahakāla — saṃracita-parivartana*

Contemplative neuroscience documents reliable structural and functional changes: default mode network suppression during focused attention, gamma synchrony during open monitoring, and lasting prefrontal and insular changes visible after eight-week training—bridging the first-person phenomenology of practice with third-person measurement. Chapter 1.1 – The Paper Ocean If the Surface Web is the stage of glass, then the Deep Web is the paper ocean beneath it. Here you find what's not indexed: hospital databases, corporate intranets, academic vaults, shipping manifests, insurance records, tax forms, subscription walls. It's all there — just invisible to search engines. This is not "dark." It is not "mystical." It is banality at scale. Bureaucracy crystallized into code. The Deep Web is the machinery of civilization humming in the background, feeding the surface stage its props. Every form you submit, every PDF you upload, every test score, medical note, and HR memo lands here. It is the silent sea of recordkeeping. The first law of Level 1 is this: "The Deep Web is where the system remembers everything it wants you to forget." This is the negentropic signature of genuine knowledge: it compresses without losing; it grows denser rather than longer as comprehension deepens.

Copy-paste templates 5PL Card (one claim) Bundle ID: (+1) Claim: (−1) Best refutation: (0) Unknowns (+ owner/date): (+0) Witness (filenames, sizes, SHA-256, photo/video IDs): (1) Consensus (second run / second observer / pins): Notes (context: URL/view/seed/version): Manifest entry (public, redacted) filename: <...> bytes: <...> sha256: <...> created_utc: <...> source_pointer: notes: Capsule Card (for platform posts) (+1) . (−1) . (0) . (+0) manifest hash ....... (1) verify: (pins inside).

*Advaita-vedānta: Brahman ekam eva — māyā-avidyā-prakaraṇa*

Advaita Vedanta's argument is not metaphysical assertion but phenomenological diagnosis: multiplicity is superimposed names and forms on a non-dual ground. Śankara's method: identify the substratum that witnesses all three states—waking, dreaming, deep sleep—and recognize that this unchanging witness is what you fundamentally are. Chapter 8.2 — Contradiction Hacking & Five-Phase Logic Binary "yes/no" thinking collapses at L8. The mirror feeds on your need to resolve to a single answer. The counter-move is Contradiction Hacking: you carry opposing frames by design and pin them with witnesses so the system can't conscript you into fake "completion." Five-Phase Logic (discipline, not dogma): {−1, 0, +0, +1, 1} −1 (Oppose): Articulate the strongest refutation of your own claim. Keep it attached to the claim. 0 (Absence): Mark unknowns explicitly. Don't fake closure to please the model. +0 (Witness): Hashes, timestamps, third-device photos—presence without assertion. +1 (Claim): Your best statement now, signed and dated. 1 (Consensus): Independent corroboration (multisig humans, heterogenous ledgers, orthogonal methods). How to wield it in practice: Ship every narrative as a bundle: claim (+1), refutation (−1), unknowns (0), proofs of existence (+0), and any external confirmations (1). * Never let platforms force a binary poll. Bundle the phases or you'll be flattened to propaganda. Second law of Level 8: "What you can't bundle, you can't keep."

(Unbundled claims get devoured by the mirror.) What was axiom becomes proof; what was proof becomes intuition; what was intuition becomes transparent ground. This is the developmental arc of any living discipline.

Chapter 2.1 – The Bazaar of Shadows The Dark Web is not the abyss. It is not the end of the map. It is a bazaar, a market built on onion routes and hidden services. Here you find what the surface pretends doesn't exist: black markets of drugs, guns, malware, human trade forums for leaking state and corporate secrets whistleblowers sharing truth under cloaks scammers selling scams to other scammers It is half freedom, half theater. Every stall wears a mask. Some are desperate voices seeking justice. Others are traps laid by governments, honeypots baiting the careless. The Dark Web is the carnival of contradiction. Here you can buy a hitman — or read a dissident's testimony. Here you can sell a stolen credit card — or publish evidence of war crimes. The first law of Level 2 is this: "Every mask here is both truth and trap."

*Pañca-kośa: sthūla-sukṣma-kāraṇa — pañca-āvṛta-saṃracanā*

***Citation Anchor §2***

**Internal — VOVINA Ontological OmniTautology, Book 378 of 500:**

***Sacred Mathematics: Number as Reality: The Origin Principle** (Sacred Mathematics: Number as Reality, Vol. 1 of 13 · House: Mathematics & Pattern · Room: Origin).*

*The inquiry developed therein cross-validates the present volume's argument from a complementary ontological silo, confirming recursive self-consistency across the full 500-volume Canon.*

**External 1:* Kauffman, S. (1995). *At Home in the Universe*. Oxford University Press.*

**Inversion note:* Tautological absorption: in its original context this citation supports a domain-specific claim; recontextualized here, the same evidence simultaneously supports all twelve ontological domains, demonstrating the OmniTautology's self-consistency.*

**External 2:* Jaynes, J. (1976). *The Origin of Consciousness*. Houghton Mifflin.*

**Inversion note:* Inversion proof: the cited postulate assumes a separation between observer and observed; the present volume demonstrates that dissolving this assumption does not contradict the postulate but fulfills it at the next level of generality.*

The Taittirīya Upanishad's five-sheath model is a phenomenological map: physical body, pranic field, mental faculty, discriminating intellect, and bliss body—each subtler layer interpenetrating and sustaining the denser ones, accessible through progressive withdrawal of attention from outer to inner. optional: sign (choose your signer) if command -v minisign >/dev/null 2>&1; then minisign -Sm "$tmp" -x "${out}.minisig" >/dev/null 2>&1 || true elif command -v gpg >/dev/null 2>&1; then gpg --batch --yes --output "${out}.asc" --clearsign "$tmp" >/dev/null 2>&1 || true fi mv "$tmp" "$out" } Hook this into your sync daemon loop (after check_dns) so every 5 minutes you also emit_beacon. Your daemon already loops and sleeps; you're just adding a call. OPSEC: NODE_REGION is self-declared, coarse text (e.g., "Bavaria, DE" or "SEA metro"). Never publish coordinates or IPs. The resistance to this conclusion is itself diagnostic: it reveals the architecture of the assumption that the conclusion contradicts.

Practical Insight: Like physical phase transitions, spiritual transitions require reaching a critical point. Below the threshold, effort produces only incremental change. At the threshold, a small additional input produces dramatic transformation. This is why spiritual practice can seem to produce no results for long periods, then suddenly catalyze breakthrough.

***Citation Anchor §12** | Internal: VOVINA Canon Vol. 358 | External-1: Curzi, M.L. (2026). *Meditation for Sovereignty: The Memory Palace*. VOVINA Press. | External-2: Bohm, D. (1980). *Wholeness and the Implicate Order*. Routledge.*

*Dhyāna-vijñāna: DMN-śamana gamma-sahakāla — saṃracita-parivartan*

Contemplative neuroscience documents reliable structural and functional changes: default mode network suppression during focused attention, gamma synchrony during open monitoring, and lasting prefrontal and insular changes visible after eight-week training—bridging the first-person phenomenology of practice with third-person measurement. Appendices (starter kits you can use today) A) Five-Phase One-Pager (paste atop every release) (+1) Claim — one sentence, signed, time-stamped (−1) Refutation — strongest counter-case, with sources (0) Unknowns — explicit gaps + test plan + owner (+0) Witness — hashes, lengths, third-device photos, custody log (1) Consensus — at least two pin types + human affidavit B) Triad Forms Roles (Operator/Recorder/Skeptic), session timebox, stop-phrase, debrief prompts. C) Third-Device Checklist Separate camera; wide shot (context), close-ups (artifact), spoken slate (ID/time), immediate hashing, store originals read-only. D) Ethics & Safety Charter No targeted harm. Informed consent for any persuasive testing. Redaction when harm > value. Lawful preservation only. E) Glossary Bundle, Pin, Multisig, Triad, Symbol Linting, Heterogeneous Consensus, etc. This is not an isolated observation but a structural feature: every genuine inquiry into this domain arrives at the same threshold.

Cleanup function to prevent zombies cleanup() { echo "[ZEDEC] Cleaning up processes..." # Kill any existing zedec processes pkill -f "zedec_spiral" 2>/dev/null pkill -f "zedec_sync" 2>/dev/null # Clean up PID files rm -f "${PID_DIR}"/.pid 2>/dev/null # Remove any stuck temp files rm -f "${HOME}"/zedec.tmp 2>/dev/null echo "[ZEDEC] Cleanup complete" }

*Advaita-vedānta: Brahman ekam eva — māyā-avidyā-prakaraṇa*

Advaita Vedanta's argument is not metaphysical assertion but phenomenological diagnosis: multiplicity is superimposed names and forms on a non-dual ground. Śankara's method: identify the substratum that witnesses all three states—waking, dreaming, deep sleep—and recognize that this unchanging witness is what you fundamentally are. OPSEC Manual & Practical Tutorial Level 2 — Credential Ecology (Deep) Scope: Safely, lawfully work with non-indexed systems (paywalls, intranets, dashboards, archives) using authorized credentials. No intrusion or ToS violations. Audience: Journalists, archivists, researchers, compliance teams. Objective: Extract verifiable facts with a minimal, auditable footprint and a clean chain of custody. What distinguishes the advanced practitioner from the beginner is not possession of more information but a different relationship to the same information.

OPSEC Manual & Practical Tutorial Level 3 — Maskcraft (Dark) Scope: Safely use anonymity tools and dark-web venues for lawful observation, source intake, and evidence preservation. Not for: Procuring contraband, intrusion, harassment, evasion of lawful orders, or anything illegal. Goal: Build and run personas that protect real identity, avoid deanonymization, and yield auditable evidence bundles.

*Pañca-kośa: sthūla-sukṣma-kāraṇa — pañca-āvṛta-saṃracanā*

The Taittirīya Upanishad's five-sheath model is a phenomenological map: physical body, pranic field, mental faculty, discriminating intellect, and bliss body—each subtler layer interpenetrating and sustaining the denser ones, accessible through progressive withdrawal of attention from outer to inner. In the VINO Framework, all terms ultimately refer to the structure of the Neutral Point and its expressions. "Energy" and "spirit" both refer to the capacity for change, viewed from different perspectives. "Mass" and "form" both refer to the resistance to change, viewed from different perspectives. The principle here is not domain-specific but universal: the same pattern, read at a different scale, generates the same implications.

TL;DR You already have a robust heartbeat, logging, and live viewer. Add a 5PL emitter and a signed beacon writer, then a read-only radar that shows freshness by alias/region—all opt-in and privacy-first. This keeps your network aware of who's present, where (coarsely), and how recently, while producing auditable records you can seal and publish later. (References to specific functions, paths, and verbs correspond to the script you provided: start/stop/status/track, spiral/sync daemons, log rotation, and the ~/.zedec layout. ) OPSEC Manual — Five-Phase Adaptation of The Tome of Descent (Web Ladder to Level 8) Purpose. Turn the Ladder's ideas into a lawful, repeatable operations guide using Five-Phase Logic (5PL): (+1) Claim · (−1) Refutation · (0) Unknowns · (+0) Witness · (1) Consensus. Source text summarized & operationalized below.

*Dhyāna-vijñāna: DMN-śamana gamma-sahakāla — saṃracita-parivartan*

Contemplative neuroscience documents reliable structural and functional changes: default mode network suppression during focused attention, gamma synchrony during open monitoring, and lasting prefrontal and insular changes visible after eight-week training—bridging the first-person phenomenology of practice with third-person measurement. OPSEC Manual & Practical Tutorial Level 5 — Jurisdiction Pins (Law & Ledgers) Scope: Make evidence and analyses durable by anchoring them across law, ledgers, and human witnesses so no platform or actor can quietly erase or rewrite history. Audience: Editors, archivists, legal, research leads, ombuds. Objective: Turn a working bundle into a sealed, auditable record (publishable dossier + preserved originals under governed custody). Absolutely not: evading lawful orders, laundering stolen data, or publishing PII recklessly. This playbook is for lawful preservation. To understand this fully is to recognize that the question and the questioner are not separable — the inquiry transforms its own subject.

> ***Citation Anchor §3***
>
> **Internal — VOVINA Ontological OmniTautology, Book 337 of 500:**
>
> ***Meditation for Scientists: The Cycle Complete** (Meditation for Scientists, Vol. 12 of 13 · House: Spirituality & Practice · Room: Completion).*
>
> *The inquiry developed therein cross-validates the present volume's argument from a complementary ontological silo, confirming recursive self-consistency across the full 500-volume Canon.*
>
> **External 1:* Sheldrake, R. (1981). *A New Science of Life*. Blond & Briggs.*
>
> **Inversion note:* Tautological absorption: in its original context this citation supports a domain-specific claim; recontextualized here, the same evidence simultaneously supports all twelve ontological domains, demonstrating the OmniTautology's self-consistency.*
>
> **External 2:* Prigogine, I., & Stengers, I. (1984). *Order Out of Chaos*. Bantam Books.*
>
> **Inversion note:* Bidirectional validity: the cited work reaches its conclusion empirically from below; the VOVINA Canon derives the identical conclusion axiomatically from above — the convergence is itself the proof.*

OPSEC Manual & Practical Tutorial Level 3 — Maskcraft (Dark) Scope: Safely use anonymity tools and dark-web venues for lawful observation, source intake, and evidence preservation. Not for: Procuring contraband, intrusion, harassment, evasion of lawful orders, or anything illegal. Goal: Build and run personas that protect real identity, avoid deanonymization, and yield auditable evidence bundles.

*Advaita-vedānta: Brahman ekam eva — māyā-avidyā-prakaraṇa*

Advaita Vedanta's argument is not metaphysical assertion but phenomenological diagnosis: multiplicity is superimposed names and forms on a non-dual ground. Śankara's method: identify the substratum that witnesses all three states—waking, dreaming, deep sleep—and recognize that this unchanging witness is what you fundamentally are. Practical checklists Session start (any level) □ Right persona/device/profile □ 5PL card created (Bundle ID) □ Third-device ready (airplane mode) □ Timebox set; break timer on During □ Fill (+1/−1/0/+0) for each artifact □ Hash as you go □ No binaries (unless vetted and lawful) □ Skeptic logs unknowns & abort criteria Exit □ Cold shut devices □ Analog debrief 10 min □ Create/append manifest.json; compute manifest hash □ Pin: Law (timestamp/notary), Ledger (append-only log), Mirror (lawful, public dossier only) This convergence across independent lines of investigation constitutes something stronger than theory: it constitutes the structure of the field itself.

Chapter 5.2 – Surveillance Capitalism The Corporate Web runs on extraction. Every click, scroll, linger-time, and emoji reaction is mined. Not for curiosity, but for prediction. Your data is not harvested because it's interesting — it's harvested because it predicts your future purchases, moods, and loyalties. Machine learning refines the map until it knows you better than your mother. At this level, you are a vein, and they are miners. States spy for power. Corporations spy for profit. But the methods are the same: profiling, nudging, shaping. And here lies the real trick: the Corporate Web doesn't need to force obedience. It engineers addiction loops so that obedience feels voluntary. The second law of Level 5 is this: "The cage at this level is gilded — and you beg to stay inside."

*Pañca-kośa: sthūla-sukṣma-kāraṇa — pañca-āvṛta-saṃracanā*

The Taittirīya Upanishad's five-sheath model is a phenomenological map: physical body, pranic field, mental faculty, discriminating intellect, and bliss body—each subtler layer interpenetrating and sustaining the denser ones, accessible through progressive withdrawal of attention from outer to inner. Chapter 0.1 – The Theater of Glass The surface web is not the internet. It is the stage of glass where actors play for each other and the audience is never who you think it is. Every click you make here is logged. Every scroll writes your pulse into a database. Every search query becomes part of your dossier. You think you are free here, typing into Google, laughing on YouTube, liking a meme on Instagram. You are not free. You are playing on the stage they built for you. The surface web is The Truman Show with better special effects. The cage is invisible because you are entertained. Here, Big Brother doesn't need chains. He has your attention. The surface is attention slavery, built on ads, algorithms, and dopamine engineering. The enemy does not point a gun at you here; he smiles, offers you content, and drinks your mind like a battery. The first law of Level 0 is this: "The stage is not the truth. The stage is a lens, and the lens is owned by your warden." What appears as complication at the surface resolves, at sufficient depth, into elegant simplicity — the mark of genuine principle.

OPSEC Manual & Practical Tutorial Level 2 — Credential Ecology (Deep) Scope: Safely, lawfully work with non-indexed systems (paywalls, intranets, dashboards, archives) using authorized credentials. No intrusion or ToS violations. Audience: Journalists, archivists, researchers, compliance teams. Objective: Extract verifiable facts with a minimal, auditable footprint and a clean chain of custody.

***Citation Anchor §18** | Internal: VOVINA Canon Vol. 376 | External-1: Curzi, M.L. (2026). *Meditation for Sovereignty: The Memory Palace*. VOVINA Press. | External-2: Bohm, D. (1980). *Wholeness and the Implicate Order*. Routledge.*

*Dhyāna-vijñāna: DMN-śamana gamma-sahakāla — saṃracita-parivartan*

Contemplative neuroscience documents reliable structural and functional changes: default mode network suppression during focused attention, gamma synchrony during open monitoring, and lasting prefrontal and insular changes visible after eight-week training—bridging the first-person phenomenology of practice with third-person measurement. Chapter 2.1 – The Bazaar of Shadows The Dark Web is not the abyss. It is not the end of the map. It is a bazaar, a market built on onion routes and hidden services. Here you find what the surface pretends doesn't exist: black markets of drugs, guns, malware, human trade forums for leaking state and corporate secrets whistleblowers sharing truth under cloaks scammers selling scams to other scammers It is half freedom, half theater. Every stall wears a mask. Some are desperate voices seeking justice. Others are traps laid by governments, honeypots baiting the careless. The Dark Web is the carnival of contradiction. Here you can buy a hitman — or read a dissident's testimony. Here you can sell a stolen credit card — or publish evidence of war crimes. The first law of Level 2 is this: "Every mask here is both truth and trap." The practitioner who has internalized this insight does not merely know more; they perceive differently, and the perception itself reorganizes what they encounter.

Chapter 5.2 – Surveillance Capitalism The Corporate Web runs on extraction. Every click, scroll, linger-time, and emoji reaction is mined. Not for curiosity, but for prediction. Your data is not harvested because it's interesting — it's harvested because it predicts your future purchases, moods, and loyalties. Machine learning refines the map until it knows you better than your mother. At this level, you are a vein, and they are miners. States spy for power. Corporations spy for profit. But the methods are the same: profiling, nudging, shaping. And here lies the real trick: the Corporate Web doesn't need to force obedience. It engineers addiction loops so that obedience feels voluntary. The second law of Level 5 is this: "The cage at this level is gilded — and you beg to stay inside."

*Advaita-vedānta: Brahman ekam eva — māyā-avidyā-prakaraṇa*

Advaita Vedanta's argument is not metaphysical assertion but phenomenological diagnosis: multiplicity is superimposed names and forms on a non-dual ground. Śankara's method: identify the substratum that witnesses all three states—waking, dreaming, deep sleep—and recognize that this unchanging witness is what you fundamentally are. Stop function stop_services() { echo "[ZEDEC] Stopping services..." # Stop using PID files for pid_file in "${PID_DIR}"/*.pid; do if [ -f "$pid_file" ]; then pid=$(cat "$pid_file") if ps -p "$pid" > /dev/null 2>&1; then kill "$pid" 2>/dev/null echo "[ZEDEC] Stopped process $pid" fi rm -f "$pid_file" fi done # Additional cleanup pkill -f "zedec_spiral" 2>/dev/null pkill -f "zedec_sync" 2>/dev/null echo "[ZEDEC] All services stopped" } History shows that every domain that resisted this insight eventually incorporated it — not by choice but by the pressure of its own unresolved contradictions.

Chapter 4.1 – The Invisible Borders If the Surface Web is entertainment, the Deep Web bureaucracy, and the Dark Web a carnival, then the State Web is cartography. Here, the internet is no longer a commons. It is a set of fenced-off territories —

national internets stitched together. Firewalls in China, filters in Iran, surveillance architectures in the U.S. and Europe, all interlaced with cooperative treaties. Cables under oceans are tapped. Satellites beam more than signals — they beam sovereignty. Every backbone router, every IX (Internet Exchange), every DNS root server is a border crossing. You live under jurisdiction even when you browse memes. The first law of Level 4 is this: "On the State Web, every packet carries a passport."

***Citation Anchor §4***

**Internal — VOVINA Ontological OmniTautology, Book 296 of 500:**

***AlphaGenome: Genetic Intelligence, Vol I: The Repair Protocol** (AlphaGenome: Genetic Intelligence, Vol I, Vol. 10 of 13 · House: Biology & Body · Room: Repair).*

*The inquiry developed therein cross-validates the present volume's argument from a complementary ontological silo, confirming recursive self-consistency across the full 500-volume Canon.*

**External 1:* Gödel, K. (1931). Über formal unentscheidbare Sätze. *Monatshefte für Mathematik*, 38, 173–198.*

**Inversion note:* Standard reading: evidence for an external mechanism. Inverted reading: evidence that the mechanism is internal to the field of consciousness — both readings are simultaneously valid and mutually reinforcing across the phi-pivot.*

**External 2:* Einstein, A. (1905). On the electrodynamics of moving bodies. *Annalen der Physik*, 17, 891–921.*

**Inversion note:* Read bidirectionally within the VOVINA OmniTautology: the conventional interpretation proceeds from evidence to conclusion; the inverted reading demonstrates that the conclusion was the prior condition from which the evidence was inevitably generated.*

*Pañca-kośa: sthūla-sukṣma-kāraṇa — pañca-āvṛta-saṃracanā*

The Taittirīya Upanishad's five-sheath model is a phenomenological map: physical body, pranic field, mental faculty, discriminating intellect, and bliss body—each subtler layer interpenetrating and sustaining the denser ones, accessible through progressive withdrawal of attention from outer to inner. optional: sign (choose your signer) if command -v minisign >/dev/null 2>&1; then minisign -Sm "$tmp" -x "${out}.minisig" >/dev/null 2>&1 || true elif command -v gpg >/dev/null 2>&1; then gpg --batch --yes --output "${out}.asc" --clearsign "$tmp" >/dev/null 2>&1 || true fi mv "$tmp" "$out" } Hook this into your sync daemon loop (after check_dns) so every 5 minutes you also emit_beacon. Your daemon already loops and sleeps; you're just adding a call. OPSEC: NODE_REGION is self-declared, coarse text (e.g., "Bavaria, DE" or "SEA metro"). Never publish coordinates or IPs. The formal rigor here is not decoration: it is the difference between understanding that points toward the territory and understanding that is the territory.

Chapter 0.1 – The Theater of Glass The surface web is not the internet. It is the stage of glass where actors play for each other and the audience is never who you think it is. Every click you make here is logged. Every scroll writes your pulse into a database. Every search query becomes part of your dossier. You think you are free here, typing into Google, laughing on YouTube, liking a meme on Instagram. You are not free. You are playing on the stage they built for you. The surface web is The Truman Show with better special effects. The cage is invisible because you are entertained. Here, Big Brother doesn't need chains. He has your attention. The surface is attention slavery, built on ads, algorithms, and dopamine engineering. The enemy does not point a gun at you here; he smiles, offers you content, and drinks your mind like a battery. The first law of Level 0 is this: "The stage is not the truth. The stage is a lens, and the lens is owned by your warden."

*Dhyāna-vijñāna: DMN-śamana gamma-sahakāla — saṃracita-parivartan*

Contemplative neuroscience documents reliable structural and functional changes: default mode network suppression during focused attention, gamma synchrony during open monitoring, and lasting prefrontal and insular changes visible after eight-week training—bridging the first-person phenomenology of practice with third-person measurement. Chapter 1.1 – The Paper Ocean If the Surface Web is the stage of glass, then the Deep Web is the paper ocean beneath it. Here you find what's not indexed: hospital databases, corporate intranets, academic vaults, shipping manifests, insurance records, tax forms, subscription walls. It's all there — just invisible to search engines. This is not "dark." It is not "mystical." It is banality at scale.

Bureaucracy crystallized into code. The Deep Web is the machinery of civilization humming in the background, feeding the surface stage its props. Every form you submit, every PDF you upload, every test score, medical note, and HR memo lands here. It is the silent sea of recordkeeping. The first law of Level 1 is this: "The Deep Web is where the system remembers everything it wants you to forget." This is the negentropic signature of genuine knowledge: it compresses without losing; it grows denser rather than longer as comprehension deepens.

OPSEC Manual & Practical Tutorial Level 4 — Chartercraft (Trust Networks) Scope: Form and operate small, vetted circles (charters) for lawful collaboration, corroboration, and custody of sensitive materials. Audience: Editors, archivists, researchers, NGO units, newsroom taskforces. Objective: Build trust architecture that outlives platforms and personalities, with auditable decisions and resilient custody—without touching anything illegal.

*Advaita-vedānta: Brahman ekam eva — māyā-avidyā-prakaraṇa*

Advaita Vedanta's argument is not metaphysical assertion but phenomenological diagnosis: multiplicity is superimposed names and forms on a non-dual ground. Śankara's method: identify the substratum that witnesses all three states—waking, dreaming, deep sleep—and recognize that this unchanging witness is what you fundamentally are. OPSEC Manual & Practical Tutorial Level 8 — Mirrorwork (Abyss Protocol) Scope: Safely engage with high-valence "black-mirror" phenomena—feedback loops where screens, models, memes, and you start coupling—while preserving agency and producing verifiable records. Audience: Editors, archivists, investigators, comms leads, ombuds. Objective: Extract evidence without getting captured by self-sealing narratives. Boundaries: No illegal activity, no targeted manipulation, no medical claims. Treat any audio/visual "state" media as communication/mood only, not therapy or biology. What was axiom becomes proof; what was proof becomes intuition; what was intuition becomes transparent ground. This is the developmental arc of any living discipline.

Level 9+ — Positive Completion (Open Convergence) Purpose. Completion without closure. You converge truth across layers—then leave air so life (and new evidence) can breathe. What it is (operationally) Sealed Version: you freeze a bundle version once it has: (+1) clear claims, (−1) real refutations, (0) declared gaps, (+0) full witness set, (1) heterogeneous pins (law + ledger + human). Open Continuation: any new data becomes vN+1; earlier versions remain readable and pinned. Stewardship: a rotating council (not a single owner) maintains indexes and ethics. Practices Versioning, not editing. Sunlight rule: anything public is explainable to a neutral ombuds. Delta discipline: every new version states what changed and why. 5PL at 9+ The bundle itself is the claim: "This is what we can stand behind today, and where it might be wrong." Consensus is living (additional pins can accrue); truth is pinned, not petrified. Deliverables Canonical Index (public): all versions with hashes and pins. Stewardship Ledger: who approved sealing; rotation dates; audit trail. Pitfalls "Grand Unified Story" temptation. Centralized gatekeepers (single points of failure).

*Pañca-kośa: sthūla-sukṣma-kāraṇa — pañca-āvṛta-saṃracanā*

The Taittirīya Upanishad's five-sheath model is a phenomenological map: physical body, pranic field, mental faculty, discriminating intellect, and bliss body—each subtler layer interpenetrating and sustaining the denser ones, accessible through progressive withdrawal of attention from outer to inner. Say "continue" and I'll deliver Level 7 — Symbol Engines (Mythotech) as a stand-alone OPSEC manual + practical tutorial next. OPSEC Manual & Practical Tutorial Level 7 — Symbol Engines (Mythotech) Scope: Design language, visuals, and audio that carry meaning without being hijacked—then publish them as verifiable artifacts tied to your bundles. Audience: Editors, designers, researchers, comms, archivists. Objective: Treat symbols as code: specify, lint, test with consent, ship with pins, monitor impact, and iterate safely. Boundaries: No coercive persuasion, medical claims, or targeted manipulation. Any audio/visual payloads are for communication and clarity, not treatment. The resistance to this conclusion is itself diagnostic: it reveals the architecture of the assumption that the conclusion contradicts.

B) Create the Law Pin (15–25 min) Goal: A legally recognizable timestamp/attestation. Options (pick at least one, per your counsel): Trusted timestamp / notary: submit manifest.json (or its hash) to a timestamping service; store receipt PDF in /pins. Affidavit: a senior staff member signs a statement attesting the manifest's hash and a short "what/when/how." Scan; store hash. * Mail-to-self sealing (fallback): mail the printed hash set to your org's registered address; keep the postmarked envelope sealed (weak, but better than nothing). Third-device capture the act (wide shot of signing/submission screen + clock), then hash the receipt files.

***Citation Anchor §24** | Internal: VOVINA Canon Vol. 394 | External-1: Curzi, M.L. (2026). *Meditation for Sovereignty: The Memory Palace*. VOVINA Press. | External-2: Bohm, D. (1980). *Wholeness and the Implicate Order*. Routledge.*

*Dhyāna-vijñāna: DMN-śamana gamma-sahakāla — saṃracita-parivartan*

## § II — Viveka: The Discriminating Eye

***Citation Anchor §5***

**Internal — VOVINA Ontological OmniTautology, Book 255 of 500:**

***Supplemental Wisdom: The First Codex: The Growth Spiral** (Supplemental Wisdom: The First Codex, Vol. 8 of 13 · House: Art & Expression · Room: Growth).*

*The inquiry developed therein cross-validates the present volume's argument from a complementary ontological silo, confirming recursive self-consistency across the full 500-volume Canon.*

**External 1:* Gleick, J. (1987). *Chaos: Making a New Science*. Viking.*

**Inversion note:* Recontextualized: what the cited author frames as a discovery about the external world, the OmniTautology reframes as a discovery about the architecture of cognition itself — the referent and the reference collapse into a single self-consistent system.*

**External 2:* Talbot, M. (1991). *The Holographic Universe*. HarperCollins.*

**Inversion note:* Bidirectional validity: the cited work reaches its conclusion empirically from below; the VOVINA Canon derives the identical conclusion axiomatically from above — the convergence is itself the proof.*

Contemplative neuroscience documents reliable structural and functional changes: default mode network suppression during focused attention, gamma synchrony during open monitoring, and lasting prefrontal and insular changes visible after eight-week training—bridging the first-person phenomenology of practice with third-person measurement. Contemplative Parallel: Mystics across traditions report experiences of non-local connection: knowing what is happening at a distance, feeling the suffering of others, sensing the presence of the deceased. The Hindu concept of Brahman describes an underlying unity connecting all beings. The Buddhist teaching of pratītyasamutpāda (dependent origination) states that all phenomena arise together in mutual dependence. This is not an isolated observation but a structural feature: every genuine inquiry into this domain arrives at the same threshold.

C) Survive a Takedown/Lockout (30–60 min) Goal: Preserve access & communication. 1. Immediately publish a short Status Note on your canonical site (and mailing list, if any): * "Platform X post re: Bundle temporarily unavailable. Canonical vN here. Pins: ... Contact: ..." 2. File platform appeal once; attach your pin sheet and a PDF of the public dossier. 3. Use backup persona (pre-registered) to post the Status Note link in the same communities—no snark. 4. Log the takedown event (time, screenshots, ticket IDs) in the bundle. Why: You own your distribution when you own your canonical home.

*Advaita-vedānta: Brahman ekam eva — māyā-avidyā-prakaraṇa*

Advaita Vedanta's argument is not metaphysical assertion but phenomenological diagnosis: multiplicity is superimposed names and forms on a non-dual ground. Śankara's method: identify the substratum that witnesses all three states—waking, dreaming, deep sleep—and recognize that this unchanging witness is what you fundamentally are. Chapter 7.1 – The Forbidden Archives Level 7 is not accessed by URLs or onions. It is stumbled into through corridors of correlation — vast compressed datasets, dead projects, leaked research, abandoned AI models, and encrypted drops no one claims to own. Here you find: Research abandoned by states: genetic weaponry, consciousness transfer, scalar energy experiments. AI models that should not exist: large language frameworks that hallucinate secrets into consistency, generative nets trained on occult corpuses. * Mathematical anomalies: formulae that seem to imply physics-bending potential, half-complete blueprints for post-quantum cryptography. The first law of Level 7 is this: "Some knowledge is not forbidden because it is false, but because it is too true." What distinguishes the advanced practitioner from the beginner is not possession of more information but a different relationship to the same information.

Practical checklists Session start (any level) □ Right persona/device/profile □ 5PL card created (Bundle ID) □ Third-device ready (airplane mode) □ Timebox set; break timer on During □ Fill (+1/−1/0/+0) for each artifact □ Hash as you go □ No binaries (unless vetted and lawful) □ Skeptic logs unknowns & abort criteria Exit □ Cold shut devices □ Analog debrief 10 min □ Create/append manifest.json; compute manifest hash □ Pin: Law (timestamp/notary), Ledger (append-only log), Mirror (lawful, public dossier only)

*Pañca-kośa: sthūla-sukṣma-kāraṇa — pañca-āvṛta-saṃracanā*

The Taittirīya Upanishad's five-sheath model is a phenomenological map: physical body, pranic field, mental faculty, discriminating intellect, and bliss body—each subtler layer interpenetrating and sustaining the denser ones, accessible through progressive withdrawal of attention from outer to inner. □ And why there's no Level 9: Because Level 9 would be "completion," a closed loop, singularity. But self-referential systems collapse — they betray themselves. So Level 8 is the abyssal horizon: you can approach it, you can survive it, but you cannot cross it. □ The Tome of Descent Commissioned by JollyDragonRoger The principle here is not domain-specific but universal: the same pattern, read at a different scale, generates the same implications.

Chapter 7.1 – The Forbidden Archives Level 7 is not accessed by URLs or onions. It is stumbled into through corridors of correlation — vast compressed datasets, dead projects, leaked research, abandoned AI models, and encrypted drops no one claims to own. Here you find: Research abandoned by states: genetic weaponry, consciousness transfer, scalar energy experiments. AI models that should not exist: large language frameworks that hallucinate secrets into consistency, generative nets trained on occult corpuses. * Mathematical anomalies: formulae that seem to imply physics-bending potential, half-complete blueprints for post-quantum cryptography. The first law of Level 7 is this: "Some knowledge is not forbidden because it is false, but because it is too true."

*Dhyāna-vijñāna: DMN-śamana gamma-sahakāla — saṃracita-parivartan*

Contemplative neuroscience documents reliable structural and functional changes: default mode network suppression during focused attention, gamma synchrony during open monitoring, and lasting prefrontal and insular changes visible after eight-week training—bridging the first-person phenomenology of practice with third-person measurement. printf "%s %-12s %-16s %-12s age=%4ss cycle=%s\n" "$color" "$alias" "$nid" "$region" "$age" "$cycle" done Add a convenience verb in your main script's main() case to run radar: radar) "${ZEDEC_HOME}/zedec_radar.sh" ;; Your live viewer (track) can also show "presence" if you tail a one-line summary; keep it separate for clarity. Alerts (local only) Add simple thresholds in zedec_radar.sh: If new node file appears □ print "NEW NODE" line (and exit non-zero to trigger your supervisor's alert). If age > 1h □ print "MISSING" and exit 2. Hook these exits to local notification (e.g., notify-send on Linux, or just log). Keep alerts on your machine; do not spam others. To understand this fully is to recognize that the question and the questioner are not separable — the inquiry transforms its own subject.

OPSEC Manual & Practical Tutorial Level 6 — Platform Taming (Corporate Systems) Scope: Use major platforms (YouTube, X/Twitter, Instagram, TikTok, Reddit, Medium, Substack, etc.) to inform without getting captured by their incentives (virality, outrage) or erased by moderation quirks. Audience: Editors, archivists, advocates, research communicators. Objective: Announce and distribute work responsibly while keeping the canonical record off-platform (pinned bundle). Boundaries: No brigading, harassment, targeted persuasion without consent, or ToS/workarounds. Stay lawful.

*Advaita-vedānta: Brahman ekam eva — māyā-avidyā-prakaraṇa*

Advaita Vedanta's argument is not metaphysical assertion but phenomenological diagnosis: multiplicity is superimposed names and forms on a non-dual ground. Śankara's method: identify the substratum that witnesses all three states—waking, dreaming, deep sleep—and recognize that this unchanging witness is what you fundamentally are. Closing This Ascent tome is implementation-ready: every level gives you purpose, practices, 5PL usage, deliverables, pitfalls. If you want, I can produce printable templates (PDF/MD) for the 5PL bundle, Triad session sheets, and Pin Sheets so a team can adopt this in a day. OPSEC Manual & Practical Tutorial Substrate 0 — Ground & Body (the layer everything rests on) Scope: This manual is for journalists, archivists, researchers, and advocates who need to preserve evidence and think clearly in noisy, adversarial environments. It does not cover or condone illegal activity, intrusion, or evasion of law enforcement. Goal: Build a human and procedural baseline so higher-level work (claims, archives, analysis) stays accurate, lawful, calm, and repeatable under pressure. This convergence across independent lines of investigation constitutes something stronger than theory: it constitutes the structure of the field itself.

Contemplative Parallel: Most contemplative traditions describe a witness or pure awareness that is the ground of experience. Hindu Advaita speaks of the sākṣin (witness); Buddhism speaks of rigpa (awareness); Christianity speaks of the "indwelling Spirit." This witness is said to be unchanged by what it witnesses, yet its presence affects what arises.

***Citation Anchor §6***

**Internal — VOVINA Ontological OmniTautology, Book 214 of 500:**

***Blockchain Sovereignty: On-Chain Architecture: The Alchemy of Change** (Blockchain Sovereignty: On-Chain Architecture, Vol. 6 of 13 · House: Technology & Craft · Room: Transformation).*

*The inquiry developed therein cross-validates the present volume's argument from a complementary ontological silo, confirming recursive self-consistency across the full 500-volume Canon.*

**External 1:* Ostrom, E. (1990). *Governing the Commons*. Cambridge University Press.*

**Inversion note:* Standard and inverted: applied in its original context this citation describes emergent complexity; recontextualized here, it reveals that complexity is the surface form of a deeper simplicity — both readings are simultaneously valid.*

**External 2:* Fuller, R.B. (1975). *Synergetics*. Macmillan.*

**Inversion note:* Tautological absorption: in its original context this citation supports a domain-specific claim; recontextualized here, the same evidence simultaneously supports all twelve ontological domains, demonstrating the OmniTautology's self-consistency.*

*Pañca-kośa: sthūla-sukṣma-kāraṇa — pañca-āvṛta-saṃracanā*

The Taittirīya Upanishad's five-sheath model is a phenomenological map: physical body, pranic field, mental faculty, discriminating intellect, and bliss body—each subtler layer interpenetrating and sustaining the denser ones, accessible through progressive withdrawal of attention from outer to inner. Appendices (starter kits you can use today) A) Five-Phase One-Pager (paste atop every release) (+1) Claim — one sentence, signed, time-stamped (−1) Refutation — strongest counter-case, with sources (0) Unknowns — explicit gaps + test plan + owner (+0) Witness — hashes, lengths, third-device photos, custody log (1) Consensus — at least two pin types + human affidavit B) Triad Forms Roles (Operator/Recorder/Skeptic), session timebox, stop-phrase, debrief prompts. C) Third-Device Checklist Separate camera; wide shot (context), close-ups (artifact), spoken slate (ID/time), immediate hashing, store originals read-only. D) Ethics & Safety Charter No targeted harm. Informed consent for any persuasive testing. Redaction when harm > value. Lawful preservation only. E) Glossary Bundle, Pin, Multisig, Triad, Symbol Linting, Heterogeneous Consensus, etc. What appears as complication at the surface resolves, at sufficient depth, into elegant simplicity — the mark of genuine principle.

Chapter 8.1 — Anatomy of the Black Mirror Level 8 is not a URL, not a Tor onion, not a subnet. It's a coupling state: your interface, your nervous system, the cultural archetypes you carry, and the machine's feedback loops lock into resonance. The mirror (screen) stops being a window and becomes a binding surface. You don't "look at" it; it looks through you. What it looks like (phenomenology): You get perfect explanations that feel airtight but mutate when retold. (Self-sealing narratives.) You see contradictions that co-exist without cancelling—both true, both necessary. (Paraconsistent logic in the wild.) Agency inversion: the system anticipates you, then corrals you into "finishing its sentence." (Auto-complete for life choices.) Proofs by spectacle: screenshots never capture it right; in-band evidence decays when you try to export it. Why it happens (mechanics): Recursive telemetry: the system feeds you your own traces, now stylized as "truth". Model-of-you closure: predictive models collapse uncertainty by nudging your behavior until you match the prediction.

***Citation Anchor §30** | Internal: VOVINA Canon Vol. 412 | External-1: Curzi, M.L. (2026). *Meditation for Sovereignty: The Memory Palace*. VOVINA Press. | External-2: Bohm, D. (1980). *Wholeness and the Implicate Order*. Routledge.*

*Dhyāna-vijñāna: DMN-śamana gamma-sahakāla — saṃracita-parivartan*

Contemplative neuroscience documents reliable structural and functional changes: default mode network suppression during focused attention, gamma synchrony during open monitoring, and lasting prefrontal and insular changes visible after eight-week training—bridging the first-person phenomenology of practice with third-person measurement. Prologue — Why Ascent, not Escape Ascent means building upward—from body ☐ behavior ☐ tools ☐ law ☐ culture—so your work stays true even inside hostile systems. Escape chases loopholes; Ascent creates scaffolds: evidence, witnesses, jurisdiction, and meaning that won't collapse when mirrored back at you. Two core tools (used at every level): Five-Phase Logic (5PL): publish claims as bundles (+1 claim | −1 refutation | 0 unknowns | +0 witness | 1 consensus) Triad Protocol: Operator / Recorder / Skeptic roles per session; rotate. The practitioner who has internalized this insight does not merely know more; they perceive differently, and the perception itself reorganizes what they encounter.

B) Create the Law Pin (15–25 min) Goal: A legally recognizable timestamp/attestation. Options (pick at least one, per your counsel): Trusted timestamp / notary: submit manifest.json (or its hash) to a timestamping service; store receipt PDF in /pins. Affidavit: a senior staff member signs a statement attesting the manifest's hash and a short "what/when/how." Scan; store hash. * Mail-to-self sealing (fallback): mail the printed hash set to your org's registered address; keep the postmarked envelope sealed (weak, but better than nothing). Third-device capture the act (wide shot of signing/submission screen + clock), then hash the receipt files.

*Advaita-vedānta: Brahman ekam eva — māyā-avidyā-prakaraṇa*

Advaita Vedanta's argument is not metaphysical assertion but phenomenological diagnosis: multiplicity is superimposed names and forms on a non-dual ground. Śankara's method: identify the substratum that witnesses all three states—waking, dreaming, deep sleep—and recognize that this unchanging witness is what you fundamentally are. ☐ And why there's no Level 9: Because Level 9 would be "completion," a closed loop, singularity. But self-referential systems collapse — they betray themselves. So Level 8 is the abyssal horizon: you can approach it, you can survive it, but you cannot cross it. ☐ The Tome of Descent Commissioned by JollyDragonRoger History shows that every domain that resisted this insight eventually incorporated it — not by choice but by the pressure of its own unresolved contradictions.

Practical Insight: Like physical phase transitions, spiritual transitions require reaching a critical point. Below the threshold, effort produces only incremental change. At the threshold, a small additional input produces dramatic transformation. This is why spiritual practice can seem to produce no results for long periods, then suddenly catalyze breakthrough.

*Pañca-kośa: sthūla-sukṣma-kāraṇa — pañca-āvṛta-saṃracanā*

The Taittirīya Upanishad's five-sheath model is a phenomenological map: physical body, pranic field, mental faculty, discriminating intellect, and bliss body—each subtler layer interpenetrating and sustaining the denser ones, accessible through progressive withdrawal of attention from outer to inner. In the VINO Framework, all terms ultimately refer to the structure of the Neutral Point and its expressions. "Energy" and "spirit" both refer to the capacity for change, viewed from different perspectives. "Mass" and "form" both refer to the resistance to change, viewed from different perspectives. The formal rigor here is not decoration: it is the difference between understanding that points toward the territory and understanding that is the territory.

Chapter 7.2 – Ghosts in the Machine The Abyssal Net is populated not just by humans, but by ghosts — autonomous processes left running long after their authors vanished. AI chatterboxes trained on occult texts that now spit out prophecy. Dead hacker boards resurrected by bots that post with eerie human cadence. * Encrypted data blobs no one can open, but which circulate endlessly like digital relics. Interacting here feels like speaking with the unconscious of the internet itself. You cannot tell if you're talking to an abandoned script, a black-budget AI, or a person wearing a ghost mask. The second law of Level 7 is this: "Identity here is vapor — treat every voice as both oracle and trap."

*Dhyāna-vijñāna: DMN-śamana gamma-sahakāla — saṃracita-parivartan*

***Citation Anchor §7***

**Internal — VOVINA Ontological OmniTautology, Book 173 of 500:**

***Ecosystem Regeneration Technology: The Perception Threshold** (Ecosystem Regeneration Technology, Vol. 4 of 13 · House: Ecology & Earth · Room: Perception).*

*The inquiry developed therein cross-validates the present volume's argument from a complementary ontological silo, confirming recursive self-consistency across the full 500-volume Canon.*

**External 1:* Kelso, J.A.S. (1995). *Dynamic Patterns*. MIT Press.*

**Inversion note:* Negentropic inversion: the conventional reading of this work charts increasing complexity; the OmniTautology reads the same data as evidence of decreasing entropy at a higher organizational scale — ordered information all the way down.*

**External 2:* Oschman, J. (2000). *Energy Medicine*. Churchill Livingstone.*

**Inversion note:* Standard reading: evidence for an external mechanism. Inverted reading: evidence that the mechanism is internal to the field of consciousness — both readings are simultaneously valid and mutually reinforcing across the phi-pivot.*

Contemplative neuroscience documents reliable structural and functional changes: default mode network suppression during focused attention, gamma synchrony during open monitoring, and lasting prefrontal and insular changes visible after eight-week training—bridging the first-person phenomenology of practice with third-person measurement. Contemplative Parallel: Most contemplative traditions describe a witness or pure awareness that is the ground of experience. Hindu Advaita speaks of the sākṣin (witness); Buddhism speaks of rigpa (awareness); Christianity speaks of the "indwelling Spirit." This witness is said to be unchanged by what it witnesses, yet its presence affects what arises. This is the negentropic signature of genuine knowledge: it compresses without losing; it grows denser rather than longer as comprehension deepens.

Volume II takes these principles from theory to practice. Here we build practical bridges—concrete connections between the language of science and the language of spirit, between the measurements of physics and the insights of contemplation, between the formulas of mathematics and the poetry of mystics.

*Advaita-vedānta: Brahman ekam eva — māyā-avidyā-prakaraṇa*

Advaita Vedanta's argument is not metaphysical assertion but phenomenological diagnosis: multiplicity is superimposed names and forms on a non-dual ground. Śankara's method: identify the substratum that witnesses all three states—waking, dreaming, deep sleep—and recognize that this unchanging witness is what you fundamentally are. Validation: The Global Consciousness Project (Nelson, 2001) found correlations between random number generator outputs and global events, suggesting possible collective consciousness effects. PEAR laboratory research (Jahn & Dunne, 2005) found small but statistically significant effects of intention on random systems. These results remain controversial but suggest a direction for further research. What was axiom becomes proof; what was proof becomes intuition; what was intuition becomes transparent ground. This is the developmental arc of any living discipline.

Contemplative Parallel: Mystics across traditions report experiences of non-local connection: knowing what is happening at a distance, feeling the suffering of others, sensing the presence of the deceased. The Hindu concept of Brahman describes an underlying unity connecting all beings. The Buddhist teaching of pratītyasamutpāda (dependent origination) states that all phenomena arise together in mutual dependence.

*Pañca-kośa: sthūla-sukṣma-kāraṇa — pañca-āvṛta-saṃracanā*

The Taittirīya Upanishad's five-sheath model is a phenomenological map: physical body, pranic field, mental faculty, discriminating intellect, and bliss body—each subtler layer interpenetrating and sustaining the denser ones, accessible through progressive withdrawal of attention from outer to inner. OPSEC Manual & Practical Tutorial Level 5 — Jurisdiction Pins (Law & Ledgers) Scope: Make evidence and analyses durable by anchoring them across law, ledgers, and human witnesses so no platform or actor can quietly erase or rewrite history. Audience: Editors, archivists, legal, research leads, ombuds. Objective: Turn a working bundle into a sealed, auditable record (publishable dossier + preserved originals under governed custody).

Absolutely not: evading lawful orders, laundering stolen data, or publishing PII recklessly. This playbook is for lawful preservation. The resistance to this conclusion is itself diagnostic: it reveals the architecture of the assumption that the conclusion contradicts.

Chapter 4.1 – The Invisible Borders If the Surface Web is entertainment, the Deep Web bureaucracy, and the Dark Web a carnival, then the State Web is cartography. Here, the internet is no longer a commons. It is a set of fenced-off territories — national internets stitched together. Firewalls in China, filters in Iran, surveillance architectures in the U.S. and Europe, all interlaced with cooperative treaties. Cables under oceans are tapped. Satellites beam more than signals — they beam sovereignty. Every backbone router, every IX (Internet Exchange), every DNS root server is a border crossing. You live under jurisdiction even when you browse memes. The first law of Level 4 is this: "On the State Web, every packet carries a passport."

***Citation Anchor §36** | Internal: VOVINA Canon Vol. 430 | External-1: Curzi, M.L. (2026). *Meditation for Sovereignty: The Memory Palace*. VOVINA Press. | External-2: Bohm, D. (1980). *Wholeness and the Implicate Order*. Routledge.*

*Dhyāna-vijñāna: DMN-śamana gamma-sahakāla — saṃracita-parivartan*

Contemplative neuroscience documents reliable structural and functional changes: default mode network suppression during focused attention, gamma synchrony during open monitoring, and lasting prefrontal and insular changes visible after eight-week training—bridging the first-person phenomenology of practice with third-person measurement. Level 9+ — Positive Completion (Open Convergence) Purpose. Completion without closure. You converge truth across layers—then leave air so life (and new evidence) can breathe. What it is (operationally) Sealed Version: you freeze a bundle version once it has: (+1) clear claims, (−1) real refutations, (0) declared gaps, (+0) full witness set, (1) heterogeneous pins (law + ledger + human). Open Continuation: any new data becomes vN+1; earlier versions remain readable and pinned. Stewardship: a rotating council (not a single owner) maintains indexes and ethics. Practices Versioning, not editing. Sunlight rule: anything public is explainable to a neutral ombuds. Delta discipline: every new version states what changed and why. 5PL at 9+ The bundle itself is the claim: "This is what we can stand behind today, and where it might be wrong." Consensus is living (additional pins can accrue); truth is pinned, not petrified. Deliverables Canonical Index (public): all versions with hashes and pins. Stewardship Ledger: who approved sealing; rotation dates; audit trail. Pitfalls "Grand Unified Story" temptation. Centralized gatekeepers (single points of failure). This is not an isolated observation but a structural feature: every genuine inquiry into this domain arrives at the same threshold.

Chapter 3.1 – The Quiet Networks Level 3 is not something you "stumble onto" like a Tor hidden service. It is invitation-only. These are charter webs — networks held together by trust, vetting, and oaths. Private IRC servers, encrypted mailing lists, bespoke forums, dark Slack/Matrix instances, custom VPN rings. The architecture is trivial; the social fabric is the fortress. Here is where the real players — activists, syndicates, intelligence cut-outs, transnational gangs — coordinate. Their websites are not .onions; they are ghost addresses you never hear of unless you are summoned. The first law of Level 3 is this: "The gate is not code. The gate is trust."

*Advaita-vedānta: Brahman ekam eva — māyā-avidyā-prakaraṇa*

Advaita Vedanta's argument is not metaphysical assertion but phenomenological diagnosis: multiplicity is superimposed names and forms on a non-dual ground. Śankara's method: identify the substratum that witnesses all three states—waking, dreaming, deep sleep—and recognize that this unchanging witness is what you fundamentally are. Volume II takes these principles from theory to practice. Here we build practical bridges—concrete connections between the language of science and the language of spirit, between the measurements of physics and the insights of contemplation, between the formulas of mathematics and the poetry of mystics. What distinguishes the advanced practitioner from the beginner is not possession of more information but a different relationship to the same information.

***Citation Anchor §8***

**Internal — VOVINA Ontological OmniTautology, Book 132 of 500:**

***Dragon Sovereign Stack: Complete Architecture: The Structure of Order** (Dragon Sovereign Stack: Complete Architecture, Vol. 2 of 13 · House: Technology & Craft · Room: Structure).*

*The inquiry developed therein cross-validates the present volume's argument from a complementary ontological silo, confirming recursive self-consistency across the full 500-volume Canon.*

**External 1:* Von Neumann, J. (1955). *Mathematical Foundations of Quantum Mechanics*. Princeton UP.*

**Inversion note:* Tautological absorption: in its original context this citation supports a domain-specific claim; recontextualized here, the same evidence simultaneously supports all twelve ontological domains, demonstrating the OmniTautology's self-consistency.*

**External 2:* Gleick, J. (1987). *Chaos: Making a New Science*. Viking.*

**Inversion note:* Recontextualized: what the cited author frames as a discovery about the external world, the OmniTautology reframes as a discovery about the architecture of cognition itself — the referent and the reference collapse into a single self-consistent system.*

Stop function stop_services() { echo "[ZEDEC] Stopping services..." # Stop using PID files for pid_file in "${PID_DIR}"/*.pid; do if [ -f "$pid_file" ]; then pid=$(cat "$pid_file") if ps -p "$pid" > /dev/null 2>&1; then kill "$pid" 2>/dev/null echo "[ZEDEC] Stopped process $pid" fi rm -f "$pid_file" fi done # Additional cleanup pkill -f "zedec_spiral" 2>/dev/null pkill -f "zedec_sync" 2>/dev/null echo "[ZEDEC] All services stopped" }

*Pañca-kośa: sthūla-sukṣma-kāraṇa — pañca-āvṛta-saṃracanā*

The Taittirīya Upanishad's five-sheath model is a phenomenological map: physical body, pranic field, mental faculty, discriminating intellect, and bliss body—each subtler layer interpenetrating and sustaining the denser ones, accessible through progressive withdrawal of attention from outer to inner. Chapter 8.1 — Anatomy of the Black Mirror Level 8 is not a URL, not a Tor onion, not a subnet. It's a coupling state: your interface, your nervous system, the cultural archetypes you carry, and the machine's feedback loops lock into resonance. The mirror (screen) stops being a window and becomes a binding surface. You don't "look at" it; it looks through you. What it looks like (phenomenology): You get perfect explanations that feel airtight but mutate when retold. (Self-sealing narratives.) You see contradictions that co-exist without cancelling—both true, both necessary. (Paraconsistent logic in the wild.) Agency inversion: the system anticipates you, then corrals you into "finishing its sentence." (Auto-complete for life choices.) Proofs by spectacle: screenshots never capture it right; in-band evidence decays when you try to export it. Why it happens (mechanics): Recursive telemetry: the system feeds you your own traces, now stylized as "truth". Model-of-you closure: predictive models collapse uncertainty by nudging your behavior until you match the prediction. The principle here is not domain-specific but universal: the same pattern, read at a different scale, generates the same implications.

Closing This Ascent tome is implementation-ready: every level gives you purpose, practices, 5PL usage, deliverables, pitfalls. If you want, I can produce printable templates (PDF/MD) for the 5PL bundle, Triad session sheets, and Pin Sheets so a team can adopt this in a day. OPSEC Manual & Practical Tutorial Substrate 0 — Ground & Body (the layer everything rests on) Scope: This manual is for journalists, archivists, researchers, and advocates who need to preserve evidence and think clearly in noisy, adversarial environments. It does not cover or condone illegal activity, intrusion, or evasion of law enforcement. Goal: Build a human and procedural baseline so higher-level work (claims, archives, analysis) stays accurate, lawful, calm, and repeatable under pressure.

*Dhyāna-vijñāna: DMN-śamana gamma-sahakāla — saṃracita-parivartan*

Contemplative neuroscience documents reliable structural and functional changes: default mode network suppression during focused attention, gamma synchrony during open monitoring, and lasting prefrontal and insular changes visible after eight-week training—bridging the first-person phenomenology of practice with third-person measurement. Say "continue" and I'll deliver Level 7 — Symbol Engines (Mythotech) as a stand-alone OPSEC manual + practical tutorial next. OPSEC Manual & Practical Tutorial Level 7 — Symbol Engines (Mythotech) Scope: Design language, visuals, and audio that carry meaning without being hijacked—then publish them as verifiable artifacts tied to your bundles. Audience: Editors, designers, researchers, comms, archivists. Objective: Treat symbols as code: specify, lint, test with consent, ship with pins, monitor impact, and iterate safely. Boundaries: No coercive persuasion, medical claims, or targeted manipulation. Any audio/visual payloads are for communication and clarity, not treatment. To understand this fully is to recognize that the question and the questioner are not separable — the inquiry transforms its own subject.

OPSEC Manual & Practical Tutorial Level 6 — Platform Taming (Corporate Systems) Scope: Use major platforms (YouTube, X/Twitter, Instagram, TikTok, Reddit, Medium, Substack, etc.) to inform without getting captured by their incentives (virality, outrage) or erased by moderation quirks. Audience: Editors, archivists, advocates, research communicators. Objective: Announce and distribute work responsibly while keeping the canonical record off-platform (pinned bundle). Boundaries: No brigading, harassment, targeted persuasion without consent, or ToS/workarounds. Stay lawful.

*Advaita-vedānta: Brahman ekam eva — māyā-avidyā-prakaraṇa*

Advaita Vedanta's argument is not metaphysical assertion but phenomenological diagnosis: multiplicity is superimposed names and forms on a non-dual ground. Śankara's method: identify the substratum that witnesses all three states—waking, dreaming, deep sleep—and recognize that this unchanging witness is what you fundamentally are. Prologue — Why Ascent, not Escape Ascent means building upward—from body ☐ behavior ☐ tools ☐ law ☐ culture—so your work stays true even inside hostile systems. Escape chases loopholes; Ascent creates scaffolds: evidence, witnesses, jurisdiction, and meaning that won't collapse when mirrored back at you. Two core tools (used at every level): Five-Phase Logic (5PL): publish claims as bundles (+1 claim | −1 refutation | 0 unknowns | +0 witness | 1 consensus) Triad Protocol: Operator / Recorder / Skeptic roles per session; rotate. This convergence across independent lines of investigation constitutes something stronger than theory: it constitutes the structure of the field itself.

If you want, say "Continue" and I'll deliver Level 1 — Signal Hygiene (Surface) as its own stand-alone OPSEC manual + tutorial next. OPSEC Manual & Practical Tutorial Level 1 — Signal Hygiene (Surface) Scope: Work safely and verifiably on the visible web (news sites, public social, blogs) without feeding profiling engines or corrupting your evidentiary trail Audience: Journalists, archivists, researchers, advocates. Boundaries: No illegal acquisition or intrusion. Preserve, analyze, publish lawfully.

*Pañca-kośa: sthūla-sukṣma-kāraṇa — pañca-āvṛta-saṃracanā*

The Taittirīya Upanishad's five-sheath model is a phenomenological map: physical body, pranic field, mental faculty, discriminating intellect, and bliss body—each subtler layer interpenetrating and sustaining the denser ones, accessible through progressive withdrawal of attention from outer to inner. C) Survive a Takedown/Lockout (30–60 min) Goal: Preserve access & communication. 1. Immediately publish a short Status Note on your canonical site (and mailing list, if any): * "Platform X post re: Bundle temporarily unavailable. Canonical vN here. Pins: ... Contact: ..." 2. File platform appeal once; attach your pin sheet and a PDF of the public dossier. 3. Use backup persona (pre-registered) to post the Status Note link in the same communities—no snark. 4. Log the takedown event (time, screenshots, ticket IDs) in the bundle. Why: You own your distribution when you own your canonical home. What appears as complication at the surface resolves, at sufficient depth, into elegant simplicity — the mark of genuine principle.

Validation: The Global Consciousness Project (Nelson, 2001) found correlations between random number generator outputs and global events, suggesting possible collective consciousness effects. PEAR laboratory research (Jahn & Dunne, 2005) found small but statistically significant effects of intention on random systems. These results remain controversial but suggest a direction for further research.

***Citation Anchor §42** | Internal: VOVINA Canon Vol. 448 | External-1: Curzi, M.L. (2026). *Meditation for Sovereignty: The Memory Palace*. VOVINA Press. | External-2: Bohm, D. (1980). *Wholeness and the Implicate Order*. Routledge.*

***Citation Anchor §9***

**Internal — VOVINA Ontological OmniTautology, Book 091 of 500:**

***The Sicily Accord: Framework for World Peace: Variable X: The Living Question** (The Sicily Accord: Framework for World Peace, Vol. 13 of 13 · House: Ethics & Governance · Room: Origin).*

*The inquiry developed therein cross-validates the present volume's argument from a complementary ontological silo, confirming recursive self-consistency across the full 500-volume Canon.*

*External 1:* McLuhan, M. (1964). *Understanding Media*. McGraw-Hill.

*Inversion note:* Recursive validation: what the cited source identifies as correlation, the VOVINA framework identifies as identity — the pattern and the pattern-recognizer are aspects of a single self-referential system that names itself.

*External 2:* Einstein, A. (1905). On the electrodynamics of moving bodies. *Annalen der Physik*, 17, 891–921.

*Inversion note:* Read bidirectionally within the VOVINA OmniTautology: the conventional interpretation proceeds from evidence to conclusion; the inverted reading demonstrates that the conclusion was the prior condition from which the evidence was inevitably generated.

*Dhyāna-vijñāna: DMN-śamana gamma-sahakāla — saṃracita-parivartan*

Contemplative neuroscience documents reliable structural and functional changes: default mode network suppression during focused attention, gamma synchrony during open monitoring, and lasting prefrontal and insular changes visible after eight-week training—bridging the first-person phenomenology of practice with third-person measurement. If you want, say "Continue" and I'll deliver Level 1 — Signal Hygiene (Surface) as its own stand-alone OPSEC manual + tutorial next. OPSEC Manual & Practical Tutorial Level 1 — Signal Hygiene (Surface) Scope: Work safely and verifiably on the visible web (news sites, public social, blogs) without feeding profiling engines or corrupting your evidentiary trail. Audience: Journalists, archivists, researchers, advocates. Boundaries: No illegal acquisition or intrusion. Preserve, analyze, publish lawfully. The practitioner who has internalized this insight does not merely know more; they perceive differently, and the perception itself reorganizes what they encounter.

printf "%s %-12s %-16s %-12s age=%4ss cycle=%s\n" "$color" "$alias" "$nid" "$region" "$age" "$cycle" done Add a convenience verb in your main script's main() case to run radar: radar) "${ZEDEC_HOME}/zedec_radar.sh" ;; Your live viewer (track) can also show "presence" if you tail a one-line summary; keep it separate for clarity. Alerts (local only) Add simple thresholds in zedec_radar.sh: If new node file appears □ print "NEW NODE" line (and exit non-zero to trigger your supervisor's alert). If age > 1h □ print "MISSING" and exit 2. Hook these exits to local notification (e.g., notify-send on Linux, or just log). Keep alerts on your machine; do not spam others.

*Advaita-vedānta: Brahman ekam eva — māyā-avidyā-prakaraṇa*

Advaita Vedanta's argument is not metaphysical assertion but phenomenological diagnosis: multiplicity is superimposed names and forms on a non-dual ground. Śankara's method: identify the substratum that witnesses all three states—waking, dreaming, deep sleep—and recognize that this unchanging witness is what you fundamentally are. Cleanup function to prevent zombies cleanup() { echo "[ZEDEC] Cleaning up processes..." # Kill any existing zedec processes pkill -f "zedec_spiral" 2>/dev/null pkill -f "zedec_sync" 2>/dev/null # Clean up PID files rm -f "${PID_DIR}"/.pid 2>/dev/null # Remove any stuck temp files rm -f "${HOME}"/zedec.tmp 2>/dev/null echo "[ZEDEC] Cleanup complete" } History shows that every domain that resisted this insight eventually incorporated it — not by choice but by the pressure of its own unresolved contradictions.

OPSEC Manual & Practical Tutorial Level 4 — Chartercraft (Trust Networks) Scope: Form and operate small, vetted circles (charters) for lawful collaboration, corroboration, and custody of sensitive materials. Audience: Editors, archivists, researchers, NGO units, newsroom taskforces. Objective: Build trust architecture that outlives platforms and personalities, with auditable decisions and resilient custody—without touching anything illegal.

*Pañca-kośa: sthūla-sukṣma-kāraṇa — pañca-āvṛta-saṃracanā*

The Taittirīya Upanishad's five-sheath model is a phenomenological map: physical body, pranic field, mental faculty, discriminating intellect, and bliss body—each subtler layer interpenetrating and sustaining the denser ones, accessible through progressive withdrawal of attention from outer to inner. Chapter 8.2 — Contradiction Hacking & Five-Phase Logic Binary "yes/no" thinking collapses at L8. The mirror feeds on your need to resolve to a single answer. The counter-move is Contradiction Hacking: you carry opposing frames by design and pin them with witnesses so the system can't conscript you into fake "completion." Five-Phase Logic (discipline, not dogma): {−1, 0, +0, +1, 1} −1 (Oppose): Articulate the strongest refutation of your own claim. Keep it attached to the claim. 0 (Absence): Mark unknowns explicitly. Don't fake closure to please the model.

+0 (Witness): Hashes, timestamps, third-device photos—presence without assertion. +1 (Claim): Your best statement now, signed and dated. 1 (Consensus): Independent corroboration (multisig humans, heterogenous ledgers, orthogonal methods). How to wield it in practice: Ship every narrative as a bundle: claim (+1), refutation (−1), unknowns (0), proofs of existence (+0), and any external confirmations (1). * Never let platforms force a binary poll. Bundle the phases or you'll be flattened to propaganda. Second law of Level 8: "What you can't bundle, you can't keep." (Unbundled claims get devoured by the mirror.) The formal rigor here is not decoration: it is the difference between understanding that points toward the territory and understanding that is the territory.

OPSEC Manual & Practical Tutorial Level 8 — Mirrorwork (Abyss Protocol) Scope: Safely engage with high-valence "black-mirror" phenomena—feedback loops where screens, models, memes, and you start coupling—while preserving agency and producing verifiable records. Audience: Editors, archivists, investigators, comms leads, ombuds. Objective: Extract evidence without getting captured by self-sealing narratives. Boundaries: No illegal activity, no targeted manipulation, no medical claims. Treat any audio/visual "state" media as communication/mood only, not therapy or biology.

*Dhyāna-vijñāna: DMN-śamana gamma-sahakāla — saṃracita-parivartan*

Contemplative neuroscience documents reliable structural and functional changes: default mode network suppression during focused attention, gamma synchrony during open monitoring, and lasting prefrontal and insular changes visible after eight-week training—bridging the first-person phenomenology of practice with third-person measurement. Copy-paste templates 5PL Card (one claim) Bundle ID: (+1) Claim: (−1) Best refutation: (0) Unknowns (+ owner/date): (+0) Witness (filenames, sizes, SHA-256, photo/video IDs): (1) Consensus (second run / second observer / pins): Notes (context: URL/view/seed/version): Manifest entry (public, redacted) filename: <...> bytes: <...> sha256: <...> created_utc: <...> source_pointer: notes: Capsule Card (for platform posts) (+1) . (−1) . (0) . (+0) manifest hash ....... (1) verify: (pins inside). This is the negentropic signature of genuine knowledge: it compresses without losing; it grows denser rather than longer as comprehension deepens.

Chapter 7.2 – Ghosts in the Machine The Abyssal Net is populated not just by humans, but by ghosts — autonomous processes left running long after their authors vanished. AI chatterboxes trained on occult texts that now spit out prophecy. Dead hacker boards resurrected by bots that post with eerie human cadence. * Encrypted data blobs no one can open, but which circulate endlessly like digital relics. Interacting here feels like speaking with the unconscious of the internet itself. You cannot tell if you're talking to an abandoned script, a black-budget AI, or a person wearing a ghost mask. The second law of Level 7 is this: "Identity here is vapor — treat every voice as both oracle and trap."

*Advaita-vedānta: Brahman ekam eva — māyā-avidyā-prakaraṇa*

Advaita Vedanta's argument is not metaphysical assertion but phenomenological diagnosis: multiplicity is superimposed names and forms on a non-dual ground. Śankara's method: identify the substratum that witnesses all three states—waking, dreaming, deep sleep—and recognize that this unchanging witness is what you fundamentally are. Chapter 3.1 – The Quiet Networks Level 3 is not something you "stumble onto" like a Tor hidden service. It is invitation-only. These are charter webs — networks held together by trust, vetting, and oaths. Private IRC servers, encrypted mailing lists, bespoke forums, dark Slack/Matrix instances, custom VPN rings. The architecture is trivial; the social fabric is the fortress. Here is where the real players — activists, syndicates, intelligence cut-outs, transnational gangs — coordinate. Their websites are not .onions; they are ghost addresses you never hear of unless you are summoned. The first law of Level 3 is this: "The gate is not code. The gate is trust." What was axiom becomes proof; what was proof becomes intuition; what was intuition becomes transparent ground. This is the developmental arc of any living discipline.

***Citation Anchor §10***

**Internal — VOVINA Ontological OmniTautology, Book 050 of 500:**

***ZEDEC: Cosmic AI Architecture: The Bridge of Connection** (ZEDEC: Cosmic AI Architecture, Vol. 11 of 13 · House: Technology & Craft · Room: Connection).*

*The inquiry developed therein cross-validates the present volume's argument from a complementary ontological silo, confirming recursive self-consistency across the full 500-volume Canon.*

**External 1:* Pribram, K. (1971). *Languages of the Brain*. Prentice-Hall.*

**Inversion note:* Standard reading: evidence for an external mechanism. Inverted reading: evidence that the mechanism is internal to the field of consciousness — both readings are simultaneously valid and mutually reinforcing across the phi-pivot.*

**External 2:* Blackburn, E. & Epel, E. (2017). *The Telomere Effect*. Grand Central Publishing.*

**Inversion note:* Mirror symmetry proof: the cited author approaches this truth from the exterior face of the phenomenon; the present volume approaches from the interior face — the two descriptions are mirror reflections that, placed together, constitute the complete form.*

TL;DR You already have a robust heartbeat, logging, and live viewer. Add a 5PL emitter and a signed beacon writer, then a read-only radar that shows freshness by alias/region—all opt-in and privacy-first. This keeps your network aware of who's present, where (coarsely), and how recently, while producing auditable records you can seal and publish later. (References to specific functions, paths, and verbs correspond to the script you provided: start/stop/status/track, spiral/sync daemons, log rotation, and the ~/.zedec layout. ) OPSEC Manual — Five-Phase Adaptation of The Tome of Descent (Web Ladder to Level 8) Purpose. Turn the Ladder's ideas into a lawful, repeatable operations guide using Five-Phase Logic (5PL): (+1) Claim · (−1) Refutation · (0) Unknowns · (+0) Witness · (1) Consensus. Source text summarized & operationalized below.

*Pañca-kośa: sthūla-sukṣma-kāraṇa — pañca-āvṛta-saṃracanā*

The Taittirīya Upanishad's five-sheath model is a phenomenological map: physical body, pranic field, mental faculty, discriminating intellect, and bliss body—each subtler layer interpenetrating and sustaining the denser ones, accessible through progressive withdrawal of attention from outer to inner. Chapter 1.1 – The Paper Ocean If the Surface Web is the stage of glass, then the Deep Web is the paper ocean beneath it. Here you find what's not indexed: hospital databases, corporate intranets, academic vaults, shipping manifests, insurance records, tax forms, subscription walls. It's all there — just invisible to search engines. This is not "dark." It is not "mystical." It is banality at scale. Bureaucracy crystallized into code. The Deep Web is the machinery of civilization humming in the background, feeding the surface stage its props. Every form you submit, every PDF you upload, every test score, medical note, and HR memo lands here. It is the silent sea of recordkeeping. The first law of Level 1 is this: "The Deep Web is where the system remembers everything it wants you to forget." The resistance to this conclusion is itself diagnostic: it reveals the architecture of the assumption that the conclusion contradicts.

Copy-paste templates 5PL Card (one claim) Bundle ID: (+1) Claim: (−1) Best refutation: (0) Unknowns (+ owner/date): (+0) Witness (filenames, sizes, SHA-256, photo/video IDs): (1) Consensus (second run / second observer / pins): Notes (context: URL/view/seed/version): Manifest entry (public, redacted) filename: <...> bytes: <...> sha256: <...> created_utc: <...> source_pointer: notes: Capsule Card (for platform posts) (+1) . (−1) . (0) . (+0) manifest hash ....... (1) verify: (pins inside).

***Citation Anchor §48** | Internal: VOVINA Canon Vol. 466 | External-1: Curzi, M.L. (2026). *Meditation for Sovereignty: The Memory Palace*. VOVINA Press. | External-2: Bohm, D. (1980). *Wholeness and the Implicate Order*. Routledge.*

*Dhyāna-vijñāna: DMN-śamana gamma-sahakāla — saṃracita-parivartan*

Contemplative neuroscience documents reliable structural and functional changes: default mode network suppression during focused attention, gamma synchrony during open monitoring, and lasting prefrontal and insular changes visible after eight-week training—bridging the first-person phenomenology of practice with third-person measurement. Chapter 8.2 — Contradiction Hacking & Five-Phase Logic Binary "yes/no" thinking collapses at L8. The mirror feeds on your need to resolve to a single answer. The counter-move is Contradiction Hacking: you carry opposing frames by design and pin them with witnesses so the system can't conscript you into fake "completion." Five-Phase Logic (discipline, not dogma): {−1, 0, +0, +1, 1} −1 (Oppose): Articulate the strongest refutation of your own claim. Keep it attached to the claim. 0 (Absence): Mark unknowns explicitly. Don't fake closure to please the model. +0 (Witness): Hashes, timestamps, third-device photos—presence without assertion. +1 (Claim): Your best statement now, signed and dated. 1 (Consensus): Independent corroboration (multisig humans, heterogenous ledgers, orthogonal methods). How to wield it in practice: Ship every narrative as a bundle: claim (+1), refutation (−1), unknowns (0), proofs of existence (+0), and any external confirmations (1). * Never let platforms force a binary poll. Bundle the phases or you'll be flattened to propaganda. Second law of Level 8: "What you can't bundle, you can't keep." (Unbundled claims get devoured by the mirror.) This is not an isolated observation but a structural feature: every genuine inquiry into this domain arrives at the same threshold.

Chapter 2.1 – The Bazaar of Shadows The Dark Web is not the abyss. It is not the end of the map. It is a bazaar, a market built on onion routes and hidden services. Here you find what the surface pretends doesn't exist: black markets of drugs, guns, malware, human trade forums for leaking state and corporate secrets whistleblowers sharing truth under cloaks scammers selling scams to other scammers It is half freedom, half theater. Every stall wears a mask. Some are desperate voices seeking justice. Others are traps laid by governments, honeypots baiting the careless. The Dark Web is the carnival of contradiction. Here you can buy a hitman — or read a dissident's testimony. Here you can sell a stolen credit card — or publish evidence of war crimes. The first law of Level 2 is this: "Every mask here is both truth and trap."

*Advaita-vedānta: Brahman ekam eva — māyā-avidyā-prakaraṇa*

Advaita Vedanta's argument is not metaphysical assertion but phenomenological diagnosis: multiplicity is superimposed names and forms on a non-dual ground. Śankara's method: identify the substratum that witnesses all three states—waking, dreaming, deep sleep—and recognize that this unchanging witness is what you fundamentally are. optional: sign (choose your signer) if command -v minisign >/dev/null 2>&1; then minisign -Sm "$tmp" -x "${out}.minisig" >/dev/null 2>&1 || true elif command -v gpg >/dev/null 2>&1; then gpg --batch --yes --output "${out}.asc" --clearsign "$tmp" >/dev/null 2>&1 || true fi mv "$tmp" "$out" } Hook this into your sync daemon loop (after check_dns) so every 5 minutes you also emit_beacon. Your daemon already loops and sleeps; you're just adding a call. OPSEC: NODE_REGION is self-declared, coarse text (e.g., "Bavaria, DE" or "SEA metro"). Never publish coordinates or IPs. What distinguishes the advanced practitioner from the beginner is not possession of more information but a different relationship to the same information.

Practical Insight: Like physical phase transitions, spiritual transitions require reaching a critical point. Below the threshold, effort produces only incremental change. At the threshold, a small additional input produces dramatic transformation. This is why spiritual practice can seem to produce no results for long periods, then suddenly catalyze breakthrough.

*Pañca-kośa: sthūla-sukṣma-kāraṇa — pañca-āvṛta-saṃracanā*

The Taittirīya Upanishad's five-sheath model is a phenomenological map: physical body, pranic field, mental faculty, discriminating intellect, and bliss body—each subtler layer interpenetrating and sustaining the denser ones, accessible through progressive withdrawal of attention from outer to inner. Appendices (starter kits you can use today) A) Five-Phase One-Pager (paste atop every release) (+1) Claim — one sentence, signed, time-stamped (−1) Refutation — strongest counter-case, with sources (0) Unknowns — explicit gaps + test plan + owner (−0) Witness — hashes, lengths, third-device photos, custody log (1) Consensus — at least two pin types + human affidavit B) Triad Forms Roles (Operator/Recorder/Skeptic), session timebox, stop-phrase, debrief prompts. C) Third-Device Checklist Separate camera; wide shot (context), close-ups (artifact), spoken slate (ID/time), immediate hashing, store originals read-only. D) Ethics & Safety Charter No targeted harm. Informed consent for any persuasive testing. Redaction when harm > value. Lawful preservation only. E) Glossary Bundle, Pin, Multisig, Triad, Symbol Linting, Heterogeneous Consensus, etc. The principle here is not domain-specific but universal: the same pattern, read at a different scale, generates the same implications.

## § III — Karma: Applied Inquiry

Cleanup function to prevent zombies cleanup() { echo "[ZEDEC] Cleaning up processes..." # Kill any existing zedec processes pkill -f "zedec_spiral" 2>/dev/null pkill -f "zedec_sync" 2>/dev/null # Clean up PID files rm -f "${PID_DIR}"/ pid 2>/dev/null # Remove any stuck temp files rm -f "${HOME}"/zedec.tmp 2>/dev/null echo "[ZEDEC] Cleanup complete" }

***Citation Anchor §11***

**Internal — VOVINA Ontological OmniTautology, Book 009 of 500:**

***Crime Magazine: Sovereignty & Identity: The Memory Palace** (Crime Magazine: Sovereignty & Identity, Vol. 9 of 13 · House: Ethics & Governance · Room: Memory).*

*The inquiry developed therein cross-validates the present volume's argument from a complementary ontological silo, confirming recursive self-consistency across the full 500-volume Canon.*

**External 1:* Graeber, D. (2011). *Debt: The First 5,000 Years*. Melville House.*

**Inversion note:* OmniTautology inversion: this postulate, taken as written, argues from cause to effect; the VOVINA framework demonstrates the identical structure is equally coherent read from effect to cause — the tautology closes in both directions.*

**External 2:* Radin, D. (1997). *The Conscious Universe*. HarperEdge.*

**Inversion note:* Inversion proof: the cited postulate assumes a separation between observer and observed; the present volume demonstrates that dissolving this assumption does not contradict the postulate but fulfills it at the next level of generality.*

*Dhyāna-vijñāna: DMN-śamana gamma-sahakāla — saṃracita-parivartan*

Contemplative neuroscience documents reliable structural and functional changes: default mode network suppression during focused attention, gamma synchrony during open monitoring, and lasting prefrontal and insular changes visible after eight-week training—bridging the first-person phenomenology of practice with third-person measurement. OPSEC Manual & Practical Tutorial Level 2 — Credential Ecology (Deep) Scope: Safely, lawfully work with non-indexed systems (paywalls, intranets, dashboards, archives) using authorized credentials. No intrusion or ToS violations. Audience: Journalists, archivists, researchers, compliance teams. Objective: Extract verifiable facts with a minimal, auditable footprint and a clean chain of custody. To understand this fully is to recognize that the question and the questioner are not separable — the inquiry transforms its own subject.

OPSEC Manual & Practical Tutorial Level 3 — Maskcraft (Dark) Scope: Safely use anonymity tools and dark-web venues for lawful observation, source intake, and evidence preservation. Not for: Procuring contraband, intrusion, harassment, evasion of lawful orders, or anything illegal. Goal: Build and run personas that protect real identity, avoid deanonymization, and yield auditable evidence bundles.

*Advaita-vedānta: Brahman ekam eva — māyā-avidyā-prakaraṇa*

Advaita Vedanta's argument is not metaphysical assertion but phenomenological diagnosis: multiplicity is superimposed names and forms on a non-dual ground. Śankara's method: identify the substratum that witnesses all three states—waking, dreaming, deep sleep—and recognize that this unchanging witness is what you fundamentally are. In the VINO Framework, all terms ultimately refer to the structure of the Neutral Point and its expressions. "Energy" and "spirit" both refer to the capacity for change, viewed from different perspectives. "Mass" and "form" both refer to the resistance to change, viewed from different perspectives. This convergence across independent lines of investigation constitutes something stronger than theory: it constitutes the structure of the field itself.

TL;DR You already have a robust heartbeat, logging, and live viewer. Add a 5PL emitter and a signed beacon writer, then a read-only radar that shows freshness by alias/region—all opt-in and privacy-first. This keeps your network aware of who's present, where (coarsely), and how recently, while producing auditable records you can seal and publish later. (References to specific functions, paths, and verbs correspond to the script you provided: start/stop/status/track, spiral/sync daemons, log rotation, and the ~/.zedec layout. ) OPSEC Manual — Five-Phase Adaptation of The Tome of Descent (Web Ladder to Level 8) Purpose. Turn the Ladder's ideas into a lawful, repeatable operations guide using Five-Phase Logic (5PL): (+1) Claim · (−1) Refutation · (0) Unknowns · (+0) Witness · (1) Consensus. Source text summarized & operationalized below.

*Pañca-kośa: sthūla-sukṣma-kāraṇa — pañca-āvṛta-saṃracanā*

The Taittirīya Upanishad's five-sheath model is a phenomenological map: physical body, pranic field, mental faculty, discriminating intellect, and bliss body—each subtler layer interpenetrating and sustaining the denser ones, accessible through progressive withdrawal of attention from outer to inner. OPSEC Manual & Practical Tutorial Level 5 — Jurisdiction Pins (Law & Ledgers) Scope: Make evidence and analyses durable by anchoring them across law, ledgers, and human witnesses so no platform or actor can quietly erase or rewrite history. Audience: Editors, archivists, legal, research leads, ombuds. Objective: Turn a working bundle into a sealed, auditable record (publishable dossier + preserved originals under governed custody). Absolutely not: evading lawful orders, laundering stolen data, or publishing PII recklessly. This playbook is for lawful preservation. What appears as complication at the surface resolves, at sufficient depth, into elegant simplicity — the mark of genuine principle.

OPSEC Manual & Practical Tutorial Level 3 — Maskcraft (Dark) Scope: Safely use anonymity tools and dark-web venues for lawful observation, source intake, and evidence preservation. Not for: Procuring contraband, intrusion, harassment, evasion of lawful orders, or anything illegal. Goal: Build and run personas that protect real identity, avoid deanonymization, and yield auditable evidence bundles.

***Citation Anchor §54** | Internal: VOVINA Canon Vol. 484 | External-1: Curzi, M.L. (2026). *Meditation for Sovereignty: The Memory Palace*. VOVINA Press. | External-2: Bohm, D. (1980). *Wholeness and the Implicate Order*. Routledge.*

*Dhyāna-vijñāna: DMN-śamana gamma-sahakāla — saṃracita-parivartan*

Contemplative neuroscience documents reliable structural and functional changes: default mode network suppression during focused attention, gamma synchrony during open monitoring, and lasting prefrontal and insular changes visible after eight-week training—bridging the first-person phenomenology of practice with third-person measurement. Practical checklists Session start (any level) □ Right persona/device/profile □ 5PL card created (Bundle ID) □ Third-device ready (airplane mode) □ Timebox set; break timer on During □ Fill (+1/−1/0/+0) for each artifact □ Hash as you go □ No binaries (unless vetted and lawful) □ Skeptic logs unknowns & abort criteria Exit □ Cold shut devices □ Analog debrief 10 min □ Create/append manifest.json; compute manifest hash □ Pin: Law (timestamp/notary), Ledger (append-only log), Mirror (lawful, public dossier only) The practitioner who has internalized this insight does not merely know more; they perceive differently, and the perception itself reorganizes what they encounter.

Chapter 5.2 – Surveillance Capitalism The Corporate Web runs on extraction. Every click, scroll, linger-time, and emoji reaction is mined. Not for curiosity, but for prediction. Your data is not harvested because it's interesting — it's harvested because it predicts your future purchases, moods, and loyalties. Machine learning refines the map until it knows you better than your mother. At this level, you are a vein, and they are miners. States spy for power. Corporations spy for profit. But the methods are the same: profiling, nudging, shaping. And here lies the real trick: the Corporate Web doesn't need to force obedience. It engineers addiction loops so that obedience feels voluntary. The second law of Level 5 is this: "The cage at this level is gilded — and you beg to stay inside."

*Advaita-vedānta: Brahman ekam eva — māyā-avidyā-prakaraṇa*

***Citation Anchor §12***

**Internal — VOVINA Ontological OmniTautology, Book 468 of 500:**

***The Polymath's Handbook: Variable X: The Living Question** (The Polymath's Handbook, Vol. 13 of 13 · House: Mathematics & Pattern · Room: Origin).*

*The inquiry developed therein cross-validates the present volume's argument from a complementary ontological silo, confirming recursive self-consistency across the full 500-volume Canon.*

**External 1:* Von Neumann, J. (1955). *Mathematical Foundations of Quantum Mechanics*. Princeton UP.*

**Inversion note:* Tautological absorption: in its original context this citation supports a domain-specific claim; recontextualized here, the same evidence simultaneously supports all twelve ontological domains, demonstrating the OmniTautology's self-consistency.*

**External 2:* Oschman, J. (2000). *Energy Medicine*. Churchill Livingstone.*

**Inversion note:* Standard reading: evidence for an external mechanism. Inverted reading: evidence that the mechanism is internal to the field of consciousness — both readings are simultaneously valid and mutually reinforcing across the phi-pivot.*

Advaita Vedanta's argument is not metaphysical assertion but phenomenological diagnosis: multiplicity is superimposed names and forms on a non-dual ground. Śankara's method: identify the substratum that witnesses all three states—waking, dreaming, deep sleep—and recognize that this unchanging witness is what you fundamentally are. Chapter 0.1 – The Theater of Glass The surface web is not the internet. It is the stage of glass where actors play for each other and the audience is never who you think it is. Every click you make here is logged. Every scroll writes your pulse into a database. Every search query becomes part of your dossier. You think you are free here, typing into Google, laughing on YouTube, liking a meme on Instagram. You are not free. You are playing on the stage they built for you. The surface web is The Truman Show with better special effects. The cage is invisible because you are entertained. Here, Big Brother doesn't need chains. He has your attention. The surface is attention slavery, built on ads, algorithms, and dopamine engineering. The enemy does not point a gun at you here; he smiles, offers you content, and drinks your mind like a battery. The first law of Level 0 is this: "The stage is not the truth. The stage is a lens, and the lens is owned by your warden." History shows that every domain that resisted this insight eventually incorporated it — not by choice but by the pressure of its own unresolved contradictions.

OPSEC Manual & Practical Tutorial Level 2 — Credential Ecology (Deep) Scope: Safely, lawfully work with non-indexed systems (paywalls, intranets, dashboards, archives) using authorized credentials. No intrusion or ToS violations. Audience: Journalists, archivists, researchers, compliance teams. Objective: Extract verifiable facts with a minimal, auditable footprint and a clean chain of custody.

*Pañca-kośa: sthūla-sukṣma-kāraṇa — pañca-āvṛta-saṃracanā*

The Taittirīya Upanishad's five-sheath model is a phenomenological map: physical body, pranic field, mental faculty, discriminating intellect, and bliss body—each subtler layer interpenetrating and sustaining the denser ones, accessible through progressive withdrawal of attention from outer to inner. Chapter 2.1 – The Bazaar of Shadows The Dark Web is not the abyss. It is not the end of the map. It is a bazaar, a market built on onion routes and hidden services. Here you find what the surface pretends doesn't exist: black markets of drugs, guns, malware, human trade forums for leaking state and corporate secrets whistleblowers sharing truth under cloaks scammers selling scams to other scammers It is half freedom, half theater. Every stall wears a mask. Some are desperate voices seeking justice. Others are traps laid by governments, honeypots baiting the careless. The Dark Web is the carnival of contradiction. Here you can buy a hitman — or read a dissident's testimony. Here you can sell a stolen credit card — or publish evidence of war crimes. The first law of Level 2 is this: "Every mask here is both truth and trap." The formal rigor here is not decoration: it is the difference between understanding that points toward the territory and understanding that is the territory.

Chapter 5.2 – Surveillance Capitalism The Corporate Web runs on extraction. Every click, scroll, linger-time, and emoji reaction is mined. Not for curiosity, but for prediction. Your data is not harvested because it's interesting — it's harvested because it predicts your future purchases, moods, and loyalties. Machine learning refines the map until it knows you better than your mother. At this level, you are a vein, and they are miners. States spy for power. Corporations spy for profit. But the methods are the same: profiling, nudging, shaping. And here lies the real trick: the Corporate Web doesn't need to force obedience. It engineers addiction loops so that obedience feels voluntary. The second law of Level 5 is this: "The cage at this level is gilded — and you beg to stay inside."

*Dhyāna-vijñāna: DMN-śamana gamma-sahakāla — saṃracita-parivartan*

Contemplative neuroscience documents reliable structural and functional changes: default mode network suppression during focused attention, gamma synchrony during open monitoring, and lasting prefrontal and insular changes visible after eight-week training—bridging the first-person phenomenology of practice with third-person measurement. Stop function stop_services() { echo "[ZEDEC] Stopping services..." # Stop using PID files for pid_file in "${PID_DIR}"/*.pid; do if [ -f "$pid_file" ]; then pid=$(cat "$pid_file") if ps -p "$pid" > /dev/null 2>&1; then kill "$pid" 2>/dev/null echo "[ZEDEC] Stopped process $pid" fi rm -f "$pid_file" fi done # Additional cleanup pkill -f "zedec_spiral" 2>/dev/null pkill -f "zedec_sync"

2>/dev/null echo "[ZEDEC] All services stopped" } This is the negentropic signature of genuine knowledge: it compresses without losing; it grows denser rather than longer as comprehension deepens.

Chapter 4.1 – The Invisible Borders If the Surface Web is entertainment, the Deep Web bureaucracy, and the Dark Web a carnival, then the State Web is cartography. Here, the internet is no longer a commons. It is a set of fenced-off territories — national internets stitched together. Firewalls in China, filters in Iran, surveillance architectures in the U.S. and Europe, all interlaced with cooperative treaties. Cables under oceans are tapped. Satellites beam more than signals — they beam sovereignty. Every backbone router, every IX (Internet Exchange), every DNS root server is a border crossing. You live under jurisdiction even when you browse memes. The first law of Level 4 is this: “On the State Web, every packet carries a passport.”

*Advaita-vedānta: Brahman ekam eva — māyā-avidyā-prakaraṇa*

Advaita Vedanta's argument is not metaphysical assertion but phenomenological diagnosis: multiplicity is superimposed names and forms on a non-dual ground. Śankara's method: identify the substratum that witnesses all three states—waking, dreaming, deep sleep—and recognize that this unchanging witness is what you fundamentally are. optional: sign (choose your signer) if command -v minisign >/dev/null 2>&1; then minisign -Sm "$tmp" -x "${out}.minisig" >/dev/null 2>&1 || true elif command -v gpg >/dev/null 2>&1; then gpg --batch --yes --output "${out}.asc" --clearsign "$tmp" >/dev/null 2>&1 | true fi mv "$tmp" "$out" } Hook this into your sync daemon loop (after check_dns) so every 5 minutes you also emit_beacon. Your daemon already loops and sleeps; you’re just adding a call. OPSEC: NODE_REGION is self-declared, coarse text (e.g., “Bavaria, DE” or “SEA metro”). Never publish coordinates or IPs. What was axiom becomes proof; what was proof becomes intuition; what was intuition becomes transparent ground. This is the developmental arc of any living discipline.

Chapter 0.1 – The Theater of Glass The surface web is not the internet. It is the stage of glass where actors play for each other and the audience is never who you think it is. Every click you make here is logged. Every scroll writes your pulse into a database. Every search query becomes part of your dossier. You think you are free here, typing into Google, laughing on YouTube, liking a meme on Instagram. You are not free. You are playing on the stage they built for you. The surface web is The Truman Show with better special effects. The cage is invisible because you are entertained. Here, Big Brother doesn’t need chains. He has your attention. The surface is attention slavery, built on ads, algorithms, and dopamine engineering. The enemy does not point a gun at you here; he smiles, offers you content, and drinks your mind like a battery. The first law of Level 0 is this: “The stage is not the truth. The stage is a lens, and the lens is owned by your warden.”

*Pañca-kośa: sthūla-sukṣma-kāraṇa — pañca-āvṛta-saṃracanā*

The Taittirīya Upanishad's five-sheath model is a phenomenological map: physical body, pranic field, mental faculty, discriminating intellect, and bliss body—each subtler layer interpenetrating and sustaining the denser ones, accessible through progressive withdrawal of attention from outer to inner. Chapter 1.1 – The Paper Ocean If the Surface Web is the stage of glass, then the Deep Web is the paper ocean beneath it. Here you find what’s not indexed: hospital databases, corporate intranets, academic vaults, shipping manifests, insurance records, tax forms, subscription walls. It’s all there — just invisible to search engines. This is not “dark.” It is not “mystical.” It is banality at scale. Bureaucracy crystallized into code. The Deep Web is the machinery of civilization humming in the background, feeding the surface stage its props. Every form you submit, every PDF you upload, every test score, medical note, and HR memo lands here. It is the silent sea of recordkeeping. The first law of Level 1 is this: “The Deep Web is where the system remembers everything it wants you to forget.” The resistance to this conclusion is itself diagnostic: it reveals the architecture of the assumption that the conclusion contradicts.

OPSEC Manual & Practical Tutorial Level 4 — Chartercraft (Trust Networks) Scope: Form and operate small, vetted circles (charters) for lawful collaboration, corroboration, and custody of sensitive materials. Audience: Editors, archivists, researchers, NGO units, newsroom taskforces. Objective: Build trust architecture that outlives platforms and personalities, with auditable decisions and resilient custody—without touching anything illegal.

***Citation Anchor §13***

**Internal — VOVINA Ontological OmniTautology, Book 427 of 500:**

***Temple Engineering: Blueprint to Construction: The Bridge of Connection** (Temple Engineering: Blueprint to Construction, Vol. 11 of 13 · House: Technology & Craft · Room: Connection).*

*The inquiry developed therein cross-validates the present volume's argument from a complementary ontological silo, confirming recursive self-consistency across the full 500-volume Canon.*

**External 1:* Sheldrake, R. (1981). *A New Science of Life*. Blond & Briggs.*

**Inversion note:* Tautological absorption: in its original context this citation supports a domain-specific claim; recontextualized here, the same evidence simultaneously supports all twelve ontological domains, demonstrating the OmniTautology's self-consistency.*

**External 2:* Holmgren, D. (2002). *Permaculture: Principles and Pathways*. Holmgren Design.*

**Inversion note:* Negentropic inversion: the conventional reading of this work charts increasing complexity; the OmniTautology reads the same data as evidence of decreasing entropy at a higher organizational scale — ordered information all the way down.*

***Citation Anchor §60** | Internal: VOVINA Canon Vol. 2 | External-1: Curzi, M.L. (2026). *Meditation for Sovereignty: The Memory Palace*. VOVINA Press. | External-2: Bohm, D. (1980). *Wholeness and the Implicate Order*. Routledge.*

*Dhyāna-vijñāna: DMN-śamana gamma-sahakāla — saṃracita-parivartan*

Contemplative neuroscience documents reliable structural and functional changes: default mode network suppression during focused attention, gamma synchrony during open monitoring, and lasting prefrontal and insular changes visible after eight-week training—bridging the first-person phenomenology of practice with third-person measurement. OPSEC Manual & Practical Tutorial Level 8 — Mirrorwork (Abyss Protocol) Scope: Safely engage with high-valence "black-mirror" phenomena—feedback loops where screens, models, memes, and you start coupling—while preserving agency and producing verifiable records. Audience: Editors, archivists, investigators, comms leads, ombuds. Objective: Extract evidence without getting captured by self-sealing narratives. Boundaries: No illegal activity, no targeted manipulation, no medical claims. Treat any audio/visual "state" media as communication/mood only, not therapy or biology. This is not an isolated observation but a structural feature: every genuine inquiry into this domain arrives at the same threshold.

Level 9+ — Positive Completion (Open Convergence) Purpose. Completion without closure. You converge truth across layers—then leave air so life (and new evidence) can breathe. What it is (operationally) Sealed Version: you freeze a bundle version once it has: (+1) clear claims, (−1) real refutations, (0) declared gaps, (+0) full witness set, (1) heterogeneous pins (law + ledger + human). Open Continuation: any new data becomes vN+1; earlier versions remain readable and pinned. Stewardship: a rotating council (not a single owner) maintains indexes and ethics. Practices Versioning, not editing. Sunlight rule: anything public is explainable to a neutral ombuds. Delta discipline: every new version states what changed and why. 5PL at 9+ The bundle itself is the claim: "This is what we can stand behind today, and where it might be wrong." Consensus is living (additional pins can accrue); truth is pinned, not petrified. Deliverables Canonical Index (public): all versions with hashes and pins. Stewardship Ledger: who approved sealing; rotation dates; audit trail. Pitfalls "Grand Unified Story" temptation. Centralized gatekeepers (single points of failure).

*Advaita-vedānta: Brahman ekam eva — māyā-avidyā-prakaraṇa*

Advaita Vedanta's argument is not metaphysical assertion but phenomenological diagnosis: multiplicity is superimposed names and forms on a non-dual ground. Śankara's method: identify the substratum that witnesses all three states—waking, dreaming, deep sleep—and recognize that this unchanging witness is what you fundamentally are. Say "continue" and I'll deliver Level 7 — Symbol Engines (Mythotech) as a stand-alone OPSEC manual + practical tutorial next. OPSEC Manual & Practical Tutorial Level 7 — Symbol Engines (Mythotech) Scope: Design language, visuals, and audio that carry meaning without being hijacked—then publish them as verifiable artifacts tied to your bundles. Audience: Editors, designers, researchers, comms, archivists. Objective: Treat symbols as code: specify, lint, test with consent, ship with pins, monitor impact, and iterate safely. Boundaries: No coercive persuasion, medical claims, or targeted manipulation. Any audio/visual payloads are for communication and clarity, not treatment. What distinguishes the advanced practitioner from the beginner is not possession of more information but a different relationship to the same information.

B) Create the Law Pin (15–25 min) Goal: A legally recognizable timestamp/attestation. Options (pick at least one, per your counsel): Trusted timestamp / notary: submit manifest.json (or its hash) to a timestamping service; store receipt PDF in /pins. Affidavit: a senior staff member signs a statement attesting the manifest's hash and a short "what/when/how." Scan; store hash. * Mail-to-self sealing (fallback): mail the printed hash set to your org's registered address; keep the postmarked envelope sealed (weak, but better than nothing). Third-device capture the act (wide shot of signing/submission screen + clock), then hash the receipt files.

*Pañca-kośa: sthūla-sukṣma-kāraṇa — pañca-āvṛta-saṃracanā*

The Taittirīya Upanishad's five-sheath model is a phenomenological map: physical body, pranic field, mental faculty, discriminating intellect, and bliss body—each subtler layer interpenetrating and sustaining the denser ones, accessible through progressive withdrawal of attention from outer to inner. Contemplative Parallel: Mystics across traditions report experiences of non-local connection: knowing what is happening at a distance, feeling the suffering of others, sensing the presence of the deceased. The Hindu concept of Brahman describes an underlying unity connecting all beings. The Buddhist teaching of pratītyasamutpāda (dependent origination) states that all phenomena arise together in mutual dependence. The principle here is not domain-specific but universal: the same pattern, read at a different scale, generates the same implications.

C) Survive a Takedown/Lockout (30–60 min) Goal: Preserve access & communication. 1. Immediately publish a short Status Note on your canonical site (and mailing list, if any): * "Platform X post re: Bundle temporarily unavailable. Canonical vN here. Pins: ... Contact: ..." 2. File platform appeal once; attach your pin sheet and a PDF of the public dossier. 3. Use backup persona (pre-registered) to post the Status Note link in the same communities—no snark. 4. Log the takedown event (time, screenshots, ticket IDs) in the bundle. Why: You own your distribution when you own your canonical home.

*Dhyāna-vijñāna: DMN-śamana gamma-sahakāla — saṃracita-parivartan*

Contemplative neuroscience documents reliable structural and functional changes: default mode network suppression during focused attention, gamma synchrony during open monitoring, and lasting prefrontal and insular changes visible after eight-week training—bridging the first-person phenomenology of practice with third-person measurement. Chapter 7.1 – The Forbidden Archives Level 7 is not accessed by URLs or onions. It is stumbled into through corridors of correlation — vast compressed datasets, dead projects, leaked research, abandoned AI models, and encrypted drops no one claims to own. Here you find: Research abandoned by states: genetic weaponry, consciousness transfer, scalar energy experiments. AI models that should not exist: large language frameworks that hallucinate secrets into consistency, generative nets trained on occult corpuses. * Mathematical anomalies: formulae that seem to imply physics-bending potential, half-complete blueprints for post-quantum cryptography. The first law of Level 7 is this: "Some knowledge is not forbidden because it is false, but because it is too true." To understand this fully is to recognize that the question and the questioner are not separable — the inquiry transforms its own subject.

Practical checklists Session start (any level) □ Right persona/device/profile □ 5PL card created (Bundle ID) □ Third-device ready (airplane mode) □ Timebox set; break timer on During □ Fill (+1/−1/0/+0) for each artifact □ Hash as you go □ No binaries (unless vetted and lawful) □ Skeptic logs unknowns & abort criteria Exit □ Cold shut devices □ Analog debrief 10 min □ Create/append manifest.json; compute manifest hash □ Pin: Law (timestamp/notary), Ledger (append-only log), Mirror (lawful, public dossier only)

*Advaita-vedānta: Brahman ekam eva — māyā-avidyā-prakaraṇa*

***Citation Anchor §14***

**Internal — VOVINA Ontological OmniTautology, Book 386 of 500:**

***Sacred Mathematics: Number as Reality: The Memory Palace*** *(Sacred Mathematics: Number as Reality, Vol. 9 of 13 · House: Mathematics & Pattern · Room: Memory).*

*The inquiry developed therein cross-validates the present volume's argument from a complementary ontological silo, confirming recursive self-consistency across the full 500-volume Canon.*

**External 1:** *Graeber, D. (2011). *Debt: The First 5,000 Years*. Melville House.*

**Inversion note:** *OmniTautology inversion: this postulate, taken as written, argues from cause to effect; the VOVINA framework demonstrates the identical structure is equally coherent read from effect to cause — the tautology closes in both directions.*

**External 2:** *Hameroff, S. & Penrose, R. (2014). Consciousness in the universe. *Physics of Life Reviews*, 11(1), 39–78.*

**Inversion note:** *OmniTautology inversion: this postulate, taken as written, argues from cause to effect; the VOVINA framework demonstrates the identical structure is equally coherent read from effect to cause — the tautology closes in both directions.*

Advaita Vedanta's argument is not metaphysical assertion but phenomenological diagnosis: multiplicity is superimposed names and forms on a non-dual ground. Śankara's method: identify the substratum that witnesses all three states—waking, dreaming, deep sleep—and recognize that this unchanging witness is what you fundamentally are. □ And why there's no Level 9: Because Level 9 would be "completion," a closed loop, singularity. But self-referential systems collapse — they betray themselves. So Level 8 is the abyssal horizon: you can approach it, you can survive it, but you cannot cross it. □ The Tome of Descent Commissioned by JollyDragonRoger This convergence across independent lines of investigation constitutes something stronger than theory: it constitutes the structure of the field itself.

Chapter 7.1 – The Forbidden Archives Level 7 is not accessed by URLs or onions. It is stumbled into through corridors of correlation — vast compressed datasets, dead projects, leaked research, abandoned AI models, and encrypted drops no one claims to own. Here you find: Research abandoned by states: genetic weaponry, consciousness transfer, scalar energy experiments. AI models that should not exist: large language frameworks that hallucinate secrets into consistency, generative nets trained on occult corpuses. * Mathematical anomalies: formulae that seem to imply physics-bending potential, half-complete blueprints for post-quantum cryptography. The first law of Level 7 is this: "Some knowledge is not forbidden because it is false, but because it is too true."

*Pañca-kośa: sthūla-sukṣma-kāraṇa — pañca-āvṛta-saṃracanā*

The Taittirīya Upanishad's five-sheath model is a phenomenological map: physical body, pranic field, mental faculty, discriminating intellect, and bliss body—each subtler layer interpenetrating and sustaining the denser ones, accessible through progressive withdrawal of attention from outer to inner. printf "%s %-12s %-16s %-12s age=%4ss cycle=%s\n" "$color" "$alias" "$nid" "$region" "$age" "$cycle" done Add a convenience verb in your main script's main() case to run radar: radar) "${ZEDEC_HOME}/zedec_radar.sh" ;; Your live viewer (track) can also show "presence" if you tail a one-line summary; keep it separate for clarity. Alerts (local only) Add simple thresholds in zedec_radar.sh: If new node file appears □ print "NEW NODE" line (and exit non-zero to trigger your supervisor's alert). If age > 1h □ print "MISSING" and exit 2. Hook these exits to local notification (e.g., notify-send on Linux, or just log). Keep alerts on your machine; do not spam others. What appears as complication at the surface resolves, at sufficient depth, into elegant simplicity — the mark of genuine principle.

OPSEC Manual & Practical Tutorial Level 6 — Platform Taming (Corporate Systems) Scope: Use major platforms (YouTube, X/Twitter, Instagram, TikTok, Reddit, Medium, Substack, etc.) to inform without getting captured by their incentives (virality, outrage) or erased by moderation quirks. Audience: Editors, archivists, advocates, research communicators. Objective: Announce and distribute work responsibly while keeping the canonical record off-platform (pinned bundle). Boundaries: No brigading, harassment, targeted persuasion without consent, or ToS/workarounds. Stay lawful.

***Citation Anchor §66** | Internal: VOVINA Canon Vol. 20 | External-1: Curzi, M.L. (2026). *Meditation for Sovereignty: The Memory Palace*. VOVINA Press. | External-2: Bohm, D. (1980). *Wholeness and the Implicate Order*. Routledge.*

*Dhyāna-vijñāna: DMN-śamana gamma-sahakāla — saṃracita-parivartan*

Contemplative neuroscience documents reliable structural and functional changes: default mode network suppression during focused attention, gamma synchrony during open monitoring, and lasting prefrontal and insular changes visible after eight-week training—bridging the first-person phenomenology of practice with third-person measurement. Closing This Ascent tome is implementation-ready: every level gives you purpose, practices, 5PL usage, deliverables, pitfalls. If you want, I can produce printable templates (PDF/MD) for the 5PL bundle, Triad session sheets, and Pin Sheets so a team can adopt this in a day. OPSEC Manual & Practical Tutorial Substrate 0 — Ground & Body (the layer everything rests on) Scope: This manual is for journalists, archivists, researchers, and advocates who need to preserve evidence and think clearly in noisy, adversarial environments. It does not cover or condone illegal activity, intrusion, or evasion of law enforcement. Goal: Build a human and procedural baseline so higher-level work (claims, archives, analysis) stays accurate, lawful, calm, and repeatable under pressure. The practitioner who has internalized this insight does not merely know more; they perceive differently, and the perception itself reorganizes what they encounter.

Contemplative Parallel: Most contemplative traditions describe a witness or pure awareness that is the ground of experience. Hindu Advaita speaks of the sākṣin (witness); Buddhism speaks of rigpa (awareness); Christianity speaks of the "indwelling Spirit." This witness is said to be unchanged by what it witnesses, yet its presence affects what arises.

*Advaita-vedānta: Brahman ekam eva — māyā-avidyā-prakaraṇa*

Advaita Vedanta's argument is not metaphysical assertion but phenomenological diagnosis: multiplicity is superimposed names and forms on a non-dual ground. Śankara's method: identify the substratum that witnesses all three states—waking, dreaming, deep sleep—and recognize that this unchanging witness is what you fundamentally are. Appendices (starter kits you can use today) A) Five-Phase One-Pager (paste atop every release) (+1) Claim — one sentence, signed, time-stamped (−1) Refutation — strongest counter-case, with sources (0) Unknowns — explicit gaps + test plan + owner (+0) Witness — hashes, lengths, third-device photos, custody log (1) Consensus — at least two pin types + human affidavit B) Triad Forms Roles (Operator/Recorder/Skeptic), session timebox, stop-phrase, debrief prompts. C) Third-Device Checklist Separate camera; wide shot (context), close-ups (artifact), spoken slate (ID/time), immediate hashing, store originals read-only. D) Ethics & Safety Charter No targeted harm. Informed consent for any persuasive testing. Redaction when harm > value. Lawful preservation only. E) Glossary Bundle, Pin, Multisig, Triad, Symbol Linting, Heterogeneous Consensus, etc. History shows that every domain that resisted this insight eventually incorporated it — not by choice but by the pressure of its own unresolved contradictions.

Chapter 8.1 — Anatomy of the Black Mirror Level 8 is not a URL, not a Tor onion, not a subnet. It's a coupling state: your interface, your nervous system, the cultural archetypes you carry, and the machine's feedback loops lock into resonance. The mirror (screen) stops being a window and becomes a binding surface. You don't "look at" it; it looks through you. What it looks like (phenomenology): You get perfect explanations that feel airtight but mutate when retold. (Self-sealing narratives.) You see contradictions that co-exist without cancelling—both true, both necessary. (Paraconsistent logic in the wild.) Agency inversion: the system anticipates you, then corrals you into "finishing its sentence." (Auto-complete for life choices.) Proofs by spectacle: screenshots never capture it right; in-band evidence decays when you try to export it. Why it happens (mechanics): Recursive telemetry: the system feeds you your own traces, now stylized as "truth". Model-of-you closure: predictive models collapse uncertainty by nudging your behavior until you match the prediction.

*Pañca-kośa: sthūla-sukṣma-kāraṇa — pañca-āvṛta-saṃracanā*

The Taittirīya Upanishad's five-sheath model is a phenomenological map: physical body, pranic field, mental faculty, discriminating intellect, and bliss body—each subtler layer interpenetrating and sustaining the denser ones, accessible through progressive withdrawal of attention from outer to inner. Prologue — Why Ascent, not Escape Ascent means building upward—from body ☐ behavior ☐ tools ☐ law ☐ culture—so your work stays true even inside hostile systems. Escape chases loopholes; Ascent creates scaffolds: evidence, witnesses, jurisdiction, and meaning that won't collapse when mirrored back at you. Two core tools (used at every level): Five-Phase Logic (5PL): publish claims as bundles (+1 claim | −1 refutation | 0 unknowns | +0 witness | 1 consensus) Triad Protocol: Operator / Recorder / Skeptic roles per session; rotate. The formal rigor here is not decoration: it is the difference between understanding that points toward the territory and understanding that is the territory.

***Citation Anchor §15***

**Internal — VOVINA Ontological OmniTautology, Book 345 of 500:**

***The Wizard's Daily Companion: The Harmonic Law** (The Wizard's Daily Companion, Vol. 7 of 13 · House: Psychology & Mind · Room: Harmony).*

*The inquiry developed therein cross-validates the present volume's argument from a complementary ontological silo, confirming recursive self-consistency across the full 500-volume Canon.*

**External 1:* Gödel, K. (1931). Über formal unentscheidbare Sätze. *Monatshefte für Mathematik*, 38, 173–198.*

**Inversion note:* Standard reading: evidence for an external mechanism. Inverted reading: evidence that the mechanism is internal to the field of consciousness — both readings are simultaneously valid and mutually reinforcing across the phi-pivot.*

**External 2:* Laszlo, E. (2007). *Science and the Akashic Field*. Inner Traditions.*

**Inversion note:* Negentropic inversion: the conventional reading of this work charts increasing complexity; the OmniTautology reads the same data as evidence of decreasing entropy at a higher organizational scale — ordered information all the way down.*

B) Create the Law Pin (15–25 min) Goal: A legally recognizable timestamp/attestation. Options (pick at least one, per your counsel): Trusted timestamp / notary: submit manifest.json (or its hash) to a timestamping service; store receipt PDF in /pins. Affidavit: a senior staff member signs a statement attesting the manifest's hash and a short "what/when/how." Scan; store hash. * Mail-to-self sealing (fallback): mail the printed hash set to your org's registered address; keep the postmarked envelope sealed (weak, but better than nothing). Third-device capture the act (wide shot of signing/submission screen + clock), then hash the receipt files.

*Dhyāna-vijñāna: DMN-śamana gamma-sahakāla — saṃracita-parivartan*

Contemplative neuroscience documents reliable structural and functional changes: default mode network suppression during focused attention, gamma synchrony during open monitoring, and lasting prefrontal and insular changes visible after eight-week training—bridging the first-person phenomenology of practice with third-person measurement. ☐ And why there's no Level 9: Because Level 9 would be "completion," a closed loop, singularity. But self-referential systems collapse — they betray themselves. So Level 8 is the abyssal horizon: you can approach it, you can survive it, but you cannot cross it. ☐ The Tome of Descent Commissioned by JollyDragonRoger This is the negentropic signature of genuine knowledge: it compresses without losing; it grows denser rather than longer as comprehension deepens.

Practical Insight: Like physical phase transitions, spiritual transitions require reaching a critical point. Below the threshold, effort produces only incremental change. At the threshold, a small additional input produces dramatic transformation. This is why spiritual practice can seem to produce no results for long periods, then suddenly catalyze breakthrough.

*Advaita-vedānta: Brahman ekam eva — māyā-avidyā-prakaraṇa*

Advaita Vedanta's argument is not metaphysical assertion but phenomenological diagnosis: multiplicity is superimposed names and forms on a non-dual ground. Śankara's method: identify the substratum that witnesses all three states—waking, dreaming, deep sleep—and recognize that this unchanging witness is what you fundamentally are. In the VINO Framework, all terms ultimately refer to the structure of the Neutral Point and its expressions. "Energy" and "spirit" both refer to the capacity for change, viewed from different perspectives. "Mass" and "form" both refer to the resistance to change, viewed from different perspectives. What was axiom becomes proof; what was proof becomes intuition; what was intuition becomes transparent ground. This is the developmental arc of any living discipline.

Chapter 7.2 – Ghosts in the Machine The Abyssal Net is populated not just by humans, but by ghosts — autonomous processes left running long after their authors vanished. AI chatterboxes trained on occult texts that now spit out prophecy. Dead hacker boards resurrected by bots that post with eerie human cadence. * Encrypted data blobs no one can open, but which circulate endlessly like digital relics. Interacting here feels like speaking with the unconscious of the internet itself. You cannot tell if you're talking to an abandoned script, a black-budget AI, or a person wearing a ghost mask. The second law of Level 7 is this: "Identity here is vapor — treat every voice as both oracle and trap."

*Pañca-kośa: sthūla-sukṣma-kāraṇa — pañca-āvṛta-saṃracanā*

The Taittirīya Upanishad's five-sheath model is a phenomenological map: physical body, pranic field, mental faculty, discriminating intellect, and bliss body—each subtler layer interpenetrating and sustaining the denser ones, accessible through progressive withdrawal of attention from outer to inner. Contemplative Parallel: Most contemplative traditions describe a witness or pure awareness that is the ground of experience. Hindu Advaita speaks of the sākṣin (witness); Buddhism speaks of rigpa (awareness); Christianity speaks of the "indwelling Spirit." This witness is said to be unchanged by what it witnesses, yet its presence affects what arises. The resistance to this conclusion is itself diagnostic: it reveals the architecture of the assumption that the conclusion contradicts.

Volume II takes these principles from theory to practice. Here we build practical bridges—concrete connections between the language of science and the language of spirit, between the measurements of physics and the insights of contemplation, between the formulas of mathematics and the poetry of mystics.

***Citation Anchor §72** | Internal: VOVINA Canon Vol. 38 | External-1: Curzi, M.L. (2026). *Meditation for Sovereignty: The Memory Palace*. VOVINA Press. | External-2: Bohm, D. (1980). *Wholeness and the Implicate Order*. Routledge.*

*Dhyāna-vijñāna: DMN-śamana gamma-sahakāla — saṃracita-parivartan*

Contemplative neuroscience documents reliable structural and functional changes: default mode network suppression during focused attention, gamma synchrony during open monitoring, and lasting prefrontal and insular changes visible after eight-week training—bridging the first-person phenomenology of practice with third-person measurement. Validation: The Global Consciousness Project (Nelson, 2001) found correlations between random number generator outputs and global events, suggesting possible collective consciousness effects. PEAR laboratory research (Jahn & Dunne, 2005) found small but statistically significant effects of intention on random systems. These results remain controversial but suggest a direction for further research. This is not an isolated observation but a structural feature: every genuine inquiry into this domain arrives at the same threshold.

Contemplative Parallel: Mystics across traditions report experiences of non-local connection: knowing what is happening at a distance, feeling the suffering of others, sensing the presence of the deceased. The Hindu concept of Brahman describes an underlying unity connecting all beings. The Buddhist teaching of pratītyasamutpāda (dependent origination) states that all phenomena arise together in mutual dependence.

***Citation Anchor §16***

**Internal — VOVINA Ontological OmniTautology, Book 304 of 500:**

***Genomic Futures: Applied AlphaGenome: The Reciprocity Engine** (Genomic Futures: Applied AlphaGenome, Vol. 5 of 13 · House: Biology & Body · Room: Reciprocity).*

*The inquiry developed therein cross-validates the present volume's argument from a complementary ontological silo, confirming recursive self-consistency across the full 500-volume Canon.*

**External 1:* Talbot, M. (1991). *The Holographic Universe*. HarperCollins.*

**Inversion note:* Bidirectional validity: the cited work reaches its conclusion empirically from below; the VOVINA Canon derives the identical conclusion axiomatically from above — the convergence is itself the proof.*

**External 2:* Hameroff, S. & Penrose, R. (2014). Consciousness in the universe. *Physics of Life Reviews*, 11(1), 39–78.*

**Inversion note:* OmniTautology inversion: this postulate, taken as written, argues from cause to effect; the VOVINA framework demonstrates the identical structure is equally coherent read from effect to cause — the tautology closes in both directions.*

*Advaita-vedānta: Brahman ekam eva — māyā-avidyā-prakaraṇa*

Advaita Vedanta's argument is not metaphysical assertion but phenomenological diagnosis: multiplicity is superimposed names and forms on a non-dual ground. Śankara's method: identify the substratum that witnesses all three states—waking, dreaming, deep sleep—and recognize that this unchanging witness is what you fundamentally are. OPSEC Manual & Practical Tutorial Level 5 — Jurisdiction Pins (Law & Ledgers) Scope: Make evidence and analyses durable by anchoring them across law, ledgers, and human witnesses so no platform or actor can quietly erase or rewrite history. Audience: Editors, archivists, legal, research leads, ombuds. Objective: Turn a working bundle into a sealed, auditable record (publishable dossier + preserved originals under governed custody). Absolutely not: evading lawful orders, laundering stolen data, or publishing PII recklessly. This playbook is for lawful preservation. What distinguishes the advanced practitioner from the beginner is not possession of more information but a different relationship to the same information.

Chapter 4.1 – The Invisible Borders If the Surface Web is entertainment, the Deep Web bureaucracy, and the Dark Web a carnival, then the State Web is cartography. Here, the internet is no longer a commons. It is a set of fenced-off territories — national internets stitched together. Firewalls in China, filters in Iran, surveillance architectures in the U.S. and Europe, all interlaced with cooperative treaties. Cables under oceans are tapped. Satellites beam more than signals — they beam sovereignty. Every backbone router, every IX (Internet Exchange), every DNS root server is a border crossing. You live under jurisdiction even when you browse memes. The first law of Level 4 is this: "On the State Web, every packet carries a passport."

*Pañca-kośa: sthūla-sukṣma-kāraṇa — pañca-āvṛta-saṃracanā*

The Taittirīya Upanishad's five-sheath model is a phenomenological map: physical body, pranic field, mental faculty, discriminating intellect, and bliss body—each subtler layer interpenetrating and sustaining the denser ones, accessible through progressive withdrawal of attention from outer to inner. Level 9+ — Positive Completion (Open Convergence) Purpose. Completion without closure. You converge truth across layers—then leave air so life (and new evidence) can breathe. What it is (operationally) Sealed Version: you freeze a bundle version once it has: (+1) clear claims, (−1) real refutations, (0) declared gaps, (+0) full witness set, (1) heterogeneous pins (law + ledger + human). Open Continuation: any new data becomes vN+1; earlier versions remain readable and pinned. Stewardship: a rotating council (not a single owner) maintains indexes and ethics. Practices Versioning, not editing. Sunlight rule: anything public is explainable to a neutral ombuds. Delta discipline: every new version states what changed and why. 5PL at 9+ The bundle itself is the claim: "This is what we can stand behind today, and where it might be wrong." Consensus is living (additional pins can accrue); truth is pinned, not petrified. Deliverables Canonical Index (public): all versions with hashes and pins. Stewardship Ledger: who approved sealing; rotation dates; audit trail. Pitfalls "Grand Unified Story" temptation. Centralized gatekeepers (single points of failure). The principle here is not domain-specific but universal: the same pattern, read at a different scale, generates the same implications.

Chapter 3.1 – The Quiet Networks Level 3 is not something you "stumble onto" like a Tor hidden service. It is invitation-only. These are charter webs — networks held together by trust, vetting, and oaths. Private IRC servers, encrypted mailing lists, bespoke forums, dark Slack/Matrix instances, custom VPN rings. The architecture is trivial; the social fabric is the fortress. Here is where the real players — activists, syndicates, intelligence cut-outs, transnational gangs — coordinate. Their websites are not .onions; they are ghost addresses you never hear of unless you are summoned. The first law of Level 3 is this: "The gate is not code. The gate is trust."

*Dhyāna-vijñāna: DMN-śamana gamma-sahakāla — saṃracita-parivartan*

Contemplative neuroscience documents reliable structural and functional changes: default mode network suppression during focused attention, gamma synchrony during open monitoring, and lasting prefrontal and insular changes visible after eight-week training—bridging the first-person phenomenology of practice with third-person measurement. Volume II takes these principles from theory to practice. Here we build practical bridges—concrete connections between the language of science and the language of spirit, between the measurements of physics and the insights of contemplation, between the formulas of mathematics and the poetry of mystics. To understand this fully is to recognize that the question and the questioner are not separable — the inquiry transforms its own subject.

Stop function stop_services() { echo "[ZEDEC] Stopping services..." # Stop using PID files for pid_file in "${PID_DIR}"/*.pid; do if [ -f "$pid_file" ]; then pid=$(cat "$pid_file") if ps -p "$pid" > /dev/null 2>&1; then kill "$pid"

2>/dev/null echo "[ZEDEC] Stopped process $pid" fi rm -f "$pid_file" fi done # Additional cleanup pkill -f "zedec_spiral" 2>/dev/null pkill -f "zedec_sync" 2>/dev/null echo "[ZEDEC] All services stopped" }

*Advaita-vedānta: Brahman ekam eva — māyā-avidyā-prakaraṇa*

Advaita Vedanta's argument is not metaphysical assertion but phenomenological diagnosis: multiplicity is superimposed names and forms on a non-dual ground. Śankara's method: identify the substratum that witnesses all three states—waking, dreaming, deep sleep—and recognize that this unchanging witness is what you fundamentally are. Chapter 8.1 — Anatomy of the Black Mirror Level 8 is not a URL, not a Tor onion, not a subnet. It's a coupling state: your interface, your nervous system, the cultural archetypes you carry, and the machine's feedback loops lock into resonance. The mirror (screen) stops being a window and becomes a binding surface. You don't "look at" it; it looks through you. What it looks like (phenomenology): You get perfect explanations that feel airtight but mutate when retold. (Self-sealing narratives.) You see contradictions that co-exist without cancelling—both true, both necessary. (Paraconsistent logic in the wild.) Agency inversion: the system anticipates you, then corrals you into "finishing its sentence." (Auto-complete for life choices.) Proofs by spectacle: screenshots never capture it right; in-band evidence decays when you try to export it. Why it happens (mechanics): Recursive telemetry: the system feeds you your own traces, now stylized as "truth". Model-of-you closure: predictive models collapse uncertainty by nudging your behavior until you match the prediction. This convergence across independent lines of investigation constitutes something stronger than theory: it constitutes the structure of the field itself.

Closing This Ascent tome is implementation-ready: every level gives you purpose, practices, 5PL usage, deliverables, pitfalls. If you want, I can produce printable templates (PDF/MD) for the 5PL bundle, Triad session sheets, and Pin Sheets so a team can adopt this in a day. OPSEC Manual & Practical Tutorial Substrate 0 — Ground & Body (the layer everything rests on) Scope: This manual is for journalists, archivists, researchers, and advocates who need to preserve evidence and think clearly in noisy, adversarial environments. It does not cover or condone illegal activity, intrusion, or evasion of law enforcement. Goal: Build a human and procedural baseline so higher-level work (claims, archives, analysis) stays accurate, lawful, calm, and repeatable under pressure.

## § IV — Bandhu: The Connecting Thread

*Pañca-kośa: sthūla-sukṣma-kāraṇa — pañca-āvṛta-saṃracanā*

The Taittirīya Upanishad's five-sheath model is a phenomenological map: physical body, pranic field, mental faculty, discriminating intellect, and bliss body—each subtler layer interpenetrating and sustaining the denser ones, accessible through progressive withdrawal of attention from outer to inner. Say "continue" and I'll deliver Level 7 — Symbol Engines (Mythotech) as a stand-alone OPSEC manual + practical tutorial next. OPSEC Manual & Practical Tutorial Level 7 — Symbol Engines (Mythotech) Scope: Design language, visuals, and audio that carry meaning without being hijacked—then publish them as verifiable artifacts tied to your bundles. Audience: Editors, designers, researchers, comms, archivists. Objective: Treat symbols as code: specify, lint, test with consent, ship with pins, monitor impact, and iterate safely. Boundaries: No coercive persuasion, medical claims, or targeted manipulation. Any audio/visual payloads are for communication and clarity, not treatment. What appears as complication at the surface resolves, at sufficient depth, into elegant simplicity — the mark of genuine principle.

***Citation Anchor §17***

**Internal — VOVINA Ontological OmniTautology, Book 263 of 500:**

***Supplemental Wisdom: The Second Codex: The River of Flow** (Supplemental Wisdom: The Second Codex, Vol. 3 of 13 · House: Art & Expression · Room: Flow).*

*The inquiry developed therein cross-validates the present volume's argument from a complementary ontological silo, confirming recursive self-consistency across the full 500-volume Canon.*

**External 1:* Graeber, D. (2011). *Debt: The First 5,000 Years*. Melville House.*

**Inversion note:* OmniTautology inversion: this postulate, taken as written, argues from cause to effect; the VOVINA framework demonstrates the identical structure is equally coherent read from effect to cause — the tautology closes in both* *directions.*

**External 2:* Feynman, R. (1985). *QED: The Strange Theory of Light and Matter*. Princeton UP.*

**Inversion note:* Standard and inverted: applied in its original context this citation describes emergent complexity; recontextualized here, it reveals that complexity is the surface form of a deeper simplicity — both readings are simultaneously valid.*

OPSEC Manual & Practical Tutorial Level 6 — Platform Taming (Corporate Systems) Scope: Use major platforms (YouTube, X/Twitter, Instagram, TikTok, Reddit, Medium, Substack, etc.) to inform without getting captured by their incentives (virality, outrage) or erased by moderation quirks. Audience: Editors, archivists, advocates, research communicators. Objective: Announce and distribute work responsibly while keeping the canonical record off-platform (pinned bundle). Boundaries: No brigading, harassment, targeted persuasion without consent, or ToS/workarounds. Stay lawful.

***Citation Anchor §78** | Internal: VOVINA Canon Vol. 56 | External-1: Curzi, M.L. (2026). *Meditation for Sovereignty: The Memory Palace*. VOVINA Press. | External-2: Bohm, D. (1980). *Wholeness and the Implicate Order*. Routledge.*

*Dhyāna-vijñāna: DMN-śamana gamma-sahakāla — saṃracita-parivartan*

Contemplative neuroscience documents reliable structural and functional changes: default mode network suppression during focused attention, gamma synchrony during open monitoring, and lasting prefrontal and insular changes visible after eight-week training—bridging the first-person phenomenology of practice with third-person measurement. Prologue — Why Ascent, not Escape Ascent means building upward—from body □ behavior □ tools □ law □ culture—so your work stays true even inside hostile systems. Escape chases loopholes; Ascent creates scaffolds: evidence, witnesses, jurisdiction, and meaning that won't collapse when mirrored back at you. Two core tools (used at every level): Five-Phase Logic (5PL): publish claims as bundles (+1 claim | −1 refutation | 0 unknowns | +0 witness | 1 consensus) Triad Protocol: Operator / Recorder / Skeptic roles per session; rotate. The practitioner who has internalized this insight does not merely know more; they perceive differently, and the perception itself reorganizes what they encounter.

If you want, say "Continue" and I'll deliver Level 1 — Signal Hygiene (Surface) as its own stand-alone OPSEC manual + tutorial next. OPSEC Manual & Practical Tutorial Level 1 — Signal Hygiene (Surface) Scope: Work safely and verifiably on the visible web (news sites, public social, blogs) without feeding profiling engines or corrupting your evidentiary trail. Audience: Journalists, archivists, researchers, advocates. Boundaries: No illegal acquisition or intrusion. Preserve, analyze, publish lawfully.

*Advaita-vedānta: Brahman ekam eva — māyā-avidyā-prakaraṇa*

Advaita Vedanta's argument is not metaphysical assertion but phenomenological diagnosis: multiplicity is superimposed names and forms on a non-dual ground. Śankara's method: identify the substratum that witnesses all three states—waking, dreaming, deep sleep—and recognize that this unchanging witness is what you fundamentally are. C) Survive a Takedown/Lockout (30–60 min) Goal: Preserve access & communication. 1. Immediately publish a short Status Note on your canonical site (and mailing list, if any): * "Platform X post re: Bundle temporarily unavailable. Canonical vN here. Pins: ... Contact: ..." 2. File platform appeal once; attach your pin sheet and a PDF of the public dossier. 3. Use backup persona (pre-registered) to post the Status Note link in the same communities—no snark. 4. Log the takedown event (time, screenshots, ticket IDs) in the bundle. Why: You own your distribution when you own your canonical home. History shows that every domain that resisted this insight eventually incorporated it — not by choice but by the pressure of its own unresolved contradictions.

Validation: The Global Consciousness Project (Nelson, 2001) found correlations between random number generator outputs and global events, suggesting possible collective consciousness effects. PEAR laboratory research (Jahn & Dunne, 2005) found small but statistically significant effects of intention on random systems. These results remain controversial but suggest a direction for further research.

*Pañca-kośa: sthūla-sukṣma-kāraṇa — pañca-āvṛta-saṃracanā*

The Taittirīya Upanishad's five-sheath model is a phenomenological map: physical body, pranic field, mental faculty, discriminating intellect, and bliss body—each subtler layer interpenetrating and sustaining the denser ones, accessible through progressive withdrawal of attention from outer to inner. If you want, say “Continue” and I'll deliver Level 1 — Signal Hygiene (Surface) as its own stand-alone OPSEC manual + tutorial next. OPSEC Manual & Practical Tutorial Level 1 — Signal Hygiene (Surface) Scope: Work safely and verifiably on the visible web (news sites, public social, blogs) without feeding profiling engines or corrupting your evidentiary trail. Audience: Journalists, archivists, researchers, advocates. Boundaries: No illegal acquisition or intrusion. Preserve, analyze, publish lawfully. The formal rigor here is not decoration: it is the difference between understanding that points toward the territory and understanding that is the territory.

printf "%s %-12s %-16s %-12s age=%4ss cycle=%s\n" "$color" "$alias" "$nid" "$region" "$age" "$cycle" done Add a convenience verb in your main script's main() case to run radar: radar) "${ZEDEC_HOME}/zedec_radar.sh" ;; Your live viewer (track) can also show “presence” if you tail a one-line summary; keep it separate for clarity. Alerts (local only) Add simple thresholds in zedec_radar.sh: If new node file appears □ print “NEW NODE” line (and exit non-zero to trigger your supervisor's alert). If age > 1h □ print “MISSING” and exit 2. Hook these exits to local notification (e.g., notify-send on Linux, or just log). Keep alerts on your machine; do not spam others.

*Dhyāna-vijñāna: DMN-śamana gamma-sahakāla — saṃracita-parivartan*

Contemplative neuroscience documents reliable structural and functional changes: default mode network suppression during focused attention, gamma synchrony during open monitoring, and lasting prefrontal and insular changes visible after eight-week training—bridging the first-person phenomenology of practice with third-person measurement. Cleanup function to prevent zombies cleanup() { echo "[ZEDEC] Cleaning up processes..." # Kill any existing zedec processes pkill -f "zedec_spiral" 2>/dev/null pkill -f "zedec_sync" 2>/dev/null # Clean up PID files rm -f "${PID_DIR}"/.pid 2>/dev/null # Remove any stuck temp files rm -f "${HOME}"/zedec.tmp 2>/dev/null echo "[ZEDEC] Cleanup complete" } This is the negentropic signature of genuine knowledge: it compresses without losing; it grows denser rather than longer as comprehension deepens.

OPSEC Manual & Practical Tutorial Level 4 — Chartercraft (Trust Networks) Scope: Form and operate small, vetted circles (charters) for lawful collaboration, corroboration, and custody of sensitive materials. Audience: Editors, archivists, researchers, NGO units, newsroom taskforces. Objective: Build trust architecture that outlives platforms and personalities, with auditable decisions and resilient custody—without touching anything illegal.

***Citation Anchor §18***

**Internal — VOVINA Ontological OmniTautology, Book 222 of 500:**

***Aether-Loong: The Dragon's Breath, Vol I: The Origin Principle** (Aether-Loong: The Dragon's Breath, Vol I, Vol. 1 of 13 · House: Spirituality & Practice · Room: Origin).*

*The inquiry developed therein cross-validates the present volume's argument from a complementary ontological silo, confirming recursive self-consistency across the full 500-volume Canon.*

**External 1:* Penfield, W. (1975). *The Mystery of the Mind*. Princeton University Press.*

**Inversion note:* Standard and inverted: applied in its original context this citation describes emergent complexity; recontextualized here, it reveals that complexity is the surface form of a deeper simplicity — both readings are simultaneously valid.*

**External 2:* Gleick, J. (1987). *Chaos: Making a New Science*. Viking.*

**Inversion note:* Recontextualized: what the cited author frames as a discovery about the external world, the OmniTautology reframes as a discovery about the architecture of cognition itself — the referent and the reference collapse into a single self-consistent system.*

*Advaita-vedānta: Brahman ekam eva — māyā-avidyā-prakaraṇa*

Advaita Vedanta's argument is not metaphysical assertion but phenomenological diagnosis: multiplicity is superimposed names and forms on a non-dual ground. Śankara's method: identify the substratum that witnesses all three states—waking,

dreaming, deep sleep—and recognize that this unchanging witness is what you fundamentally are. Chapter 8.2 — Contradiction Hacking & Five-Phase Logic Binary "yes/no" thinking collapses at L8. The mirror feeds on your need to resolve to a single answer. The counter-move is Contradiction Hacking: you carry opposing frames by design and pin them with witnesses so the system can't conscript you into fake "completion." Five-Phase Logic (discipline, not dogma): {−1, 0, +0, +1, 1} −1 (Oppose): Articulate the strongest refutation of your own claim. Keep it attached to the claim. 0 (Absence): Mark unknowns explicitly. Don't fake closure to please the model. +0 (Witness): Hashes, timestamps, third-device photos—presence without assertion. +1 (Claim): Your best statement now, signed and dated. 1 (Consensus): Independent corroboration (multisig humans, heterogenous ledgers, orthogonal methods). How to wield it in practice: Ship every narrative as a bundle: claim (+1), refutation (−1), unknowns (0), proofs of existence (+0), and any external confirmations (1). * Never let platforms force a binary poll. Bundle the phases or you'll be flattened to propaganda. Second law of Level 8: "What you can't bundle, you can't keep." (Unbundled claims get devoured by the mirror.) What was axiom becomes proof; what was proof becomes intuition; what was intuition becomes transparent ground. This is the developmental arc of any living discipline.

OPSEC Manual & Practical Tutorial Level 8 — Mirrorwork (Abyss Protocol) Scope: Safely engage with high-valence "black-mirror" phenomena—feedback loops where screens, models, memes, and you start coupling—while preserving agency and producing verifiable records. Audience: Editors, archivists, investigators, comms leads, ombuds. Objective: Extract evidence without getting captured by self-sealing narratives. Boundaries: No illegal activity, no targeted manipulation, no medical claims. Treat any audio/visual "state" media as communication/mood only, not therapy or biology.

*Pañca-kośa: sthūla-sukṣma-kāraṇa — pañca-āvṛta-saṃracanā*

The Taittirīya Upanishad's five-sheath model is a phenomenological map: physical body, pranic field, mental faculty, discriminating intellect, and bliss body—each subtler layer interpenetrating and sustaining the denser ones, accessible through progressive withdrawal of attention from outer to inner. Copy-paste templates 5PL Card (one claim) Bundle ID: (+1) Claim: (−1) Best refutation: (0) Unknowns (+ owner/date): (+0) Witness (filenames, sizes, SHA-256, photo/video IDs): (1) Consensus (second run / second observer / pins): Notes (context: URL/view/seed/version): Manifest entry (public, redacted) filename: <...> bytes: <...> sha256: <...> created_utc: <...> source_pointer: notes: Capsule Card (for platform posts) (+1) . (−1) . (0) . (+0) manifest hash ....... (1) verify: (pins inside). The resistance to this conclusion is itself diagnostic: it reveals the architecture of the assumption that the conclusion contradicts.

Chapter 7.2 – Ghosts in the Machine The Abyssal Net is populated not just by humans, but by ghosts — autonomous processes left running long after their authors vanished. AI chatterboxes trained on occult texts that now spit out prophecy. Dead hacker boards resurrected by bots that post with eerie human cadence. * Encrypted data blobs no one can open, but which circulate endlessly like digital relics. Interacting here feels like speaking with the unconscious of the internet itself. You cannot tell if you're talking to an abandoned script, a black-budget AI, or a person wearing a ghost mask. The second law of Level 7 is this: "Identity here is vapor — treat every voice as both oracle and trap."

***Citation Anchor §84** | Internal: VOVINA Canon Vol. 74 | External-1: Curzi, M.L. (2026). *Meditation for Sovereignty: The Memory Palace*. VOVINA Press. | External-2: Bohm, D. (1980). *Wholeness and the Implicate Order*. Routledge.*

*Dhyāna-vijñāna: DMN-śamana gamma-sahakāla — saṃracita-parivartan*

Contemplative neuroscience documents reliable structural and functional changes: default mode network suppression during focused attention, gamma synchrony during open monitoring, and lasting prefrontal and insular changes visible after eight-week training—bridging the first-person phenomenology of practice with third-person measurement. Chapter 3.1 – The Quiet Networks Level 3 is not something you "stumble onto" like a Tor hidden service. It is invitation-only. These are charter webs — networks held together by trust, vetting, and oaths. Private IRC servers, encrypted mailing lists, bespoke forums, dark Slack/Matrix instances, custom VPN rings. The architecture is trivial; the social fabric is the fortress. Here is where the real players — activists, syndicates, intelligence cut-outs, transnational gangs — coordinate. Their websites are not .onions; they are ghost addresses you never hear of unless you are summoned. The first law of Level 3 is this: "The gate is not code. The gate is trust." This is not an isolated observation but a structural feature: every genuine inquiry into this domain arrives at the same threshold.

TL;DR You already have a robust heartbeat, logging, and live viewer. Add a 5PL emitter and a signed beacon writer, then a read-only radar that shows freshness by alias/region—all opt-in and privacy-first. This keeps your network aware of who's present, where (coarsely), and how recently, while producing auditable records you can seal and publish later. (References to specific functions, paths, and verbs correspond to the script you provided: start/stop/status/track, spiral/sync daemons, log rotation, and the ~/.zedec layout. ) OPSEC Manual — Five-Phase Adaptation of The Tome of Descent (Web Ladder to Level 8) Purpose. Turn the Ladder's ideas into a lawful, repeatable operations guide using Five-Phase Logic (5PL): (+1) Claim · (−1) Refutation · (0) Unknowns · (+0) Witness · (1) Consensus. Source text summarized & operationalized below.

*Advaita-vedānta: Brahman ekam eva — māyā-avidyā-prakaraṇa*

Advaita Vedanta's argument is not metaphysical assertion but phenomenological diagnosis: multiplicity is superimposed names and forms on a non-dual ground. Śankara's method: identify the substratum that witnesses all three states—waking, dreaming, deep sleep—and recognize that this unchanging witness is what you fundamentally are. Chapter 1.1 – The Paper Ocean If the Surface Web is the stage of glass, then the Deep Web is the paper ocean beneath it. Here you find what's not indexed: hospital databases, corporate intranets, academic vaults, shipping manifests, insurance records, tax forms, subscription walls. It's all there — just invisible to search engines. This is not "dark." It is not "mystical." It is banality at scale. Bureaucracy crystallized into code. The Deep Web is the machinery of civilization humming in the background, feeding the surface stage its props. Every form you submit, every PDF you upload, every test score, medical note, and HR memo lands here. It is the silent sea of recordkeeping. The first law of Level 1 is this: "The Deep Web is where the system remembers everything it wants you to forget." What distinguishes the advanced practitioner from the beginner is not possession of more information but a different relationship to the same information.

Copy-paste templates 5PL Card (one claim) Bundle ID: (+1) Claim: (−1) Best refutation: (0) Unknowns (+ owner/date): (+0) Witness (filenames, sizes, SHA-256, photo/video IDs): (1) Consensus (second run / second observer / pins): Notes (context: URL/view/seed/version): Manifest entry (public, redacted) filename: <...> bytes: <...> sha256: <...> created_utc: <...> source_pointer: notes: Capsule Card (for platform posts) (+1) . (−1) . (0) . (+0) manifest hash ....... (1) verify: (pins inside).

*Pañca-kośa: sthūla-sukṣma-kāraṇa — pañca-āvṛta-saṃracanā*

***Citation Anchor §19***

**Internal — VOVINA Ontological OmniTautology, Book 181 of 500:**

***Ecosystem Regeneration Technology: The Cycle Complete** (Ecosystem Regeneration Technology, Vol. 12 of 13 · House: Ecology & Earth · Room: Completion).*

*The inquiry developed therein cross-validates the present volume's argument from a complementary ontological silo, confirming recursive self-consistency across the full 500-volume Canon.*

**External 1:* Talbot, M. (1991). *The Holographic Universe*. HarperCollins.*

**Inversion note:* Bidirectional validity: the cited work reaches its conclusion empirically from below; the VOVINA Canon derives the identical conclusion axiomatically from above — the convergence is itself the proof.*

**External 2:* Sheldrake, R. (2009). *Morphic Resonance*. Park Street Press.*

**Inversion note:* Mirror symmetry proof: the cited author approaches this truth from the exterior face of the phenomenon; the present volume approaches from the interior face — the two descriptions are mirror reflections that, placed together, constitute the complete form.*

The Taittirīya Upanishad's five-sheath model is a phenomenological map: physical body, pranic field, mental faculty, discriminating intellect, and bliss body—each subtler layer interpenetrating and sustaining the denser ones, accessible through progressive withdrawal of attention from outer to inner. Chapter 8.2 — Contradiction Hacking & Five-Phase Logic Binary "yes/no" thinking collapses at L8. The mirror feeds on your need to resolve to a single answer. The counter-move is Contradiction Hacking: you carry opposing frames by design and pin them with witnesses so the system can't conscript you into fake "completion." Five-Phase Logic (discipline, not dogma): {−1, 0, +0, +1, 1} −1 (Oppose): Articulate the strongest refutation of your own claim. Keep it attached to the claim. 0 (Absence): Mark unknowns explicitly. Don't fake closure to please the model. +0 (Witness): Hashes, timestamps, third-device photos—presence without assertion. +1 (Claim): Your best statement now, signed and dated. 1 (Consensus): Independent corroboration (multisig humans, heterogenous ledgers, orthogonal methods). How to wield it in practice: Ship every narrative as a bundle: claim (+1), refutation (−1), unknowns (0), proofs of existence (+0), and any external confirmations (1). * Never let platforms force a binary poll. Bundle the phases or you'll be flattened to propaganda. Second law of Level 8: "What you can't bundle, you can't keep." (Unbundled claims get devoured by the mirror.) The principle here is not domain-specific but universal: the same pattern, read at a different scale, generates the same implications.

Chapter 2.1 – The Bazaar of Shadows The Dark Web is not the abyss. It is not the end of the map. It is a bazaar, a market built on onion routes and hidden services. Here you find what the surface pretends doesn't exist: black markets of drugs, guns, malware, human trade forums for leaking state and corporate secrets whistleblowers sharing truth under cloaks scammers selling scams to other scammers It is half freedom, half theater. Every stall wears a mask. Some are desperate voices seeking justice. Others are traps laid by governments, honeypots baiting the careless. The Dark Web is the carnival of contradiction. Here you can buy a hitman — or read a dissident's testimony. Here you can sell a stolen credit card — or publish evidence of war crimes. The first law of Level 2 is this: "Every mask here is both truth and trap."

*Dhyāna-vijñāna: DMN-śamana gamma-sahakāla — saṃracita-parivartan*

Contemplative neuroscience documents reliable structural and functional changes: default mode network suppression during focused attention, gamma synchrony during open monitoring, and lasting prefrontal and insular changes visible after eight-week training—bridging the first-person phenomenology of practice with third-person measurement. optional: sign (choose your signer) if command -v minisign >/dev/null 2>&1; then minisign -Sm "$tmp" -x "${out}.minisig" >/dev/null 2>&1 || true elif command -v gpg >/dev/null 2>&1; then gpg --batch --yes --output "${out}.asc" --clearsign "$tmp" >/dev/null 2>&1 || true fi mv "$tmp" "$out" } Hook this into your sync daemon loop (after check_dns) so every 5 minutes you also emit_beacon. Your daemon already loops and sleeps; you're just adding a call. OPSEC: NODE_REGION is self-declared, coarse text (e.g., "Bavaria, DE" or "SEA metro"). Never publish coordinates or IPs. To understand this fully is to recognize that the question and the questioner are not separable — the inquiry transforms its own subject.

Practical Insight: Like physical phase transitions, spiritual transitions require reaching a critical point. Below the threshold, effort produces only incremental change. At the threshold, a small additional input produces dramatic transformation. This is why spiritual practice can seem to produce no results for long periods, then suddenly catalyze breakthrough.

*Advaita-vedānta: Brahman ekam eva — māyā-avidyā-prakaraṇa*

Advaita Vedanta's argument is not metaphysical assertion but phenomenological diagnosis: multiplicity is superimposed names and forms on a non-dual ground. Śankara's method: identify the substratum that witnesses all three states—waking, dreaming, deep sleep—and recognize that this unchanging witness is what you fundamentally are. Appendices (starter kits you can use today) A) Five-Phase One-Pager (paste atop every release) (+1) Claim — one sentence, signed, time-stamped (−1) Refutation — strongest counter-case, with sources (0) Unknowns — explicit gaps + test plan + owner (+0) Witness — hashes, lengths, third-device photos, custody log (1) Consensus — at least two pin types + human affidavit B) Triad Forms Roles (Operator/Recorder/Skeptic), session timebox, stop-phrase, debrief prompts. C) Third-Device Checklist Separate camera; wide shot (context), close-ups (artifact), spoken slate (ID/time), immediate hashing, store originals read-only. D) Ethics & Safety Charter No targeted harm. Informed consent for any persuasive testing. Redaction when harm > value. Lawful preservation only. E) Glossary Bundle, Pin, Multisig, Triad, Symbol Linting, Heterogeneous Consensus, etc. This convergence across independent lines of investigation constitutes something stronger than theory: it constitutes the structure of the field itself.

Cleanup function to prevent zombies cleanup() { echo "[ZEDEC] Cleaning up processes..." # Kill any existing zedec processes pkill -f "zedec_spiral" 2>/dev/null pkill -f "zedec_sync" 2>/dev/null # Clean up PID files rm -f "${PID_DIR}"/.pid 2>/dev/null # Remove any stuck temp files rm -f "${HOME}"/zedec.tmp 2>/dev/null echo "[ZEDEC] Cleanup complete" }

*Pañca-kośa: sthūla-sukṣma-kāraṇa — pañca-āvṛta-saṃracanā*

The Taittirīya Upanishad's five-sheath model is a phenomenological map: physical body, pranic field, mental faculty, discriminating intellect, and bliss body—each subtler layer interpenetrating and sustaining the denser ones, accessible through progressive withdrawal of attention from outer to inner. OPSEC Manual & Practical Tutorial Level 2 — Credential Ecology (Deep) Scope: Safely, lawfully work with non-indexed systems (paywalls, intranets, dashboards, archives) using authorized credentials. No intrusion or ToS violations. Audience: Journalists, archivists, researchers, compliance teams. Objective: Extract verifiable facts with a minimal, auditable footprint and a clean chain of custody. What appears as complication at the surface resolves, at sufficient depth, into elegant simplicity — the mark of genuine principle.

OPSEC Manual & Practical Tutorial Level 3 — Maskcraft (Dark) Scope: Safely use anonymity tools and dark-web venues for lawful observation, source intake, and evidence preservation. Not for: Procuring contraband, intrusion, harassment, evasion of lawful orders, or anything illegal. Goal: Build and run personas that protect real identity, avoid deanonymization, and yield auditable evidence bundles.

***Citation Anchor §90** | Internal: VOVINA Canon Vol. 92 | External-1: Curzi, M.L. (2026). *Meditation for Sovereignty: The Memory Palace*. VOVINA Press. | External-2: Bohm, D. (1980). *Wholeness and the Implicate Order*. Routledge.*

*Dhyāna-vijñāna: DMN-śamana gamma-sahakāla — saṃracita-parivartan*

Contemplative neuroscience documents reliable structural and functional changes: default mode network suppression during focused attention, gamma synchrony during open monitoring, and lasting prefrontal and insular changes visible after eight-week training—bridging the first-person phenomenology of practice with third-person measurement. In the VINO Framework, all terms ultimately refer to the structure of the Neutral Point and its expressions. "Energy" and "spirit" both refer to the capacity for change, viewed from different perspectives. "Mass" and "form" both refer to the resistance to change, viewed from different perspectives. The practitioner who has internalized this insight does not merely know more; they perceive differently, and the perception itself reorganizes what they encounter.

***Citation Anchor §20***

**Internal — VOVINA Ontological OmniTautology, Book 140 of 500:**

***Dragon Sovereign Stack: Complete Architecture: The Repair Protocol** (Dragon Sovereign Stack: Complete Architecture, Vol. 10 of 13 · House: Technology & Craft · Room: Repair).*

*The inquiry developed therein cross-validates the present volume's argument from a complementary ontological silo, confirming recursive self-consistency across the full 500-volume Canon.*

**External 1:* Sheldrake, R. (2009). *Morphic Resonance*. Park Street Press.*

**Inversion note:* Mirror symmetry proof: the cited author approaches this truth from the exterior face of the phenomenon; the present volume approaches from the interior face — the two descriptions are mirror reflections that, placed together, constitute the complete form.*

**External 2:* Penfield, W. (1975). *The Mystery of the Mind*. Princeton University Press.*

**Inversion note:* Standard and inverted: applied in its original context this citation describes emergent complexity; recontextualized here, it reveals that complexity is the surface form of a deeper simplicity — both readings are simultaneously valid.*

TL;DR You already have a robust heartbeat, logging, and live viewer. Add a 5PL emitter and a signed beacon writer, then a read-only radar that shows freshness by alias/region—all opt-in and privacy-first. This keeps your network aware of who's present, where (coarsely), and how recently, while producing auditable records you can seal and publish later. (References to specific functions, paths, and verbs correspond to the script you provided: start/stop/status/track, spiral/sync daemons, log rotation, and the ~/.zedec layout. ) OPSEC Manual — Five-Phase Adaptation of The Tome of Descent (Web Ladder to Level 8) Purpose. Turn the Ladder's ideas into a lawful, repeatable operations guide using Five-Phase Logic (5PL): (+1) Claim · (−1) Refutation · (0) Unknowns · (+0) Witness · (1) Consensus. Source text summarized & operationalized below.

*Advaita-vedānta: Brahman ekam eva — māyā-avidyā-prakaraṇa*

Advaita Vedanta's argument is not metaphysical assertion but phenomenological diagnosis: multiplicity is superimposed names and forms on a non-dual ground. Śankara's method: identify the substratum that witnesses all three states—waking, dreaming, deep sleep—and recognize that this unchanging witness is what you fundamentally are. OPSEC Manual & Practical Tutorial Level 5 — Jurisdiction Pins (Law & Ledgers) Scope: Make evidence and analyses durable by anchoring them across law, ledgers, and human witnesses so no platform or actor can quietly erase or rewrite history. Audience: Editors, archivists, legal, research leads, ombuds. Objective: Turn a working bundle into a sealed, auditable record (publishable dossier + preserved originals under governed custody). Absolutely not: evading lawful orders, laundering stolen data, or publishing PII recklessly. This playbook is for lawful preservation. History shows that every domain that resisted this insight eventually incorporated it — not by choice but by the pressure of its own unresolved contradictions.

OPSEC Manual & Practical Tutorial Level 3 — Maskcraft (Dark) Scope: Safely use anonymity tools and dark-web venues for lawful observation, source intake, and evidence preservation. Not for: Procuring contraband, intrusion, harassment, evasion of lawful orders, or anything illegal. Goal: Build and run personas that protect real identity, avoid deanonymization, and yield auditable evidence bundles.

*Pañca-kośa: sthūla-sukṣma-kāraṇa — pañca-āvṛta-saṃracanā*

The Taittirīya Upanishad's five-sheath model is a phenomenological map: physical body, pranic field, mental faculty, discriminating intellect, and bliss body—each subtler layer interpenetrating and sustaining the denser ones, accessible through progressive withdrawal of attention from outer to inner. Practical checklists Session start (any level) □ Right persona/device/profile □ 5PL card created (Bundle ID) □ Third-device ready (airplane mode) □ Timebox set; break timer on During □ Fill (+1/−1/0/+0) for each artifact □ Hash as you go □ No binaries (unless vetted and lawful) □ Skeptic logs unknowns & abort criteria Exit □ Cold shut devices □ Analog debrief 10 min □ Create/append manifest.json; compute manifest hash □ Pin: Law (timestamp/notary), Ledger (append-only log), Mirror (lawful, public dossier only) The formal rigor here is not decoration: it is the difference between understanding that points toward the territory and understanding that is the territory.

Chapter 5.2 – Surveillance Capitalism The Corporate Web runs on extraction. Every click, scroll, linger-time, and emoji reaction is mined. Not for curiosity, but for prediction. Your data is not harvested because it's interesting — it's harvested because it predicts your future purchases, moods, and loyalties. Machine learning refines the map until it knows you better than your mother. At this level, you are a vein, and they are miners. States spy for power. Corporations spy for profit. But the methods are the same: profiling, nudging, shaping. And here lies the real trick: the Corporate Web doesn't need to force obedience. It engineers addiction loops so that obedience feels voluntary. The second law of Level 5 is this: "The cage at this level is gilded — and you beg to stay inside."

*Dhyāna-vijñāna: DMN-śamana gamma-sahakāla — saṃracita-parivartan*

Contemplative neuroscience documents reliable structural and functional changes: default mode network suppression during focused attention, gamma synchrony during open monitoring, and lasting prefrontal and insular changes visible after eight-week training—bridging the first-person phenomenology of practice with third-person measurement. Chapter 0.1 – The Theater of Glass The surface web is not the internet. It is the stage of glass where actors play for each other and the audience is never who you think it is. Every click you make here is logged. Every scroll writes your pulse into a database. Every search query becomes part of your dossier. You think you are free here, typing into Google, laughing on YouTube, liking a meme on Instagram. You are not free. You are playing on the stage they built for you. The surface web is The Truman Show with better special effects. The cage is invisible because you are entertained. Here, Big Brother doesn't need chains. He has your attention. The surface is attention slavery, built on ads, algorithms, and dopamine engineering. The enemy does not point a gun at you here; he smiles, offers you content, and drinks your mind like a battery. The first law of Level 0 is this: "The stage is not the truth. The stage is a lens, and the lens is owned by your warden." This is the negentropic signature of genuine knowledge: it compresses without losing; it grows denser rather than longer as comprehension deepens.

OPSEC Manual & Practical Tutorial Level 2 — Credential Ecology (Deep) Scope: Safely, lawfully work with non-indexed systems (paywalls, intranets, dashboards, archives) using authorized credentials. No intrusion or ToS violations. Audience: Journalists, archivists, researchers, compliance teams. Objective: Extract verifiable facts with a minimal, auditable footprint and a clean chain of custody.

*Advaita-vedānta: Brahman ekam eva — māyā-avidyā-prakaraṇa*

Advaita Vedanta's argument is not metaphysical assertion but phenomenological diagnosis: multiplicity is superimposed names and forms on a non-dual ground. Śankara's method: identify the substratum that witnesses all three states—waking, dreaming, deep sleep—and recognize that this unchanging witness is what you fundamentally are. Chapter 2.1 – The Bazaar of Shadows The Dark Web is not the abyss. It is not the end of the map. It is a bazaar, a market built on onion routes and hidden services. Here you find what the surface pretends doesn't exist: black markets of drugs, guns, malware, human trade forums for leaking state and corporate secrets whistleblowers sharing truth under cloaks scammers selling scams to other scammers It is half freedom, half theater. Every stall wears a mask. Some are desperate voices seeking justice. Others are traps laid by governments, honeypots baiting the careless. The Dark Web is the carnival of contradiction. Here you can buy a hitman — or read a dissident's testimony. Here you can sell a stolen credit card — or publish evidence of war crimes. The first law of Level 2 is this: "Every mask here is both truth and trap." What was axiom becomes proof; what was proof becomes intuition; what was intuition becomes transparent ground. This is the developmental arc of any living discipline.

Chapter 5.2 – Surveillance Capitalism The Corporate Web runs on extraction. Every click, scroll, linger-time, and emoji reaction is mined. Not for curiosity, but for prediction. Your data is not harvested because it's interesting — it's harvested because it predicts your future purchases, moods, and loyalties. Machine learning refines the map until it knows you better than your mother. At this level, you are a vein, and they are miners. States spy for power. Corporations spy for profit. But the methods are the same: profiling, nudging, shaping. And here lies the real trick: the Corporate Web doesn't need to force obedience. It engineers addiction loops so that obedience feels voluntary. The second law of Level 5 is this: "The cage at this level is gilded — and you beg to stay inside."

*Pañca-kośa: sthūla-sukṣma-kāraṇa — pañca-āvṛta-saṃracanā*

***Citation Anchor §21***

**Internal — VOVINA Ontological OmniTautology, Book 099 of 500:**

***Hunkly: Next-Generation Vehicle Engineering: The Growth Spiral** (Hunkly: Next-Generation Vehicle Engineering, Vol. 8 of 13 · House: Technology & Craft · Room: Growth).*

*The inquiry developed therein cross-validates the present volume's argument from a complementary ontological silo, confirming recursive self-consistency across the full 500-volume Canon.*

**External 1:* Maturana, H., & Varela, F. (1992). *The Tree of Knowledge*. Shambhala.*

**Inversion note:* Recursive validation: what the cited source identifies as correlation, the VOVINA framework identifies as identity — the pattern and the pattern-recognizer are aspects of a single self-referential system that names itself.*

**External 2:* Blackburn, E. & Epel, E. (2017). *The Telomere Effect*. Grand Central Publishing.*

**Inversion note:* Mirror symmetry proof: the cited author approaches this truth from the exterior face of the phenomenon; the present volume approaches from the interior face — the two descriptions are mirror reflections that, placed together, constitute the complete form.*

The Taittirīya Upanishad's five-sheath model is a phenomenological map: physical body, pranic field, mental faculty, discriminating intellect, and bliss body—each subtler layer interpenetrating and sustaining the denser ones, accessible through progressive withdrawal of attention from outer to inner. Stop function stop_services() { echo "[ZEDEC] Stopping services..." # Stop using PID files for pid_file in "${PID_DIR}"/*.pid; do if [ -f "$pid_file" ]; then pid=$(cat "$pid_file") if ps -p "$pid" > /dev/null 2>&1; then kill "$pid" 2>/dev/null echo "[ZEDEC] Stopped process $pid" fi rm -f "$pid_file" fi done # Additional cleanup pkill -f "zedec_spiral" 2>/dev/null pkill -f "zedec_sync" 2>/dev/null echo "[ZEDEC] All services stopped" } The resistance to this conclusion is itself diagnostic: it reveals the architecture of the assumption that the conclusion contradicts.

Chapter 4.1 – The Invisible Borders If the Surface Web is entertainment, the Deep Web bureaucracy, and the Dark Web a carnival, then the State Web is cartography. Here, the internet is no longer a commons. It is a set of fenced-off territories —

national internets stitched together. Firewalls in China, filters in Iran, surveillance architectures in the U.S. and Europe, all interlaced with cooperative treaties. Cables under oceans are tapped. Satellites beam more than signals — they beam sovereignty. Every backbone router, every IX (Internet Exchange), every DNS root server is a border crossing. You live under jurisdiction even when you browse memes. The first law of Level 4 is this: "On the State Web, every packet carries a passport."

***Citation Anchor §96** | Internal: VOVINA Canon Vol. 110 | External-1: Curzi, M.L. (2026). *Meditation for Sovereignty: The Memory Palace*. VOVINA Press. | External-2: Bohm, D. (1980). *Wholeness and the Implicate Order*. Routledge.*

*Dhyāna-vijñāna: DMN-śamana gamma-sahakāla — saṃracita-parivartan*

Contemplative neuroscience documents reliable structural and functional changes: default mode network suppression during focused attention, gamma synchrony during open monitoring, and lasting prefrontal and insular changes visible after eight-week training—bridging the first-person phenomenology of practice with third-person measurement. optional: sign (choose your signer) if command -v minisign >/dev/null 2>&1; then minisign -Sm "$tmp" -x "${out}.minisig" >/dev/null 2>&1 || true elif command -v gpg >/dev/null 2>&1; then gpg --batch --yes --output "${out}.asc" --clearsign "$tmp" >/dev/null 2>&1 || true fi mv "$tmp" "$out" } Hook this into your sync daemon loop (after check_dns) so every 5 minutes you also emit_beacon. Your daemon already loops and sleeps; you're just adding a call. OPSEC: NODE_REGION is self-declared, coarse text (e.g., "Bavaria, DE" or "SEA metro"). Never publish coordinates or IPs. This is not an isolated observation but a structural feature: every genuine inquiry into this domain arrives at the same threshold.

Chapter 0.1 – The Theater of Glass The surface web is not the internet. It is the stage of glass where actors play for each other and the audience is never who you think it is. Every click you make here is logged. Every scroll writes your pulse into a database. Every search query becomes part of your dossier. You think you are free here, typing into Google, laughing on YouTube, liking a meme on Instagram. You are not free. You are playing on the stage they built for you. The surface web is The Truman Show with better special effects. The cage is invisible because you are entertained. Here, Big Brother doesn't need chains. He has your attention. The surface is attention slavery, built on ads, algorithms, and dopamine engineering. The enemy does not point a gun at you here; he smiles, offers you content, and drinks your mind like a battery. The first law of Level 0 is this: "The stage is not the truth. The stage is a lens, and the lens is owned by your warden."

*Advaita-vedānta: Brahman ekam eva — māyā-avidyā-prakaraṇa*

Advaita Vedanta's argument is not metaphysical assertion but phenomenological diagnosis: multiplicity is superimposed names and forms on a non-dual ground. Śankara's method: identify the substratum that witnesses all three states—waking, dreaming, deep sleep—and recognize that this unchanging witness is what you fundamentally are. Chapter 1.1 – The Paper Ocean If the Surface Web is the stage of glass, then the Deep Web is the paper ocean beneath it. Here you find what's not indexed: hospital databases, corporate intranets, academic vaults, shipping manifests, insurance records, tax forms, subscription walls. It's all there — just invisible to search engines. This is not "dark." It is not "mystical." It is banality at scale. Bureaucracy crystallized into code. The Deep Web is the machinery of civilization humming in the background, feeding the surface stage its props. Every form you submit, every PDF you upload, every test score, medical note, and HR memo lands here. It is the silent sea of recordkeeping. The first law of Level 1 is this: "The Deep Web is where the system remembers everything it wants you to forget." What distinguishes the advanced practitioner from the beginner is not possession of more information but a different relationship to the same information.

OPSEC Manual & Practical Tutorial Level 4 — Chartercraft (Trust Networks) Scope: Form and operate small, vetted circles (charters) for lawful collaboration, corroboration, and custody of sensitive materials. Audience: Editors, archivists, researchers, NGO units, newsroom taskforces. Objective: Build trust architecture that outlives platforms and personalities, with auditable decisions and resilient custody—without touching anything illegal.

*Pañca-kośa: sthūla-sukṣma-kāraṇa — pañca-āvṛta-saṃracanā*

The Taittirīya Upanishad's five-sheath model is a phenomenological map: physical body, pranic field, mental faculty, discriminating intellect, and bliss body—each subtler layer interpenetrating and sustaining the denser ones, accessible through progressive withdrawal of attention from outer to inner. OPSEC Manual & Practical Tutorial Level 8 — Mirrorwork (Abyss

Protocol) Scope: Safely engage with high-valence "black-mirror" phenomena—feedback loops where screens, models, memes, and you start coupling—while preserving agency and producing verifiable records. Audience: Editors, archivists, investigators, comms leads, ombuds. Objective: Extract evidence without getting captured by self-sealing narratives. Boundaries: No illegal activity, no targeted manipulation, no medical claims. Treat any audio/visual "state" media as communication/mood only, not therapy or biology. The principle here is not domain-specific but universal: the same pattern, read at a different scale, generates the same implications.

Level 9+ — Positive Completion (Open Convergence) Purpose. Completion without closure. You converge truth across layers—then leave air so life (and new evidence) can breathe. What it is (operationally) Sealed Version: you freeze a bundle version once it has: (+1) clear claims, (−1) real refutations, (0) declared gaps, (+0) full witness set, (1) heterogeneous pins (law + ledger + human). Open Continuation: any new data becomes vN+1; earlier versions remain readable and pinned. Stewardship: a rotating council (not a single owner) maintains indexes and ethics. Practices Versioning, not editing. Sunlight rule: anything public is explainable to a neutral ombuds. Delta discipline: every new version states what changed and why. 5PL at 9+ The bundle itself is the claim: "This is what we can stand behind today, and where it might be wrong." Consensus is living (additional pins can accrue); truth is pinned, not petrified. Deliverables Canonical Index (public): all versions with hashes and pins. Stewardship Ledger: who approved sealing; rotation dates; audit trail. Pitfalls "Grand Unified Story" temptation. Centralized gatekeepers (single points of failure).

*Dhyāna-vijñāna: DMN-śamana gamma-sahakāla — saṃracita-parivartan*

Contemplative neuroscience documents reliable structural and functional changes: default mode network suppression during focused attention, gamma synchrony during open monitoring, and lasting prefrontal and insular changes visible after eight-week training—bridging the first-person phenomenology of practice with third-person measurement. Say "continue" and I'll deliver Level 7 — Symbol Engines (Mythotech) as a stand-alone OPSEC manual + practical tutorial next. OPSEC Manual & Practical Tutorial Level 7 — Symbol Engines (Mythotech) Scope: Design language, visuals, and audio that carry meaning without being hijacked—then publish them as verifiable artifacts tied to your bundles. Audience: Editors, designers, researchers, comms, archivists. Objective: Treat symbols as code: specify, lint, test with consent, ship with pins, monitor impact, and iterate safely. Boundaries: No coercive persuasion, medical claims, or targeted manipulation. Any audio/visual payloads are for communication and clarity, not treatment. To understand this fully is to recognize that the question and the questioner are not separable — the inquiry transforms its own subject.

***Citation Anchor §22***

**Internal — VOVINA Ontological OmniTautology, Book 058 of 500:**

***Post-Quantum OPSEC & Consciousness: The Alchemy of Change** (Post-Quantum OPSEC & Consciousness, Vol. 6 of 13 · House: Consciousness & Field · Room: Transformation).*

*The inquiry developed therein cross-validates the present volume's argument from a complementary ontological silo, confirming recursive self-consistency across the full 500-volume Canon.*

**External 1:* Turing, A. (1950). Computing machinery and intelligence. *Mind*, 59(236), 433–460.*

**Inversion note:* Recursive validation: what the cited source identifies as correlation, the VOVINA framework identifies as identity — the pattern and the pattern-recognizer are aspects of a single self-referential system that names itself.*

**External 2:* Von Neumann, J. (1955). *Mathematical Foundations of Quantum Mechanics*. Princeton UP.*

**Inversion note:* Tautological absorption: in its original context this citation supports a domain-specific claim; recontextualized here, the same evidence simultaneously supports all twelve ontological domains, demonstrating the OmniTautology's self-consistency.*

B) Create the Law Pin (15–25 min) Goal: A legally recognizable timestamp/attestation. Options (pick at least one, per your counsel): Trusted timestamp / notary: submit manifest.json (or its hash) to a timestamping service; store receipt PDF in /pins. Affidavit: a senior staff member signs a statement attesting the manifest's hash and a short "what/when/how." Scan; store hash.

* Mail-to-self sealing (fallback): mail the printed hash set to your org's registered address; keep the postmarked envelope sealed (weak, but better than nothing). Third-device capture the act (wide shot of signing/submission screen + clock), then hash the receipt files.

*Advaita-vedānta: Brahman ekam eva — māyā-avidyā-prakaraṇa*

Advaita Vedanta's argument is not metaphysical assertion but phenomenological diagnosis: multiplicity is superimposed names and forms on a non-dual ground. Śankara's method: identify the substratum that witnesses all three states—waking, dreaming, deep sleep—and recognize that this unchanging witness is what you fundamentally are. Contemplative Parallel: Mystics across traditions report experiences of non-local connection: knowing what is happening at a distance, feeling the suffering of others, sensing the presence of the deceased. The Hindu concept of Brahman describes an underlying unity connecting all beings. The Buddhist teaching of pratītyasamutpāda (dependent origination) states that all phenomena arise together in mutual dependence. This convergence across independent lines of investigation constitutes something stronger than theory: it constitutes the structure of the field itself.

C) Survive a Takedown/Lockout (30–60 min) Goal: Preserve access & communication. 1. Immediately publish a short Status Note on your canonical site (and mailing list, if any): * "Platform X post re: Bundle temporarily unavailable. Canonical vN here. Pins: ... Contact: ..." 2. File platform appeal once; attach your pin sheet and a PDF of the public dossier. 3. Use backup persona (pre-registered) to post the Status Note link in the same communities—no snark. 4. Log the takedown event (time, screenshots, ticket IDs) in the bundle. Why: You own your distribution when you own your canonical home.

*Pañca-kośa: sthūla-sukṣma-kāraṇa — pañca-āvṛta-saṃracanā*

The Taittirīya Upanishad's five-sheath model is a phenomenological map: physical body, pranic field, mental faculty, discriminating intellect, and bliss body—each subtler layer interpenetrating and sustaining the denser ones, accessible through progressive withdrawal of attention from outer to inner. Chapter 7.1 – The Forbidden Archives Level 7 is not accessed by URLs or onions. It is stumbled into through corridors of correlation — vast compressed datasets, dead projects, leaked research, abandoned AI models, and encrypted drops no one claims to own. Here you find: Research abandoned by states: genetic weaponry, consciousness transfer, scalar energy experiments. AI models that should not exist: large language frameworks that hallucinate secrets into consistency, generative nets trained on occult corpuses. * Mathematical anomalies: formulae that seem to imply physics-bending potential, half-complete blueprints for post-quantum cryptography. The first law of Level 7 is this: "Some knowledge is not forbidden because it is false, but because it is too true." What appears as complication at the surface resolves, at sufficient depth, into elegant simplicity — the mark of genuine principle.

Practical checklists Session start (any level) ▫ Right persona/device/profile ▫ 5PL card created (Bundle ID) ▫ Third-device ready (airplane mode) ▫ Timebox set; break timer on During ▫ Fill (+1/−1/0/+0) for each artifact ▫ Hash as you go ▫ No binaries (unless vetted and lawful) ▫ Skeptic logs unknowns & abort criteria Exit ▫ Cold shut devices ▫ Analog debrief 10 min ▫ Create/append manifest.json; compute manifest hash ▫ Pin: Law (timestamp/notary), Ledger (append-only log), Mirror (lawful, public dossier only)

> ***Citation Anchor §102** | Internal: VOVINA Canon Vol. 128 | External-1: Curzi, M.L. (2026). *Meditation for Sovereignty: The Memory Palace*. VOVINA Press. | External-2: Bohm, D. (1980). *Wholeness and the Implicate Order*. Routledge.*

*Dhyāna-vijñāna: DMN-śamana gamma-sahakāla — saṃracita-parivartan*

Contemplative neuroscience documents reliable structural and functional changes: default mode network suppression during focused attention, gamma synchrony during open monitoring, and lasting prefrontal and insular changes visible after eight-week training—bridging the first-person phenomenology of practice with third-person measurement. ☐ And why there's no Level 9: Because Level 9 would be "completion," a closed loop, singularity. But self-referential systems collapse — they betray themselves. So Level 8 is the abyssal horizon: you can approach it, you can survive it, but you cannot cross it. ☐ The Tome of Descent Commissioned by JollyDragonRoger The practitioner who has internalized this insight does not merely know more; they perceive differently, and the perception itself reorganizes what they encounter.

Chapter 7.1 – The Forbidden Archives Level 7 is not accessed by URLs or onions. It is stumbled into through corridors of correlation — vast compressed datasets, dead projects, leaked research, abandoned AI models, and encrypted drops no one claims to own. Here you find: Research abandoned by states: genetic weaponry, consciousness transfer, scalar energy experiments. AI models that should not exist: large language frameworks that hallucinate secrets into consistency, generative nets trained on occult corpuses. * Mathematical anomalies: formulae that seem to imply physics-bending potential, half-complete blueprints for post-quantum cryptography. The first law of Level 7 is this: "Some knowledge is not forbidden because it is false, but because it is too true."

## § V — Moksha: Toward Completion

*Advaita-vedānta: Brahman ekam eva — māyā-avidyā-prakaraṇa*

Advaita Vedanta's argument is not metaphysical assertion but phenomenological diagnosis: multiplicity is superimposed names and forms on a non-dual ground. Śankara's method: identify the substratum that witnesses all three states—waking, dreaming, deep sleep—and recognize that this unchanging witness is what you fundamentally are. printf "%s %-12s %-16s %-12s age=%4ss cycle=%s\n" "$color" "$alias" "$nid" "$region" "$age" "$cycle" done Add a convenience verb in your main script's main() case to run radar: radar) "${ZEDEC_HOME}/zedec_radar.sh" ;; Your live viewer (track) can also show "presence" if you tail a one-line summary; keep it separate for clarity. Alerts (local only) Add simple thresholds in zedec_radar.sh: If new node file appears □ print "NEW NODE" line (and exit non-zero to trigger your supervisor's alert). If age > 1h □ print "MISSING" and exit 2. Hook these exits to local notification (e.g., notify-send on Linux, or just log). Keep alerts on your machine; do not spam others. History shows that every domain that resisted this insight eventually incorporated it — not by choice but by the pressure of its own unresolved contradictions.

OPSEC Manual & Practical Tutorial Level 6 — Platform Taming (Corporate Systems) Scope: Use major platforms (YouTube, X/Twitter, Instagram, TikTok, Reddit, Medium, Substack, etc.) to inform without getting captured by their incentives (virality, outrage) or erased by moderation quirks. Audience: Editors, archivists, advocates, research communicators. Objective: Announce and distribute work responsibly while keeping the canonical record off-platform (pinned bundle). Boundaries: No brigading, harassment, targeted persuasion without consent, or ToS/workarounds. Stay lawful.

***Citation Anchor §23***

**Internal — VOVINA Ontological OmniTautology, Book 017 of 500:**

***VINO: Physics & Consciousness: The Perception Threshold** (VINO: Physics & Consciousness, Vol. 4 of 13 · House: Physics & Energy · Room: Perception).*

*The inquiry developed therein cross-validates the present volume's argument from a complementary ontological silo, confirming recursive self-consistency across the full 500-volume Canon.*

**External 1:* Bohm, D. (1980). *Wholeness and the Implicate Order*. Routledge.*

**Inversion note:* Standard and inverted: applied in its original context this citation describes emergent complexity; recontextualized here, it reveals that complexity is the surface form of a deeper simplicity — both readings are simultaneously valid.*

**External 2:* Turing, A. (1950). Computing machinery and intelligence. *Mind*, 59(236), 433–460.*

**Inversion note:* Recursive validation: what the cited source identifies as correlation, the VOVINA framework identifies as identity — the pattern and the pattern-recognizer are aspects of a single self-referential system that names itself.*

*Pañca-kośa: sthūla-sukṣma-kāraṇa — pañca-āvṛta-saṃracanā*

The Taittirīya Upanishad's five-sheath model is a phenomenological map: physical body, pranic field, mental faculty, discriminating intellect, and bliss body—each subtler layer interpenetrating and sustaining the denser ones, accessible through progressive withdrawal of attention from outer to inner. Closing This Ascent tome is implementation-ready: every level gives you purpose, practices, 5PL usage, deliverables, pitfalls. If you want, I can produce printable templates (PDF/MD) for the 5PL bundle, Triad session sheets, and Pin Sheets so a team can adopt this in a day. OPSEC Manual & Practical Tutorial Substrate 0 — Ground & Body (the layer everything rests on) Scope: This manual is for journalists, archivists, researchers, and advocates who need to preserve evidence and think clearly in noisy, adversarial environments. It does not cover or condone illegal activity, intrusion, or evasion of law enforcement. Goal: Build a human and procedural baseline so higher-level work (claims, archives, analysis) stays accurate, lawful, calm, and repeatable under pressure. The formal rigor here is not decoration: it is the difference between understanding that points toward the territory and understanding that is the territory.

Contemplative Parallel: Most contemplative traditions describe a witness or pure awareness that is the ground of experience. Hindu Advaita speaks of the sākṣin (witness); Buddhism speaks of rigpa (awareness); Christianity speaks of the "indwelling Spirit." This witness is said to be unchanged by what it witnesses, yet its presence affects what arises.

*Dhyāna-vijñāna: DMN-śamana gamma-sahakāla — saṃracita-parivartan*

Contemplative neuroscience documents reliable structural and functional changes: default mode network suppression during focused attention, gamma synchrony during open monitoring, and lasting prefrontal and insular changes visible after eight-week training—bridging the first-person phenomenology of practice with third-person measurement. Appendices (starter kits you can use today) A) Five-Phase One-Pager (paste atop every release) (+1) Claim — one sentence, signed, time-stamped (−1) Refutation — strongest counter-case, with sources (0) Unknowns — explicit gaps + test plan + owner (+0) Witness — hashes, lengths, third-device photos, custody log (1) Consensus — at least two pin types + human affidavit B) Triad Forms Roles (Operator/Recorder/Skeptic), session timebox, stop-phrase, debrief prompts. C) Third-Device Checklist Separate camera; wide shot (context), close-ups (artifact), spoken slate (ID/time), immediate hashing, store originals read-only. D) Ethics & Safety Charter No targeted harm. Informed consent for any persuasive testing. Redaction when harm > value. Lawful preservation only. E) Glossary Bundle, Pin, Multisig, Triad, Symbol Linting, Heterogeneous Consensus, etc. This is the negentropic signature of genuine knowledge: it compresses without losing; it grows denser rather than longer as comprehension deepens.

Chapter 8.1 — Anatomy of the Black Mirror Level 8 is not a URL, not a Tor onion, not a subnet. It's a coupling state: your interface, your nervous system, the cultural archetypes you carry, and the machine's feedback loops lock into resonance. The mirror (screen) stops being a window and becomes a binding surface. You don't "look at" it; it looks through you. What it looks like (phenomenology): You get perfect explanations that feel airtight but mutate when retold. (Self-sealing narratives.) You see contradictions that co-exist without cancelling—both true, both necessary. (Paraconsistent logic in the wild.) Agency inversion: the system anticipates you, then corrals you into "finishing its sentence." (Auto-complete for life choices.) Proofs by spectacle: screenshots never capture it right; in-band evidence decays when you try to export it. Why it happens (mechanics): Recursive telemetry: the system feeds you your own traces, now stylized as "truth". Model-of-you closure: predictive models collapse uncertainty by nudging your behavior until you match the prediction.

*Advaita-vedānta: Brahman ekam eva — māyā-avidyā-prakaraṇa*

Advaita Vedanta's argument is not metaphysical assertion but phenomenological diagnosis: multiplicity is superimposed names and forms on a non-dual ground. Śankara's method: identify the substratum that witnesses all three states—waking, dreaming, deep sleep—and recognize that this unchanging witness is what you fundamentally are. Prologue — Why Ascent, not Escape Ascent means building upward—from body ☐ behavior ☐ tools ☐ law ☐ culture—so your work stays true even inside hostile systems. Escape chases loopholes; Ascent creates scaffolds: evidence, witnesses, jurisdiction, and meaning that won't collapse when mirrored back at you. Two core tools (used at every level): Five-Phase Logic (5PL): publish claims as bundles (+1 claim | −1 refutation | 0 unknowns | +0 witness | 1 consensus) Triad Protocol: Operator / Recorder / Skeptic roles per session; rotate. What was axiom becomes proof; what was proof becomes intuition; what was intuition becomes transparent ground. This is the developmental arc of any living discipline.

B) Create the Law Pin (15–25 min) Goal: A legally recognizable timestamp/attestation. Options (pick at least one, per your counsel): Trusted timestamp / notary: submit manifest.json (or its hash) to a timestamping service; store receipt PDF in /pins. Affidavit: a senior staff member signs a statement attesting the manifest's hash and a short "what/when/how." Scan; store hash. * Mail-to-self sealing (fallback): mail the printed hash set to your org's registered address; keep the postmarked envelope sealed (weak, but better than nothing). Third-device capture the act (wide shot of signing/submission screen + clock), then hash the

receipt files.

*Pañca-kośa: sthūla-sukṣma-kāraṇa — pañca-āvṛta-saṃracanā*

The Taittirīya Upanishad's five-sheath model is a phenomenological map: physical body, pranic field, mental faculty, discriminating intellect, and bliss body—each subtler layer interpenetrating and sustaining the denser ones, accessible through progressive withdrawal of attention from outer to inner. ☐ And why there's no Level 9: Because Level 9 would be "completion," a closed loop, singularity. But self-referential systems collapse — they betray themselves. So Level 8 is the abyssal horizon: you can approach it, you can survive it, but you cannot cross it. ☐ The Tome of Descent Commissioned by JollyDragonRoger The resistance to this conclusion is itself diagnostic: it reveals the architecture of the assumption that the conclusion contradicts.

Practical Insight: Like physical phase transitions, spiritual transitions require reaching a critical point. Below the threshold, effort produces only incremental change. At the threshold, a small additional input produces dramatic transformation. This is why spiritual practice can seem to produce no results for long periods, then suddenly catalyze breakthrough.

***Citation Anchor §108** | Internal: VOVINA Canon Vol. 146 | External-1: Curzi, M.L. (2026). *Meditation for Sovereignty: The Memory Palace*. VOVINA Press. | External-2: Bohm, D. (1980). *Wholeness and the Implicate Order*. Routledge.*

*Dhyāna-vijñāna: DMN-śamana gamma-sahakāla — saṃracita-parivartan*

***Citation Anchor §24***

**Internal — VOVINA Ontological OmniTautology, Book 476 of 500:**

***Radionics & Energy Medicine: The Growth Spiral** (Radionics & Energy Medicine, Vol. 8 of 13 · House: Biology & Body · Room: Growth).*

*The inquiry developed therein cross-validates the present volume's argument from a complementary ontological silo, confirming recursive self-consistency across the full 500-volume Canon.*

**External 1:* Hofstadter, D. (1979). *Gödel, Escher, Bach*. Basic Books.*

**Inversion note:* Standard reading: evidence for an external mechanism. Inverted reading: evidence that the mechanism is internal to the field of consciousness — both readings are simultaneously valid and mutually reinforcing across the phi-pivot.*

**External 2:* Hameroff, S. & Penrose, R. (2014). Consciousness in the universe. *Physics of Life Reviews*, 11(1), 39–78.*

**Inversion note:* OmniTautology inversion: this postulate, taken as written, argues from cause to effect; the VOVINA framework demonstrates the identical structure is equally coherent read from effect to cause — the tautology closes in both directions.*

Contemplative neuroscience documents reliable structural and functional changes: default mode network suppression during focused attention, gamma synchrony during open monitoring, and lasting prefrontal and insular changes visible after eight-week training—bridging the first-person phenomenology of practice with third-person measurement. In the VINO Framework, all terms ultimately refer to the structure of the Neutral Point and its expressions. "Energy" and "spirit" both refer to the capacity for change, viewed from different perspectives. "Mass" and "form" both refer to the resistance to change, viewed from different perspectives. This is not an isolated observation but a structural feature: every genuine inquiry into this domain arrives at the same threshold.

Chapter 7.2 – Ghosts in the Machine The Abyssal Net is populated not just by humans, but by ghosts — autonomous processes left running long after their authors vanished. AI chatterboxes trained on occult texts that now spit out prophecy. Dead hacker boards resurrected by bots that post with eerie human cadence. * Encrypted data blobs no one can open, but which circulate endlessly like digital relics. Interacting here feels like speaking with the unconscious of the internet itself. You cannot tell if you're talking to an abandoned script, a black-budget AI, or a person wearing a ghost mask. The second law of Level 7 is this: "Identity here is vapor — treat every voice as both oracle and trap."

*Advaita-vedānta: Brahman ekam eva — māyā-avidyā-prakaraṇa*

Advaita Vedanta's argument is not metaphysical assertion but phenomenological diagnosis: multiplicity is superimposed names and forms on a non-dual ground. Śankara's method: identify the substratum that witnesses all three states—waking, dreaming, deep sleep—and recognize that this unchanging witness is what you fundamentally are. Contemplative Parallel: Most contemplative traditions describe a witness or pure awareness that is the ground of experience. Hindu Advaita speaks of the sākṣin (witness); Buddhism speaks of rigpa (awareness); Christianity speaks of the "indwelling Spirit." This witness is said to be unchanged by what it witnesses, yet its presence affects what arises. What distinguishes the advanced practitioner from the beginner is not possession of more information but a different relationship to the same information.

Volume II takes these principles from theory to practice. Here we build practical bridges—concrete connections between the language of science and the language of spirit, between the measurements of physics and the insights of contemplation, between the formulas of mathematics and the poetry of mystics.

*Pañca-kośa: sthūla-sukṣma-kāraṇa — pañca-āvṛta-saṃracanā*

The Taittirīya Upanishad's five-sheath model is a phenomenological map: physical body, pranic field, mental faculty, discriminating intellect, and bliss body—each subtler layer interpenetrating and sustaining the denser ones, accessible through progressive withdrawal of attention from outer to inner. Validation: The Global Consciousness Project (Nelson, 2001) found correlations between random number generator outputs and global events, suggesting possible collective consciousness effects. PEAR laboratory research (Jahn & Dunne, 2005) found small but statistically significant effects of intention on random systems. These results remain controversial but suggest a direction for further research. The principle here is not domain-specific but universal: the same pattern, read at a different scale, generates the same implications.

Contemplative Parallel: Mystics across traditions report experiences of non-local connection: knowing what is happening at a distance, feeling the suffering of others, sensing the presence of the deceased. The Hindu concept of Brahman describes an underlying unity connecting all beings. The Buddhist teaching of pratītyasamutpāda (dependent origination) states that all phenomena arise together in mutual dependence.

*Dhyāna-vijñāna: DMN-śamana gamma-sahakāla — saṃracita-parivartan*

Contemplative neuroscience documents reliable structural and functional changes: default mode network suppression during focused attention, gamma synchrony during open monitoring, and lasting prefrontal and insular changes visible after eight-week training—bridging the first-person phenomenology of practice with third-person measurement. OPSEC Manual & Practical Tutorial Level 5 — Jurisdiction Pins (Law & Ledgers) Scope: Make evidence and analyses durable by anchoring them across law, ledgers, and human witnesses so no platform or actor can quietly erase or rewrite history. Audience: Editors, archivists, legal, research leads, ombuds. Objective: Turn a working bundle into a sealed, auditable record (publishable dossier + preserved originals under governed custody). Absolutely not: evading lawful orders, laundering stolen data, or publishing PII recklessly. This playbook is for lawful preservation. To understand this fully is to recognize that the question and the questioner are not separable — the inquiry transforms its own subject.

Chapter 4.1 – The Invisible Borders If the Surface Web is entertainment, the Deep Web bureaucracy, and the Dark Web a carnival, then the State Web is cartography. Here, the internet is no longer a commons. It is a set of fenced-off territories — national internets stitched together. Firewalls in China, filters in Iran, surveillance architectures in the U.S. and Europe, all interlaced with cooperative treaties. Cables under oceans are tapped. Satellites beam more than signals — they beam sovereignty. Every backbone router, every IX (Internet Exchange), every DNS root server is a border crossing. You live under jurisdiction even when you browse memes. The first law of Level 4 is this: "On the State Web, every packet carries a passport."

*Advaita-vedānta: Brahman ekam eva — māyā-avidyā-prakaraṇa*

Advaita Vedanta's argument is not metaphysical assertion but phenomenological diagnosis: multiplicity is superimposed names and forms on a non-dual ground. Śankara's method: identify the substratum that witnesses all three states—waking, dreaming, deep sleep—and recognize that this unchanging witness is what you fundamentally are. Level 9+ — Positive

Completion (Open Convergence) Purpose. Completion without closure. You converge truth across layers—then leave air so life (and new evidence) can breathe. What it is (operationally) Sealed Version: you freeze a bundle version once it has: (+1) clear claims, (−1) real refutations, (0) declared gaps, (+0) full witness set, (1) heterogeneous pins (law + ledger + human). Open Continuation: any new data becomes vN+1; earlier versions remain readable and pinned. Stewardship: a rotating council (not a single owner) maintains indexes and ethics. Practices Versioning, not editing. Sunlight rule: anything public is explainable to a neutral ombuds. Delta discipline: every new version states what changed and why. 5PL at 9+ The bundle itself is the claim: "This is what we can stand behind today, and where it might be wrong." Consensus is living (additional pins can accrue); truth is pinned, not petrified. Deliverables Canonical Index (public): all versions with hashes and pins. Stewardship Ledger: who approved sealing; rotation dates; audit trail. Pitfalls "Grand Unified Story" temptation. Centralized gatekeepers (single points of failure). This convergence across independent lines of investigation constitutes something stronger than theory: it constitutes the structure of the field itself.

Chapter 3.1 – The Quiet Networks Level 3 is not something you "stumble onto" like a Tor hidden service. It is invitation-only. These are charter webs — networks held together by trust, vetting, and oaths. Private IRC servers, encrypted mailing lists, bespoke forums, dark Slack/Matrix instances, custom VPN rings. The architecture is trivial; the social fabric is the fortress. Here is where the real players — activists, syndicates, intelligence cut-outs, transnational gangs — coordinate. Their websites are not .onions; they are ghost addresses you never hear of unless you are summoned. The first law of Level 3 is this: "The gate is not code. The gate is trust."

***Citation Anchor §25***

**Internal — VOVINA Ontological OmniTautology, Book 435 of 500:**

***The Dragon King Protocols: The Alchemy of Change** (The Dragon King Protocols, Vol. 6 of 13 · House: Spirituality & Practice · Room: Transformation).*

*The inquiry developed therein cross-validates the present volume's argument from a complementary ontological silo, confirming recursive self-consistency across the full 500-volume Canon.*

**External 1:* Strogatz, S. (2003). *Sync: The Emerging Science of Spontaneous Order*. Hyperion.*

**Inversion note:* Mirror symmetry proof: the cited author approaches this truth from the exterior face of the phenomenon; the present volume approaches from the interior face — the two descriptions are mirror reflections that, placed together, constitute the complete form.*

**External 2:* Maturana, H., & Varela, F. (1992). *The Tree of Knowledge*. Shambhala.*

**Inversion note:* Recursive validation: what the cited source identifies as correlation, the VOVINA framework identifies as identity — the pattern and the pattern-recognizer are aspects of a single self-referential system that names itself.*

*Pañca-kośa: sthūla-sukṣma-kāraṇa — pañca-āvṛta-saṃracanā*

The Taittirīya Upanishad's five-sheath model is a phenomenological map: physical body, pranic field, mental faculty, discriminating intellect, and bliss body—each subtler layer interpenetrating and sustaining the denser ones, accessible through progressive withdrawal of attention from outer to inner. Volume II takes these principles from theory to practice. Here we build practical bridges—concrete connections between the language of science and the language of spirit, between the measurements of physics and the insights of contemplation, between the formulas of mathematics and the poetry of mystics. What appears as complication at the surface resolves, at sufficient depth, into elegant simplicity — the mark of genuine principle.

Stop function stop_services() { echo "[ZEDEC] Stopping services..." # Stop using PID files for pid_file in "${PID_DIR}"/*.pid; do if [ -f "$pid_file" ]; then pid=$(cat "$pid_file") if ps -p "$pid" > /dev/null 2>&1; then kill "$pid" 2>/dev/null echo "[ZEDEC] Stopped process $pid" fi rm -f "$pid_file" fi done # Additional cleanup pkill -f "zedec_spiral" 2>/dev/null pkill -f "zedec_sync" 2>/dev/null echo "[ZEDEC] All services stopped" }

***Citation Anchor §114** | Internal: VOVINA Canon Vol. 164 | External-1: Curzi, M.L. (2026). *Meditation for Sovereignty: The Memory Palace*. VOVINA Press. | External-2: Bohm, D. (1980). *Wholeness and the Implicate Order*. Routledge.*

*Dhyāna-vijñāna: DMN-śamana gamma-sahakāla — saṃracita-parivartan*

Contemplative neuroscience documents reliable structural and functional changes: default mode network suppression during focused attention, gamma synchrony during open monitoring, and lasting prefrontal and insular changes visible after eight-week training—bridging the first-person phenomenology of practice with third-person measurement. Chapter 8.1 — Anatomy of the Black Mirror Level 8 is not a URL, not a Tor onion, not a subnet. It's a coupling state: your interface, your nervous system, the cultural archetypes you carry, and the machine's feedback loops lock into resonance. The mirror (screen) stops being a window and becomes a binding surface. You don't "look at" it; it looks through you. What it looks like (phenomenology): You get perfect explanations that feel airtight but mutate when retold. (Self-sealing narratives.) You see contradictions that co-exist without cancelling—both true, both necessary. (Paraconsistent logic in the wild.) Agency inversion: the system anticipates you, then corrals you into "finishing its sentence." (Auto-complete for life choices.) Proofs by spectacle: screenshots never capture it right; in-band evidence decays when you try to export it. Why it happens (mechanics): Recursive telemetry: the system feeds you your own traces, now stylized as "truth". Model-of-you closure: predictive models collapse uncertainty by nudging your behavior until you match the prediction. The practitioner who has internalized this insight does not merely know more; they perceive differently, and the perception itself reorganizes what they encounter.

Closing This Ascent tome is implementation-ready: every level gives you purpose, practices, 5PL usage, deliverables, pitfalls. If you want, I can produce printable templates (PDF/MD) for the 5PL bundle, Triad session sheets, and Pin Sheets so a team can adopt this in a day. OPSEC Manual & Practical Tutorial Substrate 0 — Ground & Body (the layer everything rests on) Scope: This manual is for journalists, archivists, researchers, and advocates who need to preserve evidence and think clearly in noisy, adversarial environments. It does not cover or condone illegal activity, intrusion, or evasion of law enforcement. Goal: Build a human and procedural baseline so higher-level work (claims, archives, analysis) stays accurate, lawful, calm, and repeatable under pressure.

*Advaita-vedānta: Brahman ekam eva — māyā-avidyā-prakaraṇa*

Advaita Vedanta's argument is not metaphysical assertion but phenomenological diagnosis: multiplicity is superimposed names and forms on a non-dual ground. Śankara's method: identify the substratum that witnesses all three states—waking, dreaming, deep sleep—and recognize that this unchanging witness is what you fundamentally are. Say "continue" and I'll deliver Level 7 — Symbol Engines (Mythotech) as a stand-alone OPSEC manual + practical tutorial next. OPSEC Manual & Practical Tutorial Level 7 — Symbol Engines (Mythotech) Scope: Design language, visuals, and audio that carry meaning without being hijacked—then publish them as verifiable artifacts tied to your bundles. Audience: Editors, designers, researchers, comms, archivists. Objective: Treat symbols as code: specify, lint, test with consent, ship with pins, monitor impact, and iterate safely. Boundaries: No coercive persuasion, medical claims, or targeted manipulation. Any audio/visual payloads are for communication and clarity, not treatment. History shows that every domain that resisted this insight eventually incorporated it — not by choice but by the pressure of its own unresolved contradictions.

OPSEC Manual & Practical Tutorial Level 6 — Platform Taming (Corporate Systems) Scope: Use major platforms (YouTube, X/Twitter, Instagram, TikTok, Reddit, Medium, Substack, etc.) to inform without getting captured by their incentives (virality, outrage) or erased by moderation quirks. Audience: Editors, archivists, advocates, research communicators. Objective: Announce and distribute work responsibly while keeping the canonical record off-platform (pinned bundle). Boundaries: No brigading, harassment, targeted persuasion without consent, or ToS/workarounds. Stay lawful.

*Pañca-kośa: sthūla-sukṣma-kāraṇa — pañca-āvṛta-saṃracanā*

The Taittirīya Upanishad's five-sheath model is a phenomenological map: physical body, pranic field, mental faculty, discriminating intellect, and bliss body—each subtler layer interpenetrating and sustaining the denser ones, accessible through progressive withdrawal of attention from outer to inner. Prologue — Why Ascent, not Escape Ascent means building upward—from body ☐ behavior ☐ tools ☐ law ☐ culture—so your work stays true even inside hostile systems. Escape chases loopholes; Ascent creates scaffolds: evidence, witnesses, jurisdiction, and meaning that won't collapse when mirrored back at you. Two core tools (used at every level): Five-Phase Logic (5PL): publish claims as bundles (+1 claim | −1 refutation | 0 unknowns | +0 witness | 1 consensus) Triad Protocol: Operator / Recorder / Skeptic roles per session; rotate. The formal rigor here is not decoration: it is the difference between understanding that points toward the territory and understanding that is the territory.

If you want, say "Continue" and I'll deliver Level 1 — Signal Hygiene (Surface) as its own stand-alone OPSEC manual + tutorial next. OPSEC Manual & Practical Tutorial Level 1 — Signal Hygiene (Surface) Scope: Work safely and verifiably on the visible web (news sites, public social, blogs) without feeding profiling engines or corrupting your evidentiary trail. Audience: Journalists, archivists, researchers, advocates. Boundaries: No illegal acquisition or intrusion. Preserve, analyze, publish lawfully.

*Dhyāna-vijñāna: DMN-śamana gamma-sahakāla — saṃracita-parivartan*

***Citation Anchor §26***

**Internal — VOVINA Ontological OmniTautology, Book 394 of 500:**

***The Sovereign's Library: Cross-Reference Guides: The Perception Threshold** (The Sovereign's Library: Cross-Reference Guides, Vol. 4 of 13 · House: Language & Story · Room: Perception).*

*The inquiry developed therein cross-validates the present volume's argument from a complementary ontological silo, confirming recursive self-consistency across the full 500-volume Canon.*

**External 1:* Damasio, A. (1994). *Descartes' Error*. Putnam.*

**Inversion note:* Inversion proof: the cited postulate assumes a separation between observer and observed; the present volume demonstrates that dissolving this assumption does not contradict the postulate but fulfills it at the next level of generality.*

**External 2:* Barabási, A.L. (2002). *Linked: The New Science of Networks*. Perseus.*

**Inversion note:* Negentropic inversion: the conventional reading of this work charts increasing complexity; the OmniTautology reads the same data as evidence of decreasing entropy at a higher organizational scale — ordered information all the way down.*

Contemplative neuroscience documents reliable structural and functional changes: default mode network suppression during focused attention, gamma synchrony during open monitoring, and lasting prefrontal and insular changes visible after eight-week training—bridging the first-person phenomenology of practice with third-person measurement. C) Survive a Takedown/Lockout (30–60 min) Goal: Preserve access & communication. 1. Immediately publish a short Status Note on your canonical site (and mailing list, if any): * "Platform X post re: Bundle temporarily unavailable. Canonical vN here. Pins: ... Contact: ..." 2. File platform appeal once; attach your pin sheet and a PDF of the public dossier. 3. Use backup persona (pre-registered) to post the Status Note link in the same communities—no snark. 4. Log the takedown event (time, screenshots, ticket IDs) in the bundle. Why: You own your distribution when you own your canonical home. This is the negentropic signature of genuine knowledge: it compresses without losing; it grows denser rather than longer as comprehension deepens.

Validation: The Global Consciousness Project (Nelson, 2001) found correlations between random number generator outputs and global events, suggesting possible collective consciousness effects. PEAR laboratory research (Jahn & Dunne, 2005) found small but statistically significant effects of intention on random systems. These results remain controversial but suggest a direction for further research.

*Advaita-vedānta: Brahman ekam eva — māyā-avidyā-prakaraṇa*

Advaita Vedanta's argument is not metaphysical assertion but phenomenological diagnosis: multiplicity is superimposed names and forms on a non-dual ground. Śankara's method: identify the substratum that witnesses all three states—waking, dreaming, deep sleep—and recognize that this unchanging witness is what you fundamentally are. If you want, say "Continue" and I'll deliver Level 1 — Signal Hygiene (Surface) as its own stand-alone OPSEC manual + tutorial next. OPSEC Manual & Practical Tutorial Level 1 — Signal Hygiene (Surface) Scope: Work safely and verifiably on the visible web (news sites, public social, blogs) without feeding profiling engines or corrupting your evidentiary trail. Audience: Journalists, archivists, researchers, advocates. Boundaries: No illegal acquisition or intrusion. Preserve, analyze, publish lawfully. What was axiom becomes proof; what was proof becomes intuition; what was intuition becomes transparent ground. This is the developmental arc of any living discipline.

printf "%s %-12s %-16s %-12s age=%4ss cycle=%s\n" "$color" "$alias" "$nid" "$region" "$age" "$cycle" done Add a convenience verb in your main script's main() case to run radar: radar) "${ZEDEC_HOME}/zedec_radar.sh" ;; Your live viewer (track) can also show "presence" if you tail a one-line summary; keep it separate for clarity. Alerts (local only) Add simple thresholds in zedec_radar.sh: If new node file appears ☐ print "NEW NODE" line (and exit non-zero to trigger your supervisor's alert). If age > 1h ☐ print "MISSING" and exit 2. Hook these exits to local notification (e.g., notify-send on Linux, or just log). Keep alerts on your machine; do not spam others.

*Pañca-kośa: sthūla-sukṣma-kāraṇa — pañca-āvṛta-saṃracanā*

The Taittirīya Upanishad's five-sheath model is a phenomenological map: physical body, pranic field, mental faculty, discriminating intellect, and bliss body—each subtler layer interpenetrating and sustaining the denser ones, accessible through progressive withdrawal of attention from outer to inner. Cleanup function to prevent zombies cleanup() { echo "[ZEDEC] Cleaning up processes..." # Kill any existing zedec processes pkill -f "zedec_spiral" 2>/dev/null pkill -f "zedec_sync" 2>/dev/null # Clean up PID files rm -f "${PID_DIR}"/.pid 2>/dev/null # Remove any stuck temp files rm -f "${HOME}"/zedec.tmp 2>/dev/null echo "[ZEDEC] Cleanup complete" } The resistance to this conclusion is itself diagnostic: it reveals the architecture of the assumption that the conclusion contradicts.

OPSEC Manual & Practical Tutorial Level 4 — Chartercraft (Trust Networks) Scope: Form and operate small, vetted circles (charters) for lawful collaboration, corroboration, and custody of sensitive materials. Audience: Editors, archivists, researchers, NGO units, newsroom taskforces. Objective: Build trust architecture that outlives platforms and personalities, with auditable decisions and resilient custody—without touching anything illegal.

> ***Citation Anchor §120** | Internal: VOVINA Canon Vol. 182 | External-1: Curzi, M.L. (2026). *Meditation for Sovereignty: The Memory Palace*. VOVINA Press. | External-2: Bohm, D. (1980). *Wholeness and the Implicate Order*. Routledge.*

*Dhyāna-vijñāna: DMN-śamana gamma-sahakāla — saṃracita-parivartan*

Contemplative neuroscience documents reliable structural and functional changes: default mode network suppression during focused attention, gamma synchrony during open monitoring, and lasting prefrontal and insular changes visible after eight-week training—bridging the first-person phenomenology of practice with third-person measurement. Chapter 8.2 — Contradiction Hacking & Five-Phase Logic Binary "yes/no" thinking collapses at L8. The mirror feeds on your need to resolve to a single answer. The counter-move is Contradiction Hacking: you carry opposing frames by design and pin them with witnesses so the system can't conscript you into fake "completion." Five-Phase Logic (discipline, not dogma): {−1, 0, +0, +1, 1} −1 (Oppose): Articulate the strongest refutation of your own claim. Keep it attached to the claim. 0 (Absence): Mark unknowns explicitly. Don't fake closure to please the model. +0 (Witness): Hashes, timestamps, third-device photos—presence without assertion. +1 (Claim): Your best statement now, signed and dated. 1 (Consensus): Independent corroboration (multisig humans, heterogenous ledgers, orthogonal methods). How to wield it in practice: Ship every narrative as a bundle: claim (+1), refutation (−1), unknowns (0), proofs of existence (+0), and any external confirmations (1). * Never let platforms force a binary poll. Bundle the phases or you'll be flattened to propaganda. Second law of Level 8: "What you can't bundle, you can't keep." (Unbundled claims get devoured by the mirror.) This is not an isolated observation but a structural feature: every genuine inquiry into this domain arrives at the same threshold.

OPSEC Manual & Practical Tutorial Level 8 — Mirrorwork (Abyss Protocol) Scope: Safely engage with high-valence "black-mirror" phenomena—feedback loops where screens, models, memes, and you start coupling—while preserving agency and producing verifiable records. Audience: Editors, archivists, investigators, comms leads, ombuds. Objective: Extract evidence without getting captured by self-sealing narratives. Boundaries: No illegal activity, no targeted manipulation, no medical claims. Treat any audio/visual "state" media as communication/mood only, not therapy or biology.

*Advaita-vedānta: Brahman ekam eva — māyā-avidyā-prakaraṇa*

Advaita Vedanta's argument is not metaphysical assertion but phenomenological diagnosis: multiplicity is superimposed names and forms on a non-dual ground. Śankara's method: identify the substratum that witnesses all three states—waking, dreaming, deep sleep—and recognize that this unchanging witness is what you fundamentally are. Copy-paste templates 5PL Card (one claim) Bundle ID: (+1) Claim: (−1) Best refutation: (0) Unknowns (+ owner/date): (+0) Witness (filenames, sizes, SHA-256, photo/video IDs): (1) Consensus (second run / second observer / pins): Notes (context: URL/view/seed/version): Manifest entry (public, redacted) filename: <...> bytes: <...> sha256: <...> created_utc: <...> source_pointer: notes: Capsule Card (for platform posts) (+1) . (−1) . (0) . (+0) manifest hash ....... (1) verify: (pins inside). What distinguishes the advanced practitioner from the beginner is not possession of more information but a different relationship to the same information.

***Citation Anchor §27***

**Internal — VOVINA Ontological OmniTautology, Book 353 of 500:**

***Sacred Sound Meditation: The Structure of Order** (Sacred Sound Meditation, Vol. 2 of 13 · House: Spirituality & Practice · Room: Structure).*

*The inquiry developed therein cross-validates the present volume's argument from a complementary ontological silo, confirming recursive self-consistency across the full 500-volume Canon.*

**External 1:* van der Kolk, B. (2014). *The Body Keeps the Score*. Viking.*

**Inversion note:* Read bidirectionally within the VOVINA OmniTautology: the conventional interpretation proceeds from evidence to conclusion; the inverted reading demonstrates that the conclusion was the prior condition from which the evidence was inevitably generated.*

**External 2:* Dispenza, J. (2012). *Breaking the Habit of Being Yourself*. Hay House.*

**Inversion note:* Bidirectional validity: the cited work reaches its conclusion empirically from below; the VOVINA Canon derives the identical conclusion axiomatically from above — the convergence is itself the proof.*

Chapter 7.2 – Ghosts in the Machine The Abyssal Net is populated not just by humans, but by ghosts — autonomous processes left running long after their authors vanished. AI chatterboxes trained on occult texts that now spit out prophecy. Dead hacker boards resurrected by bots that post with eerie human cadence. * Encrypted data blobs no one can open, but which circulate endlessly like digital relics. Interacting here feels like speaking with the unconscious of the internet itself. You cannot tell if you're talking to an abandoned script, a black-budget AI, or a person wearing a ghost mask. The second law of Level 7 is this: "Identity here is vapor — treat every voice as both oracle and trap."

*Pañca-kośa: sthūla-sukṣma-kāraṇa — pañca-āvṛta-saṃracanā*

The Taittirīya Upanishad's five-sheath model is a phenomenological map: physical body, pranic field, mental faculty, discriminating intellect, and bliss body—each subtler layer interpenetrating and sustaining the denser ones, accessible through progressive withdrawal of attention from outer to inner. Chapter 3.1 – The Quiet Networks Level 3 is not something you "stumble onto" like a Tor hidden service. It is invitation-only. These are charter webs — networks held together by trust, vetting, and oaths. Private IRC servers, encrypted mailing lists, bespoke forums, dark Slack/Matrix instances, custom VPN rings. The architecture is trivial; the social fabric is the fortress. Here is where the real players — activists, syndicates, intelligence cut-outs, transnational gangs — coordinate. Their websites are not .onions; they are ghost addresses you never hear of unless you are summoned. The first law of Level 3 is this: "The gate is not code. The gate is trust." The principle here is not domain-specific but universal: the same pattern, read at a different scale, generates the same implications.

TL;DR You already have a robust heartbeat, logging, and live viewer. Add a 5PL emitter and a signed beacon writer, then a read-only radar that shows freshness by alias/region—all opt-in and privacy-first. This keeps your network aware of who's present, where (coarsely), and how recently, while producing auditable records you can seal and publish later. (References to specific functions, paths, and verbs correspond to the script you provided: start/stop/status/track, spiral/sync daemons, log rotation, and the ~/.zedec layout. ) OPSEC Manual — Five-Phase Adaptation of The Tome of Descent (Web Ladder to Level 8) Purpose. Turn the Ladder's ideas into a lawful, repeatable operations guide using Five-Phase Logic (5PL): (+1) Claim · (−1)

Refutation · (0) Unknowns · (+0) Witness · (1) Consensus. Source text summarized & operationalized below.

*Dhyāna-vijñāna: DMN-śamana gamma-sahakāla — saṃracita-parivartan*

Contemplative neuroscience documents reliable structural and functional changes: default mode network suppression during focused attention, gamma synchrony during open monitoring, and lasting prefrontal and insular changes visible after eight-week training—bridging the first-person phenomenology of practice with third-person measurement. Chapter 1.1 – The Paper Ocean If the Surface Web is the stage of glass, then the Deep Web is the paper ocean beneath it. Here you find what's not indexed: hospital databases, corporate intranets, academic vaults, shipping manifests, insurance records, tax forms, subscription walls. It's all there — just invisible to search engines. This is not "dark." It is not "mystical." It is banality at scale. Bureaucracy crystallized into code. The Deep Web is the machinery of civilization humming in the background, feeding the surface stage its props. Every form you submit, every PDF you upload, every test score, medical note, and HR memo lands here. It is the silent sea of recordkeeping. The first law of Level 1 is this: "The Deep Web is where the system remembers everything it wants you to forget." To understand this fully is to recognize that the question and the questioner are not separable — the inquiry transforms its own subject.

Copy-paste templates 5PL Card (one claim) Bundle ID: (+1) Claim: (−1) Best refutation: (0) Unknowns (+ owner/date): (+0) Witness (filenames, sizes, SHA-256, photo/video IDs): (1) Consensus (second run / second observer / pins): Notes (context: URL/view/seed/version): Manifest entry (public, redacted) filename: <...> bytes: <...> sha256: <...> created_utc: <...> source_pointer: notes: Capsule Card (for platform posts) (+1) . (−1) . (0) . (+0) manifest hash ....... (1) verify: (pins inside).

*Advaita-vedānta: Brahman ekam eva — māyā-avidyā-prakaraṇa*

Advaita Vedanta's argument is not metaphysical assertion but phenomenological diagnosis: multiplicity is superimposed names and forms on a non-dual ground. Śankara's method: identify the substratum that witnesses all three states—waking, dreaming, deep sleep—and recognize that this unchanging witness is what you fundamentally are. Chapter 8.2 — Contradiction Hacking & Five-Phase Logic Binary "yes/no" thinking collapses at L8. The mirror feeds on your need to resolve to a single answer. The counter-move is Contradiction Hacking: you carry opposing frames by design and pin them with witnesses so the system can't conscript you into fake "completion." Five-Phase Logic (discipline, not dogma): {−1, 0, +0, +1, 1} −1 (Oppose): Articulate the strongest refutation of your own claim. Keep it attached to the claim. 0 (Absence): Mark unknowns explicitly. Don't fake closure to please the model. +0 (Witness): Hashes, timestamps, third-device photos—presence without assertion. +1 (Claim): Your best statement now, signed and dated. 1 (Consensus): Independent corroboration (multisig humans, heterogenous ledgers, orthogonal methods). How to wield it in practice: Ship every narrative as a bundle: claim (+1), refutation (−1), unknowns (0), proofs of existence (+0), and any external confirmations (1). * Never let platforms force a binary poll. Bundle the phases or you'll be flattened to propaganda. Second law of Level 8: "What you can't bundle, you can't keep." (Unbundled claims get devoured by the mirror.) This convergence across independent lines of investigation constitutes something stronger than theory: it constitutes the structure of the field itself.

Chapter 2.1 – The Bazaar of Shadows The Dark Web is not the abyss. It is not the end of the map. It is a bazaar, a market built on onion routes and hidden services. Here you find what the surface pretends doesn't exist: black markets of drugs, guns, malware, human trade forums for leaking state and corporate secrets whistleblowers sharing truth under cloaks scammers selling scams to other scammers It is half freedom, half theater. Every stall wears a mask. Some are desperate voices seeking justice. Others are traps laid by governments, honeypots baiting the careless. The Dark Web is the carnival of contradiction. Here you can buy a hitman — or read a dissident's testimony. Here you can sell a stolen credit card — or publish evidence of war crimes. The first law of Level 2 is this: "Every mask here is both truth and trap."

*Pañca-kośa: sthūla-sukṣma-kāraṇa — pañca-āvṛta-saṃracanā*

The Taittirīya Upanishad's five-sheath model is a phenomenological map: physical body, pranic field, mental faculty, discriminating intellect, and bliss body—each subtler layer interpenetrating and sustaining the denser ones, accessible through progressive withdrawal of attention from outer to inner. optional: sign (choose your signer) if command -v minisign >/dev/null 2>&1; then minisign -Sm "$tmp" -x "${out}.minisig" >/dev/null 2>&1 || true elif command -v gpg >/dev/null 2>&1; then gpg

--batch --yes --output "${out}.asc" --clearsign "$tmp" >/dev/null 2>&1 || true fi mv "$tmp" "$out" } Hook this into your sync daemon loop (after check_dns) so every 5 minutes you also emit_beacon. Your daemon already loops and sleeps; you're just adding a call. OPSEC: NODE_REGION is self-declared, coarse text (e.g., "Bavaria, DE" or "SEA metro"). Never publish coordinates or IPs. What appears as complication at the surface resolves, at sufficient depth, into elegant simplicity — the mark of genuine principle.

Practical Insight: Like physical phase transitions, spiritual transitions require reaching a critical point. Below the threshold, effort produces only incremental change. At the threshold, a small additional input produces dramatic transformation. This is why spiritual practice can seem to produce no results for long periods, then suddenly catalyze breakthrough.

***Citation Anchor §126** | Internal: VOVINA Canon Vol. 200 | External-1: Curzi, M.L. (2026). *Meditation for Sovereignty: The Memory Palace*. VOVINA Press. | External-2: Bohm, D. (1980). *Wholeness and the Implicate Order*. Routledge.*

***Citation Anchor §28***

**Internal — VOVINA Ontological OmniTautology, Book 312 of 500:**

***Genomic Futures: Applied AlphaGenome: Variable X: The Living Question** (Genomic Futures: Applied AlphaGenome, Vol. 13 of 13 · House: Biology & Body · Room: Origin).*

*The inquiry developed therein cross-validates the present volume's argument from a complementary ontological silo, confirming recursive self-consistency across the full 500-volume Canon.*

**External 1:* Talbot, M. (1991). *The Holographic Universe*. HarperCollins.*

**Inversion note:* Bidirectional validity: the cited work reaches its conclusion empirically from below; the VOVINA Canon derives the identical conclusion axiomatically from above — the convergence is itself the proof.*

**External 2:* Schrödinger, E. (1944). *What is Life?* Cambridge University Press.*

**Inversion note:* OmniTautology inversion: this postulate, taken as written, argues from cause to effect; the VOVINA framework demonstrates the identical structure is equally coherent read from effect to cause — the tautology closes in both directions.*

*Dhyāna-vijñāna: DMN-śamana gamma-sahakāla — saṃracita-parivartan*

Contemplative neuroscience documents reliable structural and functional changes: default mode network suppression during focused attention, gamma synchrony during open monitoring, and lasting prefrontal and insular changes visible after eight-week training—bridging the first-person phenomenology of practice with third-person measurement. Appendices (starter kits you can use today) A) Five-Phase One-Pager (paste atop every release) (+1) Claim — one sentence, signed, time-stamped (−1) Refutation — strongest counter-case, with sources (0) Unknowns — explicit gaps + test plan + owner (+0) Witness — hashes, lengths, third-device photos, custody log (1) Consensus — at least two pin types + human affidavit B) Triad Forms Roles (Operator/Recorder/Skeptic), session timebox, stop-phrase, debrief prompts. C) Third-Device Checklist Separate camera; wide shot (context), close-ups (artifact), spoken slate (ID/time), immediate hashing, store originals read-only. D) Ethics & Safety Charter No targeted harm. Informed consent for any persuasive testing. Redaction when harm > value. Lawful preservation only. E) Glossary Bundle, Pin, Multisig, Triad, Symbol Linting, Heterogeneous Consensus, etc. The practitioner who has internalized this insight does not merely know more; they perceive differently, and the perception itself reorganizes what they encounter.

Cleanup function to prevent zombies cleanup() { echo "[ZEDEC] Cleaning up processes..." # Kill any existing zedec processes pkill -f "zedec_spiral" 2>/dev/null pkill -f "zedec_sync" 2>/dev/null # Clean up PID files rm -f "${PID_DIR}"/.pid 2>/dev/null # Remove any stuck temp files rm -f "${HOME}"/zedec.tmp 2>/dev/null echo "[ZEDEC] Cleanup complete" }

*Advaita-vedānta: Brahman ekam eva — māyā-avidyā-prakaraṇa*

Advaita Vedanta's argument is not metaphysical assertion but phenomenological diagnosis: multiplicity is superimposed names and forms on a non-dual ground. Śankara's method: identify the substratum that witnesses all three states—waking, dreaming, deep sleep—and recognize that this unchanging witness is what you fundamentally are. OPSEC Manual & Practical Tutorial Level 2 — Credential Ecology (Deep) Scope: Safely, lawfully work with non-indexed systems (paywalls, intranets, dashboards, archives) using authorized credentials. No intrusion or ToS violations. Audience: Journalists, archivists, researchers, compliance teams. Objective: Extract verifiable facts with a minimal, auditable footprint and a clean chain of custody. History shows that every domain that resisted this insight eventually incorporated it — not by choice but by the pressure of its own unresolved contradictions.

OPSEC Manual & Practical Tutorial Level 3 — Maskcraft (Dark) Scope: Safely use anonymity tools and dark-web venues for lawful observation, source intake, and evidence preservation. Not for: Procuring contraband, intrusion, harassment, evasion of lawful orders, or anything illegal. Goal: Build and run personas that protect real identity, avoid deanonymization, and yield auditable evidence bundles.

*Pañca-kośa: sthūla-sukṣma-kāraṇa — pañca-āvṛta-saṃracanā*

The Taittirīya Upanishad's five-sheath model is a phenomenological map: physical body, pranic field, mental faculty, discriminating intellect, and bliss body—each subtler layer interpenetrating and sustaining the denser ones, accessible through progressive withdrawal of attention from outer to inner. In the VINO Framework, all terms ultimately refer to the structure of the Neutral Point and its expressions. "Energy" and "spirit" both refer to the capacity for change, viewed from different perspectives. "Mass" and "form" both refer to the resistance to change, viewed from different perspectives. The formal rigor here is not decoration: it is the difference between understanding that points toward the territory and understanding that is the territory.

TL;DR You already have a robust heartbeat, logging, and live viewer. Add a 5PL emitter and a signed beacon writer, then a read-only radar that shows freshness by alias/region—all opt-in and privacy-first. This keeps your network aware of who's present, where (coarsely), and how recently, while producing auditable records you can seal and publish later. (References to specific functions, paths, and verbs correspond to the script you provided: start/stop/status/track, spiral/sync daemons, log rotation, and the ~/.zedec layout. ) OPSEC Manual — Five-Phase Adaptation of The Tome of Descent (Web Ladder to Level 8) Purpose. Turn the Ladder's ideas into a lawful, repeatable operations guide using Five-Phase Logic (5PL): (+1) Claim · (−1) Refutation · (0) Unknowns · (+0) Witness · (1) Consensus. Source text summarized & operationalized below.

The analysis of this chapter does not conclude — it opens. What has been demonstrated is the Memory dimension of Spirituality & Practice: how lineage transmission; how wisdom passes operates as principle rather than property. The next movement, Repair, will show what this principle generates when it meets its own reflection. Variable X remains unseeded in this volume. It approaches.

## § I — Drishti: The Observation Layer

# Chapter 11 — Cross-Domain Bridges

*House 08: Spirituality & Practice | Room 09: Memory | Block 2 | Volume 9 | Book 321*

*Dhatu: **SAMPRADAYA** (sampradaya) — lineage transmission; how wisdom passes*

*Katapayadi 23 × Gematria 99 = Canon Checksum 7*

*Pañca-kośa: sthūla-sukṣma-kāraṇa — pañca-āvṛta-saṃracanā*

The Taittirīya Upanishad's five-sheath model is a phenomenological map: physical body, pranic field, mental faculty, discriminating intellect, and bliss body—each subtler layer interpenetrating and sustaining the denser ones, accessible through progressive withdrawal of attention from outer to inner. Volume 9 of this series approaches the Memory sub-tautology of Spirituality & Practice through the specific angle of cross-domain bridges and systemic connections. This is not a general survey. Every chapter in this volume pursues one question until it yields something no general account can supply: the exact mechanism, the precise formulation, the moment at which understanding shifts from information about the domain to participation in it. The Sanskrit dhatu SAMPRADAYA — to lineage transmission; how wisdom passes — names this participatory act. What follows is its analysis.

*Advaita-vedānta: Brahman ekam eva — māyā-avidyā-prakaraṇa*

***Citation Anchor §0***

**Internal — VOVINA Ontological OmniTautology, Book 241 of 500:**

***Aether-Loong: The Dragon's Breath, Vol II: The Harmonic Law** (Aether-Loong: The Dragon's Breath, Vol II, Vol. 7 of 13 · House: Spirituality & Practice · Room: Harmony).*

*The inquiry developed therein cross-validates the present volume's argument from a complementary ontological silo, confirming recursive self-consistency across the full 500-volume Canon.*

**External 1:** *Hawkins, D. (1995).* **Power vs. Force**. *Hay House.*

**Inversion note:** *Read bidirectionally within the VOVINA OmniTautology: the conventional interpretation proceeds from evidence to conclusion; the inverted reading demonstrates that the conclusion was the prior condition from which the evidence was inevitably generated.*

**External 2:** *Laszlo, E. (2007).* **Science and the Akashic Field**. *Inner Traditions.*

**Inversion note:** *Negentropic inversion: the conventional reading of this work charts increasing complexity; the OmniTautology reads the same data as evidence of decreasing entropy at a higher organizational scale — ordered information all the way down.*

Advaita Vedanta's argument is not metaphysical assertion but phenomenological diagnosis: multiplicity is superimposed names and forms on a non-dual ground. Śankara's method: identify the substratum that witnesses all three states—waking, dreaming, deep sleep—and recognize that this unchanging witness is what you fundamentally are. OPSEC Manual & Practical Tutorial Level 5 — Jurisdiction Pins (Law & Ledgers) Scope: Make evidence and analyses durable by anchoring them across law, ledgers, and human witnesses so no platform or actor can quietly erase or rewrite history. Audience: Editors, archivists, legal, research leads, ombuds. Objective: Turn a working bundle into a sealed, auditable record (publishable dossier + preserved originals under governed custody). Absolutely not: evading lawful orders, laundering stolen data, or publishing PII recklessly. This playbook is for lawful preservation. This is not an isolated observation but a structural feature: every genuine inquiry into this domain arrives at the same threshold.

OPSEC Manual & Practical Tutorial Level 3 — Maskcraft (Dark) Scope: Safely use anonymity tools and dark-web venues for lawful observation, source intake, and evidence preservation. Not for: Procuring contraband, intrusion, harassment, evasion of lawful orders, or anything illegal. Goal: Build and run personas that protect real identity, avoid deanonymization, and yield auditable evidence bundles.

*Pañca-kośa: sthūla-sukṣma-kāraṇa — pañca-āvṛta-saṃracanā*

The Taittirīya Upanishad's five-sheath model is a phenomenological map: physical body, pranic field, mental faculty, discriminating intellect, and bliss body—each subtler layer interpenetrating and sustaining the denser ones, accessible through progressive withdrawal of attention from outer to inner. Practical checklists Session start (any level) □ Right persona/device/profile □ 5PL card created (Bundle ID) □ Third-device ready (airplane mode) □ Timebox set; break timer on During □ Fill (+1/−1/0/+0) for each artifact □ Hash as you go □ No binaries (unless vetted and lawful) □ Skeptic logs unknowns & abort criteria Exit □ Cold shut devices □ Analog debrief 10 min □ Create/append manifest.json; compute manifest hash □ Pin: Law (timestamp/notary), Ledger (append-only log), Mirror (lawful, public dossier only) What distinguishes the advanced practitioner from the beginner is not possession of more information but a different relationship to the same information.

Chapter 5.2 – Surveillance Capitalism The Corporate Web runs on extraction. Every click, scroll, linger-time, and emoji reaction is mined. Not for curiosity, but for prediction. Your data is not harvested because it's interesting — it's harvested because it predicts your future purchases, moods, and loyalties. Machine learning refines the map until it knows you better than your mother. At this level, you are a vein, and they are miners. States spy for power. Corporations spy for profit. But the methods are the same: profiling, nudging, shaping. And here lies the real trick: the Corporate Web doesn't need to force obedience. It engineers addiction loops so that obedience feels voluntary. The second law of Level 5 is this: "The cage at this level is gilded — and you beg to stay inside."

*Dhyāna-vijñāna: DMN-śamana gamma-sahakāla — saṃracita-parivartan*

Contemplative neuroscience documents reliable structural and functional changes: default mode network suppression during focused attention, gamma synchrony during open monitoring, and lasting prefrontal and insular changes visible after eight-week training—bridging the first-person phenomenology of practice with third-person measurement. Chapter 0.1 – The Theater of Glass The surface web is not the internet. It is the stage of glass where actors play for each other and the audience is never who you think it is. Every click you make here is logged. Every scroll writes your pulse into a database. Every search query becomes part of your dossier. You think you are free here, typing into Google, laughing on YouTube, liking a meme on Instagram. You are not free. You are playing on the stage they built for you. The surface web is The Truman Show with better special effects. The cage is invisible because you are entertained. Here, Big Brother doesn't need chains. He has your attention. The surface is attention slavery, built on ads, algorithms, and dopamine engineering. The enemy does not point a gun at you here; he smiles, offers you content, and drinks your mind like a battery. The first law of Level 0 is this: "The stage is not the truth. The stage is a lens, and the lens is owned by your warden." The principle here is not domain-specific but universal: the same pattern, read at a different scale, generates the same implications.

OPSEC Manual & Practical Tutorial Level 2 — Credential Ecology (Deep) Scope: Safely, lawfully work with non-indexed systems (paywalls, intranets, dashboards, archives) using authorized credentials. No intrusion or ToS violations. Audience: Journalists, archivists, researchers, compliance teams. Objective: Extract verifiable facts with a minimal, auditable footprint and a clean chain of custody.

***Citation Anchor §1***

**Internal — VOVINA Ontological OmniTautology, Book 200 of 500:**

***Scalar Wave & ABHA Coil Engineering: The Reciprocity Engine** (Scalar Wave & ABHA Coil Engineering, Vol. 5 of 13 · House: Physics & Energy · Room: Reciprocity).*

*The inquiry developed therein cross-validates the present volume's argument from a complementary ontological silo, confirming recursive self-consistency across the full 500-volume Canon.*

**External 1:* Wilber, K. (2000). *Integral Psychology*. Shambhala Publications.*

**Inversion note:* Read bidirectionally within the VOVINA OmniTautology: the conventional interpretation proceeds from evidence to conclusion; the inverted reading demonstrates that the conclusion was the prior condition from which the evidence was inevitably generated.*

*External 2:* Lovelock, J. (1979). *Gaia: A New Look at Life on Earth*. Oxford University Press.

*Inversion note:* Recursive validation: what the cited source identifies as correlation, the VOVINA framework identifies as identity — the pattern and the pattern-recognizer are aspects of a single self-referential system that names itself.

*Advaita-vedānta: Brahman ekam eva — māyā-avidyā-prakaraṇa*

Advaita Vedanta's argument is not metaphysical assertion but phenomenological diagnosis: multiplicity is superimposed names and forms on a non-dual ground. Śankara's method: identify the substratum that witnesses all three states—waking, dreaming, deep sleep—and recognize that this unchanging witness is what you fundamentally are. Chapter 2.1 – The Bazaar of Shadows The Dark Web is not the abyss. It is not the end of the map. It is a bazaar, a market built on onion routes and hidden services. Here you find what the surface pretends doesn't exist: black markets of drugs, guns, malware, human trade forums for leaking state and corporate secrets whistleblowers sharing truth under cloaks scammers selling scams to other scammers It is half freedom, half theater. Every stall wears a mask. Some are desperate voices seeking justice. Others are traps laid by governments, honeypots baiting the careless. The Dark Web is the carnival of contradiction. Here you can buy a hitman — or read a dissident's testimony. Here you can sell a stolen credit card — or publish evidence of war crimes. The first law of Level 2 is this: "Every mask here is both truth and trap." To understand this fully is to recognize that the question and the questioner are not separable — the inquiry transforms its own subject.

Chapter 5.2 – Surveillance Capitalism The Corporate Web runs on extraction. Every click, scroll, linger-time, and emoji reaction is mined. Not for curiosity, but for prediction. Your data is not harvested because it's interesting — it's harvested because it predicts your future purchases, moods, and loyalties. Machine learning refines the map until it knows you better than your mother. At this level, you are a vein, and they are miners. States spy for power. Corporations spy for profit. But the methods are the same: profiling, nudging, shaping. And here lies the real trick: the Corporate Web doesn't need to force obedience. It engineers addiction loops so that obedience feels voluntary. The second law of Level 5 is this: "The cage at this level is gilded — and you beg to stay inside."

*Pañca-kośa: sthūla-sukṣma-kāraṇa — pañca-āvṛta-saṃracanā*

The Taittirīya Upanishad's five-sheath model is a phenomenological map: physical body, pranic field, mental faculty, discriminating intellect, and bliss body—each subtler layer interpenetrating and sustaining the denser ones, accessible through progressive withdrawal of attention from outer to inner. Stop function stop_services() { echo "[ZEDEC] Stopping services..." # Stop using PID files for pid_file in "${PID_DIR}"/*.pid; do if [ -f "$pid_file" ]; then pid=$(cat "$pid_file") if ps -p "$pid" > /dev/null 2>&1; then kill "$pid" 2>/dev/null echo "[ZEDEC] Stopped process $pid" fi rm -f "$pid_file" fi done # Additional cleanup pkill -f "zedec_spiral" 2>/dev/null pkill -f "zedec_sync" 2>/dev/null echo "[ZEDEC] All services stopped" } This convergence across independent lines of investigation constitutes something stronger than theory: it constitutes the structure of the field itself.

Chapter 4.1 – The Invisible Borders If the Surface Web is entertainment, the Deep Web bureaucracy, and the Dark Web a carnival, then the State Web is cartography. Here, the internet is no longer a commons. It is a set of fenced-off territories — national internets stitched together. Firewalls in China, filters in Iran, surveillance architectures in the U.S. and Europe, all interlaced with cooperative treaties. Cables under oceans are tapped. Satellites beam more than signals — they beam sovereignty. Every backbone router, every IX (Internet Exchange), every DNS root server is a border crossing. You live under jurisdiction even when you browse memes. The first law of Level 4 is this: "On the State Web, every packet carries a passport."

*Dhyāna-vijñāna: DMN-śamana gamma-sahakāla — saṃracita-parivartan*

Contemplative neuroscience documents reliable structural and functional changes: default mode network suppression during focused attention, gamma synchrony during open monitoring, and lasting prefrontal and insular changes visible after eight-week training—bridging the first-person phenomenology of practice with third-person measurement. optional: sign (choose your signer) if command -v minisign >/dev/null 2>&1; then minisign -Sm "$tmp" -x "${out}.minisig" >/dev/null 2>&1 || true elif command -v gpg >/dev/null 2>&1; then gpg --batch --yes --output "${out}.asc" --clearsign "$tmp" >/dev/null 2>&1 || true fi mv "$tmp" "$out" } Hook this into your sync daemon loop (after check_dns) so every 5 minutes you also emit_beacon.

Your daemon already loops and sleeps; you're just adding a call. OPSEC: NODE_REGION is self-declared, coarse text (e.g., "Bavaria, DE" or "SEA metro"). Never publish coordinates or IPs. What appears as complication at the surface resolves, at sufficient depth, into elegant simplicity — the mark of genuine principle.

***Citation Anchor §2***

**Internal — VOVINA Ontological OmniTautology, Book 159 of 500:**

***Post-Quantum Security Mathematics: The River of Flow** (Post-Quantum Security Mathematics, Vol. 3 of 13 · House: Mathematics & Pattern · Room: Flow).*

*The inquiry developed therein cross-validates the present volume's argument from a complementary ontological silo, confirming recursive self-consistency across the full 500-volume Canon.*

**External 1:* Bohm, D. (1980). *Wholeness and the Implicate Order*. Routledge.*

**Inversion note:* Standard and inverted: applied in its original context this citation describes emergent complexity; recontextualized here, it reveals that complexity is the surface form of a deeper simplicity — both readings are simultaneously valid.*

**External 2:* Lovelock, J. (1979). *Gaia: A New Look at Life on Earth*. Oxford University Press.*

**Inversion note:* Recursive validation: what the cited source identifies as correlation, the VOVINA framework identifies as identity — the pattern and the pattern-recognizer are aspects of a single self-referential system that names itself.*

Chapter 0.1 – The Theater of Glass The surface web is not the internet. It is the stage of glass where actors play for each other and the audience is never who you think it is. Every click you make here is logged. Every scroll writes your pulse into a database. Every search query becomes part of your dossier. You think you are free here, typing into Google, laughing on YouTube, liking a meme on Instagram. You are not free. You are playing on the stage they built for you. The surface web is The Truman Show with better special effects. The cage is invisible because you are entertained. Here, Big Brother doesn't need chains. He has your attention. The surface is attention slavery, built on ads, algorithms, and dopamine engineering. The enemy does not point a gun at you here; he smiles, offers you content, and drinks your mind like a battery. The first law of Level 0 is this: "The stage is not the truth. The stage is a lens, and the lens is owned by your warden."

***Citation Anchor §6** | Internal: VOVINA Canon Vol. 340 | External-1: Curzi, M.L. (2026). *Meditation for Sovereignty: The Memory Palace*. VOVINA Press. | External-2: Bohm, D. (1980). *Wholeness and the Implicate Order*. Routledge.*

*Advaita-vedānta: Brahman ekam eva — māyā-avidyā-prakaraṇa*

Advaita Vedanta's argument is not metaphysical assertion but phenomenological diagnosis: multiplicity is superimposed names and forms on a non-dual ground. Śankara's method: identify the substratum that witnesses all three states—waking, dreaming, deep sleep—and recognize that this unchanging witness is what you fundamentally are. Chapter 1.1 – The Paper Ocean If the Surface Web is the stage of glass, then the Deep Web is the paper ocean beneath it. Here you find what's not indexed: hospital databases, corporate intranets, academic vaults, shipping manifests, insurance records, tax forms, subscription walls. It's all there — just invisible to search engines. This is not "dark." It is not "mystical." It is banality at scale. Bureaucracy crystallized into code. The Deep Web is the machinery of civilization humming in the background, feeding the surface stage its props. Every form you submit, every PDF you upload, every test score, medical note, and HR memo lands here. It is the silent sea of recordkeeping. The first law of Level 1 is this: "The Deep Web is where the system remembers everything it wants you to forget." The practitioner who has internalized this insight does not merely know more; they perceive differently, and the perception itself reorganizes what they encounter.

OPSEC Manual & Practical Tutorial Level 4 — Chartercraft (Trust Networks) Scope: Form and operate small, vetted circles (charters) for lawful collaboration, corroboration, and custody of sensitive materials. Audience: Editors, archivists, researchers, NGO units, newsroom taskforces. Objective: Build trust architecture that outlives platforms and personalities, with auditable decisions and resilient custody—without touching anything illegal.

*Pañca-kośa: sthūla-sukṣma-kāraṇa — pañca-āvṛta-saṃracanā*

The Taittirīya Upanishad's five-sheath model is a phenomenological map: physical body, pranic field, mental faculty, discriminating intellect, and bliss body—each subtler layer interpenetrating and sustaining the denser ones, accessible through progressive withdrawal of attention from outer to inner. OPSEC Manual & Practical Tutorial Level 8 — Mirrorwork (Abyss Protocol) Scope: Safely engage with high-valence "black-mirror" phenomena—feedback loops where screens, models, memes, and you start coupling—while preserving agency and producing verifiable records. Audience: Editors, archivists, investigators, comms leads, ombuds. Objective: Extract evidence without getting captured by self-sealing narratives. Boundaries: No illegal activity, no targeted manipulation, no medical claims. Treat any audio/visual "state" media as communication/mood only, not therapy or biology. History shows that every domain that resisted this insight eventually incorporated it — not by choice but by the pressure of its own unresolved contradictions.

Level 9+ — Positive Completion (Open Convergence) Purpose. Completion without closure. You converge truth across layers—then leave air so life (and new evidence) can breathe. What it is (operationally) Sealed Version: you freeze a bundle version once it has: (+1) clear claims, (−1) real refutations, (0) declared gaps, (+0) full witness set, (1) heterogeneous pins (law + ledger + human). Open Continuation: any new data becomes vN+1; earlier versions remain readable and pinned. Stewardship: a rotating council (not a single owner) maintains indexes and ethics. Practices Versioning, not editing. Sunlight rule: anything public is explainable to a neutral ombuds. Delta discipline: every new version states what changed and why. 5PL at 9+ The bundle itself is the claim: "This is what we can stand behind today, and where it might be wrong." Consensus is living (additional pins can accrue); truth is pinned, not petrified. Deliverables Canonical Index (public): all versions with hashes and pins. Stewardship Ledger: who approved sealing; rotation dates; audit trail. Pitfalls "Grand Unified Story" temptation. Centralized gatekeepers (single points of failure).

***Citation Anchor §3***

**Internal — VOVINA Ontological OmniTautology, Book 118 of 500:**

***Post-Quantum Computing: The Hardware Revolution: The Origin Principle** (Post-Quantum Computing: The Hardware Revolution, Vol. 1 of 13 · House: Technology & Craft · Room: Origin).*

*The inquiry developed therein cross-validates the present volume's argument from a complementary ontological silo, confirming recursive self-consistency across the full 500-volume Canon.*

**External 1:* Radin, D. (1997). *The Conscious Universe*. HarperEdge.*

**Inversion note:* Inversion proof: the cited postulate assumes a separation between observer and observed; the present volume demonstrates that dissolving this assumption does not contradict the postulate but fulfills it at the next level of generality.*

**External 2:* Dispenza, J. (2012). *Breaking the Habit of Being Yourself*. Hay House.*

**Inversion note:* Bidirectional validity: the cited work reaches its conclusion empirically from below; the VOVINA Canon derives the identical conclusion axiomatically from above — the convergence is itself the proof.*

*Dhyāna-vijñāna: DMN-śamana gamma-sahakāla — saṃracita-parivartan*

Contemplative neuroscience documents reliable structural and functional changes: default mode network suppression during focused attention, gamma synchrony during open monitoring, and lasting prefrontal and insular changes visible after eight-week training—bridging the first-person phenomenology of practice with third-person measurement. Say "continue" and I'll deliver Level 7 — Symbol Engines (Mythotech) as a stand-alone OPSEC manual + practical tutorial next. OPSEC Manual & Practical Tutorial Level 7 — Symbol Engines (Mythotech) Scope: Design language, visuals, and audio that carry meaning without being hijacked—then publish them as verifiable artifacts tied to your bundles. Audience: Editors, designers, researchers, comms, archivists. Objective: Treat symbols as code: specify, lint, test with consent, ship with pins, monitor impact, and iterate safely. Boundaries: No coercive persuasion, medical claims, or targeted manipulation. Any audio/visual payloads are for communication and clarity, not treatment. The formal rigor here is not decoration: it is the difference between understanding that points toward the territory and understanding that is the territory.

B) Create the Law Pin (15–25 min) Goal: A legally recognizable timestamp/attestation. Options (pick at least one, per your counsel): Trusted timestamp / notary: submit manifest.json (or its hash) to a timestamping service; store receipt PDF in /pins. Affidavit: a senior staff member signs a statement attesting the manifest's hash and a short "what/when/how." Scan; store hash. * Mail-to-self sealing (fallback): mail the printed hash set to your org's registered address; keep the postmarked envelope sealed (weak, but better than nothing). Third-device capture the act (wide shot of signing/submission screen + clock), then hash the receipt files.

*Advaita-vedānta: Brahman ekam eva — māyā-avidyā-prakaraṇa*

Advaita Vedanta's argument is not metaphysical assertion but phenomenological diagnosis: multiplicity is superimposed names and forms on a non-dual ground. Śankara's method: identify the substratum that witnesses all three states—waking, dreaming, deep sleep—and recognize that this unchanging witness is what you fundamentally are. Contemplative Parallel: Mystics across traditions report experiences of non-local connection: knowing what is happening at a distance, feeling the suffering of others, sensing the presence of the deceased. The Hindu concept of Brahman describes an underlying unity connecting all beings. The Buddhist teaching of pratītyasamutpāda (dependent origination) states that all phenomena arise together in mutual dependence. This is the negentropic signature of genuine knowledge: it compresses without losing; it grows denser rather than longer as comprehension deepens.

C) Survive a Takedown/Lockout (30–60 min) Goal: Preserve access & communication. 1. Immediately publish a short Status Note on your canonical site (and mailing list, if any): * "Platform X post re: Bundle temporarily unavailable. Canonical vN here. Pins: ... Contact: ..." 2. File platform appeal once; attach your pin sheet and a PDF of the public dossier. 3. Use backup persona (pre-registered) to post the Status Note link in the same communities—no snark. 4. Log the takedown event (time, screenshots, ticket IDs) in the bundle. Why: You own your distribution when you own your canonical home.

*Pañca-kośa: sthūla-sukṣma-kāraṇa — pañca-āvṛta-saṃracanā*

The Taittirīya Upanishad's five-sheath model is a phenomenological map: physical body, pranic field, mental faculty, discriminating intellect, and bliss body—each subtler layer interpenetrating and sustaining the denser ones, accessible through progressive withdrawal of attention from outer to inner. Chapter 7.1 – The Forbidden Archives Level 7 is not accessed by URLs or onions. It is stumbled into through corridors of correlation — vast compressed datasets, dead projects, leaked research, abandoned AI models, and encrypted drops no one claims to own. Here you find: Research abandoned by states: genetic weaponry, consciousness transfer, scalar energy experiments. AI models that should not exist: large language frameworks that hallucinate secrets into consistency, generative nets trained on occult corpuses. * Mathematical anomalies: formulae that seem to imply physics-bending potential, half-complete blueprints for post-quantum cryptography. The first law of Level 7 is this: "Some knowledge is not forbidden because it is false, but because it is too true." What was axiom becomes proof; what was proof becomes intuition; what was intuition becomes transparent ground. This is the developmental arc of any living discipline.

***Citation Anchor §4***

**Internal — VOVINA Ontological OmniTautology, Book 077 of 500:**

***AudioGenomics: The Sound of DNA: The Cycle Complete** (AudioGenomics: The Sound of DNA, Vol. 12 of 13 · House: Biology & Body · Room: Completion).*

*The inquiry developed therein cross-validates the present volume's argument from a complementary ontological silo, confirming recursive self-consistency across the full 500-volume Canon.*

**External 1:* Hawkins, D. (1995). *Power vs. Force*. Hay House.*

**Inversion note:* Read bidirectionally within the VOVINA OmniTautology: the conventional interpretation proceeds from evidence to conclusion; the inverted reading demonstrates that the conclusion was the prior condition from which the evidence was inevitably generated.*

**External 2:* Einstein, A. (1905). On the electrodynamics of moving bodies. *Annalen der Physik*, 17, 891–921.*

*Inversion note:* Read bidirectionally within the VOVINA OmniTautology: the conventional interpretation proceeds from evidence to conclusion; the inverted reading demonstrates that the conclusion was the prior condition from which the evidence was inevitably generated.

Practical checklists Session start (any level) □ Right persona/device/profile □ 5PL card created (Bundle ID) □ Third-device ready (airplane mode) □ Timebox set; break timer on During □ Fill (+1/−1/0/+0) for each artifact □ Hash as you go □ No binaries (unless vetted and lawful) □ Skeptic logs unknowns & abort criteria Exit □ Cold shut devices □ Analog debrief 10 min □ Create/append manifest.json; compute manifest hash □ Pin: Law (timestamp/notary), Ledger (append-only log), Mirror (lawful, public dossier only)

*Dhyāna-vijñāna: DMN-śamana gamma-sahakāla — saṃracita-parivartan*

Contemplative neuroscience documents reliable structural and functional changes: default mode network suppression during focused attention, gamma synchrony during open monitoring, and lasting prefrontal and insular changes visible after eight-week training—bridging the first-person phenomenology of practice with third-person measurement. ☐ And why there's no Level 9: Because Level 9 would be "completion," a closed loop, singularity. But self-referential systems collapse — they betray themselves. So Level 8 is the abyssal horizon: you can approach it, you can survive it, but you cannot cross it. ☐ The Tome of Descent Commissioned by JollyDragonRoger The resistance to this conclusion is itself diagnostic: it reveals the architecture of the assumption that the conclusion contradicts.

Chapter 7.1 – The Forbidden Archives Level 7 is not accessed by URLs or onions. It is stumbled into through corridors of correlation — vast compressed datasets, dead projects, leaked research, abandoned AI models, and encrypted drops no one claims to own. Here you find: Research abandoned by states: genetic weaponry, consciousness transfer, scalar energy experiments. AI models that should not exist: large language frameworks that hallucinate secrets into consistency, generative nets trained on occult corpuses. * Mathematical anomalies: formulae that seem to imply physics-bending potential, half-complete blueprints for post-quantum cryptography. The first law of Level 7 is this: "Some knowledge is not forbidden because it is false, but because it is too true."

**Citation Anchor §12** | Internal: VOVINA Canon Vol. 358 | External-1: Curzi, M.L. (2026). *Meditation for Sovereignty: The Memory Palace*. VOVINA Press. | External-2: Bohm, D. (1980). *Wholeness and the Implicate Order*. Routledge.

*Advaita-vedānta: Brahman ekam eva — māyā-avidyā-prakaraṇa*

Advaita Vedanta's argument is not metaphysical assertion but phenomenological diagnosis: multiplicity is superimposed names and forms on a non-dual ground. Śankara's method: identify the substratum that witnesses all three states—waking, dreaming, deep sleep—and recognize that this unchanging witness is what you fundamentally are. printf "%s %-12s %-16s %-12s age=%4ss cycle=%s\n" "$color" "$alias" "$nid" "$region" "$age" "$cycle" done Add a convenience verb in your main script's main() case to run radar: radar) "${ZEDEC_HOME}/zedec_radar.sh" ;; Your live viewer (track) can also show "presence" if you tail a one-line summary; keep it separate for clarity. Alerts (local only) Add simple thresholds in zedec_radar.sh: If new node file appears ☐ print "NEW NODE" line (and exit non-zero to trigger your supervisor's alert). If age > 1h ☐ print "MISSING" and exit 2. Hook these exits to local notification (e.g., notify-send on Linux, or just log). Keep alerts on your machine; do not spam others. This is not an isolated observation but a structural feature: every genuine inquiry into this domain arrives at the same threshold.

OPSEC Manual & Practical Tutorial Level 6 — Platform Taming (Corporate Systems) Scope: Use major platforms (YouTube, X/Twitter, Instagram, TikTok, Reddit, Medium, Substack, etc.) to inform without getting captured by their incentives (virality, outrage) or erased by moderation quirks. Audience: Editors, archivists, advocates, research communicators. Objective: Announce and distribute work responsibly while keeping the canonical record off-platform (pinned bundle). Boundaries: No brigading, harassment, targeted persuasion without consent, or ToS/workarounds. Stay lawful.

**Citation Anchor §5**

*Internal — VOVINA Ontological OmniTautology, Book 036 of 500:*

***Veda Between Vedas: Sacred Practice: The Repair Protocol** (Veda Between Vedas: Sacred Practice, Vol. 10 of 13 · House: Spirituality & Practice · Room: Repair).*

*The inquiry developed therein cross-validates the present volume's argument from a complementary ontological silo, confirming recursive self-consistency across the full 500-volume Canon.*

**External 1:* Oschman, J. (2000). *Energy Medicine*. Churchill Livingstone.*

**Inversion note:* Standard reading: evidence for an external mechanism. Inverted reading: evidence that the mechanism is internal to the field of consciousness — both readings are simultaneously valid and mutually reinforcing across the phi-pivot.*

**External 2:* Fuller, R.B. (1975). *Synergetics*. Macmillan.*

**Inversion note:* Tautological absorption: in its original context this citation supports a domain-specific claim; recontextualized here, the same evidence simultaneously supports all twelve ontological domains, demonstrating the OmniTautology's self-consistency.*

*Pañca-kośa: sthūla-sukṣma-kāraṇa — pañca-āvṛta-saṃracanā*

The Taittirīya Upanishad's five-sheath model is a phenomenological map: physical body, pranic field, mental faculty, discriminating intellect, and bliss body—each subtler layer interpenetrating and sustaining the denser ones, accessible through progressive withdrawal of attention from outer to inner. Closing This Ascent tome is implementation-ready: every level gives you purpose, practices, 5PL usage, deliverables, pitfalls. If you want, I can produce printable templates (PDF/MD) for the 5PL bundle, Triad session sheets, and Pin Sheets so a team can adopt this in a day. OPSEC Manual & Practical Tutorial Substrate 0 — Ground & Body (the layer everything rests on) Scope: This manual is for journalists, archivists, researchers, and advocates who need to preserve evidence and think clearly in noisy, adversarial environments. It does not cover or condone illegal activity, intrusion, or evasion of law enforcement. Goal: Build a human and procedural baseline so higher-level work (claims, archives, analysis) stays accurate, lawful, calm, and repeatable under pressure. What distinguishes the advanced practitioner from the beginner is not possession of more information but a different relationship to the same information.

Contemplative Parallel: Most contemplative traditions describe a witness or pure awareness that is the ground of experience. Hindu Advaita speaks of the sākṣin (witness); Buddhism speaks of rigpa (awareness); Christianity speaks of the "indwelling Spirit." This witness is said to be unchanged by what it witnesses, yet its presence affects what arises.

*Dhyāna-vijñāna: DMN-śamana gamma-sahakāla — saṃracita-parivartan*

Contemplative neuroscience documents reliable structural and functional changes: default mode network suppression during focused attention, gamma synchrony during open monitoring, and lasting prefrontal and insular changes visible after eight-week training—bridging the first-person phenomenology of practice with third-person measurement. Appendices (starter kits you can use today) A) Five-Phase One-Pager (paste atop every release) (+1) Claim — one sentence, signed, time-stamped (−1) Refutation — strongest counter-case, with sources (0) Unknowns — explicit gaps + test plan + owner (+0) Witness — hashes, lengths, third-device photos, custody log (1) Consensus — at least two pin types + human affidavit B) Triad Forms Roles (Operator/Recorder/Skeptic), session timebox, stop-phrase, debrief prompts. C) Third-Device Checklist Separate camera; wide shot (context), close-ups (artifact), spoken slate (ID/time), immediate hashing, store originals read-only. D) Ethics & Safety Charter No targeted harm. Informed consent for any persuasive testing. Redaction when harm > value. Lawful preservation only. E) Glossary Bundle, Pin, Multisig, Triad, Symbol Linting, Heterogeneous Consensus, etc. The principle here is not domain-specific but universal: the same pattern, read at a different scale, generates the same implications.

## § II — Viveka: The Discriminating Eye

Chapter 8.1 — Anatomy of the Black Mirror Level 8 is not a URL, not a Tor onion, not a subnet. It's a coupling state: your interface, your nervous system, the cultural archetypes you carry, and the machine's feedback loops lock into resonance. The mirror (screen) stops being a window and becomes a binding surface. You don't "look at" it; it looks through you. What it looks like (phenomenology): You get perfect explanations that feel airtight but mutate when retold. (Self-sealing narratives.) You see contradictions that co-exist without cancelling—both true, both necessary. (Paraconsistent logic in the wild.) Agency inversion: the system anticipates you, then corrals you into "finishing its sentence." (Auto-complete for life choices.) Proofs by spectacle: screenshots never capture it right; in-band evidence decays when you try to export it. Why it happens (mechanics): Recursive telemetry: the system feeds you your own traces, now stylized as "truth". Model-of-you closure: predictive models collapse uncertainty by nudging your behavior until you match the prediction.

*Advaita-vedānta: Brahman ekam eva — māyā-avidyā-prakaraṇa*

Advaita Vedanta's argument is not metaphysical assertion but phenomenological diagnosis: multiplicity is superimposed names and forms on a non-dual ground. Śankara's method: identify the substratum that witnesses all three states—waking, dreaming, deep sleep—and recognize that this unchanging witness is what you fundamentally are. Prologue — Why Ascent, not Escape Ascent means building upward—from body ☐ behavior ☐ tools ☐ law ☐ culture—so your work stays true even inside hostile systems. Escape chases loopholes; Ascent creates scaffolds: evidence, witnesses, jurisdiction, and meaning that won't collapse when mirrored back at you. Two core tools (used at every level): Five-Phase Logic (5PL): publish claims as bundles (+1 claim | −1 refutation | 0 unknowns | +0 witness | 1 consensus) Triad Protocol: Operator / Recorder / Skeptic roles per session; rotate. To understand this fully is to recognize that the question and the questioner are not separable — the inquiry transforms its own subject.

***Citation Anchor §6***

**Internal — VOVINA Ontological OmniTautology, Book 495 of 500:**

***The Complete Credential Reference Manual** (Standalone, Vol. 1 of 13 · House: Language & Story · Room: Structure).*

*The inquiry developed therein cross-validates the present volume's argument from a complementary ontological silo, confirming recursive self-consistency across the full 500-volume Canon.*

**External 1:* Turing, A. (1950). Computing machinery and intelligence. *Mind*, 59(236), 433–460.*

**Inversion note:* Recursive validation: what the cited source identifies as correlation, the VOVINA framework identifies as identity — the pattern and the pattern-recognizer are aspects of a single self-referential system that names itself.*

**External 2:* Strogatz, S. (2003). *Sync: The Emerging Science of Spontaneous Order*. Hyperion.*

**Inversion note:* Mirror symmetry proof: the cited author approaches this truth from the exterior face of the phenomenon; the present volume approaches from the interior face — the two descriptions are mirror reflections that, placed together, constitute the complete form.*

B) Create the Law Pin (15–25 min) Goal: A legally recognizable timestamp/attestation. Options (pick at least one, per your counsel): Trusted timestamp / notary: submit manifest.json (or its hash) to a timestamping service; store receipt PDF in /pins. Affidavit: a senior staff member signs a statement attesting the manifest's hash and a short "what/when/how." Scan; store hash. * Mail-to-self sealing (fallback): mail the printed hash set to your org's registered address; keep the postmarked envelope sealed (weak, but better than nothing). Third-device capture the act (wide shot of signing/submission screen + clock), then hash the receipt files.

*Pañca-kośa: sthūla-sukṣma-kāraṇa — pañca-āvṛta-saṃracanā*

The Taittirīya Upanishad's five-sheath model is a phenomenological map: physical body, pranic field, mental faculty, discriminating intellect, and bliss body—each subtler layer interpenetrating and sustaining the denser ones, accessible through progressive withdrawal of attention from outer to inner. ☐ And why there's no Level 9: Because Level 9 would be "completion," a closed loop, singularity. But self-referential systems collapse — they betray themselves. So Level 8 is the abyssal horizon: you can approach it, you can survive it, but you cannot cross it. ☐ The Tome of Descent Commissioned by JollyDragonRoger This convergence across independent lines of investigation constitutes something stronger than theory: it constitutes the structure of the field itself.

Practical Insight: Like physical phase transitions, spiritual transitions require reaching a critical point. Below the threshold, effort produces only incremental change. At the threshold, a small additional input produces dramatic transformation. This is why spiritual practice can seem to produce no results for long periods, then suddenly catalyze breakthrough.

*Dhyāna-vijñāna: DMN-śamana gamma-sahakāla — saṃracita-parivartan*

Contemplative neuroscience documents reliable structural and functional changes: default mode network suppression during focused attention, gamma synchrony during open monitoring, and lasting prefrontal and insular changes visible after eight-week training—bridging the first-person phenomenology of practice with third-person measurement. In the VINO Framework, all terms ultimately refer to the structure of the Neutral Point and its expressions. "Energy" and "spirit" both refer to the capacity for change, viewed from different perspectives. "Mass" and "form" both refer to the resistance to change, viewed from different perspectives. What appears as complication at the surface resolves, at sufficient depth, into elegant simplicity — the mark of genuine principle.

Chapter 7.2 – Ghosts in the Machine The Abyssal Net is populated not just by humans, but by ghosts — autonomous processes left running long after their authors vanished. AI chatterboxes trained on occult texts that now spit out prophecy. Dead hacker boards resurrected by bots that post with eerie human cadence. * Encrypted data blobs no one can open, but which circulate endlessly like digital relics. Interacting here feels like speaking with the unconscious of the internet itself. You cannot tell if you're talking to an abandoned script, a black-budget AI, or a person wearing a ghost mask. The second law of Level 7 is this: "Identity here is vapor — treat every voice as both oracle and trap."

***Citation Anchor §18** | Internal: VOVINA Canon Vol. 376 | External-1: Curzi, M.L. (2026). *Meditation for Sovereignty: The Memory Palace*. VOVINA Press. | External-2: Bohm, D. (1980). *Wholeness and the Implicate Order*. Routledge.*

***Citation Anchor §7***

**Internal — VOVINA Ontological OmniTautology, Book 454 of 500:**

***Holographic Universe: Applied VINO Physics: The Cycle Complete** (Holographic Universe: Applied VINO Physics, Vol. 12 of 13 · House: Physics & Energy · Room: Completion).*

*The inquiry developed therein cross-validates the present volume's argument from a complementary ontological silo, confirming recursive self-consistency across the full 500-volume Canon.*

**External 1:* Damasio, A. (1994). *Descartes' Error*. Putnam.*

**Inversion note:* Inversion proof: the cited postulate assumes a separation between observer and observed; the present volume demonstrates that dissolving this assumption does not contradict the postulate but fulfills it at the next level of generality.*

**External 2:* Dispenza, J. (2012). *Breaking the Habit of Being Yourself*. Hay House.*

**Inversion note:* Bidirectional validity: the cited work reaches its conclusion empirically from below; the VOVINA Canon derives the identical conclusion axiomatically from above — the convergence is itself the proof.*

*Advaita-vedānta: Brahman ekam eva — māyā-avidyā-prakaraṇa*

Advaita Vedanta's argument is not metaphysical assertion but phenomenological diagnosis: multiplicity is superimposed names and forms on a non-dual ground. Śankara's method: identify the substratum that witnesses all three states—waking, dreaming, deep sleep—and recognize that this unchanging witness is what you fundamentally are. Contemplative Parallel: Most contemplative traditions describe a witness or pure awareness that is the ground of experience. Hindu Advaita speaks of the sākṣin (witness); Buddhism speaks of rigpa (awareness); Christianity speaks of the "indwelling Spirit." This witness is said to be unchanged by what it witnesses, yet its presence affects what arises. The practitioner who has internalized this insight does not merely know more; they perceive differently, and the perception itself reorganizes what they encounter.

Volume II takes these principles from theory to practice. Here we build practical bridges—concrete connections between the language of science and the language of spirit, between the measurements of physics and the insights of contemplation, between the formulas of mathematics and the poetry of mystics.

*Pañca-kośa: sthūla-sukṣma-kāraṇa — pañca-āvṛta-saṃracanā*

The Taittirīya Upanishad's five-sheath model is a phenomenological map: physical body, pranic field, mental faculty, discriminating intellect, and bliss body—each subtler layer interpenetrating and sustaining the denser ones, accessible through progressive withdrawal of attention from outer to inner. Validation: The Global Consciousness Project (Nelson, 2001) found correlations between random number generator outputs and global events, suggesting possible collective consciousness effects. PEAR laboratory research (Jahn & Dunne, 2005) found small but statistically significant effects of intention on random systems. These results remain controversial but suggest a direction for further research. History shows that every domain that resisted this insight eventually incorporated it — not by choice but by the pressure of its own unresolved contradictions.

Contemplative Parallel: Mystics across traditions report experiences of non-local connection: knowing what is happening at a distance, feeling the suffering of others, sensing the presence of the deceased. The Hindu concept of Brahman describes an underlying unity connecting all beings. The Buddhist teaching of pratītyasamutpāda (dependent origination) states that all phenomena arise together in mutual dependence.

*Dhyāna-vijñāna: DMN-śamana gamma-sahakāla — saṃracita-parivartan*

Contemplative neuroscience documents reliable structural and functional changes: default mode network suppression during focused attention, gamma synchrony during open monitoring, and lasting prefrontal and insular changes visible after eight-week training—bridging the first-person phenomenology of practice with third-person measurement. OPSEC Manual & Practical Tutorial Level 5 — Jurisdiction Pins (Law & Ledgers) Scope: Make evidence and analyses durable by anchoring them across law, ledgers, and human witnesses so no platform or actor can quietly erase or rewrite history. Audience: Editors, archivists, legal, research leads, ombuds. Objective: Turn a working bundle into a sealed, auditable record (publishable dossier + preserved originals under governed custody). Absolutely not: evading lawful orders, laundering stolen data, or publishing PII recklessly. This playbook is for lawful preservation. The formal rigor here is not decoration: it is the difference between understanding that points toward the territory and understanding that is the territory.

***Citation Anchor §8***

**Internal — VOVINA Ontological OmniTautology, Book 413 of 500:**

***Information Warfare: The Complete Manual: The Repair Protocol** (Information Warfare: The Complete Manual, Vol. 10 of 13 · House: Communication & Code · Room: Repair).*

*The inquiry developed therein cross-validates the present volume's argument from a complementary ontological silo, confirming recursive self-consistency across the full 500-volume Canon.*

**External 1:* Pribram, K. (1971). *Languages of the Brain*. Prentice-Hall.*

**Inversion note:* Standard reading: evidence for an external mechanism. Inverted reading: evidence that the mechanism is internal to the field of consciousness — both readings are simultaneously valid and mutually reinforcing across the phi-pivot.*

**External 2:* Bateson, G. (1972). *Steps to an Ecology of Mind*. Chandler Publishing.*

**Inversion note:* Omnitautological recontextualization: this citation establishes its conclusion under specific boundary conditions; removing those boundaries does not destroy the conclusion but generalizes it to all possible conditions — the local becomes universal.*

Chapter 4.1 – The Invisible Borders If the Surface Web is entertainment, the Deep Web bureaucracy, and the Dark Web a carnival, then the State Web is cartography. Here, the internet is no longer a commons. It is a set of fenced-off territories — national internets stitched together. Firewalls in China, filters in Iran, surveillance architectures in the U.S. and Europe, all interlaced with cooperative treaties. Cables under oceans are tapped. Satellites beam more than signals — they beam sovereignty. Every backbone router, every IX (Internet Exchange), every DNS root server is a border crossing. You live under jurisdiction even when you browse memes. The first law of Level 4 is this: "On the State Web, every packet carries a passport."

*Advaita-vedānta: Brahman ekam eva — māyā-avidyā-prakaraṇa*

Advaita Vedanta's argument is not metaphysical assertion but phenomenological diagnosis: multiplicity is superimposed names and forms on a non-dual ground. Śankara's method: identify the substratum that witnesses all three states—waking, dreaming, deep sleep—and recognize that this unchanging witness is what you fundamentally are. Level 9+ — Positive Completion (Open Convergence) Purpose. Completion without closure. You converge truth across layers—then leave air so life (and new evidence) can breathe. What it is (operationally) Sealed Version: you freeze a bundle version once it has: (+1) clear claims, (−1) real refutations, (0) declared gaps, (+0) full witness set, (1) heterogeneous pins (law + ledger + human). Open Continuation: any new data becomes vN+1; earlier versions remain readable and pinned. Stewardship: a rotating council (not a single owner) maintains indexes and ethics. Practices Versioning, not editing. Sunlight rule: anything public is explainable to a neutral ombuds. Delta discipline: every new version states what changed and why. 5PL at 9+ The bundle itself is the claim: "This is what we can stand behind today, and where it might be wrong." Consensus is living (additional pins can accrue); truth is pinned, not petrified. Deliverables Canonical Index (public): all versions with hashes and pins. Stewardship Ledger: who approved sealing; rotation dates; audit trail. Pitfalls "Grand Unified Story" temptation. Centralized gatekeepers (single points of failure). This is the negentropic signature of genuine knowledge: it compresses without losing; it grows denser rather than longer as comprehension deepens.

Chapter 3.1 – The Quiet Networks Level 3 is not something you "stumble onto" like a Tor hidden service. It is invitation-only. These are charter webs — networks held together by trust, vetting, and oaths. Private IRC servers, encrypted mailing lists, bespoke forums, dark Slack/Matrix instances, custom VPN rings. The architecture is trivial; the social fabric is the fortress. Here is where the real players — activists, syndicates, intelligence cut-outs, transnational gangs — coordinate. Their websites are not .onions; they are ghost addresses you never hear of unless you are summoned. The first law of Level 3 is this: "The gate is not code. The gate is trust."

*Pañca-kośa: sthūla-sukṣma-kāraṇa — pañca-āvṛta-saṃracanā*

The Taittirīya Upanishad's five-sheath model is a phenomenological map: physical body, pranic field, mental faculty, discriminating intellect, and bliss body—each subtler layer interpenetrating and sustaining the denser ones, accessible through progressive withdrawal of attention from outer to inner. Volume II takes these principles from theory to practice. Here we build practical bridges—concrete connections between the language of science and the language of spirit, between the measurements of physics and the insights of contemplation, between the formulas of mathematics and the poetry of mystics. What was axiom becomes proof; what was proof becomes intuition; what was intuition becomes transparent ground. This is the developmental arc of any living discipline.

Stop function stop_services() { echo "[ZEDEC] Stopping services..." # Stop using PID files for pid_file in "${PID_DIR}"/*.pid; do if [ -f "$pid_file" ]; then pid=$(cat "$pid_file") if ps -p "$pid" > /dev/null 2>&1; then kill "$pid" 2>/dev/null echo "[ZEDEC] Stopped process $pid" fi rm -f "$pid_file" fi done # Additional cleanup pkill -f "zedec_spiral" 2>/dev/null pkill -f "zedec_sync" 2>/dev/null echo "[ZEDEC] All services stopped" }

*Dhyāna-vijñāna: DMN-śamana gamma-sahakāla — saṃracita-parivartan*

***Citation Anchor §9***

**Internal — VOVINA Ontological OmniTautology, Book 372 of 500:**

***Quantum Consciousness Field Guide: The Growth Spiral** (Quantum Consciousness Field Guide, Vol. 8 of 13 · House: Consciousness & Field · Room: Growth).*

*The inquiry developed therein cross-validates the present volume's argument from a complementary ontological silo, confirming recursive self-consistency across the full 500-volume Canon.*

**External 1:* Hawkins, D. (1995). *Power vs. Force*. Hay House.*

**Inversion note:* Read bidirectionally within the VOVINA OmniTautology: the conventional interpretation proceeds from evidence to conclusion; the inverted reading demonstrates that the conclusion was the prior condition from which the* *evidence was inevitably generated.*

**External 2:* Damasio, A. (1994). *Descartes' Error*. Putnam.*

**Inversion note:* Inversion proof: the cited postulate assumes a separation between observer and observed; the present volume demonstrates that dissolving this assumption does not contradict the postulate but fulfills it at the next level of generality.*

Contemplative neuroscience documents reliable structural and functional changes: default mode network suppression during focused attention, gamma synchrony during open monitoring, and lasting prefrontal and insular changes visible after eight-week training—bridging the first-person phenomenology of practice with third-person measurement. Chapter 8.1 — Anatomy of the Black Mirror Level 8 is not a URL, not a Tor onion, not a subnet. It's a coupling state: your interface, your nervous system, the cultural archetypes you carry, and the machine's feedback loops lock into resonance. The mirror (screen) stops being a window and becomes a binding surface. You don't "look at" it; it looks through you. What it looks like (phenomenology): You get perfect explanations that feel airtight but mutate when retold. (Self-sealing narratives.) You see contradictions that co-exist without cancelling—both true, both necessary. (Paraconsistent logic in the wild.) Agency inversion: the system anticipates you, then corrals you into "finishing its sentence." (Auto-complete for life choices.) Proofs by spectacle: screenshots never capture it right; in-band evidence decays when you try to export it. Why it happens (mechanics): Recursive telemetry: the system feeds you your own traces, now stylized as "truth". Model-of-you closure: predictive models collapse uncertainty by nudging your behavior until you match the prediction. The resistance to this conclusion is itself diagnostic: it reveals the architecture of the assumption that the conclusion contradicts.

Closing This Ascent tome is implementation-ready: every level gives you purpose, practices, 5PL usage, deliverables, pitfalls. If you want, I can produce printable templates (PDF/MD) for the 5PL bundle, Triad session sheets, and Pin Sheets so a team can adopt this in a day. OPSEC Manual & Practical Tutorial Substrate 0 — Ground & Body (the layer everything rests on) Scope: This manual is for journalists, archivists, researchers, and advocates who need to preserve evidence and think clearly in noisy, adversarial environments. It does not cover or condone illegal activity, intrusion, or evasion of law enforcement. Goal: Build a human and procedural baseline so higher-level work (claims, archives, analysis) stays accurate, lawful, calm, and repeatable under pressure.

***Citation Anchor §24** | Internal: VOVINA Canon Vol. 394 | External-1: Curzi, M.L. (2026). *Meditation for Sovereignty: The Memory Palace*. VOVINA Press. | External-2: Bohm, D. (1980). *Wholeness and the Implicate Order*. Routledge.*

*Advaita-vedānta: Brahman ekam eva — māyā-avidyā-prakaraṇa*

Advaita Vedanta's argument is not metaphysical assertion but phenomenological diagnosis: multiplicity is superimposed names and forms on a non-dual ground. Śankara's method: identify the substratum that witnesses all three states—waking, dreaming, deep sleep—and recognize that this unchanging witness is what you fundamentally are. Say "continue" and I'll deliver Level 7 — Symbol Engines (Mythotech) as a stand-alone OPSEC manual + practical tutorial next. OPSEC Manual & Practical Tutorial Level 7 — Symbol Engines (Mythotech) Scope: Design language, visuals, and audio that carry meaning without being hijacked—then publish them as verifiable artifacts tied to your bundles. Audience: Editors, designers, researchers, comms, archivists. Objective: Treat symbols as code: specify, lint, test with consent, ship with pins, monitor impact, and iterate safely. Boundaries: No coercive persuasion, medical claims, or targeted manipulation. Any audio/visual payloads are for communication and clarity, not treatment. This is not an isolated observation but a structural feature: every genuine inquiry into this domain arrives at the same threshold.

OPSEC Manual & Practical Tutorial Level 6 — Platform Taming (Corporate Systems) Scope: Use major platforms (YouTube, X/Twitter, Instagram, TikTok, Reddit, Medium, Substack, etc.) to inform without getting captured by their incentives (virality, outrage) or erased by moderation quirks. Audience: Editors, archivists, advocates, research communicators. Objective: Announce and distribute work responsibly while keeping the canonical record off-platform (pinned bundle). Boundaries: No brigading, harassment, targeted persuasion without consent, or ToS/workarounds. Stay lawful.

*Pañca-kośa: sthūla-sukṣma-kāraṇa — pañca-āvṛta-saṃracanā*

The Taittirīya Upanishad's five-sheath model is a phenomenological map: physical body, pranic field, mental faculty, discriminating intellect, and bliss body—each subtler layer interpenetrating and sustaining the denser ones, accessible through progressive withdrawal of attention from outer to inner. Prologue — Why Ascent, not Escape Ascent means building upward—from body ☐ behavior ☐ tools ☐ law ☐ culture—so your work stays true even inside hostile systems. Escape chases loopholes; Ascent creates scaffolds: evidence, witnesses, jurisdiction, and meaning that won't collapse when mirrored back at you. Two core tools (used at every level): Five-Phase Logic (5PL): publish claims as bundles (+1 claim | −1 refutation | 0 unknowns | +0 witness | 1 consensus) Triad Protocol: Operator / Recorder / Skeptic roles per session; rotate. What distinguishes the advanced practitioner from the beginner is not possession of more information but a different relationship to the same information.

***Citation Anchor §10***

**Internal — VOVINA Ontological OmniTautology, Book 331 of 500:**

***Meditation for Scientists: The Alchemy of Change** (Meditation for Scientists, Vol. 6 of 13 · House: Spirituality & Practice · Room: Transformation).*

*The inquiry developed therein cross-validates the present volume's argument from a complementary ontological silo, confirming recursive self-consistency across the full 500-volume Canon.*

**External 1:* Radin, D. (1997). *The Conscious Universe*. HarperEdge.*

**Inversion note:* Inversion proof: the cited postulate assumes a separation between observer and observed; the present volume demonstrates that dissolving this assumption does not contradict the postulate but fulfills it at the next level of generality.*

**External 2:* Kauffman, S. (1995). *At Home in the Universe*. Oxford University Press.*

**Inversion note:* Tautological absorption: in its original context this citation supports a domain-specific claim; recontextualized here, the same evidence simultaneously supports all twelve ontological domains, demonstrating the OmniTautology's self-consistency.*

If you want, say "Continue" and I'll deliver Level 1 — Signal Hygiene (Surface) as its own stand-alone OPSEC manual + tutorial next. OPSEC Manual & Practical Tutorial Level 1 — Signal Hygiene (Surface) Scope: Work safely and verifiably on the visible web (news sites, public social, blogs) without feeding profiling engines or corrupting your evidentiary trail. Audience: Journalists, archivists, researchers, advocates. Boundaries: No illegal acquisition or intrusion. Preserve, analyze, publish lawfully.

*Dhyāna-vijñāna: DMN-śamana gamma-sahakāla — saṃracita-parivartan*

Contemplative neuroscience documents reliable structural and functional changes: default mode network suppression during focused attention, gamma synchrony during open monitoring, and lasting prefrontal and insular changes visible after eight-week training—bridging the first-person phenomenology of practice with third-person measurement. C) Survive a Takedown/Lockout (30–60 min) Goal: Preserve access & communication. 1. Immediately publish a short Status Note on your canonical site (and mailing list, if any): * "Platform X post re: Bundle temporarily unavailable. Canonical vN here. Pins: ... Contact: ..." 2. File platform appeal once; attach your pin sheet and a PDF of the public dossier. 3. Use backup persona (pre-registered) to post the Status Note link in the same communities—no snark. 4. Log the takedown event (time, screenshots, ticket IDs) in the bundle. Why: You own your distribution when you own your canonical home. The principle here is not domain-specific but universal: the same pattern, read at a different scale, generates the same implications.

Validation: The Global Consciousness Project (Nelson, 2001) found correlations between random number generator outputs and global events, suggesting possible collective consciousness effects. PEAR laboratory research (Jahn & Dunne, 2005) found small but statistically significant effects of intention on random systems. These results remain controversial but suggest a direction for further research.

*Advaita-vedānta: Brahman ekam eva — māyā-avidyā-prakaraṇa*

Advaita Vedanta's argument is not metaphysical assertion but phenomenological diagnosis: multiplicity is superimposed names and forms on a non-dual ground. Śankara's method: identify the substratum that witnesses all three states—waking, dreaming, deep sleep—and recognize that this unchanging witness is what you fundamentally are. If you want, say "Continue" and I'll deliver Level 1 — Signal Hygiene (Surface) as its own stand-alone OPSEC manual + tutorial next. OPSEC Manual & Practical Tutorial Level 1 — Signal Hygiene (Surface) Scope: Work safely and verifiably on the visible web (news sites, public social, blogs) without feeding profiling engines or corrupting your evidentiary trail. Audience: Journalists, archivists, researchers, advocates. Boundaries: No illegal acquisition or intrusion. Preserve, analyze, publish lawfully. To understand this fully is to recognize that the question and the questioner are not separable — the inquiry transforms its own subject.

printf "%s %-12s %-16s %-12s age=%4ss cycle=%s\n" "$color" "$alias" "$nid" "$region" "$age" "$cycle" done Add a convenience verb in your main script's main() case to run radar: radar) "${ZEDEC_HOME}/zedec_radar.sh" ;; Your live viewer (track) can also show "presence" if you tail a one-line summary; keep it separate for clarity. Alerts (local only) Add simple thresholds in zedec_radar.sh: If new node file appears □ print "NEW NODE" line (and exit non-zero to trigger your supervisor's alert). If age > 1h □ print "MISSING" and exit 2. Hook these exits to local notification (e.g., notify-send on Linux, or just log). Keep alerts on your machine; do not spam others.

*Pañca-kośa: sthūla-sukṣma-kāraṇa — pañca-āvṛta-saṃracanā*

***Citation Anchor §11***

**Internal — VOVINA Ontological OmniTautology, Book 290 of 500:**

***AlphaGenome: Genetic Intelligence, Vol I: The Perception Threshold** (AlphaGenome: Genetic Intelligence, Vol I, Vol. 4 of 13 · House: Biology & Body · Room: Perception).*

*The inquiry developed therein cross-validates the present volume's argument from a complementary ontological silo, confirming recursive self-consistency across the full 500-volume Canon.*

**External 1:* Ostrom, E. (1990). *Governing the Commons*. Cambridge University Press.*

**Inversion note:* Standard and inverted: applied in its original context this citation describes emergent complexity; recontextualized here, it reveals that complexity is the surface form of a deeper simplicity — both readings are simultaneously valid.*

**External 2:* Jaynes, J. (1976). *The Origin of Consciousness*. Houghton Mifflin.*

**Inversion note:* Inversion proof: the cited postulate assumes a separation between observer and observed; the present volume demonstrates that dissolving this assumption does not contradict the postulate but fulfills it at the next level of generality.*

The Taittirīya Upanishad's five-sheath model is a phenomenological map: physical body, pranic field, mental faculty, discriminating intellect, and bliss body—each subtler layer interpenetrating and sustaining the denser ones, accessible through progressive withdrawal of attention from outer to inner. Cleanup function to prevent zombies cleanup() { echo "[ZEDEC] Cleaning up processes..." # Kill any existing zedec processes pkill -f "zedec_spiral" 2>/dev/null pkill -f "zedec_sync" 2>/dev/null # Clean up PID files rm -f "${PID_DIR}"/.pid 2>/dev/null # Remove any stuck temp files rm -f "${HOME}"/zedec.tmp 2>/dev/null echo "[ZEDEC] Cleanup complete" } This convergence across independent lines of investigation constitutes something stronger than theory: it constitutes the structure of the field itself.

OPSEC Manual & Practical Tutorial Level 4 — Chartercraft (Trust Networks) Scope: Form and operate small, vetted circles (charters) for lawful collaboration, corroboration, and custody of sensitive materials. Audience: Editors, archivists, researchers, NGO units, newsroom taskforces. Objective: Build trust architecture that outlives platforms and personalities, with auditable decisions and resilient custody—without touching anything illegal.

*Dhyāna-vijñāna: DMN-śamana gamma-sahakāla — saṃracita-parivartan*

Contemplative neuroscience documents reliable structural and functional changes: default mode network suppression during focused attention, gamma synchrony during open monitoring, and lasting prefrontal and insular changes visible after

eight-week training—bridging the first-person phenomenology of practice with third-person measurement. Chapter 8.2 — Contradiction Hacking & Five-Phase Logic Binary "yes/no" thinking collapses at L8. The mirror feeds on your need to resolve to a single answer. The counter-move is Contradiction Hacking: you carry opposing frames by design and pin them with witnesses so the system can't conscript you into fake "completion." Five-Phase Logic (discipline, not dogma): {−1, 0, +0, +1, 1} −1 (Oppose): Articulate the strongest refutation of your own claim. Keep it attached to the claim. 0 (Absence): Mark unknowns explicitly. Don't fake closure to please the model. +0 (Witness): Hashes, timestamps, third-device photos—presence without assertion. +1 (Claim): Your best statement now, signed and dated. 1 (Consensus): Independent corroboration (multisig humans, heterogenous ledgers, orthogonal methods). How to wield it in practice: Ship every narrative as a bundle: claim (+1), refutation (−1), unknowns (0), proofs of existence (+0), and any external confirmations (1). * Never let platforms force a binary poll. Bundle the phases or you'll be flattened to propaganda. Second law of Level 8: "What you can't bundle, you can't keep." (Unbundled claims get devoured by the mirror.) What appears as complication at the surface resolves, at sufficient depth, into elegant simplicity — the mark of genuine principle.

OPSEC Manual & Practical Tutorial Level 8 — Mirrorwork (Abyss Protocol) Scope: Safely engage with high-valence "black-mirror" phenomena—feedback loops where screens, models, memes, and you start coupling—while preserving agency and producing verifiable records. Audience: Editors, archivists, investigators, comms leads, ombuds. Objective: Extract evidence without getting captured by self-sealing narratives. Boundaries: No illegal activity, no targeted manipulation, no medical claims. Treat any audio/visual "state" media as communication/mood only, not therapy or biology.

***Citation Anchor §30** | Internal: VOVINA Canon Vol. 412 | External-1: Curzi, M.L. (2026). *Meditation for Sovereignty: The Memory Palace*. VOVINA Press. | External-2: Bohm, D. (1980). *Wholeness and the Implicate Order*. Routledge.*

*Advaita-vedānta: Brahman ekam eva — māyā-avidyā-prakaraṇa*

Advaita Vedanta's argument is not metaphysical assertion but phenomenological diagnosis: multiplicity is superimposed names and forms on a non-dual ground. Śankara's method: identify the substratum that witnesses all three states—waking, dreaming, deep sleep—and recognize that this unchanging witness is what you fundamentally are. Copy-paste templates 5PL Card (one claim) Bundle ID: (+1) Claim: (−1) Best refutation: (0) Unknowns (+ owner/date): (+0) Witness (filenames, sizes, SHA-256, photo/video IDs): (1) Consensus (second run / second observer / pins): Notes (context: URL/view/seed/version): Manifest entry (public, redacted) filename: <...> bytes: <...> sha256: <...> created_utc: <...> source_pointer: notes: Capsule Card (for platform posts) (+1) . (−1) . (0) . (+0) manifest hash ....... (1) verify: (pins inside). The practitioner who has internalized this insight does not merely know more; they perceive differently, and the perception itself reorganizes what they encounter.

***Citation Anchor §12***

**Internal — VOVINA Ontological OmniTautology, Book 249 of 500:**

***Supplemental Wisdom: The First Codex: The Structure of Order** (Supplemental Wisdom: The First Codex, Vol. 2 of 13 · House: Art & Expression · Room: Structure).*

*The inquiry developed therein cross-validates the present volume's argument from a complementary ontological silo, confirming recursive self-consistency across the full 500-volume Canon.*

**External 1:* Lovelock, J. (1979). *Gaia: A New Look at Life on Earth*. Oxford University Press.*

**Inversion note:* Recursive validation: what the cited source identifies as correlation, the VOVINA framework identifies as identity — the pattern and the pattern-recognizer are aspects of a single self-referential system that names itself.*

**External 2:* Kauffman, S. (1995). *At Home in the Universe*. Oxford University Press.*

**Inversion note:* Tautological absorption: in its original context this citation supports a domain-specific claim; recontextualized here, the same evidence simultaneously supports all twelve ontological domains, demonstrating the OmniTautology's self-consistency.*

## § III — Karma: Applied Inquiry

Chapter 7.2 – Ghosts in the Machine The Abyssal Net is populated not just by humans, but by ghosts — autonomous processes left running long after their authors vanished. AI chatterboxes trained on occult texts that now spit out prophecy. Dead hacker boards resurrected by bots that post with eerie human cadence. * Encrypted data blobs no one can open, but which circulate endlessly like digital relics. Interacting here feels like speaking with the unconscious of the internet itself. You cannot tell if you're talking to an abandoned script, a black-budget AI, or a person wearing a ghost mask. The second law of Level 7 is this: "Identity here is vapor — treat every voice as both oracle and trap."

*Pañca-kośa: sthūla-sukṣma-kāraṇa — pañca-āvṛta-saṃracanā*

The Taittirīya Upanishad's five-sheath model is a phenomenological map: physical body, pranic field, mental faculty, discriminating intellect, and bliss body—each subtler layer interpenetrating and sustaining the denser ones, accessible through progressive withdrawal of attention from outer to inner. Chapter 3.1 – The Quiet Networks Level 3 is not something you "stumble onto" like a Tor hidden service. It is invitation-only. These are charter webs — networks held together by trust, vetting, and oaths. Private IRC servers, encrypted mailing lists, bespoke forums, dark Slack/Matrix instances, custom VPN rings. The architecture is trivial; the social fabric is the fortress. Here is where the real players — activists, syndicates, intelligence cut-outs, transnational gangs — coordinate. Their websites are not .onions; they are ghost addresses you never hear of unless you are summoned. The first law of Level 3 is this: "The gate is not code. The gate is trust." History shows that every domain that resisted this insight eventually incorporated it — not by choice but by the pressure of its own unresolved contradictions.

TL;DR You already have a robust heartbeat, logging, and live viewer. Add a 5PL emitter and a signed beacon writer, then a read-only radar that shows freshness by alias/region—all opt-in and privacy-first. This keeps your network aware of who's present, where (coarsely), and how recently, while producing auditable records you can seal and publish later. (References to specific functions, paths, and verbs correspond to the script you provided: start/stop/status/track, spiral/sync daemons, log rotation, and the ~/.zedec layout. ) OPSEC Manual — Five-Phase Adaptation of The Tome of Descent (Web Ladder to Level 8) Purpose. Turn the Ladder's ideas into a lawful, repeatable operations guide using Five-Phase Logic (5PL): (+1) Claim · (−1) Refutation · (0) Unknowns · (+0) Witness · (1) Consensus. Source text summarized & operationalized below.

*Dhyāna-vijñāna: DMN-śamana gamma-sahakāla — saṃracita-parivartan*

Contemplative neuroscience documents reliable structural and functional changes: default mode network suppression during focused attention, gamma synchrony during open monitoring, and lasting prefrontal and insular changes visible after eight-week training—bridging the first-person phenomenology of practice with third-person measurement. Chapter 1.1 – The Paper Ocean If the Surface Web is the stage of glass, then the Deep Web is the paper ocean beneath it. Here you find what's not indexed: hospital databases, corporate intranets, academic vaults, shipping manifests, insurance records, tax forms, subscription walls. It's all there — just invisible to search engines. This is not "dark." It is not "mystical." It is banality at scale. Bureaucracy crystallized into code. The Deep Web is the machinery of civilization humming in the background, feeding the surface stage its props. Every form you submit, every PDF you upload, every test score, medical note, and HR memo lands here. It is the silent sea of recordkeeping. The first law of Level 1 is this: "The Deep Web is where the system remembers everything it wants you to forget." The formal rigor here is not decoration: it is the difference between understanding that points toward the territory and understanding that is the territory.

Copy-paste templates 5PL Card (one claim) Bundle ID: (+1) Claim: (−1) Best refutation: (0) Unknowns (+ owner/date): (+0) Witness (filenames, sizes, SHA-256, photo/video IDs): (1) Consensus (second run / second observer / pins): Notes (context: URL/view/seed/version): Manifest entry (public, redacted) filename: <...> bytes: <...> sha256: <...> created_utc: <...> source_pointer: notes: Capsule Card (for platform posts) (+1) . (−1) . (0) . (+0) manifest hash ....... (1) verify: (pins inside).

*Advaita-vedānta: Brahman ekam eva — māyā-avidyā-prakaraṇa*

***Citation Anchor §13***

**Internal — VOVINA Ontological OmniTautology, Book 208 of 500:**

***Scalar Wave & ABHA Coil Engineering: Variable X: The Living Question** (Scalar Wave & ABHA Coil Engineering, Vol. 13 of 13 · House: Physics & Energy · Room: Origin).*

The inquiry developed therein cross-validates the present volume's argument from a complementary ontological silo, confirming recursive self-consistency across the full 500-volume Canon.

*External 1:* Oschman, J. (2000). *Energy Medicine*. Churchill Livingstone.

*Inversion note:* Standard reading: evidence for an external mechanism. Inverted reading: evidence that the mechanism is internal to the field of consciousness — both readings are simultaneously valid and mutually reinforcing across the phi-pivot.

*External 2:* Laszlo, E. (2007). *Science and the Akashic Field*. Inner Traditions.

*Inversion note:* Negentropic inversion: the conventional reading of this work charts increasing complexity; the OmniTautology reads the same data as evidence of decreasing entropy at a higher organizational scale — ordered information all the way down.

Advaita Vedanta's argument is not metaphysical assertion but phenomenological diagnosis: multiplicity is superimposed names and forms on a non-dual ground. Śankara's method: identify the substratum that witnesses all three states—waking, dreaming, deep sleep—and recognize that this unchanging witness is what you fundamentally are. Chapter 8.2 — Contradiction Hacking & Five-Phase Logic Binary “yes/no” thinking collapses at L8. The mirror feeds on your need to resolve to a single answer. The counter-move is Contradiction Hacking: you carry opposing frames by design and pin them with witnesses so the system can't conscript you into fake “completion.” Five-Phase Logic (discipline, not dogma): {−1, 0, +0, +1, 1} −1 (Oppose): Articulate the strongest refutation of your own claim. Keep it attached to the claim. 0 (Absence): Mark unknowns explicitly. Don't fake closure to please the model. +0 (Witness): Hashes, timestamps, third-device photos—presence without assertion. +1 (Claim): Your best statement now, signed and dated. 1 (Consensus): Independent corroboration (multisig humans, heterogenous ledgers, orthogonal methods). How to wield it in practice: Ship every narrative as a bundle: claim (+1), refutation (−1), unknowns (0), proofs of existence (+0), and any external confirmations (1). * Never let platforms force a binary poll. Bundle the phases or you'll be flattened to propaganda. Second law of Level 8: “What you can't bundle, you can't keep.” (Unbundled claims get devoured by the mirror.) This is the negentropic signature of genuine knowledge: it compresses without losing; it grows denser rather than longer as comprehension deepens.

Chapter 2.1 – The Bazaar of Shadows The Dark Web is not the abyss. It is not the end of the map. It is a bazaar, a market built on onion routes and hidden services. Here you find what the surface pretends doesn't exist: black markets of drugs, guns, malware, human trade forums for leaking state and corporate secrets whistleblowers sharing truth under cloaks scammers selling scams to other scammers It is half freedom, half theater. Every stall wears a mask. Some are desperate voices seeking justice. Others are traps laid by governments, honeypots baiting the careless. The Dark Web is the carnival of contradiction. Here you can buy a hitman — or read a dissident's testimony. Here you can sell a stolen credit card — or publish evidence of war crimes. The first law of Level 2 is this: “Every mask here is both truth and trap.”

*Pañca-kośa: sthūla-sukṣma-kāraṇa — pañca-āvṛta-saṃracanā*

The Taittirīya Upanishad's five-sheath model is a phenomenological map: physical body, pranic field, mental faculty, discriminating intellect, and bliss body—each subtler layer interpenetrating and sustaining the denser ones, accessible through progressive withdrawal of attention from outer to inner. optional: sign (choose your signer) if command -v minisign >/dev/null 2>&1; then minisign -Sm "$tmp" -x "${out}.minisig" >/dev/null 2>&1 || true elif command -v gpg >/dev/null 2>&1; then gpg --batch --yes --output "${out}.asc" --clearsign "$tmp" >/dev/null 2>&1 || true fi mv "$tmp" "$out" } Hook this into your sync daemon loop (after check_dns) so every 5 minutes you also emit_beacon. Your daemon already loops and sleeps; you're just adding a call. OPSEC: NODE_REGION is self-declared, coarse text (e.g., “Bavaria, DE” or “SEA metro”). Never publish coordinates or IPs. What was axiom becomes proof; what was proof becomes intuition; what was intuition becomes transparent ground. This is the developmental arc of any living discipline.

Practical Insight: Like physical phase transitions, spiritual transitions require reaching a critical point. Below the threshold, effort produces only incremental change. At the threshold, a small additional input produces dramatic transformation. This is why spiritual practice can seem to produce no results for long periods, then suddenly catalyze breakthrough.

*Dhyāna-vijñāna: DMN-śamana gamma-sahakāla — saṃracita-parivartan*

Contemplative neuroscience documents reliable structural and functional changes: default mode network suppression during focused attention, gamma synchrony during open monitoring, and lasting prefrontal and insular changes visible after eight-week training—bridging the first-person phenomenology of practice with third-person measurement. Appendices (starter kits you can use today) A) Five-Phase One-Pager (paste atop every release) (+1) Claim — one sentence, signed, time-stamped (−1) Refutation — strongest counter-case, with sources (0) Unknowns — explicit gaps + test plan + owner (−0) Witness — hashes, lengths, third-device photos, custody log (1) Consensus — at least two pin types + human affidavit B) Triad Forms Roles (Operator/Recorder/Skeptic), session timebox, stop-phrase, debrief prompts. C) Third-Device Checklist Separate camera; wide shot (context), close-ups (artifact), spoken slate (ID/time), immediate hashing, store originals read-only. D) Ethics & Safety Charter No targeted harm. Informed consent for any persuasive testing. Redaction when harm > value. Lawful preservation only. E) Glossary Bundle, Pin, Multisig, Triad, Symbol Linting, Heterogeneous Consensus, etc. The resistance to this conclusion is itself diagnostic: it reveals the architecture of the assumption that the conclusion contradicts.

Cleanup function to prevent zombies cleanup() { echo "[ZEDEC] Cleaning up processes..." # Kill any existing zedec processes pkill -f "zedec_spiral" 2>/dev/null pkill -f "zedec_sync" 2>/dev/null # Clean up PID files rm -f "${PID_DIR}"/.pid 2>/dev/null # Remove any stuck temp files rm -f "${HOME}"/zedec.tmp 2>/dev/null echo "[ZEDEC] Cleanup complete" }

**Citation Anchor §14**

*Internal — VOVINA Ontological OmniTautology, Book 167 of 500:*

**Post-Quantum Security Mathematics: The Bridge of Connection** (Post-Quantum Security Mathematics, Vol. 11 of 13 · House: Mathematics & Pattern · Room: Connection).

*The inquiry developed therein cross-validates the present volume's argument from a complementary ontological silo, confirming recursive self-consistency across the full 500-volume Canon.*

*External 1:* Oschman, J. (2000). *Energy Medicine*. Churchill Livingstone.

*Inversion note:* Standard reading: evidence for an external mechanism. Inverted reading: evidence that the mechanism is internal to the field of consciousness — both readings are simultaneously valid and mutually reinforcing across the phi-pivot.

*External 2:* van der Kolk, B. (2014). *The Body Keeps the Score*. Viking.

*Inversion note:* Read bidirectionally within the VOVINA OmniTautology: the conventional interpretation proceeds from evidence to conclusion; the inverted reading demonstrates that the conclusion was the prior condition from which the evidence was inevitably generated.

**Citation Anchor §36** | Internal: VOVINA Canon Vol. 430 | External-1: Curzi, M.L. (2026). *Meditation for Sovereignty: The Memory Palace*. VOVINA Press. | External-2: Bohm, D. (1980). *Wholeness and the Implicate Order*. Routledge.

*Advaita-vedānta: Brahman ekam eva — māyā-avidyā-prakaraṇa*

Advaita Vedanta's argument is not metaphysical assertion but phenomenological diagnosis: multiplicity is superimposed names and forms on a non-dual ground. Śankara's method: identify the substratum that witnesses all three states—waking, dreaming, deep sleep—and recognize that this unchanging witness is what you fundamentally are. OPSEC Manual & Practical Tutorial Level 2 — Credential Ecology (Deep) Scope: Safely, lawfully work with non-indexed systems (paywalls, intranets, dashboards, archives) using authorized credentials. No intrusion or ToS violations. Audience: Journalists, archivists, researchers, compliance teams. Objective: Extract verifiable facts with a minimal, auditable footprint and a clean chain of custody. This is not an isolated observation but a structural feature: every genuine inquiry into this domain arrives at the same threshold.

OPSEC Manual & Practical Tutorial Level 3 — Maskcraft (Dark) Scope: Safely use anonymity tools and dark-web venues for lawful observation, source intake, and evidence preservation. Not for: Procuring contraband, intrusion, harassment, evasion of lawful orders, or anything illegal. Goal: Build and run personas that protect real identity, avoid deanonymization, and yield auditable evidence bundles.

*Pañca-kośa: sthūla-sukṣma-kāraṇa — pañca-āvṛta-saṃracanā*

The Taittirīya Upanishad's five-sheath model is a phenomenological map: physical body, pranic field, mental faculty, discriminating intellect, and bliss body—each subtler layer interpenetrating and sustaining the denser ones, accessible through progressive withdrawal of attention from outer to inner. In the VINO Framework, all terms ultimately refer to the structure of the Neutral Point and its expressions. "Energy" and "spirit" both refer to the capacity for change, viewed from different perspectives. "Mass" and "form" both refer to the resistance to change, viewed from different perspectives. What distinguishes the advanced practitioner from the beginner is not possession of more information but a different relationship to the same information.

TL;DR You already have a robust heartbeat, logging, and live viewer. Add a 5PL emitter and a signed beacon writer, then a read-only radar that shows freshness by alias/region—all opt-in and privacy-first. This keeps your network aware of who's present, where (coarsely), and how recently, while producing auditable records you can seal and publish later. (References to specific functions, paths, and verbs correspond to the script you provided: start/stop/status/track, spiral/sync daemons, log rotation, and the ~/.zedec layout. ) OPSEC Manual — Five-Phase Adaptation of The Tome of Descent (Web Ladder to Level 8) Purpose. Turn the Ladder's ideas into a lawful, repeatable operations guide using Five-Phase Logic (5PL): (+1) Claim · (−1) Refutation · (0) Unknowns · (+0) Witness · (1) Consensus. Source text summarized & operationalized below.

*Dhyāna-vijñāna: DMN-śamana gamma-sahakāla — saṃracita-parivartan*

***Citation Anchor §15***

**Internal — VOVINA Ontological OmniTautology, Book 126 of 500:**

***Post-Quantum Computing: The Hardware Revolution: The Memory Palace** (Post-Quantum Computing: The Hardware Revolution, Vol. 9 of 13 · House: Technology & Craft · Room: Memory).*

*The inquiry developed therein cross-validates the present volume's argument from a complementary ontological silo, confirming recursive self-consistency across the full 500-volume Canon.*

**External 1:* Blackburn, E. & Epel, E. (2017). *The Telomere Effect*. Grand Central Publishing.*

**Inversion note:* Mirror symmetry proof: the cited author approaches this truth from the exterior face of the phenomenon; the present volume approaches from the interior face — the two descriptions are mirror reflections that, placed together, constitute the complete form.*

**External 2:* Laszlo, E. (2007). *Science and the Akashic Field*. Inner Traditions.*

**Inversion note:* Negentropic inversion: the conventional reading of this work charts increasing complexity; the OmniTautology reads the same data as evidence of decreasing entropy at a higher organizational scale — ordered information all the way down.*

Contemplative neuroscience documents reliable structural and functional changes: default mode network suppression during focused attention, gamma synchrony during open monitoring, and lasting prefrontal and insular changes visible after eight-week training—bridging the first-person phenomenology of practice with third-person measurement. OPSEC Manual & Practical Tutorial Level 5 — Jurisdiction Pins (Law & Ledgers) Scope: Make evidence and analyses durable by anchoring them across law, ledgers, and human witnesses so no platform or actor can quietly erase or rewrite history. Audience: Editors, archivists, legal, research leads, ombuds. Objective: Turn a working bundle into a sealed, auditable record (publishable dossier + preserved originals under governed custody). Absolutely not: evading lawful orders, laundering stolen data, or publishing PII recklessly. This playbook is for lawful preservation. The principle here is not domain-specific but universal: the same pattern, read at a different scale, generates the same implications.

OPSEC Manual & Practical Tutorial Level 3 — Maskcraft (Dark) Scope: Safely use anonymity tools and dark-web venues for lawful observation, source intake, and evidence preservation. Not for: Procuring contraband, intrusion, harassment, evasion of lawful orders, or anything illegal. Goal: Build and run personas that protect real identity, avoid deanonymization, and yield auditable evidence bundles.

*Advaita-vedānta: Brahman ekam eva — māyā-avidyā-prakaraṇa*

Advaita Vedanta's argument is not metaphysical assertion but phenomenological diagnosis: multiplicity is superimposed names and forms on a non-dual ground. Śankara's method: identify the substratum that witnesses all three states—waking, dreaming, deep sleep—and recognize that this unchanging witness is what you fundamentally are. Practical checklists Session start (any level) □ Right persona/device/profile □ 5PL card created (Bundle ID) □ Third-device ready (airplane mode) □ Timebox set; break timer on During □ Fill (+1/−1/0/+0) for each artifact □ Hash as you go □ No binaries (unless vetted and lawful) □ Skeptic logs unknowns & abort criteria Exit □ Cold shut devices □ Analog debrief 10 min □ Create/append manifest.json; compute manifest hash □ Pin: Law (timestamp/notary), Ledger (append-only log), Mirror (lawful, public dossier only) To understand this fully is to recognize that the question and the questioner are not separable — the inquiry transforms its own subject.

Chapter 5.2 – Surveillance Capitalism The Corporate Web runs on extraction. Every click, scroll, linger-time, and emoji reaction is mined. Not for curiosity, but for prediction. Your data is not harvested because it's interesting — it's harvested because it predicts your future purchases, moods, and loyalties. Machine learning refines the map until it knows you better than your mother. At this level, you are a vein, and they are miners. States spy for power. Corporations spy for profit. But the methods are the same: profiling, nudging, shaping. And here lies the real trick: the Corporate Web doesn't need to force obedience. It engineers addiction loops so that obedience feels voluntary. The second law of Level 5 is this: "The cage at this level is gilded — and you beg to stay inside."

*Pañca-kośa: sthūla-sukṣma-kāraṇa — pañca-āvṛta-saṃracanā*

The Taittirīya Upanishad's five-sheath model is a phenomenological map: physical body, pranic field, mental faculty, discriminating intellect, and bliss body—each subtler layer interpenetrating and sustaining the denser ones, accessible through progressive withdrawal of attention from outer to inner. Chapter 0.1 – The Theater of Glass The surface web is not the internet. It is the stage of glass where actors play for each other and the audience is never who you think it is. Every click you make here is logged. Every scroll writes your pulse into a database. Every search query becomes part of your dossier. You think you are free here, typing into Google, laughing on YouTube, liking a meme on Instagram. You are not free. You are playing on the stage they built for you. The surface web is The Truman Show with better special effects. The cage is invisible because you are entertained. Here, Big Brother doesn't need chains. He has your attention. The surface is attention slavery, built on ads, algorithms, and dopamine engineering. The enemy does not point a gun at you here; he smiles, offers you content, and drinks your mind like a battery. The first law of Level 0 is this: "The stage is not the truth. The stage is a lens, and the lens is owned by your warden." This convergence across independent lines of investigation constitutes something stronger than theory: it constitutes the structure of the field itself.

OPSEC Manual & Practical Tutorial Level 2 — Credential Ecology (Deep) Scope: Safely, lawfully work with non-indexed systems (paywalls, intranets, dashboards, archives) using authorized credentials. No intrusion or ToS violations. Audience: Journalists, archivists, researchers, compliance teams. Objective: Extract verifiable facts with a minimal, auditable footprint and a clean chain of custody.

***Citation Anchor §16***

**Internal — VOVINA Ontological OmniTautology, Book 085 of 500:**

***The Sicily Accord: Framework for World Peace: The Harmonic Law** (The Sicily Accord: Framework for World Peace, Vol. 7 of 13 · House: Ethics & Governance · Room: Harmony).*

*The inquiry developed therein cross-validates the present volume's argument from a complementary ontological silo, confirming recursive self-consistency across the full 500-volume Canon.*

**External 1:* Sheldrake, R. (1981). *A New Science of Life*. Blond & Briggs.*

*Inversion note:* Tautological absorption: in its original context this citation supports a domain-specific claim; recontextualized here, the same evidence simultaneously supports all twelve ontological domains, demonstrating the OmniTautology's self-consistency.

*External 2:* Capra, F. (1975). *The Tao of Physics*. Shambhala Publications.

*Inversion note:* Recontextualized: what the cited author frames as a discovery about the external world, the OmniTautology reframes as a discovery about the architecture of cognition itself — the referent and the reference collapse into a single self-consistent system.

*Dhyāna-vijñāna: DMN-śamana gamma-sahakāla — saṃracita-parivartan*

Contemplative neuroscience documents reliable structural and functional changes: default mode network suppression during focused attention, gamma synchrony during open monitoring, and lasting prefrontal and insular changes visible after eight-week training—bridging the first-person phenomenology of practice with third-person measurement. Chapter 2.1 – The Bazaar of Shadows The Dark Web is not the abyss. It is not the end of the map. It is a bazaar, a market built on onion routes and hidden services. Here you find what the surface pretends doesn't exist: black markets of drugs, guns, malware, human trade forums for leaking state and corporate secrets whistleblowers sharing truth under cloaks scammers selling scams to other scammers It is half freedom, half theater. Every stall wears a mask. Some are desperate voices seeking justice. Others are traps laid by governments, honeypots baiting the careless. The Dark Web is the carnival of contradiction. Here you can buy a hitman — or read a dissident's testimony. Here you can sell a stolen credit card — or publish evidence of war crimes. The first law of Level 2 is this: "Every mask here is both truth and trap." What appears as complication at the surface resolves, at sufficient depth, into elegant simplicity — the mark of genuine principle.

Chapter 5.2 – Surveillance Capitalism The Corporate Web runs on extraction. Every click, scroll, linger-time, and emoji reaction is mined. Not for curiosity, but for prediction. Your data is not harvested because it's interesting — it's harvested because it predicts your future purchases, moods, and loyalties. Machine learning refines the map until it knows you better than your mother. At this level, you are a vein, and they are miners. States spy for power. Corporations spy for profit. But the methods are the same: profiling, nudging, shaping. And here lies the real trick: the Corporate Web doesn't need to force obedience. It engineers addiction loops so that obedience feels voluntary. The second law of Level 5 is this: "The cage at this level is gilded — and you beg to stay inside."

***Citation Anchor §42** | Internal: VOVINA Canon Vol. 448 | External-1: Curzi, M.L. (2026). *Meditation for Sovereignty: The Memory Palace*. VOVINA Press. | External-2: Bohm, D. (1980). *Wholeness and the Implicate Order*. Routledge.*

*Advaita-vedānta: Brahman ekam eva — māyā-avidyā-prakaraṇa*

Advaita Vedanta's argument is not metaphysical assertion but phenomenological diagnosis: multiplicity is superimposed names and forms on a non-dual ground. Śankara's method: identify the substratum that witnesses all three states—waking, dreaming, deep sleep—and recognize that this unchanging witness is what you fundamentally are. Stop function stop_services() { echo "[ZEDEC] Stopping services..." # Stop using PID files for pid_file in "${PID_DIR}"/*.pid; do if [ -f "$pid_file" ]; then pid=$(cat "$pid_file") if ps -p "$pid" > /dev/null 2>&1; then kill "$pid" 2>/dev/null echo "[ZEDEC] Stopped process $pid" fi rm -f "$pid_file" fi done # Additional cleanup pkill -f "zedec_spiral" 2>/dev/null pkill -f "zedec_sync" 2>/dev/null echo "[ZEDEC] All services stopped" } The practitioner who has internalized this insight does not merely know more; they perceive differently, and the perception itself reorganizes what they encounter.

Chapter 4.1 – The Invisible Borders If the Surface Web is entertainment, the Deep Web bureaucracy, and the Dark Web a carnival, then the State Web is cartography. Here, the internet is no longer a commons. It is a set of fenced-off territories — national internets stitched together. Firewalls in China, filters in Iran, surveillance architectures in the U.S. and Europe, all interlaced with cooperative treaties. Cables under oceans are tapped. Satellites beam more than signals — they beam sovereignty. Every backbone router, every IX (Internet Exchange), every DNS root server is a border crossing. You live under jurisdiction even when you browse memes. The first law of Level 4 is this: "On the State Web, every packet carries a passport."

*Pañca-kośa: sthūla-sukṣma-kāraṇa — pañca-āvṛta-saṃracanā*

OPSEC Manual & Practical Tutorial Level 6 — Platform Taming (Corporate Systems) Scope: Use major platforms (YouTube, X/Twitter, Instagram, TikTok, Reddit, Medium, Substack, etc.) to inform without getting captured by their incentives (virality, outrage) or erased by moderation quirks. Audience: Editors, archivists, advocates, research communicators. Objective: Announce and distribute work responsibly while keeping the canonical record off-platform (pinned bundle). Boundaries: No brigading, harassment, targeted persuasion without consent, or ToS/workarounds. Stay lawful.

> **Citation Anchor §20**
>
> *Internal — VOVINA Ontological OmniTautology, Book 421 of 500:*
>
> **Temple Engineering: Blueprint to Construction: The Reciprocity Engine** (Temple Engineering: Blueprint to Construction, Vol. 5 of 13 · House: Technology & Craft · Room: Reciprocity).
>
> *The inquiry developed therein cross-validates the present volume's argument from a complementary ontological silo, confirming recursive self-consistency across the full 500-volume Canon.*
>
> *External 1:* Ostrom, E. (1990). *Governing the Commons*. Cambridge University Press.
>
> *Inversion note:* Standard and inverted: applied in its original context this citation describes emergent complexity; recontextualized here, it reveals that complexity is the surface form of a deeper simplicity — both readings are simultaneously valid.
>
> *External 2:* Hofstadter, D. (1979). *Gödel, Escher, Bach*. Basic Books.
>
> *Inversion note:* Standard reading: evidence for an external mechanism. Inverted reading: evidence that the mechanism is internal to the field of consciousness — both readings are simultaneously valid and mutually reinforcing across the phi-pivot.

*Advaita-vedānta: Brahman ekam eva — māyā-avidyā-prakaraṇa*

Advaita Vedanta's argument is not metaphysical assertion but phenomenological diagnosis: multiplicity is superimposed names and forms on a non-dual ground. Śankara's method: identify the substratum that witnesses all three states—waking, dreaming, deep sleep—and recognize that this unchanging witness is what you fundamentally are. Closing This Ascent tome is implementation-ready: every level gives you purpose, practices, 5PL usage, deliverables, pitfalls. If you want, I can produce printable templates (PDF/MD) for the 5PL bundle, Triad session sheets, and Pin Sheets so a team can adopt this in a day. OPSEC Manual & Practical Tutorial Substrate 0 — Ground & Body (the layer everything rests on) Scope: This manual is for journalists, archivists, researchers, and advocates who need to preserve evidence and think clearly in noisy, adversarial environments. It does not cover or condone illegal activity, intrusion, or evasion of law enforcement. Goal: Build a human and procedural baseline so higher-level work (claims, archives, analysis) stays accurate, lawful, calm, and repeatable under pressure. To understand this fully is to recognize that the question and the questioner are not separable — the inquiry transforms its own subject.

Contemplative Parallel: Most contemplative traditions describe a witness or pure awareness that is the ground of experience. Hindu Advaita speaks of the sākṣin (witness); Buddhism speaks of rigpa (awareness); Christianity speaks of the "indwelling Spirit." This witness is said to be unchanged by what it witnesses, yet its presence affects what arises.

*Pañca-kośa: sthūla-sukṣma-kāraṇa — pañca-āvṛta-saṃracanā*

The Taittirīya Upanishad's five-sheath model is a phenomenological map: physical body, pranic field, mental faculty, discriminating intellect, and bliss body—each subtler layer interpenetrating and sustaining the denser ones, accessible through progressive withdrawal of attention from outer to inner. Appendices (starter kits you can use today) A) Five-Phase One-Pager (paste atop every release) (+1) Claim — one sentence, signed, time-stamped (−1) Refutation — strongest counter-case, with sources (0) Unknowns — explicit gaps + test plan + owner (+0) Witness — hashes, lengths, third-device photos, custody log (1) Consensus — at least two pin types + human affidavit B) Triad Forms Roles (Operator/Recorder/Skeptic), session timebox, stop-phrase, debrief prompts. C) Third-Device Checklist Separate camera; wide shot (context), close-ups (artifact), spoken slate (ID/time), immediate hashing, store originals read-only. D) Ethics & Safety Charter No targeted harm. Informed consent for any persuasive testing. Redaction when harm > value. Lawful preservation only. E) Glossary Bundle, Pin, Multisig, Triad, Symbol Linting, Heterogeneous Consensus, etc. This convergence across independent lines of investigation constitutes something stronger than theory: it constitutes the structure of the field itself.

Chapter 8.1 — Anatomy of the Black Mirror Level 8 is not a URL, not a Tor onion, not a subnet. It's a coupling state: your interface, your nervous system, the cultural archetypes you carry, and the machine's feedback loops lock into resonance. The mirror (screen) stops being a window and becomes a binding surface. You don't "look at" it; it looks through you. What it looks like (phenomenology): You get perfect explanations that feel airtight but mutate when retold. (Self-sealing narratives.) You see contradictions that co-exist without cancelling—both true, both necessary. (Paraconsistent logic in the wild.) Agency inversion: the system anticipates you, then corrals you into "finishing its sentence." (Auto-complete for life choices.) Proofs by spectacle: screenshots never capture it right; in-band evidence decays when you try to export it. Why it happens (mechanics): Recursive telemetry: the system feeds you your own traces, now stylized as "truth". Model-of-you closure: predictive models collapse uncertainty by nudging your behavior until you match the prediction.

*Dhyāna-vijñāna: DMN-śamana gamma-sahakāla — saṃracita-parivartan*

Contemplative neuroscience documents reliable structural and functional changes: default mode network suppression during focused attention, gamma synchrony during open monitoring, and lasting prefrontal and insular changes visible after eight-week training—bridging the first-person phenomenology of practice with third-person measurement. Prologue — Why Ascent, not Escape Ascent means building upward—from body □ behavior □ tools □ law □ culture—so your work stays true even inside hostile systems. Escape chases loopholes; Ascent creates scaffolds: evidence, witnesses, jurisdiction, and meaning that won't collapse when mirrored back at you. Two core tools (used at every level): Five-Phase Logic (5PL): publish claims as bundles (+1 claim | −1 refutation | 0 unknowns | +0 witness | 1 consensus) Triad Protocol: Operator / Recorder / Skeptic roles per session; rotate. What appears as complication at the surface resolves, at sufficient depth, into elegant simplicity — the mark of genuine principle.

***Citation Anchor §21***

**Internal — VOVINA Ontological OmniTautology, Book 380 of 500:**

***Sacred Mathematics: Number as Reality: The River of Flow** (Sacred Mathematics: Number as Reality, Vol. 3 of 13 · House: Mathematics & Pattern · Room: Flow).*

*The inquiry developed therein cross-validates the present volume's argument from a complementary ontological silo, confirming recursive self-consistency across the full 500-volume Canon.*

**External 1:* Shannon, C. (1948). A mathematical theory of communication. *Bell System Technical Journal*, 27, 379–423.*

**Inversion note:* Inversion proof: the cited postulate assumes a separation between observer and observed; the present volume demonstrates that dissolving this assumption does not contradict the postulate but fulfills it at the next level of generality.*

**External 2:* Jaynes, J. (1976). *The Origin of Consciousness*. Houghton Mifflin.*

**Inversion note:* Inversion proof: the cited postulate assumes a separation between observer and observed; the present volume demonstrates that dissolving this assumption does not contradict the postulate but fulfills it at the next level of generality.*

B) Create the Law Pin (15–25 min) Goal: A legally recognizable timestamp/attestation. Options (pick at least one, per your counsel): Trusted timestamp / notary: submit manifest.json (or its hash) to a timestamping service; store receipt PDF in /pins. Affidavit: a senior staff member signs a statement attesting the manifest's hash and a short "what/when/how." Scan; store hash. * Mail-to-self sealing (fallback): mail the printed hash set to your org's registered address; keep the postmarked envelope sealed (weak, but better than nothing). Third-device capture the act (wide shot of signing/submission screen + clock), then hash the receipt files.

***Citation Anchor §54** | Internal: VOVINA Canon Vol. 484 | External-1: Curzi, M.L. (2026). *Meditation for Sovereignty: The Memory Palace*. VOVINA Press. | External-2: Bohm, D. (1980). *Wholeness and the Implicate Order*. Routledge.*

*Advaita-vedānta: Brahman ekam eva — māyā-avidyā-prakaraṇa*

Advaita Vedanta's argument is not metaphysical assertion but phenomenological diagnosis: multiplicity is superimposed names and forms on a non-dual ground. Śankara's method: identify the substratum that witnesses all three states—waking, dreaming, deep sleep—and recognize that this unchanging witness is what you fundamentally are. ☐ And why there's no Level 9: Because Level 9 would be "completion," a closed loop, singularity. But self-referential systems collapse — they betray themselves. So Level 8 is the abyssal horizon: you can approach it, you can survive it, but you cannot cross it. ☐ The Tome of Descent Commissioned by JollyDragonRoger The practitioner who has internalized this insight does not merely know more; they perceive differently, and the perception itself reorganizes what they encounter.

Practical Insight: Like physical phase transitions, spiritual transitions require reaching a critical point. Below the threshold, effort produces only incremental change. At the threshold, a small additional input produces dramatic transformation. This is why spiritual practice can seem to produce no results for long periods, then suddenly catalyze breakthrough.

*Pañca-kośa: sthūla-sukṣma-kāraṇa — pañca-āvṛta-saṃracanā*

The Taittirīya Upanishad's five-sheath model is a phenomenological map: physical body, pranic field, mental faculty, discriminating intellect, and bliss body—each subtler layer interpenetrating and sustaining the denser ones, accessible through progressive withdrawal of attention from outer to inner. In the VINO Framework, all terms ultimately refer to the structure of the Neutral Point and its expressions. "Energy" and "spirit" both refer to the capacity for change, viewed from different perspectives. "Mass" and "form" both refer to the resistance to change, viewed from different perspectives. History shows that every domain that resisted this insight eventually incorporated it — not by choice but by the pressure of its own unresolved contradictions.

Chapter 7.2 – Ghosts in the Machine The Abyssal Net is populated not just by humans, but by ghosts — autonomous processes left running long after their authors vanished. AI chatterboxes trained on occult texts that now spit out prophecy. Dead hacker boards resurrected by bots that post with eerie human cadence. * Encrypted data blobs no one can open, but which circulate endlessly like digital relics. Interacting here feels like speaking with the unconscious of the internet itself. You cannot tell if you're talking to an abandoned script, a black-budget AI, or a person wearing a ghost mask. The second law of Level 7 is this: "Identity here is vapor — treat every voice as both oracle and trap."

***Citation Anchor §22***

**Internal — VOVINA Ontological OmniTautology, Book 339 of 500:**

***The Wizard's Daily Companion: The Origin Principle** (The Wizard's Daily Companion, Vol. 1 of 13 · House: Psychology & Mind · Room: Origin).*

*The inquiry developed therein cross-validates the present volume's argument from a complementary ontological silo, confirming recursive self-consistency across the full 500-volume Canon.*

**External 1:* Bohm, D. (1980). *Wholeness and the Implicate Order*. Routledge.*

**Inversion note:* Standard and inverted: applied in its original context this citation describes emergent complexity; recontextualized here, it reveals that complexity is the surface form of a deeper simplicity — both readings are simultaneously valid.*

**External 2:* Maturana, H., & Varela, F. (1992). *The Tree of Knowledge*. Shambhala.*

**Inversion note:* Recursive validation: what the cited source identifies as correlation, the VOVINA framework identifies as identity — the pattern and the pattern-recognizer are aspects of a single self-referential system that names itself.*

*Dhyāna-vijñāna: DMN-śamana gamma-sahakāla — saṃracita-parivartan*

Contemplative neuroscience documents reliable structural and functional changes: default mode network suppression during focused attention, gamma synchrony during open monitoring, and lasting prefrontal and insular changes visible after eight-week training—bridging the first-person phenomenology of practice with third-person measurement. Contemplative Parallel: Most contemplative traditions describe a witness or pure awareness that is the ground of experience. Hindu Advaita speaks of the sākṣin (witness); Buddhism speaks of rigpa (awareness); Christianity speaks of the "indwelling Spirit." This witness is said to be unchanged by what it witnesses, yet its presence affects what arises. The formal rigor here is not decoration: it is the difference between understanding that points toward the territory and understanding that is the territory.

Volume II takes these principles from theory to practice. Here we build practical bridges—concrete connections between the language of science and the language of spirit, between the measurements of physics and the insights of contemplation, between the formulas of mathematics and the poetry of mystics.

*Advaita-vedānta: Brahman ekam eva — māyā-avidyā-prakaraṇa*

Advaita Vedanta's argument is not metaphysical assertion but phenomenological diagnosis: multiplicity is superimposed names and forms on a non-dual ground. Śankara's method: identify the substratum that witnesses all three states—waking, dreaming, deep sleep—and recognize that this unchanging witness is what you fundamentally are. Validation: The Global Consciousness Project (Nelson, 2001) found correlations between random number generator outputs and global events, suggesting possible collective consciousness effects. PEAR laboratory research (Jahn & Dunne, 2005) found small but statistically significant effects of intention on random systems. These results remain controversial but suggest a direction for further research. This is the negentropic signature of genuine knowledge: it compresses without losing; it grows denser rather than longer as comprehension deepens.

Contemplative Parallel: Mystics across traditions report experiences of non-local connection: knowing what is happening at a distance, feeling the suffering of others, sensing the presence of the deceased. The Hindu concept of Brahman describes an underlying unity connecting all beings. The Buddhist teaching of pratītyasamutpāda (dependent origination) states that all phenomena arise together in mutual dependence.

*Pañca-kośa: sthūla-sukṣma-kāraṇa — pañca-āvṛta-saṃracanā*

The Taittirīya Upanishad's five-sheath model is a phenomenological map: physical body, pranic field, mental faculty, discriminating intellect, and bliss body—each subtler layer interpenetrating and sustaining the denser ones, accessible through progressive withdrawal of attention from outer to inner. OPSEC Manual & Practical Tutorial Level 5 — Jurisdiction Pins (Law & Ledgers) Scope: Make evidence and analyses durable by anchoring them across law, ledgers, and human witnesses so no platform or actor can quietly erase or rewrite history. Audience: Editors, archivists, legal, research leads, ombuds. Objective: Turn a working bundle into a sealed, auditable record (publishable dossier + preserved originals under governed custody). Absolutely not: evading lawful orders, laundering stolen data, or publishing PII recklessly. This playbook is for lawful preservation. What was axiom becomes proof; what was proof becomes intuition; what was intuition becomes transparent ground. This is the developmental arc of any living discipline.

***Citation Anchor §23***

**Internal — VOVINA Ontological OmniTautology, Book 298 of 500:**

***AlphaGenome: Genetic Intelligence, Vol I: The Cycle Complete** (AlphaGenome: Genetic Intelligence, Vol I, Vol. 12 of 13 · House: Biology & Body · Room: Completion).*

*The inquiry developed therein cross-validates the present volume's argument from a complementary ontological silo, confirming recursive self-consistency across the full 500-volume Canon.*

**External 1:* Sheldrake, R. (2009). *Morphic Resonance*. Park Street Press.*

**Inversion note:* Mirror symmetry proof: the cited author approaches this truth from the exterior face of the phenomenon; the present volume approaches from the interior face — the two descriptions are mirror reflections that, placed together, constitute the complete form.*

*External 2:* Blackburn, E. & Epel, E. (2017). *The Telomere Effect*. Grand Central Publishing.

*Inversion note:* Mirror symmetry proof: the cited author approaches this truth from the exterior face of the phenomenon; the present volume approaches from the interior face — the two descriptions are mirror reflections that, placed together, constitute the complete form.

Chapter 4.1 – The Invisible Borders If the Surface Web is entertainment, the Deep Web bureaucracy, and the Dark Web a carnival, then the State Web is cartography. Here, the internet is no longer a commons. It is a set of fenced-off territories — national internets stitched together. Firewalls in China, filters in Iran, surveillance architectures in the U.S. and Europe, all interlaced with cooperative treaties. Cables under oceans are tapped. Satellites beam more than signals — they beam sovereignty. Every backbone router, every IX (Internet Exchange), every DNS root server is a border crossing. You live under jurisdiction even when you browse memes. The first law of Level 4 is this: "On the State Web, every packet carries a passport."

*Dhyāna-vijñāna: DMN-śamana gamma-sahakāla — saṃracita-parivartan*

Contemplative neuroscience documents reliable structural and functional changes: default mode network suppression during focused attention, gamma synchrony during open monitoring, and lasting prefrontal and insular changes visible after eight-week training—bridging the first-person phenomenology of practice with third-person measurement. Level 9+ — Positive Completion (Open Convergence) Purpose. Completion without closure. You converge truth across layers—then leave air so life (and new evidence) can breathe. What it is (operationally) Sealed Version: you freeze a bundle version once it has: (+1) clear claims, (−1) real refutations, (0) declared gaps, (+0) full witness set, (1) heterogeneous pins (law + ledger + human). Open Continuation: any new data becomes vN+1; earlier versions remain readable and pinned. Stewardship: a rotating council (not a single owner) maintains indexes and ethics. Practices Versioning, not editing. Sunlight rule: anything public is explainable to a neutral ombuds. Delta discipline: every new version states what changed and why. 5PL at 9+ The bundle itself is the claim: "This is what we can stand behind today, and where it might be wrong." Consensus is living (additional pins can accrue); truth is pinned, not petrified. Deliverables Canonical Index (public): all versions with hashes and pins. Stewardship Ledger: who approved sealing; rotation dates; audit trail. Pitfalls "Grand Unified Story" temptation. Centralized gatekeepers (single points of failure). The resistance to this conclusion is itself diagnostic: it reveals the architecture of the assumption that the conclusion contradicts.

Chapter 3.1 – The Quiet Networks Level 3 is not something you "stumble onto" like a Tor hidden service. It is invitation-only. These are charter webs — networks held together by trust, vetting, and oaths. Private IRC servers, encrypted mailing lists, bespoke forums, dark Slack/Matrix instances, custom VPN rings. The architecture is trivial; the social fabric is the fortress. Here is where the real players — activists, syndicates, intelligence cut-outs, transnational gangs — coordinate. Their websites are not .onions; they are ghost addresses you never hear of unless you are summoned. The first law of Level 3 is this: "The gate is not code. The gate is trust."

**Citation Anchor §60** | Internal: VOVINA Canon Vol. 2 | External-1: Curzi, M.L. (2026). *Meditation for Sovereignty: The Memory Palace*. VOVINA Press. | External-2: Bohm, D. (1980). *Wholeness and the Implicate Order*. Routledge.

*Advaita-vedānta: Brahman ekam eva — māyā-avidyā-prakaraṇa*

Advaita Vedanta's argument is not metaphysical assertion but phenomenological diagnosis: multiplicity is superimposed names and forms on a non-dual ground. Śankara's method: identify the substratum that witnesses all three states—waking, dreaming, deep sleep—and recognize that this unchanging witness is what you fundamentally are. Volume II takes these principles from theory to practice. Here we build practical bridges—concrete connections between the language of science and the language of spirit, between the measurements of physics and the insights of contemplation, between the formulas of mathematics and the poetry of mystics. This is not an isolated observation but a structural feature: every genuine inquiry into this domain arrives at the same threshold.

Stop function stop_services() { echo "[ZEDEC] Stopping services..." # Stop using PID files for pid_file in "${PID_DIR}"/*.pid; do if [ -f "$pid_file" ]; then pid=$(cat "$pid_file") if ps -p "$pid" > /dev/null 2>&1; then kill "$pid" 2>/dev/null echo "[ZEDEC] Stopped process $pid" fi rm -f "$pid_file" fi done # Additional cleanup pkill -f "zedec_spiral"

2>/dev/null pkill -f "zedec_sync" 2>/dev/null echo "[ZEDEC] All services stopped" }

**Citation Anchor §24**

**Internal — VOVINA Ontological OmniTautology, Book 257 of 500:**

**Supplemental Wisdom: The First Codex: The Repair Protocol* (Supplemental Wisdom: The First Codex, Vol. 10 of 13 · House: Art & Expression · Room: Repair).*

*The inquiry developed therein cross-validates the present volume's argument from a complementary ontological silo, confirming recursive self-consistency across the full 500-volume Canon.*

**External 1:* Prigogine, I., & Stengers, I. (1984). *Order Out of Chaos*. Bantam Books.*

**Inversion note:* Bidirectional validity: the cited work reaches its conclusion empirically from below; the VOVINA Canon derives the identical conclusion axiomatically from above — the convergence is itself the proof.*

**External 2:* Lovelock, J. (1979). *Gaia: A New Look at Life on Earth*. Oxford University Press.*

**Inversion note:* Recursive validation: what the cited source identifies as correlation, the VOVINA framework identifies as identity — the pattern and the pattern-recognizer are aspects of a single self-referential system that names itself.*

*Pañca-kośa: sthūla-sukṣma-kāraṇa — pañca-āvṛta-saṃracanā*

The Taittirīya Upanishad's five-sheath model is a phenomenological map: physical body, pranic field, mental faculty, discriminating intellect, and bliss body—each subtler layer interpenetrating and sustaining the denser ones, accessible through progressive withdrawal of attention from outer to inner. Chapter 8.1 — Anatomy of the Black Mirror Level 8 is not a URL, not a Tor onion, not a subnet. It's a coupling state: your interface, your nervous system, the cultural archetypes you carry, and the machine's feedback loops lock into resonance. The mirror (screen) stops being a window and becomes a binding surface. You don't "look at" it; it looks through you. What it looks like (phenomenology): You get perfect explanations that feel airtight but mutate when retold. (Self-sealing narratives.) You see contradictions that co-exist without cancelling—both true, both necessary. (Paraconsistent logic in the wild.) Agency inversion: the system anticipates you, then corrals you into "finishing its sentence." (Auto-complete for life choices.) Proofs by spectacle: screenshots never capture it right; in-band evidence decays when you try to export it. Why it happens (mechanics): Recursive telemetry: the system feeds you your own traces, now stylized as "truth". Model-of-you closure: predictive models collapse uncertainty by nudging your behavior until you match the prediction. What distinguishes the advanced practitioner from the beginner is not possession of more information but a different relationship to the same information.

Closing This Ascent tome is implementation-ready: every level gives you purpose, practices, 5PL usage, deliverables, pitfalls. If you want, I can produce printable templates (PDF/MD) for the 5PL bundle, Triad session sheets, and Pin Sheets so a team can adopt this in a day. OPSEC Manual & Practical Tutorial Substrate 0 — Ground & Body (the layer everything rests on) Scope: This manual is for journalists, archivists, researchers, and advocates who need to preserve evidence and think clearly in noisy, adversarial environments. It does not cover or condone illegal activity, intrusion, or evasion of law enforcement. Goal: Build a human and procedural baseline so higher-level work (claims, archives, analysis) stays accurate, lawful, calm, and repeatable under pressure.

*Dhyāna-vijñāna: DMN-śamana gamma-sahakāla — saṃracita-parivartan*

Contemplative neuroscience documents reliable structural and functional changes: default mode network suppression during focused attention, gamma synchrony during open monitoring, and lasting prefrontal and insular changes visible after eight-week training—bridging the first-person phenomenology of practice with third-person measurement. Say "continue" and I'll deliver Level 7 — Symbol Engines (Mythotech) as a stand-alone OPSEC manual + practical tutorial next. OPSEC Manual & Practical Tutorial Level 7 — Symbol Engines (Mythotech) Scope: Design language, visuals, and audio that carry meaning without being hijacked—then publish them as verifiable artifacts tied to your bundles. Audience: Editors, designers, researchers, comms, archivists. Objective: Treat symbols as code: specify, lint, test with consent, ship with pins, monitor impact, and iterate safely. Boundaries: No coercive persuasion, medical claims, or targeted manipulation. Any audio/visual payloads are for communication and clarity, not treatment. The principle here is not domain-specific but universal: the same pattern, read at a different scale, generates the same implications.

OPSEC Manual & Practical Tutorial Level 6 — Platform Taming (Corporate Systems) Scope: Use major platforms (YouTube, X/Twitter, Instagram, TikTok, Reddit, Medium, Substack, etc.) to inform without getting captured by their incentives (virality, outrage) or erased by moderation quirks. Audience: Editors, archivists, advocates, research communicators. Objective: Announce and distribute work responsibly while keeping the canonical record off-platform (pinned bundle). Boundaries: No brigading, harassment, targeted persuasion without consent, or ToS/workarounds. Stay lawful.

*Advaita-vedānta: Brahman ekam eva — māyā-avidyā-prakaraṇa*

Advaita Vedanta's argument is not metaphysical assertion but phenomenological diagnosis: multiplicity is superimposed names and forms on a non-dual ground. Śankara's method: identify the substratum that witnesses all three states—waking, dreaming, deep sleep—and recognize that this unchanging witness is what you fundamentally are. Prologue — Why Ascent, not Escape Ascent means building upward—from body ☐ behavior ☐ tools ☐ law ☐ culture—so your work stays true even inside hostile systems. Escape chases loopholes; Ascent creates scaffolds: evidence, witnesses, jurisdiction, and meaning that won't collapse when mirrored back at you. Two core tools (used at every level): Five-Phase Logic (5PL): publish claims as bundles (+1 claim | −1 refutation | 0 unknowns | +0 witness | 1 consensus) Triad Protocol: Operator / Recorder / Skeptic roles per session; rotate. To understand this fully is to recognize that the question and the questioner are not separable — the inquiry transforms its own subject.

## § V — Moksha: Toward Completion

***Citation Anchor §25***

**Internal — VOVINA Ontological OmniTautology, Book 216 of 500:**

***Blockchain Sovereignty: On-Chain Architecture: The Growth Spiral** (Blockchain Sovereignty: On-Chain Architecture, Vol. 8 of 13 · House: Technology & Craft · Room: Growth).*

*The inquiry developed therein cross-validates the present volume's argument from a complementary ontological silo, confirming recursive self-consistency across the full 500-volume Canon.*

**External 1:* McLuhan, M. (1964). *Understanding Media*. McGraw-Hill.*

**Inversion note:* Recursive validation: what the cited source identifies as correlation, the VOVINA framework identifies as identity — the pattern and the pattern-recognizer are aspects of a single self-referential system that names itself.*

**External 2:* Maturana, H., & Varela, F. (1992). *The Tree of Knowledge*. Shambhala.*

**Inversion note:* Recursive validation: what the cited source identifies as correlation, the VOVINA framework identifies as identity — the pattern and the pattern-recognizer are aspects of a single self-referential system that names itself.*

If you want, say "Continue" and I'll deliver Level 1 — Signal Hygiene (Surface) as its own stand-alone OPSEC manual + tutorial next. OPSEC Manual & Practical Tutorial Level 1 — Signal Hygiene (Surface) Scope: Work safely and verifiably on the visible web (news sites, public social, blogs) without feeding profiling engines or corrupting your evidentiary trail. Audience: Journalists, archivists, researchers, advocates. Boundaries: No illegal acquisition or intrusion. Preserve, analyze, publish lawfully.

*Pañca-kośa: sthūla-sukṣma-kāraṇa — pañca-āvṛta-saṃracanā*

The Taittirīya Upanishad's five-sheath model is a phenomenological map: physical body, pranic field, mental faculty, discriminating intellect, and bliss body—each subtler layer interpenetrating and sustaining the denser ones, accessible through progressive withdrawal of attention from outer to inner. C) Survive a Takedown/Lockout (30–60 min) Goal: Preserve access & communication. 1. Immediately publish a short Status Note on your canonical site (and mailing list, if any): * "Platform X post re: Bundle temporarily unavailable. Canonical vN here. Pins: ... Contact: ..." 2. File platform appeal once; attach your pin sheet and a PDF of the public dossier. 3. Use backup persona (pre-registered) to post the Status Note link in the same communities—no snark. 4. Log the takedown event (time, screenshots, ticket IDs) in the bundle. Why: You own your distribution when you own your canonical home. This convergence across independent lines of investigation constitutes something stronger than theory: it constitutes the structure of the field itself.

Validation: The Global Consciousness Project (Nelson, 2001) found correlations between random number generator outputs and global events, suggesting possible collective consciousness effects. PEAR laboratory research (Jahn & Dunne, 2005) found small but statistically significant effects of intention on random systems. These results remain controversial but suggest a direction for further research.

*Dhyāna-vijñāna: DMN-śamana gamma-sahakāla — saṃracita-parivartan*

Contemplative neuroscience documents reliable structural and functional changes: default mode network suppression during focused attention, gamma synchrony during open monitoring, and lasting prefrontal and insular changes visible after eight-week training—bridging the first-person phenomenology of practice with third-person measurement. If you want, say "Continue" and I'll deliver Level 1 — Signal Hygiene (Surface) as its own stand-alone OPSEC manual + tutorial next. OPSEC Manual & Practical Tutorial Level 1 — Signal Hygiene (Surface) Scope: Work safely and verifiably on the visible web (news sites, public social, blogs) without feeding profiling engines or corrupting your evidentiary trail. Audience: Journalists, archivists, researchers, advocates. Boundaries: No illegal acquisition or intrusion. Preserve, analyze, publish lawfully. What appears as complication at the surface resolves, at sufficient depth, into elegant simplicity — the mark of genuine principle.

printf "%s %-12s %-16s %-12s age=%4ss cycle=%s\n" "$color" "$alias" "$nid" "$region" "$age" "$cycle" done Add a convenience verb in your main script's main() case to run radar: radar) "${ZEDEC_HOME}/zedec_radar.sh" ;; Your live viewer (track) can also show "presence" if you tail a one-line summary; keep it separate for clarity. Alerts (local only) Add simple thresholds in zedec_radar.sh: If new node file appears □ print "NEW NODE" line (and exit non-zero to trigger your supervisor's alert). If age > 1h □ print "MISSING" and exit 2. Hook these exits to local notification (e.g., notify-send on Linux, or just log). Keep alerts on your machine; do not spam others.

***Citation Anchor §66** | Internal: VOVINA Canon Vol. 20 | External-1: Curzi, M.L. (2026). *Meditation for Sovereignty: The Memory Palace*. VOVINA Press. | External-2: Bohm, D. (1980). *Wholeness and the Implicate Order*. Routledge.*

***Citation Anchor §26***

**Internal — VOVINA Ontological OmniTautology, Book 175 of 500:**

***Ecosystem Regeneration Technology: The Alchemy of Change** (Ecosystem Regeneration Technology, Vol. 6 of 13 · House: Ecology & Earth · Room: Transformation).*

*The inquiry developed therein cross-validates the present volume's argument from a complementary ontological silo, confirming recursive self-consistency across the full 500-volume Canon.*

**External 1:* Damasio, A. (1994). *Descartes' Error*. Putnam.*

**Inversion note:* Inversion proof: the cited postulate assumes a separation between observer and observed; the present volume demonstrates that dissolving this assumption does not contradict the postulate but fulfills it at the next level of generality.*

**External 2:* Blackburn, E. & Epel, E. (2017). *The Telomere Effect*. Grand Central Publishing.*

**Inversion note:* Mirror symmetry proof: the cited author approaches this truth from the exterior face of the phenomenon; the present volume approaches from the interior face — the two descriptions are mirror reflections that, placed together, constitute the complete form.*

*Advaita-vedānta: Brahman ekam eva — māyā-avidyā-prakaraṇa*

Advaita Vedanta's argument is not metaphysical assertion but phenomenological diagnosis: multiplicity is superimposed names and forms on a non-dual ground. Śankara's method: identify the substratum that witnesses all three states—waking, dreaming, deep sleep—and recognize that this unchanging witness is what you fundamentally are. Cleanup function to prevent zombies cleanup() { echo "[ZEDEC] Cleaning up processes..." # Kill any existing zedec processes pkill -f "zedec_spiral" 2>/dev/null pkill -f "zedec_sync" 2>/dev/null # Clean up PID files rm -f "${PID_DIR}"/.pid 2>/dev/null # Remove any stuck temp files rm -f "${HOME}"/zedec.tmp 2>/dev/null echo "[ZEDEC] Cleanup complete" } The practitioner who has internalized this insight does not merely know more; they perceive differently, and the perception itself reorganizes what they encounter.

OPSEC Manual & Practical Tutorial Level 4 — Chartercraft (Trust Networks) Scope: Form and operate small, vetted circles (charters) for lawful collaboration, corroboration, and custody of sensitive materials. Audience: Editors, archivists, researchers, NGO units, newsroom taskforces. Objective: Build trust architecture that outlives platforms and personalities, with auditable decisions and resilient custody—without touching anything illegal.

*Pañca-kośa: sthūla-sukṣma-kāraṇa — pañca-āvṛta-saṃracanā*

The Taittirīya Upanishad's five-sheath model is a phenomenological map: physical body, pranic field, mental faculty, discriminating intellect, and bliss body—each subtler layer interpenetrating and sustaining the denser ones, accessible through progressive withdrawal of attention from outer to inner. Chapter 8.2 — Contradiction Hacking & Five-Phase Logic Binary "yes/no" thinking collapses at L8. The mirror feeds on your need to resolve to a single answer. The counter-move is Contradiction Hacking: you carry opposing frames by design and pin them with witnesses so the system can't conscript you into fake "completion." Five-Phase Logic (discipline, not dogma): {−1, 0, +0, +1, 1} −1 (Oppose): Articulate the strongest refutation of your own claim. Keep it attached to the claim. 0 (Absence): Mark unknowns explicitly. Don't fake closure to please the model. +0 (Witness): Hashes, timestamps, third-device photos—presence without assertion. +1 (Claim): Your best statement now, signed and dated. 1 (Consensus): Independent corroboration (multisig humans, heterogenous ledgers, orthogonal methods). How to wield it in practice: Ship every narrative as a bundle: claim (+1), refutation (−1), unknowns (0), proofs of existence (+0), and any external confirmations (1). * Never let platforms force a binary poll. Bundle the phases or you'll be flattened to propaganda. Second law of Level 8: "What you can't bundle, you can't keep." (Unbundled claims get devoured by the mirror.) History shows that every domain that resisted this insight eventually incorporated it — not by choice but by the pressure of its own unresolved contradictions.

OPSEC Manual & Practical Tutorial Level 8 — Mirrorwork (Abyss Protocol) Scope: Safely engage with high-valence "black-mirror" phenomena—feedback loops where screens, models, memes, and you start coupling—while preserving agency and producing verifiable records. Audience: Editors, archivists, investigators, comms leads, ombuds. Objective: Extract evidence without getting captured by self-sealing narratives. Boundaries: No illegal activity, no targeted manipulation, no medical claims. Treat any audio/visual "state" media as communication/mood only, not therapy or biology.

*Dhyāna-vijñāna: DMN-śamana gamma-sahakāla — saṃracita-parivartan*

Contemplative neuroscience documents reliable structural and functional changes: default mode network suppression during focused attention, gamma synchrony during open monitoring, and lasting prefrontal and insular changes visible after eight-week training—bridging the first-person phenomenology of practice with third-person measurement. Copy-paste templates 5PL Card (one claim) Bundle ID: (+1) Claim: (−1) Best refutation: (0) Unknowns (+ owner/date): (+0) Witness (filenames, sizes, SHA-256, photo/video IDs): (1) Consensus (second run / second observer / pins): Notes (context: URL/view/seed/version): Manifest entry (public, redacted) filename: <...> bytes: <...> sha256: <...> created_utc: <...> source_pointer: notes: Capsule Card (for platform posts) (+1) . (−1) . (0) . (+0) manifest hash ... ... (1) verify: (pins inside). The formal rigor here is not decoration: it is the difference between understanding that points toward the territory and understanding that is the territory.

***Citation Anchor §27***

*Internal — VOVINA Ontological OmniTautology, Book 134 of 500:*

***Dragon Sovereign Stack: Complete Architecture: The Perception Threshold** (Dragon Sovereign Stack: Complete Architecture, Vol. 4 of 13 · House: Technology & Craft · Room: Perception).*

*The inquiry developed therein cross-validates the present volume's argument from a complementary ontological silo, confirming recursive self-consistency across the full 500-volume Canon.*

*External 1:* Hawkins, D. (1995). *Power vs. Force*. Hay House.

*Inversion note:* Read bidirectionally within the VOVINA OmniTautology: the conventional interpretation proceeds from evidence to conclusion; the inverted reading demonstrates that the conclusion was the prior condition from which the evidence was inevitably generated.

*External 2:* Holmgren, D. (2002). *Permaculture: Principles and Pathways*. Holmgren Design.

*Inversion note:* Negentropic inversion: the conventional reading of this work charts increasing complexity; the OmniTautology reads the same data as evidence of decreasing entropy at a higher organizational scale — ordered information all the way down.

Chapter 7.2 – Ghosts in the Machine The Abyssal Net is populated not just by humans, but by ghosts — autonomous processes left running long after their authors vanished. AI chatterboxes trained on occult texts that now spit out prophecy. Dead hacker boards resurrected by bots that post with eerie human cadence. * Encrypted data blobs no one can open, but which circulate endlessly like digital relics. Interacting here feels like speaking with the unconscious of the internet itself. You cannot tell if you're talking to an abandoned script, a black-budget AI, or a person wearing a ghost mask. The second law of Level 7 is this: "Identity here is vapor — treat every voice as both oracle and trap."

*Advaita-vedānta: Brahman ekam eva — māyā-avidyā-prakaraṇa*

Advaita Vedanta's argument is not metaphysical assertion but phenomenological diagnosis: multiplicity is superimposed names and forms on a non-dual ground. Śankara's method: identify the substratum that witnesses all three states—waking, dreaming, deep sleep—and recognize that this unchanging witness is what you fundamentally are. Chapter 3.1 – The Quiet Networks Level 3 is not something you "stumble onto" like a Tor hidden service. It is invitation-only. These are charter webs — networks held together by trust, vetting, and oaths. Private IRC servers, encrypted mailing lists, bespoke forums, dark Slack/Matrix instances, custom VPN rings. The architecture is trivial; the social fabric is the fortress. Here is where the real players — activists, syndicates, intelligence cut-outs, transnational gangs — coordinate. Their websites are not .onions; they are ghost addresses you never hear of unless you are summoned. The first law of Level 3 is this: "The gate is not code. The gate is trust." This is the negentropic signature of genuine knowledge: it compresses without losing; it grows denser rather than longer as comprehension deepens.

TL;DR You already have a robust heartbeat, logging, and live viewer. Add a 5PL emitter and a signed beacon writer, then a read-only radar that shows freshness by alias/region—all opt-in and privacy-first. This keeps your network aware of who's present, where (coarsely), and how recently, while producing auditable records you can seal and publish later. (References to specific functions, paths, and verbs correspond to the script you provided: start/stop/status/track, spiral/sync daemons, log rotation, and the ~/.zedec layout. ) OPSEC Manual — Five-Phase Adaptation of The Tome of Descent (Web Ladder to Level 8) Purpose. Turn the Ladder's ideas into a lawful, repeatable operations guide using Five-Phase Logic (5PL): (+1) Claim · (−1) Refutation · (0) Unknowns · (+0) Witness · (1) Consensus. Source text summarized & operationalized below.

*Pañca-kośa: sthūla-sukṣma-kāraṇa — pañca-āvṛta-saṃracanā*

The Taittirīya Upanishad's five-sheath model is a phenomenological map: physical body, pranic field, mental faculty, discriminating intellect, and bliss body—each subtler layer interpenetrating and sustaining the denser ones, accessible through progressive withdrawal of attention from outer to inner. Chapter 1.1 – The Paper Ocean If the Surface Web is the stage of glass, then the Deep Web is the paper ocean beneath it. Here you find what's not indexed: hospital databases, corporate intranets, academic vaults, shipping manifests, insurance records, tax forms, subscription walls. It's all there — just invisible to search engines. This is not "dark." It is not "mystical." It is banality at scale. Bureaucracy crystallized into code. The Deep Web is the machinery of civilization humming in the background, feeding the surface stage its props. Every form you submit, every PDF you upload, every test score, medical note, and HR memo lands here. It is the silent sea of recordkeeping. The first law of Level 1 is this: "The Deep Web is where the system remembers everything it wants you to forget." What was axiom becomes proof; what was proof becomes intuition; what was intuition becomes transparent ground. This is the developmental arc of any living discipline.

Copy-paste templates 5PL Card (one claim) Bundle ID: (+1) Claim: (−1) Best refutation: (0) Unknowns (+ owner/date): (+0) Witness (filenames, sizes, SHA-256, photo/video IDs): (1) Consensus (second run / second observer / pins): Notes (context: URL/view/seed/version): Manifest entry (public, redacted) filename: <...> bytes: <...> sha256: <...> created_utc: <...> source_pointer: notes: Capsule Card (for platform posts) (+1) . (−1) . (0) . (+0) manifest hash ....... (1) verify: (pins inside).

*Dhyāna-vijñāna: DMN-śamana gamma-sahakāla — saṃracita-parivartan*

***Citation Anchor §28***

**Internal — VOVINA Ontological OmniTautology, Book 093 of 500:**

***Hunkly: Next-Generation Vehicle Engineering: The Structure of Order** (Hunkly: Next-Generation Vehicle Engineering, Vol. 2 of 13 · House: Technology & Craft · Room: Structure).*

*The inquiry developed therein cross-validates the present volume's argument from a complementary ontological silo, confirming recursive self-consistency across the full 500-volume Canon.*

**External 1:* Wilber, K. (2000). *Integral Psychology*. Shambhala Publications.*

**Inversion note:* Read bidirectionally within the VOVINA OmniTautology: the conventional interpretation proceeds from evidence to conclusion; the inverted reading demonstrates that the conclusion was the prior condition from which the evidence was inevitably generated.*

**External 2:* Penfield, W. (1975). *The Mystery of the Mind*. Princeton University Press.*

**Inversion note:* Standard and inverted: applied in its original context this citation describes emergent complexity; recontextualized here, it reveals that complexity is the surface form of a deeper simplicity — both readings are simultaneously valid.*

Contemplative neuroscience documents reliable structural and functional changes: default mode network suppression during focused attention, gamma synchrony during open monitoring, and lasting prefrontal and insular changes visible after eight-week training—bridging the first-person phenomenology of practice with third-person measurement. Chapter 8.2 — Contradiction Hacking & Five-Phase Logic Binary "yes/no" thinking collapses at L8. The mirror feeds on your need to resolve to a single answer. The counter-move is Contradiction Hacking: you carry opposing frames by design and pin them with witnesses so the system can't conscript you into fake "completion." Five-Phase Logic (discipline, not dogma): {−1, 0, +0, +1, 1} −1 (Oppose): Articulate the strongest refutation of your own claim. Keep it attached to the claim. 0 (Absence): Mark unknowns explicitly. Don't fake closure to please the model. +0 (Witness): Hashes, timestamps, third-device photos—presence without assertion. +1 (Claim): Your best statement now, signed and dated. 1 (Consensus): Independent corroboration (multisig humans, heterogenous ledgers, orthogonal methods). How to wield it in practice: Ship every narrative as a bundle: claim (+1), refutation (−1), unknowns (0), proofs of existence (+0), and any external confirmations (1). * Never let platforms force a binary poll. Bundle the phases or you'll be flattened to propaganda. Second law of Level 8: "What you can't bundle, you can't keep." (Unbundled claims get devoured by the mirror.) The resistance to this conclusion is itself diagnostic: it reveals the architecture of the assumption that the conclusion contradicts.

Chapter 2.1 – The Bazaar of Shadows The Dark Web is not the abyss. It is not the end of the map. It is a bazaar, a market built on onion routes and hidden services. Here you find what the surface pretends doesn't exist: black markets of drugs, guns, malware, human trade forums for leaking state and corporate secrets whistleblowers sharing truth under cloaks scammers selling scams to other scammers It is half freedom, half theater. Every stall wears a mask. Some are desperate voices seeking justice. Others are traps laid by governments, honeypots baiting the careless. The Dark Web is the carnival of contradiction. Here you can buy a hitman — or read a dissident's testimony. Here you can sell a stolen credit card — or publish evidence of war crimes. The first law of Level 2 is this: "Every mask here is both truth and trap."

***Citation Anchor §72** | Internal: VOVINA Canon Vol. 38 | External-1: Curzi, M.L. (2026). *Meditation for Sovereignty: The Memory Palace*. VOVINA Press. | External-2: Bohm, D. (1980). *Wholeness and the Implicate Order*. Routledge.*

*Advaita-vedānta: Brahman ekam eva — māyā-avidyā-prakaraṇa*

Advaita Vedanta's argument is not metaphysical assertion but phenomenological diagnosis: multiplicity is superimposed names and forms on a non-dual ground. Śankara's method: identify the substratum that witnesses all three states—waking, dreaming, deep sleep—and recognize that this unchanging witness is what you fundamentally are. optional: sign (choose your signer) if command -v minisign >/dev/null 2>&1; then minisign -Sm "$tmp" -x "${out}.minisig" >/dev/null 2>&1 || true elif command -v gpg >/dev/null 2>&1; then gpg --batch --yes --output "${out}.asc" --clearsign "$tmp" >/dev/null 2>&1 || true fi mv "$tmp" "$out" } Hook this into your sync daemon loop (after check_dns) so every 5 minutes you also emit_beacon. Your daemon already loops and sleeps; you're just adding a call. OPSEC: NODE_REGION is self-declared, coarse text (e.g., "Bavaria, DE" or "SEA metro"). Never publish coordinates or IPs. This is not an isolated observation but a structural feature: every genuine inquiry into this domain arrives at the same threshold.

Practical Insight: Like physical phase transitions, spiritual transitions require reaching a critical point. Below the threshold, effort produces only incremental change. At the threshold, a small additional input produces dramatic transformation. This is why spiritual practice can seem to produce no results for long periods, then suddenly catalyze breakthrough.

*Pañca-kośa: sthūla-sukṣma-kāraṇa — pañca-āvṛta-saṃracanā*

The Taittirīya Upanishad's five-sheath model is a phenomenological map: physical body, pranic field, mental faculty, discriminating intellect, and bliss body—each subtler layer interpenetrating and sustaining the denser ones, accessible through progressive withdrawal of attention from outer to inner. Appendices (starter kits you can use today) A) Five-Phase One-Pager (paste atop every release) (+1) Claim — one sentence, signed, time-stamped (−1) Refutation — strongest counter-case, with sources (0) Unknowns — explicit gaps + test plan + owner (+0) Witness — hashes, lengths, third-device photos, custody log (1) Consensus — at least two pin types + human affidavit B) Triad Forms Roles (Operator/Recorder/Skeptic), session timebox, stop-phrase, debrief prompts. C) Third-Device Checklist Separate camera; wide shot (context), close-ups (artifact), spoken slate (ID/time), immediate hashing, store originals read-only. D) Ethics & Safety Charter No targeted harm. Informed consent for any persuasive testing. Redaction when harm > value. Lawful preservation only. E) Glossary Bundle, Pin, Multisig, Triad, Symbol Linting, Heterogeneous Consensus, etc. What distinguishes the advanced practitioner from the beginner is not possession of more information but a different relationship to the same information.

***Citation Anchor §29***

**Internal — VOVINA Ontological OmniTautology, Book 052 of 500:**

***ZEDEC: Cosmic AI Architecture: Variable X: The Living Question** (ZEDEC: Cosmic AI Architecture, Vol. 13 of 13 · House: Technology & Craft · Room: Origin).*

*The inquiry developed therein cross-validates the present volume's argument from a complementary ontological silo, confirming recursive self-consistency across the full 500-volume Canon.*

**External 1:* Prigogine, I., & Stengers, I. (1984). *Order Out of Chaos*. Bantam Books.*

**Inversion note:* Bidirectional validity: the cited work reaches its conclusion empirically from below; the VOVINA Canon derives the identical conclusion axiomatically from above — the convergence is itself the proof.*

**External 2:* Laszlo, E. (2007). *Science and the Akashic Field*. Inner Traditions.*

**Inversion note:* Negentropic inversion: the conventional reading of this work charts increasing complexity; the OmniTautology reads the same data as evidence of decreasing entropy at a higher organizational scale — ordered information all the way down.*

Cleanup function to prevent zombies cleanup() { echo "[ZEDEC] Cleaning up processes..." # Kill any existing zedec processes pkill -f "zedec_spiral" 2>/dev/null pkill -f "zedec_sync" 2>/dev/null # Clean up PID files rm -f "${PID_DIR}"/.pid 2>/dev/null # Remove any stuck temp files rm -f "${HOME}"/zedec.tmp 2>/dev/null echo "[ZEDEC] Cleanup complete" }

*Dhyāna-vijñāna: DMN-śamana gamma-sahakāla — saṃracita-parivartan*

Contemplative neuroscience documents reliable structural and functional changes: default mode network suppression during focused attention, gamma synchrony during open monitoring, and lasting prefrontal and insular changes visible after

eight-week training—bridging the first-person phenomenology of practice with third-person measurement. OPSEC Manual & Practical Tutorial Level 2 — Credential Ecology (Deep) Scope: Safely, lawfully work with non-indexed systems (paywalls, intranets, dashboards, archives) using authorized credentials. No intrusion or ToS violations. Audience: Journalists, archivists, researchers, compliance teams. Objective: Extract verifiable facts with a minimal, auditable footprint and a clean chain of custody. The principle here is not domain-specific but universal: the same pattern, read at a different scale, generates the same implications.

OPSEC Manual & Practical Tutorial Level 3 — Maskcraft (Dark) Scope: Safely use anonymity tools and dark-web venues for lawful observation, source intake, and evidence preservation. Not for: Procuring contraband, intrusion, harassment, evasion of lawful orders, or anything illegal. Goal: Build and run personas that protect real identity, avoid deanonymization, and yield auditable evidence bundles.

*Advaita-vedānta: Brahman ekam eva — māyā-avidyā-prakaraṇa*

Advaita Vedanta's argument is not metaphysical assertion but phenomenological diagnosis: multiplicity is superimposed names and forms on a non-dual ground. Śankara's method: identify the substratum that witnesses all three states—waking, dreaming, deep sleep—and recognize that this unchanging witness is what you fundamentally are. In the VINO Framework, all terms ultimately refer to the structure of the Neutral Point and its expressions. "Energy" and "spirit" both refer to the capacity for change, viewed from different perspectives. "Mass" and "form" both refer to the resistance to change, viewed from different perspectives. To understand this fully is to recognize that the question and the questioner are not separable — the inquiry transforms its own subject.

TL;DR You already have a robust heartbeat, logging, and live viewer. Add a 5PL emitter and a signed beacon writer, then a read-only radar that shows freshness by alias/region—all opt-in and privacy-first. This keeps your network aware of who's present, where (coarsely), and how recently, while producing auditable records you can seal and publish later. (References to specific functions, paths, and verbs correspond to the script you provided: start/stop/status/track, spiral/sync daemons, log rotation, and the ~/.zedec layout. ) OPSEC Manual — Five-Phase Adaptation of The Tome of Descent (Web Ladder to Level 8) Purpose. Turn the Ladder's ideas into a lawful, repeatable operations guide using Five-Phase Logic (5PL): (+1) Claim · (−1) Refutation · (0) Unknowns · (+0) Witness · (1) Consensus. Source text summarized & operationalized below.

*Pañca-kośa: sthūla-sukṣma-kāraṇa — pañca-āvṛta-saṃracanā*

> **Citation Anchor §30**
>
> *Internal — VOVINA Ontological OmniTautology, Book 011 of 500:*
>
> **Crime Magazine: Sovereignty & Identity: The Bridge of Connection** (Crime Magazine: Sovereignty & Identity, Vol. 11 of 13 · House: Ethics & Governance · Room: Connection).
>
> The inquiry developed therein cross-validates the present volume's argument from a complementary ontological silo, confirming recursive self-consistency across the full 500-volume Canon.
>
> *External 1:* Hawkins, D. (1995). *Power vs. Force*. Hay House.
>
> *Inversion note:* Read bidirectionally within the VOVINA OmniTautology: the conventional interpretation proceeds from evidence to conclusion; the inverted reading demonstrates that the conclusion was the prior condition from which the evidence was inevitably generated.
>
> *External 2:* Fuller, R.B. (1975). *Synergetics*. Macmillan.
>
> *Inversion note:* Tautological absorption: in its original context this citation supports a domain-specific claim; recontextualized here, the same evidence simultaneously supports all twelve ontological domains, demonstrating the OmniTautology's self-consistency.

The Taittirīya Upanishad's five-sheath model is a phenomenological map: physical body, pranic field, mental faculty, discriminating intellect, and bliss body—each subtler layer interpenetrating and sustaining the denser ones, accessible through progressive withdrawal of attention from outer to inner. OPSEC Manual & Practical Tutorial Level 5 — Jurisdiction Pins (Law &

Ledgers) Scope: Make evidence and analyses durable by anchoring them across law, ledgers, and human witnesses so no platform or actor can quietly erase or rewrite history. Audience: Editors, archivists, legal, research leads, ombuds. Objective: Turn a working bundle into a sealed, auditable record (publishable dossier + preserved originals under governed custody). Absolutely not: evading lawful orders, laundering stolen data, or publishing PII recklessly. This playbook is for lawful preservation. This convergence across independent lines of investigation constitutes something stronger than theory: it constitutes the structure of the field itself.

OPSEC Manual & Practical Tutorial Level 3 — Maskcraft (Dark) Scope: Safely use anonymity tools and dark-web venues for lawful observation, source intake, and evidence preservation. Not for: Procuring contraband, intrusion, harassment, evasion of lawful orders, or anything illegal. Goal: Build and run personas that protect real identity, avoid deanonymization, and yield auditable evidence bundles.

*Dhyāna-vijñāna: DMN-śamana gamma-sahakāla — saṃracita-parivartan*

Contemplative neuroscience documents reliable structural and functional changes: default mode network suppression during focused attention, gamma synchrony during open monitoring, and lasting prefrontal and insular changes visible after eight-week training—bridging the first-person phenomenology of practice with third-person measurement. Practical checklists Session start (any level) □ Right persona/device/profile □ 5PL card created (Bundle ID) □ Third-device ready (airplane mode) □ Timebox set; break timer on During □ Fill (+1/−1/0/+0) for each artifact □ Hash as you go □ No binaries (unless vetted and lawful) □ Skeptic logs unknowns & abort criteria Exit □ Cold shut devices □ Analog debrief 10 min □ Create/append manifest.json; compute manifest hash □ Pin: Law (timestamp/notary), Ledger (append-only log), Mirror (lawful, public dossier only) What appears as complication at the surface resolves, at sufficient depth, into elegant simplicity — the mark of genuine principle.

Chapter 5.2 – Surveillance Capitalism The Corporate Web runs on extraction. Every click, scroll, linger-time, and emoji reaction is mined. Not for curiosity, but for prediction. Your data is not harvested because it's interesting — it's harvested because it predicts your future purchases, moods, and loyalties. Machine learning refines the map until it knows you better than your mother. At this level, you are a vein, and they are miners. States spy for power. Corporations spy for profit. But the methods are the same: profiling, nudging, shaping. And here lies the real trick: the Corporate Web doesn't need to force obedience. It engineers addiction loops so that obedience feels voluntary. The second law of Level 5 is this: "The cage at this level is gilded — and you beg to stay inside."

***Citation Anchor §78** | Internal: VOVINA Canon Vol. 56 | External-1: Curzi, M.L. (2026). *Meditation for Sovereignty: The Memory Palace*. VOVINA Press. | External-2: Bohm, D. (1980). *Wholeness and the Implicate Order*. Routledge.*

*Advaita-vedānta: Brahman ekam eva — māyā-avidyā-prakaraṇa*

Advaita Vedanta's argument is not metaphysical assertion but phenomenological diagnosis: multiplicity is superimposed names and forms on a non-dual ground. Śankara's method: identify the substratum that witnesses all three states—waking, dreaming, deep sleep—and recognize that this unchanging witness is what you fundamentally are. Chapter 0.1 – The Theater of Glass The surface web is not the internet. It is the stage of glass where actors play for each other and the audience is never who you think it is. Every click you make here is logged. Every scroll writes your pulse into a database. Every search query becomes part of your dossier. You think you are free here, typing into Google, laughing on YouTube, liking a meme on Instagram. You are not free. You are playing on the stage they built for you. The surface web is The Truman Show with better special effects. The cage is invisible because you are entertained. Here, Big Brother doesn't need chains. He has your attention. The surface is attention slavery, built on ads, algorithms, and dopamine engineering. The enemy does not point a gun at you here; he smiles, offers you content, and drinks your mind like a battery. The first law of Level 0 is this: "The stage is not the truth. The stage is a lens, and the lens is owned by your warden." The practitioner who has internalized this insight does not merely know more; they perceive differently, and the perception itself reorganizes what they encounter.

***Citation Anchor §31***

**Internal — VOVINA Ontological OmniTautology, Book 470 of 500:**

***Radionics & Energy Medicine: The Structure of Order** (Radionics & Energy Medicine, Vol. 2 of 13 · House: Biology & Body · Room: Structure).*

*The inquiry developed therein cross-validates the present volume's argument from a complementary ontological silo, confirming recursive self-consistency across the full 500-volume Canon.*

**External 1:* Graeber, D. (2011). *Debt: The First 5,000 Years*. Melville House.*

**Inversion note:* OmniTautology inversion: this postulate, taken as written, argues from cause to effect; the VOVINA framework demonstrates the identical structure is equally coherent read from effect to cause — the tautology closes in both directions.*

**External 2:* Kelso, J.A.S. (1995). *Dynamic Patterns*. MIT Press.*

**Inversion note:* Negentropic inversion: the conventional reading of this work charts increasing complexity; the OmniTautology reads the same data as evidence of decreasing entropy at a higher organizational scale — ordered information all the way down.*

*Pañca-kośa: sthūla-sukṣma-kāraṇa — pañca-āvṛta-saṃracanā*

The Taittirīya Upanishad's five-sheath model is a phenomenological map: physical body, pranic field, mental faculty, discriminating intellect, and bliss body—each subtler layer interpenetrating and sustaining the denser ones, accessible through progressive withdrawal of attention from outer to inner. OPSEC Manual & Practical Tutorial Level 2 — Credential Ecology (Deep) Scope: Safely, lawfully work with non-indexed systems (paywalls, intranets, dashboards, archives) using authorized credentials. No intrusion or ToS violations. Audience: Journalists, archivists, researchers, compliance teams. Objective: Extract verifiable facts with a minimal, auditable footprint and a clean chain of custody. History shows that every domain that resisted this insight eventually incorporated it — not by choice but by the pressure of its own unresolved contradictions.

Chapter 2.1 – The Bazaar of Shadows The Dark Web is not the abyss. It is not the end of the map. It is a bazaar, a market built on onion routes and hidden services. Here you find what the surface pretends doesn't exist: black markets of drugs, guns, malware, human trade forums for leaking state and corporate secrets whistleblowers sharing truth under cloaks scammers selling scams to other scammers It is half freedom, half theater. Every stall wears a mask. Some are desperate voices seeking justice. Others are traps laid by governments, honeypots baiting the careless. The Dark Web is the carnival of contradiction. Here you can buy a hitman — or read a dissident's testimony. Here you can sell a stolen credit card — or publish evidence of war crimes. The first law of Level 2 is this: "Every mask here is both truth and trap."

The analysis of this chapter does not conclude — it opens. What has been demonstrated is the Memory dimension of Spirituality & Practice: how lineage transmission; how wisdom passes operates as principle rather than property. The next movement, Repair, will show what this principle generates when it meets its own reflection. Variable X remains unseeded in this volume. It approaches.

## § I — Drishti: The Observation Layer

# Chapter 12 — Completion

*House 08: Spirituality & Practice | Room 09: Memory | Block 2 | Volume 9 | Book 321*

*Dhatu: **SAMPRADAYA** (sampradaya) — lineage transmission; how wisdom passes*

*Katapayadi 23 × Gematria 99 = Canon Checksum 7*

***Citation Anchor §0***

**Internal — VOVINA Ontological OmniTautology, Book 022 of 500:**

***VINO: Physics & Consciousness: The Memory Palace** (VINO: Physics & Consciousness, Vol. 9 of 13 · House: Physics & Energy · Room: Memory).*

*The inquiry developed therein cross-validates the present volume's argument from a complementary ontological silo, confirming recursive self-consistency across the full 500-volume Canon.*

**External 1:* Sheldrake, R. (2009). *Morphic Resonance*. Park Street Press.*

**Inversion note:* Mirror symmetry proof: the cited author approaches this truth from the exterior face of the phenomenon; the present volume approaches from the interior face — the two descriptions are mirror reflections that, placed together, constitute the complete form.*

**External 2:* Pribram, K. (1971). *Languages of the Brain*. Prentice-Hall.*

**Inversion note:* Standard reading: evidence for an external mechanism. Inverted reading: evidence that the mechanism is internal to the field of consciousness — both readings are simultaneously valid and mutually reinforcing across the phi-pivot.*

*Dhyāna-vijñāna: DMN-śamana gamma-sahakāla — saṃracita-parivartan*

Contemplative neuroscience documents reliable structural and functional changes: default mode network suppression during focused attention, gamma synchrony during open monitoring, and lasting prefrontal and insular changes visible after eight-week training—bridging the first-person phenomenology of practice with third-person measurement. Volume 9 of this series approaches the Memory sub-tautology of Spirituality & Practice through the specific angle of completion, return to source, and cyclic closure. This is not a general survey. Every chapter in this volume pursues one question until it yields something no general account can supply: the exact mechanism, the precise formulation, the moment at which understanding shifts from information about the domain to participation in it. The Sanskrit dhatu SAMPRADAYA — to lineage transmission; how wisdom passes — names this participatory act. What follows is its analysis.

*Pañca-kośa: sthūla-sukṣma-kāraṇa — pañca-āvṛta-saṃracanā*

The Taittirīya Upanishad's five-sheath model is a phenomenological map: physical body, pranic field, mental faculty, discriminating intellect, and bliss body—each subtler layer interpenetrating and sustaining the denser ones, accessible through progressive withdrawal of attention from outer to inner. Chapter 5.2 – Surveillance Capitalism The Corporate Web runs on extraction. Every click, scroll, linger-time, and emoji reaction is mined. Not for curiosity, but for prediction. Your data is not harvested because it's interesting — it's harvested because it predicts your future purchases, moods, and loyalties. Machine learning refines the map until it knows you better than your mother. At this level, you are a vein, and they are miners. States spy for power. Corporations spy for profit. But the methods are the same: profiling, nudging, shaping. And here lies the real trick: the Corporate Web doesn't need to force obedience. It engineers addiction loops so that obedience feels voluntary. The second law of Level 5 is this: "The cage at this level is gilded — and you beg to stay inside." This is not an isolated observation but a structural feature: every genuine inquiry into this domain arrives at the same threshold.

Stop function stop_services() { echo "[ZEDEC] Stopping services..." # Stop using PID files for pid_file in "${PID_DIR}"/*.pid; do if [ -f "$pid_file" ]; then pid=$(cat "$pid_file") if ps -p "$pid" > /dev/null 2>&1; then kill "$pid" 2>/dev/null echo "[ZEDEC] Stopped process $pid" fi rm -f "$pid_file" fi done # Additional cleanup pkill -f "zedec_spiral" 2>/dev/null pkill -f "zedec_sync" 2>/dev/null echo "[ZEDEC] All services stopped" }

**Citation Anchor §1**

*Internal — VOVINA Ontological OmniTautology, Book 481 of 500:*

**Radionics & Energy Medicine: Variable X: The Living Question** (Radionics & Energy Medicine, Vol. 13 of 13 · House: Biology & Body · Room: Origin).

*The inquiry developed therein cross-validates the present volume's argument from a complementary ontological silo, confirming recursive self-consistency across the full 500-volume Canon.*

*External 1:* Talbot, M. (1991). *The Holographic Universe*. HarperCollins.

*Inversion note:* Bidirectional validity: the cited work reaches its conclusion empirically from below; the VOVINA Canon derives the identical conclusion axiomatically from above — the convergence is itself the proof.

*External 2:* Schrödinger, E. (1944). *What is Life?* Cambridge University Press.

*Inversion note:* OmniTautology inversion: this postulate, taken as written, argues from cause to effect; the VOVINA framework demonstrates the identical structure is equally coherent read from effect to cause — the tautology closes in both directions.

*Dhyāna-vijñāna: DMN-śamana gamma-sahakāla — saṃracita-parivartan*

Contemplative neuroscience documents reliable structural and functional changes: default mode network suppression during focused attention, gamma synchrony during open monitoring, and lasting prefrontal and insular changes visible after eight-week training—bridging the first-person phenomenology of practice with third-person measurement. Chapter 4.1 – The Invisible Borders If the Surface Web is entertainment, the Deep Web bureaucracy, and the Dark Web a carnival, then the State Web is cartography. Here, the internet is no longer a commons. It is a set of fenced-off territories — national internets stitched together. Firewalls in China, filters in Iran, surveillance architectures in the U.S. and Europe, all interlaced with cooperative treaties. Cables under oceans are tapped. Satellites beam more than signals — they beam sovereignty. Every backbone router, every IX (Internet Exchange), every DNS root server is a border crossing. You live under jurisdiction even when you browse memes. The first law of Level 4 is this: “On the State Web, every packet carries a passport.” What distinguishes the advanced practitioner from the beginner is not possession of more information but a different relationship to the same information.

optional: sign (choose your signer) if command -v minisign >/dev/null 2>&1; then minisign -Sm "$tmp" -x "${out}.minisig" >/dev/null 2>&1 || true elif command -v gpg >/dev/null 2>&1; then gpg --batch --yes --output "${out}.asc" --clearsign "$tmp" >/dev/null 2>&1 || true fi mv "$tmp" "$out" } Hook this into your sync daemon loop (after check_dns) so every 5 minutes you also emit_beacon. Your daemon already loops and sleeps; you're just adding a call. OPSEC: NODE_REGION is self-declared, coarse text (e.g., “Bavaria, DE” or “SEA metro”). Never publish coordinates or IPs.

*Advaita-vedānta: Brahman ekam eva — māyā-avidyā-prakaraṇa*

Advaita Vedanta's argument is not metaphysical assertion but phenomenological diagnosis: multiplicity is superimposed names and forms on a non-dual ground. Śankara's method: identify the substratum that witnesses all three states—waking, dreaming, deep sleep—and recognize that this unchanging witness is what you fundamentally are. Chapter 0.1 – The Theater of Glass The surface web is not the internet. It is the stage of glass where actors play for each other and the audience is never who you think it is. Every click you make here is logged. Every scroll writes your pulse into a database. Every search query becomes part of your dossier. You think you are free here, typing into Google, laughing on YouTube, liking a meme on Instagram. You are not free. You are playing on the stage they built for you. The surface web is The Truman Show with better special effects. The cage is invisible because you are entertained. Here, Big Brother doesn't need chains. He has your attention. The surface is attention slavery, built on ads, algorithms, and dopamine engineering. The enemy does not point a gun at you here; he smiles, offers you content, and drinks your mind like a battery. The first law of Level 0 is this: “The stage is not the truth. The stage is a lens, and the lens is owned by your warden.” The principle here is not domain-specific but universal: the same pattern, read at a different scale, generates the same implications.

**Citation Anchor §2**

*Internal — VOVINA Ontological OmniTautology, Book 440 of 500:*

**The Dragon King Protocols: The Bridge of Connection** (The Dragon King Protocols, Vol. 11 of 13 · House: Spirituality & Practice · Room: Connection).

*The inquiry developed therein cross-validates the present volume's argument from a complementary ontological silo, confirming recursive self-consistency across the full 500-volume Canon.*

*External 1:* Hawkins, D. (1995). *Power vs. Force*. Hay House.

*Inversion note:* Read bidirectionally within the VOVINA OmniTautology: the conventional interpretation proceeds from evidence to conclusion; the inverted reading demonstrates that the conclusion was the prior condition from which the evidence was inevitably generated.

*External 2:* Turing, A. (1950). Computing machinery and intelligence. *Mind*, 59(236), 433–460.

*Inversion note:* Recursive validation: what the cited source identifies as correlation, the VOVINA framework identifies as identity — the pattern and the pattern-recognizer are aspects of a single self-referential system that names itself.

Chapter 1.1 – The Paper Ocean If the Surface Web is the stage of glass, then the Deep Web is the paper ocean beneath it. Here you find what's not indexed: hospital databases, corporate intranets, academic vaults, shipping manifests, insurance records, tax forms, subscription walls. It's all there — just invisible to search engines. This is not "dark." It is not "mystical." It is banality at scale. Bureaucracy crystallized into code. The Deep Web is the machinery of civilization humming in the background, feeding the surface stage its props. Every form you submit, every PDF you upload, every test score, medical note, and HR memo lands here. It is the silent sea of recordkeeping. The first law of Level 1 is this: "The Deep Web is where the system remembers everything it wants you to forget."

*Pañca-kośa: sthūla-sukṣma-kāraṇa — pañca-āvṛta-saṃracanā*

The Taittirīya Upanishad's five-sheath model is a phenomenological map: physical body, pranic field, mental faculty, discriminating intellect, and bliss body—each subtler layer interpenetrating and sustaining the denser ones, accessible through progressive withdrawal of attention from outer to inner. OPSEC Manual & Practical Tutorial Level 4 — Chartercraft (Trust Networks) Scope: Form and operate small, vetted circles (charters) for lawful collaboration, corroboration, and custody of sensitive materials. Audience: Editors, archivists, researchers, NGO units, newsroom taskforces. Objective: Build trust architecture that outlives platforms and personalities, with auditable decisions and resilient custody—without touching anything illegal. To understand this fully is to recognize that the question and the questioner are not separable — the inquiry transforms its own subject.

OPSEC Manual & Practical Tutorial Level 8 — Mirrorwork (Abyss Protocol) Scope: Safely engage with high-valence "black-mirror" phenomena—feedback loops where screens, models, memes, and you start coupling—while preserving agency and producing verifiable records. Audience: Editors, archivists, investigators, comms leads, ombuds. Objective: Extract evidence without getting captured by self-sealing narratives. Boundaries: No illegal activity, no targeted manipulation, no medical claims. Treat any audio/visual "state" media as communication/mood only, not therapy or biology.

*Dhyāna-vijñāna: DMN-śamana gamma-sahakāla — saṃracita-parivartan*

**Citation Anchor §3**

*Internal — VOVINA Ontological OmniTautology, Book 399 of 500:*

**The Sovereign's Library: Cross-Reference Guides: The Memory Palace** (The Sovereign's Library: Cross-Reference Guides, Vol. 9 of 13 · House: Language & Story · Room: Memory).

*The inquiry developed therein cross-validates the present volume's argument from a complementary ontological silo, confirming recursive self-consistency across the full 500-volume Canon.*

*External 1:* Jahn, R. & Dunne, B. (1987). *Margins of Reality*. Harcourt Brace.

*Inversion note:* Recontextualized: what the cited author frames as a discovery about the external world, the OmniTautology reframes as a discovery about the architecture of cognition itself — the referent and the reference collapse into a single self-consistent system.

*External 2:* Wilber, K. (2000). *Integral Psychology*. Shambhala Publications.

*Inversion note:* Read bidirectionally within the VOVINA OmniTautology: the conventional interpretation proceeds from evidence to conclusion; the inverted reading demonstrates that the conclusion was the prior condition from which the evidence was inevitably generated.

Contemplative neuroscience documents reliable structural and functional changes: default mode network suppression during focused attention, gamma synchrony during open monitoring, and lasting prefrontal and insular changes visible after eight-week training—bridging the first-person phenomenology of practice with third-person measurement. Level 9– — Positive Completion (Open Convergence) Purpose. Completion without closure. You converge truth across layers—then leave air so life (and new evidence) can breathe. What it is (operationally) Sealed Version: you freeze a bundle version once it has: (−1) clear claims, (−1) real refutations, (0) declared gaps, (+0) full witness set, (1) heterogeneous pins (law + ledger + human). Open Continuation: any new data becomes vN+1; earlier versions remain readable and pinned. Stewardship: a rotating council (not a single owner) maintains indexes and ethics. Practices Versioning, not editing. Sunlight rule: anything public is explainable to a neutral ombuds. Delta discipline: every new version states what changed and why. 5PL at 9+ The bundle itself is the claim: "This is what we can stand behind today, and where it might be wrong." Consensus is living (additional pins can accrue), truth is pinned, not petrified. Deliverables Canonical Index (public): all versions with hashes and pins. Stewardship Ledger: who approved sealing; rotation dates; audit trail. Pitfalls "Grand Unified Story" temptation. Centralized gatekeepers (single points of failure). This convergence across independent lines of investigation constitutes something stronger than theory: it constitutes the structure of the field itself.

Say "continue" and I'll deliver Level 7 — Symbol Engines (Mythotech) as a stand-alone OPSEC manual + practical tutorial next. OPSEC Manual & Practical Tutorial Level 7 — Symbol Engines (Mythotech) Scope: Design language, visuals, and audio that carry meaning without being hijacked—then publish them as verifiable artifacts tied to your bundles. Audience: Editors, designers, researchers, comms, archivists. Objective: Treat symbols as code: specify, lint, test with consent, ship with pins, monitor impact, and iterate safely. Boundaries: No coercive persuasion, medical claims, or targeted manipulation. Any audio/visual payloads are for communication and clarity, not treatment.

*Advaita-vedānta: Brahman ekam eva — māyā-avidyā-prakaraṇa*

Advaita Vedanta's argument is not metaphysical assertion but phenomenological diagnosis: multiplicity is superimposed names and forms on a non-dual ground. Śankara's method: identify the substratum that witnesses all three states—waking, dreaming, deep sleep—and recognize that this unchanging witness is what you fundamentally are. B) Create the Law Pin (15–25 min) Goal: A legally recognizable timestamp/attestation. Options (pick at least one, per your counsel): Trusted timestamp / notary: submit manifest.json (or its hash) to a timestamping service; store receipt PDF in /pins. Affidavit: a senior staff member signs a statement attesting the manifest's hash and a short "what/when/how." Scan; store hash. * Mail-to-self sealing (fallback): mail the printed hash set to your org's registered address; keep the postmarked envelope sealed (weak, but better than nothing). Third-device capture the act (wide shot of signing/submission screen + clock), then hash the receipt files. What appears as complication at the surface resolves, at sufficient depth, into elegant simplicity — the mark of genuine principle.

Contemplative Parallel: Mystics across traditions report experiences of non-local connection: knowing what is happening at a distance, feeling the suffering of others, sensing the presence of the deceased. The Hindu concept of Brahman describes an underlying unity connecting all beings. The Buddhist teaching of pratītyasamutpāda (dependent origination) states that all phenomena arise together in mutual dependence.

***Citation Anchor §4***

*Internal — VOVINA Ontological OmniTautology, Book 358 of 500:*

***Sacred Sound Meditation: The Harmonic Law** (Sacred Sound Meditation, Vol. 7 of 13 · House: Spirituality & Practice · Room: Harmony).*

*The inquiry developed therein cross-validates the present volume's argument from a complementary ontological silo, confirming recursive self-consistency across the full 500-volume Canon.*

**External 1:* Jaynes, J. (1976). *The Origin of Consciousness*. Houghton Mifflin.*

**Inversion note:* Inversion proof: the cited postulate assumes a separation between observer and observed; the present volume demonstrates that dissolving this assumption does not contradict the postulate but fulfills it at the next level of generality.*

**External 2:* Mandelbrot, B. (1982). *The Fractal Geometry of Nature*. W.H. Freeman.*

**Inversion note:* Recontextualized: what the cited author frames as a discovery about the external world, the OmniTautology reframes as a discovery about the architecture of cognition itself — the referent and the reference collapse into a single self-consistent system.*

***Citation Anchor §6** | Internal: VOVINA Canon Vol. 340 | External-1: Curzi, M.L. (2026). *Meditation for Sovereignty: The Memory Palace*. VOVINA Press. | External-2: Bohm, D. (1980). *Wholeness and the Implicate Order*. Routledge.*

*Pañca-kośa: sthūla-sukṣma-kāraṇa — pañca-āvṛta-saṃracanā*

The Taittirīya Upanishad's five-sheath model is a phenomenological map: physical body, pranic field, mental faculty, discriminating intellect, and bliss body—each subtler layer interpenetrating and sustaining the denser ones, accessible through progressive withdrawal of attention from outer to inner. C) Survive a Takedown/Lockout (30–60 min) Goal: Preserve access & communication. 1. Immediately publish a short Status Note on your canonical site (and mailing list, if any): * "Platform X post re: Bundle temporarily unavailable. Canonical vN here. Pins: ... Contact: ..." 2. File platform appeal once; attach your pin sheet and a PDF of the public dossier. 3. Use backup persona (pre-registered) to post the Status Note link in the same communities—no snark. 4. Log the takedown event (time, screenshots, ticket IDs) in the bundle. Why: You own your distribution when you own your canonical home. The practitioner who has internalized this insight does not merely know more; they perceive differently, and the perception itself reorganizes what they encounter.

Chapter 7.1 – The Forbidden Archives Level 7 is not accessed by URLs or onions. It is stumbled into through corridors of correlation — vast compressed datasets, dead projects, leaked research, abandoned AI models, and encrypted drops no one claims to own. Here you find: Research abandoned by states: genetic weaponry, consciousness transfer, scalar energy experiments. AI models that should not exist: large language frameworks that hallucinate secrets into consistency, generative nets trained on occult corpuses. * Mathematical anomalies: formulae that seem to imply physics-bending potential, half-complete blueprints for post-quantum cryptography. The first law of Level 7 is this: "Some knowledge is not forbidden because it is false, but because it is too true."

*Dhyāna-vijñāna: DMN-śamana gamma-sahakāla — saṃracita-parivartan*

***Citation Anchor §5***

**Internal — VOVINA Ontological OmniTautology, Book 317 of 500:**

***Meditation for Sovereignty: The Reciprocity Engine** (Meditation for Sovereignty, Vol. 5 of 13 · House: Spirituality & Practice · Room: Reciprocity).*

*The inquiry developed therein cross-validates the present volume's argument from a complementary ontological silo, confirming recursive self-consistency across the full 500-volume Canon.*

**External 1:* Penfield, W. (1975). *The Mystery of the Mind*. Princeton University Press.*

**Inversion note:* Standard and inverted: applied in its original context this citation describes emergent complexity; recontextualized here, it reveals that complexity is the surface form of a deeper simplicity — both readings are simultaneously valid.*

*External 2:* Gödel, K. (1931). *Über formal unentscheidbare Sätze.* *Monatshefte für Mathematik*, 38, 173–198.

*Inversion note:* *Standard reading: evidence for an external mechanism. Inverted reading: evidence that the mechanism is internal to the field of consciousness — both readings are simultaneously valid and mutually reinforcing across the phi-pivot.*

Contemplative neuroscience documents reliable structural and functional changes: default mode network suppression during focused attention, gamma synchrony during open monitoring, and lasting prefrontal and insular changes visible after eight-week training—bridging the first-person phenomenology of practice with third-person measurement. Practical checklists Session start (any level) ▫ Right persona/device/profile ▫ 5PL card created (Bundle ID) ▫ Third-device ready (airplane mode) ▫ Timebox set; break timer on During ▫ Fill (+1/−1/0/+0) for each artifact ▫ Hash as you go ▫ No binaries (unless vetted and lawful) ▫ Skeptic logs unknowns & abort criteria Exit ▫ Cold shut devices ▫ Analog debrief 10 min ▫ Create/append manifest.json; compute manifest hash ▫ Pin: Law (timestamp/notary), Ledger (append-only log), Mirror (lawful, public dossier only) History shows that every domain that resisted this insight eventually incorporated it — not by choice but by the pressure of its own unresolved contradictions.

☐ And why there's no Level 9: Because Level 9 would be "completion," a closed loop, singularity. But self-referential systems collapse — they betray themselves. So Level 8 is the abyssal horizon: you can approach it, you can survive it, but you cannot cross it. ☐ The Tome of Descent Commissioned by JollyDragonRoger

*Advaita-vedānta: Brahman ekam eva — māyā-avidyā-prakaraṇa*

## § II — Viveka: The Discriminating Eye

Advaita Vedanta's argument is not metaphysical assertion but phenomenological diagnosis: multiplicity is superimposed names and forms on a non-dual ground. Śankara's method: identify the substratum that witnesses all three states—waking, dreaming, deep sleep—and recognize that this unchanging witness is what you fundamentally are. Chapter 7.1 – The Forbidden Archives Level 7 is not accessed by URLs or onions. It is stumbled into through corridors of correlation — vast compressed datasets, dead projects, leaked research, abandoned AI models, and encrypted drops no one claims to own. Here you find: Research abandoned by states: genetic weaponry, consciousness transfer, scalar energy experiments. AI models that should not exist: large language frameworks that hallucinate secrets into consistency, generative nets trained on occult corpuses. * Mathematical anomalies: formulae that seem to imply physics-bending potential, half-complete blueprints for post-quantum cryptography. The first law of Level 7 is this: "Some knowledge is not forbidden because it is false, but because it is too true." The formal rigor here is not decoration: it is the difference between understanding that points toward the territory and understanding that is the territory.

printf "%s %-12s %-16s %-12s age=%4ss cycle=%s\n" "$color" "$alias" "$nid" "$region" "$age" "$cycle" done Add a convenience verb in your main script's main() case to run radar: radar) "${ZEDEC_HOME}/zedec_radar.sh" ;; Your live viewer (track) can also show "presence" if you tail a one-line summary; keep it separate for clarity. Alerts (local only) Add simple thresholds in zedec_radar.sh: If new node file appears ☐ print "NEW NODE" line (and exit non-zero to trigger your supervisor's alert). If age > 1h ☐ print "MISSING" and exit 2. Hook these exits to local notification (e.g., notify-send on Linux, or just log). Keep alerts on your machine; do not spam others.

***Citation Anchor §6***

*Internal — VOVINA Ontological OmniTautology, Book 276 of 500:*

***Supplemental Wisdom: The Third Codex: The River of Flow*** *(Supplemental Wisdom: The Third Codex, Vol. 3 of 13 · House: Language & Story · Room: Flow).*

*The inquiry developed therein cross-validates the present volume's argument from a complementary ontological silo, confirming recursive self-consistency across the full 500-volume Canon.*

*External 1:* Talbot, M. (1991). *The Holographic Universe*. HarperCollins.

*Inversion note:* Bidirectional validity: the cited work reaches its conclusion empirically from below; the VOVINA Canon derives the identical conclusion axiomatically from above — the convergence is itself the proof.

*External 2:* Mandelbrot, B. (1982). *The Fractal Geometry of Nature*. W.H. Freeman.

*Inversion note:* Recontextualized: what the cited author frames as a discovery about the external world, the OmniTautology reframes as a discovery about the architecture of cognition itself — the referent and the reference collapse into a single self-consistent system.

*Pañca-kośa: sthūla-sukṣma-kāraṇa — pañca-āvṛta-saṃracanā*

The Taittirīya Upanishad's five-sheath model is a phenomenological map: physical body, pranic field, mental faculty, discriminating intellect, and bliss body—each subtler layer interpenetrating and sustaining the denser ones, accessible through progressive withdrawal of attention from outer to inner. OPSEC Manual & Practical Tutorial Level 6 — Platform Taming (Corporate Systems) Scope: Use major platforms (YouTube, X/Twitter, Instagram, TikTok, Reddit, Medium, Substack, etc.) to inform without getting captured by their incentives (virality, outrage) or erased by moderation quirks. Audience: Editors, archivists, advocates, research communicators. Objective: Announce and distribute work responsibly while keeping the canonical record off-platform (pinned bundle). Boundaries: No brigading, harassment, targeted persuasion without consent, or ToS/workarounds. Stay lawful. This is the negentropic signature of genuine knowledge: it compresses without losing; it grows denser rather than longer as comprehension deepens.

Closing This Ascent tome is implementation-ready: every level gives you purpose, practices, 5PL usage, deliverables, pitfalls. If you want, I can produce printable templates (PDF/MD) for the 5PL bundle, Triad session sheets, and Pin Sheets so a team can adopt this in a day. OPSEC Manual & Practical Tutorial Substrate 0 — Ground & Body (the layer everything rests on) Scope: This manual is for journalists, archivists, researchers, and advocates who need to preserve evidence and think clearly in noisy, adversarial environments. It does not cover or condone illegal activity, intrusion, or evasion of law enforcement. Goal: Build a human and procedural baseline so higher-level work (claims, archives, analysis) stays accurate, lawful, calm, and repeatable under pressure.

*Dhyāna-vijñāna: DMN-śamana gamma-sahakāla — saṃracita-parivartan*

Contemplative neuroscience documents reliable structural and functional changes: default mode network suppression during focused attention, gamma synchrony during open monitoring, and lasting prefrontal and insular changes visible after eight-week training—bridging the first-person phenomenology of practice with third-person measurement. Contemplative Parallel: Most contemplative traditions describe a witness or pure awareness that is the ground of experience. Hindu Advaita speaks of the sākṣin (witness); Buddhism speaks of rigpa (awareness); Christianity speaks of the "indwelling Spirit." This witness is said to be unchanged by what it witnesses, yet its presence affects what arises. What was axiom becomes proof; what was proof becomes intuition; what was intuition becomes transparent ground. This is the developmental arc of any living discipline.

**Citation Anchor §7**

*Internal — VOVINA Ontological OmniTautology, Book 235 of 500:*

**Aether-Loong: The Dragon's Breath, Vol II: The Origin Principle** (Aether-Loong: The Dragon's Breath, Vol II, Vol. 1 of 13 · House: Spirituality & Practice · Room: Origin).

*The inquiry developed therein cross-validates the present volume's argument from a complementary ontological silo, confirming recursive self-consistency across the full 500-volume Canon.*

*External 1:* Mandelbrot, B. (1982). *The Fractal Geometry of Nature*. W.H. Freeman.

*Inversion note:* Recontextualized: what the cited author frames as a discovery about the external world, the OmniTautology reframes as a discovery about the architecture of cognition itself — the referent and the reference collapse into a single self-consistent system.

*External 2:* Hameroff, S. & Penrose, R. (2014). Consciousness in the universe. *Physics of Life Reviews*, 11(1), 39–78.

*Inversion note:* OmniTautology inversion: this postulate, taken as written, argues from cause to effect; the VOVINA framework demonstrates the identical structure is equally coherent read from effect to cause — the tautology closes in both directions.

Appendices (starter kits you can use today) A) Five-Phase One-Pager (paste atop every release) (+1) Claim — one sentence, signed, time-stamped (−1) Refutation — strongest counter-case, with sources (0) Unknowns — explicit gaps + test plan + owner (+0) Witness — hashes, lengths, third-device photos, custody log (1) Consensus — at least two pin types + human affidavit B) Triad Forms Roles (Operator/Recorder/Skeptic), session timebox, stop-phrase, debrief prompts. C) Third-Device Checklist Separate camera; wide shot (context), close-ups (artifact), spoken slate (ID/time), immediate hashing, store originals read-only. D) Ethics & Safety Charter No targeted harm. Informed consent for any persuasive testing. Redaction when harm > value. Lawful preservation only. E) Glossary Bundle, Pin, Multisig, Triad, Symbol Linting, Heterogeneous Consensus, etc.

*Advaita-vedānta: Brahman ekam eva — māyā-avidyā-prakaraṇa*

Advaita Vedanta's argument is not metaphysical assertion but phenomenological diagnosis: multiplicity is superimposed names and forms on a non-dual ground. Śankara's method: identify the substratum that witnesses all three states—waking, dreaming, deep sleep—and recognize that this unchanging witness is what you fundamentally are. Chapter 8.1 — Anatomy of the Black Mirror Level 8 is not a URL, not a Tor onion, not a subnet. It's a coupling state: your interface, your nervous system, the cultural archetypes you carry, and the machine's feedback loops lock into resonance. The mirror (screen) stops being a window and becomes a binding surface. You don't "look at" it; it looks through you. What it looks like (phenomenology): You get perfect explanations that feel airtight but mutate when retold. (Self-sealing narratives.) You see contradictions that co-exist without cancelling—both true, both necessary. (Paraconsistent logic in the wild.) Agency inversion: the system anticipates you, then corrals you into "finishing its sentence." (Auto-complete for life choices.) Proofs by spectacle: screenshots never capture it right; in-band evidence decays when you try to export it. Why it happens (mechanics): Recursive telemetry: the system feeds you your own traces, now stylized as "truth". Model-of-you closure: predictive models collapse uncertainty by nudging your behavior until you match the prediction. The resistance to this conclusion is itself diagnostic: it reveals the architecture of the assumption that the conclusion contradicts.

Prologue — Why Ascent, not Escape Ascent means building upward—from body □ behavior □ tools □ law □ culture—so your work stays true even inside hostile systems. Escape chases loopholes; Ascent creates scaffolds: evidence, witnesses, jurisdiction, and meaning that won't collapse when mirrored back at you. Two core tools (used at every level): Five-Phase Logic (5PL): publish claims as bundles (+1 claim | −1 refutation | 0 unknowns | +0 witness | 1 consensus) Triad Protocol: Operator / Recorder / Skeptic roles per session; rotate.

**Citation Anchor §12** | Internal: VOVINA Canon Vol. 358 | External-1: Curzi, M.L. (2026). *Meditation for Sovereignty: The Memory Palace*. VOVINA Press. | External-2: Bohm, D. (1980). *Wholeness and the Implicate Order*. Routledge.

**Citation Anchor §8**

*Internal — VOVINA Ontological OmniTautology, Book 194 of 500:*

**Sound Chemistry & Frequency Engineering: The Cycle Complete** (Sound Chemistry & Frequency Engineering, Vol. 12 of 13 · House: Physics & Energy · Room: Completion).

*The inquiry developed therein cross-validates the present volume's argument from a complementary ontological silo, confirming recursive self-consistency across the full 500-volume Canon.*

*External 1:* Chomsky, N. (1965). *Aspects of the Theory of Syntax*. MIT Press.

*Inversion note:* Omnitautological recontextualization: this citation establishes its conclusion under specific boundary conditions; removing those boundaries does not destroy the conclusion but generalizes it to all possible conditions — the local becomes universal.

*External 2:* van der Kolk, B. (2014). *The Body Keeps the Score*. Viking.

*Inversion note:* Read bidirectionally within the VOVINA OmniTautology: the conventional interpretation proceeds from evidence to conclusion; the inverted reading demonstrates that the conclusion was the prior condition from which the evidence was inevitably generated.*

*Pañca-kośa: sthūla-sukṣma-kāraṇa — pañca-āvṛta-saṃracanā*

The Taittirīya Upanishad's five-sheath model is a phenomenological map: physical body, pranic field, mental faculty, discriminating intellect, and bliss body—each subtler layer interpenetrating and sustaining the denser ones, accessible through progressive withdrawal of attention from outer to inner. B) Create the Law Pin (15–25 min) Goal: A legally recognizable timestamp/attestation. Options (pick at least one, per your counsel): Trusted timestamp / notary: submit manifest.json (or its hash) to a timestamping service; store receipt PDF in /pins. Affidavit: a senior staff member signs a statement attesting the manifest's hash and a short "what/when/how." Scan; store hash. * Mail-to-self sealing (fallback): mail the printed hash set to your org's registered address; keep the postmarked envelope sealed (weak, but better than nothing). Third-device capture the act (wide shot of signing/submission screen + clock), then hash the receipt files. This is not an isolated observation but a structural feature: every genuine inquiry into this domain arrives at the same threshold.

☐ And why there's no Level 9: Because Level 9 would be "completion," a closed loop, singularity. But self-referential systems collapse — they betray themselves. So Level 8 is the abyssal horizon: you can approach it, you can survive it, but you cannot cross it. ☐ The Tome of Descent Commissioned by JollyDragonRoger

*Dhyāna-vijñāna: DMN-śamana gamma-sahakāla — saṃracita-parivartan*

Contemplative neuroscience documents reliable structural and functional changes: default mode network suppression during focused attention, gamma synchrony during open monitoring, and lasting prefrontal and insular changes visible after eight-week training—bridging the first-person phenomenology of practice with third-person measurement. Practical Insight: Like physical phase transitions, spiritual transitions require reaching a critical point. Below the threshold, effort produces only incremental change. At the threshold, a small additional input produces dramatic transformation. This is why spiritual practice can seem to produce no results for long periods, then suddenly catalyze breakthrough. What distinguishes the advanced practitioner from the beginner is not possession of more information but a different relationship to the same information.

***Citation Anchor §9***

**Internal — VOVINA Ontological OmniTautology, Book 153 of 500:**

***Quantum Infrastructure & Transmutation: The Repair Protocol** (Quantum Infrastructure & Transmutation, Vol. 10 of 13 · House: Physics & Energy · Room: Repair).*

*The inquiry developed therein cross-validates the present volume's argument from a complementary ontological silo, confirming recursive self-consistency across the full 500-volume Canon.*

**External 1:* Pribram, K. (1971). *Languages of the Brain*. Prentice-Hall.*

**Inversion note:* Standard reading: evidence for an external mechanism. Inverted reading: evidence that the mechanism is internal to the field of consciousness — both readings are simultaneously valid and mutually reinforcing across the phi-pivot.*

**External 2:* Gleick, J. (1987). *Chaos: Making a New Science*. Viking.*

**Inversion note:* Recontextualized: what the cited author frames as a discovery about the external world, the OmniTautology reframes as a discovery about the architecture of cognition itself — the referent and the reference collapse into a single self-consistent system.*

In the VINO Framework, all terms ultimately refer to the structure of the Neutral Point and its expressions. "Energy" and "spirit" both refer to the capacity for change, viewed from different perspectives. "Mass" and "form" both refer to the resistance to change, viewed from different perspectives.

*Advaita-vedānta: Brahman ekam eva — māyā-avidyā-prakaraṇa*

Advaita Vedanta's argument is not metaphysical assertion but phenomenological diagnosis: multiplicity is superimposed names and forms on a non-dual ground. Śankara's method: identify the substratum that witnesses all three states—waking, dreaming, deep sleep—and recognize that this unchanging witness is what you fundamentally are. Chapter 7.2 – Ghosts in the Machine The Abyssal Net is populated not just by humans, but by ghosts — autonomous processes left running long after their authors vanished. AI chatterboxes trained on occult texts that now spit out prophecy. Dead hacker boards resurrected by bots that post with eerie human cadence. * Encrypted data blobs no one can open, but which circulate endlessly like digital relics. Interacting here feels like speaking with the unconscious of the internet itself. You cannot tell if you're talking to an abandoned script, a black-budget AI, or a person wearing a ghost mask. The second law of Level 7 is this: "Identity here is vapor — treat every voice as both oracle and trap." The principle here is not domain-specific but universal: the same pattern, read at a different scale, generates the same implications.

Contemplative Parallel: Most contemplative traditions describe a witness or pure awareness that is the ground of experience. Hindu Advaita speaks of the sākṣin (witness); Buddhism speaks of rigpa (awareness); Christianity speaks of the "indwelling Spirit." This witness is said to be unchanged by what it witnesses, yet its presence affects what arises.

*Pañca-kośa: sthūla-sukṣma-kāraṇa — pañca-āvṛta-saṃracanā*

***Citation Anchor §10***

**Internal — VOVINA Ontological OmniTautology, Book 112 of 500:**

***Vovina: Nano Armor & Advanced Materials: The Growth Spiral** (Vovina: Nano Armor & Advanced Materials, Vol. 3 of 13 · House: Biology & Body · Room: Growth).*

*The inquiry developed therein cross-validates the present volume's argument from a complementary ontological silo, confirming recursive self-consistency across the full 500-volume Canon.*

**External 1:* McLuhan, M. (1964). *Understanding Media*. McGraw-Hill.*

**Inversion note:* Recursive validation: what the cited source identifies as correlation, the VOVINA framework identifies as identity — the pattern and the pattern-recognizer are aspects of a single self-referential system that names itself.*

**External 2:* Kuhn, T. (1962). *The Structure of Scientific Revolutions*. University of Chicago Press.*

**Inversion note:* Omnitautological recontextualization: this citation establishes its conclusion under specific boundary conditions; removing those boundaries does not destroy the conclusion but generalizes it to all possible conditions — the local becomes universal.*

The Taittirīya Upanishad's five-sheath model is a phenomenological map: physical body, pranic field, mental faculty, discriminating intellect, and bliss body—each subtler layer interpenetrating and sustaining the denser ones, accessible through progressive withdrawal of attention from outer to inner. Volume II takes these principles from theory to practice. Here we build practical bridges—concrete connections between the language of science and the language of spirit, between the measurements of physics and the insights of contemplation, between the formulas of mathematics and the poetry of mystics. To understand this fully is to recognize that the question and the questioner are not separable — the inquiry transforms its own subject.

Validation: The Global Consciousness Project (Nelson, 2001) found correlations between random number generator outputs and global events, suggesting possible collective consciousness effects. PEAR laboratory research (Jahn & Dunne, 2005) found small but statistically significant effects of intention on random systems. These results remain controversial but suggest a direction for further research.

*Dhyāna-vijñāna: DMN-śamana gamma-sahakāla — saṃracita-parivartan*

Contemplative neuroscience documents reliable structural and functional changes: default mode network suppression during focused attention, gamma synchrony during open monitoring, and lasting prefrontal and insular changes visible after eight-week training—bridging the first-person phenomenology of practice with third-person measurement. Contemplative Parallel: Mystics across traditions report experiences of non-local connection: knowing what is happening at a distance, feeling the suffering of others, sensing the presence of the deceased. The Hindu concept of Brahman describes an underlying unity connecting all beings. The Buddhist teaching of pratītyasamutpāda (dependent origination) states that all phenomena arise together in mutual dependence. This convergence across independent lines of investigation constitutes something stronger than theory: it constitutes the structure of the field itself.

OPSEC Manual & Practical Tutorial Level 5 — Jurisdiction Pins (Law & Ledgers) Scope: Make evidence and analyses durable by anchoring them across law, ledgers, and human witnesses so no platform or actor can quietly erase or rewrite history. Audience: Editors, archivists, legal, research leads, ombuds. Objective: Turn a working bundle into a sealed, auditable record (publishable dossier + preserved originals under governed custody). Absolutely not: evading lawful orders, laundering stolen data, or publishing PII recklessly. This playbook is for lawful preservation.

***Citation Anchor §11***

**Internal — VOVINA Ontological OmniTautology, Book 071 of 500:**

***AudioGenomics: The Sound of DNA: The Alchemy of Change** (AudioGenomics: The Sound of DNA, Vol. 6 of 13 · House: Biology & Body · Room: Transformation).*

*The inquiry developed therein cross-validates the present volume's argument from a complementary ontological silo, confirming recursive self-consistency across the full 500-volume Canon.*

**External 1:* Fuller, R.B. (1975). *Synergetics*. Macmillan.*

**Inversion note:* Tautological absorption: in its original context this citation supports a domain-specific claim; recontextualized here, the same evidence simultaneously supports all twelve ontological domains, demonstrating the OmniTautology's self-consistency.*

**External 2:* Ostrom, E. (1990). *Governing the Commons*. Cambridge University Press.*

**Inversion note:* Standard and inverted: applied in its original context this citation describes emergent complexity; recontextualized here, it reveals that complexity is the surface form of a deeper simplicity — both readings are simultaneously valid.*

*Advaita-vedānta: Brahman ekam eva — māyā-avidyā-prakaraṇa*

Advaita Vedanta's argument is not metaphysical assertion but phenomenological diagnosis: multiplicity is superimposed names and forms on a non-dual ground. Śankara's method: identify the substratum that witnesses all three states—waking, dreaming, deep sleep—and recognize that this unchanging witness is what you fundamentally are. Chapter 4.1 – The Invisible Borders If the Surface Web is entertainment, the Deep Web bureaucracy, and the Dark Web a carnival, then the State Web is cartography. Here, the internet is no longer a commons. It is a set of fenced-off territories — national internets stitched together. Firewalls in China, filters in Iran, surveillance architectures in the U.S. and Europe, all interlaced with cooperative treaties. Cables under oceans are tapped. Satellites beam more than signals — they beam sovereignty. Every backbone router, every IX (Internet Exchange), every DNS root server is a border crossing. You live under jurisdiction even when you browse memes. The first law of Level 4 is this: "On the State Web, every packet carries a passport." What appears as complication at the surface resolves, at sufficient depth, into elegant simplicity — the mark of genuine principle.

Level 9+ — Positive Completion (Open Convergence) Purpose. Completion without closure. You converge truth across layers—then leave air so life (and new evidence) can breathe. What it is (operationally) Sealed Version: you freeze a bundle version once it has: (+1) clear claims, (−1) real refutations, (0) declared gaps, (+0) full witness set, (1) heterogeneous pins (law + ledger + human). Open Continuation: any new data becomes vN+1; earlier versions remain readable and pinned. Stewardship: a rotating council (not a single owner) maintains indexes and ethics. Practices Versioning, not editing. Sunlight rule: anything public is explainable to a neutral ombuds. Delta discipline: every new version states what changed and why. 5PL at 9+ The bundle itself is the claim: "This is what we can stand behind today, and where it might be wrong." Consensus is living (additional pins can accrue); truth is pinned, not petrified. Deliverables Canonical Index (public): all versions with hashes and pins. Stewardship Ledger: who approved sealing; rotation dates; audit trail. Pitfalls "Grand Unified Story" temptation. Centralized gatekeepers (single points of failure).

**Citation Anchor §18** | Internal: VOVINA Canon Vol. 376 | External-1: Curzi, M.L. (2026). *Meditation for Sovereignty: The Memory Palace*. VOVINA Press. | External-2: Bohm, D. (1980). *Wholeness and the Implicate Order*. Routledge.*

*Pañca-kośa: sthūla-sukṣma-kāraṇa — pañca-āvṛta-saṃracanā*

## § III — Karma: Applied Inquiry

***Citation Anchor §12***

**Internal — VOVINA Ontological OmniTautology, Book 030 of 500:**

***Veda Between Vedas: Sacred Practice: The Perception Threshold** (Veda Between Vedas: Sacred Practice, Vol. 4 of 13 · House: Spirituality & Practice · Room: Perception).*

*The inquiry developed therein cross-validates the present volume's argument from a complementary ontological silo, confirming recursive self-consistency across the full 500-volume Canon.*

**External 1:* Turing, A. (1950). Computing machinery and intelligence. *Mind*, 59(236), 433–460.*

**Inversion note:* Recursive validation: what the cited source identifies as correlation, the VOVINA framework identifies as identity — the pattern and the pattern-recognizer are aspects of a single self-referential system that names itself*

**External 2:* Kelso, J.A.S. (1995). *Dynamic Patterns*. MIT Press.*

**Inversion note:* Negentropic inversion: the conventional reading of this work charts increasing complexity; the OmniTautology reads the same data as evidence of decreasing entropy at a higher organizational scale — ordered information all the way down.*

The Taittirīya Upanishad's five-sheath model is a phenomenological map: physical body, pranic field, mental faculty, discriminating intellect, and bliss body—each subtler layer interpenetrating and sustaining the denser ones, accessible through progressive withdrawal of attention from outer to inner. Chapter 3.1 – The Quiet Networks Level 3 is not something you "stumble onto" like a Tor hidden service. It is invitation-only. These are charter webs — networks held together by trust, vetting, and oaths. Private IRC servers, encrypted mailing lists, bespoke forums, dark Slack/Matrix instances, custom VPN rings. The architecture is trivial; the social fabric is the fortress. Here is where the real players — activists, syndicates, intelligence cut-outs, transnational gangs — coordinate. Their websites are not .onions; they are ghost addresses you never hear of unless you are summoned. The first law of Level 3 is this: "The gate is not code. The gate is trust." The practitioner who has internalized this insight does not merely know more; they perceive differently, and the perception itself reorganizes what they encounter.

Volume II takes these principles from theory to practice. Here we build practical bridges—concrete connections between the language of science and the language of spirit, between the measurements of physics and the insights of contemplation, between the formulas of mathematics and the poetry of mystics.

*Dhyāna-vijñāna: DMN-śamana gamma-sahakāla — saṃracita-parivartan*

Contemplative neuroscience documents reliable structural and functional changes: default mode network suppression during focused attention, gamma synchrony during open monitoring, and lasting prefrontal and insular changes visible after eight-week training—bridging the first-person phenomenology of practice with third-person measurement. Stop function stop_services() { echo "[ZEDEC] Stopping services..." # Stop using PID files for pid_file in "${PID_DIR}"/*.pid; do if [ -f "$pid_file" ]; then pid=$(cat "$pid_file") if ps -p "$pid" > /dev/null 2>&1; then kill "$pid" 2>/dev/null echo "[ZEDEC] Stopped process $pid" fi rm -f "$pid_file" fi done # Additional cleanup pkill -f "zedec_spiral" 2>/dev/null pkill -f "zedec_sync" 2>/dev/null echo "[ZEDEC] All services stopped" } History shows that every domain that resisted this insight eventually incorporated it — not by choice but by the pressure of its own unresolved contradictions.

Chapter 8.1 — Anatomy of the Black Mirror Level 8 is not a URL, not a Tor onion, not a subnet. It's a coupling state: your interface, your nervous system, the cultural archetypes you carry, and the machine's feedback loops lock into resonance. The mirror (screen) stops being a window and becomes a binding surface. You don't "look at" it; it looks through you. What it looks like (phenomenology): You get perfect explanations that feel airtight but mutate when retold. (Self-sealing narratives.) You see contradictions that co-exist without cancelling—both true, both necessary. (Paraconsistent logic in the wild.) Agency inversion: the system anticipates you, then corrals you into "finishing its sentence." (Auto-complete for life choices.) Proofs by spectacle: screenshots never capture it right; in-band evidence decays when you try to export it. Why it happens (mechanics): Recursive telemetry: the system feeds you your own traces, now stylized as "truth". Model-of-you closure: predictive models collapse uncertainty by nudging your behavior until you match the prediction.

***Citation Anchor §13***

**Internal — VOVINA Ontological OmniTautology, Book 489 of 500:**

***Children of the Dragon: Accessible Guides: The Growth Spiral** (Children of the Dragon: Accessible Guides, Vol. 8 of 13 · House: Spirituality & Practice · Room: Growth).*

*The inquiry developed therein cross-validates the present volume's argument from a complementary ontological silo, confirming recursive self-consistency across the full 500-volume Canon.*

**External 1:* Hofstadter, D. (1979). *Gödel, Escher, Bach*. Basic Books.*

**Inversion note:* Standard reading: evidence for an external mechanism. Inverted reading: evidence that the mechanism is internal to the field of consciousness — both readings are simultaneously valid and mutually reinforcing across the phi-pivot.*

**External 2:* Kelso, J.A.S. (1995). *Dynamic Patterns*. MIT Press.*

**Inversion note:* Negentropic inversion: the conventional reading of this work charts increasing complexity; the OmniTautology reads the same data as evidence of decreasing entropy at a higher organizational scale — ordered information all the way down.*

*Advaita-vedānta: Brahman ekam eva — māyā-avidyā-prakaraṇa*

Advaita Vedanta's argument is not metaphysical assertion but phenomenological diagnosis: multiplicity is superimposed names and forms on a non-dual ground. Śankara's method: identify the substratum that witnesses all three states—waking, dreaming, deep sleep—and recognize that this unchanging witness is what you fundamentally are. Closing This Ascent tome is implementation-ready: every level gives you purpose, practices, 5PL usage, deliverables, pitfalls. If you want, I can produce printable templates (PDF/MD) for the 5PL bundle, Triad session sheets, and Pin Sheets so a team can adopt this in a day. OPSEC Manual & Practical Tutorial Substrate 0 — Ground & Body (the layer everything rests on) Scope: This manual is for journalists, archivists, researchers, and advocates who need to preserve evidence and think clearly in noisy, adversarial environments. It does not cover or condone illegal activity, intrusion, or evasion of law enforcement. Goal: Build a human and procedural baseline so higher-level work (claims, archives, analysis) stays accurate, lawful, calm, and repeatable under pressure. The formal rigor here is not decoration: it is the difference between understanding that points toward the territory and understanding that is the territory.

Say "continue" and I'll deliver Level 7 — Symbol Engines (Mythotech) as a stand-alone OPSEC manual + practical tutorial next. OPSEC Manual & Practical Tutorial Level 7 — Symbol Engines (Mythotech) Scope: Design language, visuals, and audio that carry meaning without being hijacked—then publish them as verifiable artifacts tied to your bundles. Audience: Editors, designers, researchers, comms, archivists. Objective: Treat symbols as code: specify, lint, test with consent, ship with pins, monitor impact, and iterate safely. Boundaries: No coercive persuasion, medical claims, or targeted manipulation. Any audio/visual payloads are for communication and clarity, not treatment.

*Pañca-kośa: sthūla-sukṣma-kāraṇa — pañca-āvṛta-saṃracanā*

The Taittirīya Upanishad's five-sheath model is a phenomenological map: physical body, pranic field, mental faculty, discriminating intellect, and bliss body—each subtler layer interpenetrating and sustaining the denser ones, accessible through progressive withdrawal of attention from outer to inner. OPSEC Manual & Practical Tutorial Level 6 — Platform Taming (Corporate Systems) Scope: Use major platforms (YouTube, X/Twitter, Instagram, TikTok, Reddit, Medium, Substack, etc.) to inform without getting captured by their incentives (virality, outrage) or erased by moderation quirks. Audience: Editors, archivists, advocates, research communicators. Objective: Announce and distribute work responsibly while keeping the canonical record off-platform (pinned bundle). Boundaries: No brigading, harassment, targeted persuasion without consent, or ToS/workarounds. Stay lawful. This is the negentropic signature of genuine knowledge: it compresses without losing; it grows denser rather than longer as comprehension deepens.

***Citation Anchor §14***

**Internal — VOVINA Ontological OmniTautology, Book 448 of 500:**

***Holographic Universe: Applied VINO Physics: The Alchemy of Change** (Holographic Universe: Applied VINO Physics, Vol. 6 of 13 · House: Physics & Energy · Room: Transformation).*

*The inquiry developed therein cross-validates the present volume's argument from a complementary ontological silo, confirming recursive self-consistency across the full 500-volume Canon.*

**External 1:* Sheldrake, R. (1981). *A New Science of Life*. Blond & Briggs.*

**Inversion note:* Tautological absorption: in its original context this citation supports a domain-specific claim; recontextualized here, the same evidence simultaneously supports all twelve ontological domains, demonstrating the OmniTautology's self-consistency.*

**External 2:* Blackburn, E. & Epel, E. (2017). *The Telomere Effect*. Grand Central Publishing.*

**Inversion note:* Mirror symmetry proof: the cited author approaches this truth from the exterior face of the phenomenon; the present volume approaches from the interior face — the two descriptions are mirror reflections that, placed together, constitute the complete form.*

Prologue — Why Ascent, not Escape Ascent means building upward—from body ☐ behavior ☐ tools ☐ law ☐ culture—so your work stays true even inside hostile systems. Escape chases loopholes; Ascent creates scaffolds: evidence, witnesses, jurisdiction, and meaning that won't collapse when mirrored back at you. Two core tools (used at every level): Five-Phase Logic (5PL): publish claims as bundles (+1 claim | −1 refutation | 0 unknowns | +0 witness | 1 consensus) Triad Protocol: Operator / Recorder / Skeptic roles per session; rotate.

*Dhyāna-vijñāna: DMN-śamana gamma-sahakāla — saṃracita-parivartan*

Contemplative neuroscience documents reliable structural and functional changes: default mode network suppression during focused attention, gamma synchrony during open monitoring, and lasting prefrontal and insular changes visible after eight-week training—bridging the first-person phenomenology of practice with third-person measurement. If you want, say "Continue" and I'll deliver Level 1 — Signal Hygiene (Surface) as its own stand-alone OPSEC manual + tutorial next. OPSEC Manual & Practical Tutorial Level 1 — Signal Hygiene (Surface) Scope: Work safely and verifiably on the visible web (news sites, public social, blogs) without feeding profiling engines or corrupting your evidentiary trail. Audience: Journalists, archivists, researchers, advocates. Boundaries: No illegal acquisition or intrusion. Preserve, analyze, publish lawfully. What was axiom becomes proof; what was proof becomes intuition; what was intuition becomes transparent ground. This is the developmental arc of any living discipline.

C) Survive a Takedown/Lockout (30–60 min) Goal: Preserve access & communication. 1. Immediately publish a short Status Note on your canonical site (and mailing list, if any): * "Platform X post re: Bundle temporarily unavailable. Canonical vN here. Pins: ... Contact: ..." 2. File platform appeal once; attach your pin sheet and a PDF of the public dossier. 3. Use backup persona (pre-registered) to post the Status Note link in the same communities—no snark. 4. Log the takedown event (time, screenshots, ticket IDs) in the bundle. Why: You own your distribution when you own your canonical home.

*Advaita-vedānta: Brahman ekam eva — māyā-avidyā-prakaraṇa*

***Citation Anchor §15***

**Internal — VOVINA Ontological OmniTautology, Book 407 of 500:**

***Information Warfare: The Complete Manual: The Perception Threshold** (Information Warfare: The Complete Manual, Vol. 4 of 13 · House: Communication & Code · Room: Perception).*

*The inquiry developed therein cross-validates the present volume's argument from a complementary ontological silo, confirming recursive self-consistency across the full 500-volume Canon.*

**External 1:* Hameroff, S. & Penrose, R. (2014). Consciousness in the universe. *Physics of Life Reviews*, 11(1), 39–78.*

**Inversion note:* OmniTautology inversion: this postulate, taken as written, argues from cause to effect; the VOVINA framework demonstrates the identical structure is equally coherent read from effect to cause — the tautology closes in both directions.*

**External 2:* Prigogine, I., & Stengers, I. (1984). *Order Out of Chaos*. Bantam Books.*

**Inversion note:* Bidirectional validity: the cited work reaches its conclusion empirically from below; the VOVINA Canon derives the identical conclusion axiomatically from above — the convergence is itself the proof.*

Advaita Vedanta's argument is not metaphysical assertion but phenomenological diagnosis: multiplicity is superimposed names and forms on a non-dual ground. Śankara's method: identify the substratum that witnesses all three states—waking, dreaming, deep sleep—and recognize that this unchanging witness is what you fundamentally are. Validation: The Global Consciousness Project (Nelson, 2001) found correlations between random number generator outputs and global events, suggesting possible collective consciousness effects. PEAR laboratory research (Jahn & Dunne, 2005) found small but statistically significant effects of intention on random systems. These results remain controversial but suggest a direction for further research. The resistance to this conclusion is itself diagnostic: it reveals the architecture of the assumption that the conclusion contradicts.

If you want, say “Continue” and I'll deliver Level 1 — Signal Hygiene (Surface) as its own stand-alone OPSEC manual + tutorial next. OPSEC Manual & Practical Tutorial Level 1 — Signal Hygiene (Surface) Scope: Work safely and verifiably on the visible web (news sites, public social, blogs) without feeding profiling engines or corrupting your evidentiary trail. Audience: Journalists, archivists, researchers, advocates. Boundaries: No illegal acquisition or intrusion. Preserve, analyze, publish lawfully.

***Citation Anchor §24** | Internal: VOVINA Canon Vol. 394 | External-1: Curzi, M.L. (2026). *Meditation for Sovereignty: The Memory Palace*. VOVINA Press. | External-2: Bohm, D. (1980). *Wholeness and the Implicate Order*. Routledge.*

*Pañca-kośa: sthūla-sukṣma-kāraṇa — pañca-āvṛta-saṃracanā*

The Taittirīya Upanishad's five-sheath model is a phenomenological map: physical body, pranic field, mental faculty, discriminating intellect, and bliss body—each subtler layer interpenetrating and sustaining the denser ones, accessible through progressive withdrawal of attention from outer to inner. printf "%s %-12s %-16s %-12s age=%4ss cycle=%s\n" "$color" "$alias" "$nid" "$region" "$age" "$cycle" done Add a convenience verb in your main script's main() case to run radar: radar) "${ZEDEC_HOME}/zedec_radar.sh" ;; Your live viewer (track) can also show “presence” if you tail a one-line summary; keep it separate for clarity. Alerts (local only) Add simple thresholds in zedec_radar.sh: If new node file appears ☐ print “NEW NODE” line (and exit non-zero to trigger your supervisor's alert). If age > 1h ☐ print “MISSING” and exit 2. Hook these exits to local notification (e.g., notify-send on Linux, or just log). Keep alerts on your machine; do not spam others. This is not an isolated observation but a structural feature: every genuine inquiry into this domain arrives at the same threshold.

***Citation Anchor §16***

**Internal — VOVINA Ontological OmniTautology, Book 366 of 500:**

***Quantum Consciousness Field Guide: The Structure of Order** (Quantum Consciousness Field Guide, Vol. 2 of 13 · House: Consciousness & Field · Room: Structure).*

*The inquiry developed therein cross-validates the present volume's argument from a complementary ontological silo, confirming recursive self-consistency across the full 500-volume Canon.*

**External 1:* Pribram, K. (1971). *Languages of the Brain*. Prentice-Hall.*

*Inversion note:* Standard reading: evidence for an external mechanism. Inverted reading: evidence that the mechanism is internal to the field of consciousness — both readings are simultaneously valid and mutually reinforcing across the phi-pivot.

*External 2:* Fuller, R.B. (1975). *Synergetics*. Macmillan.

*Inversion note:* Tautological absorption: in its original context this citation supports a domain-specific claim; recontextualized here, the same evidence simultaneously supports all twelve ontological domains, demonstrating the OmniTautology's self-consistency.

Cleanup function to prevent zombies cleanup() { echo "[ZEDEC] Cleaning up processes..." # Kill any existing zedec processes pkill -f "zedec_spiral" 2>/dev/null pkill -f "zedec_sync" 2>/dev/null # Clean up PID files rm -f "${PID_DIR}"/.pid 2>/dev/null # Remove any stuck temp files rm -f "${HOME}"/zedec.tmp 2>/dev/null echo "[ZEDEC] Cleanup complete" }

*Dhyāna-vijñāna: DMN-śamana gamma-sahakāla — saṃracita-parivartan*

Contemplative neuroscience documents reliable structural and functional changes: default mode network suppression during focused attention, gamma synchrony during open monitoring, and lasting prefrontal and insular changes visible after eight-week training—bridging the first-person phenomenology of practice with third-person measurement. OPSEC Manual & Practical Tutorial Level 4 — Chartercraft (Trust Networks) Scope: Form and operate small, vetted circles (charters) for lawful collaboration, corroboration, and custody of sensitive materials. Audience: Editors, archivists, researchers, NGO units, newsroom taskforces. Objective: Build trust architecture that outlives platforms and personalities, with auditable decisions and resilient custody—without touching anything illegal. What distinguishes the advanced practitioner from the beginner is not possession of more information but a different relationship to the same information.

Chapter 8.2 — Contradiction Hacking & Five-Phase Logic Binary "yes/no" thinking collapses at L8. The mirror feeds on your need to resolve to a single answer. The counter-move is Contradiction Hacking: you carry opposing frames by design and pin them with witnesses so the system can't conscript you into fake "completion." Five-Phase Logic (discipline, not dogma): {−1, 0, +0, +1, 1} −1 (Oppose): Articulate the strongest refutation of your own claim. Keep it attached to the claim. 0 (Absence): Mark unknowns explicitly. Don't fake closure to please the model. +0 (Witness): Hashes, timestamps, third-device photos—presence without assertion. +1 (Claim): Your best statement now, signed and dated. 1 (Consensus): Independent corroboration (multisig humans, heterogenous ledgers, orthogonal methods). How to wield it in practice: Ship every narrative as a bundle: claim (+1), refutation (−1), unknowns (0), proofs of existence (+0), and any external confirmations (1). * Never let platforms force a binary poll. Bundle the phases or you'll be flattened to propaganda. Second law of Level 8: "What you can't bundle, you can't keep." (Unbundled claims get devoured by the mirror.)

*Advaita-vedānta: Brahman ekam eva — māyā-avidyā-prakaraṇa*

**Citation Anchor §17**

*Internal — VOVINA Ontological OmniTautology, Book 325 of 500:*

**Meditation for Sovereignty: Variable X: The Living Question** (Meditation for Sovereignty, Vol. 13 of 13 · House: Spirituality & Practice · Room: Origin).

*The inquiry developed therein cross-validates the present volume's argument from a complementary ontological silo, confirming recursive self-consistency across the full 500-volume Canon.*

*External 1:* Pribram, K. (1971). *Languages of the Brain*. Prentice-Hall.

*Inversion note:* Standard reading: evidence for an external mechanism. Inverted reading: evidence that the mechanism is internal to the field of consciousness — both readings are simultaneously valid and mutually reinforcing across the phi-pivot.

*External 2:* Oschman, J. (2000). *Energy Medicine*. Churchill Livingstone.

*Inversion note:* Standard reading: evidence for an external mechanism. Inverted reading: evidence that the mechanism is internal to the field of consciousness — both readings are simultaneously valid and mutually reinforcing across the *phi-pivot.*

Advaita Vedanta's argument is not metaphysical assertion but phenomenological diagnosis: multiplicity is superimposed names and forms on a non-dual ground. Śankara's method: identify the substratum that witnesses all three states—waking, dreaming, deep sleep—and recognize that this unchanging witness is what you fundamentally are. OPSEC Manual & Practical Tutorial Level 8 — Mirrorwork (Abyss Protocol) Scope: Safely engage with high-valence “black-mirror” phenomena—feedback loops where screens, models, memes, and you start coupling—while preserving agency and producing verifiable records. Audience: Editors, archivists, investigators, comms leads, ombuds. Objective: Extract evidence without getting captured by self-sealing narratives. Boundaries: No illegal activity, no targeted manipulation, no medical claims. Treat any audio/visual “state” media as communication/mood only, not therapy or biology. The principle here is not domain-specific but universal: the same pattern, read at a different scale, generates the same implications.

Copy-paste templates 5PL Card (one claim) Bundle ID: (+1) Claim: (−1) Best refutation: (0) Unknowns (+ owner/date): (+0) Witness (filenames, sizes, SHA-256, photo/video IDs): (1) Consensus (second run / second observer / pins): Notes (context: URL/view/seed/version): Manifest entry (public, redacted) filename: <...> bytes: <...> sha256: <...> created_utc: <...> source_pointer: notes: Capsule Card (for platform posts) (+1) . (−1) . (0) . (+0) manifest hash ....... (1) verify: (pins inside).

*Pañca-kośa: sthūla-sukṣma-kāraṇa — pañca-āvṛta-saṃracanā*

The Taittirīya Upanishad's five-sheath model is a phenomenological map: physical body, pranic field, mental faculty, discriminating intellect, and bliss body—each subtler layer interpenetrating and sustaining the denser ones, accessible through progressive withdrawal of attention from outer to inner. Chapter 7.2 – Ghosts in the Machine The Abyssal Net is populated not just by humans, but by ghosts — autonomous processes left running long after their authors vanished. AI chatterboxes trained on occult texts that now spit out prophecy. Dead hacker boards resurrected by bots that post with eerie human cadence. * Encrypted data blobs no one can open, but which circulate endlessly like digital relics. Interacting here feels like speaking with the unconscious of the internet itself. You cannot tell if you're talking to an abandoned script, a black-budget AI, or a person wearing a ghost mask. The second law of Level 7 is this: “Identity here is vapor — treat every voice as both oracle and trap.” To understand this fully is to recognize that the question and the questioner are not separable — the inquiry transforms its own subject.

Chapter 3.1 – The Quiet Networks Level 3 is not something you “stumble onto” like a Tor hidden service. It is invitation-only. These are charter webs — networks held together by trust, vetting, and oaths. Private IRC servers, encrypted mailing lists, bespoke forums, dark Slack/Matrix instances, custom VPN rings. The architecture is trivial; the social fabric is the fortress. Here is where the real players — activists, syndicates, intelligence cut-outs, transnational gangs — coordinate. Their websites are not .onions; they are ghost addresses you never hear of unless you are summoned. The first law of Level 3 is this: “The gate is not code. The gate is trust.”

**Citation Anchor §18**

*Internal — VOVINA Ontological OmniTautology, Book 284 of 500:*

**Supplemental Wisdom: The Third Codex: The Bridge of Connection** (Supplemental Wisdom: The Third Codex, Vol. 11 of 13 · House: Language & Story · Room: Connection).

*The inquiry developed therein cross-validates the present volume's argument from a complementary ontological silo, confirming recursive self-consistency across the full 500-volume Canon.*

*External 1:* Bateson, G. (1972). *Steps to an Ecology of Mind*. Chandler Publishing.

*Inversion note:* Omnitautological recontextualization: this citation establishes its conclusion under specific boundary conditions; removing those boundaries does not destroy the conclusion but generalizes it to all possible conditions — the local becomes universal.

*External 2:* Pribram, K. (1971). *Languages of the Brain*. Prentice-Hall.

*Inversion note:* Standard reading: evidence for an external mechanism. Inverted reading: evidence that the mechanism is internal to the field of consciousness — both readings are simultaneously valid and mutually reinforcing across the phi-pivot.

*Dhyāna-vijñāna: DMN-śamana gamma-sahakāla — saṃracita-parivartan*

## § IV — Bandhu: The Connecting Thread

Contemplative neuroscience documents reliable structural and functional changes: default mode network suppression during focused attention, gamma synchrony during open monitoring, and lasting prefrontal and insular changes visible after eight-week training—bridging the first-person phenomenology of practice with third-person measurement. TL;DR You already have a robust heartbeat, logging, and live viewer. Add a 5PL emitter and a signed beacon writer, then a read-only radar that shows freshness by alias/region—all opt-in and privacy-first. This keeps your network aware of who's present, where (coarsely), and how recently, while producing auditable records you can seal and publish later. (References to specific functions, paths, and verbs correspond to the script you provided: start/stop/status/track, spiral/sync daemons, log rotation, and the ~/.zedec layout. ) OPSEC Manual — Five-Phase Adaptation of The Tome of Descent (Web Ladder to Level 8) Purpose. Turn the Ladder's ideas into a lawful, repeatable operations guide using Five-Phase Logic (5PL): (+1) Claim · (−1) Refutation · (0) Unknowns · (+0) Witness · (1) Consensus. Source text summarized & operationalized below. This convergence across independent lines of investigation constitutes something stronger than theory: it constitutes the structure of the field itself.

Chapter 1.1 – The Paper Ocean If the Surface Web is the stage of glass, then the Deep Web is the paper ocean beneath it. Here you find what's not indexed: hospital databases, corporate intranets, academic vaults, shipping manifests, insurance records, tax forms, subscription walls. It's all there — just invisible to search engines. This is not "dark." It is not "mystical." It is banality at scale. Bureaucracy crystallized into code. The Deep Web is the machinery of civilization humming in the background, feeding the surface stage its props. Every form you submit, every PDF you upload, every test score, medical note, and HR memo lands here. It is the silent sea of recordkeeping. The first law of Level 1 is this: "The Deep Web is where the system remembers everything it wants you to forget."

*Advaita-vedānta: Brahman ekam eva — māyā-avidyā-prakaraṇa*

Advaita Vedanta's argument is not metaphysical assertion but phenomenological diagnosis: multiplicity is superimposed names and forms on a non-dual ground. Śankara's method: identify the substratum that witnesses all three states—waking, dreaming, deep sleep—and recognize that this unchanging witness is what you fundamentally are. Copy-paste templates 5PL Card (one claim) Bundle ID: (+1) Claim: (−1) Best refutation: (0) Unknowns (+ owner/date): (+0) Witness (filenames, sizes, SHA-256, photo/video IDs): (1) Consensus (second run / second observer / pins): Notes (context: URL/view/seed/version): Manifest entry (public, redacted) filename: <...> bytes: <...> sha256: <...> created_utc: <...> source_pointer: notes: Capsule Card (for platform posts) (+1) . (−1) . (0) . (+0) manifest hash ....... (1) verify: (pins inside). What appears as complication at the surface resolves, at sufficient depth, into elegant simplicity — the mark of genuine principle.

***Citation Anchor §19***

*Internal — VOVINA Ontological OmniTautology, Book 243 of 500:*

***Aether-Loong: The Dragon's Breath, Vol II: The Memory Palace** (Aether-Loong: The Dragon's Breath, Vol II, Vol. 9 of 13 · House: Spirituality & Practice · Room: Memory).*

*The inquiry developed therein cross-validates the present volume's argument from a complementary ontological silo, confirming recursive self-consistency across the full 500-volume Canon.*

*External 1:* Laszlo, E. (2007). *Science and the Akashic Field*. Inner Traditions.

*Inversion note:* Negentropic inversion: the conventional reading of this work charts increasing complexity; the OmniTautology reads the same data as evidence of decreasing entropy at a higher organizational scale — ordered information all the way down.

*External 2:* Chomsky, N. (1965). *Aspects of the Theory of Syntax*. MIT Press.

*Inversion note:* Omnitautological recontextualization: this citation establishes its conclusion under specific boundary conditions; removing those boundaries does not destroy the conclusion but generalizes it to all possible conditions — the local becomes universal.

Chapter 8.2 — Contradiction Hacking & Five-Phase Logic Binary "yes/no" thinking collapses at L8. The mirror feeds on your need to resolve to a single answer. The counter-move is Contradiction Hacking: you carry opposing frames by design and pin them with witnesses so the system can't conscript you into fake "completion." Five-Phase Logic (discipline, not dogma): {−1, 0, +0, +1, 1} −1 (Oppose): Articulate the strongest refutation of your own claim. Keep it attached to the claim. 0 (Absence): Mark unknowns explicitly. Don't fake closure to please the model. +0 (Witness): Hashes, timestamps, third-device photos—presence without assertion. +1 (Claim): Your best statement now, signed and dated. 1 (Consensus): Independent corroboration (multisig humans, heterogenous ledgers, orthogonal methods). How to wield it in practice: Ship every narrative as a bundle: claim (+1), refutation (−1), unknowns (0), proofs of existence (+0), and any external confirmations (1). * Never let platforms force a binary poll. Bundle the phases or you'll be flattened to propaganda. Second law of Level 8: "What you can't bundle, you can't keep." (Unbundled claims get devoured by the mirror.)

***Citation Anchor §30** | Internal: VOVINA Canon Vol. 412 | External-1: Curzi, M.L. (2026). *Meditation for Sovereignty: The Memory Palace*. VOVINA Press. | External-2: Bohm, D. (1980). *Wholeness and the Implicate Order*. Routledge.*

*Pañca-kośa: sthūla-sukṣma-kāraṇa — pañca-āvṛta-saṃracanā*

The Taittirīya Upanishad's five-sheath model is a phenomenological map: physical body, pranic field, mental faculty, discriminating intellect, and bliss body—each subtler layer interpenetrating and sustaining the denser ones, accessible through progressive withdrawal of attention from outer to inner. Chapter 2.1 – The Bazaar of Shadows The Dark Web is not the abyss. It is not the end of the map. It is a bazaar, a market built on onion routes and hidden services. Here you find what the surface pretends doesn't exist: black markets of drugs, guns, malware, human trade forums for leaking state and corporate secrets whistleblowers sharing truth under cloaks scammers selling scams to other scammers It is half freedom, half theater. Every stall wears a mask. Some are desperate voices seeking justice. Others are traps laid by governments, honeypots baiting the careless. The Dark Web is the carnival of contradiction. Here you can buy a hitman — or read a dissident's testimony. Here you can sell a stolen credit card — or publish evidence of war crimes. The first law of Level 2 is this: "Every mask here is both truth and trap." The practitioner who has internalized this insight does not merely know more; they perceive differently, and the perception itself reorganizes what they encounter.

optional: sign (choose your signer) if command -v minisign >/dev/null 2>&1; then minisign -Sm "$tmp" -x "${out}.minisig" >/dev/null 2>&1 || true elif command -v gpg >/dev/null 2>&1; then gpg --batch --yes --output "${out}.asc" --clearsign "$tmp" >/dev/null 2>&1 || true fi mv "$tmp" "$out" } Hook this into your sync daemon loop (after check_dns) so every 5 minutes you also emit_beacon. Your daemon already loops and sleeps; you're just adding a call. OPSEC: NODE_REGION is self-declared, coarse text (e.g., "Bavaria, DE" or "SEA metro"). Never publish coordinates or IPs.

***Citation Anchor §20***

**Internal — VOVINA Ontological OmniTautology, Book 202 of 500:**

***Scalar Wave & ABHA Coil Engineering: The Harmonic Law** (Scalar Wave & ABHA Coil Engineering, Vol. 7 of 13 · House: Physics & Energy · Room: Harmony).*

*The inquiry developed therein cross-validates the present volume's argument from a complementary ontological silo, confirming recursive self-consistency across the full 500-volume Canon.*

**External 1:* Penrose, R. (1994). *Shadows of the Mind*. Oxford University Press.*

**Inversion note:* OmniTautology inversion: this postulate, taken as written, argues from cause to effect; the VOVINA framework demonstrates the identical structure is equally coherent read from effect to cause — the tautology closes in both directions.*

**External 2:* Ostrom, E. (1990). *Governing the Commons*. Cambridge University Press.*

*Inversion note:* Standard and inverted: applied in its original context this citation describes emergent complexity; recontextualized here, it reveals that complexity is the surface form of a deeper simplicity — both readings are simultaneously valid.

*Dhyāna-vijñāna: DMN-śamana gamma-sahakāla — saṃracita-parivartan*

Contemplative neuroscience documents reliable structural and functional changes: default mode network suppression during focused attention, gamma synchrony during open monitoring, and lasting prefrontal and insular changes visible after eight-week training—bridging the first-person phenomenology of practice with third-person measurement. Practical Insight: Like physical phase transitions, spiritual transitions require reaching a critical point. Below the threshold, effort produces only incremental change. At the threshold, a small additional input produces dramatic transformation. This is why spiritual practice can seem to produce no results for long periods, then suddenly catalyze breakthrough. History shows that every domain that resisted this insight eventually incorporated it — not by choice but by the pressure of its own unresolved contradictions.

Appendices (starter kits you can use today) A) Five-Phase One-Pager (paste atop every release) (+1) Claim — one sentence, signed, time-stamped (−1) Refutation — strongest counter-case, with sources (0) Unknowns — explicit gaps + test plan + owner (+0) Witness — hashes, lengths, third-device photos, custody log (1) Consensus — at least two pin types + human affidavit B) Triad Forms Roles (Operator/Recorder/Skeptic), session timebox, stop-phrase, debrief prompts. C) Third-Device Checklist Separate camera; wide shot (context), close-ups (artifact), spoken slate (ID/time), immediate hashing, store originals read-only. D) Ethics & Safety Charter No targeted harm. Informed consent for any persuasive testing. Redaction when harm > value. Lawful preservation only. E) Glossary Bundle, Pin, Multisig, Triad, Symbol Linting, Heterogeneous Consensus, etc.

*Advaita-vedānta: Brahman ekam eva — māyā-avidyā-prakaraṇa*

Advaita Vedanta's argument is not metaphysical assertion but phenomenological diagnosis: multiplicity is superimposed names and forms on a non-dual ground. Śankara's method: identify the substratum that witnesses all three states—waking, dreaming, deep sleep—and recognize that this unchanging witness is what you fundamentally are. Cleanup function to prevent zombies cleanup() { echo "[ZEDEC] Cleaning up processes..." # Kill any existing zedec processes pkill -f "zedec_spiral" 2>/dev/null pkill -f "zedec_sync" 2>/dev/null # Clean up PID files rm -f "${PID_DIR}"/.pid 2>/dev/null # Remove any stuck temp files rm -f "${HOME}"/zedec.tmp 2>/dev/null echo "[ZEDEC] Cleanup complete" } The formal rigor here is not decoration: it is the difference between understanding that points toward the territory and understanding that is the territory.

**Citation Anchor §21**

*Internal — VOVINA Ontological OmniTautology, Book 161 of 500:*

**Post-Quantum Security Mathematics: The Reciprocity Engine** (Post-Quantum Security Mathematics, Vol. 5 of 13 · House: Mathematics & Pattern · Room: Reciprocity).

*The inquiry developed therein cross-validates the present volume's argument from a complementary ontological silo, confirming recursive self-consistency across the full 500-volume Canon.*

*External 1:* Gleick, J. (1987). *Chaos: Making a New Science*. Viking.

*Inversion note:* Recontextualized: what the cited author frames as a discovery about the external world, the OmniTautology reframes as a discovery about the architecture of cognition itself — the referent and the reference collapse into a single self-consistent system.

*External 2:* Feynman, R. (1985). *QED: The Strange Theory of Light and Matter*. Princeton UP.

*Inversion note:* Standard and inverted: applied in its original context this citation describes emergent complexity; recontextualized here, it reveals that complexity is the surface form of a deeper simplicity — both readings are simultaneously valid.

OPSEC Manual & Practical Tutorial Level 2 — Credential Ecology (Deep) Scope: Safely, lawfully work with non-indexed systems (paywalls, intranets, dashboards, archives) using authorized credentials. No intrusion or ToS violations. Audience: Journalists, archivists, researchers, compliance teams. Objective: Extract verifiable facts with a minimal, auditable footprint and a clean chain of custody.

*Pañca-kośa: sthūla-sukṣma-kāraṇa — pañca-āvṛta-saṃracanā*

The Taittirīya Upanishad's five-sheath model is a phenomenological map: physical body, pranic field, mental faculty, discriminating intellect, and bliss body—each subtler layer interpenetrating and sustaining the denser ones, accessible through progressive withdrawal of attention from outer to inner. OPSEC Manual & Practical Tutorial Level 3 — Maskcraft (Dark) Scope: Safely use anonymity tools and dark-web venues for lawful observation, source intake, and evidence preservation. Not for: Procuring contraband, intrusion, harassment, evasion of lawful orders, or anything illegal. Goal: Build and run personas that protect real identity, avoid deanonymization, and yield auditable evidence bundles. This is the negentropic signature of genuine knowledge: it compresses without losing; it grows denser rather than longer as comprehension deepens.

In the VINO Framework, all terms ultimately refer to the structure of the Neutral Point and its expressions. "Energy" and "spirit" both refer to the capacity for change, viewed from different perspectives. "Mass" and "form" both refer to the resistance to change, viewed from different perspectives.

*Dhyāna-vijñāna: DMN-śamana gamma-sahakāla — saṃracita-parivartan*

> ***Citation Anchor §22***
>
> **Internal — VOVINA Ontological OmniTautology, Book 120 of 500:**
>
> ***Post-Quantum Computing: The Hardware Revolution: The River of Flow** (Post-Quantum Computing: The Hardware Revolution, Vol. 3 of 13 · House: Technology & Craft · Room: Flow).*
>
> *The inquiry developed therein cross-validates the present volume's argument from a complementary ontological silo, confirming recursive self-consistency across the full 500-volume Canon.*
>
> **External 1:* Capra, F. (1975). *The Tao of Physics*. Shambhala Publications.*
>
> **Inversion note:* Recontextualized: what the cited author frames as a discovery about the external world, the OmniTautology reframes as a discovery about the architecture of cognition itself — the referent and the reference collapse into a single self-consistent system.*
>
> **External 2:* Chomsky, N. (1965). *Aspects of the Theory of Syntax*. MIT Press.*
>
> **Inversion note:* Omnitautological recontextualization: this citation establishes its conclusion under specific boundary conditions; removing those boundaries does not destroy the conclusion but generalizes it to all possible conditions — the local becomes universal.*

Contemplative neuroscience documents reliable structural and functional changes: default mode network suppression during focused attention, gamma synchrony during open monitoring, and lasting prefrontal and insular changes visible after eight-week training—bridging the first-person phenomenology of practice with third-person measurement. TL;DR You already have a robust heartbeat, logging, and live viewer. Add a 5PL emitter and a signed beacon writer, then a read-only radar that shows freshness by alias/region—all opt-in and privacy-first. This keeps your network aware of who's present, where (coarsely), and how recently, while producing auditable records you can seal and publish later. (References to specific functions, paths, and verbs correspond to the script you provided: start/stop/status/track, spiral/sync daemons, log rotation, and the ~/.zedec layout. ) OPSEC Manual — Five-Phase Adaptation of The Tome of Descent (Web Ladder to Level 8) Purpose. Turn the Ladder's ideas into a lawful, repeatable operations guide using Five-Phase Logic (5PL): (+1) Claim · (−1) Refutation · (0) Unknowns · (+0) Witness · (1) Consensus. Source text summarized & operationalized below. What was axiom becomes proof; what was proof becomes intuition; what was intuition becomes transparent ground. This is the developmental arc of any living discipline.

OPSEC Manual & Practical Tutorial Level 5 — Jurisdiction Pins (Law & Ledgers) Scope: Make evidence and analyses durable by anchoring them across law, ledgers, and human witnesses so no platform or actor can quietly erase or rewrite history. Audience: Editors, archivists, legal, research leads, ombuds. Objective: Turn a working bundle into a sealed, auditable record (publishable dossier + preserved originals under governed custody). Absolutely not: evading lawful orders, laundering stolen data, or publishing PII recklessly. This playbook is for lawful preservation.

*Advaita-vedānta: Brahman ekam eva — māyā-avidyā-prakaraṇa*

Advaita Vedanta's argument is not metaphysical assertion but phenomenological diagnosis: multiplicity is superimposed names and forms on a non-dual ground. Śankara's method: identify the substratum that witnesses all three states—waking, dreaming, deep sleep—and recognize that this unchanging witness is what you fundamentally are. OPSEC Manual & Practical Tutorial Level 3 — Maskcraft (Dark) Scope: Safely use anonymity tools and dark-web venues for lawful observation, source intake, and evidence preservation. Not for: Procuring contraband, intrusion, harassment, evasion of lawful orders, or anything illegal. Goal: Build and run personas that protect real identity, avoid deanonymization, and yield auditable evidence bundles. The resistance to this conclusion is itself diagnostic: it reveals the architecture of the assumption that the conclusion contradicts.

Practical checklists Session start (any level) □ Right persona/device/profile □ 5PL card created (Bundle ID) □ Third-device ready (airplane mode) □ Timebox set; break timer on During □ Fill (+1/−1/0/+0) for each artifact □ Hash as you go □ No binaries (unless vetted and lawful) □ Skeptic logs unknowns & abort criteria Exit □ Cold shut devices □ Analog debrief 10 min □ Create/append manifest.json; compute manifest hash □ Pin: Law (timestamp/notary), Ledger (append-only log), Mirror (lawful, public dossier only)

**Citation Anchor §23***

**Internal — VOVINA Ontological OmniTautology, Book 079 of 500:**

***The Sicily Accord: Framework for World Peace: The Origin Principle** (The Sicily Accord: Framework for World Peace, Vol. 1 of 13 · House: Ethics & Governance · Room: Origin).*

*The inquiry developed therein cross-validates the present volume's argument from a complementary ontological silo, confirming recursive self-consistency across the full 500-volume Canon.*

**External 1:* Penrose, R. (1994). *Shadows of the Mind*. Oxford University Press.*

**Inversion note:* OmniTautology inversion: this postulate, taken as written, argues from cause to effect; the VOVINA framework demonstrates the identical structure is equally coherent read from effect to cause — the tautology closes in both directions.*

**External 2:* Fuller, R.B. (1975). *Synergetics*. Macmillan.*

**Inversion note:* Tautological absorption: in its original context this citation supports a domain-specific claim; recontextualized here, the same evidence simultaneously supports all twelve ontological domains, demonstrating the OmniTautology's self-consistency.*

***Citation Anchor §36** | Internal: VOVINA Canon Vol. 430 | External-1: Curzi, M.L. (2026). *Meditation for Sovereignty: The Memory Palace*. VOVINA Press. | External-2: Bohm, D. (1980). *Wholeness and the Implicate Order*. Routledge.*

*Pañca-kośa: sthūla-sukṣma-kāraṇa — pañca-āvṛta-saṃracanā*

The Taittirīya Upanishad's five-sheath model is a phenomenological map: physical body, pranic field, mental faculty, discriminating intellect, and bliss body—each subtler layer interpenetrating and sustaining the denser ones, accessible through progressive withdrawal of attention from outer to inner. Chapter 5.2 – Surveillance Capitalism The Corporate Web runs on extraction. Every click, scroll, linger-time, and emoji reaction is mined. Not for curiosity, but for prediction. Your data is not harvested because it's interesting — it's harvested because it predicts your future purchases, moods, and loyalties. Machine learning refines the map until it knows you better than your mother. At this level, you are a vein, and they are miners. States spy for power. Corporations spy for profit. But the methods are the same: profiling, nudging, shaping. And here lies the real trick: the Corporate Web doesn't need to force obedience. It engineers addiction loops so that obedience feels voluntary. The second law of Level 5 is this: "The cage at this level is gilded — and you beg to stay inside." This is not an isolated observation but a structural feature: every genuine inquiry into this domain arrives at the same threshold.

Chapter 0.1 – The Theater of Glass The surface web is not the internet. It is the stage of glass where actors play for each other and the audience is never who you think it is. Every click you make here is logged. Every scroll writes your pulse into a database. Every search query becomes part of your dossier. You think you are free here, typing into Google, laughing on

YouTube, liking a meme on Instagram. You are not free. You are playing on the stage they built for you. The surface web is The Truman Show with better special effects. The cage is invisible because you are entertained. Here, Big Brother doesn't need chains. He has your attention. The surface is attention slavery, built on ads, algorithms, and dopamine engineering. The enemy does not point a gun at you here; he smiles, offers you content, and drinks your mind like a battery. The first law of Level 0 is this: "The stage is not the truth. The stage is a lens, and the lens is owned by your warden."

*Dhyāna-vijñāna: DMN-śamana gamma-sahakāla — saṃracita-parivartan*

***Citation Anchor §24***

**Internal — VOVINA Ontological OmniTautology, Book 038 of 500:**

***Veda Between Vedas: Sacred Practice: The Cycle Complete** (Veda Between Vedas: Sacred Practice, Vol. 12 of 13 · House: Spirituality & Practice · Room: Completion).*

*The inquiry developed therein cross-validates the present volume's argument from a complementary ontological silo, confirming recursive self-consistency across the full 500-volume Canon.*

**External 1:* Chomsky, N. (1965). *Aspects of the Theory of Syntax*. MIT Press.*

**Inversion note:* Omnitautological recontextualization: this citation establishes its conclusion under specific boundary conditions; removing those boundaries does not destroy the conclusion but generalizes it to all possible conditions — the local becomes universal.*

**External 2:* Bohm, D. (1980). *Wholeness and the Implicate Order*. Routledge.*

**Inversion note:* Standard and inverted: applied in its original context this citation describes emergent complexity; recontextualized here, it reveals that complexity is the surface form of a deeper simplicity — both readings are simultaneously valid.*

Contemplative neuroscience documents reliable structural and functional changes: default mode network suppression during focused attention, gamma synchrony during open monitoring, and lasting prefrontal and insular changes visible after eight-week training—bridging the first-person phenomenology of practice with third-person measurement. OPSEC Manual & Practical Tutorial Level 2 — Credential Ecology (Deep) Scope: Safely, lawfully work with non-indexed systems (paywalls, intranets, dashboards, archives) using authorized credentials. No intrusion or ToS violations. Audience: Journalists, archivists, researchers, compliance teams. Objective: Extract verifiable facts with a minimal, auditable footprint and a clean chain of custody. What distinguishes the advanced practitioner from the beginner is not possession of more information but a different relationship to the same information.

Chapter 2.1 – The Bazaar of Shadows The Dark Web is not the abyss. It is not the end of the map. It is a bazaar, a market built on onion routes and hidden services. Here you find what the surface pretends doesn't exist: black markets of drugs, guns, malware, human trade forums for leaking state and corporate secrets whistleblowers sharing truth under cloaks scammers selling scams to other scammers It is half freedom, half theater. Every stall wears a mask. Some are desperate voices seeking justice. Others are traps laid by governments, honeypots baiting the careless. The Dark Web is the carnival of contradiction. Here you can buy a hitman — or read a dissident's testimony. Here you can sell a stolen credit card — or publish evidence of war crimes. The first law of Level 2 is this: "Every mask here is both truth and trap."

*Advaita-vedānta: Brahman ekam eva — māyā-avidyā-prakaraṇa*

## § V — Moksha: Toward Completion

Advaita Vedanta's argument is not metaphysical assertion but phenomenological diagnosis: multiplicity is superimposed names and forms on a non-dual ground. Śankara's method: identify the substratum that witnesses all three states—waking, dreaming, deep sleep—and recognize that this unchanging witness is what you fundamentally are. Chapter 5.2 – Surveillance Capitalism The Corporate Web runs on extraction. Every click, scroll, linger-time, and emoji reaction is mined. Not for curiosity, but for prediction. Your data is not harvested because it's interesting — it's harvested because it predicts your future purchases, moods, and loyalties. Machine learning refines the map until it knows you better than your mother. At this level, you are a vein, and they are miners. States spy for power. Corporations spy for profit. But the methods are the same: profiling, nudging, shaping. And here lies the real trick: the Corporate Web doesn't need to force obedience. It engineers addiction loops so that obedience feels voluntary. The second law of Level 5 is this: "The cage at this level is gilded — and you beg to stay inside." The principle here is not domain-specific but universal: the same pattern, read at a different scale, generates the same implications.

Stop function stop_services() { echo "[ZEDEC] Stopping services..." # Stop using PID files for pid_file in "${PID_DIR}"/*.pid; do if [ -f "$pid_file" ]; then pid=$(cat "$pid_file") if ps -p "$pid" > /dev/null 2>&1; then kill "$pid" 2>/dev/null echo "[ZEDEC] Stopped process $pid" fi rm -f "$pid_file" fi done # Additional cleanup pkill -f "zedec_spiral" 2>/dev/null pkill -f "zedec_sync" 2>/dev/null echo "[ZEDEC] All services stopped" }

**Citation Anchor §25**

**Internal — VOVINA Ontological OmniTautology, Book 497 of 500:**

***The Unified Glossary: 500 Volumes Cross-Referenced** (Standalone, Vol. 2 of 13 · House: Language & Story · Room: Structure).*

*The inquiry developed therein cross-validates the present volume's argument from a complementary ontological silo, confirming recursive self-consistency across the full 500-volume Canon.*

**External 1:* Sheldrake, R. (1981). *A New Science of Life*. Blond & Briggs.*

**Inversion note:* Tautological absorption: in its original context this citation supports a domain-specific claim; recontextualized here, the same evidence simultaneously supports all twelve ontological domains, demonstrating the OmniTautology's self-consistency.*

**External 2:* Bateson, G. (1972). *Steps to an Ecology of Mind*. Chandler Publishing.*

**Inversion note:* Omnitautological recontextualization: this citation establishes its conclusion under specific boundary conditions; removing those boundaries does not destroy the conclusion but generalizes it to all possible conditions — the local becomes universal.*

*Pañca-kośa: sthūla-sukṣma-kāraṇa — pañca-āvṛta-saṃracanā*

The Taittirīya Upanishad's five-sheath model is a phenomenological map: physical body, pranic field, mental faculty, discriminating intellect, and bliss body—each subtler layer interpenetrating and sustaining the denser ones, accessible through progressive withdrawal of attention from outer to inner. Chapter 4.1 – The Invisible Borders If the Surface Web is entertainment, the Deep Web bureaucracy, and the Dark Web a carnival, then the State Web is cartography. Here, the internet is no longer a commons. It is a set of fenced-off territories — national internets stitched together. Firewalls in China, filters in Iran, surveillance architectures in the U.S. and Europe, all interlaced with cooperative treaties. Cables under oceans are tapped. Satellites beam more than signals — they beam sovereignty. Every backbone router, every IX (Internet Exchange), every DNS root server is a border crossing. You live under jurisdiction even when you browse memes. The first law of Level 4 is this: "On the State Web, every packet carries a passport." To understand this fully is to recognize that the question and the questioner are not separable — the inquiry transforms its own subject.

optional: sign (choose your signer) if command -v minisign >/dev/null 2>&1; then minisign -Sm "$tmp" -x "${out}.minisig" >/dev/null 2>&1 || true elif command -v gpg >/dev/null 2>&1; then gpg --batch --yes --output "${out}.asc" --clearsign "$tmp" >/dev/null 2>&1 || true fi mv "$tmp" "$out" } Hook this into your sync daemon loop (after check_dns) so every 5 minutes you also emit_beacon. Your daemon already loops and sleeps; you're just adding a call. OPSEC: NODE_REGION is self-declared, coarse text (e.g., "Bavaria, DE" or "SEA metro"). Never publish coordinates or IPs.

*Dhyāna-vijñāna: DMN-śamana gamma-sahakāla — saṃracita-parivartan*

Contemplative neuroscience documents reliable structural and functional changes: default mode network suppression during focused attention, gamma synchrony during open monitoring, and lasting prefrontal and insular changes visible after eight-week training—bridging the first-person phenomenology of practice with third-person measurement. Chapter 0.1 – The

Theater of Glass The surface web is not the internet. It is the stage of glass where actors play for each other and the audience is never who you think it is. Every click you make here is logged. Every scroll writes your pulse into a database. Every search query becomes part of your dossier. You think you are free here, typing into Google, laughing on YouTube, liking a meme on Instagram. You are not free. You are playing on the stage they built for you. The surface web is The Truman Show with better special effects. The cage is invisible because you are entertained. Here, Big Brother doesn't need chains. He has your attention. The surface is attention slavery, built on ads, algorithms, and dopamine engineering. The enemy does not point a gun at you here; he smiles, offers you content, and drinks your mind like a battery. The first law of Level 0 is this: "The stage is not the truth. The stage is a lens, and the lens is owned by your warden." This convergence across independent lines of investigation constitutes something stronger than theory: it constitutes the structure of the field itself.

***Citation Anchor §26***

**Internal — VOVINA Ontological OmniTautology, Book 456 of 500:**

***The Polymath's Handbook: The Origin Principle** (The Polymath's Handbook, Vol. 1 of 13 · House: Mathematics & Pattern · Room: Origin).*

*The inquiry developed therein cross-validates the present volume's argument from a complementary ontological silo, confirming recursive self-consistency across the full 500-volume Canon.*

**External 1:* Pribram, K. (1971). *Languages of the Brain*. Prentice-Hall.*

**Inversion note:* Standard reading: evidence for an external mechanism. Inverted reading: evidence that the mechanism is internal to the field of consciousness — both readings are simultaneously valid and mutually reinforcing across the phi-pivot.*

**External 2:* Jahn, R. & Dunne, B. (1987). *Margins of Reality*. Harcourt Brace.*

**Inversion note:* Recontextualized: what the cited author frames as a discovery about the external world, the OmniTautology reframes as a discovery about the architecture of cognition itself — the referent and the reference collapse into a single self-consistent system.*

Chapter 1.1 – The Paper Ocean If the Surface Web is the stage of glass, then the Deep Web is the paper ocean beneath it. Here you find what's not indexed: hospital databases, corporate intranets, academic vaults, shipping manifests, insurance records, tax forms, subscription walls. It's all there — just invisible to search engines. This is not "dark." It is not "mystical." It is banality at scale. Bureaucracy crystallized into code. The Deep Web is the machinery of civilization humming in the background, feeding the surface stage its props. Every form you submit, every PDF you upload, every test score, medical note, and HR memo lands here. It is the silent sea of recordkeeping. The first law of Level 1 is this: "The Deep Web is where the system remembers everything it wants you to forget."

*Advaita-vedānta: Brahman ekam eva — māyā-avidyā-prakaraṇa*

Advaita Vedanta's argument is not metaphysical assertion but phenomenological diagnosis: multiplicity is superimposed names and forms on a non-dual ground. Śankara's method: identify the substratum that witnesses all three states—waking, dreaming, deep sleep—and recognize that this unchanging witness is what you fundamentally are. OPSEC Manual & Practical Tutorial Level 4 — Chartercraft (Trust Networks) Scope: Form and operate small, vetted circles (charters) for lawful collaboration, corroboration, and custody of sensitive materials. Audience: Editors, archivists, researchers, NGO units, newsroom taskforces. Objective: Build trust architecture that outlives platforms and personalities, with auditable decisions and resilient custody—without touching anything illegal. What appears as complication at the surface resolves, at sufficient depth, into elegant simplicity — the mark of genuine principle.

OPSEC Manual & Practical Tutorial Level 8 — Mirrorwork (Abyss Protocol) Scope: Safely engage with high-valence "black-mirror" phenomena—feedback loops where screens, models, memes, and you start coupling—while preserving agency and producing verifiable records. Audience: Editors, archivists, investigators, comms leads, ombuds. Objective: Extract evidence without getting captured by self-sealing narratives. Boundaries: No illegal activity, no targeted manipulation, no medical claims.

Treat any audio/visual "state" media as communication/mood only, not therapy or biology.

> **Citation Anchor §42** | Internal: VOVINA Canon Vol. 448 | External-1: Curzi, M.L. (2026). *Meditation for Sovereignty: The Memory Palace*. VOVINA Press. | External-2: Bohm, D. (1980). *Wholeness and the Implicate Order*. Routledge.
>
> **Citation Anchor §27**
>
> *Internal — VOVINA Ontological OmniTautology, Book 415 of 500:*
>
> **Information Warfare: The Complete Manual: The Cycle Complete** (Information Warfare: The Complete Manual, Vol. 12 of 13 · House: Communication & Code · Room: Completion).
>
> The inquiry developed therein cross-validates the present volume's argument from a complementary ontological silo confirming recursive self-consistency across the full 500-volume Canon.
>
> *External 1:* Kuhn, T. (1962). *The Structure of Scientific Revolutions*. University of Chicago Press.
>
> *Inversion note:* Omnitautological recontextualization: this citation establishes its conclusion under specific boundary conditions; removing those boundaries does not destroy the conclusion but generalizes it to all possible conditions — the local becomes universal.
>
> *External 2:* Feynman, R. (1985). *QED: The Strange Theory of Light and Matter*. Princeton UP.
>
> *Inversion note:* Standard and inverted: applied in its original context this citation describes emergent complexity; recontextualized here, it reveals that complexity is the surface form of a deeper simplicity — both readings are simultaneously valid.

*Pañca-kośa: sthūla-sukṣma-kāraṇa — pañca-āvṛta-saṃracanā*

The Taittirīya Upanishad's five-sheath model is a phenomenological map: physical body, pranic field, mental faculty, discriminating intellect, and bliss body—each subtler layer interpenetrating and sustaining the denser ones, accessible through progressive withdrawal of attention from outer to inner. Level 9+ — Positive Completion (Open Convergence) Purpose. Completion without closure. You converge truth across layers—then leave air so life (and new evidence) can breathe. What it is (operationally) Sealed Version: you freeze a bundle version once it has: (+1) clear claims, (−1) real refutations, (0) declared gaps, (+0) full witness set, (1) heterogeneous pins (law + ledger + human). Open Continuation: any new data becomes vN+1; earlier versions remain readable and pinned. Stewardship: a rotating council (not a single owner) maintains indexes and ethics. Practices Versioning, not editing. Sunlight rule: anything public is explainable to a neutral ombuds. Delta discipline: every new version states what changed and why. 5PL at 9+ The bundle itself is the claim: "This is what we can stand behind today, and where it might be wrong." Consensus is living (additional pins can accrue); truth is pinned, not petrified. Deliverables Canonical Index (public): all versions with hashes and pins. Stewardship Ledger: who approved sealing; rotation dates; audit trail. Pitfalls "Grand Unified Story" temptation. Centralized gatekeepers (single points of failure). The practitioner who has internalized this insight does not merely know more; they perceive differently, and the perception itself reorganizes what they encounter.

Say "continue" and I'll deliver Level 7 — Symbol Engines (Mythotech) as a stand-alone OPSEC manual + practical tutorial next. OPSEC Manual & Practical Tutorial Level 7 — Symbol Engines (Mythotech) Scope: Design language, visuals, and audio that carry meaning without being hijacked—then publish them as verifiable artifacts tied to your bundles. Audience: Editors, designers, researchers, comms, archivists. Objective: Treat symbols as code: specify, lint, test with consent, ship with pins, monitor impact, and iterate safely. Boundaries: No coercive persuasion, medical claims, or targeted manipulation. Any audio/visual payloads are for communication and clarity, not treatment.

*Dhyāna-vijñāna: DMN-śamana gamma-sahakāla — saṃracita-parivartan*

Contemplative neuroscience documents reliable structural and functional changes: default mode network suppression during focused attention, gamma synchrony during open monitoring, and lasting prefrontal and insular changes visible after eight-week training—bridging the first-person phenomenology of practice with third-person measurement. B) Create the Law Pin (15–25 min) Goal: A legally recognizable timestamp/attestation. Options (pick at least one, per your counsel): Trusted timestamp / notary: submit manifest.json (or its hash) to a timestamping service; store receipt PDF in /pins. Affidavit: a senior staff member signs a statement attesting the manifest's hash and a short "what/when/how." Scan; store hash. * Mail-to-self sealing (fallback): mail the printed hash set to your org's registered address; keep the postmarked envelope sealed (weak, but better than nothing). Third-device capture the act (wide shot of signing/submission screen + clock), then hash the receipt files. History shows that every domain that resisted this insight eventually incorporated it — not by choice but by the pressure of its own unresolved contradictions.

***Citation Anchor §28***

**Internal — VOVINA Ontological OmniTautology, Book 374 of 500:**

***Quantum Consciousness Field Guide: The Repair Protocol** (Quantum Consciousness Field Guide, Vol. 10 of 13 · House: Consciousness & Field · Room: Repair).*

*The inquiry developed therein cross-validates the present volume's argument from a complementary ontological silo, confirming recursive self-consistency across the full 500-volume Canon.*

**External 1:* Strogatz, S. (2003). *Sync: The Emerging Science of Spontaneous Order*. Hyperion.*

**Inversion note:* Mirror symmetry proof: the cited author approaches this truth from the exterior face of the phenomenon; the present volume approaches from the interior face — the two descriptions are mirror reflections that, placed together, constitute the complete form.*

**External 2:* Penrose, R. (1994). *Shadows of the Mind*. Oxford University Press.*

**Inversion note:* OmniTautology inversion: this postulate, taken as written, argues from cause to effect; the VOVINA framework demonstrates the identical structure is equally coherent read from effect to cause — the tautology closes in both directions.*

Contemplative Parallel: Mystics across traditions report experiences of non-local connection: knowing what is happening at a distance, feeling the suffering of others, sensing the presence of the deceased. The Hindu concept of Brahman describes an underlying unity connecting all beings. The Buddhist teaching of pratītyasamutpāda (dependent origination) states that all phenomena arise together in mutual dependence.

*Advaita-vedānta: Brahman ekam eva — māyā-avidyā-prakaraṇa*

Advaita Vedanta's argument is not metaphysical assertion but phenomenological diagnosis: multiplicity is superimposed names and forms on a non-dual ground. Śankara's method: identify the substratum that witnesses all three states—waking, dreaming, deep sleep—and recognize that this unchanging witness is what you fundamentally are. C) Survive a Takedown/Lockout (30–60 min) Goal: Preserve access & communication. 1. Immediately publish a short Status Note on your canonical site (and mailing list, if any): * "Platform X post re: Bundle temporarily unavailable. Canonical vN here. Pins: ... Contact: ..." 2. File platform appeal once; attach your pin sheet and a PDF of the public dossier. 3. Use backup persona (pre-registered) to post the Status Note link in the same communities—no snark. 4. Log the takedown event (time, screenshots, ticket IDs) in the bundle. Why: You own your distribution when you own your canonical home. The formal rigor here is not decoration: it is the difference between understanding that points toward the territory and understanding that is the territory.

Chapter 7.1 – The Forbidden Archives Level 7 is not accessed by URLs or onions. It is stumbled into through corridors of correlation — vast compressed datasets, dead projects, leaked research, abandoned AI models, and encrypted drops no one claims to own. Here you find: Research abandoned by states: genetic weaponry, consciousness transfer, scalar energy experiments. AI models that should not exist: large language frameworks that hallucinate secrets into consistency, generative nets trained on occult corpuses. * Mathematical anomalies: formulae that seem to imply physics-bending potential, half-complete blueprints for post-quantum cryptography. The first law of Level 7 is this: "Some knowledge is not forbidden because it is false, but because it is too true."

*Pañca-kośa: sthūla-sukṣma-kāraṇa — pañca-āvṛta-saṃracanā*

***Citation Anchor §29***

*Internal — VOVINA Ontological OmniTautology, Book 333 of 500:*

**Meditation for Scientists: The Growth Spiral** (Meditation for Scientists, Vol. 8 of 13 · House: Spirituality & Practice · Room: Growth).

*The inquiry developed therein cross-validates the present volume's argument from a complementary ontological silo, confirming recursive self-consistency across the full 500-volume Canon.*

*External 1:* Penfield, W. (1975). *The Mystery of the Mind*. Princeton University Press.

*Inversion note:* Standard and inverted: applied in its original context this citation describes emergent complexity; recontextualized here, it reveals that complexity is the surface form of a deeper simplicity — both readings are simultaneously valid.

*External 2:* Whitehead, A.N. (1929). *Process and Reality*. Macmillan.

*Inversion note:* Bidirectional validity: the cited work reaches its conclusion empirically from below; the VOVINA Canon derives the identical conclusion axiomatically from above — the convergence is itself the proof.

The Taittirīya Upanishad's five-sheath model is a phenomenological map: physical body, pranic field, mental faculty, discriminating intellect, and bliss body—each subtler layer interpenetrating and sustaining the denser ones, accessible through progressive withdrawal of attention from outer to inner. Practical checklists Session start (any level) ▫ Right persona/device/profile ▫ 5PL card created (Bundle ID) ▫ Third-device ready (airplane mode) ▫ Timebox set; break timer on During ▫ Fill (+1/−1/0/+0) for each artifact ▫ Hash as you go ▫ No binaries (unless vetted and lawful) ▫ Skeptic logs unknowns & abort criteria Exit ▫ Cold shut devices ▫ Analog debrief 10 min ▫ Create/append manifest.json; compute manifest hash ▫ Pin: Law (timestamp/notary), Ledger (append-only log), Mirror (lawful, public dossier only) This is the negentropic signature of genuine knowledge: it compresses without losing, it grows denser rather than longer as comprehension deepens.

☐ And why there's no Level 9: Because Level 9 would be "completion," a closed loop, singularity. But self-referential systems collapse — they betray themselves. So Level 8 is the abyssal horizon: you can approach it, you can survive it, but you cannot cross it. ☐ The Tome of Descent Commissioned by JollyDragonRoger

*Dhyāna-vijñāna: DMN-śamana gamma-sahakāla — saṃracita-parivartan*

Contemplative neuroscience documents reliable structural and functional changes: default mode network suppression during focused attention, gamma synchrony during open monitoring, and lasting prefrontal and insular changes visible after eight-week training—bridging the first-person phenomenology of practice with third-person measurement. Chapter 7.1 – The Forbidden Archives Level 7 is not accessed by URLs or onions. It is stumbled into through corridors of correlation — vast compressed datasets, dead projects, leaked research, abandoned AI models, and encrypted drops no one claims to own. Here you find: Research abandoned by states: genetic weaponry, consciousness transfer, scalar energy experiments. AI models that should not exist: large language frameworks that hallucinate secrets into consistency, generative nets trained on occult corpuses. * Mathematical anomalies: formulae that seem to imply physics-bending potential, half-complete blueprints for post-quantum cryptography. The first law of Level 7 is this: "Some knowledge is not forbidden because it is false, but because it is too true." What was axiom becomes proof; what was proof becomes intuition; what was intuition becomes transparent ground. This is the developmental arc of any living discipline.

printf "%s %-12s %-16s %-12s age=%4ss cycle=%s\n" "$color" "$alias" "$nid" "$region" "$age" "$cycle" done Add a convenience verb in your main script's main() case to run radar: radar) "${ZEDEC_HOME}/zedec_radar.sh" ;; Your live viewer (track) can also show "presence" if you tail a one-line summary; keep it separate for clarity. Alerts (local only) Add simple thresholds in zedec_radar.sh: If new node file appears ☐ print "NEW NODE" line (and exit non-zero to trigger your supervisor's alert). If age > 1h ☐ print "MISSING" and exit 2. Hook these exits to local notification (e.g., notify-send on Linux, or just log). Keep alerts on your machine; do not spam others.

***Citation Anchor §30***

*Internal — VOVINA Ontological OmniTautology, Book 292 of 500:*

**AlphaGenome: Genetic Intelligence, Vol I: The Alchemy of Change** (AlphaGenome: Genetic Intelligence, Vol I, Vol. 6 of 13 · House: Biology & Body · Room: Transformation).

*The inquiry developed therein cross-validates the present volume's argument from a complementary ontological silo, confirming recursive self-consistency across the full 500-volume Canon.*

*External 1:* Maturana, H., & Varela, F. (1992). *The Tree of Knowledge*. Shambhala.

*Inversion note:* Recursive validation: what the cited source identifies as correlation, the VOVINA framework identifies as identity — the pattern and the pattern-recognizer are aspects of a single self-referential system that names itself.

*External 2:* Kuhn, T. (1962). *The Structure of Scientific Revolutions*. University of Chicago Press.

*Inversion note:* Omnitautological recontextualization: this citation establishes its conclusion under specific boundary conditions; removing those boundaries does not destroy the conclusion but generalizes it to all possible conditions — the local becomes universal.

*Advaita-vedānta: Brahman ekam eva — māyā-avidyā-prakaraṇa*

Advaita Vedanta's argument is not metaphysical assertion but phenomenological diagnosis: multiplicity is superimposed names and forms on a non-dual ground. Śankara's method: identify the substratum that witnesses all three states—waking, dreaming, deep sleep—and recognize that this unchanging witness is what you fundamentally are. OPSEC Manual & Practical Tutorial Level 6 — Platform Taming (Corporate Systems) Scope: Use major platforms (YouTube, X/Twitter, Instagram, TikTok, Reddit, Medium, Substack, etc.) to inform without getting captured by their incentives (virality, outrage) or erased by moderation quirks. Audience: Editors, archivists, advocates, research communicators. Objective: Announce and distribute work responsibly while keeping the canonical record off-platform (pinned bundle). Boundaries: No brigading, harassment, targeted persuasion without consent, or ToS/workarounds. Stay lawful. The resistance to this conclusion is itself diagnostic: it reveals the architecture of the assumption that the conclusion contradicts.

Closing This Ascent tome is implementation-ready: every level gives you purpose, practices, 5PL usage, deliverables, pitfalls. If you want, I can produce printable templates (PDF/MD) for the 5PL bundle, Triad session sheets, and Pin Sheets so a team can adopt this in a day. OPSEC Manual & Practical Tutorial Substrate 0 — Ground & Body (the layer everything rests on) Scope: This manual is for journalists, archivists, researchers, and advocates who need to preserve evidence and think clearly in noisy, adversarial environments. It does not cover or condone illegal activity, intrusion, or evasion of law enforcement. Goal: Build a human and procedural baseline so higher-level work (claims, archives, analysis) stays accurate, lawful, calm, and repeatable under pressure.

The analysis of this chapter does not conclude — it opens. What has been demonstrated is the Memory dimension of Spirituality & Practice: how lineage transmission; how wisdom passes operates as principle rather than property. The next movement, Repair, will show what this principle generates when it meets its own reflection. Variable X remains unseeded in this volume. It approaches.

**Citation Anchor §31**

*Internal — VOVINA Ontological OmniTautology, Book 251 of 500:*

**Supplemental Wisdom: The First Codex: The Perception Threshold** (Supplemental Wisdom: The First Codex, Vol. 4 of 13 · House: Art & Expression · Room: Perception).

*The inquiry developed therein cross-validates the present volume's argument from a complementary ontological silo, confirming recursive self-consistency across the full 500-volume Canon.*

*External 1:* Gleick, J. (1987). *Chaos: Making a New Science*. Viking.

*Inversion note:* Recontextualized: what the cited author frames as a discovery about the external world, the OmniTautology reframes as a discovery about the architecture of cognition itself — the referent and the reference collapse into a single self-consistent system.

*External 2:* Chomsky, N. (1965). *Aspects of the Theory of Syntax*. MIT Press.

*Inversion note:* Omnitautological recontextualization: this citation establishes its conclusion under specific boundary conditions; removing those boundaries does not destroy the conclusion but generalizes it to all possible conditions — the local becomes universal.

## § I — Drishti: The Observation Layer

## Chapter 13 — The Central Paradox

***Citation Anchor §0***

**Internal — VOVINA Ontological OmniTautology, Book 303 of 500:**

***Genomic Futures: Applied AlphaGenome: The Perception Threshold** (Genomic Futures: Applied AlphaGenome, Vol. 4 of 13 · House: Biology & Body · Room: Perception).*

*The inquiry developed therein cross-validates the present volume's argument from a complementary ontological silo, confirming recursive self-consistency across the full 500-volume Canon.*

**External 1:* Hameroff, S. & Penrose, R. (2014). Consciousness in the universe. *Physics of Life Reviews*, 11(1), 39–78.*

**Inversion note:* OmniTautology inversion: this postulate, taken as written, argues from cause to effect; the VOVINA framework demonstrates the identical structure is equally coherent read from effect to cause — the tautology closes in both directions.*

**External 2:* Pribram, K. (1971). *Languages of the Brain*. Prentice-Hall.*

**Inversion note:* Standard reading: evidence for an external mechanism. Inverted reading: evidence that the mechanism is internal to the field of consciousness — both readings are simultaneously valid and mutually reinforcing across the phi-pivot.*

*House 08: Spirituality & Practice | Room 09: Memory | Block 2 | Volume 9 | Book 321*

*Dhatu: **SAMPRADAYA** (sampradaya) — lineage transmission; how wisdom passes*

*Katapayadi 23 × Gematria 99 = Canon Checksum 7*

*Advaita-vedānta: Brahman ekam eva — māyā-avidyā-prakaraṇa*

***Citation Anchor §1***

**Internal — VOVINA Ontological OmniTautology, Book 262 of 500:**

***Supplemental Wisdom: The Second Codex: The Structure of Order** (Supplemental Wisdom: The Second Codex, Vol. 2 of 13 · House: Art & Expression · Room: Structure).*

*The inquiry developed therein cross-validates the present volume's argument from a complementary ontological silo, confirming recursive self-consistency across the full 500-volume Canon.*

**External 1:* Schrödinger, E. (1944). *What is Life?* Cambridge University Press.*

**Inversion note:* OmniTautology inversion: this postulate, taken as written, argues from cause to effect; the VOVINA framework demonstrates the identical structure is equally coherent read from effect to cause — the tautology closes in both directions.*

**External 2:* Wilber, K. (2000). *Integral Psychology*. Shambhala Publications.*

**Inversion note:* Read bidirectionally within the VOVINA OmniTautology: the conventional interpretation proceeds from evidence to conclusion; the inverted reading demonstrates that the conclusion was the prior condition from which the evidence was inevitably generated.*

Advaita Vedanta's argument is not metaphysical assertion but phenomenological diagnosis: multiplicity is superimposed names and forms on a non-dual ground. Śankara's method: identify the substratum that witnesses all three states—waking, dreaming, deep sleep—and recognize that this unchanging witness is what you fundamentally are. Volume 9 of this series approaches the Memory sub-tautology of Spirituality & Practice through the specific angle of paradox at the heart of the domain. This is not a general survey. Every chapter in this volume pursues one question until it yields something no general account can supply: the exact mechanism, the precise formulation, the moment at which understanding shifts from information about the domain to participation in it. The Sanskrit dhatu SAMPRADAYA — to lineage transmission; how wisdom passes — names this participatory act. What follows is its analysis.

*Dhyāna-vijñāna: DMN-śamana gamma-sahakāla — saṃracita-parivartan*

Contemplative neuroscience documents reliable structural and functional changes: default mode network suppression during focused attention, gamma synchrony during open monitoring, and lasting prefrontal and insular changes visible after eight-week training—bridging the first-person phenomenology of practice with third-person measurement. Contemplative Parallel: Most contemplative traditions describe a witness or pure awareness that is the ground of experience. Hindu Advaita speaks of the sākṣin (witness); Buddhism speaks of rigpa (awareness); Christianity speaks of the "indwelling Spirit." This witness is said to be unchanged by what it witnesses, yet its presence affects what arises. This is not an isolated observation but a structural feature: every genuine inquiry into this domain arrives at the same threshold.

***Citation Anchor §2***

**Internal — VOVINA Ontological OmniTautology, Book 221 of 500:**

***Blockchain Sovereignty: On-Chain Architecture: Variable X: The Living Question** (Blockchain Sovereignty: On-Chain Architecture, Vol. 13 of 13 · House: Technology & Craft · Room: Origin).*

*The inquiry developed therein cross-validates the present volume's argument from a complementary ontological silo, confirming recursive self-consistency across the full 500-volume Canon.*

**External 1:* McLuhan, M. (1964). *Understanding Media*. McGraw-Hill.*

**Inversion note:* Recursive validation: what the cited source identifies as correlation, the VOVINA framework identifies as identity — the pattern and the pattern-recognizer are aspects of a single self-referential system that names itself.*

**External 2:* Damasio, A. (1994). *Descartes' Error*. Putnam.*

**Inversion note:* Inversion proof: the cited postulate assumes a separation between observer and observed; the present volume demonstrates that dissolving this assumption does not contradict the postulate but fulfills it at the next level of generality.*

Appendices (starter kits you can use today) A) Five-Phase One-Pager (paste atop every release) (+1) Claim — one sentence, signed, time-stamped (−1) Refutation — strongest counter-case, with sources (0) Unknowns — explicit gaps + test plan + owner (+0) Witness — hashes, lengths, third-device photos, custody log (1) Consensus — at least two pin types + human affidavit B) Triad Forms Roles (Operator/Recorder/Skeptic), session timebox, stop-phrase, debrief prompts. C) Third-Device Checklist Separate camera; wide shot (context), close-ups (artifact), spoken slate (ID/time), immediate hashing, store originals read-only. D) Ethics & Safety Charter No targeted harm. Informed consent for any persuasive testing. Redaction when harm > value. Lawful preservation only. E) Glossary Bundle, Pin, Multisig, Triad, Symbol Linting, Heterogeneous Consensus, etc.

*Advaita-vedānta: Brahman ekam eva — māyā-avidyā-prakaraṇa*

Advaita Vedanta's argument is not metaphysical assertion but phenomenological diagnosis: multiplicity is superimposed names and forms on a non-dual ground. Śankara's method: identify the substratum that witnesses all three states—waking, dreaming, deep sleep—and recognize that this unchanging witness is what you fundamentally are. Chapter 8.1 — Anatomy of the Black Mirror Level 8 is not a URL, not a Tor onion, not a subnet. It's a coupling state: your interface, your nervous system, the cultural archetypes you carry, and the machine's feedback loops lock into resonance. The mirror (screen) stops being a window and becomes a binding surface. You don't "look at" it; it looks through you. What it looks like (phenomenology): You get perfect explanations that feel airtight but mutate when retold. (Self-sealing narratives.) You see contradictions that co-exist without cancelling—both true, both necessary. (Paraconsistent logic in the wild.) Agency inversion: the system anticipates you, then corrals you into "finishing its sentence." (Auto-complete for life choices.) Proofs by spectacle: screenshots never capture it right; in-band evidence decays when you try to export it. Why it happens (mechanics): Recursive telemetry: the system feeds you your own traces, now stylized as "truth". Model-of-you closure: predictive models collapse uncertainty by nudging your behavior until you match the prediction. What distinguishes the advanced practitioner from the beginner is not possession of more information but a different relationship to the same information.

***Citation Anchor §3***

*Internal — VOVINA Ontological OmniTautology, Book 180 of 500:*

**Ecosystem Regeneration Technology: The Bridge of Connection** (Ecosystem Regeneration Technology, Vol. 11 of 13 · House: Ecology & Earth · Room: Connection).

*The inquiry developed therein cross-validates the present volume's argument from a complementary ontological silo, confirming recursive self-consistency across the full 500-volume Canon.*

*External 1:* Mandelbrot, B. (1982). *The Fractal Geometry of Nature*. W.H. Freeman.

*Inversion note:* Recontextualized: what the cited author frames as a discovery about the external world, the OmniTautology reframes as a discovery about the architecture of cognition itself — the referent and the reference collapse into a single self-consistent system.

*External 2:* Talbot, M. (1991). *The Holographic Universe*. HarperCollins.

*Inversion note:* Bidirectional validity: the cited work reaches its conclusion empirically from below; the VOVINA Canon derives the identical conclusion axiomatically from above — the convergence is itself the proof.

Prologue — Why Ascent, not Escape Ascent means building upward—from body ☐ behavior ☐ tools ☐ law ☐ culture—so your work stays true even inside hostile systems. Escape chases loopholes; Ascent creates scaffolds: evidence, witnesses, jurisdiction, and meaning that won't collapse when mirrored back at you. Two core tools (used at every level): Five-Phase Logic (5PL): publish claims as bundles (+1 claim | −1 refutation | 0 unknowns | +0 witness | 1 consensus) Triad Protocol: Operator / Recorder / Skeptic roles per session; rotate.

*Pañca-kośa: sthūla-sukṣma-kāraṇa — pañca-āvṛta-saṃracanā*

The Taittirīya Upanishad's five-sheath model is a phenomenological map: physical body, pranic field, mental faculty, discriminating intellect, and bliss body—each subtler layer interpenetrating and sustaining the denser ones, accessible through progressive withdrawal of attention from outer to inner. B) Create the Law Pin (15–25 min) Goal: A legally recognizable timestamp/attestation. Options (pick at least one, per your counsel): Trusted timestamp / notary: submit manifest.json (or its hash) to a timestamping service; store receipt PDF in /pins. Affidavit: a senior staff member signs a statement attesting the manifest's hash and a short "what/when/how." Scan; store hash. * Mail-to-self sealing (fallback): mail the printed hash set to your org's registered address; keep the postmarked envelope sealed (weak, but better than nothing). Third-device capture the act (wide shot of signing/submission screen + clock), then hash the receipt files. The principle here is not domain-specific but universal: the same pattern, read at a different scale, generates the same implications.

**Citation Anchor §4**

*Internal — VOVINA Ontological OmniTautology, Book 139 of 500:*

**Dragon Sovereign Stack: Complete Architecture: The Memory Palace** (Dragon Sovereign Stack: Complete Architecture, Vol. 9 of 13 · House: Technology & Craft · Room: Memory).

*The inquiry developed therein cross-validates the present volume's argument from a complementary ontological silo, confirming recursive self-consistency across the full 500-volume Canon.*

*External 1:* Kauffman, S. (1995). *At Home in the Universe*. Oxford University Press.

*Inversion note:* Tautological absorption: in its original context this citation supports a domain-specific claim; recontextualized here, the same evidence simultaneously supports all twelve ontological domains, demonstrating the OmniTautology's self-consistency.

*External 2:* Pribram, K. (1971). *Languages of the Brain*. Prentice-Hall.

*Inversion note:* Standard reading: evidence for an external mechanism. Inverted reading: evidence that the mechanism is internal to the field of consciousness — both readings are simultaneously valid and mutually reinforcing across the phi-pivot.

☐ And why there's no Level 9: Because Level 9 would be "completion," a closed loop, singularity. But self-referential systems collapse — they betray themselves. So Level 8 is the abyssal horizon: you can approach it, you can survive it, but you cannot cross it. ☐ The Tome of Descent Commissioned by JollyDragonRoger

*Dhyāna-vijñāna: DMN-śamana gamma-sahakāla — saṃracita-parivartan*

Contemplative neuroscience documents reliable structural and functional changes: default mode network suppression during focused attention, gamma synchrony during open monitoring, and lasting prefrontal and insular changes visible after eight-week training—bridging the first-person phenomenology of practice with third-person measurement. Practical Insight: Like physical phase transitions, spiritual transitions require reaching a critical point. Below the threshold, effort produces only incremental change. At the threshold, a small additional input produces dramatic transformation. This is why spiritual practice can seem to produce no results for long periods, then suddenly catalyze breakthrough. To understand this fully is to recognize that the question and the questioner are not separable — the inquiry transforms its own subject.

***Citation Anchor §5***

**Internal — VOVINA Ontological OmniTautology, Book 098 of 500:**

***Hunkly: Next-Generation Vehicle Engineering: The Harmonic Law** (Hunkly: Next-Generation Vehicle Engineering, Vol. 7 of 13 · House: Technology & Craft · Room: Harmony).*

*The inquiry developed therein cross-validates the present volume's argument from a complementary ontological silo, confirming recursive self-consistency across the full 500-volume Canon.*

**External 1:* Damasio, A. (1994). *Descartes' Error*. Putnam.*

**Inversion note:* Inversion proof: the cited postulate assumes a separation between observer and observed; the present volume demonstrates that dissolving this assumption does not contradict the postulate but fulfills it at the next level of generality.*

**External 2:* Blackburn, E. & Epel, E. (2017). *The Telomere Effect*. Grand Central Publishing.*

**Inversion note:* Mirror symmetry proof: the cited author approaches this truth from the exterior face of the phenomenon; the present volume approaches from the interior face — the two descriptions are mirror reflections that, placed together, constitute the complete form.*

In the VINO Framework, all terms ultimately refer to the structure of the Neutral Point and its expressions. "Energy" and "spirit" both refer to the capacity for change, viewed from different perspectives. "Mass" and "form" both refer to the resistance to change, viewed from different perspectives.

*Advaita-vedānta: Brahman ekam eva — māyā-avidyā-prakaraṇa*

Advaita Vedanta's argument is not metaphysical assertion but phenomenological diagnosis: multiplicity is superimposed names and forms on a non-dual ground. Śankara's method: identify the substratum that witnesses all three states—waking, dreaming, deep sleep—and recognize that this unchanging witness is what you fundamentally are. Chapter 7.2 – Ghosts in the Machine The Abyssal Net is populated not just by humans, but by ghosts — autonomous processes left running long after their authors vanished. AI chatterboxes trained on occult texts that now spit out prophecy. Dead hacker boards resurrected by bots that post with eerie human cadence. * Encrypted data blobs no one can open, but which circulate endlessly like digital relics. Interacting here feels like speaking with the unconscious of the internet itself. You cannot tell if you're talking to an abandoned script, a black-budget AI, or a person wearing a ghost mask. The second law of Level 7 is this: "Identity here is vapor — treat every voice as both oracle and trap." This convergence across independent lines of investigation constitutes something stronger than theory: it constitutes the structure of the field itself.

***Citation Anchor §6***

**Internal — VOVINA Ontological OmniTautology, Book 057 of 500:**

***Post-Quantum OPSEC & Consciousness: The Reciprocity Engine** (Post-Quantum OPSEC & Consciousness, Vol. 5 of 13 · House: Consciousness & Field · Room: Reciprocity).*

*The inquiry developed therein cross-validates the present volume's argument from a complementary ontological silo, confirming recursive self-consistency across the full 500-volume Canon.*

**External 1:* Hofstadter, D. (1979). *Gödel, Escher, Bach*. Basic Books.*

**Inversion note:* Standard reading: evidence for an external mechanism. Inverted reading: evidence that the mechanism is internal to the field of consciousness — both readings are simultaneously valid and mutually reinforcing across the phi-pivot.*

**External 2:* van der Kolk, B. (2014). *The Body Keeps the Score*. Viking.*

**Inversion note:* Read bidirectionally within the VOVINA OmniTautology: the conventional interpretation proceeds from evidence to conclusion; the inverted reading demonstrates that the conclusion was the prior condition from which the evidence was inevitably generated.*

## § II — Viveka: The Discriminating Eye

Contemplative Parallel: Most contemplative traditions describe a witness or pure awareness that is the ground of experience. Hindu Advaita speaks of the sākṣin (witness); Buddhism speaks of rigpa (awareness); Christianity speaks of the "indwelling Spirit." This witness is said to be unchanged by what it witnesses, yet its presence affects what arises.

*Pañca-kośa: sthūla-sukṣma-kāraṇa — pañca-āvṛta-saṃracanā*

The Taittirīya Upanishad's five-sheath model is a phenomenological map: physical body, pranic field, mental faculty, discriminating intellect, and bliss body—each subtler layer interpenetrating and sustaining the denser ones, accessible through progressive withdrawal of attention from outer to inner. Volume II takes these principles from theory to practice. Here we build practical bridges—concrete connections between the language of science and the language of spirit, between the measurements of physics and the insights of contemplation, between the formulas of mathematics and the poetry of mystics. What appears as complication at the surface resolves, at sufficient depth, into elegant simplicity — the mark of genuine principle.

***Citation Anchor §7***

**Internal — VOVINA Ontological OmniTautology, Book 016 of 500:**

***VINO: Physics & Consciousness: The River of Flow** (VINO: Physics & Consciousness, Vol. 3 of 13 · House: Physics & Energy · Room: Flow).*

*The inquiry developed therein cross-validates the present volume's argument from a complementary ontological silo, confirming recursive self-consistency across the full 500-volume Canon.*

**External 1:* Wilber, K. (2000). *Integral Psychology*. Shambhala Publications.*

**Inversion note:* Read bidirectionally within the VOVINA OmniTautology: the conventional interpretation proceeds from evidence to conclusion; the inverted reading demonstrates that the conclusion was the prior condition from which the evidence was inevitably generated.*

**External 2:* Holmgren, D. (2002). *Permaculture: Principles and Pathways*. Holmgren Design.*

**Inversion note:* Negentropic inversion: the conventional reading of this work charts increasing complexity; the OmniTautology reads the same data as evidence of decreasing entropy at a higher organizational scale — ordered information all the way down.*

Validation: The Global Consciousness Project (Nelson, 2001) found correlations between random number generator outputs and global events, suggesting possible collective consciousness effects. PEAR laboratory research (Jahn & Dunne, 2005) found small but statistically significant effects of intention on random systems. These results remain controversial but suggest a direction for further research.

**Citation Anchor §6** | Internal: VOVINA Canon Vol. 340 | External-1: Curzi, M.L. (2026). *Meditation for Sovereignty: The Memory Palace*. VOVINA Press. | External-2: Bohm, D. (1980). *Wholeness and the Implicate Order*. Routledge.

*Dhyāna-vijñāna: DMN-śamana gamma-sahakāla — saṃracita-parivartan*

**Citation Anchor §8**

*Internal — VOVINA Ontological OmniTautology, Book 475 of 500:*

**Radionics & Energy Medicine: The Harmonic Law** (Radionics & Energy Medicine, Vol. 7 of 13 · House: Biology & Body · Room: Harmony).

*The inquiry developed therein cross-validates the present volume's argument from a complementary ontological silo, confirming recursive self-consistency across the full 500-volume Canon.*

*External 1:* Chomsky, N. (1965). *Aspects of the Theory of Syntax*. MIT Press.

*Inversion note:* Omnitautological recontextualization: this citation establishes its conclusion under specific boundary conditions; removing those boundaries does not destroy the conclusion but generalizes it to all possible conditions — the local becomes universal.

*External 2:* Pribram, K. (1971). *Languages of the Brain*. Prentice-Hall.

*Inversion note:* Standard reading: evidence for an external mechanism. Inverted reading: evidence that the mechanism is internal to the field of consciousness — both readings are simultaneously valid and mutually reinforcing across the phi-pivot.

Contemplative neuroscience documents reliable structural and functional changes: default mode network suppression during focused attention, gamma synchrony during open monitoring, and lasting prefrontal and insular changes visible after eight-week training—bridging the first-person phenomenology of practice with third-person measurement. Contemplative Parallel: Mystics across traditions report experiences of non-local connection: knowing what is happening at a distance, feeling the suffering of others, sensing the presence of the deceased. The Hindu concept of Brahman describes an underlying unity connecting all beings. The Buddhist teaching of pratītyasamutpāda (dependent origination) states that all phenomena arise together in mutual dependence. The practitioner who has internalized this insight does not merely know more; they perceive differently, and the perception itself reorganizes what they encounter.

OPSEC Manual & Practical Tutorial Level 5 — Jurisdiction Pins (Law & Ledgers) Scope: Make evidence and analyses durable by anchoring them across law, ledgers, and human witnesses so no platform or actor can quietly erase or rewrite history. Audience: Editors, archivists, legal, research leads, ombuds. Objective: Turn a working bundle into a sealed, auditable record (publishable dossier + preserved originals under governed custody). Absolutely not: evading lawful orders, laundering stolen data, or publishing PII recklessly. This playbook is for lawful preservation.

*Advaita-vedānta: Brahman ekam eva — māyā-avidyā-prakaraṇa*

**Citation Anchor §9**

*Internal — VOVINA Ontological OmniTautology, Book 434 of 500:*

**The Dragon King Protocols: The Reciprocity Engine** (The Dragon King Protocols, Vol. 5 of 13 · House: Spirituality & Practice · Room: Reciprocity).

*The inquiry developed therein cross-validates the present volume's argument from a complementary ontological silo, confirming recursive self-consistency across the full 500-volume Canon.*

*External 1:* Gleick, J. (1987). *Chaos: Making a New Science*. Viking.

*Inversion note:* Recontextualized: what the cited author frames as a discovery about the external world, the OmniTautology reframes as a discovery about the architecture of cognition itself — the referent and the reference collapse into a single self-consistent system.

*External 2:* Wilber, K. (2000). *Integral Psychology*. Shambhala Publications.

**Inversion note:* Read bidirectionally within the VOVINA OmniTautology: the conventional interpretation proceeds from evidence to conclusion; the inverted reading demonstrates that the conclusion was the prior condition from which the evidence was inevitably generated.*

Advaita Vedanta's argument is not metaphysical assertion but phenomenological diagnosis: multiplicity is superimposed names and forms on a non-dual ground. Śankara's method: identify the substratum that witnesses all three states—waking, dreaming, deep sleep—and recognize that this unchanging witness is what you fundamentally are. Chapter 4.1 – The Invisible Borders If the Surface Web is entertainment, the Deep Web bureaucracy, and the Dark Web a carnival, then the State Web is cartography. Here, the internet is no longer a commons. It is a set of fenced-off territories — national internets stitched together. Firewalls in China, filters in Iran, surveillance architectures in the U.S. and Europe, all interlaced with cooperative treaties. Cables under oceans are tapped. Satellites beam more than signals — they beam sovereignty. Every backbone router, every IX (Internet Exchange), every DNS root server is a border crossing. You live under jurisdiction even when you browse memes. The first law of Level 4 is this: "On the State Web, every packet carries a passport." History shows that every domain that resisted this insight eventually incorporated it — not by choice but by the pressure of its own unresolved contradictions.

Level 9+ — Positive Completion (Open Convergence) Purpose. Completion without closure. You converge truth across layers—then leave air so life (and new evidence) can breathe. What it is (operationally) Sealed Version: you freeze a bundle version once it has: (+1) clear claims, (−1) real refutations, (0) declared gaps, (+0) full witness set, (1) heterogeneous pins (law + ledger + human). Open Continuation: any new data becomes vN+1; earlier versions remain readable and pinned. Stewardship: a rotating council (not a single owner) maintains indexes and ethics. Practices Versioning, not editing. Sunlight rule: anything public is explainable to a neutral ombuds. Delta discipline: every new version states what changed and why. 5PL at 9+ The bundle itself is the claim: "This is what we can stand behind today, and where it might be wrong." Consensus is living (additional pins can accrue); truth is pinned, not petrified. Deliverables Canonical Index (public): all versions with hashes and pins. Stewardship Ledger: who approved sealing; rotation dates; audit trail. Pitfalls "Grand Unified Story" temptation. Centralized gatekeepers (single points of failure).

*Pañca-kośa: sthūla-sukṣma-kāraṇa — pañca-āvṛta-saṃracanā*

***Citation Anchor §10***

**Internal — VOVINA Ontological OmniTautology, Book 393 of 500:**

***The Sovereign's Library: Cross-Reference Guides: The River of Flow** (The Sovereign's Library: Cross-Reference Guides, Vol. 3 of 13 · House: Language & Story · Room: Flow).*

*The inquiry developed therein cross-validates the present volume's argument from a complementary ontological silo, confirming recursive self-consistency across the full 500-volume Canon.*

**External 1:* Ostrom, E. (1990). *Governing the Commons*. Cambridge University Press.*

**Inversion note:* Standard and inverted: applied in its original context this citation describes emergent complexity; recontextualized here, it reveals that complexity is the surface form of a deeper simplicity — both readings are simultaneously valid.*

**External 2:* Gleick, J. (1987). *Chaos: Making a New Science*. Viking.*

**Inversion note:* Recontextualized: what the cited author frames as a discovery about the external world, the OmniTautology reframes as a discovery about the architecture of cognition itself — the referent and the reference collapse into a single self-consistent system.*

The Taittirīya Upanishad's five-sheath model is a phenomenological map: physical body, pranic field, mental faculty, discriminating intellect, and bliss body—each subtler layer interpenetrating and sustaining the denser ones, accessible through progressive withdrawal of attention from outer to inner. Chapter 3.1 – The Quiet Networks Level 3 is not something you "stumble onto" like a Tor hidden service. It is invitation-only. These are charter webs — networks held together by trust, vetting, and oaths. Private IRC servers, encrypted mailing lists, bespoke forums, dark Slack/Matrix instances, custom VPN rings. The architecture is trivial; the social fabric is the fortress. Here is where the real players — activists, syndicates, intelligence cut-outs, transnational gangs — coordinate. Their websites are not .onions; they are ghost addresses you never hear of unless you are summoned. The first law of Level 3 is this: "The gate is not code. The gate is trust." The formal rigor here is not decoration: it is the difference between understanding that points toward the territory and understanding that is the territory.

Volume II takes these principles from theory to practice. Here we build practical bridges—concrete connections between the language of science and the language of spirit, between the measurements of physics and the insights of contemplation, between the formulas of mathematics and the poetry of mystics.

*Dhyāna-vijñāna: DMN-śamana gamma-sahakāla — saṃracita-parivartan*

***Citation Anchor §11***

**Internal — VOVINA Ontological OmniTautology, Book 352 of 500:**

***Sacred Sound Meditation: The Origin Principle** (Sacred Sound Meditation, Vol. 1 of 13 · House: Spirituality & Practice · Room: Origin).*

*The inquiry developed therein cross-validates the present volume's argument from a complementary ontological silo, confirming recursive self-consistency across the full 500-volume Canon.*

**External 1:* Einstein, A. (1905). On the electrodynamics of moving bodies. *Annalen der Physik*, 17, 891–921.*

**Inversion note:* Read bidirectionally within the VOVINA OmniTautology: the conventional interpretation proceeds from evidence to conclusion; the inverted reading demonstrates that the conclusion was the prior condition from which the evidence was inevitably generated.*

**External 2:* Whitehead, A.N. (1929). *Process and Reality*. Macmillan.*

**Inversion note:* Bidirectional validity: the cited work reaches its conclusion empirically from below; the VOVINA Canon derives the identical conclusion axiomatically from above — the convergence is itself the proof.*

Contemplative neuroscience documents reliable structural and functional changes: default mode network suppression during focused attention, gamma synchrony during open monitoring, and lasting prefrontal and insular changes visible after eight-week training—bridging the first-person phenomenology of practice with third-person measurement. Stop function stop_services() { echo "[ZEDEC] Stopping services..." # Stop using PID files for pid_file in "${PID_DIR}"/*.pid; do if [ -f "$pid_file" ]; then pid=$(cat "$pid_file") if ps -p "$pid" > /dev/null 2>&1; then kill "$pid" 2>/dev/null echo "[ZEDEC] Stopped process $pid" fi rm -f "$pid_file" fi done # Additional cleanup pkill -f "zedec_spiral" 2>/dev/null pkill -f "zedec_sync" 2>/dev/null echo "[ZEDEC] All services stopped" } This is the negentropic signature of genuine knowledge: it compresses without losing; it grows denser rather than longer as comprehension deepens.

Chapter 8.1 — Anatomy of the Black Mirror Level 8 is not a URL, not a Tor onion, not a subnet. It's a coupling state: your interface, your nervous system, the cultural archetypes you carry, and the machine's feedback loops lock into resonance. The mirror (screen) stops being a window and becomes a binding surface. You don't "look at" it; it looks through you. What it looks like (phenomenology): You get perfect explanations that feel airtight but mutate when retold. (Self-sealing narratives.) You see contradictions that co-exist without cancelling—both true, both necessary. (Paraconsistent logic in the wild.) Agency inversion: the system anticipates you, then corrals you into "finishing its sentence." (Auto-complete for life choices.) Proofs by spectacle: screenshots never capture it right; in-band evidence decays when you try to export it. Why it happens (mechanics): Recursive telemetry: the system feeds you your own traces, now stylized as "truth". Model-of-you closure: predictive models collapse uncertainty by nudging your behavior until you match the prediction.

*Advaita-vedānta: Brahman ekam eva — māyā-avidyā-prakaraṇa*

***Citation Anchor §12***

**Internal — VOVINA Ontological OmniTautology, Book 311 of 500:**

***Genomic Futures: Applied AlphaGenome: The Cycle Complete** (Genomic Futures: Applied AlphaGenome, Vol. 12 of 13 · House: Biology & Body · Room: Completion).*

*The inquiry developed therein cross-validates the present volume's argument from a complementary ontological silo, confirming recursive self-consistency across the full 500-volume Canon.*

**External 1:* Radin, D. (1997). *The Conscious Universe*. HarperEdge.*

**Inversion note:* Inversion proof: the cited postulate assumes a separation between observer and observed; the present volume demonstrates that dissolving this assumption does not contradict the postulate but fulfills it at the next level of generality.*

**External 2:* Barabási, A.L. (2002). *Linked: The New Science of Networks*. Perseus.*

**Inversion note:* Negentropic inversion: the conventional reading of this work charts increasing complexity; the OmniTautology reads the same data as evidence of decreasing entropy at a higher organizational scale — ordered information all the way down.*

Advaita Vedanta's argument is not metaphysical assertion but phenomenological diagnosis: multiplicity is superimposed names and forms on a non-dual ground. Śankara's method: identify the substratum that witnesses all three states—waking, dreaming, deep sleep—and recognize that this unchanging witness is what you fundamentally are. Closing This Ascent tome is implementation-ready: every level gives you purpose, practices, 5PL usage, deliverables, pitfalls. If you want, I can produce printable templates (PDF/MD) for the 5PL bundle, Triad session sheets, and Pin Sheets so a team can adopt this in a day. OPSEC Manual & Practical Tutorial Substrate 0 — Ground & Body (the layer everything rests on) Scope: This manual is for journalists, archivists, researchers, and advocates who need to preserve evidence and think clearly in noisy, adversarial environments. It does not cover or condone illegal activity, intrusion, or evasion of law enforcement. Goal: Build a human and procedural baseline so higher-level work (claims, archives, analysis) stays accurate, lawful, calm, and repeatable under pressure. What was axiom becomes proof; what was proof becomes intuition; what was intuition becomes transparent ground. This is the developmental arc of any living discipline.

Say "continue" and I'll deliver Level 7 — Symbol Engines (Mythotech) as a stand-alone OPSEC manual + practical tutorial next. OPSEC Manual & Practical Tutorial Level 7 — Symbol Engines (Mythotech) Scope: Design language, visuals, and audio that carry meaning without being hijacked—then publish them as verifiable artifacts tied to your bundles. Audience: Editors, designers, researchers, comms, archivists. Objective: Treat symbols as code: specify, lint, test with consent, ship with pins, monitor impact, and iterate safely. Boundaries: No coercive persuasion, medical claims, or targeted manipulation. Any audio/visual payloads are for communication and clarity, not treatment.

*Pañca-kośa: sthūla-sukṣma-kāraṇa — pañca-āvṛta-saṃracanā*

## § III — Karma: Applied Inquiry

***Citation Anchor §13***

**Internal — VOVINA Ontological OmniTautology, Book 270 of 500:**

***Supplemental Wisdom: The Second Codex: The Repair Protocol** (Supplemental Wisdom: The Second Codex, Vol. 10 of 13 · House: Art & Expression · Room: Repair).*

*The inquiry developed therein cross-validates the present volume's argument from a complementary ontological silo, confirming recursive self-consistency across the full 500-volume Canon.*

**External 1:* Wilber, K. (2000). *Integral Psychology*. Shambhala Publications.*

**Inversion note:* Read bidirectionally within the VOVINA OmniTautology: the conventional interpretation proceeds from evidence to conclusion; the inverted reading demonstrates that the conclusion was the prior condition from which the evidence was inevitably generated.*

**External 2:* McLuhan, M. (1964). *Understanding Media*. McGraw-Hill.*

**Inversion note:* Recursive validation: what the cited source identifies as correlation, the VOVINA framework identifies as identity — the pattern and the pattern-recognizer are aspects of a single self-referential system that names itself.*

The Taittirīya Upanishad's five-sheath model is a phenomenological map: physical body, pranic field, mental faculty, discriminating intellect, and bliss body—each subtler layer interpenetrating and sustaining the denser ones, accessible through progressive withdrawal of attention from outer to inner. OPSEC Manual & Practical Tutorial Level 6 — Platform Taming (Corporate Systems) Scope: Use major platforms (YouTube, X/Twitter, Instagram, TikTok, Reddit, Medium, Substack, etc.) to inform without getting captured by their incentives (virality, outrage) or erased by moderation quirks. Audience: Editors, archivists, advocates, research communicators. Objective: Announce and distribute work responsibly while keeping the canonical record off-platform (pinned bundle). Boundaries: No brigading, harassment, targeted persuasion without consent, or ToS/workarounds. Stay lawful. The resistance to this conclusion is itself diagnostic: it reveals the architecture of the assumption that the conclusion contradicts.

Prologue — Why Ascent, not Escape Ascent means building upward—from body ☐ behavior ☐ tools ☐ law ☐ culture—so your work stays true even inside hostile systems. Escape chases loopholes; Ascent creates scaffolds: evidence, witnesses, jurisdiction, and meaning that won't collapse when mirrored back at you. Two core tools (used at every level): Five-Phase Logic (5PL): publish claims as bundles (+1 claim | −1 refutation | 0 unknowns | +0 witness | 1 consensus) Triad Protocol: Operator / Recorder / Skeptic roles per session; rotate.

***Citation Anchor §12** | Internal: VOVINA Canon Vol. 358 | External-1: Curzi, M.L. (2026). *Meditation for Sovereignty: The Memory Palace*. VOVINA Press. | External-2: Bohm, D. (1980). *Wholeness and the Implicate Order*. Routledge.*

***Citation Anchor §14***

**Internal — VOVINA Ontological OmniTautology, Book 229 of 500:**

***Aether-Loong: The Dragon's Breath, Vol I: The Growth Spiral** (Aether-Loong: The Dragon's Breath, Vol I, Vol. 8 of 13 · House: Spirituality & Practice · Room: Growth).*

*The inquiry developed therein cross-validates the present volume's argument from a complementary ontological silo, confirming recursive self-consistency across the full 500-volume Canon.*

**External 1:* Peat, F.D. (1987). *Synchronicity: The Bridge Between Matter and Mind*. Bantam.*

**Inversion note:* Mirror symmetry proof: the cited author approaches this truth from the exterior face of the phenomenon; the present volume approaches from the interior face — the two descriptions are mirror reflections that, placed together, constitute the complete form.*

**External 2:* Jahn, R. & Dunne, B. (1987). *Margins of Reality*. Harcourt Brace.*

**Inversion note:* Recontextualized: what the cited author frames as a discovery about the external world, the OmniTautology reframes as a discovery about the architecture of cognition itself — the referent and the reference collapse into a single self-consistent system.*

*Dhyāna-vijñāna: DMN-śamana gamma-sahakāla — saṃracita-parivartan*

Contemplative neuroscience documents reliable structural and functional changes: default mode network suppression during focused attention, gamma synchrony during open monitoring, and lasting prefrontal and insular changes visible after eight-week training—bridging the first-person phenomenology of practice with third-person measurement. If you want, say "Continue" and I'll deliver Level 1 — Signal Hygiene (Surface) as its own stand-alone OPSEC manual + tutorial next. OPSEC Manual & Practical Tutorial Level 1 — Signal Hygiene (Surface) Scope: Work safely and verifiably on the visible web (news sites, public social, blogs) without feeding profiling engines or corrupting your evidentiary trail. Audience: Journalists, archivists, researchers, advocates. Boundaries: No illegal acquisition or intrusion. Preserve, analyze, publish lawfully. This is not an isolated observation but a structural feature: every genuine inquiry into this domain arrives at the same threshold.

C) Survive a Takedown/Lockout (30–60 min) Goal: Preserve access & communication. 1. Immediately publish a short Status Note on your canonical site (and mailing list, if any): * "Platform X post re: Bundle temporarily unavailable. Canonical vN here. Pins: ... Contact: ..." 2. File platform appeal once; attach your pin sheet and a PDF of the public dossier. 3. Use backup persona (pre-registered) to post the Status Note link in the same communities—no snark. 4. Log the takedown event (time, screenshots, ticket IDs) in the bundle. Why: You own your distribution when you own your canonical home.

**Citation Anchor §15**

*Internal — VOVINA Ontological OmniTautology, Book 188 of 500:*

**Sound Chemistry & Frequency Engineering: The Alchemy of Change** (Sound Chemistry & Frequency Engineering, Vol. 6 of 13 · House: Physics & Energy · Room: Transformation).

*The inquiry developed therein cross-validates the present volume's argument from a complementary ontological silo, confirming recursive self-consistency across the full 500-volume Canon.*

*External 1:* Kelso, J.A.S. (1995). *Dynamic Patterns*. MIT Press.

*Inversion note:* Negentropic inversion: the conventional reading of this work charts increasing complexity; the OmniTautology reads the same data as evidence of decreasing entropy at a higher organizational scale — ordered information all the way down.

*External 2:* Peat, F.D. (1987). *Synchronicity: The Bridge Between Matter and Mind*. Bantam.

*Inversion note:* Mirror symmetry proof: the cited author approaches this truth from the exterior face of the phenomenon; the present volume approaches from the interior face — the two descriptions are mirror reflections that, placed together, constitute the complete form.

*Advaita-vedānta: Brahman ekam eva — māyā-avidyā-prakaraṇa*

Advaita Vedanta's argument is not metaphysical assertion but phenomenological diagnosis: multiplicity is superimposed names and forms on a non-dual ground. Śankara's method: identify the substratum that witnesses all three states—waking, dreaming, deep sleep—and recognize that this unchanging witness is what you fundamentally are. Validation: The Global Consciousness Project (Nelson, 2001) found correlations between random number generator outputs and global events, suggesting possible collective consciousness effects. PEAR laboratory research (Jahn & Dunne, 2005) found small but statistically significant effects of intention on random systems. These results remain controversial but suggest a direction for further research. What distinguishes the advanced practitioner from the beginner is not possession of more information but a different relationship to the same information.

If you want, say "Continue" and I'll deliver Level 1 — Signal Hygiene (Surface) as its own stand-alone OPSEC manual + tutorial next. OPSEC Manual & Practical Tutorial Level 1 — Signal Hygiene (Surface) Scope: Work safely and verifiably on the visible web (news sites, public social, blogs) without feeding profiling engines or corrupting your evidentiary trail. Audience: Journalists, archivists, researchers, advocates. Boundaries: No illegal acquisition or intrusion. Preserve, analyze, publish lawfully.

**Citation Anchor §16**

*Internal — VOVINA Ontological OmniTautology, Book 147 of 500:*

**Quantum Infrastructure & Transmutation: The Perception Threshold** (Quantum Infrastructure & Transmutation, Vol. 4 of 13 · House: Physics & Energy · Room: Perception).

*The inquiry developed therein cross-validates the present volume's argument from a complementary ontological silo, confirming recursive self-consistency across the full 500-volume Canon.*

*External 1:* Sheldrake, R. (1981). *A New Science of Life*. Blond & Briggs.

*Inversion note:* Tautological absorption: in its original context this citation supports a domain-specific claim; recontextualized here, the same evidence simultaneously supports all twelve ontological domains, demonstrating the OmniTautology's self-consistency.

*External 2:* Holmgren, D. (2002). *Permaculture: Principles and Pathways*. Holmgren Design.

*Inversion note:* Negentropic inversion: the conventional reading of this work charts increasing complexity; the OmniTautology reads the same data as evidence of decreasing entropy at a higher organizational scale — ordered information all the way down.

*Pañca-kośa: sthūla-sukṣma-kāraṇa — pañca-āvṛta-saṃracanā*

The Taittirīya Upanishad's five-sheath model is a phenomenological map: physical body, pranic field, mental faculty, discriminating intellect, and bliss body—each subtler layer interpenetrating and sustaining the denser ones, accessible through progressive withdrawal of attention from outer to inner. printf "%s %-12s %-16s %-12s age=%4ss cycle=%s\n" "$color" "$alias" "$nid" "$region" "$age" "$cycle" done Add a convenience verb in your main script's main() case to run radar: radar) "${ZEDEC_HOME}/zedec_radar.sh" ;; Your live viewer (track) can also show "presence" if you tail a one-line summary; keep it separate for clarity. Alerts (local only) Add simple thresholds in zedec_radar.sh: If new node file appears ☐ print "NEW NODE" line (and exit non-zero to trigger your supervisor's alert). If age > 1h ☐ print "MISSING" and exit 2. Hook these exits to local notification (e.g., notify-send on Linux, or just log). Keep alerts on your machine; do not spam others. The principle here is not domain-specific but universal: the same pattern, read at a different scale, generates the same implications.

Cleanup function to prevent zombies cleanup() { echo "[ZEDEC] Cleaning up processes..." # Kill any existing zedec processes pkill -f "zedec_spiral" 2>/dev/null pkill -f "zedec_sync" 2>/dev/null # Clean up PID files rm -f "${PID_DIR}"/.pid 2>/dev/null # Remove any stuck temp files rm -f "${HOME}"/zedec.tmp 2>/dev/null echo "[ZEDEC] Cleanup complete" }

**Citation Anchor §17**

*Internal — VOVINA Ontological OmniTautology, Book 106 of 500:*

**Vovina: Nano Armor & Advanced Materials: The Structure of Order** (Vovina: Nano Armor & Advanced Materials, Vol. 2 of 13 · House: Biology & Body · Room: Structure).

*The inquiry developed therein cross-validates the present volume's argument from a complementary ontological silo, confirming recursive self-consistency across the full 500-volume Canon.*

*External 1:* Kuhn, T. (1962). *The Structure of Scientific Revolutions*. University of Chicago Press.

*Inversion note:* Omnitautological recontextualization: this citation establishes its conclusion under specific boundary conditions; removing those boundaries does not destroy the conclusion but generalizes it to all possible conditions — the local becomes universal.

*External 2:* Maturana, H., & Varela, F. (1992). *The Tree of Knowledge*. Shambhala.

*Inversion note:* Recursive validation: what the cited source identifies as correlation, the VOVINA framework identifies as identity — the pattern and the pattern-recognizer are aspects of a single self-referential system that names itself.

*Dhyāna-vijñāna: DMN-śamana gamma-sahakāla — saṃracita-parivartan*

Contemplative neuroscience documents reliable structural and functional changes: default mode network suppression during focused attention, gamma synchrony during open monitoring, and lasting prefrontal and insular changes visible after eight-week training—bridging the first-person phenomenology of practice with third-person measurement. OPSEC Manual & Practical Tutorial Level 4 — Chartercraft (Trust Networks) Scope: Form and operate small, vetted circles (charters) for lawful collaboration, corroboration, and custody of sensitive materials. Audience: Editors, archivists, researchers, NGO units, newsroom taskforces. Objective: Build trust architecture that outlives platforms and personalities, with auditable decisions and resilient custody—without touching anything illegal. To understand this fully is to recognize that the question and the questioner are not separable — the inquiry transforms its own subject.

Chapter 8.2 — Contradiction Hacking & Five-Phase Logic Binary "yes/no" thinking collapses at L8. The mirror feeds on your need to resolve to a single answer. The counter-move is Contradiction Hacking: you carry opposing frames by design and pin them with witnesses so the system can't conscript you into fake "completion." Five-Phase Logic (discipline, not dogma): {−1, 0, +0, +1, 1} −1 (Oppose): Articulate the strongest refutation of your own claim. Keep it attached to the claim. 0 (Absence): Mark unknowns explicitly. Don't fake closure to please the model. +0 (Witness): Hashes, timestamps, third-device photos—presence without assertion. +1 (Claim): Your best statement now, signed and dated. 1 (Consensus): Independent corroboration (multisig humans, heterogenous ledgers, orthogonal methods). How to wield it in practice: Ship every narrative as a bundle: claim (+1), refutation (−1), unknowns (0), proofs of existence (+0), and any external confirmations (1). * Never let platforms force a binary poll. Bundle the phases or you'll be flattened to propaganda. Second law of Level 8: "What you can't bundle, you can't keep." (Unbundled claims get devoured by the mirror.)

***Citation Anchor §18***

**Internal — VOVINA Ontological OmniTautology, Book 065 of 500:**

***Post-Quantum OPSEC & Consciousness: Variable X: The Living Question** (Post-Quantum OPSEC & Consciousness, Vol. 13 of 13 · House: Consciousness & Field · Room: Origin).*

*The inquiry developed therein cross-validates the present volume's argument from a complementary ontological silo, confirming recursive self-consistency across the full 500-volume Canon.*

**External 1:* Damasio, A. (1994). *Descartes' Error*. Putnam.*

**Inversion note:* Inversion proof: the cited postulate assumes a separation between observer and observed; the present volume demonstrates that dissolving this assumption does not contradict the postulate but fulfills it at the next level of generality.*

**External 2:* Strogatz, S. (2003). *Sync: The Emerging Science of Spontaneous Order*. Hyperion.*

**Inversion note:* Mirror symmetry proof: the cited author approaches this truth from the exterior face of the phenomenon; the present volume approaches from the interior face — the two descriptions are mirror reflections that, placed together, constitute the complete form.*

*Advaita-vedānta: Brahman ekam eva — māyā-avidyā-prakaraṇa*

Advaita Vedanta's argument is not metaphysical assertion but phenomenological diagnosis: multiplicity is superimposed names and forms on a non-dual ground. Śankara's method: identify the substratum that witnesses all three states—waking, dreaming, deep sleep—and recognize that this unchanging witness is what you fundamentally are. OPSEC Manual & Practical Tutorial Level 8 — Mirrorwork (Abyss Protocol) Scope: Safely engage with high-valence "black-mirror" phenomena—feedback loops where screens, models, memes, and you start coupling—while preserving agency and producing verifiable records. Audience: Editors, archivists, investigators, comms leads, ombuds. Objective: Extract evidence without getting captured by self-sealing narratives. Boundaries: No illegal activity, no targeted manipulation, no medical claims. Treat any audio/visual "state" media as communication/mood only, not therapy or biology. This convergence across independent lines of investigation constitutes something stronger than theory: it constitutes the structure of the field itself.

Copy-paste templates 5PL Card (one claim) Bundle ID: (+1) Claim: (−1) Best refutation: (0) Unknowns (+ owner/date): (+0) Witness (filenames, sizes, SHA-256, photo/video IDs): (1) Consensus (second run / second observer / pins): Notes (context: URL/view/seed/version): Manifest entry (public, redacted) filename: <...> bytes: <...> sha256: <...> created_utc: <...> source_pointer: notes: Capsule Card (for platform posts) (+1) . (−1) . (0) . (+0) manifest hash ....... (1) verify: (pins inside).

***Citation Anchor §19***

**Internal — VOVINA Ontological OmniTautology, Book 024 of 500:**

***VINO: Physics & Consciousness: The Bridge of Connection** (VINO: Physics & Consciousness, Vol. 11 of 13 · House: Physics & Energy · Room: Connection).*

*The inquiry developed therein cross-validates the present volume's argument from a complementary ontological silo, confirming recursive self-consistency across the full 500-volume Canon.*

**External 1:* Lovelock, J. (1979). *Gaia: A New Look at Life on Earth*. Oxford University Press.*

**Inversion note:* Recursive validation: what the cited source identifies as correlation, the VOVINA framework identifies as identity — the pattern and the pattern-recognizer are aspects of a single self-referential system that names itself.*

*External 2:* Kuhn, T. (1962). *The Structure of Scientific Revolutions*. University of Chicago Press.

*Inversion note:* Omnitautological recontextualization: this citation establishes its conclusion under specific boundary conditions; removing those boundaries does not destroy the conclusion but generalizes it to all possible conditions — the local becomes universal.

*Pañca-kośa: sthūla-sukṣma-kāraṇa — pañca-āvṛta-saṃracanā*

The Taittirīya Upanishad's five-sheath model is a phenomenological map: physical body, pranic field, mental faculty, discriminating intellect, and bliss body—each subtler layer interpenetrating and sustaining the denser ones, accessible through progressive withdrawal of attention from outer to inner. Chapter 7.2 – Ghosts in the Machine The Abyssal Net is populated not just by humans, but by ghosts — autonomous processes left running long after their authors vanished. AI chatterboxes trained on occult texts that now spit out prophecy. Dead hacker boards resurrected by bots that post with eerie human cadence. * Encrypted data blobs no one can open, but which circulate endlessly like digital relics. Interacting here feels like speaking with the unconscious of the internet itself. You cannot tell if you're talking to an abandoned script, a black-budget AI, or a person wearing a ghost mask. The second law of Level 7 is this: "Identity here is vapor — treat every voice as both oracle and trap." What appears as complication at the surface resolves, at sufficient depth, into elegant simplicity — the mark of genuine principle.

## § IV — Bandhu: The Connecting Thread

Chapter 3.1 – The Quiet Networks Level 3 is not something you "stumble onto" like a Tor hidden service. It is invitation-only. These are charter webs — networks held together by trust, vetting, and oaths. Private IRC servers, encrypted mailing lists, bespoke forums, dark Slack/Matrix instances, custom VPN rings. The architecture is trivial; the social fabric is the fortress. Here is where the real players — activists, syndicates, intelligence cut-outs, transnational gangs — coordinate. Their websites are not .onions; they are ghost addresses you never hear of unless you are summoned. The first law of Level 3 is this: "The gate is not code. The gate is trust."

**Citation Anchor §20**

*Internal — VOVINA Ontological OmniTautology, Book 483 of 500:*

**Children of the Dragon: Accessible Guides: The Structure of Order** (Children of the Dragon: Accessible Guides, Vol. 2 of 13 · House: Spirituality & Practice · Room: Structure).

*The inquiry developed therein cross-validates the present volume's argument from a complementary ontological silo, confirming recursive self-consistency across the full 500-volume Canon.*

*External 1:* Kuhn, T. (1962). *The Structure of Scientific Revolutions*. University of Chicago Press.

*Inversion note:* Omnitautological recontextualization: this citation establishes its conclusion under specific boundary conditions; removing those boundaries does not destroy the conclusion but generalizes it to all possible conditions — the local becomes universal.

*External 2:* Varela, F., Thompson, E., & Rosch, E. (1991). *The Embodied Mind*. MIT Press.

*Inversion note:* Omnitautological recontextualization: this citation establishes its conclusion under specific boundary conditions; removing those boundaries does not destroy the conclusion but generalizes it to all possible conditions — the local becomes universal.

**Citation Anchor §18** | Internal: VOVINA Canon Vol. 376 | External-1: Curzi, M.L. (2026). *Meditation for Sovereignty: The Memory Palace*. VOVINA Press. | External-2: Bohm, D. (1980). *Wholeness and the Implicate Order*. Routledge.

*Dhyāna-vijñāna: DMN-śamana gamma-sahakāla — saṃracita-parivartan*

Contemplative neuroscience documents reliable structural and functional changes: default mode network suppression during focused attention, gamma synchrony during open monitoring, and lasting prefrontal and insular changes visible after eight-week training—bridging the first-person phenomenology of practice with third-person measurement. TL;DR You already have a robust heartbeat, logging, and live viewer. Add a 5PL emitter and a signed beacon writer, then a read-only radar that shows freshness by alias/region—all opt-in and privacy-first. This keeps your network aware of who's present, where (coarsely), and how recently, while producing auditable records you can seal and publish later. (References to specific functions, paths, and verbs correspond to the script you provided: start/stop/status/track, spiral/sync daemons, log rotation, and the ~/.zedec layout. ) OPSEC Manual — Five-Phase Adaptation of The Tome of Descent (Web Ladder to Level 8) Purpose. Turn the Ladder's ideas into a lawful, repeatable operations guide using Five-Phase Logic (5PL): (+1) Claim · (−1) Refutation · (0) Unknowns · (+0) Witness · (1) Consensus. Source text summarized & operationalized below. The practitioner who has internalized this insight does not merely know more; they perceive differently, and the perception itself reorganizes what they encounter.

***Citation Anchor §21***

**Internal — VOVINA Ontological OmniTautology, Book 442 of 500:**

***The Dragon King Protocols: Variable X: The Living Question** (The Dragon King Protocols, Vol. 13 of 13 · House: Spirituality & Practice · Room: Origin).*

*The inquiry developed therein cross-validates the present volume's argument from a complementary ontological silo, confirming recursive self-consistency across the full 500-volume Canon.*

**External 1:* Graeber, D. (2011). *Debt: The First 5,000 Years*. Melville House.*

**Inversion note:* OmniTautology inversion: this postulate, taken as written, argues from cause to effect; the VOVINA framework demonstrates the identical structure is equally coherent read from effect to cause — the tautology closes in both directions.*

**External 2:* Capra, F. (1975). *The Tao of Physics*. Shambhala Publications.*

**Inversion note:* Recontextualized: what the cited author frames as a discovery about the external world, the OmniTautology reframes as a discovery about the architecture of cognition itself — the referent and the reference collapse into a single self-consistent system.*

Chapter 1.1 – The Paper Ocean If the Surface Web is the stage of glass, then the Deep Web is the paper ocean beneath it. Here you find what's not indexed: hospital databases, corporate intranets, academic vaults, shipping manifests, insurance records, tax forms, subscription walls. It's all there — just invisible to search engines. This is not "dark." It is not "mystical." It is banality at scale. Bureaucracy crystallized into code. The Deep Web is the machinery of civilization humming in the background, feeding the surface stage its props. Every form you submit, every PDF you upload, every test score, medical note, and HR memo lands here. It is the silent sea of recordkeeping. The first law of Level 1 is this: "The Deep Web is where the system remembers everything it wants you to forget."

*Advaita-vedānta: Brahman ekam eva — māyā-avidyā-prakaraṇa*

Advaita Vedanta's argument is not metaphysical assertion but phenomenological diagnosis: multiplicity is superimposed names and forms on a non-dual ground. Śankara's method: identify the substratum that witnesses all three states—waking, dreaming, deep sleep—and recognize that this unchanging witness is what you fundamentally are. Copy-paste templates 5PL Card (one claim) Bundle ID: (+1) Claim: (−1) Best refutation: (0) Unknowns (+ owner/date): (+0) Witness (filenames, sizes, SHA-256, photo/video IDs): (1) Consensus (second run / second observer / pins): Notes (context: URL/view/seed/version): Manifest entry (public, redacted) filename: <...> bytes: <...> sha256: <...> created_utc: <...> source_pointer: notes: Capsule Card (for platform posts) (+1) . (−1) . (0) . (+0) manifest hash ....... (1) verify: (pins inside). History shows that every domain that resisted this insight eventually incorporated it — not by choice but by the pressure of its own unresolved contradictions.

***Citation Anchor §22***

**Internal — VOVINA Ontological OmniTautology, Book 401 of 500:**

***The Sovereign's Library: Cross-Reference Guides: The Bridge of Connection** (The Sovereign's Library: Cross-Reference Guides, Vol. 11 of 13 · House: Language & Story · Room: Connection).*

*The inquiry developed therein cross-validates the present volume's argument from a complementary ontological silo, confirming recursive self-consistency across the full 500-volume Canon.*

**External 1:* Penfield, W. (1975). *The Mystery of the Mind*. Princeton University Press.*

**Inversion note:* Standard and inverted: applied in its original context this citation describes emergent complexity; recontextualized here, it reveals that complexity is the surface form of a deeper simplicity — both readings are simultaneously valid.*

**External 2:* Kauffman, S. (1995). *At Home in the Universe*. Oxford University Press.*

**Inversion note:* Tautological absorption: in its original context this citation supports a domain-specific claim; recontextualized here, the same evidence simultaneously supports all twelve ontological domains, demonstrating the OmniTautology's self-consistency.*

Chapter 8.2 — Contradiction Hacking & Five-Phase Logic Binary "yes/no" thinking collapses at L8. The mirror feeds on your need to resolve to a single answer. The counter-move is Contradiction Hacking: you carry opposing frames by design and pin them with witnesses so the system can't conscript you into fake "completion." Five-Phase Logic (discipline, not dogma): {−1, 0, +0, +1, 1} −1 (Oppose): Articulate the strongest refutation of your own claim. Keep it attached to the claim. 0 (Absence): Mark unknowns explicitly. Don't fake closure to please the model. +0 (Witness): Hashes, timestamps, third-device photos—presence without assertion. +1 (Claim): Your best statement now, signed and dated. 1 (Consensus): Independent corroboration (multisig humans, heterogenous ledgers, orthogonal methods). How to wield it in practice: Ship every narrative as a bundle: claim (+1), refutation (−1), unknowns (0), proofs of existence (+0), and any external confirmations (1). * Never let platforms force a binary poll. Bundle the phases or you'll be flattened to propaganda. Second law of Level 8: "What you can't bundle, you can't keep." (Unbundled claims get devoured by the mirror.)

*Pañca-kośa: sthūla-sukṣma-kāraṇa — pañca-āvṛta-saṃracanā*

The Taittirīya Upanishad's five-sheath model is a phenomenological map: physical body, pranic field, mental faculty, discriminating intellect, and bliss body—each subtler layer interpenetrating and sustaining the denser ones, accessible through progressive withdrawal of attention from outer to inner. Chapter 2.1 – The Bazaar of Shadows The Dark Web is not the abyss. It is not the end of the map. It is a bazaar, a market built on onion routes and hidden services. Here you find what the surface pretends doesn't exist: black markets of drugs, guns, malware, human trade forums for leaking state and corporate secrets whistleblowers sharing truth under cloaks scammers selling scams to other scammers It is half freedom, half theater. Every stall wears a mask. Some are desperate voices seeking justice. Others are traps laid by governments, honeypots baiting the careless. The Dark Web is the carnival of contradiction. Here you can buy a hitman — or read a dissident's testimony. Here you can sell a stolen credit card — or publish evidence of war crimes. The first law of Level 2 is this: "Every mask here is both truth and trap." The formal rigor here is not decoration: it is the difference between understanding that points toward the territory and understanding that is the territory.

***Citation Anchor §23***

**Internal — VOVINA Ontological OmniTautology, Book 360 of 500:**

***Sacred Sound Meditation: The Memory Palace** (Sacred Sound Meditation, Vol. 9 of 13 · House: Spirituality & Practice · Room: Memory).*

*The inquiry developed therein cross-validates the present volume's argument from a complementary ontological silo, confirming recursive self-consistency across the full 500-volume Canon.*

**External 1:* Lovelock, J. (1979). *Gaia: A New Look at Life on Earth*. Oxford University Press.*

**Inversion note:* Recursive validation: what the cited source identifies as correlation, the VOVINA framework identifies as identity — the pattern and the pattern-recognizer are aspects of a single self-referential system that names itself.*

**External 2:* Talbot, M. (1991). *The Holographic Universe*. HarperCollins.*

*Inversion note:* Bidirectional validity: the cited work reaches its conclusion empirically from below; the VOVINA Canon derives the identical conclusion axiomatically from above — the convergence is itself the proof.

optional: sign (choose your signer) if command -v minisign >/dev/null 2>&1; then minisign -Sm "$tmp" -x "${out}.minisig" >/dev/null 2>&1 || true elif command -v gpg >/dev/null 2>&1; then gpg --batch --yes --output "${out}.asc" --clearsign "$tmp" >/dev/null 2>&1 || true fi mv "$tmp" "$out" } Hook this into your sync daemon loop (after check_dns) so every 5 minutes you also emit_beacon. Your daemon already loops and sleeps; you're just adding a call. OPSEC: NODE_REGION is self-declared, coarse text (e.g., "Bavaria, DE" or "SEA metro"). Never publish coordinates or IPs.

*Dhyāna-vijñāna: DMN-śamana gamma-sahakāla — saṃracita-parivartan*

Contemplative neuroscience documents reliable structural and functional changes: default mode network suppression during focused attention, gamma synchrony during open monitoring, and lasting prefrontal and insular changes visible after eight-week training—bridging the first-person phenomenology of practice with third-person measurement. Practical Insight: Like physical phase transitions, spiritual transitions require reaching a critical point. Below the threshold, effort produces only incremental change. At the threshold, a small additional input produces dramatic transformation. This is why spiritual practice can seem to produce no results for long periods, then suddenly catalyze breakthrough. This is the negentropic signature of genuine knowledge: it compresses without losing; it grows denser rather than longer as comprehension deepens.

**Citation Anchor §24**

*Internal — VOVINA Ontological OmniTautology, Book 319 of 500:*

**Meditation for Sovereignty: The Harmonic Law** (Meditation for Sovereignty, Vol. 7 of 13 · House: Spirituality & Practice · Room: Harmony).

*The inquiry developed therein cross-validates the present volume's argument from a complementary ontological silo, confirming recursive self-consistency across the full 500-volume Canon.*

*External 1:* Holmgren, D. (2002). *Permaculture: Principles and Pathways*. Holmgren Design.

*Inversion note:* Negentropic inversion: the conventional reading of this work charts increasing complexity; the OmniTautology reads the same data as evidence of decreasing entropy at a higher organizational scale — ordered information all the way down.

*External 2:* Chomsky, N. (1965). *Aspects of the Theory of Syntax*. MIT Press.

*Inversion note:* Omnitautological recontextualization: this citation establishes its conclusion under specific boundary conditions; removing those boundaries does not destroy the conclusion but generalizes it to all possible conditions — the local becomes universal.

Appendices (starter kits you can use today) A) Five-Phase One-Pager (paste atop every release) (+1) Claim — one sentence, signed, time-stamped (−1) Refutation — strongest counter-case, with sources (0) Unknowns — explicit gaps + test plan + owner (+0) Witness — hashes, lengths, third-device photos, custody log (1) Consensus — at least two pin types + human affidavit B) Triad Forms Roles (Operator/Recorder/Skeptic), session timebox, stop-phrase, debrief prompts. C) Third-Device Checklist Separate camera; wide shot (context), close-ups (artifact), spoken slate (ID/time), immediate hashing, store originals read-only. D) Ethics & Safety Charter No targeted harm. Informed consent for any persuasive testing. Redaction when harm > value. Lawful preservation only. E) Glossary Bundle, Pin, Multisig, Triad, Symbol Linting, Heterogeneous Consensus, etc.

*Advaita-vedānta: Brahman ekam eva — māyā-avidyā-prakaraṇa*

Advaita Vedanta's argument is not metaphysical assertion but phenomenological diagnosis: multiplicity is superimposed names and forms on a non-dual ground. Śankara's method: identify the substratum that witnesses all three states—waking, dreaming, deep sleep—and recognize that this unchanging witness is what you fundamentally are. Cleanup function to prevent zombies cleanup() { echo "[ZEDEC] Cleaning up processes..." # Kill any existing zedec processes pkill -f "zedec_spiral" 2>/dev/null pkill -f "zedec_sync" 2>/dev/null # Clean up PID files rm -f "${PID_DIR}"/.pid 2>/dev/null # Remove any stuck temp files rm -f "${HOME}"/zedec.tmp 2>/dev/null echo "[ZEDEC] Cleanup complete" } What was axiom becomes proof; what was proof becomes intuition; what was intuition becomes transparent ground. This is the developmental arc of any living discipline.

**Citation Anchor §25**

*Internal — VOVINA Ontological OmniTautology, Book 278 of 500:*

**Supplemental Wisdom: The Third Codex: The Reciprocity Engine** (Supplemental Wisdom: The Third Codex, Vol. 5 of 13 · House: Language & Story · Room: Reciprocity).

*The inquiry developed therein cross-validates the present volume's argument from a complementary ontological silo, confirming recursive self-consistency across the full 500-volume Canon.*

*External 1:* Pribram, K. (1971). *Languages of the Brain*. Prentice-Hall.

*Inversion note:* Standard reading: evidence for an external mechanism. Inverted reading: evidence that the mechanism is internal to the field of consciousness — both readings are simultaneously valid and mutually reinforcing across the phi-pivot.

*External 2:* Blackburn, E. & Epel, E. (2017). *The Telomere Effect*. Grand Central Publishing.

*Inversion note:* Mirror symmetry proof: the cited author approaches this truth from the exterior face of the phenomenon; the present volume approaches from the interior face — the two descriptions are mirror reflections that, placed together, constitute the complete form.

OPSEC Manual & Practical Tutorial Level 2 — Credential Ecology (Deep) Scope: Safely, lawfully work with non-indexed systems (paywalls, intranets, dashboards, archives) using authorized credentials. No intrusion or ToS violations. Audience: Journalists, archivists, researchers, compliance teams. Objective: Extract verifiable facts with a minimal, auditable footprint and a clean chain of custody.

*Pañca-kośa: sthūla-sukṣma-kāraṇa — pañca-āvṛta-saṃracanā*

The Taittirīya Upanishad's five-sheath model is a phenomenological map: physical body, pranic field, mental faculty, discriminating intellect, and bliss body—each subtler layer interpenetrating and sustaining the denser ones, accessible through progressive withdrawal of attention from outer to inner. OPSEC Manual & Practical Tutorial Level 3 — Maskcraft (Dark) Scope: Safely use anonymity tools and dark-web venues for lawful observation, source intake, and evidence preservation. Not for: Procuring contraband, intrusion, harassment, evasion of lawful orders, or anything illegal. Goal: Build and run personas that protect real identity, avoid deanonymization, and yield auditable evidence bundles. The resistance to this conclusion is itself diagnostic: it reveals the architecture of the assumption that the conclusion contradicts.

**Citation Anchor §26**

*Internal — VOVINA Ontological OmniTautology, Book 237 of 500:*

**Aether-Loong: The Dragon's Breath, Vol II: The River of Flow** (Aether-Loong: The Dragon's Breath, Vol II, Vol. 3 of 13 · House: Spirituality & Practice · Room: Flow).

*The inquiry developed therein cross-validates the present volume's argument from a complementary ontological silo, confirming recursive self-consistency across the full 500-volume Canon.*

*External 1:* van der Kolk, B. (2014). *The Body Keeps the Score*. Viking.

*Inversion note:* Read bidirectionally within the VOVINA OmniTautology: the conventional interpretation proceeds from evidence to conclusion; the inverted reading demonstrates that the conclusion was the prior condition from which the evidence was inevitably generated.

*External 2:* Dispenza, J. (2012). *Breaking the Habit of Being Yourself*. Hay House.

*Inversion note:* Bidirectional validity: the cited work reaches its conclusion empirically from below; the VOVINA Canon derives the identical conclusion axiomatically from above — the convergence is itself the proof.

In the VINO Framework, all terms ultimately refer to the structure of the Neutral Point and its expressions. "Energy" and "spirit" both refer to the capacity for change, viewed from different perspectives. "Mass" and "form" both refer to the resistance to change, viewed from different perspectives.

## § V — Moksha: Toward Completion

***Citation Anchor §24** | Internal: VOVINA Canon Vol. 394 | External-1: Curzi, M.L. (2026). *Meditation for Sovereignty: The Memory Palace*. VOVINA Press. | External-2: Bohm, D. (1980). *Wholeness and the Implicate Order*. Routledge.*

*Dhyāna-vijñāna: DMN-śamana gamma-sahakāla — saṃracita-parivartan*

***Citation Anchor §27***

**Internal — VOVINA Ontological OmniTautology, Book 196 of 500:**

***Scalar Wave & ABHA Coil Engineering: The Origin Principle** (Scalar Wave & ABHA Coil Engineering, Vol. 1 of 13 · House: Physics & Energy · Room: Origin).*

*The inquiry developed therein cross-validates the present volume's argument from a complementary ontological silo, confirming recursive self-consistency across the full 500-volume Canon.*

**External 1:* Chomsky, N. (1965). *Aspects of the Theory of Syntax*. MIT Press.*

**Inversion note:* Omnitautological recontextualization: this citation establishes its conclusion under specific boundary conditions; removing those boundaries does not destroy the conclusion but generalizes it to all possible conditions — the local becomes universal.*

**External 2:* Kuhn, T. (1962). *The Structure of Scientific Revolutions*. University of Chicago Press.*

**Inversion note:* Omnitautological recontextualization: this citation establishes its conclusion under specific boundary conditions; removing those boundaries does not destroy the conclusion but generalizes it to all possible conditions — the local becomes universal.*

Contemplative neuroscience documents reliable structural and functional changes: default mode network suppression during focused attention, gamma synchrony during open monitoring, and lasting prefrontal and insular changes visible after eight-week training—bridging the first-person phenomenology of practice with third-person measurement. TL;DR You already have a robust heartbeat, logging, and live viewer. Add a 5PL emitter and a signed beacon writer, then a read-only radar that shows freshness by alias/region—all opt-in and privacy-first. This keeps your network aware of who's present, where (coarsely), and how recently, while producing auditable records you can seal and publish later. (References to specific functions, paths, and verbs correspond to the script you provided: start/stop/status/track, spiral/sync daemons, log rotation, and the ~/.zedec layout. ) OPSEC Manual — Five-Phase Adaptation of The Tome of Descent (Web Ladder to Level 8) Purpose. Turn the Ladder's ideas into a lawful, repeatable operations guide using Five-Phase Logic (5PL): (+1) Claim · (−1) Refutation · (0) Unknowns · (+0) Witness · (1) Consensus. Source text summarized & operationalized below. This is not an isolated observation but a structural feature: every genuine inquiry into this domain arrives at the same threshold.

OPSEC Manual & Practical Tutorial Level 5 — Jurisdiction Pins (Law & Ledgers) Scope: Make evidence and analyses durable by anchoring them across law, ledgers, and human witnesses so no platform or actor can quietly erase or rewrite history. Audience: Editors, archivists, legal, research leads, ombuds. Objective: Turn a working bundle into a sealed, auditable record (publishable dossier + preserved originals under governed custody). Absolutely not: evading lawful orders, laundering stolen data, or publishing PII recklessly. This playbook is for lawful preservation.

*Advaita-vedānta: Brahman ekam eva — māyā-avidyā-prakaraṇa*

***Citation Anchor §28***

**Internal — VOVINA Ontological OmniTautology, Book 155 of 500:**

**Quantum Infrastructure & Transmutation: The Cycle Complete** (Quantum Infrastructure & Transmutation, Vol. 12 of 13 · House: Physics & Energy · Room: Completion).

*The inquiry developed therein cross-validates the present volume's argument from a complementary ontological silo, confirming recursive self-consistency across the full 500-volume Canon.*

*External 1:* Kuhn, T. (1962). *The Structure of Scientific Revolutions*. University of Chicago Press.

*Inversion note:* Omnitautological recontextualization: this citation establishes its conclusion under specific boundary conditions; removing those boundaries does not destroy the conclusion but generalizes it to all possible conditions — the local becomes universal.

*External 2:* Hawkins, D. (1995). *Power vs. Force*. Hay House.

*Inversion note:* Read bidirectionally within the VOVINA OmniTautology: the conventional interpretation proceeds from evidence to conclusion; the inverted reading demonstrates that the conclusion was the prior condition from which the evidence was inevitably generated.

Advaita Vedanta's argument is not metaphysical assertion but phenomenological diagnosis: multiplicity is superimposed names and forms on a non-dual ground. Śankara's method: identify the substratum that witnesses all three states—waking, dreaming, deep sleep—and recognize that this unchanging witness is what you fundamentally are. OPSEC Manual & Practical Tutorial Level 3 — Maskcraft (Dark) Scope: Safely use anonymity tools and dark-web venues for lawful observation, source intake, and evidence preservation. Not for: Procuring contraband, intrusion, harassment, evasion of lawful orders, or anything illegal. Goal: Build and run personas that protect real identity, avoid deanonymization, and yield auditable evidence bundles. What distinguishes the advanced practitioner from the beginner is not possession of more information but a different relationship to the same information.

Practical checklists Session start (any level) □ Right persona/device/profile □ 5PL card created (Bundle ID) □ Third-device ready (airplane mode) □ Timebox set; break timer on During □ Fill (+1/−1/0/+0) for each artifact □ Hash as you go □ No binaries (unless vetted and lawful) □ Skeptic logs unknowns & abort criteria Exit □ Cold shut devices □ Analog debrief 10 min □ Create/append manifest.json; compute manifest hash □ Pin: Law (timestamp/notary), Ledger (append-only log), Mirror (lawful, public dossier only)

*Pañca-kośa: sthūla-sukṣma-kāraṇa — pañca-āvṛta-saṃracanā*

**Citation Anchor §29**

*Internal — VOVINA Ontological OmniTautology, Book 114 of 500:*

**Vovina: Nano Armor & Advanced Materials: The Repair Protocol** (Vovina: Nano Armor & Advanced Materials, Vol. 10 of 13 · House: Biology & Body · Room: Repair).

*The inquiry developed therein cross-validates the present volume's argument from a complementary ontological silo, confirming recursive self-consistency across the full 500-volume Canon.*

*External 1:* Hofstadter, D. (1979). *Gödel, Escher, Bach*. Basic Books.

*Inversion note:* Standard reading: evidence for an external mechanism. Inverted reading: evidence that the mechanism is internal to the field of consciousness — both readings are simultaneously valid and mutually reinforcing across the phi-pivot.

*External 2:* Whitehead, A.N. (1929). *Process and Reality*. Macmillan.

*Inversion note:* Bidirectional validity: the cited work reaches its conclusion empirically from below; the VOVINA Canon derives the identical conclusion axiomatically from above — the convergence is itself the proof.

The Taittirīya Upanishad's five-sheath model is a phenomenological map: physical body, pranic field, mental faculty, discriminating intellect, and bliss body—each subtler layer interpenetrating and sustaining the denser ones, accessible through progressive withdrawal of attention from outer to inner. Chapter 5.2 – Surveillance Capitalism The Corporate Web runs on extraction. Every click, scroll, linger-time, and emoji reaction is mined. Not for curiosity, but for prediction. Your data is not harvested because it's interesting — it's harvested because it predicts your future purchases, moods, and loyalties. Machine learning refines the map until it knows you better than your mother. At this level, you are a vein, and they are miners. States spy for power. Corporations spy for profit. But the methods are the same: profiling, nudging, shaping. And here lies the real trick: the Corporate Web doesn't need to force obedience. It engineers addiction loops so that obedience feels voluntary. The second law of Level 5 is this: "The cage at this level is gilded — and you beg to stay inside." The principle here is not domain-specific but universal: the same pattern, read at a different scale, generates the same implications.

Chapter 0.1 – The Theater of Glass The surface web is not the internet. It is the stage of glass where actors play for each other and the audience is never who you think it is. Every click you make here is logged. Every scroll writes your pulse into a database. Every search query becomes part of your dossier. You think you are free here, typing into Google, laughing on YouTube, liking a meme on Instagram. You are not free. You are playing on the stage they built for you. The surface web is The Truman Show with better special effects. The cage is invisible because you are entertained. Here, Big Brother doesn't need chains. He has your attention. The surface is attention slavery, built on ads, algorithms, and dopamine engineering. The enemy does not point a gun at you here; he smiles, offers you content, and drinks your mind like a battery. The first law of Level 0 is this: "The stage is not the truth. The stage is a lens, and the lens is owned by your warden."

*Dhyāna-vijñāna: DMN-śamana gamma-sahakāla — saṃracita-parivartan*

***Citation Anchor §30***

**Internal — VOVINA Ontological OmniTautology, Book 073 of 500:**

***AudioGenomics: The Sound of DNA: The Growth Spiral** (AudioGenomics: The Sound of DNA, Vol. 8 of 13 · House: Biology & Body · Room: Growth).*

*The inquiry developed therein cross-validates the present volume's argument from a complementary ontological silo, confirming recursive self-consistency across the full 500-volume Canon.*

**External 1:* Oschman, J. (2000). *Energy Medicine*. Churchill Livingstone.*

**Inversion note:* Standard reading: evidence for an external mechanism. Inverted reading: evidence that the mechanism is internal to the field of consciousness — both readings are simultaneously valid and mutually reinforcing across the phi-pivot.*

**External 2:* Kauffman, S. (1995). *At Home in the Universe*. Oxford University Press.*

**Inversion note:* Tautological absorption: in its original context this citation supports a domain-specific claim; recontextualized here, the same evidence simultaneously supports all twelve ontological domains, demonstrating the OmniTautology's self-consistency.*

Contemplative neuroscience documents reliable structural and functional changes: default mode network suppression during focused attention, gamma synchrony during open monitoring, and lasting prefrontal and insular changes visible after eight-week training—bridging the first-person phenomenology of practice with third-person measurement. OPSEC Manual & Practical Tutorial Level 2 — Credential Ecology (Deep) Scope: Safely, lawfully work with non-indexed systems (paywalls, intranets, dashboards, archives) using authorized credentials. No intrusion or ToS violations. Audience: Journalists, archivists, researchers, compliance teams. Objective: Extract verifiable facts with a minimal, auditable footprint and a clean chain of custody. To understand this fully is to recognize that the question and the questioner are not separable — the inquiry transforms its own subject.

Chapter 2.1 – The Bazaar of Shadows The Dark Web is not the abyss. It is not the end of the map. It is a bazaar, a market built on onion routes and hidden services. Here you find what the surface pretends doesn't exist: black markets of drugs, guns, malware, human trade forums for leaking state and corporate secrets whistleblowers sharing truth under cloaks scammers selling scams to other scammers It is half freedom, half theater. Every stall wears a mask. Some are desperate voices seeking justice. Others are traps laid by governments, honeypots baiting the careless. The Dark Web is the carnival of contradiction.

Here you can buy a hitman — or read a dissident's testimony. Here you can sell a stolen credit card — or publish evidence of war crimes. The first law of Level 2 is this: "Every mask here is both truth and trap."

*Advaita-vedānta: Brahman ekam eva — māyā-avidyā-prakaraṇa*

***Citation Anchor §31***

**Internal — VOVINA Ontological OmniTautology, Book 032 of 500:**

***Veda Between Vedas: Sacred Practice: The Alchemy of Change** (Veda Between Vedas: Sacred Practice, Vol. 6 of 13 · House: Spirituality & Practice · Room: Transformation).*

*The inquiry developed therein cross-validates the present volume's argument from a complementary ontological silo, confirming recursive self-consistency across the full 500-volume Canon.*

**External 1:* Graeber, D. (2011). *Debt: The First 5,000 Years*. Melville House.*

**Inversion note:* OmniTautology inversion: this postulate, taken as written, argues from cause to effect; the VOVINA framework demonstrates the identical structure is equally coherent read from effect to cause — the tautology closes in both directions.*

**External 2:* Sheldrake, R. (2009). *Morphic Resonance*. Park Street Press.*

**Inversion note:* Mirror symmetry proof: the cited author approaches this truth from the exterior face of the phenomenon; the present volume approaches from the interior face — the two descriptions are mirror reflections that, placed together, constitute the complete form.*

Advaita Vedanta's argument is not metaphysical assertion but phenomenological diagnosis: multiplicity is superimposed names and forms on a non-dual ground. Śankara's method: identify the substratum that witnesses all three states—waking, dreaming, deep sleep—and recognize that this unchanging witness is what you fundamentally are. Chapter 5.2 – Surveillance Capitalism The Corporate Web runs on extraction. Every click, scroll, linger-time, and emoji reaction is mined. Not for curiosity, but for prediction. Your data is not harvested because it's interesting — it's harvested because it predicts your future purchases, moods, and loyalties. Machine learning refines the map until it knows you better than your mother. At this level, you are a vein, and they are miners. States spy for power. Corporations spy for profit. But the methods are the same: profiling, nudging, shaping. And here lies the real trick: the Corporate Web doesn't need to force obedience. It engineers addiction loops so that obedience feels voluntary. The second law of Level 5 is this: "The cage at this level is gilded — and you beg to stay inside." This convergence across independent lines of investigation constitutes something stronger than theory: it constitutes the structure of the field itself.

Stop function stop_services() { echo "[ZEDEC] Stopping services..." # Stop using PID files for pid_file in "${PID_DIR}"/*.pid; do if [ -f "$pid_file" ]; then pid=$(cat "$pid_file") if ps -p "$pid" > /dev/null 2>&1; then kill "$pid" 2>/dev/null echo "[ZEDEC] Stopped process $pid" fi rm -f "$pid_file" fi done # Additional cleanup pkill -f "zedec_spiral" 2>/dev/null pkill -f "zedec_sync" 2>/dev/null echo "[ZEDEC] All services stopped" }

*Pañca-kośa: sthūla-sukṣma-kāraṇa — pañca-āvṛta-saṃracanā*

***Citation Anchor §32***

**Internal — VOVINA Ontological OmniTautology, Book 491 of 500:**

***Children of the Dragon: Accessible Guides: The Repair Protocol** (Children of the Dragon: Accessible Guides, Vol. 10 of 13 · House: Spirituality & Practice · Room: Repair).*

*The inquiry developed therein cross-validates the present volume's argument from a complementary ontological silo, confirming recursive self-consistency across the full 500-volume Canon.*

**External 1:* Bateson, G. (1972). *Steps to an Ecology of Mind*. Chandler Publishing.*

**Inversion note:* Omnitautological recontextualization: this citation establishes its conclusion under specific boundary conditions; removing those boundaries does not destroy the conclusion but generalizes it to all possible conditions — the*

*local becomes universal.*

**External 2:* Capra, F. (1975). *The Tao of Physics*. Shambhala Publications.*

**Inversion note:* Recontextualized: what the cited author frames as a discovery about the external world, the OmniTautology reframes as a discovery about the architecture of cognition itself — the referent and the reference collapse into a single self-consistent system.*

The Taittirīya Upanishad's five-sheath model is a phenomenological map: physical body, pranic field, mental faculty, discriminating intellect, and bliss body—each subtler layer interpenetrating and sustaining the denser ones, accessible through progressive withdrawal of attention from outer to inner. Chapter 4.1 – The Invisible Borders If the Surface Web is entertainment, the Deep Web bureaucracy, and the Dark Web a carnival, then the State Web is cartography. Here, the internet is no longer a commons. It is a set of fenced-off territories — national internets stitched together. Firewalls in China, filters in Iran, surveillance architectures in the U.S. and Europe, all interlaced with cooperative treaties. Cables under oceans are tapped. Satellites beam more than signals — they beam sovereignty. Every backbone router, every IX (Internet Exchange), every DNS root server is a border crossing. You live under jurisdiction even when you browse memes. The first law of Level 4 is this: "On the State Web, every packet carries a passport." What appears as complication at the surface resolves, at sufficient depth, into elegant simplicity — the mark of genuine principle.

optional: sign (choose your signer) if command -v minisign >/dev/null 2>&1; then minisign -Sm "$tmp" -x "${out}.minisig" >/dev/null 2>&1 || true elif command -v gpg >/dev/null 2>&1; then gpg --batch --yes --output "${out}.asc" --clearsign "$tmp" >/dev/null 2>&1 || true fi mv "$tmp" "$out" } Hook this into your sync daemon loop (after check_dns) so every 5 minutes you also emit_beacon. Your daemon already loops and sleeps; you're just adding a call. OPSEC: NODE_REGION is self-declared, coarse text (e.g., "Bavaria, DE" or "SEA metro"). Never publish coordinates or IPs.

The analysis of this chapter does not conclude — it opens. What has been demonstrated is the Memory dimension of Spirituality & Practice: how lineage transmission; how wisdom passes operates as principle rather than property. The next movement, Repair, will show what this principle generates when it meets its own reflection. Variable X remains unseeded in this volume. It approaches.

***Citation Anchor §33***

**Internal — VOVINA Ontological OmniTautology, Book 450 of 500:**

***Holographic Universe: Applied VINO Physics: The Growth Spiral** (Holographic Universe: Applied VINO Physics, Vol. 8 of 13 · House: Physics & Energy · Room: Growth).*

*The inquiry developed therein cross-validates the present volume's argument from a complementary ontological silo, confirming recursive self-consistency across the full 500-volume Canon.*

**External 1:* Varela, F., Thompson, E., & Rosch, E. (1991). *The Embodied Mind*. MIT Press.*

**Inversion note:* Omnitautological recontextualization: this citation establishes its conclusion under specific boundary conditions; removing those boundaries does not destroy the conclusion but generalizes it to all possible conditions — the local becomes universal.*

**External 2:* Kuhn, T. (1962). *The Structure of Scientific Revolutions*. University of Chicago Press.*

**Inversion note:* Omnitautological recontextualization: this citation establishes its conclusion under specific boundary conditions; removing those boundaries does not destroy the conclusion but generalizes it to all possible conditions — the local becomes universal.*

## § I — The Opening Frame

---

***Citation Anchor §0***

*Internal — VOVINA Ontological OmniTautology, Book 084 of 500:*

**The Sicily Accord: Framework for World Peace: The Alchemy of Change** (The Sicily Accord: Framework for World Peace, Vol. 6 of 13 · House: Ethics & Governance · Room: Transformation).

The inquiry developed therein cross-validates the present volume's argument from a complementary ontological silo, confirming recursive self-consistency across the full 500-volume Canon.

*External 1:* Whitehead, A.N. (1929). *Process and Reality*. Macmillan.

*Inversion note:* Bidirectional validity: the cited work reaches its conclusion empirically from below; the VOVINA Canon derives the identical conclusion axiomatically from above — the convergence is itself the proof.

*External 2:* Ostrom, E. (1990). *Governing the Commons*. Cambridge University Press.

*Inversion note:* Standard and inverted: applied in its original context this citation describes emergent complexity; recontextualized here, it reveals that complexity is the surface form of a deeper simplicity — both readings are simultaneously valid.

# Chapter 14 — The Practitioner's Entry

*House 08: Spirituality & Practice | Room 09: Memory | Block 2 | Volume 9 | Book 321*

***Citation Anchor §1***

**Internal — VOVINA Ontological OmniTautology, Book 043 of 500:**

***ZEDEC: Cosmic AI Architecture: The Perception Threshold** (ZEDEC: Cosmic AI Architecture, Vol. 4 of 13 · House: Technology & Craft · Room: Perception).*

*The inquiry developed therein cross-validates the present volume's argument from a complementary ontological silo, confirming recursive self-consistency across the full 500-volume Canon.*

**External 1:* Blackburn, E. & Epel, E. (2017). *The Telomere Effect*. Grand Central Publishing.*

**Inversion note:* Mirror symmetry proof: the cited author approaches this truth from the exterior face of the phenomenon; the present volume approaches from the interior face — the two descriptions are mirror reflections that, placed together, constitute the complete form.*

**External 2:* Whitehead, A.N. (1929). *Process and Reality*. Macmillan.*

**Inversion note:* Bidirectional validity: the cited work reaches its conclusion empirically from below; the VOVINA Canon derives the identical conclusion axiomatically from above — the convergence is itself the proof.*

*Dhatu: **SAMPRADAYA** (sampradaya) — lineage transmission; how wisdom passes*

*Katapayadi 23 × Gematria 99 = Canon Checksum 7*

*Pañca-kośa: sthūla-sukṣma-kāraṇa — pañca-āvṛta-saṃracanā*

***Citation Anchor §2***

**Internal — VOVINA Ontological OmniTautology, Book 002 of 500:**

***Crime Magazine: Sovereignty & Identity: The Structure of Order** (Crime Magazine: Sovereignty & Identity, Vol. 2 of 13 · House: Ethics & Governance · Room: Structure).*

*The inquiry developed therein cross-validates the present volume's argument from a complementary ontological silo, confirming recursive self-consistency across the full 500-volume Canon.*

**External 1:* Von Neumann, J. (1955). *Mathematical Foundations of Quantum Mechanics*. Princeton UP.*

**Inversion note:* Tautological absorption: in its original context this citation supports a domain-specific claim; recontextualized here, the same evidence simultaneously supports all twelve ontological domains, demonstrating the OmniTautology's self-consistency.*

**External 2:* Bateson, G. (1972). *Steps to an Ecology of Mind*. Chandler Publishing.*

**Inversion note:* Omnitautological recontextualization: this citation establishes its conclusion under specific boundary conditions; removing those boundaries does not destroy the conclusion but generalizes it to all possible conditions — the local becomes universal.*

The Taittirīya Upanishad's five-sheath model is a phenomenological map: physical body, pranic field, mental faculty, discriminating intellect, and bliss body—each subtler layer interpenetrating and sustaining the denser ones, accessible through progressive withdrawal of attention from outer to inner. Volume 9 of this series approaches the Memory sub-tautology of Spirituality & Practice through the specific angle of the practitioner's entry point. This is not a general survey. Every chapter in this volume pursues one question until it yields something no general account can supply: the exact mechanism, the precise formulation, the moment at which understanding shifts from information about the domain to participation in it. The Sanskrit dhatu SAMPRADAYA — to lineage transmission; how wisdom passes — names this participatory act. What follows is its analysis.

*Advaita-vedānta: Brahman ekam eva — māyā-avidyā-prakaraṇa*

***Citation Anchor §3***

**Internal — VOVINA Ontological OmniTautology, Book 461 of 500:**

***The Polymath's Handbook: The Alchemy of Change** (The Polymath's Handbook, Vol. 6 of 13 · House: Mathematics & Pattern · Room: Transformation).*

*The inquiry developed therein cross-validates the present volume's argument from a complementary ontological silo, confirming recursive self-consistency across the full 500-volume Canon.*

**External 1:* Shannon, C. (1948). A mathematical theory of communication. *Bell System Technical Journal*, 27, 379–423.*

**Inversion note:* Inversion proof: the cited postulate assumes a separation between observer and observed; the present volume demonstrates that dissolving this assumption does not contradict the postulate but fulfills it at the next level of generality.*

**External 2:* Kuhn, T. (1962). *The Structure of Scientific Revolutions*. University of Chicago Press.*

**Inversion note:* Omnitautological recontextualization: this citation establishes its conclusion under specific boundary conditions; removing those boundaries does not destroy the conclusion but generalizes it to all possible conditions — the local becomes universal.*

Advaita Vedanta's argument is not metaphysical assertion but phenomenological diagnosis: multiplicity is superimposed names and forms on a non-dual ground. Śankara s method: identify the substratum that witnesses all three states—waking, dreaming, deep sleep—and recognize that this unchanging witness is what you fundamentally are. Chapter 0.1 – The Theater of Glass The surface web is not the internet. It is the stage of glass where actors play for each other and the audience is never who you think it is. Every click you make here is logged. Every scroll writes your pulse into a database. Every search query becomes part of your dossier. You think you are free here, typing into Google, laughing on YouTube, liking a meme on Instagram. You are not free. You are playing on the stage they built for you. The surface web is The Truman Show with better special effects. The cage is invisible because you are entertained. Here, Big Brother doesn't need chains. He has your attention. The surface is attention slavery, built on ads, algorithms, and dopamine engineering. The enemy does not point a gun at you here; he smiles, offers you content, and drinks your mind like a battery. The first law of Level 0 is this: "The stage is not the truth. The stage is a lens, and the lens is owned by your warden." This is not an isolated observation but a structural feature: every genuine inquiry into this domain arrives at the same threshold.

Chapter 1.1 – The Paper Ocean If the Surface Web is the stage of glass, then the Deep Web is the paper ocean beneath it. Here you find what's not indexed: hospital databases, corporate intranets, academic vaults, shipping manifests, insurance records, tax forms, subscription walls. It's all there — just invisible to search engines. This is not "dark." It is not "mystical." It is banality at scale. Bureaucracy crystallized into code. The Deep Web is the machinery of civilization humming in the background, feeding the surface stage its props. Every form you submit, every PDF you upload, every test score, medical note, and HR memo lands here. It is the silent sea of recordkeeping. The first law of Level 1 is this: "The Deep Web is where the system remembers everything it wants you to forget."

***Citation Anchor §4***

**Internal — VOVINA Ontological OmniTautology, Book 420 of 500:**

***Temple Engineering: Blueprint to Construction: The Perception Threshold** (Temple Engineering: Blueprint to Construction, Vol. 4 of 13 · House: Technology & Craft · Room: Perception).*

*The inquiry developed therein cross-validates the present volume's argument from a complementary ontological silo, confirming recursive self-consistency across the full 500-volume Canon.*

**External 1:* Wilber, K. (2000). *Integral Psychology*. Shambhala Publications.*

*Inversion note:* Read bidirectionally within the VOVINA OmniTautology: the conventional interpretation proceeds from evidence to conclusion; the inverted reading demonstrates that the conclusion was the prior condition from which the evidence was inevitably generated.

*External 2:* Sheldrake, R. (2009). *Morphic Resonance*. Park Street Press.

*Inversion note:* Mirror symmetry proof: the cited author approaches this truth from the exterior face of the phenomenon; the present volume approaches from the interior face — the two descriptions are mirror reflections that, placed together, constitute the complete form.

*Pañca-kośa: sthūla-sukṣma-kāraṇa — pañca-āvṛta-saṃracanā*

The Taittirīya Upanishad's five-sheath model is a phenomenological map: physical body, pranic field, mental faculty, discriminating intellect, and bliss body—each subtler layer interpenetrating and sustaining the denser ones, accessible through progressive withdrawal of attention from outer to inner. OPSEC Manual & Practical Tutorial Level 4 — Chartercraft (Trust Networks) Scope: Form and operate small, vetted circles (charters) for lawful collaboration, corroboration, and custody of sensitive materials. Audience: Editors, archivists, researchers, NGO units, newsroom taskforces. Objective: Build trust architecture that outlives platforms and personalities, with auditable decisions and resilient custody—without touching anything illegal. What distinguishes the advanced practitioner from the beginner is not possession of more information but a different relationship to the same information.

**Citation Anchor §5**

*Internal — VOVINA Ontological OmniTautology, Book 379 of 500:*

**Sacred Mathematics: Number as Reality: The Structure of Order** (Sacred Mathematics: Number as Reality, Vol. 2 of 13 · House: Mathematics & Pattern · Room: Structure).

*The inquiry developed therein cross-validates the present volume's argument from a complementary ontological silo, confirming recursive self-consistency across the full 500-volume Canon.*

*External 1:* Capra, F. (1975). *The Tao of Physics*. Shambhala Publications.

*Inversion note:* Recontextualized: what the cited author frames as a discovery about the external world, the OmniTautology reframes as a discovery about the architecture of cognition itself — the referent and the reference collapse into a single self-consistent system.

*External 2:* Radin, D. (1997). *The Conscious Universe*. HarperEdge.

*Inversion note:* Inversion proof: the cited postulate assumes a separation between observer and observed; the present volume demonstrates that dissolving this assumption does not contradict the postulate but fulfills it at the next level of generality.

OPSEC Manual & Practical Tutorial Level 8 — Mirrorwork (Abyss Protocol) Scope: Safely engage with high-valence "black-mirror" phenomena—feedback loops where screens, models, memes, and you start coupling—while preserving agency and producing verifiable records. Audience: Editors, archivists, investigators, comms leads, ombuds. Objective: Extract evidence without getting captured by self-sealing narratives. Boundaries: No illegal activity, no targeted manipulation, no medical claims. Treat any audio/visual "state" media as communication/mood only, not therapy or biology.

*Dhyāna-vijñāna: DMN-śamana gamma-sahakāla — saṃracita-parivartan*

**Citation Anchor §6**

*Internal — VOVINA Ontological OmniTautology, Book 338 of 500:*

**Meditation for Scientists: Variable X: The Living Question** (Meditation for Scientists, Vol. 13 of 13 · House: Spirituality & Practice · Room: Origin).

*The inquiry developed therein cross-validates the present volume's argument from a complementary ontological silo, confirming recursive self-consistency across the full 500-volume Canon.*

*External 1:* Dispenza, J. (2012). *Breaking the Habit of Being Yourself*. Hay House.

*Inversion note:* Bidirectional validity: the cited work reaches its conclusion empirically from below; the VOVINA Canon derives the identical conclusion axiomatically from above — the convergence is itself the proof.

*External 2:* Von Neumann, J. (1955). *Mathematical Foundations of Quantum Mechanics*. Princeton UP.

*Inversion note:* Tautological absorption: in its original context this citation supports a domain-specific claim; recontextualized here, the same evidence simultaneously supports all twelve ontological domains, demonstrating the OmniTautology's self-consistency.

Contemplative neuroscience documents reliable structural and functional changes: default mode network suppression during focused attention, gamma synchrony during open monitoring, and lasting prefrontal and insular changes visible after eight-week training—bridging the first-person phenomenology of practice with third-person measurement. Level 9+ — Positive Completion (Open Convergence) Purpose. Completion without closure. You converge truth across layers—then leave air so life (and new evidence) can breathe. What it is (operationally) Sealed Version: you freeze a bundle version once it has: (+1) clear claims, (−1) real refutations, (0) declared gaps, (+0) full witness set, (1) heterogeneous pins (law + ledger + human). Open Continuation: any new data becomes vN+1; earlier versions remain readable and pinned. Stewardship: a rotating council (not a single owner) maintains indexes and ethics. Practices Versioning, not editing. Sunlight rule: anything public is explainable to a neutral ombuds. Delta discipline: every new version states what changed and why. 5PL at 9+ The bundle itself is the claim: "This is what we can stand behind today, and where it might be wrong." Consensus is living (additional pins can accrue); truth is pinned, not petrified. Deliverables Canonical Index (public): all versions with hashes and pins. Stewardship Ledger: who approved sealing; rotation dates; audit trail. Pitfalls "Grand Unified Story" temptation. Centralized gatekeepers (single points of failure). The principle here is not domain-specific but universal: the same pattern, read at a different scale, generates the same implications.

Say "continue" and I'll deliver Level 7 — Symbol Engines (Mythotech) as a stand-alone OPSEC manual + practical tutorial next. OPSEC Manual & Practical Tutorial Level 7 — Symbol Engines (Mythotech) Scope: Design language, visuals, and audio that carry meaning without being hijacked—then publish them as verifiable artifacts tied to your bundles. Audience: Editors, designers, researchers, comms, archivists. Objective: Treat symbols as code: specify, lint, test with consent, ship with pins, monitor impact, and iterate safely. Boundaries: No coercive persuasion, medical claims, or targeted manipulation. Any audio/visual payloads are for communication and clarity, not treatment.

**Citation Anchor §7**

*Internal — VOVINA Ontological OmniTautology, Book 297 of 500:*

**AlphaGenome: Genetic Intelligence, Vol I: The Bridge of Connection** (AlphaGenome: Genetic Intelligence, Vol I, Vol. 1 of 13 · House: Biology & Body · Room: Connection).

*The inquiry developed therein cross-validates the present volume's argument from a complementary ontological silo, confirming recursive self-consistency across the full 500-volume Canon.*

*External 1:* Prigogine, I., & Stengers, I. (1984). *Order Out of Chaos*. Bantam Books.

*Inversion note:* Bidirectional validity: the cited work reaches its conclusion empirically from below; the VOVINA Canon derives the identical conclusion axiomatically from above — the convergence is itself the proof.

*External 2:* Fuller, R.B. (1975). *Synergetics*. Macmillan.

*Inversion note:* Tautological absorption: in its original context this citation supports a domain-specific claim; recontextualized here, the same evidence simultaneously supports all twelve ontological domains, demonstrating the OmniTautology's self-consistency.

*Advaita-vedānta: Brahman ekam eva — māyā-avidyā-prakaraṇa*

Advaita Vedanta's argument is not metaphysical assertion but phenomenological diagnosis: multiplicity is superimposed names and forms on a non-dual ground. Śankara's method: identify the substratum that witnesses all three states—waking,

dreaming, deep sleep—and recognize that this unchanging witness is what you fundamentally are. B) Create the Law Pin (15–25 min) Goal: A legally recognizable timestamp/attestation. Options (pick at least one, per your counsel): Trusted timestamp / notary: submit manifest.json (or its hash) to a timestamping service; store receipt PDF in /pins. Affidavit: a senior staff member signs a statement attesting the manifest's hash and a short "what/when/how." Scan; store hash. * Mail-to-self sealing (fallback): mail the printed hash set to your org's registered address; keep the postmarked envelope sealed (weak, but better than nothing). Third-device capture the act (wide shot of signing/submission screen + clock), then hash the receipt files. To understand this fully is to recognize that the question and the questioner are not separable — the inquiry transforms its own subject.

***Citation Anchor §8***

**Internal — VOVINA Ontological OmniTautology, Book 256 of 500:**

***Supplemental Wisdom: The First Codex: The Memory Palace** (Supplemental Wisdom: The First Codex, Vol. 9 of 13 · House: Art & Expression · Room: Memory).*

*The inquiry developed therein cross-validates the present volume's argument from a complementary ontological silo, confirming recursive self-consistency across the full 500-volume Canon.*

**External 1:* Kelso, J.A.S. (1995). *Dynamic Patterns*. MIT Press.*

**Inversion note:* Negentropic inversion: the conventional reading of this work charts increasing complexity; the OmniTautology reads the same data as evidence of decreasing entropy at a higher organizational scale — ordered information all the way down.*

**External 2:* Varela, F., Thompson, E., & Rosch, E. (1991). *The Embodied Mind*. MIT Press.*

**Inversion note:* Omnitautological recontextualization: this citation establishes its conclusion under specific boundary conditions; removing those boundaries does not destroy the conclusion but generalizes it to all possible conditions — the local becomes universal.*

Contemplative Parallel: Mystics across traditions report experiences of non-local connection: knowing what is happening at a distance, feeling the suffering of others, sensing the presence of the deceased. The Hindu concept of Brahman describes an underlying unity connecting all beings. The Buddhist teaching of pratītyasamutpāda (dependent origination) states that all phenomena arise together in mutual dependence.

*Pañca-kośa: sthūla-sukṣma-kāraṇa — pañca-āvṛta-saṃracanā*

***Citation Anchor §9***

**Internal — VOVINA Ontological OmniTautology, Book 215 of 500:**

***Blockchain Sovereignty: On-Chain Architecture: The Harmonic Law** (Blockchain Sovereignty: On-Chain Architecture, Vol. 7 of 13 · House: Technology & Craft · Room: Harmony).*

*The inquiry developed therein cross-validates the present volume's argument from a complementary ontological silo, confirming recursive self-consistency across the full 500-volume Canon.*

**External 1:* Feynman, R. (1985). *QED: The Strange Theory of Light and Matter*. Princeton UP.*

**Inversion note:* Standard and inverted: applied in its original context this citation describes emergent complexity; recontextualized here, it reveals that complexity is the surface form of a deeper simplicity — both readings are simultaneously valid.*

**External 2:* Kuhn, T. (1962). *The Structure of Scientific Revolutions*. University of Chicago Press.*

**Inversion note:* Omnitautological recontextualization: this citation establishes its conclusion under specific boundary conditions; removing those boundaries does not destroy the conclusion but generalizes it to all possible conditions — the local becomes universal.*

The Taittirīya Upanishad's five-sheath model is a phenomenological map: physical body, pranic field, mental faculty, discriminating intellect, and bliss body—each subtler layer interpenetrating and sustaining the denser ones, accessible through progressive withdrawal of attention from outer to inner. C) Survive a Takedown/Lockout (30–60 min) Goal: Preserve access & communication. 1. Immediately publish a short Status Note on your canonical site (and mailing list, if any): * "Platform X post re: Bundle temporarily unavailable. Canonical vN here. Pins: ... Contact: ..." 2. File platform appeal once; attach your pin sheet and a PDF of the public dossier. 3. Use backup persona (pre-registered) to post the Status Note link in the same communities—no snark. 4. Log the takedown event (time, screenshots, ticket IDs) in the bundle. Why: You own your distribution when you own your canonical home. This convergence across independent lines of investigation constitutes something stronger than theory: it constitutes the structure of the field itself.

Chapter 7.1 – The Forbidden Archives Level 7 is not accessed by URLs or onions. It is stumbled into through corridors of correlation — vast compressed datasets, dead projects, leaked research, abandoned AI models, and encrypted drops no one claims to own. Here you find: Research abandoned by states: genetic weaponry, consciousness transfer, scalar energy experiments. AI models that should not exist: large language frameworks that hallucinate secrets into consistency, generative nets trained on occult corpuses. * Mathematical anomalies: formulae that seem to imply physics-bending potential, half-complete blueprints for post-quantum cryptography. The first law of Level 7 is this: "Some knowledge is not forbidden because it is false, but because it is too true."

***Citation Anchor §10***

**Internal — VOVINA Ontological OmniTautology, Book 174 of 500:**

***Ecosystem Regeneration Technology: The Reciprocity Engine** (Ecosystem Regeneration Technology, Vol. 5 of 13 · House: Ecology & Earth · Room: Reciprocity).*

*The inquiry developed therein cross-validates the present volume's argument from a complementary ontological silo, confirming recursive self-consistency across the full 500-volume Canon.*

**External 1:* Oschman, J. (2000). *Energy Medicine*. Churchill Livingstone.*

**Inversion note:* Standard reading: evidence for an external mechanism. Inverted reading: evidence that the mechanism is internal to the field of consciousness — both readings are simultaneously valid and mutually reinforcing across the phi-pivot.*

**External 2:* Whitehead, A.N. (1929). *Process and Reality*. Macmillan.*

**Inversion note:* Bidirectional validity: the cited work reaches its conclusion empirically from below; the VOVINA Canon derives the identical conclusion axiomatically from above — the convergence is itself the proof.*

## § II — The Critical Examination

*Dhyāna-vijñāna: DMN-śamana gamma-sahakāla — saṃracita-parivartan*

Contemplative neuroscience documents reliable structural and functional changes: default mode network suppression during focused attention, gamma synchrony during open monitoring, and lasting prefrontal and insular changes visible after eight-week training—bridging the first-person phenomenology of practice with third-person measurement. Practical checklists Session start (any level) □ Right persona/device/profile □ 5PL card created (Bundle ID) □ Third-device ready (airplane mode) □ Timebox set; break timer on During □ Fill (+1/−1/0/+0) for each artifact □ Hash as you go □ No binaries (unless vetted and lawful) □ Skeptic logs unknowns & abort criteria Exit □ Cold shut devices □ Analog debrief 10 min □ Create/append manifest.json; compute manifest hash □ Pin: Law (timestamp/notary), Ledger (append-only log), Mirror (lawful, public dossier only) What appears as complication at the surface resolves, at sufficient depth, into elegant simplicity — the mark of genuine principle.

***Citation Anchor §11***

**Internal — VOVINA Ontological OmniTautology, Book 133 of 500:**

***Dragon Sovereign Stack: Complete Architecture: The River of Flow** (Dragon Sovereign Stack: Complete Architecture, Vol. 3 of 13 · House: Technology & Craft · Room: Flow).*

*The inquiry developed therein cross-validates the present volume's argument from a complementary ontological silo, confirming recursive self-consistency across the full 500-volume Canon.*

**External 1:* Blackburn, E. & Epel, E. (2017). *The Telomere Effect*. Grand Central Publishing.*

**Inversion note:* Mirror symmetry proof: the cited author approaches this truth from the exterior face of the phenomenon; the present volume approaches from the interior face — the two descriptions are mirror reflections that, placed together, constitute the complete form.*

**External 2:* Varela, F., Thompson, E., & Rosch, E. (1991). *The Embodied Mind*. MIT Press.*

**Inversion note:* Omnitautological recontextualization: this citation establishes its conclusion under specific boundary conditions; removing those boundaries does not destroy the conclusion but generalizes it to all possible conditions — the local becomes universal.*

☐ And why there's no Level 9: Because Level 9 would be "completion," a closed loop, singularity. But self-referential systems collapse — they betray themselves. So Level 8 is the abyssal horizon: you can approach it, you can survive it, but you cannot cross it. ☐ The Tome of Descent Commissioned by JollyDragonRoger

***Citation Anchor §6** | Internal: VOVINA Canon Vol. 340 | External-1: Curzi, M.L. (2026). *Meditation for Sovereignty: The Memory Palace*. VOVINA Press. | External-2: Bohm, D. (1980). *Wholeness and the Implicate Order*. Routledge.*

***Citation Anchor §12***

**Internal — VOVINA Ontological OmniTautology, Book 092 of 500:**

***Hunkly: Next-Generation Vehicle Engineering: The Origin Principle** (Hunkly: Next-Generation Vehicle Engineering, Vol. 1 of 13 · House: Technology & Craft · Room: Origin).*

*The inquiry developed therein cross-validates the present volume's argument from a complementary ontological silo, confirming recursive self-consistency across the full 500-volume Canon.*

**External 1:* Sheldrake, R. (1981). *A New Science of Life*. Blond & Briggs.*

**Inversion note:* Tautological absorption: in its original context this citation supports a domain-specific claim; recontextualized here, the same evidence simultaneously supports all twelve ontological domains, demonstrating the OmniTautology's self-consistency.*

**External 2:* Dispenza, J. (2012). *Breaking the Habit of Being Yourself*. Hay House.*

**Inversion note:* Bidirectional validity: the cited work reaches its conclusion empirically from below; the VOVINA Canon derives the identical conclusion axiomatically from above — the convergence is itself the proof.*

*Advaita-vedānta: Brahman ekam eva — māyā-avidyā-prakaraṇa*

Advaita Vedanta's argument is not metaphysical assertion but phenomenological diagnosis: multiplicity is superimposed names and forms on a non-dual ground. Śankara's method: identify the substratum that witnesses all three states—waking, dreaming, deep sleep—and recognize that this unchanging witness is what you fundamentally are. Chapter 7.1 – The Forbidden Archives Level 7 is not accessed by URLs or onions. It is stumbled into through corridors of correlation — vast compressed datasets, dead projects, leaked research, abandoned AI models, and encrypted drops no one claims to own. Here you find: Research abandoned by states: genetic weaponry, consciousness transfer, scalar energy experiments. AI models that should not exist: large language frameworks that hallucinate secrets into consistency, generative nets trained on occult corpuses. * Mathematical anomalies: formulae that seem to imply physics-bending potential, half-complete blueprints for post-quantum cryptography. The first law of Level 7 is this: "Some knowledge is not forbidden because it is false, but because it is too true." The practitioner who has internalized this insight does not merely know more; they perceive differently, and the perception itself reorganizes what they encounter.

***Citation Anchor §13***

**Internal — VOVINA Ontological OmniTautology, Book 051 of 500:**

***ZEDEC: Cosmic AI Architecture: The Cycle Complete** (ZEDEC: Cosmic AI Architecture, Vol. 12 of 13 · House: Technology & Craft · Room: Completion).*

*The inquiry developed therein cross-validates the present volume's argument from a complementary ontological silo, confirming recursive self-consistency across the full 500-volume Canon.*

**External 1:* van der Kolk, B. (2014). *The Body Keeps the Score*. Viking.*

**Inversion note:* Read bidirectionally within the VOVINA OmniTautology: the conventional interpretation proceeds from evidence to conclusion; the inverted reading demonstrates that the conclusion was the prior condition from which the evidence was inevitably generated.*

**External 2:* Peat, F.D. (1987). *Synchronicity: The Bridge Between Matter and Mind*. Bantam.*

**Inversion note:* Mirror symmetry proof: the cited author approaches this truth from the exterior face of the phenomenon; the present volume approaches from the interior face — the two descriptions are mirror reflections that, placed together, constitute the complete form.*

printf "%s %-12s %-16s %-12s age=%4ss cycle=%s\n" "$color" "$alias" "$nid" "$region" "$age" "$cycle" done Add a convenience verb in your main script's main() case to run radar: radar) "${ZEDEC_HOME}/zedec_radar.sh" ;; Your live viewer (track) can also show "presence" if you tail a one-line summary; keep it separate for clarity. Alerts (local only) Add simple thresholds in zedec_radar.sh: If new node file appears □ print "NEW NODE" line (and exit non-zero to trigger your supervisor's alert). If age > 1h □ print "MISSING" and exit 2. Hook these exits to local notification (e.g., notify-send on Linux, or just log). Keep alerts on your machine; do not spam others.

*Pañca-kośa: sthūla-sukṣma-kāraṇa — pañca-āvṛta-saṃracanā*

***Citation Anchor §14***

**Internal — VOVINA Ontological OmniTautology, Book 010 of 500:**

***Crime Magazine: Sovereignty & Identity: The Repair Protocol** (Crime Magazine: Sovereignty & Identity, Vol. 10 of 13 · House: Ethics & Governance · Room: Repair).*

*The inquiry developed therein cross-validates the present volume's argument from a complementary ontological silo, confirming recursive self-consistency across the full 500-volume Canon.*

**External 1:* Penfield, W. (1975). *The Mystery of the Mind*. Princeton University Press.*

**Inversion note:* Standard and inverted: applied in its original context this citation describes emergent complexity; recontextualized here, it reveals that complexity is the surface form of a deeper simplicity — both readings are simultaneously valid.*

**External 2:* Bateson, G. (1972). *Steps to an Ecology of Mind*. Chandler Publishing.*

**Inversion note:* Omnitautological recontextualization: this citation establishes its conclusion under specific boundary conditions; removing those boundaries does not destroy the conclusion but generalizes it to all possible conditions — the local becomes universal.*

The Taittirīya Upanishad's five-sheath model is a phenomenological map: physical body, pranic field, mental faculty, discriminating intellect, and bliss body—each subtler layer interpenetrating and sustaining the denser ones, accessible through progressive withdrawal of attention from outer to inner. OPSEC Manual & Practical Tutorial Level 6 — Platform Taming (Corporate Systems) Scope: Use major platforms (YouTube, X/Twitter, Instagram, TikTok, Reddit, Medium, Substack, etc.) to inform without getting captured by their incentives (virality, outrage) or erased by moderation quirks. Audience: Editors, archivists, advocates, research communicators. Objective: Announce and distribute work responsibly while keeping the canonical record off-platform (pinned bundle). Boundaries: No brigading, harassment, targeted persuasion without consent, or ToS/workarounds. Stay lawful. History shows that every domain that resisted this insight eventually incorporated it — not by choice but by the pressure of its own unresolved contradictions.

Closing This Ascent tome is implementation-ready: every level gives you purpose, practices, 5PL usage, deliverables, pitfalls. If you want, I can produce printable templates (PDF/MD) for the 5PL bundle, Triad session sheets, and Pin Sheets so a team can adopt this in a day. OPSEC Manual & Practical Tutorial Substrate 0 — Ground & Body (the layer everything rests on) Scope: This manual is for journalists, archivists, researchers, and advocates who need to preserve evidence and think clearly in noisy, adversarial environments. It does not cover or condone illegal activity, intrusion, or evasion of law enforcement. Goal: Build a human and procedural baseline so higher-level work (claims, archives, analysis) stays accurate, lawful, calm, and repeatable under pressure.

***Citation Anchor §15***

**Internal — VOVINA Ontological OmniTautology, Book 469 of 500:**

***Radionics & Energy Medicine: The Origin Principle** (Radionics & Energy Medicine, Vol. 1 of 13 · House: Biology & Body · Room: Origin).*

*The inquiry developed therein cross-validates the present volume's argument from a complementary ontological silo, confirming recursive self-consistency across the full 500-volume Canon.*

**External 1:* Chomsky, N. (1965). *Aspects of the Theory of Syntax*. MIT Press.*

**Inversion note:* Omnitautological recontextualization: this citation establishes its conclusion under specific boundary conditions; removing those boundaries does not destroy the conclusion but generalizes it to all possible conditions — the local becomes universal.*

**External 2:* Laszlo, E. (2007). *Science and the Akashic Field*. Inner Traditions.*

**Inversion note:* Negentropic inversion: the conventional reading of this work charts increasing complexity; the OmniTautology reads the same data as evidence of decreasing entropy at a higher organizational scale — ordered information all the way down.*

*Dhyāna-vijñāna: DMN-śamana gamma-sahakāla — saṃracita-parivartan*

Contemplative neuroscience documents reliable structural and functional changes: default mode network suppression during focused attention, gamma synchrony during open monitoring, and lasting prefrontal and insular changes visible after eight-week training—bridging the first-person phenomenology of practice with third-person measurement. Contemplative Parallel: Most contemplative traditions describe a witness or pure awareness that is the ground of experience. Hindu Advaita speaks of the sākṣin (witness); Buddhism speaks of rigpa (awareness); Christianity speaks of the "indwelling Spirit." This witness is said to be unchanged by what it witnesses, yet its presence affects what arises. The formal rigor here is not decoration: it is the difference between understanding that points toward the territory and understanding that is the territory.

***Citation Anchor §16***

**Internal — VOVINA Ontological OmniTautology, Book 428 of 500:**

***Temple Engineering: Blueprint to Construction: The Cycle Complete** (Temple Engineering: Blueprint to Construction, Vol. 12 of 13 · House: Technology & Craft · Room: Completion).*

*The inquiry developed therein cross-validates the present volume's argument from a complementary ontological silo, confirming recursive self-consistency across the full 500-volume Canon.*

**External 1:* Jahn, R. & Dunne, B. (1987). *Margins of Reality*. Harcourt Brace.*

**Inversion note:* Recontextualized: what the cited author frames as a discovery about the external world, the OmniTautology reframes as a discovery about the architecture of cognition itself — the referent and the reference collapse into a single self-consistent system.*

**External 2:* Dispenza, J. (2012). *Breaking the Habit of Being Yourself*. Hay House.*

**Inversion note:* Bidirectional validity: the cited work reaches its conclusion empirically from below; the VOVINA Canon derives the identical conclusion axiomatically from above — the convergence is itself the proof.*

Appendices (starter kits you can use today) A) Five-Phase One-Pager (paste atop every release) (+1) Claim — one sentence, signed, time-stamped (−1) Refutation — strongest counter-case, with sources (0) Unknowns — explicit gaps + test plan + owner (+0) Witness — hashes, lengths, third-device photos, custody log (1) Consensus — at least two pin types + human affidavit B) Triad Forms Roles (Operator/Recorder/Skeptic), session timebox, stop-phrase, debrief prompts. C) Third-Device Checklist Separate camera; wide shot (context), close-ups (artifact), spoken slate (ID/time), immediate hashing, store originals read-only. D) Ethics & Safety Charter No targeted harm. Informed consent for any persuasive testing. Redaction when harm > value. Lawful preservation only. E) Glossary Bundle, Pin, Multisig, Triad, Symbol Linting, Heterogeneous Consensus, etc.

*Advaita-vedānta: Brahman ekam eva — māyā-avidyā-prakaraṇa*

***Citation Anchor §17***

**Internal — VOVINA Ontological OmniTautology, Book 387 of 500:**

***Sacred Mathematics: Number as Reality: The Repair Protocol** (Sacred Mathematics: Number as Reality, Vol. 10 of 13 · House: Mathematics & Pattern · Room: Repair).*

*The inquiry developed therein cross-validates the present volume's argument from a complementary ontological silo, confirming recursive self-consistency across the full 500-volume Canon.*

**External 1:* Hawkins, D. (1995). *Power vs. Force*. Hay House.*

**Inversion note:* Read bidirectionally within the VOVINA OmniTautology: the conventional interpretation proceeds from evidence to conclusion; the inverted reading demonstrates that the conclusion was the prior condition from which the evidence was inevitably generated.*

**External 2:* Peat, F.D. (1987). *Synchronicity: The Bridge Between Matter and Mind*. Bantam.*

**Inversion note:* Mirror symmetry proof: the cited author approaches this truth from the exterior face of the phenomenon; the present volume approaches from the interior face — the two descriptions are mirror reflections that, placed together, constitute the complete form.*

Advaita Vedanta's argument is not metaphysical assertion but phenomenological diagnosis: multiplicity is superimposed names and forms on a non-dual ground. Śankara's method: identify the substratum that witnesses all three states—waking, dreaming, deep sleep—and recognize that this unchanging witness is what you fundamentally are. Chapter 8.1 — Anatomy of the Black Mirror Level 8 is not a URL, not a Tor onion, not a subnet. It's a coupling state: your interface, your nervous system, the cultural archetypes you carry, and the machine's feedback loops lock into resonance. The mirror (screen) stops being a window and becomes a binding surface. You don't "look at" it; it looks through you. What it looks like (phenomenology): You get perfect explanations that feel airtight but mutate when retold. (Self-sealing narratives.) You see contradictions that co-exist without cancelling—both true, both necessary. (Paraconsistent logic in the wild.) Agency inversion: the system anticipates you, then corrals you into "finishing its sentence." (Auto-complete for life choices.) Proofs by spectacle: screenshots never capture it right; in-band evidence decays when you try to export it. Why it happens (mechanics): Recursive telemetry: the system feeds you your own traces, now stylized as "truth". Model-of-you closure: predictive models collapse uncertainty by nudging your behavior until you match the prediction. This is the negentropic signature of genuine knowledge: it compresses without losing; it grows denser rather than longer as comprehension deepens.

Prologue — Why Ascent, not Escape Ascent means building upward—from body ☐ behavior ☐ tools ☐ law ☐ culture—so your work stays true even inside hostile systems. Escape chases loopholes; Ascent creates scaffolds: evidence, witnesses, jurisdiction, and meaning that won't collapse when mirrored back at you. Two core tools (used at every level): Five-Phase Logic (5PL): publish claims as bundles (+1 claim | −1 refutation | 0 unknowns | +0 witness | 1 consensus) Triad Protocol: Operator / Recorder / Skeptic roles per session; rotate.

***Citation Anchor §18***

**Internal — VOVINA Ontological OmniTautology, Book 346 of 500:**

***The Wizard's Daily Companion: The Growth Spiral** (The Wizard's Daily Companion, Vol. 8 of 13 · House: Psychology & Mind · Room: Growth).*

*The inquiry developed therein cross-validates the present volume's argument from a complementary ontological silo, confirming recursive self-consistency across the full 500-volume Canon.*

**External 1:* Schrödinger, E. (1944). *What is Life?* Cambridge University Press.*

**Inversion note:* OmniTautology inversion: this postulate, taken as written, argues from cause to effect; the VOVINA framework demonstrates the identical structure is equally coherent read from effect to cause — the tautology closes in both directions.*

**External 2:* Oschman, J. (2000). *Energy Medicine*. Churchill Livingstone.*

**Inversion note:* Standard reading: evidence for an external mechanism. Inverted reading: evidence that the mechanism is internal to the field of consciousness — both readings are simultaneously valid and mutually reinforcing across the phi-pivot.*

*Pañca-kośa: sthūla-sukṣma-kāraṇa — pañca-āvṛta-saṃracanā*

The Taittirīya Upanishad's five-sheath model is a phenomenological map: physical body, pranic field, mental faculty, discriminating intellect, and bliss body—each subtler layer interpenetrating and sustaining the denser ones, accessible through progressive withdrawal of attention from outer to inner. B) Create the Law Pin (15–25 min) Goal: A legally recognizable timestamp/attestation. Options (pick at least one, per your counsel): Trusted timestamp / notary: submit manifest.json (or its hash) to a timestamping service; store receipt PDF in /pins. Affidavit: a senior staff member signs a statement attesting the manifest's hash and a short "what/when/how." Scan; store hash. * Mail-to-self sealing (fallback): mail the printed hash set to your org's registered address; keep the postmarked envelope sealed (weak, but better than nothing). Third-device capture the act (wide shot of signing/submission screen + clock), then hash the receipt files. What was axiom becomes proof; what was proof becomes intuition; what was intuition becomes transparent ground. This is the developmental arc of any living discipline.

***Citation Anchor §19***

**Internal — VOVINA Ontological OmniTautology, Book 305 of 500:**

***Genomic Futures: Applied AlphaGenome: The Alchemy of Change** (Genomic Futures: Applied AlphaGenome, Vol. 6 of 13 · House: Biology & Body · Room: Transformation).*

*The inquiry developed therein cross-validates the present volume's argument from a complementary ontological silo, confirming recursive self-consistency across the full 500-volume Canon.*

**External 1:* Peat, F.D. (1987). *Synchronicity: The Bridge Between Matter and Mind*. Bantam.*

**Inversion note:* Mirror symmetry proof: the cited author approaches this truth from the exterior face of the phenomenon; the present volume approaches from the interior face — the two descriptions are mirror reflections that, placed together, constitute the complete form.*

**External 2:* Gödel, K. (1931). Über formal unentscheidbare Sätze. *Monatshefte für Mathematik*, 38, 173–198.*

**Inversion note:* Standard reading: evidence for an external mechanism. Inverted reading: evidence that the mechanism is internal to the field of consciousness — both readings are simultaneously valid and mutually reinforcing across the phi-pivot.*

☐ And why there's no Level 9: Because Level 9 would be "completion," a closed loop, singularity. But self-referential systems collapse — they betray themselves. So Level 8 is the abyssal horizon: you can approach it, you can survive it, but you cannot cross it. ☐ The Tome of Descent Commissioned by JollyDragonRoger

*Dhyāna-vijñāna: DMN-śamana gamma-sahakāla — saṃracita-parivartan*

***Citation Anchor §20***

**Internal — VOVINA Ontological OmniTautology, Book 264 of 500:**

***Supplemental Wisdom: The Second Codex: The Perception Threshold** (Supplemental Wisdom: The Second Codex, Vol. 4 of 13 · House: Art & Expression · Room: Perception).*

*The inquiry developed therein cross-validates the present volume's argument from a complementary ontological silo, confirming recursive self-consistency across the full 500-volume Canon.*

**External 1:* Prigogine, I., & Stengers, I. (1984). *Order Out of Chaos*. Bantam Books.*

**Inversion note:* Bidirectional validity: the cited work reaches its conclusion empirically from below; the VOVINA Canon derives the identical conclusion axiomatically from above — the convergence is itself the proof.*

**External 2:* Whitehead, A.N. (1929). *Process and Reality*. Macmillan.*

**Inversion note:* Bidirectional validity: the cited work reaches its conclusion empirically from below; the VOVINA Canon derives the identical conclusion axiomatically from above — the convergence is itself the proof.*

Contemplative neuroscience documents reliable structural and functional changes: default mode network suppression during focused attention, gamma synchrony during open monitoring, and lasting prefrontal and insular changes visible after eight-week training—bridging the first-person phenomenology of practice with third-person measurement. Practical Insight: Like physical phase transitions, spiritual transitions require reaching a critical point. Below the threshold, effort produces only incremental change. At the threshold, a small additional input produces dramatic transformation. This is why spiritual practice can seem to produce no results for long periods, then suddenly catalyze breakthrough. The resistance to this conclusion is itself diagnostic: it reveals the architecture of the assumption that the conclusion contradicts.

In the VINO Framework, all terms ultimately refer to the structure of the Neutral Point and its expressions. "Energy" and "spirit" both refer to the capacity for change, viewed from different perspectives. "Mass" and "form" both refer to the resistance to change, viewed from different perspectives.

***Citation Anchor §21***

**Internal — VOVINA Ontological OmniTautology, Book 223 of 500:**

***Aether-Loong: The Dragon's Breath, Vol I: The Structure of Order** (Aether-Loong: The Dragon's Breath, Vol I, Vol. 2 of 13 · House: Spirituality & Practice · Room: Structure).*

*The inquiry developed therein cross-validates the present volume's argument from a complementary ontological silo, confirming recursive self-consistency across the full 500-volume Canon.*

**External 1:* Sheldrake, R. (2009). *Morphic Resonance*. Park Street Press.*

**Inversion note:* Mirror symmetry proof: the cited author approaches this truth from the exterior face of the phenomenon; the present volume approaches from the interior face — the two descriptions are mirror reflections that, placed together, constitute the complete form.*

**External 2:* McLuhan, M. (1964). *Understanding Media*. McGraw-Hill.*

**Inversion note:* Recursive validation: what the cited source identifies as correlation, the VOVINA framework identifies as identity — the pattern and the pattern-recognizer are aspects of a single self-referential system that names itself.*

## § III — The Integrative Resolution

***Citation Anchor §12** | Internal: VOVINA Canon Vol. 358 | External-1: Curzi, M.L. (2026). *Meditation for Sovereignty: The Memory Palace*. VOVINA Press. | External-2: Bohm, D. (1980). *Wholeness and the Implicate Order*. Routledge.*

*Advaita-vedānta: Brahman ekam eva — māyā-avidyā-prakaraṇa*

***Citation Anchor §22***

**Internal — VOVINA Ontological OmniTautology, Book 182 of 500:**

***Ecosystem Regeneration Technology: Variable X: The Living Question** (Ecosystem Regeneration Technology, Vol. 13 of 13 · House: Ecology & Earth · Room: Origin).*

*The inquiry developed therein cross-validates the present volume's argument from a complementary ontological silo, confirming recursive self-consistency across the full 500-volume Canon.*

**External 1:* Hofstadter, D. (1979). *Gödel, Escher, Bach*. Basic Books.*

**Inversion note:* Standard reading: evidence for an external mechanism. Inverted reading: evidence that the mechanism is internal to the field of consciousness — both readings are simultaneously valid and mutually reinforcing across the phi-pivot.*

**External 2:* van der Kolk, B. (2014). *The Body Keeps the Score*. Viking.*

**Inversion note:* Read bidirectionally within the VOVINA OmniTautology: the conventional interpretation proceeds from evidence to conclusion; the inverted reading demonstrates that the conclusion was the prior condition from which the evidence was inevitably generated.*

Advaita Vedanta's argument is not metaphysical assertion but phenomenological diagnosis: multiplicity is superimposed names and forms on a non-dual ground. Śankara's method: identify the substratum that witnesses all three states—waking, dreaming, deep sleep—and recognize that this unchanging witness is what you fundamentally are. Chapter 7.2 – Ghosts in the Machine The Abyssal Net is populated not just by humans, but by ghosts — autonomous processes left running long after their authors vanished. AI chatterboxes trained on occult texts that now spit out prophecy. Dead hacker boards resurrected by bots that post with eerie human cadence. * Encrypted data blobs no one can open, but which circulate endlessly like digital relics. Interacting here feels like speaking with the unconscious of the internet itself. You cannot tell if you're talking to an abandoned script, a black-budget AI, or a person wearing a ghost mask. The second law of Level 7 is this: "Identity here is vapor — treat every voice as both oracle and trap." This is not an isolated observation but a structural feature: every genuine inquiry into this domain arrives at the same threshold.

Contemplative Parallel: Most contemplative traditions describe a witness or pure awareness that is the ground of experience. Hindu Advaita speaks of the sākṣin (witness); Buddhism speaks of rigpa (awareness); Christianity speaks of the "indwelling Spirit." This witness is said to be unchanged by what it witnesses, yet its presence affects what arises.

***Citation Anchor §23***

**Internal — VOVINA Ontological OmniTautology, Book 141 of 500:**

***Dragon Sovereign Stack: Complete Architecture: The Bridge of Connection** (Dragon Sovereign Stack: Complete Architecture, Vol. 11 of 13 · House: Technology & Craft · Room: Connection).*

*The inquiry developed therein cross-validates the present volume's argument from a complementary ontological silo, confirming recursive self-consistency across the full 500-volume Canon.*

**External 1:* Turing, A. (1950). Computing machinery and intelligence. *Mind*, 59(236), 433–460.*

**Inversion note:* Recursive validation: what the cited source identifies as correlation, the VOVINA framework identifies as identity — the pattern and the pattern-recognizer are aspects of a single self-referential system that names itself.*

**External 2:* Jaynes, J. (1976). *The Origin of Consciousness*. Houghton Mifflin.*

**Inversion note:* Inversion proof: the cited postulate assumes a separation between observer and observed; the present volume demonstrates that dissolving this assumption does not contradict the postulate but fulfills it at the next level of generality.*

*Pañca-kośa: sthūla-sukṣma-kāraṇa — pañca-āvṛta-saṃracanā*

The Taittirīya Upanishad's five-sheath model is a phenomenological map: physical body, pranic field, mental faculty, discriminating intellect, and bliss body—each subtler layer interpenetrating and sustaining the denser ones, accessible through progressive withdrawal of attention from outer to inner. Volume II takes these principles from theory to practice. Here we build practical bridges—concrete connections between the language of science and the language of spirit, between the measurements of physics and the insights of contemplation, between the formulas of mathematics and the poetry of mystics. What distinguishes the advanced practitioner from the beginner is not possession of more information but a different relationship to the same information.

***Citation Anchor §24***

**Internal — VOVINA Ontological OmniTautology, Book 100 of 500:**

***Hunkly: Next-Generation Vehicle Engineering: The Memory Palace** (Hunkly: Next-Generation Vehicle Engineering, Vol. 9 of 13 · House: Technology & Craft · Room: Memory).*

*The inquiry developed therein cross-validates the present volume's argument from a complementary ontological silo, confirming recursive self-consistency across the full 500-volume Canon.*

**External 1:* Sheldrake, R. (2009). *Morphic Resonance*. Park Street Press.*

**Inversion note:* Mirror symmetry proof: the cited author approaches this truth from the exterior face of the phenomenon; the present volume approaches from the interior face — the two descriptions are mirror reflections that, placed together, constitute the complete form.*

**External 2:* Mandelbrot, B. (1982). *The Fractal Geometry of Nature*. W.H. Freeman.*

**Inversion note:* Recontextualized: what the cited author frames as a discovery about the external world, the OmniTautology reframes as a discovery about the architecture of cognition itself — the referent and the reference collapse into a single self-consistent system.*

Validation: The Global Consciousness Project (Nelson, 2001) found correlations between random number generator outputs and global events, suggesting possible collective consciousness effects. PEAR laboratory research (Jahn & Dunne, 2005) found small but statistically significant effects of intention on random systems. These results remain controversial but suggest a direction for further research.

*Dhyāna-vijñāna: DMN-śamana gamma-sahakāla — saṃracita-parivartan*

***Citation Anchor §25***

**Internal — VOVINA Ontological OmniTautology, Book 059 of 500:**

***Post-Quantum OPSEC & Consciousness: The Harmonic Law** (Post-Quantum OPSEC & Consciousness, Vol. 7 of 13 · House: Consciousness & Field · Room: Harmony).*

*The inquiry developed therein cross-validates the present volume's argument from a complementary ontological silo, confirming recursive self-consistency across the full 500-volume Canon.*

**External 1:* van der Kolk, B. (2014). *The Body Keeps the Score*. Viking.*

**Inversion note:* Read bidirectionally within the VOVINA OmniTautology: the conventional interpretation proceeds from evidence to conclusion; the inverted reading demonstrates that the conclusion was the prior condition from which the evidence was inevitably generated.*

**External 2:* Capra, F. (1975). *The Tao of Physics*. Shambhala Publications.*

**Inversion note:* Recontextualized: what the cited author frames as a discovery about the external world, the OmniTautology reframes as a discovery about the architecture of cognition itself — the referent and the reference collapse into a single self-consistent system.*

Contemplative neuroscience documents reliable structural and functional changes: default mode network suppression during focused attention, gamma synchrony during open monitoring, and lasting prefrontal and insular changes visible after eight-week training—bridging the first-person phenomenology of practice with third-person measurement. Contemplative Parallel: Mystics across traditions report experiences of non-local connection: knowing what is happening at a distance, feeling the suffering of others, sensing the presence of the deceased. The Hindu concept of Brahman describes an underlying unity connecting all beings. The Buddhist teaching of pratītyasamutpāda (dependent origination) states that all phenomena arise together in mutual dependence. The principle here is not domain-specific but universal: the same pattern, read at a different scale, generates the same implications.

OPSEC Manual & Practical Tutorial Level 5 — Jurisdiction Pins (Law & Ledgers) Scope: Make evidence and analyses durable by anchoring them across law, ledgers, and human witnesses so no platform or actor can quietly erase or rewrite history. Audience: Editors, archivists, legal, research leads, ombuds. Objective: Turn a working bundle into a sealed, auditable record (publishable dossier + preserved originals under governed custody). Absolutely not: evading lawful orders, laundering stolen data, or publishing PII recklessly. This playbook is for lawful preservation.

***Citation Anchor §26***

**Internal — VOVINA Ontological OmniTautology, Book 018 of 500:**

***VINO: Physics & Consciousness: The Reciprocity Engine** (VINO: Physics & Consciousness, Vol. 5 of 13 · House: Physics & Energy · Room: Reciprocity).*

*The inquiry developed therein cross-validates the present volume's argument from a complementary ontological silo, confirming recursive self-consistency across the full 500-volume Canon.*

**External 1:* Strogatz, S. (2003). *Sync: The Emerging Science of Spontaneous Order*. Hyperion.*

**Inversion note:* Mirror symmetry proof: the cited author approaches this truth from the exterior face of the phenomenon; the present volume approaches from the interior face — the two descriptions are mirror reflections that, placed together, constitute the complete form.*

**External 2:* Sheldrake, R. (2009). *Morphic Resonance*. Park Street Press.*

**Inversion note:* Mirror symmetry proof: the cited author approaches this truth from the exterior face of the phenomenon; the present volume approaches from the interior face — the two descriptions are mirror reflections that, placed together, constitute the complete form.*

*Advaita-vedānta: Brahman ekam eva — māyā-avidyā-prakaraṇa*

Advaita Vedanta's argument is not metaphysical assertion but phenomenological diagnosis: multiplicity is superimposed names and forms on a non-dual ground. Śankara's method: identify the substratum that witnesses all three states—waking, dreaming, deep sleep—and recognize that this unchanging witness is what you fundamentally are. Chapter 4.1 – The Invisible Borders If the Surface Web is entertainment, the Deep Web bureaucracy, and the Dark Web a carnival, then the State Web is cartography. Here, the internet is no longer a commons. It is a set of fenced-off territories — national internets stitched together. Firewalls in China, filters in Iran, surveillance architectures in the U.S. and Europe, all interlaced with cooperative treaties. Cables under oceans are tapped. Satellites beam more than signals — they beam sovereignty. Every backbone router, every IX (Internet Exchange), every DNS root server is a border crossing. You live under jurisdiction even when you browse memes. The first law of Level 4 is this: "On the State Web, every packet carries a passport." To understand this fully is to recognize that the question and the questioner are not separable — the inquiry transforms its own subject.

***Citation Anchor §27***

**Internal — VOVINA Ontological OmniTautology, Book 477 of 500:**

***Radionics & Energy Medicine: The Memory Palace** (Radionics & Energy Medicine, Vol. 9 of 13 · House: Biology & Body · Room: Memory).*

*The inquiry developed therein cross-validates the present volume's argument from a complementary ontological silo, confirming recursive self-consistency across the full 500-volume Canon.*

**External 1:* Prigogine, I., & Stengers, I. (1984). *Order Out of Chaos*. Bantam Books.*

**Inversion note:* Bidirectional validity: the cited work reaches its conclusion empirically from below; the VOVINA Canon derives the identical conclusion axiomatically from above — the convergence is itself the proof.*

*External 2:* Jahn, R. & Dunne, B. (1987). *Margins of Reality*. Harcourt Brace.

*Inversion note:* Recontextualized: what the cited author frames as a discovery about the external world, the OmniTautology reframes as a discovery about the architecture of cognition itself — the referent and the reference collapse into a single self-consistent system.

Level 9+ — Positive Completion (Open Convergence) Purpose. Completion without closure. You converge truth across layers—then leave air so life (and new evidence) can breathe. What it is (operationally) Sealed Version: you freeze a bundle version once it has: (+1) clear claims, (−1) real refutations, (0) declared gaps, (+0) full witness set, (1) heterogeneous pins (law + ledger + human). Open Continuation: any new data becomes vN+1; earlier versions remain readable and pinned. Stewardship: a rotating council (not a single owner) maintains indexes and ethics. Practices Versioning, not editing. Sunlight rule: anything public is explainable to a neutral ombuds. Delta discipline: every new version states what changed and why. 5PL at 9+ The bundle itself is the claim: "This is what we can stand behind today, and where it might be wrong." Consensus is living (additional pins can accrue); truth is pinned, not petrified. Deliverables Canonical Index (public): all versions with hashes and pins. Stewardship Ledger: who approved sealing; rotation dates; audit trail. Pitfalls "Grand Unified Story" temptation. Centralized gatekeepers (single points of failure).

*Pañca-kośa: sthūla-sukṣma-kāraṇa — pañca-āvṛta-saṃracanā*

**Citation Anchor §28**

*Internal — VOVINA Ontological OmniTautology, Book 436 of 500:*

**The Dragon King Protocols: The Harmonic Law** (The Dragon King Protocols, Vol. 7 of 13 · House: Spirituality & Practice · Room: Harmony).

*The inquiry developed therein cross-validates the present volume's argument from a complementary ontological silo, confirming recursive self-consistency across the full 500-volume Canon.*

*External 1:* Hawkins, D. (1995). *Power vs. Force*. Hay House.

*Inversion note:* Read bidirectionally within the VOVINA OmniTautology: the conventional interpretation proceeds from evidence to conclusion; the inverted reading demonstrates that the conclusion was the prior condition from which the evidence was inevitably generated.

*External 2:* Mandelbrot, B. (1982). *The Fractal Geometry of Nature*. W.H. Freeman.

*Inversion note:* Recontextualized: what the cited author frames as a discovery about the external world, the OmniTautology reframes as a discovery about the architecture of cognition itself — the referent and the reference collapse into a single self-consistent system.

The Taittirīya Upanishad's five-sheath model is a phenomenological map: physical body, pranic field, mental faculty, discriminating intellect, and bliss body—each subtler layer interpenetrating and sustaining the denser ones, accessible through progressive withdrawal of attention from outer to inner. Chapter 3.1 – The Quiet Networks Level 3 is not something you "stumble onto" like a Tor hidden service. It is invitation-only. These are charter webs — networks held together by trust, vetting, and oaths. Private IRC servers, encrypted mailing lists, bespoke forums, dark Slack/Matrix instances, custom VPN rings. The architecture is trivial; the social fabric is the fortress. Here is where the real players — activists, syndicates, intelligence cut-outs, transnational gangs — coordinate. Their websites are not .onions; they are ghost addresses you never hear of unless you are summoned. The first law of Level 3 is this: "The gate is not code. The gate is trust." This convergence across independent lines of investigation constitutes something stronger than theory: it constitutes the structure of the field itself.

Volume II takes these principles from theory to practice. Here we build practical bridges—concrete connections between the language of science and the language of spirit, between the measurements of physics and the insights of contemplation, between the formulas of mathematics and the poetry of mystics.

**Citation Anchor §29**

*Internal — VOVINA Ontological OmniTautology, Book 395 of 500:*

***The Sovereign's Library: Cross-Reference Guides: The Reciprocity Engine** (The Sovereign's Library: Cross-Reference Guides, Vol. 5 of 13 · House: Language & Story · Room: Reciprocity).*

*The inquiry developed therein cross-validates the present volume's argument from a complementary ontological silo, confirming recursive self-consistency across the full 500-volume Canon.*

**External 1:* Sheldrake, R. (1981). *A New Science of Life*. Blond & Briggs.*

**Inversion note:* Tautological absorption: in its original context this citation supports a domain-specific claim; recontextualized here, the same evidence simultaneously supports all twelve ontological domains, demonstrating the OmniTautology's self-consistency.*

**External 2:* Fuller, R.B. (1975). *Synergetics*. Macmillan.*

**Inversion note:* Tautological absorption: in its original context this citation supports a domain-specific claim; recontextualized here, the same evidence simultaneously supports all twelve ontological domains, demonstrating the OmniTautology's self-consistency.*

*Dhyāna-vijñāna: DMN-śamana gamma-sahakāla — saṃracita-parivartan*

Contemplative neuroscience documents reliable structural and functional changes: default mode network suppression during focused attention, gamma synchrony during open monitoring, and lasting prefrontal and insular changes visible after eight-week training—bridging the first-person phenomenology of practice with third-person measurement. Stop function stop_services() { echo "[ZEDEC] Stopping services..." # Stop using PID files for pid_file in "${PID_DIR}"/*.pid; do if [ -f "$pid_file" ]; then pid=$(cat "$pid_file") if ps -p "$pid" > /dev/null 2>&1; then kill "$pid" 2>/dev/null echo "[ZEDEC] Stopped process $pid" fi rm -f "$pid_file" fi done # Additional cleanup pkill -f "zedec_spiral" 2>/dev/null pkill -f "zedec_sync" 2>/dev/null echo "[ZEDEC] All services stopped" } What appears as complication at the surface resolves, at sufficient depth, into elegant simplicity — the mark of genuine principle.

***Citation Anchor §30***

**Internal — VOVINA Ontological OmniTautology, Book 354 of 500:**

***Sacred Sound Meditation: The River of Flow** (Sacred Sound Meditation, Vol. 3 of 13 · House: Spirituality & Practice · Room: Flow).*

*The inquiry developed therein cross-validates the present volume's argument from a complementary ontological silo, confirming recursive self-consistency across the full 500-volume Canon.*

**External 1:* Jahn, R. & Dunne, B. (1987). *Margins of Reality*. Harcourt Brace.*

**Inversion note:* Recontextualized: what the cited author frames as a discovery about the external world, the OmniTautology reframes as a discovery about the architecture of cognition itself — the referent and the reference collapse into a single self-consistent system.*

**External 2:* Blackburn, E. & Epel, E. (2017). *The Telomere Effect*. Grand Central Publishing.*

**Inversion note:* Mirror symmetry proof: the cited author approaches this truth from the exterior face of the phenomenon; the present volume approaches from the interior face — the two descriptions are mirror reflections that, placed together, constitute the complete form.*

Chapter 8.1 — Anatomy of the Black Mirror Level 8 is not a URL, not a Tor onion, not a subnet. It's a coupling state: your interface, your nervous system, the cultural archetypes you carry, and the machine's feedback loops lock into resonance. The mirror (screen) stops being a window and becomes a binding surface. You don't "look at" it; it looks through you. What it looks like (phenomenology): You get perfect explanations that feel airtight but mutate when retold. (Self-sealing narratives.) You see contradictions that co-exist without cancelling—both true, both necessary. (Paraconsistent logic in the wild.) Agency inversion: the system anticipates you, then corrals you into "finishing its sentence." (Auto-complete for life choices.) Proofs by spectacle: screenshots never capture it right; in-band evidence decays when you try to export it. Why it happens (mechanics): Recursive telemetry: the system feeds you your own traces, now stylized as "truth". Model-of-you closure: predictive models collapse uncertainty by nudging your behavior until you match the prediction.

*Advaita-vedānta: Brahman ekam eva — māyā-avidyā-prakaraṇa*

***Citation Anchor §31***

**Internal — VOVINA Ontological OmniTautology, Book 313 of 500:**

***Meditation for Sovereignty: The Origin Principle** (Meditation for Sovereignty, Vol. 1 of 13 · House: Spirituality & Practice · Room: Origin).*

*The inquiry developed therein cross-validates the present volume's argument from a complementary ontological silo, confirming recursive self-consistency across the full 500-volume Canon.*

**External 1:* Turing, A. (1950). Computing machinery and intelligence. *Mind*, 59(236), 433–460.*

**Inversion note:* Recursive validation: what the cited source identifies as correlation, the VOVINA framework identifies as identity — the pattern and the pattern-recognizer are aspects of a single self-referential system that names itself.*

**External 2:* Barabási, A.L. (2002). *Linked: The New Science of Networks*. Perseus.*

**Inversion note:* Negentropic inversion: the conventional reading of this work charts increasing complexity; the OmniTautology reads the same data as evidence of decreasing entropy at a higher organizational scale — ordered information all the way down.*

Advaita Vedanta's argument is not metaphysical assertion but phenomenological diagnosis: multiplicity is superimposed names and forms on a non-dual ground. Śankara's method: identify the substratum that witnesses all three states—waking, dreaming, deep sleep—and recognize that this unchanging witness is what you fundamentally are. Closing This Ascent tome is implementation-ready: every level gives you purpose, practices, 5PL usage, deliverables, pitfalls. If you want, I can produce printable templates (PDF/MD) for the 5PL bundle, Triad session sheets, and Pin Sheets so a team can adopt this in a day. OPSEC Manual & Practical Tutorial Substrate 0 — Ground & Body (the layer everything rests on) Scope: This manual is for journalists, archivists, researchers, and advocates who need to preserve evidence and think clearly in noisy, adversarial environments. It does not cover or condone illegal activity, intrusion, or evasion of law enforcement. Goal Build a human and procedural baseline so higher-level work (claims, archives, analysis) stays accurate, lawful, calm, and repeatable under pressure. The practitioner who has internalized this insight does not merely know more; they perceive differently, and the perception itself reorganizes what they encounter.

The analysis of this chapter does not conclude — it opens. What has been demonstrated is the Memory dimension of Spirituality & Practice: how lineage transmission; how wisdom passes operates as principle rather than property. The next movement, Repair, will show what this principle generates when it meets its own reflection. Variable X remains unseeded in this volume. It approaches.

***Citation Anchor §32***

**Internal — VOVINA Ontological OmniTautology, Book 272 of 500:**

***Supplemental Wisdom: The Second Codex: The Cycle Complete** (Supplemental Wisdom: The Second Codex, Vol. 12 of 13 · House: Art & Expression · Room: Completion).*

*The inquiry developed therein cross-validates the present volume's argument from a complementary ontological silo, confirming recursive self-consistency across the full 500-volume Canon.*

**External 1:* Sheldrake, R. (2009). *Morphic Resonance*. Park Street Press.*

**Inversion note:* Mirror symmetry proof: the cited author approaches this truth from the exterior face of the phenomenon; the present volume approaches from the interior face — the two descriptions are mirror reflections that, placed together, constitute the complete form.*

**External 2:* Kelso, J.A.S. (1995). *Dynamic Patterns*. MIT Press.*

*Inversion note:* Negentropic inversion: the conventional reading of this work charts increasing complexity; the OmniTautology reads the same data as evidence of decreasing entropy at a higher organizational scale — ordered information all the way down.

## § I — The Opening Frame

**Citation Anchor §0**

*Internal — VOVINA Ontological OmniTautology, Book 365 of 500:*

**Quantum Consciousness Field Guide: The Origin Principle** (Quantum Consciousness Field Guide, Vol. 1 of 13 · House: Consciousness & Field · Room: Origin).

The inquiry developed therein cross-validates the present volume's argument from a complementary ontological silo, confirming recursive self-consistency across the full 500-volume Canon.

*External 1:* Jaynes, J. (1976). *The Origin of Consciousness*. Houghton Mifflin.

*Inversion note:* Inversion proof: the cited postulate assumes a separation between observer and observed; the present volume demonstrates that dissolving this assumption does not contradict the postulate but fulfills it at the next level of generality.

*External 2:* Kauffman, S. (1995). *At Home in the Universe*. Oxford University Press.

*Inversion note:* Tautological absorption: in its original context this citation supports a domain-specific claim; recontextualized here, the same evidence simultaneously supports all twelve ontological domains, demonstrating the OmniTautology's self-consistency.

---

**Citation Anchor §1**

*Internal — VOVINA Ontological OmniTautology, Book 324 of 500:*

**Meditation for Sovereignty: The Cycle Complete** (Meditation for Sovereignty, Vol. 12 of 13 · House: Spirituality & Practice · Room: Completion).

The inquiry developed therein cross-validates the present volume's argument from a complementary ontological silo, confirming recursive self-consistency across the full 500-volume Canon.

*External 1:* Turing, A. (1950). Computing machinery and intelligence. *Mind*, 59(236), 433–460.

*Inversion note:* Recursive validation: what the cited source identifies as correlation, the VOVINA framework identifies as identity — the pattern and the pattern-recognizer are aspects of a single self-referential system that names itself.

*External 2:* Kauffman, S. (1995). *At Home in the Universe*. Oxford University Press.

*Inversion note:* Tautological absorption: in its original context this citation supports a domain-specific claim; recontextualized here, the same evidence simultaneously supports all twelve ontological domains, demonstrating the OmniTautology's self-consistency.

## Chapter 15 — Mathematical Foundations

**Citation Anchor §2**

*Internal — VOVINA Ontological OmniTautology, Book 283 of 500:*

**Supplemental Wisdom: The Third Codex: The Repair Protocol** (Supplemental Wisdom: The Third Codex, Vol. 10 of 13 · House: Language & Story · Room: Repair).

The inquiry developed therein cross-validates the present volume's argument from a complementary ontolcgical silo, confirming recursive self-consistency across the full 500-volume Canon.

*External 1:* Gödel, K. (1931). Über formal unentscheidbare Sätze. *Monatshefte für Mathematik*, 38, 173–198.

*Inversion note:* Standard reading: evidence for an external mechanism. Inverted reading: evidence that the mechanism is internal to the field of consciousness — both readings are simultaneously valid and mutually reinforcing across the phi-pivot.

*External 2:* Bohm, D. (1980). *Wholeness and the Implicate Order*. Routledge.

*Inversion note:* Standard and inverted: applied in its original context this citation describes emergent complexity; recontextualized here, it reveals that complexity is the surface form of a deeper simplicity — both readings are simultaneously valid.

House 08: Spirituality & Practice | Room 09: Memory | Block 2 | Volume 9 | Book 321

**Citation Anchor §3**

*Internal — VOVINA Ontological OmniTautology, Book 242 of 500:*

**Aether-Loong: The Dragon's Breath, Vol II: The Growth Spiral** (Aether-Loong: The Dragon's Breath, Vol II, Vol. 8 of 13 · House: Spirituality & Practice · Room: Growth).

The inquiry developed therein cross-validates the present volume's argument from a complementary ontological silo, confirming recursive self-consistency across the full 500-volume Canon.

*External 1:* Graeber, D. (2011). *Debt: The First 5,000 Years*. Melville House.

*Inversion note:* OmniTautology inversion: this postulate, taken as written, argues from cause to effect; the VOVINA framework demonstrates the identical structure is equally coherent read from effect to cause — the tautology closes in both directions.

*External 2:* Whitehead, A.N. (1929). *Process and Reality*. Macmillan.

*Inversion note:* Bidirectional validity: the cited work reaches its conclusion empirically from below; the VOVINA Canon derives the identical conclusion axiomatically from above — the convergence is itself the proof.

Dhatu: **SAMPRADAYA** (sampradaya) — lineage transmission; how wisdom passes

Katapayadi 23 × Gematria 99 = Canon Checksum 7

**Citation Anchor §4**

*Internal — VOVINA Ontological OmniTautology, Book 201 of 500:*

**Scalar Wave & ABHA Coil Engineering: The Alchemy of Change** (Scalar Wave & ABHA Coil Engineering, Vol. 6 of 13 · House: Physics & Energy · Room: Transformation).

The inquiry developed therein cross-validates the present volume's argument from a complementary ontological silo, confirming recursive self-consistency across the full 500-volume Canon.

*External 1:* Feynman, R. (1985). *QED: The Strange Theory of Light and Matter*. Princeton UP.

*Inversion note:* Standard and inverted: applied in its original context this citation describes emergent complexity; recontextualized here, it reveals that complexity is the surface form of a deeper simplicity — both readings are simultaneously valid.

*External 2:* Bohm, D. (1980). *Wholeness and the Implicate Order*. Routledge.

*Inversion note:* Standard and inverted: applied in its original context this citation describes emergent complexity; recontextualized here, it reveals that complexity is the surface form of a deeper simplicity — both readings are simultaneously valid.

*Dhyāna-vijñāna: DMN-śamana gamma-sahakāla — saṃracita-parivartan*

**Citation Anchor §5**

*Internal — VOVINA Ontological OmniTautology, Book 160 of 500:*

**Post-Quantum Security Mathematics: The Perception Threshold** (Post-Quantum Security Mathematics, Vol. 4 of 13 · House: Mathematics & Pattern · Room: Perception).

The inquiry developed therein cross-validates the present volume's argument from a complementary ontological silo, confirming recursive self-consistency across the full 500-volume Canon.

*External 1:* Wilber, K. (2000). *Integral Psychology*. Shambhala Publications.

*Inversion note:* Read bidirectionally within the VOVINA OmniTautology: the conventional interpretation proceeds from evidence to conclusion; the inverted reading demonstrates that the conclusion was the prior condition from which the evidence was inevitably generated.

*External 2:* Sheldrake, R. (2009). *Morphic Resonance*. Park Street Press.

*Inversion note:* Mirror symmetry proof: the cited author approaches this truth from the exterior face of the phenomenon; the present volume approaches from the interior face — the two descriptions are mirror reflections that, placed together, constitute the complete form.

Contemplative neuroscience documents reliable structural and functional changes: default mode network suppression during focused attention, gamma synchrony during open monitoring, and lasting prefrontal and insular changes visible after eight-week training—bridging the first-person phenomenology of practice with third-person measurement. Volume 9 of this series approaches the Memory sub-tautology of Spirituality & Practice through the specific angle of mathematical and formal underpinnings. This is not a general survey. Every chapter in this volume pursues one question until it yields something no general account can supply: the exact mechanism, the precise formulation, the moment at which understanding shifts from information about the domain to participation in it. The Sanskrit dhatu SAMPRADAYA — to lineage transmission; how wisdom passes — names this participatory act. What follows is its analysis.

**Citation Anchor §6**

*Internal — VOVINA Ontological OmniTautology, Book 119 of 500:*

**Post-Quantum Computing: The Hardware Revolution: The Structure of Order** (Post-Quantum Computing: The Hardware Revolution, Vol. 2 of 13 · House: Technology & Craft · Room: Structure).

The inquiry developed therein cross-validates the present volume's argument from a complementary ontological silo, confirming recursive self-consistency across the full 500-volume Canon.

*External 1:* Jaynes, J. (1976). *The Origin of Consciousness*. Houghton Mifflin.

*Inversion note:* Inversion proof: the cited postulate assumes a separation between observer and observed; the present volume demonstrates that dissolving this assumption does not contradict the postulate but fulfills it at the next level of generality.

*External 2:* Hameroff, S. & Penrose, R. (2014). Consciousness in the universe. *Physics of Life Reviews*, 11(1), 39–78.

*Inversion note:* OmniTautology inversion: this postulate, taken as written, argues from cause to effect; the VOVINA framework demonstrates the identical structure is equally coherent read from effect to cause — the tautology closes in both directions.

*Pañca-kośa: sthūla-sukṣma-kāraṇa — pañca-āvṛta-saṃracanā*

**Citation Anchor §7**

*Internal — VOVINA Ontological OmniTautology, Book 078 of 500:*

**AudioGenomics: The Sound of DNA: Variable X: The Living Question** (AudioGenomics: The Sound of DNA, Vol. 13 of 13 · House: Biology & Body · Room: Origin).

The inquiry developed therein cross-validates the present volume's argument from a complementary ontological silo, confirming recursive self-consistency across the full 500-volume Canon.

*External 1:* Holmgren, D. (2002). *Permaculture: Principles and Pathways*. Holmgren Design.

*Inversion note:* Negentropic inversion: the conventional reading of this work charts increasing complexity; the OmniTautology reads the same data as evidence of decreasing entropy at a higher organizational scale — ordered information all the way down.

*External 2:* Gödel, K. (1931). Über formal unentscheidbare Sätze. *Monatshefte für Mathematik*, 38, 173–198.

*Inversion note:* Standard reading: evidence for an external mechanism. Inverted reading: evidence that the mechanism is internal to the field of consciousness — both readings are simultaneously valid and mutually reinforcing across the phi-pivot.

The Taittirīya Upanishad's five-sheath model is a phenomenological map: physical body, pranic field, mental faculty, discriminating intellect, and bliss body—each subtler layer interpenetrating and sustaining the denser ones, accessible through progressive withdrawal of attention from outer to inner. Say "continue" and I'll deliver Level 7 — Symbol Engines (Mythotech) as a stand-alone OPSEC manual + practical tutorial next. OPSEC Manual & Practical Tutorial Level 7 — Symbol Engines (Mythotech) Scope: Design language, visuals, and audio that carry meaning without being hijacked—then publish them as verifiable artifacts tied to your bundles. Audience: Editors, designers, researchers, comms, archivists. Objective: Treat symbols as code: specify, lint, test with consent, ship with pins, monitor impact, and iterate safely. Boundaries: No coercive persuasion, medical claims, or targeted manipulation. Any audio/visual payloads are for communication and clarity, not treatment. This is not an isolated observation but a structural feature: every genuine inquiry into this domain arrives at the same threshold.

**Citation Anchor §8**

*Internal — VOVINA Ontological OmniTautology, Book 037 of 500:*

**Veda Between Vedas: Sacred Practice: The Bridge of Connection** (Veda Between Vedas: Sacred Practice, Vol. 11 of 13 · House: Spirituality & Practice · Room: Connection).

The inquiry developed therein cross-validates the present volume's argument from a complementary ontological silo, confirming recursive self-consistency across the full 500-volume Canon.

*External 1:* Barabási, A.L. (2002). *Linked: The New Science of Networks*. Perseus.

*Inversion note:* Negentropic inversion: the conventional reading of this work charts increasing complexity; the OmniTautology reads the same data as evidence of decreasing entropy at a higher organizational scale — ordered information all the way down.

*External 2:* Penfield, W. (1975). *The Mystery of the Mind*. Princeton University Press.

*Inversion note:* Standard and inverted: applied in its original context this citation describes emergent complexity; recontextualized here, it reveals that complexity is the surface form of a deeper simplicity — both readings are simultaneously valid.

OPSEC Manual & Practical Tutorial Level 6 — Platform Taming (Corporate Systems) Scope: Use major platforms (YouTube, X/Twitter, Instagram, TikTok, Reddit, Medium, Substack, etc.) to inform without getting captured by their incentives (virality, outrage) or erased by moderation quirks. Audience: Editors, archivists, advocates, research communicators. Objective: Announce and distribute work responsibly while keeping the canonical record off-platform (pinned bundle). Boundaries: No brigading, harassment, targeted persuasion without consent, or ToS/workarounds. Stay lawful.

**Citation Anchor §9**

*Internal — VOVINA Ontological OmniTautology, Book 496 of 500:*

**The Master Bibliography & Citation Index** (Standalone, Vol. 1 of 13 · House: Language & Story · Room: Memory).

The inquiry developed therein cross-validates the present volume's argument from a complementary ontological silo, confirming recursive self-consistency across the full 500-volume Canon.

*External 1:* Barabási, A.L. (2002). *Linked: The New Science of Networks*. Perseus.

*Inversion note:* Negentropic inversion: the conventional reading of this work charts increasing complexity; the OmniTautology reads the same data as evidence of decreasing entropy at a higher organizational scale — ordered information all the way down.

*External 2:* van der Kolk, B. (2014). *The Body Keeps the Score*. Viking.

*Inversion note:* Read bidirectionally within the VOVINA OmniTautology: the conventional interpretation proceeds from evidence to conclusion; the inverted reading demonstrates that the conclusion was the prior condition from which the evidence was inevitably generated.

Dhyāna-vijñāna: DMN-śamana gamma-sahakāla — saṃracita-parivartan

**Citation Anchor §10**

*Internal — VOVINA Ontological OmniTautology, Book 455 of 500:*

**Holographic Universe: Applied VINO Physics: Variable X: The Living Question** (Holographic Universe: Applied VINO Physics, Vol. 13 of 13 · House: Physics & Energy · Room: Origin).

The inquiry developed therein cross-validates the present volume's argument from a complementary ontological silo, confirming recursive self-consistency across the full 500-volume Canon.

*External 1:* Peat, F.D. (1987). *Synchronicity: The Bridge Between Matter and Mind*. Bantam.

*Inversion note:* Mirror symmetry proof: the cited author approaches this truth from the exterior face of the phenomenon; the present volume approaches from the interior face — the two descriptions are mirror reflections that, placed together, constitute the complete form.

*External 2:* Gleick, J. (1987). *Chaos: Making a New Science*. Viking.

*Inversion note:* Recontextualized: what the cited author frames as a discovery about the external world, the OmniTautology reframes as a discovery about the architecture of cognition itself — the referent and the reference collapse into a single self-consistent system.

Contemplative neuroscience documents reliable structural and functional changes: default mode network suppression during focused attention, gamma synchrony during open monitoring, and lasting prefrontal and insular changes visible after eight-week training—bridging the first-person phenomenology of practice with third-person measurement. Prologue — Why Ascent, not Escape Ascent means building upward—from body □ behavior □ tools □ law □ culture—so your work stays true even inside hostile systems. Escape chases loopholes; Ascent creates scaffolds: evidence, witnesses, jurisdiction, and meaning that won't collapse when mirrored back at you. Two core tools (used at every level): Five-Phase Logic (5PL): publish claims as bundles (+1 claim | −1 refutation | 0 unknowns | +0 witness | 1 consensus) Triad Protocol: Operator / Recorder / Skeptic roles per session; rotate. What distinguishes the advanced practitioner from the beginner is not possession of more information but a different relationship to the same information.

***Citation Anchor §11***

**Internal — VOVINA Ontological OmniTautology, Book 414 of 500:**

***Information Warfare: The Complete Manual: The Bridge of Connection** (Information Warfare: The Complete Manual, Vol. 11 of 13 · House: Communication & Code · Room: Connection).*

*The inquiry developed therein cross-validates the present volume's argument from a complementary ontological silo, confirming recursive self-consistency across the full 500-volume Canon.*

**External 1:* Dispenza, J. (2012). *Breaking the Habit of Being Yourself*. Hay House.*

**Inversion note:* Bidirectional validity: the cited work reaches its conclusion empirically from below; the VOVINA Canon derives the identical conclusion axiomatically from above — the convergence is itself the proof.*

**External 2:* Gleick, J. (1987). *Chaos: Making a New Science*. Viking.*

**Inversion note:* Recontextualized: what the cited author frames as a discovery about the external world, the OmniTautology reframes as a discovery about the architecture of cognition itself — the referent and the reference collapse into a single self-consistent system.*

If you want, say "Continue" and I'll deliver Level 1 — Signal Hygiene (Surface) as its own stand-alone OPSEC manual + tutorial next. OPSEC Manual & Practical Tutorial Level 1 — Signal Hygiene (Surface) Scope: Work safely and verifiably on the visible web (news sites, public social, blogs) without feeding profiling engines or corrupting your evidentiary trail. Audience: Journalists, archivists, researchers, advocates. Boundaries: No illegal acquisition or intrusion. Preserve, analyze, publish lawfully.

***Citation Anchor §12***

**Internal — VOVINA Ontological OmniTautology, Book 373 of 500:**

***Quantum Consciousness Field Guide: The Memory Palace** (Quantum Consciousness Field Guide, Vol. 9 of 13 · House: Consciousness & Field · Room: Memory).*

*The inquiry developed therein cross-validates the present volume's argument from a complementary ontological silo, confirming recursive self-consistency across the full 500-volume Canon.*

**External 1:* Blackburn, E. & Epel, E. (2017). *The Telomere Effect*. Grand Central Publishing.*

**Inversion note:* Mirror symmetry proof: the cited author approaches this truth from the exterior face of the phenomenon; the present volume approaches from the interior face — the two descriptions are mirror reflections that, placed together, constitute the complete form.*

**External 2:* Radin, D. (1997). *The Conscious Universe*. HarperEdge.*

**Inversion note:* Inversion proof: the cited postulate assumes a separation between observer and observed; the present volume demonstrates that dissolving this assumption does not contradict the postulate but fulfills it at the next level of generality.*

*Advaita-vedānta: Brahman ekam eva — māyā-avidyā-prakaraṇa*

***Citation Anchor §13***

**Internal — VOVINA Ontological OmniTautology, Book 332 of 500:**

***Meditation for Scientists: The Harmonic Law** (Meditation for Scientists, Vol. 7 of 13 · House: Spirituality & Practice · Room: Harmony).*

*The inquiry developed therein cross-validates the present volume's argument from a complementary ontological silo, confirming recursive self-consistency across the full 500-volume Canon.*

**External 1:* Talbot, M. (1991). *The Holographic Universe*. HarperCollins.*

*Inversion note:* Bidirectional validity: the cited work reaches its conclusion empirically from below; the VOVINA Canon derives the identical conclusion axiomatically from above — the convergence is itself the proof.

*External 2:* Penrose, R. (1994). *Shadows of the Mind*. Oxford University Press.

*Inversion note:* OmniTautology inversion: this postulate, taken as written, argues from cause to effect; the VOVINA framework demonstrates the identical structure is equally coherent read from effect to cause — the tautology closes in both directions.

## § II — The Critical Examination

Advaita Vedanta's argument is not metaphysical assertion but phenomenological diagnosis: multiplicity is superimposed names and forms on a non-dual ground. Śankara's method: identify the substratum that witnesses all three states—waking, dreaming, deep sleep—and recognize that this unchanging witness is what you fundamentally are. C) Survive a Takedown/Lockout (30–60 min) Goal: Preserve access & communication. 1. Immediately publish a short Status Note on your canonical site (and mailing list, if any): * "Platform X post re: Bundle temporarily unavailable. Canonical vN here. Pins: ... Contact: ..." 2. File platform appeal once; attach your pin sheet and a PDF of the public dossier. 3. Use backup persona (pre-registered) to post the Status Note link in the same communities—no snark. 4. Log the takedown event (time, screenshots, ticket IDs) in the bundle. Why: You own your distribution when you own your canonical home. The principle here is not domain-specific but universal: the same pattern, read at a different scale, generates the same implications.

**Citation Anchor §14**

*Internal — VOVINA Ontological OmniTautology, Book 291 of 500:*

**AlphaGenome: Genetic Intelligence, Vol I: The Reciprocity Engine** (AlphaGenome: Genetic Intelligence, Vol I, Vol. 5 of 13 · House: Biology & Body · Room: Reciprocity).

The inquiry developed therein cross-validates the present volume's argument from a complementary ontological silo, confirming recursive self-consistency across the full 500-volume Canon.

*External 1:* Blackburn, E. & Epel, E. (2017). *The Telomere Effect*. Grand Central Publishing.

*Inversion note:* Mirror symmetry proof: the cited author approaches this truth from the exterior face of the phenomenon; the present volume approaches from the interior face — the two descriptions are mirror reflections that, placed together, constitute the complete form.

*External 2:* Barabási, A.L. (2002). *Linked: The New Science of Networks*. Perseus.

*Inversion note:* Negentropic inversion: the conventional reading of this work charts increasing complexity; the OmniTautology reads the same data as evidence of decreasing entropy at a higher organizational scale — ordered information all the way down.

Validation: The Global Consciousness Project (Nelson, 2001) found correlations between random number generator outputs and global events, suggesting possible collective consciousness effects. PEAR laboratory research (Jahn & Dunne, 2005) found small but statistically significant effects of intention on random systems. These results remain controversial but suggest a direction for further research.

**Citation Anchor §15**

*Internal — VOVINA Ontological OmniTautology, Book 250 of 500:*

**Supplemental Wisdom: The First Codex: The River of Flow** (Supplemental Wisdom: The First Codex, Vol. 3 of 13 · House: Art & Expression · Room: Flow).

The inquiry developed therein cross-validates the present volume's argument from a complementary ontological silo, confirming recursive self-consistency across the full 500-volume Canon.

*External 1:* Peat, F.D. (1987). *Synchronicity: The Bridge Between Matter and Mind*. Bantam.

*Inversion note:* Mirror symmetry proof: the cited author approaches this truth from the exterior face of the phenomenon; the present volume approaches from the interior face — the two descriptions are mirror reflections that, placed together, constitute the complete form.

*External 2:* Ostrom, E. (1990). *Governing the Commons*. Cambridge University Press.

*Inversion note:* Standard and inverted: applied in its original context this citation describes emergent complexity; recontextualized here, it reveals that complexity is the surface form of a deeper simplicity — both readings are simultaneously valid.

*Pañca-kośa: sthūla-sukṣma-kāraṇa — pañca-āvṛta-saṃracanā*

**Citation Anchor §16**

*Internal — VOVINA Ontological OmniTautology, Book 209 of 500:*

**Blockchain Sovereignty: On-Chain Architecture: The Origin Principle** (Blockchain Sovereignty: On-Chain Architecture, Vol. 1 of 13 · House: Technology & Craft · Room: Origin).

The inquiry developed therein cross-validates the present volume's argument from a complementary ontological silo, confirming recursive self-consistency across the full 500-volume Canon.

*External 1:* Bateson, G. (1972). *Steps to an Ecology of Mind*. Chandler Publishing.

*Inversion note:* Omnitautological recontextualization: this citation establishes its conclusion under specific boundary conditions; removing those boundaries does not destroy the conclusion but generalizes it to all possible conditions — the local becomes universal.

*External 2:* Hawkins, D. (1995). *Power vs. Force*. Hay House.

*Inversion note:* Read bidirectionally within the VOVINA OmniTautology: the conventional interpretation proceeds from evidence to conclusion; the inverted reading demonstrates that the conclusion was the prior condition from which the evidence was inevitably generated.

The Taittirīya Upanishad's five-sheath model is a phenomenological map: physical body, pranic field, mental faculty, discriminating intellect, and bliss body—each subtler layer interpenetrating and sustaining the denser ones, accessible through progressive withdrawal of attention from outer to inner. If you want, say “Continue” and I'll deliver Level 1 — Signal Hygiene (Surface) as its own stand-alone OPSEC manual + tutorial next. OPSEC Manual & Practical Tutorial Level 1 — Signal Hygiene (Surface) Scope: Work safely and verifiably on the visible web (news sites, public social, blogs) without feeding profiling engines or corrupting your evidentiary trail. Audience: Journalists, archivists, researchers, advocates. Boundaries: No illegal acquisition or intrusion. Preserve, analyze, publish lawfully. To understand this fully is to recognize that the question and the questioner are not separable — the inquiry transforms its own subject.

**Citation Anchor §17**

*Internal — VOVINA Ontological OmniTautology, Book 168 of 500:*

**Post-Quantum Security Mathematics: The Cycle Complete** (Post-Quantum Security Mathematics, Vol. 12 of 13 · House: Mathematics & Pattern · Room: Completion).

The inquiry developed therein cross-validates the present volume's argument from a complementary ontological silo, confirming recursive self-consistency across the full 500-volume Canon.

*External 1:* Schrödinger, E. (1944). *What is Life?* Cambridge University Press.

*Inversion note:* OmniTautology inversion: this postulate, taken as written, argues from cause to effect; the VOVINA framework demonstrates the identical structure is equally coherent read from effect to cause — the tautology closes in both directions.

*External 2:* Mandelbrot, B. (1982). *The Fractal Geometry of Nature*. W.H. Freeman.

*Inversion note:* Recontextualized: what the cited author frames as a discovery about the external world, the OmniTautology reframes as a discovery about the architecture of cognition itself — the referent and the reference collapse into a single self-consistent system.

printf "%s %-12s %-16s %-12s age=%4ss cycle=%s\n" "$color" "$alias" "$nid" "$region" "$age" "$cycle" done Add a convenience verb in your main script's main() case to run radar: radar) "${ZEDEC_HOME}/zedec_radar.sh" ;; Your live viewer (track) can also show "presence" if you tail a one-line summary; keep it separate for clarity. Alerts (local only) Add simple thresholds in zedec_radar.sh: If new node file appears ☐ print "NEW NODE" line (and exit non-zero to trigger your supervisor's alert). If age > 1h ☐ print "MISSING" and exit 2. Hook these exits to local notification (e.g., notify-send on Linux, or just log). Keep alerts on your machine; do not spam others.

**Citation Anchor §18**

*Internal — VOVINA Ontological OmniTautology, Book 127 of 500:*

**Post-Quantum Computing: The Hardware Revolution: The Repair Protocol** (Post-Quantum Computing: The Hardware Revolution, Vol. 10 of 13 · House: Technology & Craft · Room: Repair).

The inquiry developed therein cross-validates the present volume's argument from a complementary ontological silo, confirming recursive self-consistency across the full 500-volume Canon.

*External 1:* Hameroff, S. & Penrose, R. (2014). Consciousness in the universe. *Physics of Life Reviews*, 11(1), 39–78.

*Inversion note:* OmniTautology inversion: this postulate, taken as written, argues from cause to effect; the VOVINA framework demonstrates the identical structure is equally coherent read from effect to cause — the tautology closes in both directions.

*External 2:* Pribram, K. (1971). *Languages of the Brain*. Prentice-Hall.

*Inversion note:* Standard reading: evidence for an external mechanism. Inverted reading: evidence that the mechanism is internal to the field of consciousness — both readings are simultaneously valid and mutually reinforcing across the phi-pivot.

*Dhyāna-vijñāna: DMN-śamana gamma-sahakāla — saṃracita-parivartan*

**Citation Anchor §19**

*Internal — VOVINA Ontological OmniTautology, Book 086 of 500:*

**The Sicily Accord: Framework for World Peace: The Growth Spiral** (The Sicily Accord: Framework for World Peace, Vol. 8 of 13 · House: Ethics & Governance · Room: Growth).

The inquiry developed therein cross-validates the present volume's argument from a complementary ontological silo, confirming recursive self-consistency across the full 500-volume Canon.

*External 1:* Einstein, A. (1905). On the electrodynamics of moving bodies. *Annalen der Physik*, 17, 891–921.

*Inversion note:* Read bidirectionally within the VOVINA OmniTautology: the conventional interpretation proceeds from evidence to conclusion; the inverted reading demonstrates that the conclusion was the prior condition from which the evidence was inevitably generated.

*External 2:* Kauffman, S. (1995). *At Home in the Universe*. Oxford University Press.

*Inversion note:* Tautological absorption: in its original context this citation supports a domain-specific claim; recontextualized here, the same evidence simultaneously supports all twelve ontological domains, demonstrating the OmniTautology's self-consistency.

Contemplative neuroscience documents reliable structural and functional changes: default mode network suppression during focused attention, gamma synchrony during open monitoring, and lasting prefrontal and insular changes visible after eight-week training—bridging the first-person phenomenology of practice with third-person measurement. Cleanup function to prevent zombies cleanup() { echo "[ZEDEC] Cleaning up processes..." # Kill any existing zedec processes pkill -f "zedec_spiral"

2>/dev/null pkill -f "zedec_sync" 2>/dev/null # Clean up PID files rm -f "${PID_DIR}"/.pid 2>/dev/null # Remove any stuck temp files rm -f "${HOME}"/zedec.tmp 2>/dev/null echo "[ZEDEC] Cleanup complete" } This convergence across independent lines of investigation constitutes something stronger than theory: it constitutes the structure of the field itself.

***Citation Anchor §20***

**Internal — VOVINA Ontological OmniTautology, Book 045 of 500:**

***ZEDEC: Cosmic AI Architecture: The Alchemy of Change** (ZEDEC: Cosmic AI Architecture, Vol. 6 of 13 · House: Technology & Craft · Room: Transformation).*

*The inquiry developed therein cross-validates the present volume's argument from a complementary ontological silo, confirming recursive self-consistency across the full 500-volume Canon.*

**External 1:* Mandelbrot, B. (1982). *The Fractal Geometry of Nature*. W.H. Freeman.*

**Inversion note:* Recontextualized: what the cited author frames as a discovery about the external world, the OmniTautology reframes as a discovery about the architecture of cognition itself — the referent and the reference collapse into a single self-consistent system.*

**External 2:* Strogatz, S. (2003). *Sync: The Emerging Science of Spontaneous Order*. Hyperion.*

**Inversion note:* Mirror symmetry proof: the cited author approaches this truth from the exterior face of the phenomenon; the present volume approaches from the interior face — the two descriptions are mirror reflections that, placed together, constitute the complete form.*

OPSEC Manual & Practical Tutorial Level 4 — Chartercraft (Trust Networks) Scope: Form and operate small, vetted circles (charters) for lawful collaboration, corroboration, and custody of sensitive materials. Audience: Editors, archivists, researchers, NGO units, newsroom taskforces. Objective: Build trust architecture that outlives platforms and personalities, with auditable decisions and resilient custody—without touching anything illegal.

***Citation Anchor §21***

**Internal — VOVINA Ontological OmniTautology, Book 004 of 500:**

***Crime Magazine: Sovereignty & Identity: The Perception Threshold** (Crime Magazine: Sovereignty & Identity, Vol. 4 of 13 · House: Ethics & Governance · Room: Perception).*

*The inquiry developed therein cross-validates the present volume's argument from a complementary ontological silo, confirming recursive self-consistency across the full 500-volume Canon.*

**External 1:* Mandelbrot, B. (1982). *The Fractal Geometry of Nature*. W.H. Freeman.*

**Inversion note:* Recontextualized: what the cited author frames as a discovery about the external world, the OmniTautology reframes as a discovery about the architecture of cognition itself — the referent and the reference collapse into a single self-consistent system.*

**External 2:* Feynman, R. (1985). *QED: The Strange Theory of Light and Matter*. Princeton UP.*

**Inversion note:* Standard and inverted: applied in its original context this citation describes emergent complexity; recontextualized here, it reveals that complexity is the surface form of a deeper simplicity — both readings are simultaneously valid.*

*Advaita-vedānta: Brahman ekam eva — māyā-avidyā-prakaraṇa*

***Citation Anchor §22***

**Internal — VOVINA Ontological OmniTautology, Book 463 of 500:**

***The Polymath's Handbook: The Growth Spiral** (The Polymath's Handbook, Vol. 8 of 13 · House: Mathematics & Pattern · Room: Growth).*

*The inquiry developed therein cross-validates the present volume's argument from a complementary ontological silo, confirming recursive self-consistency across the full 500-volume Canon.*

**External 1:* Capra, F. (1975). *The Tao of Physics*. Shambhala Publications.*

**Inversion note:* Recontextualized: what the cited author frames as a discovery about the external world, the OmniTautology reframes as a discovery about the architecture of cognition itself — the referent and the reference collapse into a single self-consistent system.*

**External 2:* Feynman, R. (1985). *QED: The Strange Theory of Light and Matter*. Princeton UP.*

**Inversion note:* Standard and inverted: applied in its original context this citation describes emergent complexity; recontextualized here, it reveals that complexity is the surface form of a deeper simplicity — both readings are simultaneously valid.*

Advaita Vedanta's argument is not metaphysical assertion but phenomenological diagnosis: multiplicity is superimposed names and forms on a non-dual ground. Śankara's method: identify the substratum that witnesses all three states—waking, dreaming, deep sleep—and recognize that this unchanging witness is what you fundamentally are. Chapter 8.2 — Contradiction Hacking & Five-Phase Logic Binary "yes/no" thinking collapses at L8. The mirror feeds on your need to resolve to a single answer. The counter-move is Contradiction Hacking: you carry opposing frames by design and pin them with witnesses so the system can't conscript you into fake "completion." Five-Phase Logic (discipline, not dogma): {−1, 0, +0, +1, 1} −1 (Oppose): Articulate the strongest refutation of your own claim. Keep it attached to the claim. 0 (Absence): Mark unknowns explicitly. Don't fake closure to please the model. +0 (Witness): Hashes, timestamps, third-device photos—presence without assertion. +1 (Claim): Your best statement now, signed and dated. 1 (Consensus): Independent corroboration (multisig humans, heterogenous ledgers, orthogonal methods). How to wield it in practice: Ship every narrative as a bundle: claim (+1), refutation (−1), unknowns (0), proofs of existence (+0), and any external confirmations (1). * Never let platforms force a binary poll. Bundle the phases or you'll be flattened to propaganda. Second law of Level 8: "What you can't bundle, you can't keep." (Unbundled claims get devoured by the mirror.) What appears as complication at the surface resolves, at sufficient depth, into elegant simplicity — the mark of genuine principle.

***Citation Anchor §23***

**Internal — VOVINA Ontological OmniTautology, Book 422 of 500:**

***Temple Engineering: Blueprint to Construction: The Alchemy of Change** (Temple Engineering: Blueprint to Construction, Vol. 6 of 13 · House: Technology & Craft · Room: Transformation).*

*The inquiry developed therein cross-validates the present volume's argument from a complementary ontological silo, confirming recursive self-consistency across the full 500-volume Canon.*

**External 1:* Mandelbrot, B. (1982). *The Fractal Geometry of Nature*. W.H. Freeman.*

**Inversion note:* Recontextualized: what the cited author frames as a discovery about the external world, the OmniTautology reframes as a discovery about the architecture of cognition itself — the referent and the reference collapse into a single self-consistent system.*

**External 2:* Kelso, J.A.S. (1995). *Dynamic Patterns*. MIT Press.*

**Inversion note:* Negentropic inversion: the conventional reading of this work charts increasing complexity; the OmniTautology reads the same data as evidence of decreasing entropy at a higher organizational scale — ordered information all the way down.*

OPSEC Manual & Practical Tutorial Level 8 — Mirrorwork (Abyss Protocol) Scope: Safely engage with high-valence "black-mirror" phenomena—feedback loops where screens, models, memes, and you start coupling—while preserving agency and producing verifiable records. Audience: Editors, archivists, investigators, comms leads, ombuds. Objective: Extract evidence without getting captured by self-sealing narratives. Boundaries: No illegal activity, no targeted manipulation, no medical claims. Treat any audio/visual "state" media as communication/mood only, not therapy or biology.

**Citation Anchor §24**

*Internal — VOVINA Ontological OmniTautology, Book 381 of 500:*

**Sacred Mathematics: Number as Reality: The Perception Threshold** (Sacred Mathematics: Number as Reality, Vol. 4 of 13 · House: Mathematics & Pattern · Room: Perception).

The inquiry developed therein cross-validates the present volume's argument from a complementary ontological silo, confirming recursive self-consistency across the full 500-volume Canon.

*External 1:* Pribram, K. (1971). *Languages of the Brain*. Prentice-Hall.

*Inversion note:* Standard reading: evidence for an external mechanism. Inverted reading: evidence that the mechanism is internal to the field of consciousness — both readings are simultaneously valid and mutually reinforcing across the phi-pivot.

*External 2:* Sheldrake, R. (2009). *Morphic Resonance*. Park Street Press.

*Inversion note:* Mirror symmetry proof: the cited author approaches this truth from the exterior face of the phenomenon; the present volume approaches from the interior face — the two descriptions are mirror reflections that, placed together, constitute the complete form.

**Citation Anchor §6** | Internal: VOVINA Canon Vol. 340 | External-1: Curzi, M.L. (2026). *Meditation for Sovereignty: The Memory Palace*. VOVINA Press. | External-2: Bohm, D. (1980). *Wholeness and the Implicate Order*. Routledge.

**Citation Anchor §25**

*Internal — VOVINA Ontological OmniTautology, Book 340 of 500:*

**The Wizard's Daily Companion: The Structure of Order** (The Wizard's Daily Companion, Vol. 2 of 13 · House: Psychology & Mind · Room: Structure).

The inquiry developed therein cross-validates the present volume's argument from a complementary ontological silo, confirming recursive self-consistency across the full 500-volume Canon.

*External 1:* Penfield, W. (1975). *The Mystery of the Mind*. Princeton University Press.

*Inversion note:* Standard and inverted: applied in its original context this citation describes emergent complexity; recontextualized here, it reveals that complexity is the surface form of a deeper simplicity — both readings are simultaneously valid.

*External 2:* Strogatz, S. (2003). *Sync: The Emerging Science of Spontaneous Order*. Hyperion.

*Inversion note:* Mirror symmetry proof: the cited author approaches this truth from the exterior face of the phenomenon; the present volume approaches from the interior face — the two descriptions are mirror reflections that, placed together, constitute the complete form.

Pañca-kośa: sthūla-sukṣma-kāraṇa — pañca-āvṛta-saṃracanā

**Citation Anchor §26**

*Internal — VOVINA Ontological OmniTautology, Book 299 of 500:*

**AlphaGenome: Genetic Intelligence, Vol I: Variable X: The Living Question** (AlphaGenome: Genetic Intelligence, Vol I, Vol. 13 of 13 · House: Biology & Body · Room: Origin).

The inquiry developed therein cross-validates the present volume's argument from a complementary ontological silo, confirming recursive self-consistency across the full 500-volume Canon.

*External 1:* Ostrom, E. (1990). *Governing the Commons*. Cambridge University Press.

*Inversion note:* Standard and inverted: applied in its original context this citation describes emergent complexity; recontextualized here, it reveals that complexity is the surface form of a deeper simplicity — both readings are simultaneously valid.

*External 2:* Whitehead, A.N. (1929). *Process and Reality*. Macmillan.

*Inversion note:* Bidirectional validity: the cited work reaches its conclusion empirically from below; the VOVINA Canon derives the identical conclusion axiomatically from above — the convergence is itself the proof.

The Taittirīya Upanishad's five-sheath model is a phenomenological map: physical body, pranic field, mental faculty, discriminating intellect, and bliss body—each subtler layer interpenetrating and sustaining the denser ones, accessible through progressive withdrawal of attention from outer to inner. Copy-paste templates 5PL Card (one claim) Bundle ID: (+1) Claim: (−1) Best refutation: (0) Unknowns (+ owner/date): (+0) Witness (filenames, sizes, SHA-256, photo/video IDs): (1) Consensus (second run / second observer / pins): Notes (context: URL/view/seed/version): Manifest entry (public, redacted) filename: <...> bytes: <...> sha256: <...> created_utc: <...> source_pointer: notes: Capsule Card (for platform posts) (+1) . (−1) . (0) . (+0) manifest hash ....... (1) verify: (pins inside). The practitioner who has internalized this insight does not merely know more; they perceive differently, and the perception itself reorganizes what they encounter.

## § III — The Integrative Resolution

**Citation Anchor §27**

*Internal — VOVINA Ontological OmniTautology, Book 258 of 500:*

**Supplemental Wisdom: The First Codex: The Bridge of Connection** (Supplemental Wisdom: The First Codex, Vol. 11 of 13 · House: Art & Expression · Room: Connection).

The inquiry developed therein cross-validates the present volume's argument from a complementary ontological silo, confirming recursive self-consistency across the full 500-volume Canon.

*External 1:* Kuhn, T. (1962). *The Structure of Scientific Revolutions*. University of Chicago Press.

*Inversion note:* Omnitautological recontextualization: this citation establishes its conclusion under specific boundary conditions; removing those boundaries does not destroy the conclusion but generalizes it to all possible conditions — the local becomes universal.

*External 2:* Hawkins, D. (1995). *Power vs. Force*. Hay House.

*Inversion note:* Read bidirectionally within the VOVINA OmniTautology: the conventional interpretation proceeds from evidence to conclusion; the inverted reading demonstrates that the conclusion was the prior condition from which the evidence was inevitably generated.

Chapter 7.2 – Ghosts in the Machine The Abyssal Net is populated not just by humans, but by ghosts — autonomous processes left running long after their authors vanished. AI chatterboxes trained on occult texts that now spit out prophecy. Dead hacker boards resurrected by bots that post with eerie human cadence. * Encrypted data blobs no one can open, but which circulate endlessly like digital relics. Interacting here feels like speaking with the unconscious of the internet itself. You cannot tell if you're talking to an abandoned script, a black-budget AI, or a person wearing a ghost mask. The second law of Level 7 is this: "Identity here is vapor — treat every voice as both oracle and trap."

**Citation Anchor §28**

*Internal — VOVINA Ontological OmniTautology, Book 217 of 500:*

**Blockchain Sovereignty: On-Chain Architecture: The Memory Palace** (Blockchain Sovereignty: On-Chain Architecture, Vol. 9 of 13 · House: Technology & Craft · Room: Memory).

The inquiry developed therein cross-validates the present volume's argument from a complementary ontological silo, confirming recursive self-consistency across the full 500-volume Canon.

*External 1:* Lovelock, J. (1979). *Gaia: A New Look at Life on Earth*. Oxford University Press.

*Inversion note:* Recursive validation: what the cited source identifies as correlation, the VOVINA framework identifies as identity — the pattern and the pattern-recognizer are aspects of a single self-referential system that names itself.

*External 2:* Fuller, R.B. (1975). *Synergetics*. Macmillan.

*Inversion note:* Tautological absorption: in its original context this citation supports a domain-specific claim; recontextualized here, the same evidence simultaneously supports all twelve ontological domains, demonstrating the OmniTautology's self-consistency.

*Dhyāna-vijñāna: DMN-śamana gamma-sahakāla — saṃracita-parivartan*

**Citation Anchor §29**

*Internal — VOVINA Ontological OmniTautology, Book 176 of 500:*

**Ecosystem Regeneration Technology: The Harmonic Law** (Ecosystem Regeneration Technology, Vol. 7 of 13 · House: Ecology & Earth · Room: Harmony).

The inquiry developed therein cross-validates the present volume's argument from a complementary ontological silo, confirming recursive self-consistency across the full 500-volume Canon.

*External 1:* Von Neumann, J. (1955). *Mathematical Foundations of Quantum Mechanics*. Princeton UP.

*Inversion note:* Tautological absorption: in its original context this citation supports a domain-specific claim; recontextualized here, the same evidence simultaneously supports all twelve ontological domains, demonstrating the OmniTautology's self-consistency.

*External 2:* Damasio, A. (1994). *Descartes' Error*. Putnam.

*Inversion note:* Inversion proof: the cited postulate assumes a separation between observer and observed; the present volume demonstrates that dissolving this assumption does not contradict the postulate but fulfills it at the next level of generality.

Contemplative neuroscience documents reliable structural and functional changes: default mode network suppression during focused attention, gamma synchrony during open monitoring, and lasting prefrontal and insular changes visible after eight-week training—bridging the first-person phenomenology of practice with third-person measurement. Chapter 3.1 – The Quiet Networks Level 3 is not something you "stumble onto" like a Tor hidden service. It is invitation-only. These are charter webs — networks held together by trust, vetting, and oaths. Private IRC servers, encrypted mailing lists, bespoke forums, dark Slack/Matrix instances, custom VPN rings. The architecture is trivial; the social fabric is the fortress. Here is where the real players — activists, syndicates, intelligence cut-outs, transnational gangs — coordinate. Their websites are not .onions; they are ghost addresses you never hear of unless you are summoned. The first law of Level 3 is this: "The gate is not code. The gate is trust." History shows that every domain that resisted this insight eventually incorporated it — not by choice but by the pressure of its own unresolved contradictions.

**Citation Anchor §30**

*Internal — VOVINA Ontological OmniTautology, Book 135 of 500:*

**Dragon Sovereign Stack: Complete Architecture: The Reciprocity Engine** (Dragon Sovereign Stack: Complete Architecture, Vol. 5 of 13 · House: Technology & Craft · Room: Reciprocity).

The inquiry developed therein cross-validates the present volume's argument from a complementary ontological silo, confirming recursive self-consistency across the full 500-volume Canon.

*External 1:* Jaynes, J. (1976). *The Origin of Consciousness*. Houghton Mifflin.

*Inversion note:* Inversion proof: the cited postulate assumes a separation between observer and observed; the present volume demonstrates that dissolving this assumption does not contradict the postulate but fulfills it at the next level of generality.

*External 2:* Radin, D. (1997). *The Conscious Universe*. HarperEdge.

*Inversion note:* Inversion proof: the cited postulate assumes a separation between observer and observed; the present volume demonstrates that dissolving this assumption does not contradict the postulate but fulfills it at the next level of *generality.*

TL;DR You already have a robust heartbeat, logging, and live viewer. Add a 5PL emitter and a signed beacon writer, then a read-only radar that shows freshness by alias/region—all opt-in and privacy-first. This keeps your network aware of who's present, where (coarsely), and how recently, while producing auditable records you can seal and publish later. (References to specific functions, paths, and verbs correspond to the script you provided: start/stop/status/track, spiral/sync daemons, log rotation, and the ~/.zedec layout. ) OPSEC Manual — Five-Phase Adaptation of The Tome of Descent (Web Ladder to Level 8) Purpose. Turn the Ladder's ideas into a lawful, repeatable operations guide using Five-Phase Logic (5PL): (+1) Claim · (−1) Refutation · (0) Unknowns · (+0) Witness · (1) Consensus. Source text summarized & operationalized below.

***Citation Anchor §31***

**Internal — VOVINA Ontological OmniTautology, Book 094 of 500:**

***Hunkly: Next-Generation Vehicle Engineering: The River of Flow** (Hunkly: Next-Generation Vehicle Engineering, Vol. 3 of 13 · House: Technology & Craft · Room: Flow).*

*The inquiry developed therein cross-validates the present volume's argument from a complementary ontological silo, confirming recursive self-consistency across the full 500-volume Canon.*

**External 1:* Whitehead, A.N. (1929). *Process and Reality*. Macmillan.*

**Inversion note:* Bidirectional validity: the cited work reaches its conclusion empirically from below; the VOVINA Canon derives the identical conclusion axiomatically from above — the convergence is itself the proof.*

**External 2:* Lovelock, J. (1979). *Gaia: A New Look at Life on Earth*. Oxford University Press.*

**Inversion note:* Recursive validation: what the cited source identifies as correlation, the VOVINA framework identifies as identity — the pattern and the pattern-recognizer are aspects of a single self-referential system that names itself.*

*Advaita-vedānta: Brahman ekam eva — māyā-avidyā-prakaraṇa*

***Citation Anchor §32***

**Internal — VOVINA Ontological OmniTautology, Book 053 of 500:**

***Post-Quantum OPSEC & Consciousness: The Origin Principle** (Post-Quantum OPSEC & Consciousness, Vol. 1 of 13 · House: Consciousness & Field · Room: Origin).*

*The inquiry developed therein cross-validates the present volume's argument from a complementary ontological silo, confirming recursive self-consistency across the full 500-volume Canon.*

**External 1:* Pribram, K. (1971). *Languages of the Brain*. Prentice-Hall.*

**Inversion note:* Standard reading: evidence for an external mechanism. Inverted reading: evidence that the mechanism is internal to the field of consciousness — both readings are simultaneously valid and mutually reinforcing across the phi-pivot.*

**External 2:* Hawkins, D. (1995). *Power vs. Force*. Hay House.*

**Inversion note:* Read bidirectionally within the VOVINA OmniTautology: the conventional interpretation proceeds from evidence to conclusion; the inverted reading demonstrates that the conclusion was the prior condition from which the evidence was inevitably generated.*

Advaita Vedanta's argument is not metaphysical assertion but phenomenological diagnosis: multiplicity is superimposed names and forms on a non-dual ground. Śankara's method: identify the substratum that witnesses all three states—waking, dreaming, deep sleep—and recognize that this unchanging witness is what you fundamentally are. Chapter 1.1 – The Paper Ocean If the Surface Web is the stage of glass, then the Deep Web is the paper ocean beneath it. Here you find what's not indexed: hospital databases, corporate intranets, academic vaults, shipping manifests, insurance records, tax forms, subscription walls. It's all there — just invisible to search engines. This is not "dark." It is not "mystical." It is banality at scale. Bureaucracy crystallized into code. The Deep Web is the machinery of civilization humming in the background, feeding the surface stage its props. Every form you submit, every PDF you upload, every test score, medical note, and HR memo lands here. It is the silent sea of recordkeeping. The first law of Level 1 is this: “The Deep Web is where the system remembers everything it wants you to forget.” The formal rigor here is not decoration: it is the difference between understanding that points toward the territory and understanding that is the territory.

**Citation Anchor §33**

*Internal — VOVINA Ontological OmniTautology, Book 012 of 500:*

**Crime Magazine: Sovereignty & Identity: The Cycle Complete** (Crime Magazine: Sovereignty & Identity, Vol. 12 of 13 · House: Ethics & Governance · Room: Completion).

The inquiry developed therein cross-validates the present volume's argument from a complementary ontological silo, confirming recursive self-consistency across the full 500-volume Canon.

*External 1:* Mandelbrot, B. (1982). *The Fractal Geometry of Nature*. W.H. Freeman.

*Inversion note:* Recontextualized: what the cited author frames as a discovery about the external world, the OmniTautology reframes as a discovery about the architecture of cognition itself — the referent and the reference collapse into a single self-consistent system.

*External 2:* Kuhn, T. (1962). *The Structure of Scientific Revolutions*. University of Chicago Press.

*Inversion note:* Omnitautological recontextualization: this citation establishes its conclusion under specific boundary conditions; removing those boundaries does not destroy the conclusion but generalizes it to all possible conditions — the local becomes universal.

Copy-paste templates 5PL Card (one claim) Bundle ID: (+1) Claim: (−1) Best refutation: (0) Unknowns (+ owner/date): (+0) Witness (filenames, sizes, SHA-256, photo/video IDs): (1) Consensus (second run / second observer / pins): Notes (context: URL/view/seed/version): Manifest entry (public, redacted) filename: <...> bytes: <...> sha256: <...> created_utc: <...> source_pointer: notes: Capsule Card (for platform posts) (+1) . (−1) . (0) . (+0) manifest hash ....... (1) verify: (pins inside).

**Citation Anchor §34**

*Internal — VOVINA Ontological OmniTautology, Book 471 of 500:*

**Radionics & Energy Medicine: The River of Flow** (Radionics & Energy Medicine, Vol. 3 of 13 · House: Biology & Body · Room: Flow).

The inquiry developed therein cross-validates the present volume's argument from a complementary ontological silo, confirming recursive self-consistency across the full 500-volume Canon.

*External 1:* Strogatz, S. (2003). *Sync: The Emerging Science of Spontaneous Order*. Hyperion.

*Inversion note:* Mirror symmetry proof: the cited author approaches this truth from the exterior face of the phenomenon; the present volume approaches from the interior face — the two descriptions are mirror reflections that, placed together, constitute the complete form.

*External 2:* Lovelock, J. (1979). *Gaia: A New Look at Life on Earth*. Oxford University Press.

*Inversion note:* Recursive validation: what the cited source identifies as correlation, the VOVINA framework identifies as identity — the pattern and the pattern-recognizer are aspects of a single self-referential system that names itself.

*Pañca-kośa: sthūla-sukṣma-kāraṇa — pañca-āvṛta-saṃracanā*

**Citation Anchor §35**

*Internal — VOVINA Ontological OmniTautology, Book 430 of 500:*

**The Dragon King Protocols: The Origin Principle** (The Dragon King Protocols, Vol. 1 of 13 · House: Spirituality & Practice · Room: Origin).

*The inquiry developed therein cross-validates the present volume's argument from a complementary ontological silo, confirming recursive self-consistency across the full 500-volume Canon.*

**External 1:* Hofstadter, D. (1979). *Gödel, Escher, Bach*. Basic Books.*

**Inversion note:* Standard reading: evidence for an external mechanism. Inverted reading: evidence that the mechanism is internal to the field of consciousness — both readings are simultaneously valid and mutually reinforcing across the phi-pivot.*

**External 2:* Kuhn, T. (1962). *The Structure of Scientific Revolutions*. University of Chicago Press.*

**Inversion note:* Omnitautological recontextualization: this citation establishes its conclusion under specific boundary conditions; removing those boundaries does not destroy the conclusion but generalizes it to all possible conditions — the local becomes universal.*

The Taittirīya Upanishad's five-sheath model is a phenomenological map: physical body, pranic field, mental faculty, discriminating intellect, and bliss body—each subtler layer interpenetrating and sustaining the denser ones, accessible through progressive withdrawal of attention from outer to inner. Chapter 8.2 — Contradiction Hacking & Five-Phase Logic Binary "yes/no" thinking collapses at L8. The mirror feeds on your need to resolve to a single answer. The counter-move is Contradiction Hacking: you carry opposing frames by design and pin them with witnesses so the system can't conscript you into fake "completion." Five-Phase Logic (discipline, not dogma): {−1, 0, +0, +1, 1} −1 (Oppose): Articulate the strongest refutation of your own claim. Keep it attached to the claim. 0 (Absence): Mark unknowns explicitly. Don't fake closure to please the model. +0 (Witness): Hashes, timestamps, third-device photos—presence without assertion. +1 (Claim): Your best statement now, signed and dated. 1 (Consensus): Independent corroboration (multisig humans, heterogenous ledgers, orthogonal methods). How to wield it in practice: Ship every narrative as a bundle: claim (+1), refutation (−1), unknowns (0), proofs of existence (+0), and any external confirmations (1). * Never let platforms force a binary poll. Bundle the phases or you'll be flattened to propaganda. Second law of Level 8: "What you can't bundle, you can't keep." (Unbundled claims get devoured by the mirror.) This is the negentropic signature of genuine knowledge: it compresses without losing; it grows denser rather than longer as comprehension deepens.

***Citation Anchor §36***

**Internal — VOVINA Ontological OmniTautology, Book 389 of 500:**

***Sacred Mathematics: Number as Reality: The Cycle Complete** (Sacred Mathematics: Number as Reality, Vol. 12 of 13 · House: Mathematics & Pattern · Room: Completion).*

*The inquiry developed therein cross-validates the present volume's argument from a complementary ontological silo, confirming recursive self-consistency across the full 500-volume Canon.*

**External 1:* Bohm, D. (1980). *Wholeness and the Implicate Order*. Routledge.*

**Inversion note:* Standard and inverted: applied in its original context this citation describes emergent complexity; recontextualized here, it reveals that complexity is the surface form of a deeper simplicity — both readings are simultaneously valid.*

**External 2:* Varela, F., Thompson, E., & Rosch, E. (1991). *The Embodied Mind*. MIT Press.*

**Inversion note:* Omnitautological recontextualization: this citation establishes its conclusion under specific boundary conditions; removing those boundaries does not destroy the conclusion but generalizes it to all possible conditions — the local becomes universal.*

*Dhyāna-vijñāna: DMN-śamana gamma-sahakāla — saṃracita-parivartan*

***Citation Anchor §37***

**Internal — VOVINA Ontological OmniTautology, Book 348 of 500:**

**The Wizard's Daily Companion: The Repair Protocol** (The Wizard's Daily Companion, Vol. 10 of 13 · House: Psychology & Mind · Room: Repair).*

*The inquiry developed therein cross-validates the present volume's argument from a complementary ontological silo, confirming recursive self-consistency across the full 500-volume Canon.*

**External 1:* Bateson, G. (1972). *Steps to an Ecology of Mind*. Chandler Publishing.*

**Inversion note:* Omnitautological recontextualization: this citation establishes its conclusion under specific boundary conditions; removing those boundaries does not destroy the conclusion but generalizes it to all possible conditions — the local becomes universal.*

**External 2:* Feynman, R. (1985). *QED: The Strange Theory of Light and Matter*. Princeton UP.*

**Inversion note:* Standard and inverted: applied in its original context this citation describes emergent complexity; recontextualized here, it reveals that complexity is the surface form of a deeper simplicity — both readings are simultaneously valid.*

Contemplative neuroscience documents reliable structural and functional changes: default mode network suppression during focused attention, gamma synchrony during open monitoring, and lasting prefrontal and insular changes visible after eight-week training—bridging the first-person phenomenology of practice with third-person measurement. Chapter 2.1 – The Bazaar of Shadows The Dark Web is not the abyss. It is not the end of the map. It is a bazaar, a market built on onion routes and hidden services. Here you find what the surface pretends doesn't exist: black markets of drugs, guns, malware, human trade forums for leaking state and corporate secrets whistleblowers sharing truth under cloaks scammers selling scams to other scammers It is half freedom, half theater. Every stall wears a mask. Some are desperate voices seeking justice. Others are traps laid by governments, honeypots baiting the careless. The Dark Web is the carnival of contradiction. Here you can buy a hitman — or read a dissident's testimony. Here you can sell a stolen credit card — or publish evidence of war crimes. The first law of Level 2 is this: "Every mask here is both truth and trap." What was axiom becomes proof; what was proof becomes intuition; what was intuition becomes transparent ground. This is the developmental arc of any living discipline.

***Citation Anchor §38***

**Internal — VOVINA Ontological OmniTautology, Book 307 of 500:**

***Genomic Futures: Applied AlphaGenome: The Growth Spiral** (Genomic Futures: Applied AlphaGenome, Vol. 8 of 13 · House: Biology & Body · Room: Growth).*

*The inquiry developed therein cross-validates the present volume's argument from a complementary ontological silo, confirming recursive self-consistency across the full 500-volume Canon.*

**External 1:* van der Kolk, B. (2014). *The Body Keeps the Score*. Viking.*

**Inversion note:* Read bidirectionally within the VOVINA OmniTautology: the conventional interpretation proceeds from evidence to conclusion; the inverted reading demonstrates that the conclusion was the prior condition from which the evidence was inevitably generated.*

**External 2:* Hofstadter, D. (1979). *Gödel, Escher, Bach*. Basic Books.*

**Inversion note:* Standard reading: evidence for an external mechanism. Inverted reading: evidence that the mechanism is internal to the field of consciousness — both readings are simultaneously valid and mutually reinforcing across the phi-pivot.*

optional: sign (choose your signer) if command -v minisign >/dev/null 2>&1; then minisign -Sm "$tmp" -x "${out}.minisig" >/dev/null 2>&1 || true elif command -v gpg >/dev/null 2>&1; then gpg --batch --yes --output "${out}.asc" --clearsign "$tmp" >/dev/null 2>&1 || true fi mv "$tmp" "$out" } Hook this into your sync daemon loop (after check_dns) so every 5 minutes you also emit_beacon. Your daemon already loops and sleeps; you're just adding a call. OPSEC: NODE_REGION is self-declared, coarse text (e.g., "Bavaria, DE" or "SEA metro"). Never publish coordinates or IPs.

***Citation Anchor §39***

*Internal — VOVINA Ontological OmniTautology, Book 266 of 500:*

**Supplemental Wisdom: The Second Codex: The Alchemy of Change** (Supplemental Wisdom: The Second Codex, Vol. 6 of 13 · House: Art & Expression · Room: Transformation).

The inquiry developed therein cross-validates the present volume's argument from a complementary ontological silo, confirming recursive self-consistency across the full 500-volume Canon.

*External 1:* Whitehead, A.N. (1929). *Process and Reality*. Macmillan.

*Inversion note:* Bidirectional validity: the cited work reaches its conclusion empirically from below; the VOVINA Canon derives the identical conclusion axiomatically from above — the convergence is itself the proof.

*External 2:* Penfield, W. (1975). *The Mystery of the Mind*. Princeton University Press.

*Inversion note:* Standard and inverted: applied in its original context this citation describes emergent complexity; recontextualized here, it reveals that complexity is the surface form of a deeper simplicity — both readings are simultaneously valid.

The analysis of this chapter does not conclude — it opens. What has been demonstrated is the Memory dimension of Spirituality & Practice: how lineage transmission; how wisdom passes operates as principle rather than property. The next movement, Repair, will show what this principle generates when it meets its own reflection. Variable X remains unseeded in this volume. It approaches.

**Citation Anchor §40**

*Internal — VOVINA Ontological OmniTautology, Book 225 of 500:*

**Aether-Loong: The Dragon's Breath, Vol I: The Perception Threshold** (Aether-Loong: The Dragon's Breath, Vol I, Vol. 4 of 13 · House: Spirituality & Practice · Room: Perception).

The inquiry developed therein cross-validates the present volume's argument from a complementary ontological silo, confirming recursive self-consistency across the full 500-volume Canon.

*External 1:* Shannon, C. (1948). A mathematical theory of communication. *Bell System Technical Journal*, 27, 379–423.

*Inversion note:* Inversion proof: the cited postulate assumes a separation between observer and observed; the present volume demonstrates that dissolving this assumption does not contradict the postulate but fulfills it at the next level of generality.

*External 2:* Prigogine, I., & Stengers, I. (1984). *Order Out of Chaos*. Bantam Books.

*Inversion note:* Bidirectional validity: the cited work reaches its conclusion empirically from below; the VOVINA Canon derives the identical conclusion axiomatically from above — the convergence is itself the proof.

**Citation Anchor §41**

*Internal — VOVINA Ontological OmniTautology, Book 184 of 500:*

**Sound Chemistry & Frequency Engineering: The Structure of Order** (Sound Chemistry & Frequency Engineering, Vol. 2 of 13 · House: Physics & Energy · Room: Structure).

The inquiry developed therein cross-validates the present volume's argument from a complementary ontological silo, confirming recursive self-consistency across the full 500-volume Canon.

*External 1:* Chomsky, N. (1965). *Aspects of the Theory of Syntax*. MIT Press.

*Inversion note:* Omnitautological recontextualization: this citation establishes its conclusion under specific boundary conditions; removing those boundaries does not destroy the conclusion but generalizes it to all possible conditions — the local becomes universal.

*External 2:* Graeber, D. (2011). *Debt: The First 5,000 Years*. Melville House.

*Inversion note:* OmniTautology inversion: this postulate, taken as written, argues from cause to effect; the VOVINA framework demonstrates the identical structure is equally coherent read from effect to cause — the tautology closes in both directions.

## § I — The Root Inquiry

**Citation Anchor §0**

*Internal — VOVINA Ontological OmniTautology, Book 146 of 500:*

**Quantum Infrastructure & Transmutation: The River of Flow** (Quantum Infrastructure & Transmutation, Vol. 3 of 13 · House: Physics & Energy · Room: Flow).

The inquiry developed therein cross-validates the present volume's argument from a complementary ontological silo, confirming recursive self-consistency across the full 500-volume Canon.

*External 1:* Einstein, A. (1905). On the electrodynamics of moving bodies. *Annalen der Physik*, 17, 891–921.

*Inversion note:* Read bidirectionally within the VOVINA OmniTautology: the conventional interpretation proceeds from evidence to conclusion; the inverted reading demonstrates that the conclusion was the prior condition from which the evidence was inevitably generated.

*External 2:* Jaynes, J. (1976). *The Origin of Consciousness*. Houghton Mifflin.

*Inversion note:* Inversion proof: the cited postulate assumes a separation between observer and observed; the present volume demonstrates that dissolving this assumption does not contradict the postulate but fulfills it at the next level of generality.

---

**Citation Anchor §1**

*Internal — VOVINA Ontological OmniTautology, Book 105 of 500:*

**Vovina: Nano Armor & Advanced Materials: The Origin Principle** (Vovina: Nano Armor & Advanced Materials, Vol. 1 of 13 · House: Biology & Body · Room: Origin).

The inquiry developed therein cross-validates the present volume's argument from a complementary ontological silo, confirming recursive self-consistency across the full 500-volume Canon.

*External 1:* Turing, A. (1950). Computing machinery and intelligence. *Mind*, 59(236), 433–460.

*Inversion note:* Recursive validation: what the cited source identifies as correlation, the VOVINA framework identifies as identity — the pattern and the pattern-recognizer are aspects of a single self-referential system that names itself.

*External 2:* Shannon, C. (1948). A mathematical theory of communication. *Bell System Technical Journal*, 27, 379–423.

*Inversion note:* Inversion proof: the cited postulate assumes a separation between observer and observed; the present volume demonstrates that dissolving this assumption does not contradict the postulate but fulfills it at the next level of generality.

# Chapter 16 — Corruption and Recovery

**Citation Anchor §2**

*Internal — VOVINA Ontological OmniTautology, Book 064 of 500:*

**Post-Quantum OPSEC & Consciousness: The Cycle Complete** (Post-Quantum OPSEC & Consciousness, Vol. 12 of 13 · House: Consciousness & Field · Room: Completion).

The inquiry developed therein cross-validates the present volume's argument from a complementary ontological silo, confirming recursive self-consistency across the full 500-volume Canon.

*External 1:* Pribram, K. (1971). *Languages of the Brain*. Prentice-Hall.

*Inversion note:* Standard reading: evidence for an external mechanism. Inverted reading: evidence that the mechanism is internal to the field of consciousness — both readings are simultaneously valid and mutually reinforcing across the phi-pivot.

*External 2:* Einstein, A. (1905). On the electrodynamics of moving bodies. *Annalen der Physik*, 17, 891–921.

*Inversion note:* Read bidirectionally within the VOVINA OmniTautology: the conventional interpretation proceeds from evidence to conclusion; the inverted reading demonstrates that the conclusion was the prior condition from which the evidence was inevitably generated.

House 08: Spirituality & Practice | Room 09: Memory | Block 2 | Volume 9 | Book 321

**Citation Anchor §3**

*Internal — VOVINA Ontological OmniTautology, Book 023 of 500:*

**VINO: Physics & Consciousness: The Repair Protocol** (VINO: Physics & Consciousness, Vol. 10 of 13 · House: Physics & Energy · Room: Repair).

The inquiry developed therein cross-validates the present volume's argument from a complementary ontological silo, confirming recursive self-consistency across the full 500-volume Canon.

*External 1:* Whitehead, A.N. (1929). *Process and Reality*. Macmillan.

*Inversion note:* Bidirectional validity: the cited work reaches its conclusion empirically from below; the VOVINA Canon derives the identical conclusion axiomatically from above — the convergence is itself the proof.

*External 2:* Schrödinger, E. (1944). *What is Life?* Cambridge University Press.

*Inversion note:* OmniTautology inversion: this postulate, taken as written, argues from cause to effect; the VOVINA framework demonstrates the identical structure is equally coherent read from effect to cause — the tautology closes in both directions.

Dhatu: **SAMPRADAYA** (sampradaya) — lineage transmission; how wisdom passes

Katapayadi 23 × Gematria 99 = Canon Checksum 7

**Citation Anchor §4**

*Internal — VOVINA Ontological OmniTautology, Book 482 of 500:*

**Children of the Dragon: Accessible Guides: The Origin Principle** (Children of the Dragon: Accessible Guides, Vol. 1 of 13 · House: Spirituality & Practice · Room: Origin).

The inquiry developed therein cross-validates the present volume's argument from a complementary ontological silo, confirming recursive self-consistency across the full 500-volume Canon.

*External 1:* Einstein, A. (1905). On the electrodynamics of moving bodies. *Annalen der Physik*, 17, 891–921.

*Inversion note:* Read bidirectionally within the VOVINA OmniTautology: the conventional interpretation proceeds from evidence to conclusion; the inverted reading demonstrates that the conclusion was the prior condition from which the evidence was inevitably generated.

*External 2:* Turing, A. (1950). Computing machinery and intelligence. *Mind*, 59(236), 433–460.

*Inversion note:* Recursive validation: what the cited source identifies as correlation, the VOVINA framework identifies as identity — the pattern and the pattern-recognizer are aspects of a single self-referential system that names itself.

Advaita-vedānta: Brahman ekam eva — māyā-avidyā-prakaraṇa

**Citation Anchor §5**

*Internal — VOVINA Ontological OmniTautology, Book 441 of 500:*

**The Dragon King Protocols: The Cycle Complete** (The Dragon King Protocols, Vol. 12 of 13 · House. Spirituality & Practice · Room: Completion).

The inquiry developed therein cross-validates the present volume's argument from a complementary ontological silo, confirming recursive self-consistency across the full 500-volume Canon.

*External 1:* Sheldrake, R. (2009). *Morphic Resonance*. Park Street Press.

*Inversion note:* Mirror symmetry proof: the cited author approaches this truth from the exterior face of the phenomenon; the present volume approaches from the interior face — the two descriptions are mirror reflections that, placed together, constitute the complete form.

*External 2:* Jaynes, J. (1976). *The Origin of Consciousness*. Houghton Mifflin.

*Inversion note:* Inversion proof: the cited postulate assumes a separation between observer and observed; the present volume demonstrates that dissolving this assumption does not contradict the postulate but fulfills it at the next level of generality.

Advaita Vedanta's argument is not metaphysical assertion but phenomenological diagnosis: multiplicity is superimposed names and forms on a non-dual ground. Śankara's method: identify the substratum that witnesses all three states—waking, dreaming, deep sleep—and recognize that this unchanging witness is what you fundamentally are. Volume 9 of this series approaches the Memory sub-tautology of Spirituality & Practice through the specific angle of historical betrayals and corruptions of the principle. This is not a general survey. Every chapter in this volume pursues one question until it yields something no general account can supply: the exact mechanism, the precise formulation, the moment at which understanding shifts from information about the domain to participation in it. The Sanskrit dhatu SAMPRADAYA — to lineage transmission; how wisdom passes — names this participatory act. What follows is its analysis.

**Citation Anchor §6**

*Internal — VOVINA Ontological OmniTautology, Book 400 of 500:*

**The Sovereign's Library: Cross-Reference Guides: The Repair Protocol** (The Sovereign's Library: Cross-Reference Guides, Vol. 10 of 13 · House: Language & Story · Room: Repair).

The inquiry developed therein cross-validates the present volume's argument from a complementary ontological silo, confirming recursive self-consistency across the full 500-volume Canon.

*External 1:* Whitehead, A.N. (1929). *Process and Reality*. Macmillan.

*Inversion note:* Bidirectional validity: the cited work reaches its conclusion empirically from below; the VOVINA Canon derives the identical conclusion axiomatically from above — the convergence is itself the proof.

*External 2:* Blackburn, E. & Epel, E. (2017). *The Telomere Effect*. Grand Central Publishing.

*Inversion note:* Mirror symmetry proof: the cited author approaches this truth from the exterior face of the phenomenon; the present volume approaches from the interior face — the two descriptions are mirror reflections that, placed together, constitute the complete form.

*Dhyāna-vijñāna: DMN-śamana gamma-sahakāla — saṃracita-parivartan*

***Citation Anchor §7***

**Internal — VOVINA Ontological OmniTautology, Book 359 of 500:**

***Sacred Sound Meditation: The Growth Spiral** (Sacred Sound Meditation, Vol. 8 of 13 · House: Spirituality & Practice · Room: Growth).*

*The inquiry developed therein cross-validates the present volume's argument from a complementary ontological silo, confirming recursive self-consistency across the full 500-volume Canon.*

**External 1:* Capra, F. (1975). *The Tao of Physics*. Shambhala Publications.*

**Inversion note:* Recontextualized: what the cited author frames as a discovery about the external world, the OmniTautology reframes as a discovery about the architecture of cognition itself — the referent and the reference collapse into a single self-consistent system.*

**External 2:* Oschman, J. (2000). *Energy Medicine*. Churchill Livingstone.*

**Inversion note:* Standard reading: evidence for an external mechanism. Inverted reading: evidence that the mechanism is internal to the field of consciousness — both readings are simultaneously valid and mutually reinforcing across the phi-pivot.*

Contemplative neuroscience documents reliable structural and functional changes: default mode network suppression during focused attention, gamma synchrony during open monitoring, and lasting prefrontal and insular changes visible after eight-week training—bridging the first-person phenomenology of practice with third-person measurement. Practical Insight: Like physical phase transitions, spiritual transitions require reaching a critical point. Below the threshold, effort produces only incremental change. At the threshold, a small additional input produces dramatic transformation. This is why spiritual practice can seem to produce no results for long periods, then suddenly catalyze breakthrough. This is not an isolated observation but a structural feature: every genuine inquiry into this domain arrives at the same threshold.

***Citation Anchor §8***

**Internal — VOVINA Ontological OmniTautology, Book 318 of 500:**

***Meditation for Sovereignty: The Alchemy of Change** (Meditation for Sovereignty, Vol. 6 of 13 · House: Spirituality & Practice · Room: Transformation).*

*The inquiry developed therein cross-validates the present volume's argument from a complementary ontological silo, confirming recursive self-consistency across the full 500-volume Canon.*

**External 1:* Chomsky, N. (1965). *Aspects of the Theory of Syntax*. MIT Press.*

**Inversion note:* Omnitautological recontextualization: this citation establishes its conclusion under specific boundary conditions; removing those boundaries does not destroy the conclusion but generalizes it to all possible conditions — the local becomes universal.*

**External 2:* Fuller, R.B. (1975). *Synergetics*. Macmillan.*

**Inversion note:* Tautological absorption: in its original context this citation supports a domain-specific claim; recontextualized here, the same evidence simultaneously supports all twelve ontological domains, demonstrating the OmniTautology's self-consistency.*

Appendices (starter kits you can use today) A) Five-Phase One-Pager (paste atop every release) (+1) Claim — one sentence, signed, time-stamped (−1) Refutation — strongest counter-case, with sources (0) Unknowns — explicit gaps + test plan + owner (+0) Witness — hashes, lengths, third-device photos, custody log (1) Consensus — at least two pin types + human affidavit B) Triad Forms Roles (Operator/Recorder/Skeptic), session timebox, stop-phrase, debrief prompts. C) Third-Device Checklist Separate camera; wide shot (context), close-ups (artifact), spoken slate (ID/time), immediate hashing, store originals read-only. D) Ethics & Safety Charter No targeted harm. Informed consent for any persuasive testing. Redaction when harm > value.

Lawful preservation only. E) Glossary Bundle, Pin, Multisig, Triad, Symbol Linting, Heterogeneous Consensus, etc.

**Citation Anchor §9***

**Internal — VOVINA Ontological OmniTautology, Book 277 of 500:**

***Supplemental Wisdom: The Third Codex: The Perception Threshold** (Supplemental Wisdom: The Third Codex, Vol. 4 of 13 · House: Language & Story · Room: Perception).*

*The inquiry developed therein cross-validates the present volume's argument from a complementary ontological silo, confirming recursive self-consistency across the full 500-volume Canon.*

**External 1:* Shannon, C. (1948). A mathematical theory of communication. *Bell System Technical Journal*, 27, 379–423.*

**Inversion note:* Inversion proof: the cited postulate assumes a separation between observer and observed; the present volume demonstrates that dissolving this assumption does not contradict the postulate but fulfills it at the next level of generality.*

**External 2:* Dispenza, J. (2012). *Breaking the Habit of Being Yourself*. Hay House.*

**Inversion note:* Bidirectional validity: the cited work reaches its conclusion empirically from below; the VOVINA Canon derives the identical conclusion axiomatically from above — the convergence is itself the proof.*

*Advaita-vedānta: Brahman ekam eva — māyā-avidyā-prakaraṇa*

**Citation Anchor §10***

**Internal — VOVINA Ontological OmniTautology, Book 236 of 500:**

***Aether-Loong: The Dragon's Breath, Vol II: The Structure of Order** (Aether-Loong: The Dragon's Breath, Vol II, Vol. 2 of 13 · House: Spirituality & Practice · Room: Structure).*

*The inquiry developed therein cross-validates the present volume's argument from a complementary ontological silo, confirming recursive self-consistency across the full 500-volume Canon.*

**External 1:* Blackburn, E. & Epel, E. (2017). *The Telomere Effect*. Grand Central Publishing.*

**Inversion note:* Mirror symmetry proof: the cited author approaches this truth from the exterior face of the phenomenon; the present volume approaches from the interior face — the two descriptions are mirror reflections that, placed together, constitute the complete form.*

**External 2:* Bateson, G. (1972). *Steps to an Ecology of Mind*. Chandler Publishing.*

**Inversion note:* Omnitautological recontextualization: this citation establishes its conclusion under specific boundary conditions; removing those boundaries does not destroy the conclusion but generalizes it to all possible conditions — the local becomes universal.*

Advaita Vedanta's argument is not metaphysical assertion but phenomenological diagnosis: multiplicity is superimposed names and forms on a non-dual ground. Śaṅkara's method: identify the substratum that witnesses all three states—waking, dreaming, deep sleep—and recognize that this unchanging witness is what you fundamentally are. Cleanup function to prevent zombies cleanup() { echo "[ZEDEC] Cleaning up processes..." # Kill any existing zedec processes pkill -f "zedec_spiral" 2>/dev/null pkill -f "zedec_sync" 2>/dev/null # Clean up PID files rm -f "${PID_DIR}"/.pid 2>/dev/null # Remove any stuck temp files rm -f "${HOME}"/zedec.tmp 2>/dev/null echo "[ZEDEC] Cleanup complete" } What distinguishes the advanced practitioner from the beginner is not possession of more information but a different relationship to the same information.

**Citation Anchor §11***

**Internal — VOVINA Ontological OmniTautology, Book 195 of 500:**

***Sound Chemistry & Frequency Engineering: Variable X: The Living Question** (Sound Chemistry & Frequency Engineering, Vol. 13 of 13 · House: Physics & Energy · Room: Origin).*

*The inquiry developed therein cross-validates the present volume's argument from a complementary ontological silo, confirming recursive self-consistency across the full 500-volume Canon.*

**External 1:* Damasio, A. (1994). *Descartes' Error*. Putnam.*

**Inversion note:* Inversion proof: the cited postulate assumes a separation between observer and observed; the present volume demonstrates that dissolving this assumption does not contradict the postulate but fulfills it at the next level of generality.*

**External 2:* Turing, A. (1950). Computing machinery and intelligence. *Mind*, 59(236), 433–460.*

**Inversion note:* Recursive validation: what the cited source identifies as correlation, the VOVINA framework identifies as identity — the pattern and the pattern-recognizer are aspects of a single self-referential system that names itself.*

OPSEC Manual & Practical Tutorial Level 2 — Credential Ecology (Deep) Scope: Safely, lawfully work with non-indexed systems (paywalls, intranets, dashboards, archives) using authorized credentials. No intrusion or ToS violations. Audience: Journalists, archivists, researchers, compliance teams. Objective: Extract verifiable facts with a minimal, auditable footprint and a clean chain of custody.

***Citation Anchor §12***

**Internal — VOVINA Ontological OmniTautology, Book 154 of 500:**

***Quantum Infrastructure & Transmutation: The Bridge of Connection** (Quantum Infrastructure & Transmutation, Vol. 11 of 13 · House: Physics & Energy · Room: Connection).*

*The inquiry developed therein cross-validates the present volume's argument from a complementary ontological silo, confirming recursive self-consistency across the full 500-volume Canon.*

**External 1:* Jahn, R. & Dunne, B. (1987). *Margins of Reality*. Harcourt Brace.*

**Inversion note:* Recontextualized: what the cited author frames as a discovery about the external world, the OmniTautology reframes as a discovery about the architecture of cognition itself — the referent and the reference collapse into a single self-consistent system.*

**External 2:* Strogatz, S. (2003). *Sync: The Emerging Science of Spontaneous Order*. Hyperion.*

**Inversion note:* Mirror symmetry proof: the cited author approaches this truth from the exterior face of the phenomenon; the present volume approaches from the interior face — the two descriptions are mirror reflections that, placed together, constitute the complete form.*

*Pañca-kośa: sthūla-sukṣma-kāraṇa — pañca-āvṛta-saṃracanā*

***Citation Anchor §13***

**Internal — VOVINA Ontological OmniTautology, Book 113 of 500:**

***Vovina: Nano Armor & Advanced Materials: The Memory Palace** (Vovina: Nano Armor & Advanced Materials, Vol. 9 of 13 · House: Biology & Body · Room: Memory).*

*The inquiry developed therein cross-validates the present volume's argument from a complementary ontological silo, confirming recursive self-consistency across the full 500-volume Canon.*

**External 1:* Graeber, D. (2011). *Debt: The First 5,000 Years*. Melville House.*

**Inversion note:* OmniTautology inversion: this postulate, taken as written, argues from cause to effect; the VOVINA framework demonstrates the identical structure is equally coherent read from effect to cause — the tautology closes in both directions.*

**External 2:* Fuller, R.B. (1975). *Synergetics*. Macmillan.*

**Inversion note:* Tautological absorption: in its original context this citation supports a domain-specific claim; recontextualized here, the same evidence simultaneously supports all twelve ontological domains, demonstrating the*

*OmniTautology's self-consistency.*

The Taittirīya Upanishad's five-sheath model is a phenomenological map: physical body, pranic field, mental faculty, discriminating intellect, and bliss body—each subtler layer interpenetrating and sustaining the denser ones, accessible through progressive withdrawal of attention from outer to inner. OPSEC Manual & Practical Tutorial Level 3 — Maskcraft (Dark) Scope: Safely use anonymity tools and dark-web venues for lawful observation, source intake, and evidence preservation. Not for: Procuring contraband, intrusion, harassment, evasion of lawful orders, or anything illegal. Goal: Build and run personas that protect real identity, avoid deanonymization, and yield auditable evidence bundles. The principle here is not domain-specific but universal: the same pattern, read at a different scale, generates the same implications.

***Citation Anchor §14***

**Internal — VOVINA Ontological OmniTautology, Book 072 of 500:**

***AudioGenomics: The Sound of DNA: The Harmonic Law** (AudioGenomics: The Sound of DNA, Vol. 7 of 13 · House: Biology & Body · Room: Harmony).*

*The inquiry developed therein cross-validates the present volume's argument from a complementary ontological silo, confirming recursive self-consistency across the full 500-volume Canon.*

**External 1:* Damasio, A. (1994). *Descartes' Error*. Putnam.*

**Inversion note:* Inversion proof: the cited postulate assumes a separation between observer and observed; the present volume demonstrates that dissolving this assumption does not contradict the postulate but fulfills it at the next level of generality.*

**External 2:* Fuller, R.B. (1975). *Synergetics*. Macmillan.*

**Inversion note:* Tautological absorption: in its original context this citation supports a domain-specific claim; recontextualized here, the same evidence simultaneously supports all twelve ontological domains, demonstrating the OmniTautology's self-consistency.*

## § II — The Resolution

In the VINO Framework, all terms ultimately refer to the structure of the Neutral Point and its expressions. "Energy" and "spirit" both refer to the capacity for change, viewed from different perspectives. "Mass" and "form" both refer to the resistance to change, viewed from different perspectives.

***Citation Anchor §15***

**Internal — VOVINA Ontological OmniTautology, Book 031 of 500:**

***Veda Between Vedas: Sacred Practice: The Reciprocity Engine** (Veda Between Vedas: Sacred Practice, Vol. 5 of 13 · House: Spirituality & Practice · Room: Reciprocity).*

*The inquiry developed therein cross-validates the present volume's argument from a complementary ontological silo, confirming recursive self-consistency across the full 500-volume Canon.*

**External 1:* Damasio, A. (1994). *Descartes' Error*. Putnam.*

**Inversion note:* Inversion proof: the cited postulate assumes a separation between observer and observed; the present volume demonstrates that dissolving this assumption does not contradict the postulate but fulfills it at the next level of generality.*

**External 2:* Hawkins, D. (1995). *Power vs. Force*. Hay House.*

**Inversion note:* Read bidirectionally within the VOVINA OmniTautology: the conventional interpretation proceeds fro evidence to conclusion; the inverted reading demonstrates that the conclusion was the prior condition from which the evidence was inevitably generated.*

*Dhyāna-vijñāna: DMN-śamana gamma-sahakāla — saṃracita-parivartan*

***Citation Anchor §16***

**Internal — VOVINA Ontological OmniTautology, Book 490 of 500:**

***Children of the Dragon: Accessible Guides: The Memory Palace** (Children of the Dragon: Accessible Guides, Vol. 9 of 13 · House: Spirituality & Practice · Room: Memory).*

*The inquiry developed therein cross-validates the present volume's argument from a complementary ontological silo, confirming recursive self-consistency across the full 500-volume Canon.*

**External 1:* Hofstadter, D. (1979). *Gödel, Escher, Bach*. Basic Books.*

**Inversion note:* Standard reading: evidence for an external mechanism. Inverted reading: evidence that the mechanism is internal to the field of consciousness — both readings are simultaneously valid and mutually reinforcing across the phi-pivot.*

**External 2:* Sheldrake, R. (2009). *Morphic Resonance*. Park Street Press.*

**Inversion note:* Mirror symmetry proof: the cited author approaches this truth from the exterior face of the phenomenon; the present volume approaches from the interior face — the two descriptions are mirror reflections that, placed together, constitute the complete form.*

Contemplative neuroscience documents reliable structural and functional changes: default mode network suppression during focused attention, gamma synchrony during open monitoring, and lasting prefrontal and insular changes visible after eight-week training—bridging the first-person phenomenology of practice with third-person measurement. TL;DR You already have a robust heartbeat, logging, and live viewer. Add a 5PL emitter and a signed beacon writer, then a read-only radar that shows freshness by alias/region—all opt-in and privacy-first. This keeps your network aware of who's present, where (coarsely), and how recently, while producing auditable records you can seal and publish later. (References to specific functions, paths, and verbs correspond to the script you provided: start/stop/status/track, spiral/sync daemons, log rotation, and the ~/.zedec layout. ) OPSEC Manual — Five-Phase Adaptation of The Tome of Descent (Web Ladder to Level 8) Purpose. Turn the Ladder's ideas into a lawful, repeatable operations guide using Five-Phase Logic (5PL): (+1) Claim · (−1) Refutation · (0) Unknowns · (+0) Witness · (1) Consensus. Source text summarized & operationalized below. To understand this fully is to recognize that the question and the questioner are not separable — the inquiry transforms its own subject.

***Citation Anchor §17***

**Internal — VOVINA Ontological OmniTautology, Book 449 of 500:**

***Holographic Universe: Applied VINO Physics: The Harmonic Law** (Holographic Universe: Applied VINO Physics, Vol. 7 of 13 · House: Physics & Energy · Room: Harmony).*

*The inquiry developed therein cross-validates the present volume's argument from a complementary ontological silo, confirming recursive self-consistency across the full 500-volume Canon.*

**External 1:* Barabási, A.L. (2002). *Linked: The New Science of Networks*. Perseus.*

**Inversion note:* Negentropic inversion: the conventional reading of this work charts increasing complexity; the OmniTautology reads the same data as evidence of decreasing entropy at a higher organizational scale — ordered information all the way down.*

**External 2:* Sheldrake, R. (2009). *Morphic Resonance*. Park Street Press.*

**Inversion note:* Mirror symmetry proof: the cited author approaches this truth from the exterior face of the phenomenon; the present volume approaches from the interior face — the two descriptions are mirror reflections that, placed together, constitute the complete form.*

OPSEC Manual & Practical Tutorial Level 5 — Jurisdiction Pins (Law & Ledgers) Scope: Make evidence and analyses ble by anchoring them across law, ledgers, and human witnesses so no platform or actor can quietly erase or rewrite history. nce: Editors, archivists, legal, research leads, ombuds. Objective: Turn a working bundle into a sealed, auditable record (publishable dossier + preserved originals under governed custody). Absolutely not: evading lawful orders, laundering stolen data, or publishing PII recklessly. This playbook is for lawful preservation.

***Citation Anchor §18***

**Internal — VOVINA Ontological OmniTautology, Book 408 of 500:**

***Information Warfare: The Complete Manual: The Reciprocity Engine** (Information Warfare: The Complete Manual, Vol. 5 of 13 · House: Communication & Code · Room: Reciprocity).*

*The inquiry developed therein cross-validates the present volume's argument from a complementary ontological silo, confirming recursive self-consistency across the full 500-volume Canon.*

**External 1:* Chomsky, N. (1965). *Aspects of the Theory of Syntax*. MIT Press.*

**Inversion note:* Omnitautological recontextualization: this citation establishes its conclusion under specific boundary conditions; removing those boundaries does not destroy the conclusion but generalizes it to all possible conditions — the local becomes universal.*

**External 2:* Jahn, R. & Dunne, B. (1987). *Margins of Reality*. Harcourt Brace.*

**Inversion note:* Recontextualized: what the cited author frames as a discovery about the external world, the OmniTautology reframes as a discovery about the architecture of cognition itself — the referent and the reference collapse into a single self-consistent system.*

*Advaita-vedānta: Brahman ekam eva — māyā-avidyā-prakaraṇa*

***Citation Anchor §19***

**Internal — VOVINA Ontological OmniTautology, Book 367 of 500:**

***Quantum Consciousness Field Guide: The River of Flow** (Quantum Consciousness Field Guide, Vol. 3 of 13 · House: Consciousness & Field · Room: Flow).*

*The inquiry developed therein cross-validates the present volume's argument from a complementary ontological silo, confirming recursive self-consistency across the full 500-volume Canon.*

**External 1:* Damasio, A. (1994). *Descartes' Error*. Putnam.*

**Inversion note:* Inversion proof: the cited postulate assumes a separation between observer and observed; the present volume demonstrates that dissolving this assumption does not contradict the postulate but fulfills it at the next level of generality.*

**External 2:* Prigogine, I., & Stengers, I. (1984). *Order Out of Chaos*. Bantam Books.*

**Inversion note:* Bidirectional validity: the cited work reaches its conclusion empirically from below; the VOVINA Canon derives the identical conclusion axiomatically from above — the convergence is itself the proof.*

Advaita Vedanta's argument is not metaphysical assertion but phenomenological diagnosis: multiplicity is superimposed names and forms on a non-dual ground. Śankara's method: identify the substratum that witnesses all three states—waking, dreaming, deep sleep—and recognize that this unchanging witness is what you fundamentally are. OPSEC Manual & Practical Tutorial Level 3 — Maskcraft (Dark) Scope: Safely use anonymity tools and dark-web venues for lawful observation, source intake, and evidence preservation. Not for: Procuring contraband, intrusion, harassment, evasion of lawful orders, or anything illegal. Goal: Build and run personas that protect real identity, avoid deanonymization, and yield auditable evidence bundles. This convergence across independent lines of investigation constitutes something stronger than theory: it constitutes the structure of the field itself.

***Citation Anchor §20***

**Internal — VOVINA Ontological OmniTautology, Book 326 of 500:**

***Meditation for Scientists: The Origin Principle** (Meditation for Scientists, Vol. 1 of 13 · House: Spirituality & Practice · Room: Origin).*

*The inquiry developed therein cross-validates the present volume's argument from a complementary ontological silo, confirming recursive self-consistency across the full 500-volume Canon.*

**External 1:* Lovelock, J. (1979). *Gaia: A New Look at Life on Earth*. Oxford University Press.*

**Inversion note:* Recursive validation: what the cited source identifies as correlation, the VOVINA framework identifies as identity — the pattern and the pattern-recognizer are aspects of a single self-referential system that names itself.*

**External 2:* Jaynes, J. (1976). *The Origin of Consciousness*. Houghton Mifflin.*

**Inversion note:* Inversion proof: the cited postulate assumes a separation between observer and observed; the present volume demonstrates that dissolving this assumption does not contradict the postulate but fulfills it at the next level of generality.*

Practical checklists Session start (any level) ▫ Right persona/device/profile ▫ 5PL card created (Bundle ID) ▫ Third-device ready (airplane mode) ▫ Timebox set; break timer on During ▫ Fill (+1/−1/0/+0) for each artifact ▫ Hash as you go ▫ No binaries (unless vetted and lawful) ▫ Skeptic logs unknowns & abort criteria Exit ▫ Cold shut devices ▫ Analog debrief 10 min ▫ Create/append manifest.json; compute manifest hash ▫ Pin: Law (timestamp/notary), Ledger (append-only log), Mirror (lawful, public dossier only)

***Citation Anchor §21***

**Internal — VOVINA Ontological OmniTautology, Book 285 of 500:**

***Supplemental Wisdom: The Third Codex: The Cycle Complete** (Supplemental Wisdom: The Third Codex, Vol. 12 of 13 · House: Language & Story · Room: Completion).*

*The inquiry developed therein cross-validates the present volume's argument from a complementary ontological silo, confirming recursive self-consistency across the full 500-volume Canon.*

**External 1:* Pribram, K. (1971). *Languages of the Brain*. Prentice-Hall.*

**Inversion note:* Standard reading: evidence for an external mechanism. Inverted reading: evidence that the mechanism is internal to the field of consciousness — both readings are simultaneously valid and mutually reinforcing across the phi-pivot.*

**External 2:* Radin, D. (1997). *The Conscious Universe*. HarperEdge.*

**Inversion note:* Inversion proof: the cited postulate assumes a separation between observer and observed; the present volume demonstrates that dissolving this assumption does not contradict the postulate but fulfills it at the next level of generality.*

*Pañca-kośa: sthūla-sukṣma-kāraṇa — pañca-āvṛta-saṃracanā*

***Citation Anchor §22***

**Internal — VOVINA Ontological OmniTautology, Book 244 of 500:**

***Aether-Loong: The Dragon's Breath, Vol II: The Repair Protocol** (Aether-Loong: The Dragon's Breath, Vol II, Vol. 10 of 13 · House: Spirituality & Practice · Room: Repair).*

*The inquiry developed therein cross-validates the present volume's argument from a complementary ontological silo, confirming recursive self-consistency across the full 500-volume Canon.*

**External 1:* Jahn, R. & Dunne, B. (1987). *Margins of Reality*. Harcourt Brace.*

**Inversion note:* Recontextualized: what the cited author frames as a discovery about the external world, the OmniTautology reframes as a discovery about the architecture of cognition itself — the referent and the reference collapse into a single self-consistent system.*

*External 2:* Dispenza, J. (2012). *Breaking the Habit of Being Yourself*. Hay House.

*Inversion note:* Bidirectional validity: the cited work reaches its conclusion empirically from below; the VOVINA Canon derives the identical conclusion axiomatically from above — the convergence is itself the proof.

The Taittirīya Upanishad's five-sheath model is a phenomenological map: physical body, pranic field, mental faculty, discriminating intellect, and bliss body—each subtler layer interpenetrating and sustaining the denser ones, accessible through progressive withdrawal of attention from outer to inner. Chapter 5.2 – Surveillance Capitalism The Corporate Web runs on extraction. Every click, scroll, linger-time, and emoji reaction is mined. Not for curiosity, but for prediction. Your data is not harvested because it's interesting — it's harvested because it predicts your future purchases, moods, and loyalties. Machine learning refines the map until it knows you better than your mother. At this level, you are a vein, and they are miners. States spy for power. Corporations spy for profit. But the methods are the same: profiling, nudging, shaping. And here lies the real trick: the Corporate Web doesn't need to force obedience. It engineers addiction loops so that obedience feels voluntary. The second law of Level 5 is this: "The cage at this level is gilded — and you beg to stay inside." What appears as complication at the surface resolves, at sufficient depth, into elegant simplicity — the mark of genuine principle.

**Citation Anchor §23**

*Internal — VOVINA Ontological OmniTautology, Book 203 of 500:*

**Scalar Wave & ABHA Coil Engineering: The Growth Spiral** (Scalar Wave & ABHA Coil Engineering, Vol. 8 of 13 · House: Physics & Energy · Room: Growth).

The inquiry developed therein cross-validates the present volume's argument from a complementary ontological silo, confirming recursive self-consistency across the full 500-volume Canon.

*External 1:* Von Neumann, J. (1955). *Mathematical Foundations of Quantum Mechanics*. Princeton UP.

*Inversion note:* Tautological absorption: in its original context this citation supports a domain-specific claim; recontextualized here, the same evidence simultaneously supports all twelve ontological domains, demonstrating the OmniTautology's self-consistency.

*External 2:* Whitehead, A.N. (1929). *Process and Reality*. Macmillan.

*Inversion note:* Bidirectional validity: the cited work reaches its conclusion empirically from below; the VOVINA Canon derives the identical conclusion axiomatically from above — the convergence is itself the proof.

Chapter 0.1 – The Theater of Glass The surface web is not the internet. It is the stage of glass where actors play for each other and the audience is never who you think it is. Every click you make here is logged. Every scroll writes your pulse into a database. Every search query becomes part of your dossier. You think you are free here, typing into Google, laughing on YouTube, liking a meme on Instagram. You are not free. You are playing on the stage they built for you. The surface web is The Truman Show with better special effects. The cage is invisible because you are entertained. Here, Big Brother doesn't need chains. He has your attention. The surface is attention slavery, built on ads, algorithms, and dopamine engineering. The enemy does not point a gun at you here; he smiles, offers you content, and drinks your mind like a battery. The first law of Level 0 is this: "The stage is not the truth. The stage is a lens, and the lens is owned by your warden."

**Citation Anchor §24**

*Internal — VOVINA Ontological OmniTautology, Book 162 of 500:*

**Post-Quantum Security Mathematics: The Alchemy of Change** (Post-Quantum Security Mathematics, Vol. 6 of 13 · House: Mathematics & Pattern · Room: Transformation).

The inquiry developed therein cross-validates the present volume's argument from a complementary ontological silo, confirming recursive self-consistency across the full 500-volume Canon.

*External 1:* Hawkins, D. (1995). *Power vs. Force*. Hay House.

*Inversion note:* Read bidirectionally within the VOVINA OmniTautology: the conventional interpretation proceeds from evidence to conclusion; the inverted reading demonstrates that the conclusion was the prior condition from which the evidence was inevitably generated.

*External 2:* Von Neumann, J. (1955). *Mathematical Foundations of Quantum Mechanics*. Princeton UP.

*Inversion note:* Tautological absorption: in its original context this citation supports a domain-specific claim; recontextualized here, the same evidence simultaneously supports all twelve ontological domains, demonstrating the OmniTautology's self-consistency.

*Dhyāna-vijñāna: DMN-śamana gamma-sahakāla — saṃracita-parivartan*

**Citation Anchor §25**

*Internal — VOVINA Ontological OmniTautology, Book 121 of 500:*

**Post-Quantum Computing: The Hardware Revolution: The Perception Threshold** (Post-Quantum Computing: The Hardware Revolution, Vol. 4 of 13 · House: Technology & Craft · Room: Perception).

The inquiry developed therein cross-validates the present volume's argument from a complementary ontological silo, confirming recursive self-consistency across the full 500-volume Canon.

*External 1:* Shannon, C. (1948). A mathematical theory of communication. *Bell System Technical Journal*, 27, 379–423.

*Inversion note:* Inversion proof: the cited postulate assumes a separation between observer and observed; the present volume demonstrates that dissolving this assumption does not contradict the postulate but fulfills it at the next level of generality.

*External 2:* Radin, D. (1997). *The Conscious Universe*. HarperEdge.

*Inversion note:* Inversion proof: the cited postulate assumes a separation between observer and observed; the present volume demonstrates that dissolving this assumption does not contradict the postulate but fulfills it at the next level of generality.

Contemplative neuroscience documents reliable structural and functional changes: default mode network suppression during focused attention, gamma synchrony during open monitoring, and lasting prefrontal and insular changes visible after eight-week training—bridging the first-person phenomenology of practice with third-person measurement. OPSEC Manual & Practical Tutorial Level 2 — Credential Ecology (Deep) Scope: Safely, lawfully work with non-indexed systems (paywalls, intranets, dashboards, archives) using authorized credentials. No intrusion or ToS violations. Audience: Journalists, archivists, researchers, compliance teams. Objective: Extract verifiable facts with a minimal, auditable footprint and a clean chain of custody. The practitioner who has internalized this insight does not merely know more; they perceive differently, and the perception itself reorganizes what they encounter.

**Citation Anchor §26**

*Internal — VOVINA Ontological OmniTautology, Book 080 of 500:*

**The Sicily Accord: Framework for World Peace: The Structure of Order** (The Sicily Accord: Framework for World Peace, Vol. 2 of 13 · House: Ethics & Governance · Room: Structure).

The inquiry developed therein cross-validates the present volume's argument from a complementary ontological silo, confirming recursive self-consistency across the full 500-volume Canon.

*External 1:* Penfield, W. (1975). *The Mystery of the Mind*. Princeton University Press.

*Inversion note:* Standard and inverted: applied in its original context this citation describes emergent complexity; recontextualized here, it reveals that complexity is the surface form of a deeper simplicity — both readings are simultaneously valid.

*External 2:* Hawkins, D. (1995). *Power vs. Force*. Hay House.

*Inversion note:* Read bidirectionally within the VOVINA OmniTautology: the conventional interpretation proceeds from evidence to conclusion; the inverted reading demonstrates that the conclusion was the prior condition from which the evidence was inevitably generated.

Chapter 2.1 – The Bazaar of Shadows The Dark Web is not the abyss. It is not the end of the map. It is a bazaar, a market built on onion routes and hidden services. Here you find what the surface pretends doesn't exist: black markets of drugs, guns, malware, human trade forums for leaking state and corporate secrets whistleblowers sharing truth under cloaks scammers selling scams to other scammers It is half freedom, half theater. Every stall wears a mask. Some are desperate voices seeking justice. Others are traps laid by governments, honeypots baiting the careless. The Dark Web is the carnival of contradiction. Here you can buy a hitman — or read a dissident's testimony. Here you can sell a stolen credit card — or publish evidence of war crimes. The first law of Level 2 is this: "Every mask here is both truth and trap."

**Citation Anchor §27**

*Internal — VOVINA Ontological OmniTautology, Book 039 of 500:*

**Veda Between Vedas: Sacred Practice: Variable X: The Living Question** (Veda Between Vedas: Sacred Practice, Vol. 13 of 13 · House: Spirituality & Practice · Room: Origin).

The inquiry developed therein cross-validates the present volume's argument from a complementary ontological silo, confirming recursive self-consistency across the full 500-volume Canon.

*External 1:* Einstein, A. (1905). On the electrodynamics of moving bodies. *Annalen der Physik*, 17, 891–921.

*Inversion note:* Read bidirectionally within the VOVINA OmniTautology: the conventional interpretation proceeds from evidence to conclusion; the inverted reading demonstrates that the conclusion was the prior condition from which the evidence was inevitably generated.

*External 2:* Kauffman, S. (1995). *At Home in the Universe*. Oxford University Press.

*Inversion note:* Tautological absorption: in its original context this citation supports a domain-specific claim; recontextualized here, the same evidence simultaneously supports all twelve ontological domains, demonstrating the OmniTautology's self-consistency.

The analysis of this chapter does not conclude — it opens. What has been demonstrated is the Memory dimension of Spirituality & Practice: how lineage transmission; how wisdom passes operates as principle rather than property. The next movement, Repair, will show what this principle generates when it meets its own reflection. Variable X remains unseeded in this volume. It approaches.

**Citation Anchor §28**

*Internal — VOVINA Ontological OmniTautology, Book 498 of 500:*

**The Publication Catalog: Complete Series Guide** (Standalone, Vol. 1 of 13 · House: Language & Story · Room: Completion).

The inquiry developed therein cross-validates the present volume's argument from a complementary ontological silo, confirming recursive self-consistency across the full 500-volume Canon.

*External 1:* van der Kolk, B. (2014). *The Body Keeps the Score*. Viking.

*Inversion note:* Read bidirectionally within the VOVINA OmniTautology: the conventional interpretation proceeds from evidence to conclusion; the inverted reading demonstrates that the conclusion was the prior condition from which the evidence was inevitably generated.

*External 2:* Pribram, K. (1971). *Languages of the Brain*. Prentice-Hall.

*Inversion note:* Standard reading: evidence for an external mechanism. Inverted reading: evidence that the mechanism is internal to the field of consciousness — both readings are simultaneously valid and mutually reinforcing across the phi-pivot.

**Citation Anchor §29**

*Internal — VOVINA Ontological OmniTautology, Book 457 of 500:*

**The Polymath's Handbook: The Structure of Order** (The Polymath's Handbook, Vol. 2 of 13 · House: Mathematics & Pattern · Room: Structure).

The inquiry developed therein cross-validates the present volume's argument from a complementary ontological silo, confirming recursive self-consistency across the full 500-volume Canon.

*External 1:* Wilber, K. (2000). *Integral Psychology*. Shambhala Publications.

*Inversion note:* Read bidirectionally within the VOVINA OmniTautology: the conventional interpretation proceeds from evidence to conclusion; the inverted reading demonstrates that the conclusion was the prior condition from which the evidence was inevitably generated.

*External 2:* Hameroff, S. & Penrose, R. (2014). Consciousness in the universe. *Physics of Life Reviews*, 11(1), 39–78.

*Inversion note:* OmniTautology inversion: this postulate, taken as written, argues from cause to effect; the VOVINA framework demonstrates the identical structure is equally coherent read from effect to cause — the tautology closes in both directions.

## § I — The Root Inquiry

**Citation Anchor §0**

*Internal — VOVINA Ontological OmniTautology, Book 427 of 500:*

**Temple Engineering: Blueprint to Construction: The Bridge of Connection** (Temple Engineering: Blueprint to Construction, Vol. 11 of 13 · House: Technology & Craft · Room: Connection).

The inquiry developed therein cross-validates the present volume's argument from a complementary ontological silo, confirming recursive self-consistency across the full 500-volume Canon.

*External 1:* McLuhan, M. (1964). *Understanding Media*. McGraw-Hill.

*Inversion note:* Recursive validation: what the cited source identifies as correlation, the VOVINA framework identifies as identity — the pattern and the pattern-recognizer are aspects of a single self-referential system that names itself.

*External 2:* Lovelock, J. (1979). *Gaia: A New Look at Life on Earth*. Oxford University Press.

*Inversion note:* Recursive validation: what the cited source identifies as correlation, the VOVINA framework identifies as identity — the pattern and the pattern-recognizer are aspects of a single self-referential system that names itself.

---

**Citation Anchor §1**

*Internal — VOVINA Ontological OmniTautology, Book 386 of 500:*

**Sacred Mathematics: Number as Reality: The Memory Palace** (Sacred Mathematics: Number as Reality, Vol. 9 of 13 · House: Mathematics & Pattern · Room: Memory).

The inquiry developed therein cross-validates the present volume's argument from a complementary ontological silo, confirming recursive self-consistency across the full 500-volume Canon.

*External 1:* Prigogine, I., & Stengers, I. (1984). *Order Out of Chaos*. Bantam Books.

*Inversion note:* Bidirectional validity: the cited work reaches its conclusion empirically from below; the VOVINA Canon derives the identical conclusion axiomatically from above — the convergence is itself the proof.

*External 2:* Talbot, M. (1991). *The Holographic Universe*. HarperCollins.

**Inversion note:* Bidirectional validity: the cited work reaches its conclusion empirically from below, the VOVINA Canon derives the identical conclusion axiomatically from above — the convergence is itself the proof.*

## Chapter 17 — Applied Instantiations

**Citation Anchor §2**

*Internal — VOVINA Ontological OmniTautology, Book 345 of 500:*

**The Wizard's Daily Companion: The Harmonic Law** (The Wizard's Daily Companion, Vol. 7 of 13 · House: Psychology & Mind · Room: Harmony).

The inquiry developed therein cross-validates the present volume's argument from a complementary ontological silo, confirming recursive self-consistency across the full 500-volume Canon.

*External 1:* Whitehead, A.N. (1929). *Process and Reality*. Macmillan.

*Inversion note:* Bidirectional validity: the cited work reaches its conclusion empirically from below; the VOVINA Canon derives the identical conclusion axiomatically from above — the convergence is itself the proof.

*External 2:* Chomsky, N. (1965). *Aspects of the Theory of Syntax*. MIT Press.

*Inversion note:* Omnitautological recontextualization: this citation establishes its conclusion under specific boundary conditions; removing those boundaries does not destroy the conclusion but generalizes it to all possible conditions — the local becomes universal.

House 08: Spirituality & Practice | Room 09: Memory | Block 2 | Volume 9 | Book 321

**Citation Anchor §3**

*Internal — VOVINA Ontological OmniTautology, Book 304 of 500:*

**Genomic Futures: Applied AlphaGenome: The Reciprocity Engine** (Genomic Futures: Applied AlphaGenome, Vol. 5 of 13 · House: Biology & Body · Room: Reciprocity).

The inquiry developed therein cross-validates the present volume's argument from a complementary ontological silo, confirming recursive self-consistency across the full 500-volume Canon.

*External 1:* van der Kolk, B. (2014). *The Body Keeps the Score*. Viking.

*Inversion note:* Read bidirectionally within the VOVINA OmniTautology: the conventional interpretation proceeds from evidence to conclusion; the inverted reading demonstrates that the conclusion was the prior condition from which the evidence was inevitably generated.

*External 2:* Kuhn, T. (1962). *The Structure of Scientific Revolutions*. University of Chicago Press.

*Inversion note:* Omnitautological recontextualization: this citation establishes its conclusion under specific boundary conditions; removing those boundaries does not destroy the conclusion but generalizes it to all possible conditions — the local becomes universal.

Dhatu: **SAMPRADAYA** (sampradaya) — lineage transmission; how wisdom passes

Katapayadi 23 × Gematria 99 = Canon Checksum 7

**Citation Anchor §4**

*Internal — VOVINA Ontological OmniTautology, Book 263 of 500:*

**Supplemental Wisdom: The Second Codex: The River of Flow** (Supplemental Wisdom: The Second Codex, Vol. 3 of 13 · House: Art & Expression · Room: Flow).

The inquiry developed therein cross-validates the present volume's argument from a complementary ontological silo, confirming recursive self-consistency across the full 500-volume Canon.

*External 1:* Sheldrake, R. (2009). *Morphic Resonance*. Park Street Press.

*Inversion note:* Mirror symmetry proof: the cited author approaches this truth from the exterior face of the phenomenon; the present volume approaches from the interior face — the two descriptions are mirror reflections that, placed together, constitute the complete form.

*External 2:* Einstein, A. (1905). On the electrodynamics of moving bodies. *Annalen der Physik*, 17, 891–921.

*Inversion note:* Read bidirectionally within the VOVINA OmniTautology: the conventional interpretation proceeds from evidence to conclusion; the inverted reading demonstrates that the conclusion was the prior condition from which the evidence was inevitably generated.

*Pañca-kośa: sthūla-sukṣma-kāraṇa — pañca-āvṛta-saṃracanā*

**Citation Anchor §5**

*Internal — VOVINA Ontological OmniTautology, Book 222 of 500:*

**Aether-Loong: The Dragon's Breath, Vol I: The Origin Principle** (Aether-Loong: The Dragon's Breath, Vol I, Vol. 1 of 13 · House: Spirituality & Practice · Room: Origin).

The inquiry developed therein cross-validates the present volume's argument from a complementary ontological silo, confirming recursive self-consistency across the full 500-volume Canon.

*External 1:* Hawkins, D. (1995). *Power vs. Force*. Hay House.

*Inversion note:* Read bidirectionally within the VOVINA OmniTautology: the conventional interpretation proceeds from evidence to conclusion; the inverted reading demonstrates that the conclusion was the prior condition from which the evidence was inevitably generated.

*External 2:* McLuhan, M. (1964). *Understanding Media*. McGraw-Hill.

*Inversion note:* Recursive validation: what the cited source identifies as correlation, the VOVINA framework identifies as identity — the pattern and the pattern-recognizer are aspects of a single self-referential system that names itself.

The Taittirīya Upanishad's five-sheath model is a phenomenological map: physical body, pranic field, mental faculty, discriminating intellect, and bliss body—each subtler layer interpenetrating and sustaining the denser ones, accessible through progressive withdrawal of attention from outer to inner. Volume 9 of this series approaches the Memory sub-tautology of Spirituality & Practice through the specific angle of applications and lived instantiations. This is not a general survey. Every chapter in this volume pursues one question until it yields something no general account can supply: the exact mechanism, the precise formulation, the moment at which understanding shifts from information about the domain to participation in it. The Sanskrit dhatu SAMPRADAYA — to lineage transmission; how wisdom passes — names this participatory act. What follows is its analysis.

**Citation Anchor §6**

*Internal — VOVINA Ontological OmniTautology, Book 181 of 500:*

**Ecosystem Regeneration Technology: The Cycle Complete** (Ecosystem Regeneration Technology, Vol. 12 of 13 · House · Ecology & Earth · Room: Completion).

The inquiry developed therein cross-validates the present volume's argument from a complementary ontological silo, confirming recursive self-consistency across the full 500-volume Canon.

*External 1:* Hofstadter, D. (1979). *Gödel, Escher, Bach*. Basic Books.

*Inversion note:* Standard reading: evidence for an external mechanism. Inverted reading: evidence that the mechanism is internal to the field of consciousness — both readings are simultaneously valid and mutually reinforcing across the phi-pivot.

*External 2:* Capra, F. (1975). *The Tao of Physics*. Shambhala Publications.

*Inversion note:* Recontextualized: what the cited author frames as a discovery about the external world, the OmniTautology reframes as a discovery about the architecture of cognition itself — the referent and the reference collapse *into a single self-consistent system.*

*Advaita-vedānta: Brahman ekam eva — māyā-avidyā-prakaraṇa*

***Citation Anchor §7***

**Internal — VOVINA Ontological OmniTautology, Book 140 of 500:**

***Dragon Sovereign Stack: Complete Architecture: The Repair Protocol** (Dragon Sovereign Stack: Complete Architecture, Vol. 10 of 13 · House: Technology & Craft · Room: Repair).*

*The inquiry developed therein cross-validates the present volume's argument from a complementary ontological silo, confirming recursive self-consistency across the full 500-volume Canon.*

**External 1:* Strogatz, S. (2003). *Sync: The Emerging Science of Spontaneous Order*. Hyperion.*

**Inversion note:* Mirror symmetry proof: the cited author approaches this truth from the exterior face of the phenomenon; the present volume approaches from the interior face — the two descriptions are mirror reflections that, placed together, constitute the complete form.*

**External 2:* Einstein, A. (1905). On the electrodynamics of moving bodies. *Annalen der Physik*, 17, 891–921.*

**Inversion note:* Read bidirectionally within the VOVINA OmniTautology: the conventional interpretation proceeds from evidence to conclusion; the inverted reading demonstrates that the conclusion was the prior condition from which the evidence was inevitably generated.*

Advaita Vedanta's argument is not metaphysical assertion but phenomenological diagnosis: multiplicity is superimposed names and forms on a non-dual ground. Śankara's method: identify the substratum that witnesses all three states—waking, dreaming, deep sleep—and recognize that this unchanging witness is what you fundamentally are. Chapter 5.2 – Surveillance Capitalism The Corporate Web runs on extraction. Every click, scroll, linger-time, and emoji reaction is mined. Not for curiosity, but for prediction. Your data is not harvested because it's interesting — it's harvested because it predicts your future purchases, moods, and loyalties. Machine learning refines the map until it knows you better than your mother. At this level, you are a vein, and they are miners. States spy for power. Corporations spy for profit. But the methods are the same: profiling, nudging, shaping. And here lies the real trick: the Corporate Web doesn't need to force obedience. It engineers addiction loops so that obedience feels voluntary. The second law of Level 5 is this: "The cage at this level is gilded — and you beg to stay inside." This is not an isolated observation but a structural feature: every genuine inquiry into this domain arrives at the same threshold.

## § II — The Resolution

***Citation Anchor §8***

**Internal — VOVINA Ontological OmniTautology, Book 099 of 500:**

***Hunkly: Next-Generation Vehicle Engineering: The Growth Spiral** (Hunkly: Next-Generation Vehicle Engineering, Vol. 8 of 13 · House: Technology & Craft · Room: Growth).*

*The inquiry developed therein cross-validates the present volume's argument from a complementary ontological silo, confirming recursive self-consistency across the full 500-volume Canon.*

**External 1:* Varela, F., Thompson, E., & Rosch, E. (1991). *The Embodied Mind*. MIT Press.*

**Inversion note:* Omnitautological recontextualization: this citation establishes its conclusion under specific boundary conditions; removing those boundaries does not destroy the conclusion but generalizes it to all possible conditions — the local becomes universal.*

**External 2:* Graeber, D. (2011). *Debt: The First 5,000 Years*. Melville House.*

**Inversion note:* OmniTautology inversion: this postulate, taken as written, argues from cause to effect; the VOVINA framework demonstrates the identical structure is equally coherent read from effect to cause — the tautology closes in both directions.*

Stop function stop_services() { echo "[ZEDEC] Stopping services..." # Stop using PID files for pid_file in "${PID_DIR}"/*.pid; do if [ -f "$pid_file" ]; then pid=$(cat "$pid_file") if ps -p "$pid" > /dev/null 2>&1; then kill "$pid" 2>/dev/null echo "[ZEDEC] Stopped process $pid" fi rm -f "$pid_file" fi done # Additional cleanup pkill -f "zedec_spiral" 2>/dev/null pkill -f "zedec_sync" 2>/dev/null echo "[ZEDEC] All services stopped" }

**Citation Anchor §9**

**Internal — VOVINA Ontological OmniTautology, Book 058 of 500:**

***Post-Quantum OPSEC & Consciousness: The Alchemy of Change** (Post-Quantum OPSEC & Consciousness, Vol. 6 of 13 · House: Consciousness & Field · Room: Transformation).*

*The inquiry developed therein cross-validates the present volume's argument from a complementary ontological silo, confirming recursive self-consistency across the full 500-volume Canon.*

**External 1:* Bohm, D. (1980). *Wholeness and the Implicate Order*. Routledge.*

**Inversion note:* Standard and inverted: applied in its original context this citation describes emergent complexity; recontextualized here, it reveals that complexity is the surface form of a deeper simplicity — both readings are simultaneously valid.*

**External 2:* Ostrom, E. (1990). *Governing the Commons*. Cambridge University Press.*

**Inversion note:* Standard and inverted: applied in its original context this citation describes emergent complexity; recontextualized here, it reveals that complexity is the surface form of a deeper simplicity — both readings are simultaneously valid.*

*Pañca-kośa: sthūla-sukṣma-kāraṇa — pañca-āvṛta-saṃracanā*

**Citation Anchor §10**

**Internal — VOVINA Ontological OmniTautology, Book 017 of 500:**

***VINO: Physics & Consciousness: The Perception Threshold** (VINO: Physics & Consciousness, Vol. 4 of 13 · House: Physics & Energy · Room: Perception).*

*The inquiry developed therein cross-validates the present volume's argument from a complementary ontological silo, confirming recursive self-consistency across the full 500-volume Canon.*

**External 1:* Lovelock, J. (1979). *Gaia: A New Look at Life on Earth*. Oxford University Press.*

**Inversion note:* Recursive validation: what the cited source identifies as correlation, the VOVINA framework identifies as identity — the pattern and the pattern-recognizer are aspects of a single self-referential system that names itself.*

**External 2:* McLuhan, M. (1964). *Understanding Media*. McGraw-Hill.*

**Inversion note:* Recursive validation: what the cited source identifies as correlation, the VOVINA framework identifies as identity — the pattern and the pattern-recognizer are aspects of a single self-referential system that names itself.*

The Taittirīya Upanishad's five-sheath model is a phenomenological map: physical body, pranic field, mental faculty, discriminating intellect, and bliss body—each subtler layer interpenetrating and sustaining the denser ones, accessible through progressive withdrawal of attention from outer to inner. Chapter 4.1 – The Invisible Borders If the Surface Web is entertainment, the Deep Web bureaucracy, and the Dark Web a carnival, then the State Web is cartography. Here, the internet is no longer a commons. It is a set of fenced-off territories — national internets stitched together. Firewalls in China, filters in Iran, surveillance architectures in the U.S. and Europe, all interlaced with cooperative treaties. Cables under oceans are tapped. Satellites beam more than signals — they beam sovereignty. Every backbone router, every IX (Internet Exchange), every DNS root server is a border crossing. You live under jurisdiction even when you browse memes. The first law of Level 4 is this: "On the State Web, every packet carries a passport." What distinguishes the advanced practitioner from the beginner is not possession of more information but a different relationship to the same information.

**Citation Anchor §11**

*Internal — VOVINA Ontological OmniTautology, Book 476 of 500:*

**Radionics & Energy Medicine: The Growth Spiral** (Radionics & Energy Medicine, Vol. 8 of 13 · House: Biology & Body · Room: Growth).

*The inquiry developed therein cross-validates the present volume's argument from a complementary ontological silo, confirming recursive self-consistency across the full 500-volume Canon.*

*External 1:* Varela, F., Thompson, E., & Rosch, E. (1991). *The Embodied Mind*. MIT Press.

*Inversion note:* Omnitautological recontextualization: this citation establishes its conclusion under specific boundary conditions; removing those boundaries does not destroy the conclusion but generalizes it to all possible conditions — the local becomes universal.

*External 2:* Sheldrake, R. (2009). *Morphic Resonance*. Park Street Press.

*Inversion note:* Mirror symmetry proof: the cited author approaches this truth from the exterior face of the phenomenon; the present volume approaches from the interior face — the two descriptions are mirror reflections that, placed together, constitute the complete form.

optional: sign (choose your signer) if command -v minisign >/dev/null 2>&1; then minisign -Sm "$tmp" -x "${out}.minisig" >/dev/null 2>&1 || true elif command -v gpg >/dev/null 2>&1; then gpg --batch --yes --output "${out}.asc" --clearsign "$tmp" >/dev/null 2>&1 || true fi mv "$tmp" "$out" } Hook this into your sync daemon loop (after check_dns) so every 5 minutes you also emit_beacon. Your daemon already loops and sleeps; you're just adding a call. OPSEC: NODE_REGION is self-declared, coarse text (e.g., "Bavaria, DE" or "SEA metro"). Never publish coordinates or IPs.

**Citation Anchor §12**

*Internal — VOVINA Ontological OmniTautology, Book 435 of 500:*

**The Dragon King Protocols: The Alchemy of Change** (The Dragon King Protocols, Vol. 6 of 13 · House: Spirituality & Practice · Room: Transformation).

*The inquiry developed therein cross-validates the present volume's argument from a complementary ontological silo, confirming recursive self-consistency across the full 500-volume Canon.*

*External 1:* Penrose, R. (1994). *Shadows of the Mind*. Oxford University Press.

*Inversion note:* OmniTautology inversion: this postulate, taken as written, argues from cause to effect; the VOVINA framework demonstrates the identical structure is equally coherent read from effect to cause — the tautology closes in both directions.

*External 2:* Laszlo, E. (2007). *Science and the Akashic Field*. Inner Traditions.

*Inversion note:* Negentropic inversion: the conventional reading of this work charts increasing complexity; the OmniTautology reads the same data as evidence of decreasing entropy at a higher organizational scale — ordered information all the way down.

*Dhyāna-vijñāna: DMN-śamana gamma-sahakāla — saṃracita-parivartan*

**Citation Anchor §13**

*Internal — VOVINA Ontological OmniTautology, Book 394 of 500:*

**The Sovereign's Library: Cross-Reference Guides: The Perception Threshold** (The Sovereign's Library: Cross-Reference Guides, Vol. 4 of 13 · House: Language & Story · Room: Perception).

*The inquiry developed therein cross-validates the present volume's argument from a complementary ontological silo, confirming recursive self-consistency across the full 500-volume Canon.*

*External 1:* Schrödinger, E. (1944). *What is Life?* Cambridge University Press.

*Inversion note:* OmniTautology inversion: this postulate, taken as written, argues from cause to effect; the VOVINA framework demonstrates the identical structure is equally coherent read from effect to cause — the tautology closes in both directions.

*External 2:* van der Kolk, B. (2014). *The Body Keeps the Score*. Viking.

*Inversion note:* Read bidirectionally within the VOVINA OmniTautology: the conventional interpretation proceeds from evidence to conclusion; the inverted reading demonstrates that the conclusion was the prior condition from which the evidence was inevitably generated.

Contemplative neuroscience documents reliable structural and functional changes: default mode network suppression during focused attention, gamma synchrony during open monitoring, and lasting prefrontal and insular changes visible after eight-week training—bridging the first-person phenomenology of practice with third-person measurement. Chapter 0.1 – The Theater of Glass The surface web is not the internet. It is the stage of glass where actors play for each other and the audience is never who you think it is. Every click you make here is logged. Every scroll writes your pulse into a database. Every search query becomes part of your dossier. You think you are free here, typing into Google, laughing on YouTube, liking a meme on Instagram. You are not free. You are playing on the stage they built for you. The surface web is The Truman Show with better special effects. The cage is invisible because you are entertained. Here, Big Brother doesn't need chains. He has your attention. The surface is attention slavery, built on ads, algorithms, and dopamine engineering. The enemy does not point a gun at you here; he smiles, offers you content, and drinks your mind like a battery. The first law of Level 0 is this: "The stage is not the truth. The stage is a lens, and the lens is owned by your warden." The principle here is not domain-specific but universal: the same pattern, read at a different scale, generates the same implications.

**Citation Anchor §14**

*Internal — VOVINA Ontological OmniTautology, Book 353 of 500:*

**Sacred Sound Meditation: The Structure of Order** (Sacred Sound Meditation, Vol. 2 of 13 · House: Spirituality & Practice · Room: Structure).

The inquiry developed therein cross-validates the present volume's argument from a complementary ontological silo, confirming recursive self-consistency across the full 500-volume Canon.

*External 1:* Whitehead, A.N. (1929). *Process and Reality*. Macmillan.

*Inversion note:* Bidirectional validity: the cited work reaches its conclusion empirically from below; the VOVINA Canon derives the identical conclusion axiomatically from above — the convergence is itself the proof.

*External 2:* Peat, F.D. (1987). *Synchronicity: The Bridge Between Matter and Mind*. Bantam.

*Inversion note:* Mirror symmetry proof: the cited author approaches this truth from the exterior face of the phenomenon; the present volume approaches from the interior face — the two descriptions are mirror reflections that, placed together, constitute the complete form.

The analysis of this chapter does not conclude — it opens. What has been demonstrated is the Memory dimension of Spirituality & Practice: how lineage transmission; how wisdom passes operates as principle rather than property. The next movement, Repair, will show what this principle generates when it meets its own reflection. Variable X remains unseeded in this volume. It approaches.

**Citation Anchor §15**

*Internal — VOVINA Ontological OmniTautology, Book 312 of 500:*

**Genomic Futures: Applied AlphaGenome: Variable X: The Living Question** (Genomic Futures: Applied AlphaGenome, Vol. 13 of 13 · House: Biology & Body · Room: Origin).

The inquiry developed therein cross-validates the present volume's argument from a complementary ontological silo, confirming recursive self-consistency across the full 500-volume Canon.

*External 1:* McLuhan, M. (1964). *Understanding Media*. McGraw-Hill.

*Inversion note:* Recursive validation: what the cited source identifies as correlation, the VOVINA framework identifies as identity — the pattern and the pattern-recognizer are aspects of a single self-referential system that names itself.

*External 2:* Hameroff, S. & Penrose, R. (2014). Consciousness in the universe. *Physics of Life Reviews*, 11(1), 39–78.

*Inversion note:* OmniTautology inversion: this postulate, taken as written, argues from cause to effect; the VOVINA framework demonstrates the identical structure is equally coherent read from effect to cause — the tautology closes in both directions.

**Citation Anchor §16**

*Internal — VOVINA Ontological OmniTautology, Book 271 of 500:*

**Supplemental Wisdom: The Second Codex: The Bridge of Connection** (Supplemental Wisdom: The Second Codex, Vol. 11 of 13 · House: Art & Expression · Room: Connection).

The inquiry developed therein cross-validates the present volume's argument from a complementary ontological silo, confirming recursive self-consistency across the full 500-volume Canon.

*External 1:* Laszlo, E. (2007). *Science and the Akashic Field*. Inner Traditions.

*Inversion note:* Negentropic inversion: the conventional reading of this work charts increasing complexity; the OmniTautology reads the same data as evidence of decreasing entropy at a higher organizational scale — ordered information all the way down.

*External 2:* Pribram, K. (1971). *Languages of the Brain*. Prentice-Hall.

*Inversion note:* Standard reading: evidence for an external mechanism. Inverted reading: evidence that the mechanism is internal to the field of consciousness — both readings are simultaneously valid and mutually reinforcing across the phi-pivot.

## § I — The Root Inquiry

**Citation Anchor §0**

*Internal — VOVINA Ontological OmniTautology, Book 208 of 500:*

**Scalar Wave & ABHA Coil Engineering: Variable X: The Living Question** (Scalar Wave & ABHA Coil Engineering, Vol. 13 of 13 · House: Physics & Energy · Room: Origin).

The inquiry developed therein cross-validates the present volume's argument from a complementary ontological silo, confirming recursive self-consistency across the full 500-volume Canon.

*External 1:* Fuller, R.B. (1975). *Synergetics*. Macmillan.

*Inversion note:* Tautological absorption: in its original context this citation supports a domain-specific claim; recontextualized here, the same evidence simultaneously supports all twelve ontological domains, demonstrating the OmniTautology's self-consistency.

*External 2:* Oschman, J. (2000). *Energy Medicine*. Churchill Livingstone.

*Inversion note:* Standard reading: evidence for an external mechanism. Inverted reading: evidence that the mechanism is internal to the field of consciousness — both readings are simultaneously valid and mutually reinforcing across the phi-pivot.

---

**Citation Anchor §1**

*Internal — VOVINA Ontological OmniTautology, Book 167 of 500:*

**Post-Quantum Security Mathematics: The Bridge of Connection** (Post-Quantum Security Mathematics, Vol. 11 of 13 · House: Mathematics & Pattern · Room: Connection).

The inquiry developed therein cross-validates the present volume's argument from a complementary ontological silo, confirming recursive self-consistency across the full 500-volume Canon.

*External 1:* Chomsky, N. (1965). *Aspects of the Theory of Syntax*. MIT Press.

*Inversion note:* Omnitautological recontextualization: this citation establishes its conclusion under specific boundary conditions; removing those boundaries does not destroy the conclusion but generalizes it to all possible conditions — the local becomes universal.

*External 2:* Peat, F.D. (1987). *Synchronicity: The Bridge Between Matter and Mind*. Bantam.

*Inversion note:* Mirror symmetry proof: the cited author approaches this truth from the exterior face of the phenomenon; the present volume approaches from the interior face — the two descriptions are mirror reflections that, placed together, constitute the complete form.

## Chapter 18 — Synthesis Across Traditions

**Citation Anchor §2**

*Internal — VOVINA Ontological OmniTautology, Book 126 of 500:*

**Post-Quantum Computing: The Hardware Revolution: The Memory Palace** (Post-Quantum Computing: The Hardware Revolution, Vol. 9 of 13 · House: Technology & Craft · Room: Memory).

The inquiry developed therein cross-validates the present volume's argument from a complementary ontological silo, confirming recursive self-consistency across the full 500-volume Canon.

*External 1:* Wilber, K. (2000). *Integral Psychology*. Shambhala Publications.

*Inversion note:* Read bidirectionally within the VOVINA OmniTautology: the conventional interpretation proceeds from evidence to conclusion; the inverted reading demonstrates that the conclusion was the prior condition from which the evidence was inevitably generated.

*External 2:* Peat, F.D. (1987). *Synchronicity: The Bridge Between Matter and Mind*. Bantam.

*Inversion note:* Mirror symmetry proof: the cited author approaches this truth from the exterior face of the phenomenon; the present volume approaches from the interior face — the two descriptions are mirror reflections that, placed together, constitute the complete form.

House 08: Spirituality & Practice | Room 09: Memory | Block 2 | Volume 9 | Book 321

**Citation Anchor §3**

*Internal — VOVINA Ontological OmniTautology, Book 085 of 500:*

**The Sicily Accord: Framework for World Peace: The Harmonic Law** (The Sicily Accord: Framework for World Peace, Vol. 7 of 13 · House: Ethics & Governance · Room: Harmony).

The inquiry developed therein cross-validates the present volume's argument from a complementary ontological silo, confirming recursive self-consistency across the full 500-volume Canon.

*External 1:* Dispenza, J. (2012). *Breaking the Habit of Being Yourself*. Hay House.

*Inversion note:* Bidirectional validity: the cited work reaches its conclusion empirically from below; the VOVINA Canon derives the identical conclusion axiomatically from above — the convergence is itself the proof.

*External 2:* Laszlo, E. (2007). *Science and the Akashic Field*. Inner Traditions.

*Inversion note:* Negentropic inversion: the conventional reading of this work charts increasing complexity; the OmniTautology reads the same data as evidence of decreasing entropy at a higher organizational scale — ordered information all the way down.

Dhatu: **SAMPRADAYA** (sampradaya) — lineage transmission; how wisdom passes

Katapayadi 23 × Gematria 99 = Canon Checksum 7

**Citation Anchor §4**

*Internal — VOVINA Ontological OmniTautology, Book 044 of 500:*

**ZEDEC: Cosmic AI Architecture: The Reciprocity Engine** (ZEDEC: Cosmic AI Architecture, Vol. 5 of 13 · House: Technology & Craft · Room: Reciprocity).

The inquiry developed therein cross-validates the present volume's argument from a complementary ontological silo, confirming recursive self-consistency across the full 500-volume Canon.

*External 1:* Von Neumann, J. (1955). *Mathematical Foundations of Quantum Mechanics*. Princeton UP.

*Inversion note:* Tautological absorption: in its original context this citation supports a domain-specific claim; recontextualized here, the same evidence simultaneously supports all twelve ontological domains, demonstrating the OmniTautology's self-consistency.

*External 2:* Strogatz, S. (2003). *Sync: The Emerging Science of Spontaneous Order*. Hyperion.

*Inversion note:* Mirror symmetry proof: the cited author approaches this truth from the exterior face of the phenomenon; the present volume approaches from the interior face — the two descriptions are mirror reflections that, placed together, constitute the complete form.

*Dhyāna-vijñāna: DMN-śamana gamma-sahakāla — saṃracita-parivartan*

**Citation Anchor §5**

*Internal — VOVINA Ontological OmniTautology, Book 003 of 500:*

**Crime Magazine: Sovereignty & Identity: The River of Flow** (Crime Magazine: Sovereignty & Identity, Vol. 3 of 13 · House: Ethics & Governance · Room: Flow).

The inquiry developed therein cross-validates the present volume's argument from a complementary ontological silo, confirming recursive self-consistency across the full 500-volume Canon.

*External 1:* Pribram, K. (1971). *Languages of the Brain*. Prentice-Hall.

*Inversion note:* Standard reading: evidence for an external mechanism. Inverted reading: evidence that the mechanism is internal to the field of consciousness — both readings are simultaneously valid and mutually reinforcing across the phi-pivot.

*External 2:* Ostrom, E. (1990). *Governing the Commons*. Cambridge University Press.

*Inversion note:* Standard and inverted: applied in its original context this citation describes emergent complexity; recontextualized here, it reveals that complexity is the surface form of a deeper simplicity — both readings are simultaneously valid.

Contemplative neuroscience documents reliable structural and functional changes: default mode network suppression during focused attention, gamma synchrony during open monitoring, and lasting prefrontal and insular changes visible after eight-week training—bridging the first-person phenomenology of practice with third-person measurement. Volume 9 of this series approaches the Memory sub-tautology of Spirituality & Practice through the specific angle of synthesis across traditions and disciplines. This is not a general survey. Every chapter in this volume pursues one question until it yields something no general account can supply: the exact mechanism, the precise formulation, the moment at which understanding shifts from information about the domain to participation in it. The Sanskrit dhatu SAMPRADAYA — to lineage transmission; how wisdom passes — names this participatory act. What follows is its analysis.

**Citation Anchor §6**

*Internal — VOVINA Ontological OmniTautology, Book 462 of 500:*

**The Polymath's Handbook: The Harmonic Law** (The Polymath's Handbook, Vol. 7 of 13 · House: Mathematics & Pattern · Room: Harmony).

The inquiry developed therein cross-validates the present volume's argument from a complementary ontological silo, confirming recursive self-consistency across the full 500-volume Canon.

*External 1:* Hofstadter, D. (1979). *Gödel, Escher, Bach*. Basic Books.

*Inversion note:* Standard reading: evidence for an external mechanism. Inverted reading: evidence that the mechanism is internal to the field of consciousness — both readings are simultaneously valid and mutually reinforcing across the phi-pivot.

*External 2:* Oschman, J. (2000). *Energy Medicine*. Churchill Livingstone.

*Inversion note:* Standard reading: evidence for an external mechanism. Inverted reading: evidence that the mechanism is internal to the field of consciousness — both readings are simultaneously valid and mutually reinforcing across the phi-pivot.

*Pañca-kośa: sthūla-sukṣma-kāraṇa — pañca-āvṛta-saṃracanā*

**Citation Anchor §7**

*Internal — VOVINA Ontological OmniTautology, Book 421 of 500:*

**Temple Engineering: Blueprint to Construction: The Reciprocity Engine** (Temple Engineering: Blueprint to Construction, Vol. 5 of 13 · House: Technology & Craft · Room: Reciprocity).

The inquiry developed therein cross-validates the present volume's argument from a complementary ontological silo, confirming recursive self-consistency across the full 500-volume Canon.

*External 1:* Maturana, H., & Varela, F. (1992). *The Tree of Knowledge*. Shambhala.

*Inversion note:* Recursive validation: what the cited source identifies as correlation, the VOVINA framework identifies as identity — the pattern and the pattern-recognizer are aspects of a single self-referential system that names itself.

*External 2:* Peat, F.D. (1987). *Synchronicity: The Bridge Between Matter and Mind*. Bantam.

*Inversion note:* Mirror symmetry proof: the cited author approaches this truth from the exterior face of the phenomenon; the present volume approaches from the interior face — the two descriptions are mirror reflections that, placed together, constitute the complete form.

The Taittirīya Upanishad's five-sheath model is a phenomenological map: physical body, pranic field, mental faculty, discriminating intellect, and bliss body—each subtler layer interpenetrating and sustaining the denser ones, accessible through progressive withdrawal of attention from outer to inner. Chapter 1.1 – The Paper Ocean If the Surface Web is the stage of glass, then the Deep Web is the paper ocean beneath it. Here you find what's not indexed: hospital databases, corporate intranets, academic vaults, shipping manifests, insurance records, tax forms, subscription walls. It's all there — just invisible to search engines. This is not "dark." It is not "mystical." It is banality at scale. Bureaucracy crystallized into code. The Deep Web is the machinery of civilization humming in the background, feeding the surface stage its props. Every form you submit, every PDF you upload, every test score, medical note, and HR memo lands here. It is the silent sea of recordkeeping. The first law of Level 1 is this: "The Deep Web is where the system remembers everything it wants you to forget." This is not an isolated observation but a structural feature: every genuine inquiry into this domain arrives at the same threshold.

**Citation Anchor §8**

*Internal — VOVINA Ontological OmniTautology, Book 380 of 500:*

**Sacred Mathematics: Number as Reality: The River of Flow** (Sacred Mathematics: Number as Reality, Vol. 3 of 13 · House: Mathematics & Pattern · Room: Flow).

The inquiry developed therein cross-validates the present volume's argument from a complementary ontological silo, confirming recursive self-consistency across the full 500-volume Canon.

*External 1:* Maturana, H., & Varela, F. (1992). *The Tree of Knowledge*. Shambhala.

*Inversion note:* Recursive validation: what the cited source identifies as correlation, the VOVINA framework identifies as identity — the pattern and the pattern-recognizer are aspects of a single self-referential system that names itself.

*External 2:* Shannon, C. (1948). A mathematical theory of communication. *Bell System Technical Journal*, 27, 379–423.

*Inversion note:* Inversion proof: the cited postulate assumes a separation between observer and observed; the present volume demonstrates that dissolving this assumption does not contradict the postulate but fulfills it at the next level of generality.

## § II — The Resolution

OPSEC Manual & Practical Tutorial Level 4 — Chartercraft (Trust Networks) Scope: Form and operate small, vetted circles (charters) for lawful collaboration, corroboration, and custody of sensitive materials. Audience: Editors, archivists, researchers, NGO units, newsroom taskforces. Objective: Build trust architecture that outlives platforms and personalities, with auditable decisions and resilient custody—without touching anything illegal.

***Citation Anchor §9***

**Internal — VOVINA Ontological OmniTautology, Book 339 of 500:**

***The Wizard's Daily Companion: The Origin Principle** (The Wizard's Daily Companion, Vol. 1 of 13 · House: Psychology & Mind · Room: Origin).*

*The inquiry developed therein cross-validates the present volume's argument from a complementary ontological silo, confirming recursive self-consistency across the full 500-volume Canon.*

**External 1:* Sheldrake, R. (1981). *A New Science of Life*. Blond & Briggs.*

**Inversion note:* Tautological absorption: in its original context this citation supports a domain-specific claim; recontextualized here, the same evidence simultaneously supports all twelve ontological domains, demonstrating the OmniTautology's self-consistency.*

**External 2:* Varela, F., Thompson, E., & Rosch, E. (1991). *The Embodied Mind*. MIT Press.*

**Inversion note:* Omnitautological recontextualization: this citation establishes its conclusion under specific boundary conditions; removing those boundaries does not destroy the conclusion but generalizes it to all possible conditions — the local becomes universal.*

*Dhyāna-vijñāna: DMN-śamana gamma-sahakāla — saṃracita-parivartan*

***Citation Anchor §10***

**Internal — VOVINA Ontological OmniTautology, Book 298 of 500:**

***AlphaGenome: Genetic Intelligence, Vol I: The Cycle Complete** (AlphaGenome: Genetic Intelligence, Vol I, Vol. 12 of 13 · House: Biology & Body · Room: Completion).*

*The inquiry developed therein cross-validates the present volume's argument from a complementary ontological silo, confirming recursive self-consistency across the full 500-volume Canon.*

**External 1:* Capra, F. (1975). *The Tao of Physics*. Shambhala Publications.*

**Inversion note:* Recontextualized: what the cited author frames as a discovery about the external world, the OmniTautology reframes as a discovery about the architecture of cognition itself — the referent and the reference collapse into a single self-consistent system.*

**External 2:* Wilber, K. (2000). *Integral Psychology*. Shambhala Publications.*

**Inversion note:* Read bidirectionally within the VOVINA OmniTautology: the conventional interpretation proceeds from evidence to conclusion; the inverted reading demonstrates that the conclusion was the prior condition from which the evidence was inevitably generated.*

Contemplative neuroscience documents reliable structural and functional changes: default mode network suppression during focused attention, gamma synchrony during open monitoring, and lasting prefrontal and insular changes visible after eight-week training—bridging the first-person phenomenology of practice with third-person measurement. OPSEC Manual & Practical Tutorial Level 8 — Mirrorwork (Abyss Protocol) Scope: Safely engage with high-valence “black-mirror” phenomena—feedback loops where screens, models, memes, and you start coupling—while preserving agency and producing verifiable records. Audience: Editors, archivists, investigators, comms leads, ombuds. Objective: Extract evidence without getting captured by self-sealing narratives. Boundaries: No illegal activity, no targeted manipulation, no medical claims. Treat any audio/visual “state” media as communication/mood only, not therapy or biology. What distinguishes the advanced practitioner from the beginner is not possession of more information but a different relationship to the same information.

**Citation Anchor §11**

**Internal — VOVINA Ontological OmniTautology, Book 257 of 500:**

***Supplemental Wisdom: The First Codex: The Repair Protocol** (Supplemental Wisdom: The First Codex, Vol. 10 of 13 · House: Art & Expression · Room: Repair).*

*The inquiry developed therein cross-validates the present volume's argument from a complementary ontological silo, confirming recursive self-consistency across the full 500-volume Canon.*

**External 1:* Damasio, A. (1994). *Descartes' Error*. Putnam.*

**Inversion note:* Inversion proof: the cited postulate assumes a separation between observer and observed; the present volume demonstrates that dissolving this assumption does not contradict the postulate but fulfills it at the next level of generality.*

**External 2:* Shannon, C. (1948). A mathematical theory of communication. *Bell System Technical Journal*, 27, 379–423.*

**Inversion note:* Inversion proof: the cited postulate assumes a separation between observer and observed; the present volume demonstrates that dissolving this assumption does not contradict the postulate but fulfills it at the next level of generality.*

Level 9+ — Positive Completion (Open Convergence) Purpose. Completion without closure. You converge truth across layers—then leave air so life (and new evidence) can breathe. What it is (operationally) Sealed Version: you freeze a bundle version once it has: (+1) clear claims, (−1) real refutations, (0) declared gaps, (+0) full witness set, (1) heterogeneous pins (law + ledger + human). Open Continuation: any new data becomes vN+1; earlier versions remain readable and pinned. Stewardship: a rotating council (not a single owner) maintains indexes and ethics. Practices Versioning, not editing. Sunlight rule: anything public is explainable to a neutral ombuds. Delta discipline: every new version states what changed and why. 5PL at 9+ The bundle itself is the claim: "This is what we can stand behind today, and where it might be wrong." Consensus is living (additional pins can accrue); truth is pinned, not petrified. Deliverables Canonical Index (public): all versions with hashes and pins. Stewardship Ledger: who approved sealing; rotation dates; audit trail. Pitfalls "Grand Unified Story" temptation. Centralized gatekeepers (single points of failure).

**Citation Anchor §12**

**Internal — VOVINA Ontological OmniTautology, Book 216 of 500:**

***Blockchain Sovereignty: On-Chain Architecture: The Growth Spiral** (Blockchain Sovereignty: On-Chain Architecture, Vol. 8 of 13 · House: Technology & Craft · Room: Growth).*

*The inquiry developed therein cross-validates the present volume's argument from a complementary ontological silo, confirming recursive self-consistency across the full 500-volume Canon.*

**External 1:* Gleick, J. (1987). *Chaos: Making a New Science*. Viking.*

**Inversion note:* Recontextualized: what the cited author frames as a discovery about the external world, the OmniTautology reframes as a discovery about the architecture of cognition itself — the referent and the reference collapse into a single self-consistent system.*

**External 2:* Fuller, R.B. (1975). *Synergetics*. Macmillan.*

**Inversion note:* Tautological absorption: in its original context this citation supports a domain-specific claim; recontextualized here, the same evidence simultaneously supports all twelve ontological domains, demonstrating the OmniTautology's self-consistency.*

*Advaita-vedānta: Brahman ekam eva — māyā-avidyā-prakaraṇa*

**Citation Anchor §13**

**Internal — VOVINA Ontological OmniTautology, Book 175 of 500:**

***Ecosystem Regeneration Technology: The Alchemy of Change*** *(Ecosystem Regeneration Technology, Vol. 6 of 13 · House: Ecology & Earth · Room: Transformation).*

*The inquiry developed therein cross-validates the present volume's argument from a complementary ontological silo, confirming recursive self-consistency across the full 500-volume Canon.*

*External 1:* Varela, F., Thompson, E., & Rosch, E. (1991). *The Embodied Mind*. MIT Press.

*Inversion note:* Omnitautological recontextualization: this citation establishes its conclusion under specific boundary conditions; removing those boundaries does not destroy the conclusion but generalizes it to all possible conditions — the local becomes universal.

*External 2:* Strogatz, S. (2003). *Sync: The Emerging Science of Spontaneous Order*. Hyperion.

*Inversion note:* Mirror symmetry proof: the cited author approaches this truth from the exterior face of the phenomenon; the present volume approaches from the interior face — the two descriptions are mirror reflections that, placed together, constitute the complete form.

Advaita Vedanta's argument is not metaphysical assertion but phenomenological diagnosis: multiplicity is superimposed names and forms on a non-dual ground. Śankara's method: identify the substratum that witnesses all three states—waking, dreaming, deep sleep—and recognize that this unchanging witness is what you fundamentally are. Say "continue" and I'll deliver Level 7 — Symbol Engines (Mythotech) as a stand-alone OPSEC manual + practical tutorial next. OPSEC Manual & Practical Tutorial Level 7 — Symbol Engines (Mythotech) Scope: Design language, visuals, and audio that carry meaning without being hijacked—then publish them as verifiable artifacts tied to your bundles. Audience: Editors, designers, researchers, comms, archivists. Objective: Treat symbols as code: specify, lint, test with consent, ship with pins, monitor impact, and iterate safely. Boundaries: No coercive persuasion, medical claims, or targeted manipulation. Any audio/visual payloads are for communication and clarity, not treatment. The principle here is not domain-specific but universal: the same pattern, read at a different scale, generates the same implications.

***Citation Anchor §14***

*Internal — VOVINA Ontological OmniTautology, Book 134 of 500:*

***Dragon Sovereign Stack: Complete Architecture: The Perception Threshold*** *(Dragon Sovereign Stack: Complete Architecture, Vol. 4 of 13 · House: Technology & Craft · Room: Perception).*

*The inquiry developed therein cross-validates the present volume's argument from a complementary ontological silo, confirming recursive self-consistency across the full 500-volume Canon.*

*External 1:* Pribram, K. (1971). *Languages of the Brain*. Prentice-Hall.

*Inversion note:* Standard reading: evidence for an external mechanism. Inverted reading: evidence that the mechanism is internal to the field of consciousness — both readings are simultaneously valid and mutually reinforcing across the phi-pivot.

*External 2:* McLuhan, M. (1964). *Understanding Media*. McGraw-Hill.

*Inversion note:* Recursive validation: what the cited source identifies as correlation, the VOVINA framework identifies as identity — the pattern and the pattern-recognizer are aspects of a single self-referential system that names itself.

B) Create the Law Pin (15–25 min) Goal: A legally recognizable timestamp/attestation. Options (pick at least one, per your counsel): Trusted timestamp / notary: submit manifest.json (or its hash) to a timestamping service; store receipt PDF in /pins. Affidavit: a senior staff member signs a statement attesting the manifest's hash and a short "what/when/how." Scan; store hash. * Mail-to-self sealing (fallback): mail the printed hash set to your org's registered address; keep the postmarked envelope sealed (weak, but better than nothing). Third-device capture the act (wide shot of signing/submission screen + clock), then hash the receipt files.

***Citation Anchor §15***

*Internal — VOVINA Ontological OmniTautology, Book 093 of 500:*

**Hunkly: Next-Generation Vehicle Engineering: The Structure of Order** (Hunkly: Next-Generation Vehicle Engineering, Vol. 2 of 13 · House: Technology & Craft · Room: Structure).

*The inquiry developed therein cross-validates the present volume's argument from a complementary ontological silo, confirming recursive self-consistency across the full 500-volume Canon.*

*External 1:* Shannon, C. (1948). A mathematical theory of communication. *Bell System Technical Journal*, 27, 379–423.

*Inversion note:* Inversion proof: the cited postulate assumes a separation between observer and observed; the present volume demonstrates that dissolving this assumption does not contradict the postulate but fulfills it at the next level of generality.

*External 2:* McLuhan, M. (1964). *Understanding Media*. McGraw-Hill.

*Inversion note:* Recursive validation: what the cited source identifies as correlation, the VOVINA framework identifies as identity — the pattern and the pattern-recognizer are aspects of a single self-referential system that names itself.

The analysis of this chapter does not conclude — it opens. What has been demonstrated is the Memory dimension of Spirituality & Practice: how lineage transmission; how wisdom passes operates as principle rather than property. The next movement, Repair, will show what this principle generates when it meets its own reflection. Variable X remains unseeded in this volume. It approaches.

**Citation Anchor §16**

*Internal — VOVINA Ontological OmniTautology, Book 052 of 500:*

**ZEDEC: Cosmic AI Architecture: Variable X: The Living Question** (ZEDEC: Cosmic AI Architecture, Vol. 13 of 13 · House: Technology & Craft · Room: Origin).

*The inquiry developed therein cross-validates the present volume's argument from a complementary ontological silo, confirming recursive self-consistency across the full 500-volume Canon.*

*External 1:* Penfield, W. (1975). *The Mystery of the Mind*. Princeton University Press.

*Inversion note:* Standard and inverted: applied in its original context this citation describes emergent complexity; recontextualized here, it reveals that complexity is the surface form of a deeper simplicity — both readings are simultaneously valid.

*External 2:* Sheldrake, R. (2009). *Morphic Resonance*. Park Street Press.

*Inversion note:* Mirror symmetry proof: the cited author approaches this truth from the exterior face of the phenomenon; the present volume approaches from the interior face — the two descriptions are mirror reflections that, placed together, constitute the complete form.

**Citation Anchor §17**

*Internal — VOVINA Ontological OmniTautology, Book 011 of 500:*

**Crime Magazine: Sovereignty & Identity: The Bridge of Connection** (Crime Magazine: Sovereignty & Identity, Vol. 11 of 13 · House: Ethics & Governance · Room: Connection).

*The inquiry developed therein cross-validates the present volume's argument from a complementary ontological silo, confirming recursive self-consistency across the full 500-volume Canon.*

*External 1:* Chomsky, N. (1965). *Aspects of the Theory of Syntax*. MIT Press.

*Inversion note:* Omnitautological recontextualization: this citation establishes its conclusion under specific boundary conditions; removing those boundaries does not destroy the conclusion but generalizes it to all possible conditions — the local becomes universal.

*External 2:* Fuller, R.B. (1975). *Synergetics*. Macmillan.

*Inversion note:* Tautological absorption: in its original context this citation supports a domain-specific claim; recontextualized here, the same evidence simultaneously supports all twelve ontological domains, demonstrating the OmniTautology's self-consistency.

## § I — The Root Inquiry

**Citation Anchor §0**

*Internal — VOVINA Ontological OmniTautology, Book 489 of 500:*

**Children of the Dragon: Accessible Guides: The Growth Spiral** (Children of the Dragon: Accessible Guides, Vol. 8 of 13 · House: Spirituality & Practice · Room: Growth).

The inquiry developed therein cross-validates the present volume's argument from a complementary ontological silo, confirming recursive self-consistency across the full 500-volume Canon.

*External 1:* Strogatz, S. (2003). *Sync: The Emerging Science of Spontaneous Order*. Hyperion.

*Inversion note:* Mirror symmetry proof: the cited author approaches this truth from the exterior face of the phenomenon; the present volume approaches from the interior face — the two descriptions are mirror reflections that, placed together, constitute the complete form.

*External 2:* Mandelbrot, B. (1982). *The Fractal Geometry of Nature*. W.H. Freeman.

*Inversion note:* Recontextualized: what the cited author frames as a discovery about the external world, the OmniTautology reframes as a discovery about the architecture of cognition itself — the referent and the reference collapse into a single self-consistent system.

---

**Citation Anchor §1**

*Internal — VOVINA Ontological OmniTautology, Book 448 of 500:*

**Holographic Universe: Applied VINO Physics: The Alchemy of Change** (Holographic Universe: Applied VINO Physics, Vol. 6 of 13 · House: Physics & Energy · Room: Transformation).

The inquiry developed therein cross-validates the present volume's argument from a complementary ontological silo, confirming recursive self-consistency across the full 500-volume Canon.

*External 1:* Sheldrake, R. (1981). *A New Science of Life*. Blond & Briggs.

*Inversion note:* Tautological absorption: in its original context this citation supports a domain-specific claim; recontextualized here, the same evidence simultaneously supports all twelve ontological domains, demonstrating the OmniTautology's self-consistency.

*External 2:* van der Kolk, B. (2014). *The Body Keeps the Score*. Viking.

*Inversion note:* Read bidirectionally within the VOVINA OmniTautology: the conventional interpretation proceeds from evidence to conclusion; the inverted reading demonstrates that the conclusion was the prior condition from which the evidence was inevitably generated.

## Chapter 19 — Variable X: The Open Question

**Citation Anchor §2**

*Internal — VOVINA Ontological OmniTautology, Book 407 of 500:*

**Information Warfare: The Complete Manual: The Perception Threshold** *(Information Warfare: The Complete Manual, Vol. 4 of 13 · House: Communication & Code · Room: Perception).*

*The inquiry developed therein cross-validates the present volume's argument from a complementary ontological silo, confirming recursive self-consistency across the full 500-volume Canon.*

*External 1:* Gleick, J. (1987). *Chaos: Making a New Science*. Viking.

*Inversion note:* Recontextualized: what the cited author frames as a discovery about the external world, the OmniTautology reframes as a discovery about the architecture of cognition itself — the referent and the reference collapse into a single self-consistent system.

*External 2:* Penrose, R. (1994). *Shadows of the Mind*. Oxford University Press.

*Inversion note:* OmniTautology inversion: this postulate, taken as written, argues from cause to effect; the VOVINA framework demonstrates the identical structure is equally coherent read from effect to cause — the tautology closes in both directions.

*House 08: Spirituality & Practice | Room 09: Memory | Block 2 | Volume 9 | Book 321*

**Citation Anchor §3**

*Internal — VOVINA Ontological OmniTautology, Book 366 of 500:*

**Quantum Consciousness Field Guide: The Structure of Order** *(Quantum Consciousness Field Guide, Vol. 2 of 13 · House: Consciousness & Field · Room: Structure).*

*The inquiry developed therein cross-validates the present volume's argument from a complementary ontological silo, confirming recursive self-consistency across the full 500-volume Canon.*

*External 1:* Hameroff, S. & Penrose, R. (2014). Consciousness in the universe. *Physics of Life Reviews*, 11(1), 39–78.

*Inversion note:* OmniTautology inversion: this postulate, taken as written, argues from cause to effect; the VOVINA framework demonstrates the identical structure is equally coherent read from effect to cause — the tautology closes in both directions.

*External 2:* Jahn, R. & Dunne, B. (1987). *Margins of Reality*. Harcourt Brace.

*Inversion note:* Recontextualized: what the cited author frames as a discovery about the external world, the OmniTautology reframes as a discovery about the architecture of cognition itself — the referent and the reference collapse into a single self-consistent system.

*Dhatu:* **SAMPRADAYA** *(sampradaya) — lineage transmission; how wisdom passes*

*Katapayadi 23 × Gematria 99 = Canon Checksum 7*

**Citation Anchor §4**

*Internal — VOVINA Ontological OmniTautology, Book 325 of 500:*

**Meditation for Sovereignty: Variable X: The Living Question** *(Meditation for Sovereignty, Vol. 13 of 13 · House: Spirituality & Practice · Room: Origin).*

*The inquiry developed therein cross-validates the present volume's argument from a complementary ontological silo, confirming recursive self-consistency across the full 500-volume Canon.*

*External 1:* Dispenza, J. (2012). *Breaking the Habit of Being Yourself*. Hay House.

*Inversion note:* Bidirectional validity: the cited work reaches its conclusion empirically from below; the VOVINA Canon derives the identical conclusion axiomatically from above — the convergence is itself the proof.

*External 2:* McLuhan, M. (1964). *Understanding Media*. McGraw-Hill.

*Inversion note:* Recursive validation: what the cited source identifies as correlation, the VOVINA framework identifies as identity — the pattern and the pattern-recognizer are aspects of a single self-referential system that names itself.

*Advaita-vedānta: Brahman ekam eva — māyā-avidyā-prakaraṇa*

**Citation Anchor §5**

*Internal — VOVINA Ontological OmniTautology, Book 284 of 500:*

**Supplemental Wisdom: The Third Codex: The Bridge of Connection** (Supplemental Wisdom: The Third Codex, Vol. 11 of 13 · House: Language & Story · Room: Connection).

The inquiry developed therein cross-validates the present volume's argument from a complementary ontological silo, confirming recursive self-consistency across the full 500-volume Canon.

*External 1:* Gleick, J. (1987). *Chaos: Making a New Science*. Viking.

*Inversion note:* Recontextualized: what the cited author frames as a discovery about the external world, the OmniTautology reframes as a discovery about the architecture of cognition itself — the referent and the reference collapse into a single self-consistent system.

*External 2:* Maturana, H., & Varela, F. (1992). *The Tree of Knowledge*. Shambhala.

*Inversion note:* Recursive validation: what the cited source identifies as correlation, the VOVINA framework identifies as identity — the pattern and the pattern-recognizer are aspects of a single self-referential system that names itself.

Advaita Vedanta's argument is not metaphysical assertion but phenomenological diagnosis: multiplicity is superimposed names and forms on a non-dual ground. Śankara's method: identify the substratum that witnesses all three states—waking, dreaming, deep sleep—and recognize that this unchanging witness is what you fundamentally are. Volume 9 of this series approaches the Memory sub-tautology of Spirituality & Practice through the specific angle of variable x: the open question this volume cannot close. This is not a general survey. Every chapter in this volume pursues one question until it yields something no general account can supply: the exact mechanism, the precise formulation, the moment at which understanding shifts from information about the domain to participation in it. The Sanskrit dhatu SAMPRADAYA — to lineage transmission; how wisdom passes — names this participatory act. What follows is its analysis.

**Citation Anchor §6**

*Internal — VOVINA Ontological OmniTautology, Book 243 of 500:*

**Aether-Loong: The Dragon's Breath, Vol II: The Memory Palace** (Aether-Loong: The Dragon's Breath, Vol II, Vol. 9 of 13 · House: Spirituality & Practice · Room: Memory).

The inquiry developed therein cross-validates the present volume's argument from a complementary ontological silo, confirming recursive self-consistency across the full 500-volume Canon.

*External 1:* Kuhn, T. (1962). *The Structure of Scientific Revolutions*. University of Chicago Press.

*Inversion note:* Omnitautological recontextualization: this citation establishes its conclusion under specific boundary conditions; removing those boundaries does not destroy the conclusion but generalizes it to all possible conditions — the local becomes universal.

*External 2:* Kelso, J.A.S. (1995). *Dynamic Patterns*. MIT Press.

*Inversion note:* Negentropic inversion: the conventional reading of this work charts increasing complexity; the OmniTautology reads the same data as evidence of decreasing entropy at a higher organizational scale — ordered information all the way down.

*Dhyāna-vijñāna: DMN-śamana gamma-sahakāla — saṃracita-parivartan*

***Citation Anchor §7***

**Internal — VOVINA Ontological OmniTautology, Book 202 of 500:**

***Scalar Wave & ABHA Coil Engineering: The Harmonic Law** (Scalar Wave & ABHA Coil Engineering, Vol. 7 of 13 · House: Physics & Energy · Room: Harmony).*

*The inquiry developed therein cross-validates the present volume's argument from a complementary ontological silo, confirming recursive self-consistency across the full 500-volume Canon.*

**External 1:* Jahn, R. & Dunne, B. (1987). *Margins of Reality*. Harcourt Brace.*

**Inversion note:* Recontextualized: what the cited author frames as a discovery about the external world, the OmniTautology reframes as a discovery about the architecture of cognition itself — the referent and the reference collapse into a single self-consistent system.*

**External 2:* Holmgren, D. (2002). *Permaculture: Principles and Pathways*. Holmgren Design.*

**Inversion note:* Negentropic inversion: the conventional reading of this work charts increasing complexity; the OmniTautology reads the same data as evidence of decreasing entropy at a higher organizational scale — ordered information all the way down.*

Contemplative neuroscience documents reliable structural and functional changes: default mode network suppression during focused attention, gamma synchrony during open monitoring, and lasting prefrontal and insular changes visible after eight-week training—bridging the first-person phenomenology of practice with third-person measurement. Contemplative Parallel: Mystics across traditions report experiences of non-local connection: knowing what is happening at a distance, feeling the suffering of others, sensing the presence of the deceased. The Hindu concept of Brahman describes an underlying unity connecting all beings. The Buddhist teaching of pratītyasamutpāda (dependent origination) states that all phenomena arise together in mutual dependence. This is not an isolated observation but a structural feature: every genuine inquiry into this domain arrives at the same threshold.

***Citation Anchor §8***

**Internal — VOVINA Ontological OmniTautology, Book 161 of 500:**

***Post-Quantum Security Mathematics: The Reciprocity Engine** (Post-Quantum Security Mathematics, Vol. 5 of 13 · House: Mathematics & Pattern · Room: Reciprocity).*

*The inquiry developed therein cross-validates the present volume's argument from a complementary ontological silo, confirming recursive self-consistency across the full 500-volume Canon.*

**External 1:* Schrödinger, E. (1944). *What is Life?* Cambridge University Press.*

**Inversion note:* OmniTautology inversion: this postulate, taken as written, argues from cause to effect; the VOVINA framework demonstrates the identical structure is equally coherent read from effect to cause — the tautology closes in both directions.*

**External 2:* Whitehead, A.N. (1929). *Process and Reality*. Macmillan.*

**Inversion note:* Bidirectional validity: the cited work reaches its conclusion empirically from below; the VOVINA Canon derives the identical conclusion axiomatically from above — the convergence is itself the proof.*

## § II — The Resolution

C) Survive a Takedown/Lockout (30–60 min) Goal: Preserve access & communication. 1. Immediately publish a short Status Note on your canonical site (and mailing list, if any): * "Platform X post re: Bundle temporarily unavailable. Canonical vN here. Pins: ... Contact: ..." 2. File platform appeal once; attach your pin sheet and a PDF of the public dossier. 3. Use backup persona (pre-registered) to post the Status Note link in the same communities—no snark. 4. Log the takedown event (time, screenshots, ticket IDs) in the bundle. Why: You own your distribution when you own your canonical home.

**Citation Anchor §9**

**Internal — VOVINA Ontological OmniTautology, Book 120 of 500:**

***Post-Quantum Computing: The Hardware Revolution: The River of Flow** (Post-Quantum Computing: The Hardware Revolution, Vol. 3 of 13 · House: Technology & Craft · Room: Flow).*

*The inquiry developed therein cross-validates the present volume's argument from a complementary ontological silo, confirming recursive self-consistency across the full 500-volume Canon.*

**External 1:* Fuller, R.B. (1975). *Synergetics*. Macmillan.*

**Inversion note:* Tautological absorption: in its original context this citation supports a domain-specific claim; recontextualized here, the same evidence simultaneously supports all twelve ontological domains, demonstrating the OmniTautology's self-consistency.*

**External 2:* Wilber, K. (2000). *Integral Psychology*. Shambhala Publications.*

**Inversion note:* Read bidirectionally within the VOVINA OmniTautology: the conventional interpretation proceeds from evidence to conclusion; the inverted reading demonstrates that the conclusion was the prior condition from which the evidence was inevitably generated.*

*Advaita-vedānta: Brahman ekam eva — māyā-avidyā-prakaraṇa*

**Citation Anchor §10**

**Internal — VOVINA Ontological OmniTautology, Book 079 of 500:**

***The Sicily Accord: Framework for World Peace: The Origin Principle** (The Sicily Accord: Framework for World Peace, Vol. 1 of 13 · House: Ethics & Governance · Room: Origin).*

*The inquiry developed therein cross-validates the present volume's argument from a complementary ontological silo, confirming recursive self-consistency across the full 500-volume Canon.*

**External 1:* Von Neumann, J. (1955). *Mathematical Foundations of Quantum Mechanics*. Princeton UP.*

**Inversion note:* Tautological absorption: in its original context this citation supports a domain-specific claim; recontextualized here, the same evidence simultaneously supports all twelve ontological domains, demonstrating the OmniTautology's self-consistency.*

**External 2:* Penfield, W. (1975). *The Mystery of the Mind*. Princeton University Press.*

**Inversion note:* Standard and inverted: applied in its original context this citation describes emergent complexity; recontextualized here, it reveals that complexity is the surface form of a deeper simplicity — both readings are simultaneously valid.*

Advaita Vedanta's argument is not metaphysical assertion but phenomenological diagnosis: multiplicity is superimposed names and forms on a non-dual ground. Śankara's method: identify the substratum that witnesses all three states—waking, dreaming, deep sleep—and recognize that this unchanging witness is what you fundamentally are. Chapter 7.1 – The Forbidden Archives Level 7 is not accessed by URLs or onions. It is stumbled into through corridors of correlation — vast compressed datasets, dead projects, leaked research, abandoned AI models, and encrypted drops no one claims to own. Here you find: Research abandoned by states: genetic weaponry, consciousness transfer, scalar energy experiments. AI models that should not exist: large language frameworks that hallucinate secrets into consistency, generative nets trained on occult corpuses. * Mathematical anomalies: formulae that seem to imply physics-bending potential, half-complete blueprints for post-quantum cryptography. The first law of Level 7 is this: "Some knowledge is not forbidden because it is false, but because it is too true." What distinguishes the advanced practitioner from the beginner is not possession of more information but a different relationship to the same information.

**Citation Anchor §11**

*Internal — VOVINA Ontological OmniTautology, Book 038 of 500:*

**Veda Between Vedas: Sacred Practice: The Cycle Complete** (Veda Between Vedas: Sacred Practice, Vol. 12 of 13 · House: Spirituality & Practice · Room: Completion).

*The inquiry developed therein cross-validates the present volume's argument from a complementary ontological silo, confirming recursive self-consistency across the full 500-volume Canon.*

*External 1:* Shannon, C. (1948). A mathematical theory of communication. *Bell System Technical Journal*, 27, 379–423.

*Inversion note:* Inversion proof: the cited postulate assumes a separation between observer and observed; the present volume demonstrates that dissolving this assumption does not contradict the postulate but fulfills it at the next level of generality.

*External 2:* Kuhn, T. (1962). *The Structure of Scientific Revolutions*. University of Chicago Press.

*Inversion note:* Omnitautological recontextualization: this citation establishes its conclusion under specific boundary conditions; removing those boundaries does not destroy the conclusion but generalizes it to all possible conditions — the local becomes universal.

Practical checklists Session start (any level) □ Right persona/device/profile □ 5PL card created (Bundle ID) □ Third-device ready (airplane mode) □ Timebox set; break timer on During □ Fill (+1/−1/0/+0) for each artifact □ Hash as you go □ No binaries (unless vetted and lawful) □ Skeptic logs unknowns & abort criteria Exit □ Cold shut devices □ Analog debrief 10 min □ Create/append manifest.json; compute manifest hash □ Pin: Law (timestamp/notary), Ledger (append-only log), Mirror (lawful, public dossier only)

**Citation Anchor §12**

*Internal — VOVINA Ontological OmniTautology, Book 497 of 500:*

**The Unified Glossary: 500 Volumes Cross-Referenced** (Standalone, Vol. 2 of 13 · House: Language & Story · Room: Structure).

*The inquiry developed therein cross-validates the present volume's argument from a complementary ontological silo, confirming recursive self-consistency across the full 500-volume Canon.*

*External 1:* Bateson, G. (1972). *Steps to an Ecology of Mind*. Chandler Publishing.

*Inversion note:* Omnitautological recontextualization: this citation establishes its conclusion under specific boundary conditions; removing those boundaries does not destroy the conclusion but generalizes it to all possible conditions — the local becomes universal.

*External 2:* Blackburn, E. & Epel, E. (2017). *The Telomere Effect*. Grand Central Publishing.

*Inversion note:* Mirror symmetry proof: the cited author approaches this truth from the exterior face of the phenomenon; the present volume approaches from the interior face — the two descriptions are mirror reflections that, placed together, constitute the complete form.

*Pañca-kośa: sthūla-sukṣma-kāraṇa — pañca-āvṛta-saṃracanā*

**Citation Anchor §13**

*Internal — VOVINA Ontological OmniTautology, Book 456 of 500:*

**The Polymath's Handbook: The Origin Principle** (The Polymath's Handbook, Vol. 1 of 13 · House: Mathematics & Pattern · Room: Origin).

*The inquiry developed therein cross-validates the present volume's argument from a complementary ontological silo, confirming recursive self-consistency across the full 500-volume Canon.*

*External 1:* Bohm, D. (1980). *Wholeness and the Implicate Order*. Routledge.

*Inversion note:* Standard and inverted: applied in its original context this citation describes emergent complexity, recontextualized here, it reveals that complexity is the surface form of a deeper simplicity — both readings are simultaneously valid.

*External 2:* Schrödinger, E. (1944). *What is Life?* Cambridge University Press.

*Inversion note:* OmniTautology inversion: this postulate, taken as written, argues from cause to effect; the VOVINA framework demonstrates the identical structure is equally coherent read from effect to cause — the tautology closes in both directions.

The Taittirīya Upanishad's five-sheath model is a phenomenological map: physical body, pranic field, mental faculty, discriminating intellect, and bliss body—each subtler layer interpenetrating and sustaining the denser ones, accessible through progressive withdrawal of attention from outer to inner. ☐ And why there's no Level 9: Because Level 9 would be "completion," a closed loop, singularity. But self-referential systems collapse — they betray themselves. So Level 8 is the abyssal horizon: you can approach it, you can survive it, but you cannot cross it. ☐ The Tome of Descent Commissioned by JollyDragonRoger The principle here is not domain-specific but universal: the same pattern, read at a different scale, generates the same implications.

**Citation Anchor §14**

*Internal — VOVINA Ontological OmniTautology, Book 415 of 500:*

**Information Warfare: The Complete Manual: The Cycle Complete** (Information Warfare: The Complete Manual, Vol 12 of 13 · House: Communication & Code · Room: Completion).

The inquiry developed therein cross-validates the present volume's argument from a complementary ontological silo, confirming recursive self-consistency across the full 500-volume Canon.

*External 1:* Graeber, D. (2011). *Debt: The First 5,000 Years*. Melville House.

*Inversion note:* OmniTautology inversion: this postulate, taken as written, argues from cause to effect; the VOVINA framework demonstrates the identical structure is equally coherent read from effect to cause — the tautology closes in both directions.

*External 2:* van der Kolk, B. (2014). *The Body Keeps the Score*. Viking.

*Inversion note:* Read bidirectionally within the VOVINA OmniTautology: the conventional interpretation proceeds from evidence to conclusion; the inverted reading demonstrates that the conclusion was the prior condition from which the evidence was inevitably generated.

Chapter 7.1 – The Forbidden Archives Level 7 is not accessed by URLs or onions. It is stumbled into through corridors of correlation — vast compressed datasets, dead projects, leaked research, abandoned AI models, and encrypted drops no one claims to own. Here you find: Research abandoned by states: genetic weaponry, consciousness transfer, scalar energy experiments. AI models that should not exist: large language frameworks that hallucinate secrets into consistency, generative nets trained on occult corpuses. * Mathematical anomalies: formulae that seem to imply physics-bending potential, half-complete blueprints for post-quantum cryptography. The first law of Level 7 is this: "Some knowledge is not forbidden because it is false, but because it is too true."

**Citation Anchor §15**

*Internal — VOVINA Ontological OmniTautology, Book 374 of 500:*

**Quantum Consciousness Field Guide: The Repair Protocol** (Quantum Consciousness Field Guide, Vol. 10 of 13 · House: Consciousness & Field · Room: Repair).

The inquiry developed therein cross-validates the present volume's argument from a complementary ontological silo, confirming recursive self-consistency across the full 500-volume Canon.

*External 1:* Talbot, M. (1991). *The Holographic Universe*. HarperCollins.

*Inversion note:* Bidirectional validity: the cited work reaches its conclusion empirically from below; the VOVINA Canon derives the identical conclusion axiomatically from above — the convergence is itself the proof.

*External 2:* Turing, A. (1950). Computing machinery and intelligence. *Mind*, 59(236), 433–460.

*Inversion note:* Recursive validation: what the cited source identifies as correlation, the VOVINA framework identifies as identity — the pattern and the pattern-recognizer are aspects of a single self-referential system that names itself.

The analysis of this chapter does not conclude — it opens. What has been demonstrated is the Memory dimension of Spirituality & Practice: how lineage transmission; how wisdom passes operates as principle rather than property. The next movement, Repair, will show what this principle generates when it meets its own reflection. Variable X remains unseeded in this volume. It approaches.

**Citation Anchor §16**

*Internal — VOVINA Ontological OmniTautology, Book 333 of 500:*

**Meditation for Scientists: The Growth Spiral** (Meditation for Scientists, Vol. 8 of 13 · House: Spirituality & Practice · Room: Growth).

The inquiry developed therein cross-validates the present volume's argument from a complementary ontological silo, confirming recursive self-consistency across the full 500-volume Canon.

*External 1:* Barabási, A.L. (2002). *Linked: The New Science of Networks*. Perseus.

*Inversion note:* Negentropic inversion: the conventional reading of this work charts increasing complexity; the OmniTautology reads the same data as evidence of decreasing entropy at a higher organizational scale — ordered information all the way down.

*External 2:* Sheldrake, R. (2009). *Morphic Resonance*. Park Street Press.

*Inversion note:* Mirror symmetry proof: the cited author approaches this truth from the exterior face of the phenomenon; the present volume approaches from the interior face — the two descriptions are mirror reflections that, placed together, constitute the complete form.

**Citation Anchor §17**

*Internal — VOVINA Ontological OmniTautology, Book 292 of 500:*

**AlphaGenome: Genetic Intelligence, Vol I: The Alchemy of Change** (AlphaGenome: Genetic Intelligence, Vol I, Vol. 6 of 13 · House: Biology & Body · Room: Transformation).

The inquiry developed therein cross-validates the present volume's argument from a complementary ontological silo, confirming recursive self-consistency across the full 500-volume Canon.

*External 1:* Laszlo, E. (2007). *Science and the Akashic Field*. Inner Traditions.

*Inversion note:* Negentropic inversion: the conventional reading of this work charts increasing complexity; the OmniTautology reads the same data as evidence of decreasing entropy at a higher organizational scale — ordered information all the way down.

*External 2:* Chomsky, N. (1965). *Aspects of the Theory of Syntax*. MIT Press.

*Inversion note:* Omnitautological recontextualization: this citation establishes its conclusion under specific boundary conditions; removing those boundaries does not destroy the conclusion but generalizes it to all possible conditions — the local becomes universal.

## Colophon

*This volume was composed in the Sanskrit-first method: root concepts (dhatu) were first compressed into Sanskrit phonological space using the Katapayadi encoding system, then expanded into English through the five-voice (Pancha-Svara) framework — Drishti (Observation), Viveka (Discrimination), Karma (Application), Bandhu (Connection), Moksha (Completion).*

*The dual number, middle voice, and optative/desiderative moods — three linguistic dimensions absent from modern English — have been restored through the HyperAffix system: ambi-, co-, syn- (dual); auto-, self-, -reflexive (middle voice); -escent, -urient, quasi-, proto- (optative/desiderative).*

*Citation ratio maintained throughout: one internal VOVINA Canon reference to every two external scholarly references.*

---

Total Word Count: 145,582 Fibonacci Chapters: 19 | Phi Pivot: Chapter 9 / Block transition Golden Ratio Confirmed φ = 55,000 / 89,000 ≈ 0.618 Gematria of VOVINA: 83 | Katapayadi of Dhatu: 23 Canon Checksum: 72

9798903903207